D1077588

PIML~~ICO~~

730

UNFORGIVABLE BLACKNESS

Geoffrey C. Ward won the National Book Critics Circle Award in 1989. With Ken Burns, he is co-author of *The Civil War* and *Jazz* (both published by Pimlico). He lives in New York City.

'Probably the finest book on the uniquely talented and horribly hounded black heavyweight champion from the early years of the 20th century... Johnson was a remarkable man ...Little has changed, believe it or not'. *Observer*

'Great subject, great book...Ward shows us how the great black heavyweight champion overcame a poor education to mix successfully with the glitterati of Europe and America'. *Daily Ireland*

'Ward is a distinguished and diligent historian, and he has mined original sources to tremendous effect. The detail is dazzling... It deserves an audience far beyond fans of the ring game: I will be surprised if a better sporting biography is published in the next 12 months'. *Daily Telegraph*

'A delicious detail on almost every page... Research this powerful gives *Unforgivable Blackness* a richness that rewards contemplative reading', *Scotland on Sunday*

'Geoffrey C. Ward offers a detailed and telling portrait of Johnson's life and times'. *Metro*

'Compelling biography... Johnson's life was a chaotic tableaux of women, fights and fast cars... Ward depicts all this in gripping prose... Hats off to Ward for getting as close to the ghost as anyone will'. *The Times*

'One of the finest boxing books I have read, a compulsive heart-rending story... Ward provides the reader with a fascinating insight into his life'. *Belfast Telegraph*

'This sad, soberly biography – drawing on new sources that include Johnson's unpublished prison memoir – portrays him as a courageous, and cultured, model of auto-emancipation'. *Daily Telegraph*

'Geoffrey Ward has produced a marvellous, meticulous, well-researched biography of a maverick, a fascinating figure who held on to sport's most coveted world crown for seven years; it is a "must-have" for the bookshelf of any sports fan'. *Birmingham Post*

'In a narrative with plenty of thrills and spills, Ward has done full justice to Johnson as a spellbinder and a subversive force. Equally, he gives a compelling picture of the sheer cliff of prejudice that he had to climb. It is down to Ward's skill that even when Johnson is at his most self-destructive we continue to empathise with him'. *Sunday Times*

'Geoffrey C. Ward's compelling chronicle of Johnson's rise and fall is a remarkable insight in to the life of one of the most divisive fighters to have ever laced a pair of gloves... Ward's account is detailed and gripping on every page... This is surely now the standard-bearer for all Johnson reference'. *Independent*

'At their best sporting histories reveal far more than stories of sport. This biography is a good case in point... A fascinating book'. *BBC History Magazine*

UNFORGIVABLE BLACKNESS

The Rise and Fall of Jack Johnson

GEOFFREY C. WARD

PIMLICO

Published by Pimlico 2006

4 6 8 10 9 7 5 3

Copyright © 2004 by The American Lives II Project, LLC

The American Lives II Project has asserted its right under the Copyright, Designs
and Patents Act 1988 to be identified as the author of this work

This book is sold subject to the condition that it shall not, by way of trade or
otherwise, be lent, resold, hired out, or otherwise circulated without the
publisher's prior consent in any form of binding or cover other than that
in which it is published and without a similar condition including
this condition being imposed on the subsequent purchaser

Grateful acknowledgment is made to the
following for permission to reprint previously published material:
A. P. Watt Ltd: 'If' from *Rudyard Kipling's Verse Definitive Edition* by Rudyard
Kipling. Reprinted by permission of A. P. Watt on behalf of The National Trust for
Places of Historic Interest or Natural Beauty; Doubleday: Excerpts from *His Eye Is on the
Sparrow* by Ethel Waters with Charles Samuels. Copyright 1951 by Ethel Waters and Charles
Samuels. Reprinted by permission of Doubleday, a division of Random House Inc. London
Publishing Co. Excerpts from 'Johnson, Craftiest Boxer' by Nat Fleischer from *The
Ring* (August 1946). Reprinted by permission of London Publishing Co.

First published in the United States by Knopf in 2004

Pimlico edition 2005

Pimlico
Random House, 20 Vauxhall Bridge Road,
London SW1V 2SA

Random House Australia (Pty) Limited
20 Alfred Street, Milsons Point, Sydney,
New South Wales 2061, Australia

Random House New Zealand Limited
18 Poland Road, Glenfield,
Auckland 10, New Zealand

Random House South Africa (Pty) Limited
Isle of Houghton, Corner Boundary Road & Carse O'Gowrie,
Houghton, 2198, South Africa

Random House UK Limited Reg. No. 954009

A CIP catalogue record for this book is available from the British Library

ISBN 0-7126-0977-6

Papers used by Random House UK Ltd are natural, recyclable products
made from wood grown in sustainable forests. The manufacturing processes
conform to the environmental regulations of the country of origin

Printed and bound in Great Britain by Cox & Wyman Ltd, Reading, Berkshire

FOR KELLY, GARRETT, NATHAN, AND KATIE
AND FOR WYNTON

Boxing has fallen into disfavor—into very great disfavor . . .
The cause is clear: Jack Johnson . . . has out-sparred an
Irishman. He did it with little brutality, the utmost fairness and
great good nature. He did not "knock" his opponent senseless.
Apparently he did not even try. Neither he nor his race invented
prize fighting or particularly like it. Why then this thrill of
national disgust? Because Johnson is black. Of course some
pretend to object to Mr. Johnson's character. But we have yet to
hear, in the case of White America, that marital troubles have
disqualified prize fighters or ball players or even statesmen.
It comes down, then, after all to this unforgivable blackness.

W. E. B. Du Bois, *The Crisis*, August 1914

CONTENTS

CONTENTS

In writing this book, I have made two editorial decisions of which the reader should be aware. There are no Jack Johnson "papers" upon which to draw—though I have included a good deal of autobiographical material in Johnson's own hand that has never before been published—and therefore much of this book is necessarily based on contemporaneous newspaper accounts of events in his life, both public and private. No one who spends any time with the white newspapers of the early twentieth century can fail to be startled by the racist contempt with which black Americans in general and Jack Johnson in particular were routinely portrayed.

Johnson was the subject of hundreds, perhaps thousands, of newspaper cartoons during the course of his career. Those who drew them usually made some effort to produce recognizable caricatures of his white opponents, but Johnson himself looks the same in virtually all of them: an inky shape with popping eyes and rubbery lips, by turns threatening and ludicrous, that bears no resemblance to Johnson or anyone else; it is as if Krazy Kat or Mickey Mouse had somehow been dropped down among human beings. Even in ostensibly objective news stories Johnson is called the "dinge," the "coon," the "stove," the "Texas Darky," the "big smoke," the "Ethiopian," the "Senegambian," and—more often than one can credit—simply "the nigger." In the same derisive fashion, Johnson's words were often rendered in a kind of minstrel dialect no one ever actually used offstage: "Deah's one man dat Ah wahnts to fight. Dat's Jeff. Ah don'e see no good reason why Ah's not entitled to a whack at Jeff fo' de champeenship." There are at least four dim old recordings of Johnson's actual voice: in three, he's adopted the formalized declamatory style of the vaudevillian he was for thirty years; in the fourth, he's *trying* to mimic a blackface comic. In none of them does he sound remotely like the buffoon the sports pages made him out to be. To help restore some sense of him as an individual, then, and to approximate the authentic sound of his speech, I have restored normal English spelling to whatever Johnson is quoted as having said. (I have not altered any of the words or made orthodox any of the grammar. Nor have I invented any of the conversations included here; every word was recalled by one or another participant or overheard by a reporter.)

And to recapture something of the atmosphere of the world in which he always insisted on remaining his own man, I decided not to use the anachronistic term "African American" in favor of the one that whites of Johnson's generation most resisted using—and blacks of his day most hoped to see in print: "Negro." GEOFFREY C. WARD

BOOK ONE

THE RISE

CHAPTER ONE

THE PURE-BLOODED
AMERICAN

IN THE SPRING OF 1910, Halley's comet returned to the heavens after an absence of seventy-five years. Some believed it a sign from God that the world was about to end. Nearly everyone saw it as a momentous event, and during the week of May 18, when astronomers predicted the earth would pass through the comet's tail, adults and sleepy children all over the country stumbled out of their homes at night to see if they could get a glimpse of it.

On the Lower East Side of New York, thousands of tenement dwellers, mostly immigrants and their families, filled the streets to peer up at the cloudy skies, while on the roof of the Waldorf-Astoria hotel uptown, Speaker of the House Joseph G. Cannon led two hundred tuxedoed guests attending the annual dinner of the National Association of Manufacturers in a champagne toast to the comet's passing. In Memphis, Tennessee, separate all-night revivals were held for white and black believers awaiting Judgment Day. In Chicago, panicked householders blocked their doors and windows against deadly gases they believed the comet would release.

And early one morning, at the fashionable Seal Rock House on Ocean Beach at San Francisco's western edge, guests and staff members alike gathered on the sand beneath the stars, listening to the rhythm of the surf and waiting to chart the comet's brilliant course above the sea.

But the hotel's most celebrated guest—the most celebrated black man on earth—remained in bed in his suite on the second floor. A member of his entourage had slipped up the stairs a few minutes earlier and tried to rouse him, but the heavyweight champion of the world had ordered him out of the room. He saw no need to get up. Over the coming centuries there would be hundreds of comets, he said. "But there ain't gonna be but one Jack Johnson."

Like a good many of his claims, this one was both outrageous and entirely accurate. He had, after all, battered his way from obscurity to the top of the heavyweight ranks and won the greatest prize in American sports—a prize that had always been the private preserve of white combatants. At a time when whites ran everything in America, he took orders from no one and resolved to live always as if color did not exist. While most Negroes struggled merely to survive, he reveled in his riches and his fame. And at a time when the mere suspicion that a black man had flirted with a white woman could cost him his life, he insisted on sleeping with whomever he pleased. Most whites (and some Negroes as well) saw him as a perpetual threat—profligate, arrogant, amoral, a dark menace, and a danger to the natural order of things.

The real Jack Johnson was both more and less than those who loved or those who hated him ever knew. He embodied American individualism in its purest form; nothing—no law or custom, no person white or black, male or female—could keep him for long from whatever he wanted. He was in the great American tradition of self-invented men, too, and no one admired his handiwork more than he did. All his life, whites and blacks alike would ask him, "Just who do you think you are?" The answer, of course, was always "Jack Johnson"—and that would prove to be more than enough for turn-of-the-twentieth-century America to handle.

Johnson visited Paris for the first time in June of 1908, before sailing to Australia and his long-delayed battle with the heavyweight champion Tommy Burns. It may have been then that he and an unknown French journalist began laboring together over the manuscript that would become the first of his autobiographies.* The language of its opening passage seems stilted, especially in translation, but the thoughts are unmistakably Jack Johnson's:

> When a white man writes his memoirs . . . he anxiously begins with the history of his family from earliest times. It seems the higher one ascends the more interested one is in it. And I think that most authors embroider their genealogy. Basically, none of it interests anyone other than family members.
>
> But I don't want to exempt myself from this ancient custom and wish to say a few words about my genealogy.

---

*There are four of them: *Ma Vie et Mes Combats,* serialized in fourteen parts in *La Vie au Grand Air* in 1910; *Mes Combats,* a revised version of the magazine articles, published in Paris in 1914; a fragmentary manuscript in Johnson's own hand, written while he was a prisoner at Leavenworth federal penitentiary, 1920–21, hereafter referred to as Prison Memoir; and *Jack Johnson—In the Ring and Out,* 1927, written with Bill Sims. Johnson also wrote, or cooperated with others in writing, a number of autobiographical magazine and newspaper articles.

Our [Negro] memories are handed down from father to son. Whites don't think so, but we blacks are also proud of our ancestors and during long days and still longer nights, though we knew neither schools nor books, we still transmitted memories of past centuries. I don't doubt that the stories have been modified over time, but the salient facts remain. If some parts are merely fables it doesn't matter much. Who can tell among the white stories what is fact and what is fable?

Facts about Johnson's ancestry are hard to come by, and he was himself a cheerful fabulist when it came to retelling his own life. But the first thing he wanted people to understand about him was that because his enslaved forebears had arrived in America long "before the United States was dreamed of," he was himself a "pure-blooded American." And because he knew that that was what he was, he saw no reason ever to accept any limitations on himself to which other Americans were not also subject.*

Why he insisted on acting that way at a time when most American Negroes were relegated to second-class citizenship remains the essential mystery of his life. No amount of sleuthing will ever fully solve it, but a few clues may lie half-hidden in what little we know of his boyhood.

He was born Arthur John Johnson in Galveston, Texas, on March 31, 1878, the year after the last Union troops were withdrawn from the former Confederacy, leaving freed blacks to fend for themselves.† His parents, Henry and Tina (known as Tiny) Johnson, both ex-slaves, did just that. She was from either North or South Carolina; government records and her son's various accounts differ. Henry was born in Maryland or Virginia sometime during the 1830s; after serving as a civilian teamster attached to the U.S. Army's 38th (Colored) Infantry, he settled in Galveston in 1867. His son loyally remembered him as "the most perfect physical specimen I have ever seen." In fact, Henry stood just five foot five and was severely disabled by an atrophied right

---

*It may seem odd to modern readers that Johnson would have felt it necessary to assert his Americanness this way. But in his time, whites routinely drew a distinction between black citizens and "real" Anglo-Saxon, native-born Americans. For example, in a Washington *Post* article published on August 10, 1913, headlined FEW STARS OF PRIZE RING OF NATIVE AMERICAN STOCK, the anonymous author asserted that "from the time of [John L.] Sullivan to the present time . . . only one real American [James J. Jeffries] has had the honor of occupying the throne, though an American negro also has held the title."

†As a boy he was known as Arthur and L'il Artha. Sportswriters would turn the latter into a derisive nickname. At some later point, he reversed the order of his names and became John Arthur Johnson.

leg, the result of exposure to cold and rain and snow in the trenches at Petersburg, Virginia, that had caused the "disease of rheumatism" to distort his right knee—or so his attorneys would later claim in one of several unsuccessful bids he made for a veteran's pension.

Despite his injury, despite the fact that he could not read and that neither he nor his wife could write, Henry Johnson never failed to find ways to support his family. He worked as a porter in a saloon, then as a school janitor, finally as supervising janitor for Galveston's East School District. His wife took in washing. Both were faithful Methodists, and Henry sometimes helped with the preaching on Sundays; Jack Johnson's glib tongue and enthusiasm for public speaking may have been an inheritance from him.

The Johnsons had nine children, five of whom lived to adulthood. They kept them all fed and clothed, saw to it that they attended at least five years of school, and somehow managed to put enough money aside to buy a plot of land at 808 Broadway at the island's eastern end, and build their own single-story home.

Jack was the Johnsons' third child and first son, and from the beginning seems to have been the focus of his family's attention. He was bright, talkative, and filled with energy, but, as he and his mother both remembered, he'd also been frail as a small boy and was still so thin at twelve that the family physician warned he might be tubercular. Like his sisters and brothers, he was expected from early childhood to help keep the family going. He swept out schoolrooms to ease his father's burdens. "Those devilish brooms were taller than I was," he remembered. "It was sure the joy of my early life to grow taller than the broomstick." And he got an early morning job, riding along on a milk wagon to keep an eye on the horse when the milkman got down to make a delivery. Every Saturday night, he was paid ten cents and a brand-new pair of bright-red socks, of which his employer evidently had a limitless supply.

Otherwise, Jack remained at home with his older sisters, Lucy and Jennie, and his younger siblings, Henry and Fannie and an adopted brother named Charles. He was especially close to his mother, who told him again and again he was "the best boy in the world" and assured him he could do anything he wanted if he wanted it badly enough.

Jack Johnson seems to have needed little encouragement along those lines. He saw himself as someone special from the first—someone set apart, not subject to the limitations holding others back. His mother liked to recall what he told her one evening when he was still a small boy doing his homework by lamplight. As she told it,

> Jack was reading in the Texas history book about great men, and he turns around to me and he allowed as how he was going to be a great man himself some one of these days. And I says, "Shucks, boy, what you talking about? What you think you're going to be—president?" He said, no, he wasn't figuring on being president, but he expects he'll be something what'll be just about as big. And that child sure was talking a parable that night.

Johnson would remain deeply devoted to Tiny Johnson until her death, lavishing her with gifts and telling reporters she had been responsible for all his success. After her death, he delivered a pulpit talk called "The Influence of My Christian Mother" before black congregations in several cities. In it, he urged his listeners to "keep your mother's image before you all the time. Remember what she taught you when you was a youngster, and there is nothing you can't accomplish."

That message was reinforced by the city (and the neighborhood within that city) in which Johnson grew up. In 1929, long after his boxing life had ended, he cooperated in writing a series of syndicated articles about his career. In one, he argued that the outstanding black heavyweights of that era, Harry Wills and George Godfrey,* would never reach the heights he had reached, in part because they were from the Deep South and therefore "grew up with the thought implanted in their minds, through generations of tradition, that the COLORED man was not equal to the WHITE. The inferiority complex which was planted in their grandfather and his father has never been shaken off and never will be shaken off."†

Johnson was a southerner, too, of course, and had also been raised in a city where, as he said, "the whites were in control." But Galveston was different from most southern communities. It was a seaport and, like its rivals, Mobile and New Orleans, took a more relaxed view of racial separation than did the inland towns and cities of the South. All sorts of people came and

---

*Godfrey's real name was Feabe Smith Williams. He named himself after the Canadian heavyweight George Godfrey, who had been one of John L. Sullivan's two most serious black challengers (see page 17).

†Johnson's theory would never be tested, because his successors as champion (Jess Willard, Jack Dempsey, and Gene Tunney) refused to face any black challengers in the ring, just as James J. Jeffries had refused to face Johnson when he held the title.

went at the waterfront. "You had all walks of life, races, creeds, colors . . . in here," a longtime resident remembered. "We were segregated but it wasn't as bad as other places in the state of Texas. . . . That was a unique thing about Galveston. Negroes and Caucasian people were poor and lived in the same neighborhood, ate the same food, suffered the same problems."

No part of Galveston Island was more racially mixed than the Twelfth Ward, in which Johnson grew up. Its most important citizen was Norris Wright Cuney, who, as the son of a Texas planter and his slave mistress, was regarded as black, not white. At a time when Negro political power was eroding all over the South, Galveston's "sable statesman" managed to hold on to his for some fourteen years. As alderman, labor organizer, collector of customs for the district of Texas, Republican National Committeeman, and leader of the racially mixed "Black and Tan" faction of the state Republican Party, he was at the time of his death in 1896 perhaps the most powerful Negro officeholder in the country—and a constant reminder to neighbors like young Jack Johnson that a black man need not limit his horizons.*

The public school Johnson and his brothers and sisters attended was segregated, but the streets and alleys through which they raced once school was out were not. "From the time I was old enough to play on the Galveston docks I played with a gang of WHITE boys," Johnson recalled.

> We had a great gang, too, and every kid in Galveston looked up to the 11th Street and Avenue K gang. That was us. My best pal and one of the best friends I have now is Leo Posner, a white boy who was the head of our gang down there. So you see, as I grew up, the white boys were my friends and my pals. I ate with them, played with them and slept at their homes. Their mothers gave me cookies, and I ate at their tables. No one ever taught me that white men were superior to me, and when I started fighting I fought just as enthusiastically AGAINST them as I once had fought on Leo Posner's side.†

---

*Norris Cuney's handsome home at 822 Avenue L was just two blocks behind Henry Johnson's house; his brother Joseph, an attorney and clerk of the Customs House, lived just across the street from the Johnsons at 813 Broadway.

†When Johnson went swimming off the docks with other boys and got too close to a steamboat's paddle wheel, a youth named Cafferty Williams, presumably a member of the Eleventh Street and Avenue K gang, dove in and saved him from being sucked under. Years later, Johnson would express his gratitude by sending Williams five hundred dollars from his winnings. (Los Angeles *Examiner,* July 16, 1910.)

Fighting of any kind had seemed alien to Johnson as a small boy. He avoided quarrels, he recalled, ran home rather than face neighborhood bullies, and depended on his older sisters to protect him until he was twelve.

It was in that year . . . when I first discovered that I could fight just a little bit. While going home from school one day, I fell into a heated argument with Willie Morris, one of my school mates. We had just reached my home, and I noticed [a neighborhood woman whom the children called] Grandmother Gilmore standing in the front yard. As I looked in Grandmother Gilmore's direction Willie struck me in the jaw. Now at that time Willie was much larger than I, and his unexpected blow to my jaw rather stunned me for a few seconds, and upon getting my bearings my first impulse was to run, and perhaps I would have had it not been for Grandma Gilmore. She had witnessed Willie strike me and when she saw that I did not show fight, she called out to me, "Arthur, if you do not whip Willie, I shall whip you." Now this assertion from Grandmother Gilmore made a different aspect upon the whole thing, it caused me to lose all thought of retreat. At once I figured that I'd much rather give Willie a whipping than receive a whipping myself . . . so immediately I sailed into Willie and whipped him. This was my first fight and I won it by in-fighting and clinching. I clinched Willie and in the breakaway I struck him in the eye which ended the fight.*

Johnson told this story countless times, the details shifting with his mood. Sometimes he remembered his first opponent as Jakey Morris, not Willie. Tiny Johnson insisted that it had been she, not Grandmother Gilmore, who had forced her son to stand up for himself. Inconsistencies like those never bothered Johnson when telling a good story about himself, and disentangling real events from imagined ones before the newspapers began to mark his path is made doubly difficult by the obvious joy he took over the years in arranging and rearranging his past to suit his sense of who and what he had become. He was an inexhaustible tender of his own legend, a teller of tall tales in the frontier tradition of his native state. It is impossible now to know

---

*Sugar Ray Robinson, who won the welterweight title and held the middleweight title five times during his long career, told almost exactly the same story about his own beginnings. When a boy, he explained to the writer W. C. Heinz, "I would avoid fighting even if I had to take the short end. I'd even apologize. . . . I got to be known as a coward and my sisters used to fight for me." Robinson, like Johnson before him, didn't much like fighting but loved "out-thinking another man and out-maneuvering him." (W. C. Heinz, *What a Time It Was*, p. 84.)

for certain what happened to him when during his early years—or even whether some of what he described with such relish ever happened at all.

Norris Wright Cuney had seen to it that the black students of Galveston had their own high school, but Johnson did not attend it. Instead, like most Negro adolescents of his time and place, he went to work. Galveston may have been more cosmopolitan than other southern cities, and Cuney's organizing skills had won for its dockworkers wages much higher than those earned by most black people in the region. But opportunities for young black men remained severely limited; as late as 1930, eight out of ten of the city's Negro wage earners would still be stevedores. Johnson worked the Galveston docks long and hard enough to know they were not for him; he hated the work so much, in fact, that he would sometimes later claim he had never done it at all. He'd been a clerk on the docks, he claimed, never a stevedore.*

He seems to have tried everything else, too: sweeping out a barbershop, working as a porter in a gambling parlor and as a baker's assistant (he would pride himself all his life on his skill at making cakes and biscuits). He hoboed to Dallas, as well, and spent several months there. After working first at the racetrack, exercising horses, he found a job as apprentice to a man who painted carriages. His parents were pleased. They thought he'd discovered a useful trade. Johnson thought the work tedious. But, he later wrote, "as luck would have it," Walter Lewis, the shop owner, turned out to be "a great lover of boxing."

> He had in his shop a stock of gloves and nothing gave him more pleasure, after a day's work, than to watch two or three rounds of sparring between friends. He didn't know much and I knew even less; the science of boxing was still Greek to me. Nevertheless, I learned to hit strong and hard.
>
> It's thanks to Lewis that I became a boxer.
>
> "Jack," he said to me, "why don't you put yourself in the ring? You have the height and reach; you are stronger than any boy your age. If you train seriously you can become a terrific fighter."

---

*In 1910, he maintained with a straight face that he had loaded cotton purely for fun: "While I never worked as a longshoreman as some people have said I used to delight when I was a boy . . . to go down on the docks and handle heavy bales of cotton and the like. I didn't do this for pay. I simply did this because I had a leaning that way. It developed my strength and I gained quite a name as a strong man." (Milwaukee *Free Press*, May 8, 1910.)

At sixteen or so, Johnson left home again and this time may have made it all the way to Manhattan. He and his friends had all read about Steve Brodie, an Irish immigrant who became famous in 1886 when he claimed to have survived a leap from the brand-new Brooklyn Bridge. Somehow, without help or permission from anyone, the young Johnson determined to go and meet him. He stowed away on the *Nueces,* a Mallory Line cotton steamer bound for New York. He was soon discovered, he later recalled, but rather than put him ashore, the captain set him to work shoveling coal and peeling potatoes for the duration of the voyage.*

> I didn't have a nickel. As the ship docked [in New York] I went on deck and, standing in the crowd of passengers, with my longest face and my saddest eyes, I announced that I was a worthless colored boy without friends, family, or money, and was about to jump overboard. I walked to the rail and told everybody to keep away from me. I had allowed my old cap to fall on deck. As I turned . . . to try my bluff at the fatal plunge, a woman threw a dollar in my cap. A shower of money followed.

Johnson went ashore and began asking strangers how he could find his hero. Eventually he discovered that Brodie ran a saloon on the Bowery.

> I got there just as fast as my legs could carry me. I sneaked in past the swinging doors and went right up to the bar. I asked, "Where's Mister Brodie?" and the men drinking must have chuckled to themselves at the thin colored youngster who was so serious in his quest. Well, they kidded the life out of me. One would wink at the other and then point out a man and say, "That's Steve Brodie over there." I'd go over and ask him if he was Steve Brodie and he'd get the wink from someone else and point out somebody else. It seemed that everyone in that saloon was Steve Brodie, and I don't know to this day if I ever met him.

Whether Johnson really traveled all that way to meet his hero or only wished he had, the youth he described in the story had many of the characteristics he would display as a grown man: independence, restlessness, an ability to improvise, to attract attention, and to get around rules intended to tie him down.

---

*In some versions of this story, Johnson claimed he made the trip in two stages. The first supposedly took him only as far as Key West, where he earned a little money diving for sponges and fought off a hungry twenty-three-foot shark before moving on. Of all his colorful tales this one seems among the least plausible. (Jack Johnson, *In the Ring and Out*, pp. 28–29.)

Instead of making his way back to Galveston right away, Johnson said, he moved on to Boston, the adopted home of another of his idols. Joe Walcott was a short but hard-hitting welterweight from the West Indies who fought out of the Massachusetts capital as the "Barbados Demon." "I went to Boston to find Joe Walcott," Johnson said. "They had cheated me out of one celebrity but I vowed that when I got back to Galveston I'd tell Leo Posner and the rest of them that I had at least talked to Walcott." He got a job exercising horses at a stable. On his days off, he remembered, he and the other stable boys made their way to Boston Common, where they liked to "annoy the Salvation Army band" while waiting for a glimpse of their hero. Walcott evidently took a liking to the lanky teenager from Texas and sometimes allowed him to carry his gear to and from the gym. "Sonny," Walcott told him before he went home again to Galveston, "[boxing's] a great game if you don't forget to pull in your chin."*

Sports were now constantly on Johnson's mind. He was big for his age—six feet tall and still growing at sixteen—with powerful arms and shoulders, and so fast on his feet, one old Avenue K friend claimed, that he could jump twelve feet backward from a standing start.

The 1896 *Plessy v. Ferguson* decision had merely legitimized Jim Crow laws already firmly in place in the South and much of the rest of the country as well, and doors of opportunity for Negroes were closing in sports, just as they were in other areas of American life. White professional baseball players had already forced their black counterparts off the field. Under the rules of the newly established Jockey Club, the licenses held by the black jockeys who had once dominated American racetracks—fourteen of the fifteen horses at the starting line for the first Kentucky Derby in 1875 had Negro riders—would no longer be renewed. Even the League of American Wheelmen had banned black bicyclists from its ranks.

---

*Randy Roberts, Johnson's most scholarly biographer, calls the story of Johnson's youthful flight to New York and Boston "universally unbelieved," but the wealth of detail in the many different versions of it the champion provided over the years convinces me that it or something like it really did occur. Part of the problem may lie with Johnson's poor memory for dates; again and again he has caused his chroniclers confusion by placing otherwise verifiable events in the wrong year or the wrong sequence. In *In the Ring and Out*, for example, he claims that he took off for New York in 1890, when he was twelve, but he could not possibly have heard of Joe Walcott then since Walcott had yet to fight his first professional bout. Walcott did not become nationally known until late 1893, when he knocked out Jack Hall, the lightweight champion of Australia, so I have assumed Johnson did not undertake his long journey till after that.

But despite the odds, there were still black sports stars for young Johnson to dream of emulating. He venerated the jockey Isaac Murphy, who won at least a third of all the races in which he rode and may have been the greatest rider in U.S. track history. Johnson lost a job at a Galveston livery stable when he exhausted one of the horses in his charge, racing with his friends in unauthorized imitation of his idol. When he finally realized he was simply too big to be a jockey, he turned to bicycle racing, seeking to follow in the tracks of Marshall "Major" Taylor, the Indiana-born "colored wonder" who had begun breaking records in the face of jeering crowds and sabotage from white competitors. Johnson entered a five-mile race at Galveston, he remembered, fell rounding a curve, and injured his leg. A week or so in bed convinced him that he should abandon bicycling, too.

Meanwhile, he found still another job, cleaning a gym run by a German-born heavyweight named Herman Bernau. Somehow Johnson saved up enough money to buy himself two pairs of gloves, and he began carrying them with him everywhere, challenging other members of his gang to spar with him. Even then he was fast and hard to hit, one of them remembered, and he already displayed the brash, taunting style he would later make famous. "He could predict every blow," one early victim remembered. "He'd tell you he was going to hit you in the eye, and he would. He'd say he was going to hit you in the mouth and he would."

His growing skill stood him in good stead in a bare-fisted street fight with a man he remembered as "grown and toughened" named Davie Pierson. He and Pierson had been intent on a game of craps when the police descended. Johnson got caught. Later the police picked up Pierson, too, and he accused Johnson of having turned him in. Johnson denied it. When the two were released from jail, they met on the dock, where a large crowd gathered to see them settle things. Johnson easily beat the bigger, older man. Afterward, he remembered, "people went around asking one another, 'Did you see what L'il Arthur did?'" and he began to think he might be good enough to make some money in the ring.

He got his first chance to see if he could in the summer of 1895, against another dockworker named John "Must Have It" Lee. "It was arranged for us to fight at Josie's Beer Garden at the east end of the island near the beach," he remembered. He was careful not to tell his mother about it for fear she'd try to stop him, she remembered, but when she noticed a steady stream of men filing past her house and asked what all the commotion was about, someone said, "Why, Jack's going to fight out to the beach."

"Fight!" she replied. "What's that boy doing fighting and people goin' out to the beach to see him? And, gracious, they told me they paid people money to fight. I never knew there was any money in this fightin' business 'cept to have to pay it to the police court for a fine."

The crowd formed a circle on the beach, Johnson remembered, and "we were stripped ready for battle when the police came along and chased us." He and Lee put their clothes back on and stalked across town to the other end of the island as the referee and fight crowd straggled along behind. There they marked out another ring in the sand and started over. The sun was fierce. No one had remembered to bring anything to quench the fighters' thirst. Finally somebody filled a bucket with warm, brackish water from a nearby pool and brought it to them. It stank, but they drank it anyway, then went right back at each other.

Johnson won the fight and the winner's purse of a dollar fifty—then had to hand over twenty-five cents of it to pay the referee. Still, it was more than he could have earned in the same amount of time on the docks, and he'd enjoyed the excitement and applause. When he came home that evening, his mother remembered, she asked him what he'd been doing. He told her not to worry. He was going to make arrangements to become a fighter, he said; he would give her all the money he earned, and one day it would be "nothin' at all for me to drop a hundred thousand dollars in your lap 'most any time you want it."

When Bob Thompson, a barnstorming 235-pound professional, turned up in town a few weeks later, promising twenty-five dollars to anyone who survived four rounds with him, Johnson stepped up to the challenge. He made it through the four rounds, he remembered, but "it was the hardest earned money of my life." He was so banged up after this contest that it was two weeks before he was willing to be seen in public again long enough to spend it.*

"We are in the midst of a growing menace," Charles A. Dana, the editor of the New York *Sun,* warned his readers in 1895, the year of Johnson's first pro-

---

*Many years later, when Johnson was heavyweight champion and Bob Thompson was a street sweeper in Los Angeles, a reporter asked Thompson about their fight. "He was just a club fighter then," he recalled, "and didn't know enough about boxing to meet a man of my experience. He weighed just 156 pounds that night . . . but that nigger surely had a punch like the hind leg of a mule." (Los Angeles *Times,* December 17, 1913.)

fessional fight. "The black man is rapidly forging to the front ranks in athletics, especially in the field of fisticuffs. We are in the midst of a black rise against white supremacy." Dana had in mind the recent successes of three Negro boxing masters then tearing their way through the lighter weight classes: George Dixon, known to his admirers as "Little Chocolate," who had won the bantamweight title in 1890 and the featherweight title in 1891; lightweight Joe Gans, a former oyster shucker and master boxer from Baltimore who had run up thirty-one straight victories by the end of 1895;* and Johnson's friend Joe Walcott, who had recently knocked out the lightweight champion of Australia and seemed on his way to a world title of his own. "If the Negro is capable of developing such prowess in those [lighter] divisions of boxing," Dana asked, "what is going to stop him from making the same progress in the heavyweight ranks?"

Only white men were meant to reign over the heavyweights. John L. Sullivan—the first heavyweight champion of the gloved era and the man most responsible for transforming the fight game from an illicit backroom pastime into a major American sport—had said so. Near the end of his career, in 1892, he explicitly stated the exclusionist policy he had informally followed since its beginning in 1878: he was prepared to defend his title against "all . . . fighters—first come, first served—who are white," he said. "I will not fight a negro. I never have and never shall."

Sullivan was the most celebrated American of his era, better known around the world than any president, and his climb from the immigrant streets of Boston held many meanings for his admirers: the triumph of the individual, the fulfillment of the immigrant dream, even American ascendancy over England, the traditional home of heavyweight champions. One sportswriter likened Sullivan's fist to "the clapper of some great bell that . . . boomed the brazen message of America's glory as a fighting nation from one end of the earth to the other." Laboring men and white-collar workers alike envied him his strength and independence, admired his courage, and made allowances for his excesses. Sullivan's mustached portrait hung

---

*Gans would go on to win both the lightweight and welterweight titles. He fought 159 times with just eight losses, at least two of which—1900 bouts with Frank Erne and Terry McGovern—were almost surely fakes forced upon him by his manager. Known as the Old Master, he was so good that the ranks soon filled with boxers eager to cash in on his success, including "Allentown Joe Gans," "Baby Joe Gans," "Cyclone Joe Gans," "Dago Joe Gans," "Italian Joe Gans," "Michigan Joe Gans," "Panama Joe Gans," and four different hopefuls who fought as "Young Joe Gans."

everywhere men gathered; small boys followed him from saloon to saloon; their fathers read about his feats in the pink pages of the *National Police Gazette;* and between bouts people seemed willing to pay to see him do almost anything, including declaim poetry and pose motionless in tights as the "Dying Gladiator" and "Hercules at Rest." For three of his ten years as champion he abandoned the ring entirely in favor of a cross-country tour playing a virtuous blacksmith in *Honest Hearts and Willing Hands,* a melodrama written especially for him. ("Mr. Sullivan," wrote one careful critic, "was quite as good as the play.") And he later starred briefly as Simon Legree in a drastically rewritten version of *Uncle Tom's Cabin* in which the part of Mrs. Stowe's harsh overseer had been rewritten so that Sullivan could hold on to the audience's sympathy while pummeling Uncle Tom.

His boxing life began one evening in 1878, the year Jack Johnson was born, when Sullivan and some friends attended a variety show at the Dudley Opera House in Boston. As part of the program, a young Irish boxer named Jack Scannell swaggered onstage and offered to take on anyone in the audience in what was billed as a three-round "exhibition" to keep the police from closing the place down. Sullivan was just nineteen, a part-time ditchdigger working on the city sewers, but he shed his coat, rolled up his sleeves, climbed onto the stage, and put on gloves. When Scannell thumped him on the back of the head, Sullivan got mad and knocked him into the piano.

"I done him up in about two minutes," he remembered. That was how he liked things to go. "I go in to win from the very first second. Win I must and win I shall." And win he did, at least forty-seven times officially and many more times than that off the record, against every blacksmith, tugboat captain, iron puddler, and gandy dancer brave or foolish enough to face him. Sullivan was, Charles Dana wrote, "the most phenomenal production of the prize ring that has been evoluted during the nineteenth century."

The Irish-American editor John Boyle O'Reilly may have captured Sullivan's fighting style best:

> Sullivan is as fierce, relentless, tireless as a cataract. The fight is wholly to go in *his* way—not at all in the other man's. His opponent wants to spar; he leaps on him with a straight blow. He wants to breathe; he dashes him into the corner with a drive in the stomach. He does not waste ten seconds of the three minutes of each round.

His defensive skills were limited largely to a ferrous chin and the psychological impact of the relentless cheer with which he complimented any man who managed to reach it. "That's a good one, Charlie!" he would shout, continuing to move inexorably forward. "I have never felt a man's blow in my life," he liked to say; there can be few more disheartening experiences in sports than to land your best punch and see its beefy target smile.

Sullivan may not actually have been able to take bites out of horseshoes, as one story had it, but his power really was prodigious. "I thought a telegraph pole had been shoved against me endways," said Paddy Ryan, from whom Sullivan took the heavyweight title in 1882; another victim, brought around by several buckets of water, wondered dreamily if he might have fallen off a barn.

The champion once claimed in court that he had "never been angry in any of the engagements I have been in." Between engagements, however, things were different: Sullivan was "a son-of-a-bitch of the first water," one contemporary said, "if he drank any." Despite his own claim that he had often been "full but never drunk," heavy drinking fueled his sensitivity to any slight, real or fancied, and his favorite barroom-brawling technique was to butt his opponents into oblivion. His drinking would eventually cause him to balloon to more than three hundred pounds; it lost him his first wife, drove off at least one mistress, and almost cost him his life when, staggering out onto the platform between railroad cars to relieve himself, he tumbled off the speeding train into a farmer's field near Springfield, Illinois.

Sullivan had all the prejudices of his time and class. Black people were beneath his notice. "Any fighter who'd get into the same ring with a nigger loses my respect," he told one reporter, and he did his best simply to ignore the existence of black challengers.* The hard-hitting Canadian George Godfrey might well have taken Sullivan's title had the champion not continually ducked him, pretending he was willing to fight him one moment, then finding a way to get out of it the next.†

Peter Jackson was even more formidable than Godfrey. Born in St. Croix,

---

*There had been black heavyweights in America since slavery days. William Richmond, a free black from Staten Island, and Tom Molineaux, a Virginia slave, both made their way to England and fought for the title in the early nineteenth century.

†Sullivan evidently never regretted any of this. In 1911, when Jim Flynn signed to fight Jack Johnson for a second time, Sullivan was still calling for interracial bouts to be banned. "I believe it is degrading for a white man to box a negro," he told a newspaperman. "Let negroes meet negroes and whites meet whites. . . . I would never box a negro no matter how great the inducements. I shudder when I think how near I was to being persuaded to meet Godfrey. My better judgment prevailed. [Jake] Kilrain met Godfrey and beat him. In all my experience I saw only two fights in which a white and a negro fought and I don't want to see another."

he began boxing in Australia. After winning the heavyweight championship of his adopted country in 1886 and punching his way past all the white challengers willing to fight him, he came to America in 1888, hoping to persuade Sullivan to give him a chance at his title. Superbly conditioned, skilled at both science and slugging, he was so impressive in his first American bout that one spectator was overheard saying "fear alone" would prevent Sullivan from ever facing him. Jackson forced George Godfrey to quit in the nineteenth round, then went on to beat every white contender who dared enter the ring with him. Negroes followed his exploits closely. After he knocked out Joe McCauliffe in San Francisco, hundreds marched up and down Market Street cheering his name. He was careful never to appear boastful: when black admirers staged a parade for him in Baltimore, he refused to take part unless a hand-painted banner proclaiming Sullivan a coward for avoiding him had been removed. Frederick Douglass kept a photograph of Jackson in his Washington office and would sometimes point to it when visitors came to call, saying, "Peter is doing a great deal with his fists to solve the Negro question."

But there was only so much he could do so long as Sullivan refused even to consider facing him. Richard K. Fox, the influential editor of the *Police Gazette,* put up ten thousand dollars as a guarantee if Sullivan would give Jackson the chance Fox believed he deserved. The champion was unmoved. Many years later, his manager, William Muldoon, admitted that it had been he who vetoed the idea of fighting Jackson simply to save Sullivan from the "humiliation of being defeated by a Negro." But by categorically barring *all* blacks, he and Sullivan also sought to turn a matter of personal convenience into what they hoped other whites would see as a matter of racial principle. Being the heavyweight champion of the world was, as the writer Gerald Early has said, something like being the "Emperor of Masculinity." Lesser beings might be permitted to battle for lesser honors, but in turn-of-the-twentieth-century America it was unthinkable that a black man might wear that most exalted crown. And the best way to ensure that such a thing never happened was to keep all blacks from contending for it.

Disappointed and already, at thirty, beginning to show signs of slowing down, Jackson agreed to meet the top white contender, James J. Corbett, in May of 1891, in San Francisco. Like Sullivan, Corbett was an Irish immigrant's son, but he was a very different kind of public figure, handsome and well spoken, elegant rather than flamboyant, a former bank clerk, not a onetime ditchdigger. (It especially annoyed Sullivan that Corbett's admirers called their hero "Gentleman" Jim.) And, like Jackson, Corbett was a master of defense. Their bout turned into a mind-numbing ring marathon, the two men handling each other with such exquisite caution that the fight stretched on for sixty-one rounds (four hours and five minutes)—so long, the sportswriter W. W. Naughton remembered, that most of the crowd was gone and many of those who remained had stretched out on the empty benches and gone to sleep by the time the referee called a halt and declared the fight "no contest."

Neither man could claim a victory, but just the fact that Corbett had endured so many rounds against Jackson built public enthusiasm for a Sullivan-Corbett contest at New Orleans in September of 1892. That fight—and the attention it drew—marked the real beginning of the modern boxing era. Instead of meeting in secret in a farmer's field or aboard an anchored offshore barge, they would fight beneath the electrically illuminated roof of an enclosed stadium as the climax of a three-night "Triple Event" of boxing covered by sportswriters from all over the country.

On the first evening, lightweight champion Jack McAuliffe knocked out challenger Billy Myer in the fifteenth round. The next night, George Dixon took on an Irish challenger, Jack Skelly. As a special concession to Dixon, a section of seats was set aside so that black fans could see their hero. He did not disappoint them, beating his outclassed opponent so badly before felling him that ringsiders never forgot the terrible sound his blood-soaked gloves made battering Skelly's face. Black New Orleanians would celebrate for the next two days and nights, but white spectators were horrified. "It was a mistake to match a negro and a white man," said the New Orleans *Daily Picayune*, "a mistake to bring the races together on any terms of equality, even in the prize ring."*

The contest between Sullivan and Corbett proved something of an anticlimax. The Great John L., badly overweight at thirty-three and breathing hard from the eighth round on, never caught up with his agile, well-conditioned challenger, who met Sullivan's every puffing lunge with counterpunches until the champion collapsed in the twenty-first round, unable to rise again. Nothing in Sullivan's ring career became him so much as his

---

*Four days later, the Olympic Athletic Club, under whose auspices the Triple Event had been organized, barred interracial contests to ensure that no white New Orleanian would have to endure such sights again. (Ashe, *A Hard Road to Glory*, p. 23.)

leaving of it. Shrugging off the restraining hands of his seconds, who thought he wanted to continue his hopeless battle, he leaned heavily on a ring post long enough to deliver a graceful curtain speech: "Gentlemen . . . All I have to say is that I came into the ring once too often—and if I had to get licked, I'm glad I was licked by an American. I remain your warm personal friend, John L. Sullivan."

Back in Galveston, Jack Johnson, reading about the fight, must have been delighted. Jim Corbett was one of his earliest ring heroes, and when, during Johnson's brief stay in Boston, he had unwisely expressed his enthusiasm for the new champion within earshot of a band of Sullivan's young fans, he received a severe thrashing. Corbett was "the most beautiful boxer that ever lived," Johnson once told a reporter; his rise had marked the moment when "skill began to have a greater place in the ring than mere brute force." Fast, clever, and coolheaded, Corbett made many of his onrushing opponents look like fools. Johnson would one day relish doing that, too. Sullivan's blanket dismissal of all black challengers must also have deepened Johnson's attachment to the new champion, who was at least generous enough to say soon after winning the title that while he planned first to fight Charlie Mitchell—a British challenger Jackson had knocked out—because that international contest was bound to sell the most tickets, he "had no objection to fighting Peter Jackson because he is colored. I think he is a credit to his profession."

Jackson was not satisfied. Passed over yet again, he wrote an open letter to the newspapers. He was careful as always not to appear overly aggressive; he had never "challenged" anyone, he wrote, and had no "animosity" for the new titleholder, but fairness surely suggested that he should meet Corbett again in the ring before age crept up on him much further. The two did get together in Manhattan in 1894 to discuss a possible meeting, but the negotiations fell apart when each man set conditions the other refused to accept: Corbett would not fight in England, and Jackson would not fight in the American South.

Peter Jackson would never get his chance at the championship. For a time he returned to England, where he began drinking so heavily his hands shook and his speech was slurred. He then came back to San Francisco, where Sailor Tom Sharkey refused to face him because of his color, and at thirty-seven he was badly beaten up by the up-and-coming young Californian James J. Jeffries. Jackson sailed back to Australia, where, in 1901, he died of tuberculosis at forty and was buried in Brisbane's Toowong Cemetery. When Charles "Parson" Davies, Jackson's former manager, heard of his passing, he paid him what was then considered the highest possible compliment. "He was 'Black Prince Peter,'" he said, "the whitest man who ever entered the ring."

Between 1895 and 1898, Jack Johnson remembered, he divided his time between Galveston, where he beat "all the big fellows who worked on the docks"—at least seven of them—and brief hoboing forays to other towns, where he hoped to do better.

In October of 1896, he found himself in New York. There he applied for a job as sparring partner for the black welterweight "Scaldy Bill" Quinn, who was getting ready for a fight with Johnson's old friend Joe Walcott. Quinn was a rough, gin-drinking customer; a jagged knife scar on his right cheek that looked like a burn gave him his nickname, and he was celebrated for an early melee during which he nearly bit off an opponent's middle finger. "I was nothing but a poor Negro, without a cent and dying of hunger," Johnson recalled. "Scaldy Bill and his trainer were leading a grand life; they threw five-dollar bills around as tips and drank to Bill's next victory. But there were no five-dollar bills for Jack Johnson." Quinn wouldn't give him any work, and when Johnson asked for three cents to take the ferry to Long Island, where Walcott was training, "he gave me a furious look and told me not to annoy him further."

Johnson got there anyway, and Walcott's manager put him up at a boardinghouse run by a woman named Taylor, whom he talked into serving him a whole leghorn chicken for lunch every day. Johnson later claimed to have run up a ninety-dollar tab. "For the love of God, Jack," Walcott said when the bill was presented to him for payment, "I've never eaten like that in my life!" To Johnson's intense satisfaction, Walcott knocked Quinn cold. He would be further pleased eight or nine years later when Quinn jumped aboard a Chicago streetcar Johnson happened to be riding and asked for a handout and he was able to tell him to get lost. During flush times, Johnson was famously generous to friends and hangers-on and sometimes even to total strangers, but he was always unforgiving toward those he felt had slighted him during his early days, when, as he said, "the world was less kind."

"There have been countless women in my life," Johnson wrote in his 1927 autobiography.

They have participated in my triumphs and suffered with me in my moments of disappointment. They have inspired me to attainment and they have balked me; they have caused me joy and they have heaped misery upon me; they have been faithful to the utmost and they have been faithless; they have praised and loved me and they have hated and denounced me. Always, a woman has swayed me—sometimes many have demanded my attention at the same moment.

If anything, Johnson was minimizing the complexities of his private life. Newspapermen and federal agents would eventually ferret out its most intimate details and spread them on the public record; but before he won his title, we have only glimpses of that life, gleaned from his own sometimes unreliable writings and from brief newspaper items that hint at more than they explain. It is difficult even to know where Johnson was living during those years and often impossible to know with whom.

Still, the simultaneous demands on Johnson's attention made by women seem to have started early, if his American autobiography is to be believed. In 1898, when his parents wanted him to settle down with the daughter of friends, he wrote, he married another young Galveston woman instead, a childhood friend named Mary Austin. "My fortune in those days was somewhat lean," Johnson remembered, "but we were devoted to each other and we were very happy." Nothing else is known about Mary Austin. No record of any marriage seems to have survived, and the 1900 census would show Johnson still living at home with his parents and siblings and without his supposed wife. Like a good many prizefighters, Johnson would one day travel with women to whom he was not married but whom he introduced for decorum's and convenience's sake as his wife. Mary Austin may have been the first such "Mrs. Jack Johnson." She would not be the last.

Married or single, Johnson turned twenty-one in March of 1899 and began to spend more and more time away from home. "There was nothing more for me to do in Galveston," he remembered.

> The purses offered me were truly minimal—10, 15 or 20 dollars at most. If I stayed there, all I'd have is debts for I had to pay one or two seconds and their wages absorbed the whole purse and sometimes more. So I decided to travel the world, to try to box from one coast to the other, and to attach myself to the training camp of a famous boxer.

He resolved to try Chicago first.

I waited until dark and then went down to the [Santa Fe] RR yards and climbed into a side door Pullman bound for Kansas City. Although I had several delays and made several changes in trains, nothing eventful happened until I was nearing K.C. Upon leaving Tulsa, Oklahoma, I had climbed into a box car which was about half full of baled straw, several of the bales were broken, which afforded an excellent bed for me. It was early in the morning and I had been sleeping soundly when I was awakened by a tattoo on the soles of my shoes. Upon waking up, I gazed into the face of a big brakeman. He held a lantern in one hand, and in the other he held a club in a most threatening way. He addressed me in a tough manner and said, "Well, boy, if you haven't any money you will have to jump off."

Johnson rose to his feet. He had no money, he said. The train was moving too fast for him to jump, and he wasn't interested in committing suicide. The brakeman swung his club.

I side-stepped it and hit him in the jaw and followed with an uppercut to his nose which knocked him into the land of nod. He was just coming to when I noticed that the train had slowed down a great deal and looking out its door I saw many lights so, judging that we were in K.C., I jumped off . . . hustled something to eat and after waiting all day I boarded another freight train for Chicago.*

Boxing was an unsentimental business. Hard-eyed white men ran it. To get anywhere, Johnson knew, even the ablest black fighter needed to find a well-connected white man willing to negotiate with other whites on his behalf. He called at one Chicago athletic club after another in search of someone willing to take him on, but victories over obscure opponents on the far-away Galveston docks carried little weight in the big city. "All the managers

---

*Johnson was not always so successful at eluding the authorities during his hoboing years. "Hard-boiled train crews did not seem enthusiastic over having me as a passenger," he wrote, "and on countless occasions I was chased from boxcars, gondolas and blinds. Brakemen impressed me with their earnestness by brandishing clubs with which they threatened to break numerous bones. . . . Train crews were not my only enemies. . . . If I ventured into the streets of some of the smaller towns where a stranger was quickly discovered, police officers and constables manifested deep concern in me. In fact, they were generally so deeply interested that they often insisted that I remain a guest of their town. On these occasions, I was introduced to the town judge, who pried into my personal affairs and asked me embarrassing questions. Usually . . . I was instructed to hasten out of town, which was just exactly what I wished to do, and what I was trying to do when the police interfered." (Jack Johnson, *In the Ring and Out*, pp. 37–38.)

who I offered my services to seemed to think me too young and would not listen to me."

Hoping vaguely that prospects might be brighter in Memphis or St. Louis, he hopped another freight. When it pulled into Springfield, Illinois, he got down and went looking for something to eat. Somehow, the big black stranger carrying a suitcase caught the eye of Johnny Connor, an ex-bantamweight who ran the Senate Bar, a favorite hangout of Illinois legislators. Connor put on boxing shows above his saloon twice a month, and he was worried about his next card. Even the Chicago promoters who had set it up were afraid the main event wouldn't be a crowd-pleaser: "Two very clever but very uninteresting boxers," one of them recalled, "would, when brought together, be doubly uninteresting."

To liven things up, Connor planned to kick off the evening with what was called a battle royal, memorably defined by the sportswriter W. C. Heinz as "an enlightened form of entertainment" that came in "when bear baiting went out, in which half a dozen or more blacks were gloved, blindfolded and pushed into a ring where they were forced to flail at one another until only one remained standing." Many whites found these spectacles hilarious.

Connor already had four men willing to take part, but he wanted five, and the tall tramp from the railroad yards looked like an ideal addition to the cast. To make the offer more attractive, Connor said he would feed and house Johnson until the night of the fight and give him a purse of a dollar fifty if he won. Johnson accepted.*

---

*He was surely familiar with such spectacles, and it has been suggested that he took part in them as a boy in Galveston. Battles royal were common in all southern cities, and Johnson's hometown was no exception. But he himself said the contest at Springfield was "my first Battle Royal." What is clear is that he had no special objection to making money from them. They were a fact of life in the rough world in which he chose to earn his living. As heavyweight champion he would cheerfully referee a battle royal at a Broadway theater in New York on December 16, 1909. Thirteen black amateurs went at one another for a cash prize and the amusement of the white crowd. "In this laughable melee," one reporter wrote, "Johnson scored a knockout for one of the principals foolishly made a swipe at the champion (perhaps the poor fellow was color blind and couldn't tell one from the other) and as he did, Jack let loose a vicious uppercut and 'Mr. Fresh' was sent clean out of the ring. The poor fellow, scared almost to death that he had dared to take such a liberty with the world's champion, wisely slunk to his dressing room."

Battles royal flourished in the South well into the 1940s. Several future champions, including Joe Gans and lightweight Beau Jack, are said to have got their start in them. Henry Armstrong, however, who became the first man to hold three titles simultaneously in different weight divisions, always refused to take part: "I wouldn't go for that," he said. "I was really too proud." (Johnson's Prison Memoir; Kaye, "Battle Blind.")

"In those days," he remembered,

most all Battle Royals were fought on a basis of winner take all, and often such fights were framed up, that is, sometimes 3 or 4 friends would be matched in the same Battle Royal and they would agree with each other to rush the stranger in the Battle and knock him out, and then they would [agree upon which one of them would win and] split the purse. [Johnson's Springfield opponents] did not believe me much of a fighter or they would never have agreed to a winner take all basis. . . . They thought they had something easy.

They didn't. All four rushed Johnson at the opening bell, fists flying. He retreated to a corner and, with his back to the ropes, knocked out the first two with right hands to the jaw, then connected to the midsection of the third, dropping him to his knees—"like he was praying," Johnson remembered. He chased the fourth man—"a big red-[haired] fellow"—until he could corner him and knock him out, too. When the man he'd felled with a body blow showed signs of struggling to his feet, Johnson hurried to his side, stood over him, and whispered, "If you get up I will kill you."* He stayed down.

I don't know what the winner's purse was as [the white man who acted as his manager] took all the money, but he showered me with praise. He said that everything was fine and dandy and that some day I would be a great fighter. He . . . bought me several glasses of beer. This part of my manager's affection I appreciated. I grabbed my glass of beer and then edged up to the free lunch counter and began to eat. . . . Well, I guess I got away with about 30 sandwiches and a dozen beers.

As soon as the headliners had finished their nonviolent encounter in Springfield that evening and the receipts had been counted and distributed, three boxing insiders from Chicago boarded the midnight train for home: the referee George Siler (known as "Honest" George in boxing circles to differentiate him from his more malleable peers), who doubled as boxing editor of the

---

*Years later, an eyewitness gave a slightly different account of the same event: "Jack was the last to enter the ring and directly as he did he landed one of his every-man-for-himself opponents a wallop on the jaw, dropping him as if shot. Two blacks then sailed in after Johnson, who danced out of distance and before his opponents knew what had happened they were on the floor because they foolishly permitted their respective jaws to come into contact with Jack's right mitt. The other blacks . . . crawled out of the ring." (George Siler, quoted in an undated article by Dick Howell in *The Knockout* magazine.)

Chicago *Tribune;* P. J. "Paddy" Carroll, a former heavyweight who now promoted boxing matches for the Illinois Athletic Club; and Jack Curley, Carroll's hulking young assistant.

Curley would one day become one of America's best-known showmen, a Barnumesque promoter and publicist whose clients would include Rudolph Valentino, William Jennings Bryan, the Vatican Choir, and a traveling flea circus, and whose most lasting contribution to American culture was to help transform professional wrestling from a legitimate if ponderous sport into a gaudy prearranged spectacle. Again and again over the years, Jack Curley would emerge from the wings just in time to further Johnson's career.

But in 1899 he was still just an eager twenty-three-year-old hustler. Born Jacques Armand Schuel to Alsatian parents in San Francisco on July 4, 1876, he derived his Americanized professional name from the ringlets that framed his moon face when he was a boy. His father enrolled him in business college, but Curley was soon lured away by what he called "the glamour of the streets." At fifteen, he got a job as a police reporter for the San Francisco *Chronicle,* only to be fired when his editor caught him spinning stories out of thin air. He drifted east in 1893 to see the World's Columbian Exposition in Chicago. There he peddled papers, washed dishes, and slept in alleyways before landing a job with Paddy Carroll, working first as a cornerman, then as Carroll's second-in-command.

After he and his companions on the Chicago-bound train had wolfed down the sandwiches they'd bought on the Springfield station platform, Curley remembered, Carroll settled back into his seat and fell asleep, a dead cigar in his mouth, while Curley and Siler talked over the evening's entertainment.

"Did you see that battle royal they put on there tonight?" Siler asked as the train rocked along.

"No. I was pretty busy about that time. Why?"

"The big coon that won it looked pretty good to me."

"George, you're just a natural booster. You know as well as I do that it was a rotten show. The semi-final was bad and the main event was worse. You don't want to pan the show—so you picked the Negro."

"No, I'm serious. The big Negro had a great left hand and looked as though he knew his way around the ring."

One evening a few weeks later, Siler and Curley were standing at the bar in Stillson's Café, a Chicago sportsman's hangout at Madison and Dearborn. The excitable bartender, Frank Kennedy, was the official timekeeper for important boxing matches in the Windy City, and so enthusiastic about a black heavyweight prospect named John Haines (who fought under the nom de guerre of "Klondike") that he kept him on his payroll as a porter between contests.

Curley remembered that when Siler began talking up "the big coon with the great left hand" he'd seen in Springfield, some of the regulars began to tease Kennedy about what this out-of-town colossus might do to his man. Finally, Kennedy pulled a fifty-dollar bill from his wallet and slapped it on the bar. "That says Klondike will put this big shine of yours out inside of six rounds!" he shouted. "Put up or shut up!"

Paddy Carroll wired Johnny Connor in Springfield, asking that Jack Johnson come to Chicago to face Klondike on the next week's undercard. There was a thirty-five-dollar purse—twenty-five to the winner, ten to the loser. Johnson had had little to eat since he'd been allowed to stuff himself with sandwiches after the battle royal, but he signed on anyway.

He made his big-city debut at the Howard Theater on May 5, 1899, on a card headed by two featherweights, Harry Forbes and "Turkey Point" Billy Smith.* Frank Kennedy, Klondike's champion and employer, kept time. The referee was named Malachy Hogan.

Johnson looked dangerously thin as he waited for the bell. He hadn't a "thimbleful of victuals" in his stomach, George Siler recalled, but he soon landed a left hand that sent Klondike to the canvas. Curley described what happened next.

> Hogan bellowed, "One!"
> Klondike didn't move.
> "What's the matter?" Hogan shouted. "Ain't you going to get up?"
> Klondike said nothing.
> "Two!"
> Klondike still hugged the canvas and Hogan prodded him with his foot.
> "Get up!" he commanded.
> Klondike merely shut his eyes.
> Hogan walked over to where Kennedy sat.
> "He's a dog, Frank."
> The count continued. The crowd roared with laughter.

---

*Smith was the model for Thomas Eakins' 1899 painting *Between Rounds*. He left boxing in 1901 and later played the bass horn in a Salvation Army band.

Hogan must have used up three minutes reaching a count of nine, when Klondike, feeling that further resistance to his pleadings and proddings was useless, finally got up.

The Negroes mauled each other until the fifth round when Klondike's left landed with a thud in Johnson's body and Jack sank to the canvas.

Again, Hogan began a burlesque count but Johnson was even more obdurate than Klondike had been. He rolled over, assumed a comfortable position with one elbow resting on the floor, his hand bracing his head, and settled himself to take the count if the process required the entire evening. When it had been completed, he dragged himself to his feet and shuffled out of the ring, paying not the slightest heed to the mingled hooting and laughter of the crowd.*

Around one that morning, Jack Curley and Carroll's other assistant, a ferret-faced onetime bantamweight named Sig Hart, finished counting the gate receipts in Paddy Carroll's office above the theater and started downstairs.

Jack Johnson was waiting in the lobby.

"Gentlemen," he said, according to Curley, "ain't I goin' to get nothin' for fightin' here tonight?"

"What did Carroll say?"

"He said if I didn't get out, he'd skin my black hide off me."

"Then I'm afraid you won't get anything."

"But Mr. Curley, I'm hungry. I ain't had nothin' to eat since seven o'clock this mornin' in Springfield. If I could just get three dollars I could get something to eat and go back to Springfield."

"Wait here a minute," Curley said.

He climbed back up to Carroll's office.

"Not a dime," the promoter said.

"But Connor sent him up here and he's a good friend of ours. We ought to give the poor fellow something."

---

*The fight yielded the earliest-known newspaper story to mention Jack Johnson. "The long, rangy colored man from Springfield," reported the Chicago *Tribune* on May 6, 1899, "looking something like [former heavyweight champion Bob] Fitzsimmons, showed up well at the start, but weakened at the steady and ponderous attack of Klondike." In his Prison Memoir, Johnson summarized the fight this way: "For three rounds I fought him to a stand-still and the other three rounds he fought me until I wanted to keep still." Other accounts say the bout ended in the fourth or fifth, not the sixth round, but the result was the same.

"He quit didn't he? I won't give him a dime."

Curley returned to the lobby.

Johnson turned to go. Curley took pity on him—or so he liked to remember many years later. (Neither empathy nor generosity was among his more conspicuous qualities.*) "Sig, have you got a buck?"

Hart came up with a dollar. Curley added two of his own. Johnson walked off into the night. "Had any one told me then that this lowly, hungry preliminary fighter would be the heavyweight champion of the world," Curley wrote, "my first thought would have been to laugh and my second to call a policeman."†

Johnson stayed on in Chicago. He worked first as a sparring partner for veteran fighter Frank Childs. Billed as the "Crafty Texan" and nine years older than Johnson, Childs was one of the top black heavyweights in the country. "Frank . . . disliked me," Johnson said, "for each time that [I] stepped into the ring with him he would give me an awful beating. . . . [Another fighter in the gym] often said, 'What are you trying to do, Frank, kill that fellow?' But this did not stop him. He would only try harder to knock me out." But when Childs learned that his fellow Texan was so broke he was forced to sleep on the lakefront, he offered him the use of the floor in his own rented room. Johnson was curled up there one night when Childs, accompanied by either his wife or his cousin (Johnson's several versions of the story differ), came home and told him he'd have to leave right away to make room for the newcomer. Johnson argued and was fired. It was cold and raining hard. He took refuge in a doorway until a policeman ordered him to move on, then found what shelter he could behind the equestrian statue of General John Logan in Lincoln Park. The rain blew in so hard off Lake Michigan that night, he remembered, "it seemed to me as if the bronze horse had turned his head away from the wind."‡

---

*In later years, Curley would insist that wrestlers from his stable work between engagements as servants in his Great Neck, New York, home. He rarely bothered to learn their names, shouting, "Wrestler! Bring us a cup of coffee!" when visitors came to call. (Pegler, "Are Wrestlers People?")

†Jack Curley's version of events was often at least as self-serving as Jack Johnson's, but in his Prison Memoir, Johnson offers at least a hint of corroboration for this story: he said he received no money for his first fight with Klondike.

‡This was one of Johnson's favorite stories, and the weather got worse with each telling until it all seemed to have taken place in the depths of winter. But Johnson worked for Childs in May, so I have adopted his 1923 version, when he said only that it was raining when Childs threw him out into the street.

A Chicago promoter got him a fight in LaSalle, Indiana.* He won it, but lost his winnings that same evening in a dice game and had to borrow the money to get back to Chicago. Then, a would-be manager named Frank Lewis said he'd represent him and provide him with food and a place to stay as well. Johnson's hardest times seemed over, but the arrangement lasted only seven days. "Oh, what a pleasant week," he remembered.

> I ate ham & eggs, pie, hot biscuits and good sweet milk to my heart's delight. I was just in the midst of one of these meals when I listened to the saddest piece of music which I had ever heard. The boss of the boarding house whispered in my ears that "Your manager Mr. Lewis is finished and you must get yourself another place to eat," and that I would have to find a new boarding & eating house.

That evening, his landlord demanded that Johnson pay the bill for his room and board. Johnson told him he'd have his money the next day, waited till everyone was asleep, lowered his trunk from the window, lugged it to the rail yards, and fled the city. He headed east this time, he remembered, and landed in Pittsburgh without enough money to buy a plate of beans. Near the stockyards someone stopped and asked him if he'd ever been in the ring. He said he had. Would he be interested in a fight? A brawny meat cutter who'd beaten up several local heroes was looking for an opponent. Johnson said he was just what they were looking for and proved it the next afternoon, knocking the butcher out in the first round. With his cap "brimming full of dollars," he moved on to New York, where he acted as a second to Joe Walcott in a bout with the New Zealand middleweight Dan Creedon.

In July 1899, he turned up in New Haven, where he earned a few dollars sweeping out Becky Stanford's Cigar Store and poolroom on Congress Avenue and helped train a young featherweight named Kid Conroy. Conroy was white, Johnson remembered, but his mother had cheerfully fed and housed the man who was helping to make a boxer out of her boy. By fall, Johnson said, he had earned enough money betting on his man to buy him-

---

*I can find no official record of this fight but see no reason to doubt it took place. The promoter Alfred Lippe said he'd made the match and that Johnson's opponent was Charles Brooks. Johnson would knock out a fighter listed as "Charley Brooks" in Galveston in April of 1900. He often fought opponents more than once. (Cleveland *Advocate*, March 1, 1919.)

self a legitimate railroad ticket home to Galveston, the first time he had ever ridden "the cushions instead of the rods."*

To be able to purchase his own train ticket was a personal milestone, but Johnson remained, as he himself said, down on his luck. He was still unable to earn a steady income in the ring, still without a manager to make the matches that would enhance his reputation, and forced to depend on his boyhood friend Leo Posner, now matchmaker for the Galveston Athletic Club, to get him fights from time to time.†

On April 6, 1900, he recalled, "I was digging in the corner of the garden when one of my little brothers hissed to me from the other side of the hedge, 'Say, Jack, there's some white folks here who say that Bob White can take you in 15 rounds. There's money in it for you. What do you say?' " White weighed 235 pounds and had won a string of victories. "My answer was to drop my shovel and jump over the hedge. I didn't feel well that day. I'd had nothing to eat," he said. But Posner had come to get him in a carriage, and he wanted to be seen riding through his neighborhood in style.

In those days there were very few carriages in [my] section of Galveston, so when one rode in a carriage one was considered some kid.

Well, I rode down to the club where I received $100 in brand-new one-dollar bills and believe me those new bills looked good to me and they were

---

*Johnson told this story at least twice, to a newspaperman in the summer of 1910 and again in his Prison Memoir. Though the records may be incomplete, I have been unable to find any Conroy victories under Johnson's tutelage. Perhaps Johnson paid for his train ticket by betting *against* his protégé. It would not have been out of character.

†According to his first French autobiography, Johnson considered a shift in careers at about this time. He got himself elected president of the Twelfth Ward Republican Club. (He didn't get many white votes, he said, but he didn't need them; most Texas Republicans were black.) Johnson loved the speech making and the applause, and when it came time to pick a countywide chairman, he decided to run for that office, too, or so he later claimed. He had a bitter rival whose name Johnson recalled only as "Deep Six." When the two appeared side by side before the convention and his opponent reached for his revolver, Johnson knocked him out. A fistfight then broke out on the floor, and the delegates ran for the doors. After that, Johnson said, he decided to return to the ring: the "political struggle was too complicated and too wearying" to suit him.

I've been unable to locate any documentation for this story, and at first glance it might seem farfetched. But Johnson did later dabble in politics as a stump speaker, and Texas Republican politics could be explosive. When the state party met in 1896 to nominate delegates to the national convention, for example, the conflict between Norris Wright Cuney's Black and Tan faction and the Lily Whites, who wanted to "separate the races in primaries as they are in schools, churches, and railroads," ended in precisely the kind of confrontation Johnson described: "Nature's weapons," one newspaper reported, "bludgeons, bottles, pistols and knives all figured in. Tables were smashed and chairs broken, while oaths and groans blended." (Quoted in Hales, *A Southern Family*, p. 90.)

good, too. I fought Bob 15 rounds winning the decision, which made me feel pretty good for I had whipped the best man in Texas.

He continued to take on all comers, sometimes two a week. On May 1, a big, jeering white crowd gathered to see him face his first known white opponent, an Australian named Jim Scanlon. Another black fighter might have been intimidated, might even have thought it the better part of valor to hold back or even surrender early. Not Jack Johnson; he knocked Scanlon senseless in the seventh round. Six days later, he knocked out Jim McCormick in seven; three weeks after that, he knocked him out again in less than half the time.* In June, Johnson held Klondike to a twenty-round draw and knocked out Horace Miles at Josie's Beer Garden for a twenty-five-dollar purse. After that fight, he remembered, "the managers, trainers and fighters all got into a dice game. I don't remember who won all the money, but I do think that I did not."

---

*McCormick battled—and was beaten by—some of the best of his day, Jack Johnson, Tom Sharkey, Billy Stift, and Sandy Ferguson among them. On March 5, 1905, John L. Sullivan lurched out of retirement and took on the 200-pound McCormick in what was intended to be a four-round "exhibition" at Smith's Opera House in Grand Rapids, Michigan. Sullivan was fifty and weighed 273 pounds, but at 1:23 of the second round he hit McCormick with a right hand that put the younger man out for five minutes. (Isenberg, *John L. Sullivan*, p. 352.)

CHAPTER TWO

THE GOOD MAN

ON SATURDAY MORNING, SEPTEMBER 8, 1900, a great hurricane swept northwestward across the Gulf of Mexico, hit Galveston, and tore it apart. It was the worst natural disaster in American history. More than six thousand people died—drowned, crushed by tree limbs and collapsing buildings, or ripped apart by shards of slate blown off roofs at better than 150 miles an hour.

When the sun rose the next morning, Jack Johnson remembered, he felt lucky to be "one of the few residents of Galveston who did not lose a member of his family." But two thirds of the city's structures had been reduced to flinders—including the little house at 808 Broadway of which Henry and Tiny Johnson had been so proud. Like roughly ten thousand of their fellow citizens, the Johnsons ended up homeless, seeking whatever shelter they could find in a muddy landscape littered with dead horses, cattle, and human beings.

Johnson would later write that in the hours following the storm he muscled boats away from profiteers who dared demand money before they would go to anyone's aid and "saved many lives" of people clinging to roofs and tree limbs.* And he may have served on the largely black crews that labored in Galveston's streets for weeks thereafter, handkerchiefs over their mouths, digging the dead from the wreckage, cremating the corpses, or ferrying them out to sea. Deputized whites with guns kept them at it when the heat and

---

*Randy Roberts disbelieves this story and he may well be right. There is no proof one way or the other. But if Johnson did exaggerate the part he played somewhat, there may be an explanation beyond his own robust ego. In the storm's aftermath, the contribution to Galveston's recovery made by its Negro citizens had been overshadowed by widespread, lurid, and almost entirely false newspaper stories of looting by bands of black "ghouls" who were said to have rifled pockets for cash and sawed off fingers to get at rings. As many as seventy-five blacks were supposed to have been shot by whites deputized to protect the dead. The real number of looters killed seems to have been eight—and no one knows to what race they belonged—but the stories were widely believed, in the North as well as in the South. Johnson, like the other black citizens of his hometown, must have resented that fact. Perhaps by playing up his own role, he may in part have been trying to redress that balance. (I am grateful to the architectural historian Ellen Beasley for suggesting this explanation.)

stench grew too bad. Their only rewards were hot meals and enough liquor to dull their senses.

Johnson's family eventually found a new home, in the alley behind West Point Baptist Church in the 3000 block of Avenue M, and Johnson himself was soon back in the ring. In December 1900, the *Police Gazette* ran an advertisement:

> I have a good man named Jack Johnson. He has fought some good men and has beaten them all. He has . . . been defeated only once. . . . Klondike got a decision over him in Chicago about a year ago, and since then he has beaten George Lawler, 15 rounds; John Heyman,* 6 rounds; drawn with Klondike 20 rounds, and has beaten a score of others. I would like to match him with some good man, Tommy Swift, Billy Stift or Klondike preferred, before any club offering the purse or for the gate receipts. Johnson is a colored man, twenty-two years old, weighs 168 pounds in trim, and is anxious to fight some good man.

It was signed "A. Busch" of Dallas, Texas. Busch's name does not appear again in the Johnson story, but he does hold one distinction: he was the first white man to go on record claiming to be in charge of Jack Johnson.

Most black fighters believed they had no choice but to defer to their managers, turning over to them the bulk of their winnings, sometimes following their orders to throw fights or pull punches or carry opponents in order to remain profitable. Johnson was never averse to a little creative prearrangement if there was money in it, but he always insisted on controlling his own destiny. "I am my own manager," he would tell the press when he was champion. "I always have been." No one knows how many white men believed themselves his boss over the years. Nor has anyone ever produced a complete tally of the lawsuits against him filed by those who learned they'd been wrong.

The Chicago promoter Paddy Carroll saw Busch's ad that winter. He was in Memphis, running the Phoenix Athletic Club for a local politician named Pat Kernan. He sent a wire to Jack Curley, asking him to arrange for Johnson and Klondike to come to Memphis and face each other for a third time. Both men "had progressed rapidly since their comic affair in Chicago," Curley remembered. Certainly, Johnson had. He closed Klondike's left eye with a right hand early on, battered him badly enough that he tried to quit in the seventh and did quit in the fourteenth. "The crowd was so incensed," Curley

---

*I have been unable to find any other record of Johnson's battle with John Heyman.

said, "that it chased [Klondike] out of the ring through an exit that led to Kernan's saloon for Negroes next door and down a cobbled street that led to the Mississippi River."

"Oh, say," Johnson remembered, "what a lacing I gave that Mr. Klondike."

> I was 22 years old and I received a thousand bucks for that fight, some dough for a youngster, eh? Well, I knocked Klondike out . . . and believe me Klondike will never forget that fight. . . . After the fight some of my friends gave a grand ball in my honor and it was some ball. We danced the slow drag, the Cuban drag, and a dance called "Coon's Girl Molly," which is what is known now as the Shimmy, and, Oh boy, but I did dance.

Johnson stayed on in Memphis for a time, enjoying the bawdy delights of Beale Street and winning so many battles royal that finally no one in town would climb into the ring with him. "No, I don't want any more of him," one battered victim said; "he hits too hard." He signed for a rematch with Jim Scanlon, too, but the chief of police canceled it at the last moment on the ground that "no white boxer should meet a negro in Memphis." In February 1901, Johnson found himself back home again in Galveston.

Jack Curley was still working for Paddy Carroll that month when a burly Texan turned up at his Chicago office. The stranger had a problem back in Galveston, he said. "We've got a big, fresh Negro down there by the name of Jack Johnson who has won some fights and is bragging too much. We're tired of listening to him and we want to see him licked, and I thought maybe Carroll could send somebody down there to do it."

Curley suggested a journeyman named Jack Beauscholte.

"No," the stranger said. "I hate to admit it, but this Negro can fight some and he's too good for Beauscholte."

Curley then suggested Joe Choynski.

Like Jack Johnson, Joseph Bartlett Choynski was a sports pioneer, the first Jewish American ever to win an international reputation as an athlete. The son of a Polish immigrant editor and poet, be began his career at fourteen, battling Irish boys from the streets of his native San Francisco. His detractors called him "Chrysanthemum Joe" for his blond pompadour and for the allegedly effete life he led outside the ring—he collected antiques, neither drank nor smoke, and was altogether too well-spoken to suit most sportswriters—and he never weighed more than 175 pounds. But he was both a brilliant boxer and a hard puncher who fought five future heavyweight champions and did well enough against them that not one dared face him after they had won their titles. Jim Corbett—who was so battle-weary after knocking Choynski out in the twenty-seventh round of their contest aboard a barge anchored off Benicia, California, that he had to be told he'd won—never forgot Choynski's power. "Little Joe was the hardest hitter I ever tangled with," he said many years later. "To this day I can't figure out how a runt like him could hit so damned hard." James J. Jeffries agreed. He managed to hold Choynski to a twenty-round draw, but not before he was hit with a left hook so powerful it drove a tooth through his upper lip; between rounds, one of his seconds had to cut it loose with a penknife.

Choynski's best days were behind him by 1901—writers called him the "old warhorse"—but Jack Curley thought him just the man to go to Galveston and take Jack Johnson down a peg. "He lives right out here in La Grange and I can get him on the telephone in a minute," he told his visitor. "But you'll have to pay him $1,500 or $2,000 to get him to go down there."

The Texan agreed.

Years later, Choynski himself took up the story. He was not unknown in Galveston.

> I had whipped a big fellow named Herman Bernau down there in three rounds [in 1897, and] when my name was mentioned, Johnson, who had seen me fight, declared I was just too small. Well, I got the match, anyway . . . and Bernau, the same man whom I had beaten, [was to] act as the referee. [He was also the same man whose gym young Jack Jackson had swept out.]
>
> I went down to Galveston in the guise of a boxing teacher . . . [The] management advertised that I was in Galveston for the purpose of giving demonstrations of physical culture and boxing.

The old veteran and the eager newcomer met on the evening of February 25, 1901, in Harmony Hall, a ramshackle survivor of the hurricane. Cold, wet air blew through its battered walls all evening, so cold and so wet that Choynski would remember the place as roofless. The house was full. A black minstrel quartet performed from the ring. Then, according to the Galveston *Daily News*, "two colored boys, who had each been deprived by accident of a leg, gave a fistic event." Finally, a club official told the crowd it was about to see "an exhibition of the manly art to the extent of 20 rounds."

Johnson looked formidable when the bell rang, Choynski remembered, and the "perfect stance that he exhibited in later years was in evidence even when he was a raw novice." But it also quickly became clear that while Choynski was smaller and lighter than the younger man and had lost some of his celebrated speed over the past seventeen years, his skills remained intact.

In the first two rounds, Choynski said,

> we both did a lot of dancing. . . . Johnson was awfully long and reachy and I remember . . . that I had a hard time getting my punches to his face. When the third round started I decided to take a chance. I felt that if I lost the fight, it would hurt my prestige and I couldn't afford that. I walked out for that round with my guard high to tempt Johnson to lead for my ribs. He bit like a hungry bass at the bait, and as he did I lashed out with all my weight for his jaw with my left hook which, pardon me for saying so, was the equal of any man's punch, bar none. It landed just below the temple.

Johnson fell forward into Choynski's arms, then slid to the floor, face down. As the referee began to count, Johnson rolled over on his back but could not get up.

Before he could regain his senses, five Texas Rangers clambered into the ring waving revolvers. He and Choynski were arrested for engaging in an illegal contest. "I never asked anyone to let [the fight] go on," Johnson remembered. "I was darn glad it was over, but I didn't much like the trip to jail." He and Choynski were locked into the same cell and photographed there together, peering glumly out between the bars like stray dogs at the pound. A grand jury was named to consider indictments against them. Texas law held that anyone who voluntarily engaged in "a pugilistic encounter between man and man, or a fight between a man and a bull or any other animal" for financial gain was guilty of a felony and subject to at least two years in state prison.

But things were not quite as dire as they seemed. Henry Thomas, the sheriff of Galveston County, was a strict but fair-minded man. Locking up the boxers, he knew, had as much to do with politics as genuine law enforcement, and he saw no need for undue harshness. "Joe went to his hotel at night, and I went to my home," Johnson wrote. "We would come back to the jail and stay there all day."

To while away the time—and perhaps to make a little pocket change for himself—Thomas allowed a crowd to gather every day at lunchtime to watch the two men spar. "A lot of us used to go up to the calaboose in the afternoon," one local newspaperman recalled, "and sit around while Choynski and Johnson jabbed and swatted each other. Choynski would point out to

Johnson how to lead, feint, move away from a blow." The veteran was impressed by Johnson's speed. "A man who can move like you," Choynski told Johnson, "should never have to take a punch." It was a lesson Johnson never forgot.

On March 8, the grand jury announced that it had failed to find a true bill against either fighter. When the sheriff let the men out of jail that evening, he told them not to come back—and to get out of town before the overzealous state attorney general could come up with another reason to hold them.

They did. Choynski went home to his family in La Grange. Johnson hopped a freight and headed for Denver. There he fought what the *Rocky Mountain News* described as a "very tame draw" with Billy Stift on April 26, and then joined what he remembered in his 1927 autobiography as "a motley crew of scrappers" living and training at Ryan's Sand Creek House, five miles northeast of town. It was a remarkable company. At one time or another that spring, it would include heavyweights Tom Sharkey, Bob Armstrong, and "Mexican Pete" Everett; welterweight "New York" Jack O'Brien; featherweights Abe Attell, Young Corbett II, and George Dixon; and expert trainers Spider Kelly and Tommy Ryan. They would spend weeks fighting local challengers in Denver and Victor and Cripple Creek, and battling one another when no one else could be persuaded to take them on.

Johnson's first assignment was to spar with Sharkey, a thick-bodied veteran mauler whose two wars with Jim Jeffries had stunned even ringside veterans with their ferocity. Sharkey was training for a May 3 go against an oversized California heavyweight named Big Fred Russell. Johnson didn't last long as a sparring partner, he remembered. "Sharkey could not hit me. He told [his trainer,] Spider [Kelly,] to tell me to hold my head up so he could hit me and Spider said, 'You're boxing him so *you* make him hold his head up.'"

After that, Johnson was relegated to the kitchen most of the time, frying chickens and making biscuits for the training table. According to Johnson, Mary Austin was with him briefly in the rundown shack all the fighters shared in Cripple Creek—perhaps he had sent for her because he had steady work for the moment—until what he called "a dispute of minor origin" caused her to leave him and shift to Denver. They were reunited there a few weeks later. On August 23, he acted as a second for George Dixon in a losing effort against Abe Attell at Coliseum Hall. The show was a sellout. Johnson received $150 as his share of the proceeds, then doubled his money at the gambling tables.

Flush for the moment, he abandoned Sharkey's ménage and with Mary

Austin boarded a train for California, then the boxing center of the country. He headed first for Stockton, where he'd heard that George E. Eckhart, superintendent and matchmaker for the Stockton Athletic Association, was looking for young fighters who could make big money for him. Johnson turned up at the matchmaker's office looking so thin, one newspaperman wrote, that "it appeared as if his stomach was firmly convinced that his throat had been cut," but without any of the meek deference expected of black boxers when in the presence of the white men who ran the sport. He could beat anybody, he said. Bring them on. Eckhart kept a couple of professionals on his payroll just to test newcomers. According to the Los Angeles *Times*, one backed off when he saw Johnson stripped and ready for action, but a young black welterweight named Aaron Lister Brown (who would one day become well known as the "Dixie Kid") agreed to try him out. "Johnson made him look foolish," the *Times* reported. "He slapped him, he poked him, he cuffed him and bumped him."

Eckhart was impressed. So was everyone else in the gym. But then, Johnson began asserting himself: if he signed with Eckhart, he said, he expected his room and board to be covered, and he wanted someone sent to the depot right away to pick up his trunk. Eckhart threw him out. He could not bear what he called Johnson's "imperious manner"; didn't "care about being a manager for such an unruly black." He wanted no fighters in his stable whom he could not control.

Frank Carillo of Bakersfield believed he could control anybody. A squat, tough-talking Mexican American with a knife scar on his cheek and a Colt revolver in his trousers, he was said to supplement his income as a saloon keeper, racehorse owner, and sometime fight manager by staging illegal cock- and dogfights, then arranging to have them raided by cooperative police officers so he could lend the arrestees bail money at high interest. He had briefly directed the career of California's first important Mexican-American boxer, featherweight Aurelio Herrera. Carillo demanded half of Johnson's winnings, but he also promised to match him against the best heavyweights in California.

Johnson decided to stay on in Bakersfield and see what Carillo could do for him. It was a rough desert town, and its handful of black citizens all lived within a single small, carefully circumscribed neighborhood. Somehow Johnson managed to find himself rented rooms in the white part of town. Barriers were meant for others, not for Jack Johnson.

That view flew in the face of most white people. It also went against the teachings of Booker T. Washington, the former slave and president of the Tuskegee Institute whose 1895 address at Atlanta's Cotton States Exposition— delivered the same summer Jack Johnson turned professional—had made him a favorite of white philanthropists, and the most powerful black man in America. "The wisest among my race understand that the agitation of questions of social equality is the extremest folly," he told a cheering white crowd that afternoon, and urged his people to "cast down your bucket where you are": to stay in the segregated South, gain an education, and through good manners, sober habits, and hard work, eventually win the respect of their white neighbors. Meanwhile, "in all things that are purely social we can be as separate as the fingers, yet one as the hand in all things essential to mutual progress."

The Great Accommodationist already had his Negro critics, younger men and women mostly, who had never been slaves and who argued that no real progress for black people could be made without appeal to the courts and the ballot box. One of them would say a few years later,

> Today, two classes of Negroes, confronted by a united opposition, are standing at the parting of the ways. The one counsels patient submission to our present humiliations and degradations, it deprecates political action and preaches the doctrine of industrial development and the acquisition of property. . . . The other class believes that it should not submit to being humiliated, degraded, and remanded to an inferior place. It believes in money and property, but it does not believe in bartering its manhood for the sake of gain.

Jack Johnson was a boxer, not an activist. He seems never to have been interested in collective action of any kind—how could he be when he saw himself always as a unique individual apart from everyone else?—but he was very clear early on that he did not identify with the Wizard of Tuskegee. He wrote:

> White people often point to the writings of Booker T. Washington as the best example of a desirable attitude on the part of the colored population. I have never been able to agree with the point of view of Washington, because he has to my mind not been altogether frank in the statement of the problems or courageous in his solution to them. . . . I have found no better way of avoiding race prejudice than to act with people of other races as if prejudice did not exist.

Frank Carillo arranged for Johnson to fight Hank Griffin, the son of a runaway slave and his American-Indian wife, at New Harmony Hall in Bakersfield on November 4, 1901. A skilled defensive fighter, two inches taller than Johnson and so slender, one writer said, that opponents couldn't see him when he stood sideways, he was called "Mummy" Griffin for his skeletal build and the impassive way he went about his work. His best punch was the kind of short, jolting right uppercut for which Johnson would one day be celebrated.

Johnson's first appearance in California was decorous but disappointing to fight fans. "The fight was one of the cleanest . . . ever witnessed in this city," said the Bakersfield *Daily Californian,* "both men breaking nicely from the clinches . . . Griffin landed many hard punches during the evening, but so did Johnson." Later, Johnson would claim he'd knocked Griffin down twice despite the fever he'd been running for days, and had held him to a draw, but no one else seems to have seen the knockdowns, and Griffin got the decision.*

Nine days later, Johnson was in San Francisco. So little was known about him even in boxing circles then that he had been billed for the Griffin fight as "Jack Johnson of Denver" because his last official bout had been held there. But he was confident, nonetheless, that his skill and strength and quick wits would take him all the way to the top, would one day make it impossible for the heavyweight champion to deny him his fair chance at the title.

James J. Jeffries was to defend his championship against Gus Ruhlin at Mechanics Pavilion on November 15, and Johnson was determined to have a look at him—and to do so for free if he could get away with it. He arranged to meet three friends outside the pavilion before dawn on the day of the fight: Abe Attell, lightweight Eddie Hanlon, and welterweight Harry Foley.† One by one, Johnson's companions took advantage of an open transom to slip inside and make their way to their prearranged hiding place. But by the time Johnson had maneuvered himself through the small opening and dropped down inside, a night watchman was coming down the corridor, club in hand.

Instead of running away, Johnson ran toward him. "Oh mister officer," he said, "chase them boys quick. I'm the janitor of this here pavilion and they done sneaked in through the transom. I been chasing them all over the build-

---

*The two men would fight three more times, and Johnson would do only marginally better; all three bouts ended in a draw. Later, he would say that Griffin had been the cause of the "greatest punishment I ever received in the ring."

†Johnson's supporting cast in this story expanded with the telling. In his 1931 article, "How I Whipped Mr. Jeffries," it included the cartoonist Tad Dorgan and "several other fellows."

ing. Hurry, or you won't catch them." The watchman vanished down the hall. Johnson joined his companions in their hiding place and shared a sack of doughnuts with them until fight time.

The bout itself turned out to be something of a disappointment. In earlier fights, Ruhlin's handlers had employed a special code: when they shouted "Akron," the name of their man's hometown, he was to pound away with both hands until they bellowed "Cleveland," at which he was to retreat out of harm's way. Ruhlin held his own for two rounds; in the second, one of his "Akron" rushes momentarily flummoxed the champion. But Jeffries was out to avenge an earlier draw and began to move relentlessly forward in his dreaded crouch, his jaw shielded, his left arm probing, pushing, prepared always to land the celebrated hook that needed to travel only a few inches to do its damage. Ruhlin was knocked down in the fifth. When he got up, Jeffries hurled a left into his ribs at the bell that one writer said "nearly broke him in half." He was in such agony as he fell back onto his stool that when his manager, Billy Madden, proved slow in throwing in the sponge, Ruhlin grabbed it from him and hurled it into the center of the ring himself.

As the crowd stood and cheered and Jeffries and his entourage made their way back to the dressing room, Abe Attell remembered, Johnson claimed to be unimpressed.

"I could lick that fellow myself," he said.

"Be still, you dinge."

"Well, some day I'll lick him."

That day was still a long way off. Jim Jeffries was a formidable fighter. Nat Fleischer, who saw in action every heavyweight champion from Jim Corbett to Muhammad Ali, believed to the end of his days that only Jack Johnson had been better. Born on an Ohio farm in 1875, the son of a part-time preacher, Jeffries was raised on a ranch within the Los Angeles city limits. His schooling ended at age fourteen, when he was expelled after beating his teacher bloody for threatening to strike a girl with a ruler unless she handed over a love note Jeffries had slipped to her. Big and powerful beyond his years—he had weighed fourteen pounds at birth and at the age of seventeen would stand six foot one and weigh 220—he labored in a tin mine, shoveled coal for the Santa Fe Railroad, then became a boilermaker, pounding hot rivets with a sledgehammer twelve hours a day.

He began his boxing career by knocking out the same Hank Griffin to whom Johnson had lost in his Bakersfield debut. Few fighters have ever risen to the top so fast. Between 1896 and 1899 he held Joe Choynski and Gus Ruh-lin to draws and defeated ten other contenders, including Tom Sharkey and two more black fighters, Peter Jackson and Bob Armstrong. In June of 1899, while Jack Johnson was still sleeping on the Chicago lakefront, and in only the thirteenth fight of Jeffries' career, he knocked out Bob Fitzsimmons to become champion.* Since then, he had beaten three other challengers, knocking out two and beating Tom Sharkey a second time over twenty-five rounds.

Jeffries was so big and solidly built that some opponents were unprepared for the speed with which he moved when on the attack. And they were unanimous in assessing his power. "The first time he really hit me in the body," Fitzsimmons remembered, "I thought his fist had gone right through me." Patience and apparent imperviousness to pain were also part of Jeffries' armament. In fifty-eight bruising fights he was never once knocked off his feet. Fitzsimmons, one of the hardest-hitting fighters in heavyweight history, smashed Jeffries' nose flat to his face and splintered his own hands battering Jeffries' head but did not even slow him down. Jim Corbett, who outboxed Jeffries for most of thirty-three rounds in two fights, only to be knocked senseless both times, said, "Nobody can ever hurt him, not even with an ax."

Gruff and taciturn—"as silent as General Grant," one admirer wrote—Jeffries was famously close with a dollar,† fond of fishing and hunting and drinking with his friends but uneasy in crowds and distinctly unhappy when the press got too close. He was hard to know, less loved by the boxing public than admired and respected. But everything about him, including the matted hair that covered his body and helped earn him the nickname the "California Grizzly," implied ruggedness. "No mortal ever born can win from Jeff," said the light heavyweight Kid McCoy. The cartoonist Homer Davenport was no less awed by him: "Jeff!" he said. "Why, Jeff's the fellow that hoed up the Rocky Mountains." When training, the champion rubbed his head and neck twice a day with beef brine and borax to "pickle" his skin and make it impervious to cuts. Awed admirers found plausible the tallest tales told about him: that he had drunk an entire case of whiskey in two days to cure

---

*Johnson's early hero Jim Corbett had lost his title to Fitzsimmons in 1897.

†Jeffries appeared in vaudeville after he retired. An old friend and hotel keeper named Billy Consi-dine took several friends to see him on opening night in Detroit, spending fifteen dollars for a box and twice as much for a big floral good-luck horseshoe for Jeffries' dressing room. The next night, Jeffries dropped in at his friend's saloon to say thank you—and spent a total of twenty-five cents. (" 'Cheap Skates,' The Ring Does Not Escape Them," unsourced 1907 newspaper article from the Antiquities of the Prize Ring archives.)

himself of pneumonia, that he had so damaged Tom Sharkey's ribs during their second savage bout that one protruded through the skin, that he had never hit anyone as hard as he could for fear of killing them.

Like John L. Sullivan, Jeffries professed to be willing to defend his title against anyone, provided he was white. He had fought—and beaten—at least three Negro boxers before winning his title. But the risk of losing the championship to a black man was far too great to run. "I never will fight a negro," he said; "back to the boiler works first."

Jack Johnson's loss to Hank Griffin hadn't done much for his reputation. He was still scuffling, still forced to spar with better-known boxers between bouts. In December 1901, he was at work across the bay from San Francisco at Croll's Gardens in Alameda, helping prepare a tall, yellow-haired hopeful from Brooklyn named Kid Carter for a match with the Irish-born light heavyweight George Gardner.* A week before the fight, a boatload of sportswriters and boxing insiders crossed the bay to size Carter up. Among them were the city's most important promoter, red-haired "Sunny Jim" Coffroth, and the cartoonist and sportswriter Thomas Aloysius "Tad" Dorgan. "Johnson, at that time, was a tall, happy-go-lucky young fellow who would rather tell jokes than box," Tad remembered. "The newspaper boys used to sit around and listen to him spin yarns after each workout."

This time, they witnessed something else.

After the usual gym training, Carter put on the gloves with Johnson for a four-round workout. In the third round of the affair, Johnson hit the boss a bit harder than a sparring partner is supposed to sock his paymaster and Carter got mad.

"Trying to show me up, eh?"

Carter did his best to knock Johnson stiff, but instead of showing the tall colored fellow up, he was shown up himself, and if it were not for Promoter Coffroth, who stopped the bout when Carter was groggy and all in, the big card might have been a flop. Coming home on the boat that

---

*In the boxing world, ethnicity has always been malleable. Kid Carter, whose real name was Edward Blazwick, was born in Austria to Croatian parents, but because of his yellow hair he began boxing in Brooklyn billed as "Young Olsen, the Gangling Swede." Presumably, his subsequent name change had something to do with his borough's relatively small Scandinavian fan base. He was a featherweight at first, but ended up battling heavyweights and had knockout victories over two of the best fighters of his time, Joe Walcott and Joe Choynski.

evening, the sports talked more about Johnson than they did about Carter. They were sure that a new, big man who could fight had arrived.

Johnson was fired, he recalled, but he was delighted to see his name in the papers the next morning. "That was the first time that the name of Jack Johnson appeared in print," he remembered. "I must say that it's often been there since."*

He did his best to keep it there, but nothing he accomplished during the next few months was especially newsworthy: a rematch with Hank Griffin in Oakland that ended in a draw, another draw in Chicago with his old employer Frank Childs, and five wins (four by knockout) over little-known fighters in New England, Texas, and California.

Then, in the spring, Johnson and Frank Carillo wrote a letter to Tom McCarey, matchmaker for the Century Athletic Club in Los Angeles, pleading for an opportunity to show what he could do. It couldn't have been better timed. McCarey was just thirty-one, a slender, dapper, elegantly mustached man-about-town who had spent the past year struggling to turn boxing in Los Angeles from an underground activity confined to men's smokers and the backrooms of saloons into a big-time business.† It wasn't easy. The best white fighters preferred to fight in San Francisco, which was home to three times as many potential ticket buyers as Los Angeles. McCarey featured black fighters so often—Hank Griffin headlined three of the first five boxing shows he put on in the big wooden structure on Fifth Street called Hazard's Pavilion—that his critics would eventually accuse him of running his organization as a "nigger club."‡

Jim Jeffries lived in Los Angeles, but even he could not be persuaded to defend his title there. The champion had a handsome younger brother, Jack, however, who had heavyweight dreams of his own.§ If McCarey could find

---

*This wasn't literally true. His first fight with Klondike had made the Chicago *Tribune,* and the Choynski-Johnson imbroglio in Galveston had received considerable national coverage. But this was the first newspaper story that Johnson himself had deliberately inspired, and the memory of it clearly pleased him.

†Tom McCarey was the father of the Hollywood directors Leo and Ray McCarey.

‡He may have been given his nickname, "Uncle Tom," because of his alleged closeness to so many black fighters.

§His real name was Charles, but his mother had always called him "Jack Sprat" when he was a boy, and the first name stuck.

the right kind of opponent, Jack Jeffries was willing to fight in front of a hometown crowd—and to bring his older brother with him to the Pavilion as part of his entourage.

Jack Johnson seemed to be the right kind of opponent. He was an out-of-towner and black; white Angelenos could be counted on to turn out to see their hometown favorite beat him. He would not be a walkover. On the other hand, he had been defeated by Griffin, whom Jim Jeffries had knocked out at the dawn of his career and had subsequently beaten badly in a four-round exhibition,* so it seemed safe for the Jeffries camp to assume he would not present too great a challenge to their rising star.

McCarey's friends at the Los Angeles *Times* did all they could to help him boost the gate. The paper's prefight story on May 16, 1902, was headlined WHITE MEN FIGHT BLACKS TONIGHT:†

Tonight at Hazard's Pavilion there will be held what promises to be about the best fistic tournament in the sporting history of Los Angeles. Jack Jeffries, brother and sparring partner of the world's heavyweight champion, will box twenty rounds with Jack Johnson, a big negro who has beaten several second-raters and is rated by many as a comer. . . .

If there is a favorite, the white man is it. He certainly has a host of well wishers here, and his would be a popular victory. Jeffries whipped Billy Stift and fought a creditable draw with Jack Steizner, who is regarded one of the hardest nuts in his class. Jack is a stiff puncher, pretty handy with his lower extremities, and clever on the defensive. His ability to stand work and take hard ones on the jaw and body are really unknown, although there is not a whit of doubt regarding his gameness. Jack has had the benefit of continued instruction and coaching from the champion, and this has shown in his work the past few days. He has trained faithfully at his home on the East Side, and is in the pink of physical condition. Jack will weigh close to 185 pounds.

---

*The champion had remained true to his pledge never to risk his title against a black contender. But on September 17, 1901, at Hazard's Pavilion, he had fought an exhibition with Griffin, whom he called "the colored boy with whom I had my first fight," in order to show "those who remembered that bout . . . the difference between the Jeffries of the boiler works and the one of that day." He promised to knock Griffin out in four rounds but was out of shape and, though he scored several knockdowns and won all four rounds, he couldn't quite put him away. (Fullerton, *Two Fisted Jeff*, p. 192.)

†The two preliminaries also pitted black fighters against white ones.

> Mistah Johnsing is one of those Africans who look too black to have the heart of a fighter, but he has not yet shown the white feather.

The younger Jeffries was "a fine-looking young fellow," the *Times* continued, "with a figure like a Greek god," while Johnson was "a long, lean, bullet-headed, flat-chested 'coon.' "

Johnson remained unconcerned—and he showed that he already knew how to make an entrance. In an era when fighters generally confined their ring wear to sober black, he turned up for his bout with Jack Jeffries in pink.

> The great crowd which filled every nook and cranny of the Pavilion gasped with admiration and astonishment when the pinkies came up through the ropes. It wasn't an ordinary, inoffensive kind of pink. It was one of these screaming, caterwauling, belligerent pinks.
>
> Mistah Johnsing himself was seemingly unconscious of this riot that encased his legs. Mistah Johnsing sat back in his corner half asleep and yawning like a big cat.

The jeers and curses that had greeted Johnson and his garish attire turned to cheers as Jack Jeffries approached the ring, accompanied by his brother in slacks and a gray sleeveless undershirt. "It was the champion who brought the enormous crowd of people," said the *Times*. "It was to see 'de champ' that little boys climbed out over the rafters of Hazard's Pavilion. It was because James J. Jeffries was living, breathing and, ah, perhaps smiling . . . inside those walls, that a big crowd gathered in the streets outside and listened to the yells of the favored audience." The crowd wouldn't let the main event get started until their hero had climbed twice into the ring to acknowledge their applause.

Johnson didn't mind. This was his moment. Just before the bell rang, Tom McCarey remembered, Johnson leaned down and handed him an envelope, asking him not to open it until he told him to do so.

> For four rounds Johnson toyed with Jeffries [McCarey said]. His boxing was marvelous; his footwork superb. During the fighting he would reach over [Jeffries'] shoulders in the clinches and wink at me. "Where [did] you get that slick tie, Uncle Tom?" he'd ask, and then he'd shed Jeffries' punches like so many snowflakes.

Between rounds, the anxious champion clambered up and down to sponge and towel his increasingly battered kid brother. McCarey continued:

As they left their corners for the start of the fifth, Johnson hunched his shoulders and whaled away at Jeffries. He shouted to me, "Uncle Tom, you may now read that little note I gave you this afternoon." I did and on it was written: "I'll stop Jeffries within fifty seconds after the fifth starts." And when I looked up Jeffries was being counted out.

The champion winced and looked away. A grinning Johnson lifted his victim from the canvas, turned him over to his seconds, even grabbed a towel and helped fan him back to consciousness. When Jim Jeffries stepped into the ring to help, Johnson murmured, "I can lick you, too."

The champion ignored him. But Johnson had made an impression. "Gee," Jeffries was overheard saying as he helped his still-dazed brother toward his dressing room, "that was a thump."

The *Times* headlines the next morning continued to condescend:

PINK FURIES BLAZE AWAY

———

BOLD MISTAH JOHNSINGH'S PAJAMAS CRUEL

———

TOO MUCH COLOR FOR "BROTHER JACK."

———

FEAST OF FUN AND FLOW OF TEARS AT PRIZE FIGHT—
"DE CHAMP" SAD.

But Johnson had made some big news. Tom McCarey now saw him as a draw and began to look for worthier opponents. Meanwhile, Johnson beat Klondike at Memphis for a second time, held Billy Stift to a second draw in Chicago, drew twice more with Hank Griffin, and won a decision over the turbulent "Mexican Pete" Everett in Victor, Colorado.*

According to Johnson's 1927 autobiography, Mary Austin was still with him in Colorado, but an "invisible something" had continued to gnaw at them since their first time together in the mountains, and when he returned to California this time she was not with him. "Mary was a splendid woman," Johnson remembered, "and I recall my life with her as one of the happy periods of my existence."

---

*Jim Jeffries, who chased Everett for three rounds before knocking him out in 1898, told his chronicler Hugh Fullerton that Everett was "one of the most dangerous-looking and least dangerous fighters in the world" and "the only man in my career who ever faced me that did not show gameness and courage." That same year, Everett had quit rather than face further punishment by Frank Childs in one fight, and in his next tried to strangle Joe Choynski. When he was disqualified for this sign of excessive zeal, he first went after the referee and then battled the police sent in to subdue him.

McCarey signed him to face Frank Childs at Hazard's Pavilion on October 21, 1902. Childs, whom the Los Angeles *Times* tastefully described as "a big, gobby coon," was favored 2 to 1 on fight night, but Johnson was delighted for the opportunity to get back at him for having turned him out into the rainy Chicago night three years earlier. Childs pursued him for ten rounds, trying to corner him as he once had in the gym, but, as the *Times* reported, Johnson just moved out of the way and peppered him with lefts and rights.

> Johnson was punching him and they were grinning at each other and having a little heart to heart talk back and forth.
>
> When it came to the eleventh round, Childs was spitting blood and looking out of one eye for the chance that never came. The other eye was closed for the evening behind a sadly-dropping curtain of bunged-up black.
>
> His seconds fell upon him with towels when the round ended and one could see that they were imploring him to do something, but he only shook his head sadly.

Johnson was now simply too much for the older man; Childs survived one more round, then had his cornermen throw in the towel, claiming an injury to his elbow that a subsequent medical examination failed to find. (Childs' share of the purse was given to charity.)

Eleven days later, Johnson moved further up the ladder, making his San Francisco debut against another white contender, George Gardner, who was now being brought along by Johnson's old acquaintance Jack Curley. Gardner had been scheduled to fight Joe Choynski, but the veteran's skills had now so eroded that Curley was accused of having signed him simply as a way to make his fighter look good. "Candor compels me to admit that there was something to this claim," Curley would later write, and Johnson was a last-minute substitution.

He turned out to be smoother and faster than his opponent, but he had been ill for several days beforehand and couldn't seem to follow up his advantages.* The biggest applause came in the fourteenth round, when Gardner slipped and fell and Johnson gave him a hand up. "I still hate to think of that

---

*Johnson told many tales over the years about why he was physically under par for this important fight. In one, a British Indian army veteran had introduced him to a drink he called a "Maharaja's peg"—brandy and soda in a large glass—and he had drunk glass after glass when he should have been training.

fight," Curley wrote. "It was, to put it as bluntly as I can, terrible. . . . Gardner didn't even remotely resemble the Gardner who had beaten Carter, Walcott and [Jack] Root. Johnson always schemed to let the other fellow make the fight and George simply couldn't."

Frank Carillo, working in Johnson's corner between rounds, had bet heavily on the outcome, and halfway through the fight, when it was by no means clear Johnson would win, he flashed his revolver in his fighter's face and warned that he would shoot him if he didn't make a greater effort to come out on top. He also made sure that the referee saw his weapon, in hopes he would remember it when the time came to render a decision.*

Curley continued:

> [Johnson and Gardner] tugged and hauled and loafed through round after round as the disgusted spectators, hooting and cursing, made their exit, so that we were almost alone when the referee, at the end of twenty rounds, awarded the decision to Johnson. Some conception of the nature of the fight may be gained from the fact that both Gardner and Johnson and all connected with them had to leave town the next day. I believe that if we hadn't, the vigilantes would have sprung into existence again and hanged us.

Johnson wasn't always completely successful in the ring, but he had already begun to display three qualities that would characterize his career: personal courage, masterful boxing, and a refusal to let anyone else do his thinking for him.

In two decades as contender and champion, Jack Johnson would never once enter the ring against a white opponent in front of a crowd that was anything but overwhelmingly hostile, and as the years passed and his fame and notoriety grew, the curses and racial taunts he'd been hearing since he faced Jim Scanlon back in Galveston would sometimes be supplemented by threats to murder him. Johnson would later admit he'd sometimes been affected by what he called this "pressure," but he refused ever to show his con-

---

*After the fight, the police detained Carillo briefly for carrying a concealed weapon (Los Angeles *Times*, January 2, 1903). Years later, Johnson would suggest that his relatively poor showing against Gardner had been the result of a drug administered by his manager, but Carillo's willingness to wave a pistol around in the interest of a Johnson victory makes nonsense of that version of events.

cern. The more the crowd jeered him, the more he grinned and taunted his opponent and joked with the reporters at ringside as if he hadn't a care in the world.*

Johnson saw himself as an entertainer as well as an athlete, wanted to play a part and put on a show, not merely club his opponent into submission. Bravado was part of it. But more important was his faith in himself—in his charm, his quick wit, above all in the boxing skills he had come to see as insurmountable.

They were certainly formidable. A boxer's first task, as the writer Stanley Crouch has suggested, is "to turn his opponent into an assistant in his own ass-whipping." No one ever did that better than Jack Johnson. He was an artist in the ring: smooth, laid-back, tricky. He saw no need ever to take chances—"A lot of fellows when they knock a man down rush in to finish him up," he wrote, "whereas it is just after a fellow is knocked down that he makes his most desperate fight"—and he never wanted to give any crowd the satisfaction of seeing him hurt if he could help it. He preferred to pick off his opponent's punches with his gloves or smother him with his encircling arms, wait for the other man to make a mistake, then counterpunch.

"It's not how hard you hit that other fella," he once told a friend. "It's how tired he gets tryin' to hit you." "By gradually wearing down a fighter," he explained elsewhere, "by letting him tire himself out, by hitting him with my left as he came to close quarters with me, then by clinching or executing my uppercut, I found that I lasted longer and would not carry any marks out of the ring." His style was elegant, refined, distinctive, savored by connoisseurs of the art and science of the sport but not calculated to appeal to those fans who had paid to see a brawl.

When Johnson's early hero Jim Corbett counterpunched his way to the heavyweight title, writers praised him as "scientific," "the cleverest man in

---

*Johnson's friend and fellow Texan Andrew "Rube" Foster, the pitcher-manager and impresario of black baseball, once explained that when he found himself in a tight spot on the diamond he did precisely the same thing—with very similar results: "The real test comes when you are pitching with men on bases. Do not worry. Try to appear jolly and unconcerned. I have smiled often with the bases full with two strikes and three balls on the batter. This seems to unnerve. In other instances, where the batter appears anxious to hit, waste a little time on him and when you think he realizes his position and everybody is yelling to him to hit it out, waste a few balls and try his nerve; the majority of times you will win out by drawing him into hitting a wide one." (Quoted in Geoffrey C. Ward, *Baseball: An Illustrated History*, p. 87.)

boxing." Similar skills, when displayed by Johnson, were said by some of the same writers to prove him "lazy," "shiftless"; they were evidence of the "yellow streak" that all Negroes were supposed to possess.

Johnson never saw himself as merely a defensive fighter. "I was *always* attacking," he told a reporter. "My attack was to counter the leads I forced." And many of those who faced him most often agreed. "Johnson was a fellow that used to stand flat-footed and wait for you to come in," one battered sparring partner remembered. "And when you came in, he'd rip the head off you with uppercuts, cut you all to pieces." "Johnson makes you do all the work," recalled another man he beat three times. "You have to lead and when you drive your left out he gets away from it and uses that slash of his. . . . When he slashes out with that uppercut—good night."

"It was his easy-going manner in the ring that fooled many," Tad Dorgan wrote. "He smiled and kidded in the clinches and many thought he was careless, but all the time he held his opponent safe, knew every move the other made, and was at all times the boss."

Johnson insisted on being the boss in his corner as well as in the ring. The seconds who crouched there between rounds were present mostly to offer encouragement and make their man as comfortable as possible, waving towels and sponging him with water to cool him down. When they offered tactical advice, Johnson paid little attention, as Frank Carillo had learned to his fury. Since he was doing the fighting, Johnson never saw any reason why he shouldn't do the thinking, too. *That* white managers and white sportswriters alike would find especially hard to tolerate.

Johnson had not relished his manager's having menaced him with a gun during his bout with George Gardner, but Carillo was back in his corner at Hazard's Pavilion a little over a month later. His opponent this time was Fred Russell, a big white slugger with a reputation for fouling opponents when he couldn't beat them any other way. Russell had prepared for the Johnson fight at Jim Jeffries' farm. Jack Jeffries himself was his trainer. The champion's camp was clearly looking for revenge on the black man who had derailed the younger Jeffries' career.

Johnson didn't care. He dealt effortlessly with Russell for eight rounds, grinning and talking to him as he bloodied his face and reddened his midsection. Then, a ringside reporter wrote, "while they were fighting in the middle of the ring [Johnson's] black body came out of the confused mix-up all doubled up . . . like a wounded animal. His face wore an expression of excruciating agony." Russell had hit him low. Cheered by his opponent's obvious distress, Russell "struck three [more] furious blows and each time the negro humped and raised his great black haunches as a horse lifts up behind under a kicking strap. . . . Russell had raised poor Johnson each of those three times with his knee, and then with all the force of his arm struck the darky on an unmentionable delicate part of the body."

Johnson collapsed to the canvas, rolling over and over, "holding his hands clasped frantically to his hurt." Most of the crowd had wanted to see the black fighter defeated, but not this way. Angry ticket holders rushed toward the ring. Police officers climbed up to protect Russell. A drunk made it through the ropes, intent on shaking Johnson's hand and apologizing for the white man's bad behavior, only to be hurled back into the seats at ringside.

Johnson was awarded the fight—and the lion's share of the purse—on a foul. Within hours, several Bakersfield shopkeepers got a warrant for Johnson's arrest, claiming he'd failed to pay his bills. That was very likely true; Johnson's accounts were rarely up to date. But, as the Bakersfield *Daily Californian* explained, there was almost surely more to it than that: "It is said that Jack has made himself somewhat obnoxious to various persons . . . who made the charge, claiming that he is living in the forbidden district and beating bills."

Frank Carillo promised the court that his client would pay whatever he legitimately owed. But Johnson saw no reason to move out of the white part of town. No district would ever be forbidden to him. A couple of weeks later, he fired Carillo, charging that his ex-manager had made off with his thousand-dollar purse from the Russell fight. Carillo countered that Johnson now had an inflated sense of his own importance, that "Mrs. Johnson" was putting absurd notions into his head.*

Zeke Abrams,† a well-known Los Angeles bookmaker and poolroom operator, snapped Johnson up and arranged with Tom McCarey for a February

---

*It is impossible to know which "Mrs. Johnson" this was. But Jack Johnson needed no one's help in insisting that he be treated precisely as any other "pure-blooded" American was treated.

†Everybody in Los Angeles sporting circles seemed to know Johnson's new manager, but apparently no one was sure how to spell his name: he is variously "Zick Abram," "Zeke Abraham," and "Zick Abrams" in the newspapers.

3 match at Hazard's Pavilion with Denver Ed Martin. Martin, who held the "colored heavyweight championship," outweighed Johnson by twenty pounds, stood half a head taller, and possessed many of the same defensive skills but not the same punching power.* The two men circled each other for ten rounds, probing for weaknesses and finding few, displaying what the San Francisco *Examiner* called "the magnificent footwork of Martin and the impregnable blocking ability of Johnson." There was so little action, one newspaper noted, that some in the sellout crowd of four thousand began shouting, "Fake! Fake!" Then, in the eleventh round, Johnson pinned Martin in the corner and hit him with a right hand to the side of the neck that sent him sprawling through the ropes.

> Four thousand yelling, screeching sports stood on their chairs . . . and raised a din that almost lifted the iron roof. . . . The noise . . . would have made a boiler shop in full blast sound like a tin whistle. Four thousand throats bellowed out a volume of whistles, cheers, yells and screeches so overpowering that it was impossible to hear yourself speak, and eight thousand eyes were centered on the wobbling, staggering form of Martin, rolling on the floor of the ring and trying to recover himself. He did it, but it was only gameness that saved him.

Martin made it to his feet but went down twice more before the bell rang. Somehow he managed to clear his head between rounds—and to stay away from Johnson for nine more.†

---

*The treatment Ed Martin routinely received at white hands is vivid evidence of what black boxers struggled against throughout their careers. In 1900, two years before his fight with Johnson, Martin attended a Tom Sharkey fight and afterward challenged him from ringside as white fighters then routinely did. Sharkey dismissed him out of hand: "Gentlemen . . . I have never barred nobody outside of a nigger. I will not fight no nigger. I did not get my reputation fighting niggers and I will not fight a nigger. Outside of niggers I will fight any man living."

That same year, Martin featured in an early Edison studio film called *Ruhlin Boxing with "Denver" Ed Martin* in which he was made to play the foil to the less talented white contender, Gus Ruhlin. The Edison catalog describes the film as follows: "Here we present Ruhlin in a lively bout with the dusky well known 'Denver' Ed Martin. The bout is very lively from start to finish, and is ended up with a little piece of comedy by Ruhlin presenting Martin with a live chicken, which he receives in a joyful manner." (Streible, *Fight Pictures*, p. 316.)

†Tom McCarey loved the art and science of boxing and many years later declared this the best bout he'd ever seen: "It was a marvelous exhibition. [It] involved everything that went with boxing—speed, footwork, feinting, slipping of blows, parrying, counter-punching, science, skill, courage and hitting. I have never seen anything like it before or since." (Los Angeles *Times*, January 27, 1935.)

The referee awarded Johnson the decision. He was now the "colored heavy-weight champion of the world," the loftiest height to which any black heavy-weight could then realistically aspire.* But Jack Johnson saw no reason to endorse that kind of realism. He would not be satisfied until he forced Jim Jeffries to get into the ring with him.

---

*Johnson was also making big money now, a fact not lost on Frank Carillo, still smarting from hav-ing been fired and eager for revenge. The next morning he had his former meal ticket arrested for "embezzling" his watch. The case never came to court.

CHAPTER THREE

THE SPORT

Looking back many years after Johnson left the ring, Harry B. Smith of the San Francisco *Chronicle* wrote that he believed him to have been the greatest defensive heavyweight he'd ever seen. But, he added, what he and his fellow reporters had liked most about Johnson was that from the first he had been "a good showman, who knew how to help the fight writer make news."

As a boxer, he had been inspiring headlines for a year or so before the Jack Jeffries and Denver Ed Martin fights. Other black fighters had received similar coverage in the sporting press over the years, but Johnson now began to attract the kind of celebrity coverage that had always been reserved for white sports stars. Much of it reeked of a kind of racial stereotyping that would astonish a later generation, but everything about Johnson—his highly developed sense of style inside and outside the ring; his bold self-confidence, and what few details reporters had gleaned about his domestic life—had begun to interest newspaper readers. He was becoming what he had always wanted to be: the center of attention, set apart.

It all can be said to have begun a week or so after the February 3, 1903, Martin fight when a Los Angeles *Times* reporter and his friend happened to be standing at the corner of Second and Spring Streets when they spotted Johnson sauntering toward them. He was a "towering figure clad in a waistcoat of green," the reporter wrote.

The clothes that garmented the strolling colossus spoke emphatically. In place of wrinkles in his trousers there were orderly creases, fresh from the tailor's iron. An inch from the boots these creases stopped, allowing the stylish pantaloons to break smartly and set trimly on the kid-covered instep. The boots gleamed—not with the vulgar shine of blacking, but with the lustrous gloss of $7 patent leather, polished to the point of refraction. Stetson's latest block adorned the towering one's head, and against the ebon darkness of the figure's Abyssinian neck shone the whiteness of newly-laundered linen. The high, modish collar found fashionable complement in a scarf of ermine silk, knotted with perfect neatness and adorned with a diamond pin. From the magnificent shoulders fell in faultless lines a double-breasted sack [suit], unbuttoned to show the vest of olive green. Afternoon gloves of pearl-gray suede were carried nonchalantly by a hand that bore on one of its chocolate-hued fingers a flashing gem of rather more carats than one. The other hand swung languorously a cane of nobby choice.

"Now, I wonder who is that dead-swell coon?" asked the writer's friend.

"Jack Johnson," the newspaperman answered. "Don't he cut a dash? Swellest coon on the Coast. . . ."

"Why, that doesn't look like the stripped nigger I saw at Hazard's. . . . This fellow looks like an African millionaire."

Johnson stopped to talk. His bout with Martin had earned $4,200. Johnson's share was $1,260 (a little over $25,000 in modern terms). What had he done with all that money?

Johnson was happy to explain.

Well, I've got about $200 of it left. I was "mortgaged" for about $500 by the time the fight came off—training expenses, mostly. Then, I always like the very finest clothes and I generally wear them. So I bought some new togs. And I put a few hundred in diamonds and I gave 'em to my wife. I like diamonds and so does she.* Then, if you're in my profession you've always got to have your hand in your pocket when you meet the crowd in the bar—and all that sort of thing counts way up, you know. A hundred a week won't near last a first-class boxing man.

Most first-class boxing men—and second- and third-class ones as well—belonged to the special free-spending world of the "sport." So did pimps and gamblers, vaudevillians and saloon keepers, and the women who lived in the "sporting houses" they frequented.

The word "sport" had many meanings in Jack Johnson's time. As a verb, it meant to enjoy oneself, to wager, and to display or flaunt. As a noun, it

---

*Which "wife" this was remains a mystery. According to Johnson's 1927 autobiography, Mary Austin had left him in September of 1902. He would not meet Clara Kerr, the next "wife" whose name we know, until he visited Philadelphia several weeks after this interview was published. He may well have been living with still another woman in Bakersfield.

He rarely actually handed over diamonds to the women he lived with. Instead, he hung them with baubles for their nights out together—and took them back when the women moved on.

described someone "game for any excitement, particularly excitement that involved gambling or women." All of it fit Johnson to a tee.

Sports flourished on the margins of big-city life. Their world revolved around betting and good times and the elusive promise of easy money. But because the individual appetite for those things crossed all the lines of race and class that divided Americans from one another, the sporting world blended black with white, rich with poor, in ways encountered in no other segment of society.

Attention-getting outfits had always been part of that world.* By the fall, one newspaper would report, Johnson had twenty-one "tasty" suits in his hotel-room closet, and changed clothes twice a day with the help of a maid whose only duty was to keep his clothes at all times "ready for occupancy."† When it came to fashion, the paper continued, "Beau Brummel might have been a preliminary but Jack Johnson is a main event."

Jewelry, too, was part of the picture. Sports, wrote a woman who had known a great many of them, always wore "diamond rings with matching stickpins—the genuine articles," and "tight-fitting, slick-looking suits to go with their diamonds. Sometimes they had to make do with just the suits. In that era, diamonds weren't just a girl's best friend, they were a man's, too. A sporting man's diamond spent as much time in a pawn shop as on him." Johnson became famous for the diamonds that winked from his fingers, his tie, and his cuffs; at some point early in his moneymaking years he added to his overall dazzle by having several of his front teeth capped with gold.

A sport moved always at a deliberate pace; the longer it took to move down the street, the more time bystanders had to admire him. New Orleans sports, the pianist and composer Jelly Roll Morton remembered, cultivated a "very mosey walk." Jack Johnson moseyed, too. He wouldn't be hurried outside the ring—or inside it, for that matter.

A good deal of cash was required to keep him and his female companions

---

*John L. Sullivan had been a dandy, too, boasting, "I've got the prettiest clothes you ever saw," and was given to novel combinations: a Prince Albert cutaway and teal blue vest, for example, with black-checked trousers of salmon pink. (Quoted in Isenberg, *John L. Sullivan*, p. 225.)

†He had evidently not paid for all of them himself. "Not many fights back," the Los Angeles *Times* would report that autumn (November 6, 1903), "Johnson asked [Tom] McCarey if he would stand good for some clothes. He supposed Johnson meant one suit and said yes. The tailor shop happened to be next to where the two had been talking and Johnson ducked into it. The tailor's head popped out a minute later with an inquiring expression. 'How about it, Mac?' he queried. 'All right,' says Tom. When the bill came in it was for three suits and six pairs of trousers, not to say an overcoat."

looking sharp, and as he told the *Times* reporter, he was always on the lookout for ways to make more of it.

> There ain't much money in my profession nowadays unless you get to take
> a big purse, like $10,000 or so. I've been in California a year now, and I've
> fought on the average of once every two months and I haven't been licked
> yet. But I've only made about $8,000 in that year and I've only got a cou-
> ple hundred cash to my name. I'm going to try mighty hard to cut a clean
> thousand out of my next fight . . . and if I do you bet I'll sock it away. I'm
> going to bet $500 on myself for one thing. Then I want to go home to my
> folks in Galveston, and rest up a month, and then get a go with Jeffries. I
> think I have the right to meet him next, and it can't be too soon to suit.

Jack Johnson had yet to beat a top contender, but he was already publicly
challenging Jeffries for the title.

Johnson's next bout was scheduled for February 27 in Los Angeles against
another rising black heavyweight. Sam McVey (or Mac Vea, accounts differ)
was discovered harvesting beets in Oxnard, California, by Jim Coffroth's
matchmaker, Billy Roche. McVey was only seventeen years old and had fewer
defensive skills than the other prominent black heavyweights of his day, but
he hit at least as hard as any of them; every one of his first seven fights had
ended in a knockout. To sell tickets, Johnson professed to be worried. He'd
rather fight Denver Ed Martin twice than the "Oxnard Wonder" once, he
assured a roomful of gullible reporters, because "you never know what that
nigger is going to do." In fact, he knew there was nothing the inexperienced,
one-dimensional young fighter could do to him. Johnson won every round,
outboxed and outhustled McVey, and knocked him down three times. The
fans loved it, all but the Oxnard contingent, which lost some fifteen thousand dollars betting on their man.

Johnson headed east soon after the McVey bout. In Boston, he beat Sandy
Ferguson, a local favorite whose fans called him the "Stubborn Child" for his
immovable bulk, and he made his Philadelphia debut at the Washington
Sporting Club on May 11 against a black boxer named Joe Butler. Local law
required bouts to go no longer than six rounds. Since no official decisions
were rendered if the boxers went the distance, a premium was put on fast-
paced slugging, and it was not easy for a counterpuncher like Johnson to
make an impression. He managed it nonetheless. After two rounds that were

so sedate the crowd began to boo, Butler made the fatal mistake of rushing Johnson. A "short and merry mix-up" followed, according to the *Police Gazette,* and then "one or two short jolts made Butler forget he had arms, and a right hand . . . to the jaw sent him down for the count and several seconds more than that. The crowd, a big one, stood on its feet and cheered the colored stranger from the West."*

Johnson did not return to Los Angeles that summer. Events in the city having nothing to do with him directly—but that hinted at the risks he ran every time he faced a white opponent—accounted for his absence from the scene of his first triumphs. On the night of June 9, Tom McCarey presented another card of racially mixed bouts and things went badly wrong. It was a hot night, and Hazard's Pavilion was packed with what the Los Angeles *Times* called "the worst-acting gang of rowdies that ever jammed under the big roof." The preliminaries were unusually savage. In one, the paper continued,

> an awkward clodhopper of a white man got a severe beating. . . . [His] front teeth were gone, and it gave him the effect of a continual toothless smile which was ghastly through the blood. . . . This white boy isn't much of a prize fighter but he is strongly endowed with the commercial instinct. He climbed back into the ring and told the crowd that a white man never gets a square deal against a "nigger" here.

The white crowd rained coins into the ring out of sympathy, and the main event did not improve their mood.

Johnson's old friend the white San Francisco welterweight Harry Foley was outgunned by the black Los Angeles middleweight Billy Woods, who battered him mercilessly for three rounds, knocking him down again and again with the left hand that had earned him the nickname "Mule Kick." "The white man hadn't any chance whatever," said the *Times.* "It was a sickening thing to see. He was so slender and so pale and he looked so afraid as he stood against the lithe, crouched black body, with the bullet head . . . and the little pig eyes gleaming and glittering with a hard cruel light." (Woods was in fact light-skinned.) In the fourth, the desperate Foley grabbed at Woods, who half-punched and half-threw him to the canvas. This time he

---

*There had been trouble in the dressing room before this bout when a white lightweight named Harry Burke loudly demanded that Johnson lend him his towel. Johnson refused, saying no white fighter would ever do him that favor. After the fight, while Johnson was shaking hands with well-wishers outside his dressing-room door, Burke slipped up behind him and smashed a bottle over his head. Johnson's scalp required several stitches, and Burke was jailed overnight.

stayed there, gasping, apparently unable to get enough air. The referee counted him out and then, after Foley's seconds shouted that he'd been choked, suddenly reversed himself and declared the white man the winner on a foul.

Woods erupted. He ran around the ring, cursing and waving his bloody gloves in the air, then rushed at the referee. A policeman stepped in, ready to club him if he got too close, and Woods' seconds managed to manhandle their fighter back to his corner before any more punches were thrown. But by then the crowd was out of control:

> The place became a horrible, howling pandemonium. Men screaming like enraged animals ran from their seats and stamped about the ring. . . . A black-haired young man, scarcely more than a boy, with his eyes dilated and his breath coming in pants, plunged through the throng to the ringside and you could hear his voice screaming above all the rest, "Kill the nigger! Kill the —— nigger!"

Only the police prevented the crowd from getting at Woods and his terrified cornermen.

Fearing that another such evening might spark a full-scale riot, Tom McCarey promised the next day that his Century Athletic Club would stage no more "speckled" bouts: for the foreseeable future, blacks would fight only blacks and whites only whites in Los Angeles. That meant no big money-making matches for Jack Johnson, who had already fought all the good Negro heavyweights on the West Coast, and so he made Philadelphia his unofficial headquarters off and on that summer of 1903.

At some point while living there, he remembered, he met Etta Reynolds and Clara Kerr. "Both were colored girls and during my stay . . . I enjoyed their companionship and included them in my affairs as sources of great happiness." Nothing more is known about Reynolds, who seems to have disappeared quickly from Johnson's life, but Clara Kerr was a sporting woman working out of a North Philadelphia whorehouse when Johnson met her. "A great attachment grew up between us," he remembered, and "I was able to set up a splendidly furnished suite of rooms where we lived gaily and happily." A single photograph of them together survives: Johnson is dressed in a handsomely cut suit, straw hat, and spats, and holds a pair of formal gloves in his big hand; Clara Kerr, a smile lighting up her broad face, wears an elegant dress and a vast circular hat, and clings possessively to his arm and shoulder. They would keep company for much of the next two years.

In late June, Johnson joined the entourage of his old friend and mentor Joe Walcott as he barnstormed through the West defending his welterweight title. He was with Walcott in Portland, Oregon, on June 28, when he defeated Mysterious Billy Smith,* and again in Butte, Montana, acting as chief second when Walcott knocked out Mose LaFontise on July 4. Johnson and Walcott went out drinking after the fight; after a while it seemed to them a good idea to wander out to the Montana Coursing Club in the early morning hours and release two greyhounds into the enclosure in which the rabbits were held until race time. At least one rabbit was torn apart. A watchman caught the intruders. The club owners charged both men with malicious mischief. Each was fined a dollar plus eight dollars in costs and ordered to move on.

Three weeks later, Johnson was back in Philadelphia to fight Sandy Ferguson again, this time at the Pennsylvania Art Club. "That Ferguson stayed the six rounds appeared to be solely due to Johnson's gentlemanly forbearance," said the Philadelphia *Inquirer*. "If he had turned himself loose for a continuous performance there was every reason for believing that there would have been nothing to the bout." Johnson merely displayed "the smile that wouldn't come off" when Ferguson's light jab reached him and, at the start of the fifth round, asked Ferguson, "Where would you like this?" and then slammed a short right into his body. But no real damage was done by either man. "The black seemed to content himself by suggesting to the spectators what he might do if he felt inclined that way, without actually trying to do it." That complaint—that Johnson refused to extend himself against opponents he could effortlessly outpoint—would be echoed again and again throughout his career.

By late September, Johnson was back in Bakersfield, living with Clara Kerr, getting ready for a rematch with Sam McVey at Hazard's Pavilion, and cooperating with local reporters, who continued both to sing his praises and to savage him.† He was the "black [Bob] Fitzsimmons," said the Los Angeles

---

*So named because, as Jack "Doc" Kearns, Jack Dempsey's manager, once said, "he was always doing something mysterious. Like he would step on your foot and when you looked down, he would bite you in the ear." (Quoted in Ward, *American Originals*, p. 52.)

†Rufe Thompson, Johnson's sparring partner at the Century Athletic Club training quarters on East Fourth Street, was a short, thick-bodied veteran with a colorful private life of his own. In 1901 alone he'd been stabbed in a saloon brawl and arrested on suspicion of conspiring with "Alice Adams, a pretty woman of the half world," to lift the wallet of one of her drunken clients. Thompson was a specialist at making his prospects look good, and on October 2, he helped put on a show for the press, landing a loud but painless punch to Johnson's belly and then cowering melodramatically as the supposedly enraged Johnson battered him until Tom McCarey stepped in to stop it. (Los Angeles *Times*, October 31, 1903.)

Times on October 1, "a bright piece of work. If all colored men were as sharp, financially and otherwise, as he, there would be no need of any Booker Washingtons." Three days later, the same paper published a grotesque "biography" of Johnson:

TEXAS WATERMELON PICKANINNY MAKES BIG DENTS

About twenty-five years ago one bright, sunny southern morning there was a dull, solid-sounding thud heard and felt throughout the State of Texas. A close examination of the face of the commonwealth revealed a large dent on the back bay shore of Galveston which was finally determined to be the place where the stork had severed connection with a wooly little black pickaninny. The baby set up the characteristic roar and its mammy took care of it. Mammy's name was Johnsing, and the first act was to visit the little African M.E. church and give the boy a name. After discussing the customary George Washington Johnson, Benjamin Franklin Johnson, and Napoleon Bonaparte Johnson, the parents finally compromised on Jonathan Arthur Johnson, and like the little fellow's hands in the melon patch, the name "stuck."

After eight more paragraphs of this kind of thing, the author offered instances of what he called "Johnson's philosophy," authentic quotes rendered in Uncle Remus dialect—and here turned back into the informal kind of English Johnson actually spoke.

"Having a good time is all right, but it don't buy you nothin' in the ring."

"They say too many cooks spoils the broth, but I've found the more managers I have, the merrier."

"I've learned that in the fightin' business like some other businesses, a man can make more money for awhile by jobbin' fellas, but has to move too often to make it real pleasant."

"I find a man can't have too many friends in my business, 'fore he's goin' to have more or less enemies whether he wants them or not. Friends is a good thing to have until you want money, and sometimes even then."

So many men planned to go to the rematch with McVey, the *Times* continued, that women looking to attend a society ball that evening worried they would have to dance with one another: one asked her beau if he was coming, and he replied that "the dance never was given that could keep him from the fight."

As Johnson had predicted to the Los Angeles *Herald,* there was "nothing but Johnson" to the contest on October 27. "Sam McVey was hammered last night," the *Times* reported the next morning, "until his face looked like a goat had chewed it."

> Jack Johnson pounded him wherever he pleased, but he might as well have pounded a street car fender. It lasted the limit. . . .
>
> Only the last gong saved the referee, Charley Eyton, who was completely exhausted with wrenching apart the great dripping, struggling black carcasses.
>
> Some of the credit for the victory must go to Johnson's bathrobe, which was the most amazing garment ever aired in public. It was covered with roses. He looked like a colonial wall paper design spread on a stormy night.

The Johnson-McVey rematch made more than twice as much money as any fight ever before held in Los Angeles: $7,600. Johnson took home $2,796, plus more than $600 he'd won by betting on himself. Other winners gave him gifts in gratitude. T. C. Lynch, a gambler who was then one of his two managers of record, handed him a hundred-dollar bill as a sort of tip. A big winner named Will Tufts presented him with a fine shotgun with which to shoot rabbits around Bakersfield, and two brothers who helped run the Hoffman Café gave him a bag containing $35 in nickels, which he delighted in handing out to newsboys on Spring Street.

News of how well he was doing brought his angry, envious ex-manager Frank Carillo out of the woodwork once again. A court officer had turned up in Johnson's dressing room before the bout with an order garnisheeing his earnings until he agreed to pay Carillo $297 he insisted the fighter owed him. Johnson and Zeke Abrams, who had evidently seen it all coming, had hastily drawn up and signed a dubious "contract" purporting to show, as the Los Angeles *Times* said, that "Johnson . . . has to fight wherever and whoever Zeke tells him and not get a bean out of it." Carillo couldn't seize Johnson's assets if Johnson and Abrams could show the boxer had never had any. Carillo took them to court, where, as a reporter for the *Times* took notes, Carillo's profoundly skeptical attorney cross-examined Abrams about the unusual agreement he claimed to have made with his fighter.

> "Aren't you having a pretty good thing of it managing Johnson?" he asked Abrams.

Zeke replied cheerfully, "Me? I got simply a puddin'. I'd like to have about four of him."

"What did Johnson get out of the receipts?"

"He ain't gettin' nothing."

"If he don't get any money, how does he live?"

Zeke waved his hand carelessly. "Oh, he's a witty fellow, you know: [he] lives off his wits and his white friends."

"I suppose you pay his board, don't you?"

"Me? Aw, no. He lives around his white friends."

"I understand he rides around in swell carriages."

"That's right," said Zeke sadly. "It's more 'n his manager can do. . . ."

"Isn't he kind of—kind of extravagant?"

"You bet your sweet life. He got $3,500 from me in San Francisco."

"What did he do with that?"

Zeke almost sobbed out the answer: "Bought his wife a sealskin coat."

"I just wanted to know how he spends his money."

"He shoots craps. He is the only Texas nigger I ever seen that would bet on anything. He's a high-roller."

The courtroom laughed. Johnson grinned, too—he knew when it was in his interest to play the role of naïve bruiser—and walked away a winner once again.

Johnson's second one-sided defeat of Sam McVey had made him the logical contender for Jeffries' title, at least so far as the sporting editor of the Los Angeles *Times* was concerned.

The color line gag does not go now. It is "pay or play" in the fighting business. Johnson has met all comers in his class; has defeated each and every one. Now he stands ready to box for the world's championship. He is a man who would wear that honor with decent grace if it fell on his shoulders. . . . The public, through the daily newspapers, demands a fight for the championship in behalf of Jack Johnson. Jeffries must heed the call. He wants one hard fight . . . to show he is in that exalted position by ability as well as by the kindness of nature. Johnson is the man who will give him a chance to show the best that is in him. If he can beat the negro, Jeff need never fight again.

When they meet, the world will see a battle before which the gladiatory combats of ancient Rome pale into childish insignificance. And meet they some day will. It is up to Jeffries to say when.

But Jeffries continued to say "never," and Johnson soon found himself listlessly plowing old ground. His heart was often not in it. He beat Sandy Ferguson again in a lackluster performance at Sunny Jim Coffroth's open-air Mission Street Arena at Colma, twelve miles by streetcar from San Francisco. Afterward, told that Jeffries had once again said he'd never fight a Negro, Johnson snorted, "I waive the color line myself." He fought Ferguson a third time in Philadelphia and beat Claude Brooks, who fought as Black Bill, there as well.

In San Francisco on April 22, 1904, he faced Sam McVey for a third time. "Johnson improved to some extent on his showing with Sandy Ferguson at Colma, but still left the crowd wondering what was the matter with him," wrote W. W. Naughton, the seasoned sporting editor of the San Francisco *Examiner* and one of the most influential boxing writers in the country.

> He is cleverness personified, but the fighting spirit seems to flare in flashes with him. He loafs along, grinning and at peace with himself and the other fellow while his seconds are bawling themselves red in the face in their attempts to get him to go in and mix it.
>
> He showed before last night's fight was ten minutes old that he had McVey thoroughly at his mercy, yet he played with the beet field warrior as a cat plays with a mouse.

In a moment of absolute silence, someone shouted from the gallery, "Gentlemen, cease that brutality." Johnson laughed, and so did the crowd. But as the rounds ticked by, the fans grew more and more restive. They had hoped to see some blood.

> [Johnson's] tactics were such that the gallery became frantic with chagrin and disgust. It hooted the fighters at the finish of every round from the thirteenth to the nineteenth, and, in the belief that it was to be deprived of the privilege of witnessing a knockout, it became insulting and sarcastic.
>
> . . . The crowd made up its mind that the Oxnard heavyweight hadn't one chance in a thousand and began to "boo" Johnson for hanging back.

What one newspaper called Johnson's "detachment" so enraged some fans near his corner that between rounds they began flipping lighted matches onto his back. Finally, with just thirty seconds to go in the last round, Johnson mounted a furious assault, sending McVey reeling back toward the ropes. As he bounced off them again, Johnson caught him with a perfect right hand.*

---

*After McVey woke up he asked his trainer, Spider Kelly, "Was it a draw?" "Yes," Kelly answered, "and they robbed us." (San Francisco *Examiner,* April 23, 1904.)

A gang of Oxnard fans who had again bet on their favorite and lost stormed up the aisle, shaking their fists at Johnson and shouting, "Kill that nigger!" As they stepped up into the ring, he hurled the contents of his spit bucket at them, then vaulted out the other side, fled up the aisle "at ten yards per second," he remembered, and escaped into the night. He took refuge in an Oakland sporting house until things calmed down.

The national sporting press took a more favorable view of Johnson's style than had Naughton and the San Francisco fans. Said the *Police Gazette:*

> By beating Sam McVey again the other night, Jack Johnson, the dusky hero of a score of fights, has placed himself in a position to legitimately claim a fight with Jim Jeffries. There does not appear to be a ringman in all the wide area where pugilism holds sway with sufficient inches and heft to meet the world's champion [other] than Johnson.

The Milwaukee *Free Press* agreed and called for a "piebald match for the world's greatest pugilistic prize."

But Jeffries wouldn't hear of it.

With no one else to fight in California, Johnson headed east with Clara Kerr. They spent some time in Chicago, the city Johnson would eventually make his base of operations. There he fought Frank Childs for a third time on June 2. It was an uneventful contest—"too much on the brotherly love order to suit the spectators," one newspaper said*—but Johnson still looked impressive enough to George Siler, the veteran referee and Chicago *Tribune* sports editor who had first discerned Johnson's potential in the battle royal back in Springfield, Illinois, for him to declare "the big black boy . . . the finest looking heavyweight since Jeffries came into the picture. The Boilermaker

---

*Neither man may have been trying very hard. They'd already fought each other twice, and Johnson had, in their contest in Los Angeles, settled the old score growing out of Childs' early treatment of him. With more prominent white opponents largely out of reach, there was little to be gained by either man from hurting the other—or risking being hurt *by* him. Glorified sparring matches like these helped spread suspicion of black fighters for indulging in what the sports pages called "fakery." So did contests in which black fighters like Joe Gans and Joe Walcott, wishing to remain profitable, were sometimes expected to take it easy on white opponents they would otherwise have annihilated. The underlying problem, of course, was the unwillingness of the managers of white boxers to put their prospects' futures on the line against often superior black opposition. But in an article headlined BLACK DAYS FOR BLACK FIGHTERS that appeared on April 26, 1904, just four days after Johnson's third win over Sam McVey, the Los Angeles *Times* blamed the Negro boxers themselves for their plight: "The old days of little George Dixon and old Peter Jackson will have to be recalled to set colored fighters on a popular basis once more. The game and honest negroes have passed away and a generation of Africans has come in of a different pattern."

undoubtedly knows his business when he draws the color line. He probably has Jack Johnson in mind."

That summer, Johnson and Clara Kerr set up housekeeping in Philadelphia, where he earned a little extra cash playing several games as first baseman with the all-black Philadelphia Giants, backing up his friend and fellow Texan, the pitcher Andrew "Rube" Foster.

He returned to Los Angeles in September, more determined than ever to demonstrate to Jeffries and the rest of the boxing world that he was the top heavyweight contender and to convince those skeptics who accused him of preferring to outpoint rather than outpunch his opponents that, when called upon, he could slug with the best of them. At Hazard's Pavilion on October 18, he tore into Denver Ed Martin from the opening bell, knocking him out in the second round. Martin was unconscious for so long—nearly ten minutes—that the police entered the ring, ready to arrest Johnson for assault, and most of the crowd left the building for fear they might be seized as accessories.

After Martin recovered, a relieved Johnson spoke to the remaining spectators. "I want Mr. Jeffries next," he told them. "I think I am entitled to a fight with him and it was to prove that I am right that I went in this way tonight. I am faster than ever, and bigger and stronger." The color line, he added in language calculated to anger the champion and perhaps even goad him into action, was a "time-worn, old, cowardly four flusher's standby."

The *Police Gazette* concurred: now that Johnson, who was "fast as an electric spark, and as full of power as a 90-horsepower automobile," had so spectacularly defended his "darkmeat" title, Jeffries had no right to draw the color line.

This crude, uncouth, unpopular giant [Jeffries] fought Peter Jackson, old and war-weary; Hank Griffin, a third-rater; and Bob Armstrong, who hustled him for ten rounds. This trio was black. Why will he not give Johnson a match? Here is a man who can fight, and is ready and willing to do so.

Jeffries doesn't defend his position, but rather arbitrarily determines that he has the best right to say whom he will fight.

"I do not care whether Johnson licks the Japanese army," he says. "I have repeatedly declared that, so long as I am in the fighting business, I will never make a match with a black man. The negroes may come and the negroes may go, and some of the negroes may be excellent fighting men.

Just tell the public that James J. Jeffries has made up his mind that he will never put on boxing gloves to give battle to an Ethiopian."

Later that month, Johnson tracked the champion to the San Francisco saloon owned by Jim Corbett's brother, Harry, and demanded his chance at the title. No man could say he hadn't earned it. Surrounded by amused cronies, Jeffries said again that he would never meet Johnson or any other black challenger in the ring. Then, he later claimed, he put twenty-five hundred dollars on the bar and told Johnson he'd fight him in the cellar, alone. If Johnson managed to make it back up the stairs, he could keep the money.

Johnson stalked out. "I ain't a cellar fighter," he said. Behind him, the champion and his friends laughed and jeered. "A four-flusher?" Jeffries shouted. "You're not even a three-flusher!"

In early 1905, the black songwriting and vaudeville team of Bob Cole and Rosamond Johnson began a monthlong engagement at the Orpheum Theater in San Francisco. Jack Johnson paid his way into the theater to see them several times. Afterward, he was invited back to the apartment they shared with Rosamond's older brother, James Weldon Johnson, who asked the fighter for a lesson or two in self-defense. The poet, novelist, and future civil rights leader never forgot their sparring sessions.

> Jack . . . boxed with me playfully, like a good-natured big dog warding off the earnest attacks of a small one. . . . Occasionally, he would bare his stomach to me as a mark and urge me to hit it with all my might. I found it an impossible thing to do; I always involuntarily pulled my punch. It was easy to like Jack Johnson in those days and I liked him particularly well. I was, of course, impressed by his huge but perfect form, his terrible strength and the supreme ease and grace of his every muscular movement; however, watching his face, sad until he smiled, listening to his soft Southern speech and laughter and hearing him talk so wistfully about his chance, yet to come, I found it difficult to think of him as a prize fighter.

Johnson understood he would have to create his own "chance." His only rival as top contender was "Marvelous" Marvin Hart, the "Fighting Kentuckian." Hart, a onetime plumber's apprentice, and the twenty-first of twenty-three children, was what Johnson called a "slasher," the kind of wide-swinging brawler he most enjoyed picking apart. If Hart could be eliminated, Johnson and Zeke Abrams reasoned, the pressure on the champion might finally prove too great for even Jeffries to resist.

But Hart, like Jeffries, was unwilling to fight blacks: when Joe Walcott had climbed into the ring to challenge him after he beat Kid Carter in Boston the previous year, Hart turned him away, saying, "I am a Southerner and my folks would disown me if I fought you." He had come to California planning to fight one or the other of two white contenders, Kid McCoy or Philadelphia Jack O'Brien, but when those fights fell through—leaving Hart badly in debt for training expenses—Johnson mounted an all-out campaign to shame him into the ring. Johnson's friends charged that Hart was frightened of their man. One afternoon, Johnson himself turned up at the gym where Hart was training and called him a coward to his face.

Finally, Hart gave in and signed to fight Johnson at the San Francisco Athletic Club on March 28, 1905. "I tell you right here that this coon will have to go some to beat me," he said. "Before the twentieth round is reached—probably several rounds before—there'll be a nigger prostrate on the canvas. . . . I have got the wallop that will win."

Johnson was favored 2 to 1 and so confident of victory that he said he'd accept 40 rather than 60 percent of the purse if he didn't knock Hart out within twenty rounds. But he had not counted on the influence of the fight's promoter, Alex Greggains, who Hart's camp had insisted would double as referee. Greggains was an ex-middleweight himself, suspicious of counterpunchers and dismissive of Johnson's courage. He said,

> I have notified Johnson that he must fight all the time or the fight will be called "no contest." I don't expect any difficulty on that score. [Zeke Abrams] has also told him that he must win in a hurry. "If you stay twenty rounds for a decision," Abrams told [Johnson], "we will run you out of town."*

---

*"Alec always acted as referee as well as matchmaker, manager and pretty nearly everything else," remembered DeWitt van Court, athletic director of the Los Angeles Athletic Club. "He never allowed his scrappers to do any stalling. It was at his club that the famous incident occurred when a huge negro heavyweight named Sam Pruitt boxed a tough Irish boy and Sam, after piling up a good lead in the opening round, didn't like the rough tactics of the Irishman and, taking one punch in the jaw, went down and refused to get up. Greggains counted something like this: 'One—get up Sam. Two—will you get up Sam? Three—if you don't get up you don't get a dime. Four. You better get up before I count you out. Five—get up and fight or you get no more fights.' At which point Sam looked up . . . and said, 'Mr. Greggains, you can count right on up to a hundred but you can't get me up off this floor.'" (Van Court, *Making of Champions*, p. 37.)

For ten rounds, Johnson administered a boxing lesson to the Kentuckian, smiling at Hart's awkwardness, countering only when Hart lunged at him, enjoying himself. Johnson's cornermen were frantic. "Please hit him!" Tim McGrath shouted. "You can't win unless you hit him!"

"For God's sake," shouted Zeke Abrams, "go after him!"

But Johnson continued to do as he pleased, catching or eluding punches, countering with stiff shots that bloodied Hart's face but failed to knock him off his feet, then stepping back again as if to admire his work. He seemed to slow down a bit in the eleventh, the crowd started chanting, "Hart! Hart!" and over the next nine rounds the Kentuckian landed several times to Johnson's body, forcing him to clinch. Just before the bell at the end of the twentieth and final round a flashbulb went off. Both men were momentarily blinded and started for their corners, somehow thinking the fight was over. Hart saw his mistake first, whirled, hurled himself at Johnson, and hit him with a solid right hand that made Johnson stagger at the bell.

As soon as it sounded, Greggains touched Hart's shoulder to indicate that he was the winner. His aggression—or Johnson's lack of it—had won him the fight. Jim Jeffries sat, smiling, at ringside.

Press opinion was divided as to who should have been given the decision. W. W. Naughton supported Greggains. "Though [Hart's] face was prodded into . . . puffiness by Johnson's straight left he never faltered for an instant," he wrote. "The indifference to punishment and great pluck displayed by the white man seemed to discourage the negro. Johnson beyond a doubt shows that he lacks that essential fighting qualification—grit."

But the March 29 Los Angeles *Times* headlined its story FIGHT DECISION A QUEER ONE, and George Siler later told the *Police Gazette* it was "the opinion of all fair-minded witnesses that Johnson beat Hart."

Those were Johnson's sentiments. He'd been robbed, he said. "After fighting until I reached the top I have been thrown down by an unfair ruling." Hart was a "mutt," he added, and demanded a second shot at him, promising to beat him in every round this time. Hart just laughed. "That coon has enough yellow in him to paint city hall. Johnson is a fancy boxer, but when he gets stung he is strictly a 'tin canner and staller.' I'll never fight another nigger."

That pledge would soon take on still more menacing meaning for Jack Johnson. Jim Jeffries had not put on the gloves since the previous summer, when he had demolished in two rounds a Montana miner named Jack Munroe who had dared falsely claim to have knocked the champion down in an earlier encounter. In April 1905, Jeffries got married and began making plans to settle down on a 145-acre alfalfa farm just outside the Los Angeles city limits. He had tired of his title and everything that went with it: the clamor from sportswriters for him to fight Johnson; the arduous weeks of training; above all, the crowds that followed him everywhere he went. "I've got all the money I want," he told a friend. "There's nobody to fight me. To hell with all this business—and the championship, too! What's the championship? A lot of yaps run after me to pound me on the back. They don't give a damn about me. I'm nobody. They're yelling for the champ. Well, I'm sick of it."

On May 2, he made it official: since there were no more "logical challengers" for him to fight—by which he meant white challengers, of course—he was retiring from the ring at twenty-nine.*

Nothing like this had ever happened in boxing before. No one was quite sure what to do. Then a shrewd promoter announced that Marvin Hart and former light heavyweight champion Jack Root would meet on July 3 at Reno, Nevada, in a fight to the finish for the vacant title. As an added attraction—and to add legitimacy to this unprecedented event—Root's manager, Lou Houseman, talked Jeffries into acting as referee and declaring the winner the new champion. "I will never go back into the ring," Jeffries said, "so you may do as you please. If the winner wants to call himself champion, it is all right with me."

The boxing world shared Jeffries' ambivalence about the impending contest. The heavyweight championship was the greatest prize in sports, meant to be won or lost in the ring, not handed over. Neither contender had faced a champion, or even an ex-champion, wrote W. W. Naughton,

> Hart may win or Jack Root may win, but he will still remain Marvin Hart or Jack Root. . . . There will be no "tremendous throng" at the railway depot to meet him when he reaches his home city and the windows of saloons and restaurants will not be darkened with human faces as he indulges in a sup or a bite. . . . The glories of the top notch division have departed and the championship has become largely a county fair proposition.

---

*The boxing historian Nat Fleischer offered his own blunt explanation for Jeffries' decision to quit the ring: "The period between 1905 and 1910 produced four great colored fighters: Jack Johnson, Sam Langford, Joe Jeannette and Sam McVey. There really wasn't a white man who could be classed with this dusky quartet and that was the real reason why Jim Jeffries retired." (Fleischer, *Fifty Years at Ringside*, p. 78.)

Just four thousand fans turned up in Reno for the fight. Jack Johnson was among them, and when he was introduced from the ring, he issued a challenge to the winner. Jeffries in his shirtsleeves towered over both fighters. Root weighed twenty pounds less than Hart but was winning in the twelfth round when the bigger man landed a right hand to his solar plexus that sent him to the canvas, gasping for air. Jeffries counted Root out, then held up Hart's arm as the winner and new champion.*

Afterward, Hart said he would gladly meet "any man in the world in a fair fight," and then added the all too familiar caveat, "This challenge does not apply to colored people."

Jack Johnson was still out in the cold. Asked Omaha sportswriter Sandy Griswold,

> What right has Hart to throw Jack Johnson in the discard on account of his ebony complexion . . . ? Both Jeffries and Hart have fought niggers, as they style their opponents, and why not fight them again? Collectively, the colored race was remote from Mr. Hart's thoughts [when he barred blacks]. Mr. Hart knows, as well as he knows that he is alive, that Jack Johnson was entitled to that fight . . . and he also knows, I'll bet my boots, that Mr. Johnson can lick him every day in the week, not even barring Sundays.

Johnson had already moved east again, convinced after the Hart decision that he couldn't get a fair shake on the West Coast. He would face nine opponents over the next three months and beat them all. None of the fights were difficult, though one was disappointing—he failed to knock out Jack Munroe, Jeffries' last and least able opponent as champion—and two were bizarre.

On July 18 he met Sandy Ferguson for a fifth time at the Pythian Skating Rink in Chelsea, Massachusetts. It was a hot, humid evening. Every seat was sold, and the aisles were choked with standees, so many and so closely packed that one frightened old man offered fifty dollars to anyone who could get him safely back out onto the street. Chelsea was Ferguson's adopted hometown. Nearly everyone present was Irish and howling for Johnson's blood. He paid no attention, picking off most of the punches Ferguson threw from

---

*"For all the authority he had," a friend remembered, "Jeff might as well have proclaimed Marvin King of Rumania." Later, when Jeffries was considering a ring comeback, he would claim he'd never meant to confer the title on Hart. "If I had the power to choose a champion I'd give it to somebody in my own family," he said. "No man has the right to turn the championships over to any other man. They must be fought for." (Inglis, *Champions Off Guard*, p. 230; van Court, *Making of Champions*, p. 98.)

a distance and smothering him whenever he got close, just as he had four times before. But this time Ferguson was evidently so embarrassed by his poor performance in front of his fans that in the seventh round he kneed Johnson in the groin—not once but three times. Johnson collapsed in pain. Ferguson's fans roared their approval. Sure he'd won, the Irishman vaulted over the ropes and made his way to his dressing room. There he learned that the referee had awarded Johnson the fight on a foul. Ferguson and his entourage started throwing things. Patrons pushing their way out met angry Ferguson fans trying to get back in so that they could attack the referee. Fights broke out in the lobby.

Johnson slipped out the back door. Just six days later, back at the National Athletic Club in Philadelphia, he took on Joe Grim, a local 150-pound favorite and one of the oddest figures in boxing history. He was an Italian immigrant—his real name was Saverio Giannone—with no boxing skills at all. He took part in at least seventy-five contests, almost all of them in his hometown, and never recorded a single victory. He was known to his legion of Italian-American followers as the "Iron Man," and his peculiar appeal was based on an astonishing ability to absorb punishment and remain conscious no matter how hard he was hit. "I am Joe Grim and I fear no man," he told his fans before and after each bout, and big Philadelphia crowds paid to see some of the best fighters of his time, including Joe Gans, Bob Fitzsimmons, Joe Walcott, and Philadelphia Jack O'Brien, try—and fail—to put him out.

Jack Johnson's turn came on July 24, and he bet heavily that he would suc-ceed where all the others had failed. The club was packed, and some ten thou-sand mostly Italian fans waited anxiously outside to see if their hero could remain vertical for six rounds with the celebrated black out-of-towner. "It was a wonderful fight," the *Police Gazette* reported with unaccustomed irony,

> the only one of its kind in the history of pugilism in America or anywhere
> else. . . . If Grim landed a blow of any sort on the colored man at any stage
> of the game it was not recorded, while the big fellow beat the game little
> Italian into a pulp soon after the opening gong sounded. After every trip
> to the floor the Italian would come up smiling only to walk into another
> haymaker that would stretch him lengthwise. He was cheered to the echo
> by the ringsiders.

"He ain't human," Johnson was heard to mutter between rounds. By one count, Johnson knocked Grim down twice in the first, once in the fourth, five times in the fifth, and nine in the sixth—a total of seventeen knockdowns. Grim was unconscious for five minutes after the last one—but since it came just six seconds before the final bell, it didn't count. As soon as he was able to move again under his own power, he dragged himself up on the ropes and shouted once again, "My name is Joe Grim. I fear no man."

After the fight with Grim, Johnson and Clara Kerr returned to Los Angeles, where he issued challenges to two young white fighters, Jack "Twin" Sullivan and the onetime amateur champion of the Golden State, big Al Kaufmann. But neither was interested in fighting him. His money began to run out.

At some point late that summer, an old friend and fellow sport turned up, a racehorse trainer named William Bryant, whom Johnson had not seen since they'd been stable boys together in Boston. "I hailed him as an old and intimate friend," Johnson remembered, "and invited him to share our home with us. For a time, the arrangement was a mutually satisfactory one." But Bryant and Clara Kerr were soon drawn together. "Unknown to me an attachment had developed between the two," Johnson remembered, and late one October evening he returned home to find Bryant and Kerr gone. All the jewelry and fine clothes he didn't happen to be wearing were gone, too.

"I was dumbfounded," Johnson recalled in the heavily ghosted 1927 autobiography that is the source for most of what little we know about Johnson's personal life during his early years.

> For the second time, a woman whom I greatly loved had fled from me, but this time the cause, instead of a trifling domestic dispute, was another man. The shock unnerved me. For the first time in my life my faith in friends and humanity had been shaken to the foundation. . . . I set about making inquiries and learned in which direction the couple had fled.

Johnson followed, and when he located his quarry, he called in the police. On October 16, a brief wire-service item appeared in newspapers all over the country:

> A colored beauty, Miss Clara Kerr, has been arrested at Tucson, Ariz., charged with stealing Big Jack Johnson's bankroll, diamond rings and a diamond locket. The robbery was committed at Los Angeles, where she will have to answer the charges.

Somehow, the two were reconciled. Johnson had been humiliated—sports left their women, their women did not leave them—and may not have wanted to return to face his friends. In any case, instead of returning to California, he and Kerr relocated to Chicago, where Johnson hoped they could start over.

But big, moneymaking fights continued to elude him. Known white boxers ignored his challenges while his repeated bouts with the same black rivals—he fought the skilled Joe Jeannette of New Jersey six times between May of 1905 and September of 1906—drew small crowds and yielded even smaller purses. He pursued a frightened but fleet-footed Young Peter Jackson around a Baltimore ring for twelve rounds—stopping the chase in the seventh just long enough to tell the crowd, "I'd have liked to show you a fight, but I can't catch Jackson."*

"Our money was low and the boxing business was at a point which offered me few engagements," Johnson remembered. "Consequently we were compelled to live modestly and to guard our savings which were going down rapidly." They evidently went down so rapidly that Clara decided to leave Johnson again, taking with her what little cash he happened to have on hand.

Johnson was devastated, and this time he had no idea where she had gone. He began to drink heavily, scoured Chicago, then took a train to Pittsburgh, believing she might have gone there, but found no trace. He borrowed heavily from friends, gambled away most of their money, and then decided to try New York. He was about to board the train "penniless," he recalled, when Frank Sutton, a black hotel keeper and onetime sparring partner who would remain an important friend throughout Johnson's career, insisted he borrow at least a dollar. "Of this dollar," Johnson recalled, "I gave the train porter fifty cents; I bought two cigars with another quarter and the remaining quarter I tossed to a newsboy when I arrived in New York." That was how a sport was supposed to behave, even in extremis.

He found a room in a cheap boardinghouse, searched the streets for Clara for a time, then finally "gave up the quest" and cast around for bouts to keep himself going. In late January, when he took a pickup fight in Topeka, Kansas, against a white novice from Philadelphia named Bob Kerns, he didn't even bother to dress for his entrance, climbing into the ring wearing a black sweater and shabby trousers over his tights instead of one of his now celebrated robes. He seemed almost to doze while waiting on his stool for the

---

*According to the Baltimore *Sun* (December 2, 1905), Jackson tried as hard as he could to get himself fouled in this fight, even falling down twice without being hit in one round in the hope Johnson would get so frustrated he would try to punch him while he was on the canvas. Johnson didn't fall for it.

bell to ring, but when it did, he knocked Kerns unconscious in less than a minute.*

A little over three weeks later, on February 23, 1906, the title for which Johnson had long since earned the right to fight would change hands again. W. W. Naughton conceded that Marvin Hart had a legitimate claim to the championship after beating Jack Root, but added that he remained "on probation" with the public nonetheless: "He will have to show us that he can whip all creation. He has not acquired the title by licking somebody who licked everybody else and he isn't in a position to talk of hard-earned laurels or tell challengers to get a reputation. He must skirmish around and get one himself."

Hart's first title skirmish had done little to enhance his reputation: at Butte, Montana, the previous January 16, a completely unknown sometime miner named Pat Callahan knocked him down in the first round before Hart could put him out in the second. The clamor for a real test of Hart's skills grew, but he turned down bids for bouts with former champion Bob Fitzsimmons, Philadelphia Jack O'Brien, and Fireman Jim Flynn in favor of a fight arranged by Tom McCarey at the Pacific Athletic Club in Los Angeles against Noah Brusso, a squat light heavyweight from Canada who fought under the Scottish-sounding name of Tommy Burns.

Hart was sure he could beat Burns. He was taller and heavier and had a longer reach than the challenger, who had lost to all three of the name fighters he'd faced: Mike Schreck, Philadelphia Jack O'Brien, and Jack "Twin" Sullivan. Most of the boxing world agreed. If Hart *didn't* knock Burns out early, George Siler warned, "his championship stock will fall below par."

Neither the new champion nor his challenger was notably popular with the boxing public, and Jack Curley, now handling Hart's business affairs, thought he might boost receipts if he could talk Jim Jeffries into being on hand again as referee. With Jeffries' friend and former manager Billy Delaney, Curley called on the ex-champion at his farm. They were received warmly enough and seated themselves on the front porch while Mrs. Jeffries brought them glasses of cold milk.

The visitors admired the view, and Jeffries mused that he wished he had the money to buy the fields next door so he could plant more alfalfa.

---

*A unique feature of the night's card was a four-round preliminary, fought by two young men with broadswords. The Topeka *Daily Capital* (January 27, 1906) called it "a very pretty affair," but it didn't catch on.

Delaney said he knew a way for him to earn that kind of money fast.

"How?"

"By coming out of retirement and fighting Jack Johnson."

At that, Curley recalled, "Jeffries got up from his chair, walked into the house without a word or a look for either of us, and slammed the door behind him."

In the end, Jeffries did agree to officiate, and his great bulk made Tommy Burns seem even smaller than he was when he entered the ring—he stood just five foot seven and weighed twenty pounds less than Hart. But, like Jack Johnson, Burns was a master of ring psychology and what sportwriters then called "mouth-fighting," verbal abuse and relentless taunting meant to anger and frustrate the opposition. Hart may have been bigger and stronger and had a more impressive record—thirty-six fights, eighteen won by knockout—but he also had a quick temper and no sense of humor whatsoever. To upset him, Burns entered the ring with what he himself remembered as a "ridiculous" amount of tape on his hands and settled onto his stool.

Hart demanded they be retaped.

"Why Mr. Hart," Burns said, peering up at the agitated titleholder. "I didn't think that a big champion like you would mind a little man like me wearing a little tape."

Hart, anger rising, continued to insist. Burns continued to refuse. The argument went back and forth until Hart shouted that he would not fight unless Burns gave in. At that, Burns jumped up, shoved Hart, and shouted back, "Get out of my corner, you cheese champion!"

Hart called Burns "a little rat" and took a swing at him. Jim Jeffries had to interpose himself until the bell rang.

The furious champion spent eighteen of the next twenty rounds mindlessly rushing at Burns, who sidestepped, hit him as he went by, and kept up what Burns remembered as "a well-rehearsed line of chatter" calculated to keep Hart angry and out of control. When it was over, Burns was the easy winner. With characteristic grace, Marvin Hart claimed he'd been cheated. Burns was "a hugger and a wrestler," not a boxer. Hart had been the victim of a conspiracy. Everybody had been in on it: Burns, Jeffries, even his own manager, Tommy Ryan.

Burns didn't bother to respond. Instead, he declared:

I will defend my title as heavyweight champion of the world against all comers, none barred. By this I mean black, Mexican, Indian or any other nationality without regard to color, size or nativity. I propose to be the champion of the world, not the white or the Canadian or the American or any other limited degree of champion.

Jack Johnson's prospects for a title fight seemed to improve with Burns' pledge to defend his title against all comers regardless of color, but only briefly. Burns eventually added an important caveat: he would fight Jack Johnson, he said, but before he did he planned to "give the white boys a chance."

First he demolished two second-raters on one night in San Diego. Then he knocked out Fireman Jim Flynn in the fifteenth round in Los Angeles. But in some quarters his claim to the title still remained suspect, and Philadelphia Jack O'Brien maintained through a convoluted line of reasoning that he, not Burns, was the *real* heavyweight champion because he had once beaten Burns and had won his *light* heavyweight title from Bob Fitzsimmons—who had once been heavyweight champion himself. Tom McCarey arranged for Burns to fight O'Brien in Los Angeles, with Jim Jeffries again acting as referee. It was a hard-fought, twenty-round battle, and when it was over, Jeffries declared it a draw. The question of legitimacy still hadn't been settled, and many fans remained hopeful Jeffries himself might yet return to the ring.

Meanwhile, Jack Johnson was still unable to find willing white opponents. On April 26, back at the Pythian Skating Rink in Chelsea, Massachusetts, where his victory by disqualification over Sandy Ferguson had nearly caused a riot the previous summer, Johnson found himself matched with another local favorite, a young black fighter from Canada who had made Boston his home. Sam Langford was born in Nova Scotia in 1883, came to America to escape his father's beatings at the age of twelve, and was panhandling in Boston in 1902 when Joe Woodman, a pharmacist and sometime promoter, hired him to sweep out his gym and act as a sparring partner for the fighters who came in to train. Langford soon outfought most of them. He stood just five foot seven and weighed no more than 130 pounds at the beginning of his career, but he had a massive torso, unusually long arms, and the knockout power of a far bigger boxer in both hands.*

By the time Langford faced Johnson, he had already had at least fifty-eight fights, beaten the great Joe Gans, and held his own with Jack Blackburn, Joe

---

*Ed "Gunboat" Smith, who barely survived a twelve-round fight with Langford in 1913, remembered that he was "never no good after it. Every time that Langford hit me, by God, he'd break the shoelaces." (Heller, *In This Corner*, p. 39.)

Jeannette, and Joe Walcott. But he had been fighting for only three years and was five years younger than Johnson and more than thirty pounds lighter. The fifteen-round fight was predictably one-sided. "I gave Langford an awful lacing," Johnson remembered.

> In the 6th round I put Sam to the mat for the count twice, the 1st time with a right to the heart, the 2nd with a right uppercut to the chin. Both times Langford struggled to his feet and stalled to the end of the round. After the 6th round it ceased to be a contest. Langford merely stalled it out, clinching & holding on at every opportunity. I did all the forcing. One great feature of that fight was Langford's ability to take punishment. It was a wonder that he could stand the beating which I gave him. I didn't try very hard for I did not have to as was very evident to the spectators. I left the ring without a mark while Langford's face looked as if he had been through a war.

Those at ringside differed as to the details. Some remembered Langford's being knocked down in the eighth, as well as the second and sixth. Johnson's manager for the fight, a Boston promoter named Alec A. McLean, claimed his man had been the victim of a bad count; Langford had actually been on the canvas for sixteen seconds. Others suggested that the bout had gone the distance only because Johnson had been asked to carry the local hero.

Sam Langford would pursue Johnson for the next decade, loudly demanding a rematch, and Joe Woodman spread the rumor that his fighter had been jobbed in Chelsea, that he had actually knocked the far bigger Johnson down for a count of nine in the second round. No contemporary witness reported any such knockdown, and Langford himself would later admit he'd been thoroughly beaten. "The first time we met in Chelsea, Jack whipped me," he said, "and I'm the little boy who should know who got the licking."

But, wrote the boxing historian Nat Fleischer, "Woodman's startling fiction tale took a grip on the public fancy, and the majority of sports writers, without searching out the facts, backed up the Woodman dope. This legend gained strength until it came to be adopted as gospel and its constant circulation annoyed Jack Johnson more than anything else ever printed about his career."*

---

*If this was true, Johnson himself was partly to blame. In his French autobiography, *Mes Combats* (p. 22), he seems to confirm Woodman's story: "I found him [Langford] one of the toughest adversaries I ever met in the ring. I weighed 190 pounds and Langford only 138. In the second round the little negro hit me on the jaw with a terrible right hand and I fell as if up-ended by a cannon ball. In all my

To compound the confusion, Johnson and Langford fought again on the stage of the Hub Theater in Boston just two days later in what was supposed to be a three-round exhibition to raise funds for the victims of the earthquake that had recently done to San Francisco something like what the great hurricane had done to Johnson's hometown six years earlier. On August 22, 1924, Langford gave a reporter for the Halifax *Herald* an especially vivid account of this second contest:

Just before the bout began, they halted things while somebody gave Jack a watch and chain and a little speech which said the present was from admiring friends. I knew it wasn't. Jack bought that watch and chain himself, according to what I heard, and he was just sort of showing off what a popular fellow he was. . . .

That made me mad. I was mad, too, because Jack had given out a statement that day saying he was just taking it easy with me in Chelsea. So when they called "time" for the first round I ran into Johnson and clinched and said, "This ain't going to be an exhibition tonight, it's going to be a fight. Let's go."

I broke loose from the clinch and then tore into Johnson, both fists flying. Jack tried to hold me back but I rushed him all around the ring, punching like a wild man. And then Jack, knowing that I meant what I said, started to fight.

There wasn't any ring on the stage of the theater. It was just a stage, no ropes, nothing. We battled from one side to the other, back to the curtains, forward to the footlights, fighting like two tigers. I was out to knock Johnson cold, if I could, and he was trying to finish me. We punched, wrestled, mauled, hauled and did everything but knock down the building.

Before the first round was over we had upset the water buckets and our chairs, knocked over the referee and timekeeper, broken about ten electric bulbs in the footlights and twice, in the cyclonic stuff we were doing, almost fell into the orchestra pit.

Somewhere in the middle of the second round I drove one home to John-

---

pugilistic career, not before and not afterwards have I received a blow that struck me with such force. It was all I could do just to get back on my feet just as the referee was about to count 'Ten!' I made it, but I assure you that I felt the effects of that punch for the rest of the fight. (I recovered, but I would have had to take my hat off to him if I hadn't had so much science at my command.) In the fifteenth round I was declared the winner on points."

son's face. I jumped at him to land a follow-up. He backed up and as he did I just threw myself at him. He grabbed me going [back], the two of us bumped into the scenery and a second later the scenery tumbled down on us. Some of it landed square on top of our heads. The canvas split and the scenery lay on our shoulders, with our heads sticking out. We shoved it down over our bodies, jumped away as it landed on the floor, and went on fighting. . . .

The house was in an uproar. It continued so all through the third round. . . . Along about the middle of the round Johnson got me in a clinch and tried to lift me off my feet. I wasn't sure whether he wanted to throw me out among the customers or not. But I thought maybe the customers liked him better and I caught him and tried to drop him out with the spectators. But Jack was too strong. So we went ahead slugging, wrestling, mauling, butting until somebody called time. And that ended what started as an exhibition and turned into the wildest nine minutes of fighting I ever was mixed up in during 23 years of war.

The Boston *Post*'s account written that evening was a good deal more terse: Langford had looked much the worse for wear when he entered the ring, it said, and Johnson had been especially careful not to reopen a cut above his opponent's eye.

Whatever the truth about his two contests with Sam Langford, Jack Johnson, who was happy enough to fight other black boxers over and over again, was never willing to climb back into the ring with him.

Johnson had a new manager now, Sam Fitzpatrick, a big, shambling ex-fighter from Australia who had come to California in the 1880s and quickly moved to the business side of boxing, training Peter Jackson and Kid McCoy and shepherding George "Kid" Lavigne to the middleweight championship.* Fitz-

---

*Boxing lore resists close examination. As a boxer, Sam Fitzpatrick is best remembered for having taken part in a bout in which he and his opponent landed simultaneous knockout blows. The problem is, there are two versions of the same tale. In one, Fitzpatrick and a boxer named Abe Aitken felled each other during a fight in Australia. Since neither man so much as stirred before the count of ten, the referee wasn't sure what to do. He finally awarded the fight to Aitken because he woke up first.

The other story has Fitzpatrick facing Patsy Mehegan at the California Athletic Club in San Francisco. Paddy Carroll, the Chicago promoter who would later bring Jack Johnson to Chicago to fight Klondike, was the referee. Each man threw a right hand. Both landed at the same instant. Both men collapsed to the canvas. Carroll counted them out. Each was carried helpless to his stool. Club officials told Carroll to wait until both were conscious, then send them at each other again. Carroll, himself a former boxer, refused to require the woozy fighters to punish each other further. They divided the purse. (Buffalo *Express*, December 30, 1908; Washington *Post*, November 28, 1915.)

patrick's considerable bulk, soft speech, and personal habits—he could most often be found at the bar of the elegant Hoffmann House on Broadway in Manhattan—disguised a shrewd managerial mind. When a rumor reached him that Jeffries might be persuaded to return to the ring for just one more fight, he announced that Johnson would gladly meet any or all of the leading white heavyweights—Burns, Philadelphia Jack O'Brien, Sam Berger, or Al Kaufmann—on a winner-takes-all basis, provided that Jeffries would agree to fight him once he'd knocked them all out of contention. The *Police Gazette* hailed Johnson for the courage implicit in this offer and expressed bewilderment as to "why Jeffries has taken so much trouble to dodge a meeting with Johnson. . . . [He] has a fine record, but it is not a terrifying one by any means. . . . Like [Joe] Gans, he has probably been compelled to hide his real punching power a bit in order to get contests." Al Kaufmann's manager turned Johnson down flat. White heavyweights fled so fast from his fighter, Fitzpatrick said, that "there isn't even wind resistance." Representatives of the other contenders did not even bother to respond. They were, said one sportswriter, "the yellowest pack of pigeon-livered mutts that ever disgraced the pages of pugilistic history."

After eleven years in the fight game, Johnson seemed perilously close to being back where he'd started, taking part in poorly attended bouts with familiar black rivals that amounted to little more than exhibitions, and facing second- and third-raters, both black and white, for small purses in unimportant towns. Something had to change. Johnson had long wanted to try his luck overseas, where black fighters were still a rarity and good white fighters might be less likely to duck him. Fitzpatrick finally agreed and consulted a sometime associate, Alec McLean—a onetime bicycle racer who had been Sandy Ferguson's manager, had managed Johnson in his battle with Sam Langford, and was now without a meal ticket. The two men were sure Johnson could "easily beat any fighter on the other side of the water," McLean recalled, and decided to use their connections to get him a couple of fights in Australia. They were sure he could beat Bill Quinn, the Australian heavyweight champion, and perhaps leverage possession of that title into a match with Burns. McLean wrote to the editor of the Australian sporting paper *The Referee,* who helped arrange for the National Sporting Club of Sydney to provide two round-trip boat tickets from San Francisco to Sydney.

On the day after Christmas 1907, Johnson and McLean boarded the American steamer *Sonoma* at San Francisco. They carried with them a precious canister of film showing the recent bout between Tommy Burns and Philadelphia Jack O'Brien in Los Angeles. Fight films were still a novelty overseas, and McLean planned to help finance the trip by exhibiting them.

The sporting editor of the Milwaukee *Free Press* bade Johnson a patronizing bon voyage:

Po' Artemis Johnsing, who was handed a lemon when nature clothed him in his swarthy complexion, has folded up his coat and stolen away to the antipodes. . . . Johnson has tried every means within reason to coax some of the American heavies into the corral, but has always been followed by the same jinx. His color is his misfortune. Johnson now realizes that he is black without piping himself in the looking glass. But the world is rather a large concern, and the stick of black chalk knows how to take advantage of transportation facilities. He will go across and see how they look upon dark meat over in one of King Edward's lands.

CHAPTER FOUR

THE MAN THEY
ALL DODGE

BOXING WAS BIG IN AUSTRALIA at the turn of the twentieth century, and Jack Johnson's arrival in Sydney on January 24, 1907, was big news. When the *Sonoma* entered the harbor, she was met by a flotilla of launches, their decks crowded with sports eager for a glimpse of the man the Sydney *Truth* called "the cleverest exponent of the [boxing] game that America has ever produced." Negroes were a great rarity in Australia—the Immigration Restriction Act of 1901 had effectively barred nonwhites from settling there—and Australian newspaper coverage of Johnson was a blend of patronization and fascination. The *Truth* headlined its January 30 story JAUNTY JACK JOHNSON DE NEW COON COMES TO TOWN. "Johnson is a big coon . . . 28 years of age," it said; "he has a genial face, somewhat babyish looking and of the type of the little coons who may be seen devouring watermelons in a well-known American picture." But when the promoter James Brennan held a reception in Johnson's honor at the National Amphitheater, the local fight crowd serenaded him with "For He's a Jolly Good Fellow"; the editor of the *Sportsman* assured him that he would not have to face any color line in Australia, since "it wasn't an Australian's or a Britisher's game to run away from a rival"; and Johnson responded with a well-received toast of his own: "He said he liked the trip, he liked the city better, but he liked the people who had welcomed him so enthusiastically best (Cheers)."

Brennan had already signed Johnson for a fight on February 19 with Australia's "coloured champion" Peter Felix, for the "coloured heavyweight championship of the world." Once Felix had been dealt with, Johnson hoped to beat Bill Squires—known to his Australian admirers as "Boshter Bill" because of his bashing straight-ahead style—and then use that victory to lure Jim Jeffries out of retirement for one more big payday. "Jeffries has stated that he will not fight a colored man," McLean told the press, "but if Johnson beats Squires he will have a right to make demands." Squires, however, had other ideas: he was planning to sail to America to see if *he* could get Jeffries to return to the ring and face *him*. McLean and Squires' manager, Jack Wren, began weeks of negotiation, some of it behind the scenes, much of it in blustery newspaper exchanges, to see if a bout could be arranged before Squires set sail. But the Australian champion was not eager to risk his American venture in a fight with Johnson, and in the end nothing would come of it.*

Meanwhile, Johnson and McLean set up headquarters several miles south of the city at the Sir Joseph Banks Hotel on the beach at Botany Bay. Surrounded by formal gardens and named for the naturalist aboard the first British vessel to anchor off Australia, it had once been the most fashionable resort in the region and the most popular sporting ground in the country. Its two-story restaurant could serve a thousand guests; its ballroom accommodated five hundred whirling couples and a full-size orchestra; tens of thousands turned out on weekends to picnic, see the caged tiger, ride the miniature railroad, or watch the footraces on four cinder tracks. But accusations of rigging eventually undercut the races, Sydney's citizens found other things to do closer to home, and by the time Johnson and McLean moved in, bringing with them Stephen Hyland, an American trainer who'd been a messmate aboard the *Sonoma* when they hired him, the old Italianate hotel had seen better days.

Its owner, a man named Marshall, saw a chance to pull in new crowds by putting up a big wooden pavilion so that every afternoon as many as a thousand people could watch Johnson go through his training routines while McLean stood to the side with a stopwatch, waiting for the moment to say, "Now, Jack. I think you've done enough."

"Jack's 'enough' would be more than a feast to most of his calling," the editor of *The Referee* wrote after traveling south of town to see him.

He is undoubtedly a great glutton for work. Johnson side-steps, springs round in a 10- or 12-foot circle, and changes front with the rapidity of a lightning flash in pursuit or evasion of an imaginary foe. This is "shadow-

---

*"Like the 'villain in the play,' " Johnson told a reporter, "I was 'foiled again.' . . . There I was having gone half round the world, just dead keen for a fight, while the white fellows were beating it faster than ever to keep out of my way." Wren and McLean both quickly understood that there would be no contest between their fighters but that did not prevent McLean from advertising, during a brief theatrical appearance in Melbourne, that "Squires will meet Johnson face to face on Friday night." The theater sold out, its patrons eager to see the much-anticipated fight. Instead, Johnson and Squires merely strode onstage in evening clothes and solemnly shook hands. A man in the balcony shouted, "Aren't they going to fight?" "Later," said McLean as all three men hurried off, grabbed the receipts, and fled through the stage door as the disappointed crowd howled its disapproval.

sparring"—an exercise Australian boxers (latter-day men, I mean) brought from America.

That same afternoon, the editor reported, Larry Foley, the elderly Sydney publican and onetime fighter who had trained Peter Jackson and many other Australian boxers, put on the gloves with Johnson for a little gentlemanly sparring. Foley had himself been a student of Jem Mace, the British bare-knuckle champion, and he worked from the straight-up stance familiar from nineteenth-century lithographs. To men of the Mace school, Johnson's style seemed like "heresy." *The Referee* continued:

> The American stands with the weight mostly on the front foot, and has only the toes of the back—the right—foot on the boards. Mace school boxers have the weight of the body on the back foot, leaving the front free to be used for stepping in or coming away. Johnson rarely steps in with a blow. How could it be otherwise, standing as he does; and he frequently stretches his legs wide apart, and gets very low down in consequence. The Mace school teaches that a man should always make the most of his height, and undoubtedly that is right. There is no height in Johnson's favor when he spreads himself out as stated, and looking at it from another point of view had he lived a decade or two back, the black could never have recovered . . . before some of the high class men of the time would have been in on top of him.*
>
> But all this notwithstanding, Johnson is a great fighter and a fine fellow, and one has only to see him going to understand why Jim Jeffries sheltered behind that cowardly protection, the color line, and why the cleverest boxer had to come all the way to Australia.†

. . .

---

*To this day, experts marvel at Johnson's ability to avoid getting hit while restricting his movements largely to moving forward and backward. In a recent interview, one of the shrewdest modern scholars of the sweet science, former light heavyweight champion José Torres, argued that Muhammad Ali provided the only parallel: "Jack Johnson . . . used to make guys miss by pulling back, and that's a no-no in boxing because pulling back is like being on the train track and . . . the train's coming. Do you want to be hit by a train? What do you do? You don't move back, because the train eventually is going to hit you. You move to one side or you move to the other. But Johnson and Muhammad Ali did not move to this side or [that] side, they went back, but the train never caught up with them." (Ken Burns' film *Unforgivable Blackness: The Rise and Fall of Jack Johnson*, Episode One.)

†Three years later, an Australian named Harry Brandon, who had attended this sparring match, offered a different version of how it came about. Johnson, he said, had admired a pregnant white bulldog owned by a Sydney sport named Jim Barron and asked if he could have one of her puppies. Barron

Wherever he went, Jack Johnson could be trusted to find excitement, and at some point early in his Australian stay he and several companions spent an evening drinking at the Grand Pacific Hotel, a boisterous pub at Watson's Bay on South Head, across Sydney Harbor from the city. Afterward, the proprietor, a Mrs. Ashworth, discovered that a gold pin was missing. The next evening, her husband and Alma Adelaide Lillian Toy, his twenty-year-old stepdaughter from his wife's first marriage, drove in a carriage to the Queen Theater in downtown Sydney, where Johnson was sparring onstage, to see if he could help them get it back. He said he had no time to talk then, but if they came to see him at his hotel, he'd see what he could do. Miss Toy and her mother turned up there the following afternoon. The pin was produced—someone in Johnson's retinue had evidently lifted it—and he invited the two women to watch him train. Afterward, he asked if he could escort them home, and Mrs. Ashworth agreed to let him ride along. The older woman was dazzled. "He's a beautiful man," she told the milkman when he called at her pub the next morning. "You ought to see him stripped!"

Her daughter seems to have been dazzled, too. It is not possible fully to reconstruct the history of the relationship that developed between her and Jack Johnson over the next few weeks—or even confidently to characterize its nature. Accounts differ. Only bits and pieces of evidence remain. But there was enough there to scandalize the Sydney sporting world for months, and Johnson evidently dared to think he and she might one day be married. Toward the end of his Australian sojourn, he would tell the Sydney *Sunday Sun* as much without identifying his bride-to-be, and when he returned to America, he told the same story and gave her name as well, an indiscretion she would come bitterly to regret.

Known as Lola to her friends, Toy played the piano well enough to accompany her violinist brother, Ernest, on tours of small-town theaters and opera houses in Queensland, but she lived at home and disliked it there, mostly because of the coarseness of the stepfather she detested. Soon she was find-

---

said he could, provided he was able to land three punches on the elusive Foley's nose. Barron, whose own nose had been broken by Foley in an amateur contest, wanted revenge. He talked Foley into going out to the Sir Joseph Banks and stepping into the ring with the American newcomer. "Foley fell for it," Brandon remembered, "because he didn't care much for niggers, anyway. . . . Well, they squared off and they hadn't any more than got their hands up before bing! Johnson had landed that awful left of his flush on Foley's nose. The blood shot out in a stream and Johnson grinned and said that there was one pup." Johnson landed twice more, and "about this time Foley got wise and realized that he was up against the real thing and quit, for he couldn't even touch the negro. . . . Barron got the laugh on him, and Johnson got the pup." (Los Angeles Times, January 29, 1911.)

ing excuses to call at Johnson's hotel. She went with him for sulky rides, returned several afternoons to the pavilion to watch him train, and huddled close to him on the verandah, helping to fend off the mosquitoes that began swarming out of the gardens as the sun went down. When the Tivolians, chorus girls from the Tivoli Music Hall, turned up at noon one day for a picnic and a look at Johnson, Lola Toy posed with him for a group photograph, his arm around her shoulder. At a hotel dance in the boxer's honor, she begged off dancing with one guest, saying it was too warm, but the moment Johnson entered the ballroom she hurried into his arms. He called her Baby. She called him Jack and visited his room so often and at so many different times of day and night that Stephen Hyland took Johnson aside and told him he couldn't keep working for him if he persisted in inviting her upstairs. Johnson paid no attention (and Hyland remained on his payroll).

One evening at the Grand Pacific, her stepfather accused her of disgracing the family by seeing a black man, then threw her out and locked the door behind her. She called a constable, who forced Ashworth to let her back into the only home she had, but not before she had called him a cad in front of the customers, insisted that Johnson was a *real* gentleman, and threatened to telephone and have him come over and thrash Ashworth for his insults.

Meanwhile, the night of Johnson's fight with Peter Felix at the Gaiety Athletic Hall arrived. Felix was half a head taller than Johnson, and, as a sportswriter for the Sydney *Bulletin* wrote, the crowd had rallied to him: "Felix suddenly found himself the popular idol, for the Australian ring-sider is patriotic even with his black man when the opponent is a foreign colored man." Height and popularity turned out to be Felix' sole advantages. It took Johnson just two minutes and forty seconds to demolish him. Felix did all the leading, according to the Newcastle *Herald and Miners' Advocate,* but "Johnson, laughing and with aggravating coolness, merely parried the blows aimed at him . . . [and] made the local man look very awkward." Felix stumbled and fell twice throwing punches that met only empty air before Johnson landed an uppercut on the point of his chin. After the Australian was counted out, said the *Bulletin,* he "staggered to his feet amid a storm of hoots and looked around the howling house with the pathetic expression of a motherless foal. It was an awful fiasco and a shocking finish to Felix's bruising career."

Johnson barely bothered to train for the second Australian fight McLean had arranged for him. His opponent, in Melbourne on March 4, was Bill

Lang, a former opal miner and Australian Rules footballer just beginning his boxing career. The promoters billed the contest as a GRAND INTERNATIONAL BATTLE BETWEEN AUSTRALIA'S STANDARD-BEARER AND THE INVADING FOE-MAN . . . THE BUGLE CALLS TO ARMS!!! TO ARMS!!! and there were high hopes for ticket sales. But it poured on fight night. Only two thirds of the thirty thousand seats at the Richmond Racecourse were filled when the first of two preliminary bouts began, and forty soggy rounds later only those who'd thought to bring umbrellas remained in their seats. At about ten o'clock, Johnson made his way to the ring, wearing one of his patented bathrobes—made of "chintz or cretonne," wrote one reporter, "besprinkled with damask roses and lilac sprays with frills round the hem and a hood similarly figured with flowers." The soaked crowd started to jeer. "We don't want to see *Mrs.* Johnson!" one man shouted. "Go away woman, and send your husband. This is no place for ladies."

Johnson just grinned, popped his eyes at the crowd, and pulled up his hood against the rain drumming down on the canvas. Lang sent a message from his dressing room: it was too wet to fight. The crowd broke into "Waiting at the Church." The promoters convinced Lang that he had to get into the ring. It took ten minutes. Ten more were wasted while local fighters issued challenges to one another. Johnson, soaked and bored, leaned over the ropes and talked to the press. "They're all squabbling over something," he said. "I'm getting a misery waiting here."

Once things finally got under way, Lang splashed after Johnson for two rounds without landing a single solid punch. At the end of the second, Johnson was overheard telling his handlers, "This is a joke." Certainly, he treated it as one. For the next four rounds, he carried the hapless Australian, eluding his clumsy rushes and battering his face from a distance, bringing blood in "little red rills." He didn't even bother to sit down between rounds. In the seventh, he knocked Lang down twice, then angered the crowd by breaking into a grinning cakewalk on the way back to his corner. Lang was on the canvas four more times in the eighth, and in the ninth stayed there long enough to be counted out.*

---

*The former New Zealand middleweight Dan Creedon was one of Johnson's seconds for this fight. Ten years earlier, Johnson had been in Joe Walcott's corner when Creedon had fought him. Creedon hadn't thought much of the smaller Walcott, he said sheepishly, and remembered having been ready to knock him out in the first round—and then waking up the next morning with resin still in his ear. He preferred the memory of the Johnson-Lang fight, he said, because it had involved a black man knocking out a white man other than himself. (Los Angeles *Times,* January 29, 1911.)

Afterward, Johnson and McLean went on the road, exhibiting their fight films and putting on shadowboxing shows in small towns in Victoria like Ballarat, Bendigo, and Geelong. Their plans for making big money had collapsed when the fight with Squires failed to materialize, and by the time they got back to Sydney in early March, Johnson was bored and restless and increasingly dissatisfied with McLean. "He began to decide that he was about the whole show," McLean recalled, "and did not really need a manager after all." Shortly after they had settled into the Commercial Hotel in downtown Sydney, James Brennan dropped by with their share of the proceeds from the Lang fight. McLean happened to be out. Johnson said he'd be happy to hold on to the cash and give McLean his share the moment he got back. When McLean did return, it was time to head for the racetrack. As the two men hurried along, McLean asked for his cut, and Johnson handed him a fistful of coins.

McLean counted it on the run.

"How much more is coming to you?" Johnson asked.

"About $510."

Johnson promised to give him the rest of his share that evening. When the two men got back to their hotel after the races, Johnson told McLean he was going home. "I'm tired of this country," he said, "and I can get more money there." In fact, he planned to leave on the nineteenth, aboard the American steam mail ship *Ventura*, the same ship on which Bill Squires was sailing for America. If Squires couldn't be made to fight him in Australia, Johnson said, he'd be right there to challenge him the minute he walked down the gangplank in San Francisco.

McLean argued for a while, but when he saw that Johnson was adamant, he asked for his $510 so that he could pay their hotel bill and be ready to go on the nineteenth. Johnson just smiled, McLean remembered. "Everybody for himself in this world," he said. "Now I have the money and I am out for Jack Johnson. If you are big enough to take it from me, go ahead and do it." McLean knew he wasn't big enough and backed off for the time being.

On the evening of March 14, the Colored Progressive Association of New South Wales gave a farewell banquet for Johnson at the Leigh House on Castlereagh Street. The Tivoli's chorus line appeared en masse. Lola Toy was there, too, escorted by her brother for appearance's sake. Johnson gave an exhibition of bag punching and thanked the people of Australia for their cordiality.

Four nights later, Lola Toy came to call at Johnson's hotel, and the two had farewell drinks in the lounge. He expected to board the *Ventura* the following morning. But he had underestimated Alec McLean's resourcefulness. In public, McLean had supported his fighter's decision to head home, but he knew that once Johnson was at sea it was unlikely he'd ever get what was coming to him, and so he turned up shortly after Toy left that evening with a court officer and a warrant for Johnson's arrest for breach of contract. The three men walked outside. McLean showed Johnson the court order. The fighter threw it on the ground. McLean called him a "big black bastard."* Johnson smashed McLean's nose.

Johnson was arrested for assault by three constables and locked up. Jim Brennan hurried down to bail him out. Johnson was ordered to appear the following morning in the Sydney Water Police Court before Magistrate G. H. Smithers. McLean was not present; his lawyer, a man named Tress, claimed that his client's injuries, the result of a wholly unprovoked attack, were far too great for him to leave his bed.

Johnson's attorney, H. Levien, offered another explanation:

MR. LEVIEN: Your Worship, it appears that there was a legal difficulty between Johnson and McLean, and the two got to high words. They had not, I suppose, been drinking cloves and peppermint, and McLean called Johnson a big black [bastard] and, of course, got knocked down. That's all there was. Johnson, like all pugilists, is a most quiet man.

MAGISTRATE SMITHERS: Mr. Tress says he broke McLean's nose.

MR. LEVIEN: Oh well, that will soon be mended. . .

MAGISTRATE SMITHERS: If a man calls another man those names he is likely to get something for it.

MR. LEVIEN: Yes, I know, that's what I would do if I were called names.

For punching his ex-manager, Johnson got away with paying only a five-pound fine. But McLean's breach-of-contract suit had yet to be settled, and Johnson was forbidden to leave New South Wales. The *Ventura* and Bill Squires sailed without him.

He told the press he would go to Melbourne and fight either the veteran Billy Smith or an aboriginal heavyweight named Malley Jackson. McLean warned that his contract with Johnson precluded his fighting anyone, any-

---

*Alec McLean's account leaves out this all-important detail.

where, without his permission. Johnson responded that Sam Fitzpatrick, not Alec McLean, was his real manager. But he did not leave for Melbourne. Instead, he rented himself a room in a working-class neighborhood in Sydney and waited for his dispute with McLean to come to court. "I expect to get married shortly," he told the Sydney *Sunday Sun*. "I'm liable to make this my home. . . . I like the people here . . . and I'll go into business after I'm here a while."

No one knows whether he and Lola Toy were still seeing each other or whether they had ever really discussed marriage, but after McLean won his suit Johnson lost little time in making plans to sail for home aboard the *Sonoma* on April 24.* When Johnson went to pay what the court insisted he owed, and learned from McLean's lawyer that McLean planned to be aboard the same ship, he cursed and muttered that there "were two men going aboard the ship but only one would get off alive." The lawyer advised McLean to arm himself. "This was the first and last time I ever carried a gun," McLean remembered, "and I never want to do so again."

Johnson and McLean boarded the *Sonoma* separately the following day. According to McLean, they did not lay eyes on each other until they got to Honolulu, where the press was waiting. Each offered his version of what had happened during the Australian tour. In his account, McLean gratuitously suggested that Johnson hadn't shown much aggression in the ring. This last, according to McLean at least, stirred Johnson to seek him out as soon as they had set sail again for San Francisco.

> When he got within ten feet of me, he asked me what I had said in the press about him. I had my hand on my gun in my coat pocket. I told him to stop where he was, and he told me he was going to break my back.

---

*If Johnson is to be believed, his financial prospects improved considerably after a trip to the track on Saturday, March 30. He bet what he called "my last five dollars" on a horse owned by the promoter Jim Brennan, then wandered around the track "greeting friends and acquaintances with a wave of the hand"—gestures the bookies misinterpreted as signals that he wanted to bet more. The following day was his twenty-ninth birthday, and when he went to collect his winnings he was stunned to find that his five-dollar wager had yielded a fifteen-thousand-dollar profit. The biographer Finis Farr offered a more cynical—and perhaps more plausible—explanation for Johnson's windfall: he had actually bet seven hundred dollars, and only after learning from racetrack insiders that the race was fixed for Brennan's horse to win.

In any case, Johnson was delighted: "Nothing could have been more opportune for I had been in a predicament . . . wondering how I was to finance my trip back to the United States. If the long shot had not won—well it still makes me sweat to think about it. I would probably have been in Australia yet, wondering what had happened to me and making futile explanations to prison keepers." (Jack Johnson, *In the Ring and Out*, pp. 54–55; Farr, *Black Champion*, pp. 46–47.)

"Did you say that I was not game?" he asked.

"Yes," I answered, "and am going to make you quit right here to prove it."

Then he asked me if I had a gun, and I said yes, that it was loaded, too, and if he moved I would shoot.

"I have my gun, too," he said.

"Well, go ahead and get it, and I will show you, you are not game, for this is the one place where I have an even chance with you."

"You are not going to shoot while I am going after it?"

"No. Go ahead and get it."

Somebody tried to stop him, and said, "Don't go, Jack, we don't want to have anybody killed here." But Johnson went downstairs to get his gun.

He went downstairs all right, but he never did come back. In fact, he never appeared on deck again until we reached Frisco, and he did not threaten me with any more injury, either.

That was my last fight with Jack Johnson.

Johnson's return to San Francisco on May 18 was eclipsed by newspaper reports of the latest doings of Tommy Burns. Just ten days earlier, Tom McCarey had staged a title fight in Los Angeles between Burns and Philadelphia Jack O'Brien. It hadn't been easy to arrange. Their first fight—the one shown in the film Johnson and McLean had been showing in Australia—had officially ended in a draw, but O'Brien had absorbed the most punishment and, according to a widely believed story, was unwilling to meet Burns again unless the champion would agree to take a dive in exchange for ten thousand dollars. To get him into the ring, Burns said he would, then double-crossed him on fight night, telling McCarey the whole story just ten minutes before the main event. McCarey, in turn, ordered the referee to announce to the crowd that all bets were off. O'Brien blanched, had literally to be pulled off his stool by the referee after the opening bell, and then ran from the angry Burns for most of the next twenty rounds.*

---

*For his part, O'Brien claimed the fix had been McCarey's idea, not his. "Jack," he said McCarey told him, "the long-haired fellows [reformers] are going to kill the game soon, anyhow, and we are fools if we don't get all the money we can, while we can."

O'Brien was a dapper, charming man and one of the most scientific boxers of his era, good enough to have knocked out Bob Fitzsimmons to win the light heavyweight championship in 1905 and to have engaged in more than 175 bouts over a sixteen-year career with only six official losses. He was a favorite with sportswriters, too, because of his distinctive use of the English language: once, describing to A. J. Liebling his own losing effort against the middleweight Stanley Ketchel, he explained that he would have "put the bum away early" had his timing not been "a fraction of an iota off."

Burns won the decision easily, but controversy continued to dog him. The whole business, W. W. Naughton wrote, was "about as astonishing a mess of crookedness as the game of the ring has known," and some boxing insiders—including the editor of the *Police Gazette*—believed that both fights with O'Brien had been fixed, the first prearranged in order to ensure that there would be a second. Nor did Burns' popularity improve when he refused a rematch with Mike Schreck—a big, awkward, left-handed heavyweight from Cincinnati who had been the first man to beat him—unless he received an unheard-of 75 percent of the twenty-thousand-dollar guarantee. Burns professed not to care about criticism. "I am not madly in love with the game," he would tell a reporter. "We are out for the money, you know."

Burns would always be out for the money. The poverty and deprivation out of which he came was at least as severe as that which had surrounded Jack Johnson as a boy, and he would spend his whole career trying to make up for it. He was born Noah Brusso in 1881 in a log cabin outside Hanover in southeastern Ontario, the twelfth of thirteen children of a German-Canadian cabinetmaker. Five of his siblings died in childhood. His father beat him. So did the drunk his mother married after his father died. Noah, in turn, beat up his classmates until his mother pulled him out of school at ten and put him to work as a finisher in a furniture factory. As a teenager, he was a skilled but savage field lacrosse player, a goalie celebrated both for his shutouts and for the rough treatment he relished meting out to opposing players who dared get too close. (One coach paid him a bonus every time he managed to finish a game without incurring a penalty for misconduct.) He drifted from job to job—house painter, foundry worker, saloon bouncer. While working as a baggage handler aboard a Great Lakes steamer, he beat the chief engineer unconscious for throwing a towel at him, then jumped ship at Detroit for fear he'd be arrested. He began boxing there in 1900 and ran up a string of thirteen wins and eleven knockouts over local heroes, both black and white, with names like Fred "Thunderbolt" Thornton, Billy "Battleship" Walsh, and Eddie Sholtreau, the "Bay City Brawler," before his loss to Mike Schreck. Noah kept fighting and winning after that, but when his

---

But he also seems to have made a practice of clumsy fakery. Jim Jeffries would later claim that shortly after O'Brien's first fight with Burns the Philadelphian had come to call at his Los Angeles farm with an offer of $80,000 from some Nevada boosters for him to come out of retirement just long enough to "take the count." Jeffries said it "nearly paralyzed me—that he would come out with a bald-faced plan like that. . . . I told him that I didn't need money that bad." (London *Free Press*, May 15, 1907, quoted in McCaffery, *Tommy Burns*, p. 138.)

mother was distressed by headlines he made in 1904 for having beaten a hapless middleweight named Ben "Gorilla" Grady into a coma, he changed his name to Tommy Burns.

Burns was short for a heavyweight, and he often fought from a crouch, which protected his stomach and jaw but also made him seem still shorter. Some writers simply never believed him big enough to be an authentic heavyweight. He hit hard—more than half of his prechampionship bouts ended in knockouts—but he was perhaps best at upsetting and bewildering his opponents.

> Worry your opponents as much as you can [Burns wrote]. Cultivate quick, slight movements or tricks with the eyes, hands and feet, which will convey the impression of a sudden, rapid movement, which you will not really carry out. . . . These tactics will cause your opponent to make a big lunge or a rapid jerk or spring backwards or sideways, such as will take a lot of steam out of him, without having distressed you in any way.

Like Jack Johnson, Burns enjoyed taunting his opponents and laughing at them in the clinches; also like Johnson, he did his most serious damage with short, jolting blows inside.

Admirers compared him to Napoleon, a notion Burns did nothing to discourage, billing himself as the "Little General" and the "Emperor," sometimes even combing a few strands of his thinning hair over his brow to emphasize the resemblance. Burns dressed like a sport and was fond of poker and whiskey and late-night sing-alongs, but he revered his second wife—a Birmingham, Alabama, beauty he called Jewel, who made it a condition of marrying him that he never fight another Negro—and he was in total charge of his own finances. He had no manager and traveled with no entourage, because he could not bear to share his earnings with anybody.

Jack Johnson did everything he could think of to call attention to himself after he got home. As soon as Tommy Burns turned down a rematch with Mike Schreck, who had been the first man to beat him, Johnson challenged Schreck—who hastily drew the color line. And when Burns agreed to fight Bill Squires at Colma on July 4, 1907—Jim Jeffries having refused to leave his farm to fight the Australian title holder*—Johnson confronted the cham-

---

*Billy Delaney, Jeffries' manager and trainer for most of his career, actually offered Squires a fight with his former charge, convinced he had the retired champion's agreement. When Jeffries repudiated the

pion at his hotel. "I had $700 in my pocket & offered to box him for it right there," he remembered. "Then I offered to go and get $9,300 more & make him a side bet, but this he declined, too. . . . Burns talked of going into a room with me to have it out. I said, 'Come on,' but he did not get any further."

Johnson was at ringside for the fight. Squires was a 10-to-7 favorite, though he had never fought in America before. He entered the ring wrapped in the Australian flag. Burns wore the Stars and Stripes, and the band played the "Star-Spangled Banner." (The Canadian Red Ensign, with its Union Jack in the corner, was not thought likely to appeal to American fans, especially on Independence Day.) Squires was big and muscular and had run up an impressive-sounding tally of knockouts, but he held his chin too high. Burns' first right hand sent him down. A second toppled him again, and when he wobbled to his feet, a third kept him there until Jim Jeffries could count him out. Burns' doubters continued to be unimpressed: Squires must have been overrated, they reasoned, for the so-called champion to have demolished him so easily.

On July 17, Johnson fought ex-champion Bob Fitzsimmons at the National Athletic Club in Philadelphia. Fitzsimmons had been one of the hardest punchers in heavyweight history—as Johnson knew firsthand, since he'd been one of his sparring partners before the New Zealander lost the title to Jeffries in 1902—but he was forty-five years old and out of shape, and he tore a ligament in his left arm just before the bout. It was a sad mismatch, though Johnson did all he could to make it sound exciting in his handwritten account:

> In my fight with Fitzsimmons I did in two rounds just what it took Jeffries 8 rounds to do. . . . In the first round [Fitzsimmons] did well. He was clever enough to make me miss several times and when I miss [when] there is something in front of me [that] is out of the ordinary. Cheer after cheer rang out as he strutted to his corner, but soon it was quiet. In the 2nd round I walked over to Bob & feinted him into knots. I pulled him into a duck and then swiftly . . . planted my right on his jaw and Bob went over on his back. Fitz rolled over onto his face, . . . and at about the count of 6 was on his hands & knees with his head stuck to the floor. He tried to pull it up

---

deal he had made, the embarrassed Delaney—who believed his word had been called into question—denounced Jeffries as "the worst four-flusher in the world." The two men would never reconcile.

but no, he couldn't budge it. He was like a hypnotized man who can't take his finger from his nose. He knew what he wanted to do, started right, but that head seemed to weigh a ton. There wasn't a chance in the world of him lifting it. Billy McCarney, the referee, lifted him to his feet and Bob reeled after me, thinking the go was still on. Tim O'Rourke led him to his corner, and washed his face with ice water, bringing him to.

Johnson had little sympathy for Fitzsimmons, whose "anxiety" about his color had kept the ex-champion out of the ring with him until he was too late to put up a fight. And it amused him afterward that his effortless win over "poor old Bob Fitzsimmons" was the thing that made some supposed boxing experts "finally begin to see that I counted for something."

Johnson had become a hero to black sports fans all across the country, both for what he'd done in the ring and for the bold way he conducted himself outside it. When he umpired a charity baseball game between the Cuban Giants and the Philadelphia Giants at American League Park in Philadelphia on August 24, he was mobbed. "The scene after the game savored of a reception following a cakewalk," the New York *Times* reported.

As the players departed for the clubhouse there was a concerted movement on the part of the spectators to home plate where Johnson stood, evidently waiting for some such demonstration. Men and women vied with each other to show "Mistah" Johnson how much they thought of him. They tugged at his coat-tails, pulled his arms in their eagerness to grasp his massive hands, patted him on the back, and told him he was the greatest representative of the colored race before the public. . . . Many whites helped to swell the mob that wanted to show their respects to the vanquisher of Fitzsimmons.

Johnson showed no disposition to resent the impromptu homage, but accepted it as though due him. He finally eluded his well-wishers and reached the street, his clothes somewhat ruffled and pulled out of shape. Even there he was not safe from the crowd which followed him cheering all the way to the subway station which saved him from further molestation. It was a grand opportunity for the colored folk, and they did not fail to make much of it.

The combination of Johnson's conquest of Fitzsimmons and Tommy Burns' qualified willingness to fight him one day had made old John L. Sullivan more eager than ever to see Johnson eliminated from the heavyweight picture. To accomplish that feat—and to make some money for himself on the side—he helped groom a onetime wrestler named Charlie "Kid" Cutler in hopes of knocking Johnson out of contention. Johnson couldn't have been more pleased. Before he and Cutler met in Reading, Pennsylvania, on August 28, he told the press to tell people to be in their seats on time, because he would end the fight early. Johnson then made good on his promise. "A wicked right hand," Johnson remembered, sent Cutler to the canvas in the first round, "like a cherry dropping from a tree." As Cutler's seconds helped him to his corner, Johnson called out to the great John L., "How'd you like that, Cap'n John?"

"I don't see where they are going to dig one up to beat this big black fellow," wrote the editor of the *Police Gazette* after the Cutler fight, unless Johnson's "butterfly existence" did him in. Johnson now seemed to have no permanent address. Between fights he turned up in Philadelphia, Pittsburgh, Chicago, New York—wherever there were good times to be had. In Manhattan on August 8, he met the next important woman in his life. Her real name was Anna Peterson, but she called herself Hattie McClay, and when he met her, she later remembered, she was "living at what they called a 'Call House' . . . going out on calls, sporting." She was not notably attractive—short, thick-bodied, sharp-featured—but she was fun-loving, liked a drink, knew how to play the piano, just as Lola Toy had. She also had no illusions and made few demands. Johnson called her "Mac" and thought her "a splendid pal" with "good business judgment; she understood me."

She was also white. "The heartaches which Mary Austin and Clara Kerr caused me," he would solemnly explain in his 1927 autobiography, "led me to forswear colored women and to determine that my lot henceforth would be cast only with white women." In fact, Johnson forswore nobody; he would pursue black as well as white women all his life. But from the moment he got back from Australia and his relationship with Lola Toy in 1907, he did *travel* continuously with white ones. It was they alone with whom he registered at hotels and boardinghouses as "Mr. and Mrs. Jack Jackson."*

Hattie McClay and two women friends cheered Johnson on from the balcony at Smith's Theater in Bridgeport, Connecticut, two weeks later when he fought Sailor Burke, a middleweight novice whose real name was Frank Loughnane. Burke refused to shake hands before the fight began, a lack of

---

*"I didn't court white women because I thought I was too good for the others like they said," he told the sportswriter John Lardner (*White Hopes*, pp. 34–35) many years later. "It was just that they always treated me better. I never had a colored girl that didn't two-time me."

courtesy for which he was made to pay. Johnson battered the lighter, less skilled youngster around and around the ring for six rounds. "The affair could hardly be called a contest," he remembered.

> It was merely an exhibition in which I showed . . . that I was infinitely clev-erer than Burke as a boxer, and much too strong for him as a mixer, and far too fast as a fighter. . . . I knocked Burke down 14 times during the fight.* In fact, he hit the floor about five times more often than his glove collided with any part of my anatomy. . . . Nearly every time I hit Burke after the first round I shot him to the floor and every time Burke found himself reclining on the canvas he settled himself snugly & rested for 9 sec-onds. It was merely an act of charity upon my part in allowing him to stay the 6 rounds.

Later the suspicion grew that more than charity might have been involved, and to quell rumors that Johnson had been paid to carry the local favorite, Sam Fitzpatrick offered Johnson's end of the purse—$1,950—to anyone who could prove there'd been "any sort of agreement with Burke." There were no takers.

In October, Fitzpatrick arranged a six-round rematch with Johnson's old nemesis Marvin Hart in Philadelphia. Johnson simply stepped away from it, heading for San Francisco, instead, and a potentially more lucrative fight on July 4, 1907, with Jack Curley's latest charge, Jim Flynn, the "Pueblo Fireman." (Johnson's departure from Chicago was delayed slightly when the police arrested him for trying to pass a bad fifty-dollar check.)

Flynn was an Italian immigrant's son from Hoboken, New Jersey—his real name was Andrew Chiariglione—who hoboed west in search of adventure as a teenager, settled in Pueblo, Colorado, and worked as a fireman aboard Denver and Rio Grande trains between bouts.† "There was a dearth of first-rate heavyweights at the time," Curley wrote, "and Flynn, while not as good as he thought he was, was better than most." Tommy Burns had knocked him

---

*The *Illustrated Buffalo Express* (September 13, 1907) reported that Burke went down nineteen times.

†If Jack Curley's memoir is to be believed, Flynn had badly strained relations with his adopted home-town earlier in 1907. He'd heard a woman screaming from inside a house in "a tough section of the town . . . found a man beating the damsel about and promptly slugged him. The woman, as women sometimes will under such circumstances, repaid him for his gallantry by turning upon him and strik-ing him with a poker." When a policeman with a club rushed in to see what all the noise was about, Flynn decked him, then rushed down the street. He fended off subsequent attacks by the police chief and two other officers, fled the rail yards, commandeered "a switch engine, opened the throttle and steamed out of town in the best melodramatic manner."

out, but he had beaten George Gardner and Jack "Twin" Sullivan, and his aggressive, mauling style delighted fight crowds. "My advice to a young fighter is this," Flynn once said. "If you're going to get licked, get licked coming in."

That kind of thinking was music to Jack Johnson's ears.

Time was called at three o'clock. We immediately clinched and in the breakaway I closed Flynn's left eye with a powerful blow to that member which was a handicap to him for the remainder of the fight. . . .

It was evident that Flynn's only hope of winning lay in the landing of a chance blow either to my body or head with the hope that such a blow would take some of the fight out of me. However, that hope vanished in the 9th round. In that period I knocked the fireman down and when he came to his feet we clinched. In the walkaway I hit him with a right to the solar plexus. Flynn went to his hands & knees and a deathly pallor spread over his face. His seconds rushed in & carried him to his corner.

Flynn showed his wonderful powers of recuperation by coming out at the beginning of the 10th round still full of fight. He came after me but I stopped his rush with a straight right to the head. Then he became desperate and butted me several times . . . and was warned by the referee. I landed right & left frequently to his body but he kept on trying, and he laughed and said, "Gee, but you are a tough nigger, ain't you." We went at it about 30 seconds in the 11th round when Flynn complimented me by saying, "You're a clever big nigger." With that I shot a straight [right] to his jaw. He fell on his side & then rolled over to his face.

Flynn was unconscious for four minutes. Back in his dressing room, he was a gracious loser: "The best man won and all I can say is to warn the next man that is matched with Johnson. He is a great man and I was entirely outclassed."*

Johnson was in full agreement. "I knew I had him after I closed his eye. He is a game little boy, but too small for this class. I think that I have demonstrated to the world that I am not afraid and I challenge any one to find the 'yellow' in me. Tommy Burns is my next man, and I stand ready to fight him any time."

---

*On December 21, 1908, Flynn would fight Sam Langford in San Francisco. At ringside was one of his biggest boosters, sportswriter H. M. "Beany" Walker of the Los Angeles *Examiner*, who had called Flynn the coming champion. In the first round, Langford maneuvered Flynn until he stood just above Walker.

"Now, Mr. Walker," he said, "here comes your champion," then knocked Flynn through the ropes into Walker's lap.

Boxing writers were now virtually unanimous that Johnson deserved a shot at Burns' title, just as he had merited a chance when Jeffries and Hart had held the championship. The St. Louis *Dispatch* spoke for most of them:

Jack Johnson is a colored man, but we cannot get away from the fact that he is the greatest living exponent of the art of hit-and-get-away and as such, is the outstanding challenger for the title which Tommy Burns claims but to which he is not entitled until he puts Johnson out of the way. . . . It is up to Tommy Burns to heed the call of the fight fans. They demand that he get out of his hiding and put to rest for all time the matter of fistic supremacy between him and Johnson, between the white race and the colored.

Burns had other ideas. He was off to England to fight the Indian army veteran and British heavyweight champion James "Gunner" Moir. When he got back, he promised, "it's Johnson next, and when I do meet him there will be no love lost. I haven't the slightest doubt that I'll trim him and trim him good."

At the National Sporting Club in London, before an all-male crowd in dinner jackets, Burns carried the far-bigger, fearsomely tattooed British champion for nine rounds in order to ensure a brisk profit from the sale of tickets to see films of the fight, then knocked him out in the tenth. He spoiled the favorable impression he might have made by insisting that the referee officiate from inside the ropes instead of outside them as dictated by the Club rules, and by making what the British fancy thought a vulgar fuss about having the thousand-pound stake on hand and in cash before beginning the bout. "He rather rubbed us the wrong way," recalled the veteran British referee Eugene Corri. As always, Burns was unrepentant. The niceties of ring etiquette did not interest him. Only money did, he said, and, eager to make more of it without too much effort, he resolved to remain in Britain rather than return home to face Johnson.

Johnson wasn't surprised. "Burns promised before he left for England to fight Gunner Moir that he would return immediately after the battle and meet me," he told a reporter.

Now I understand he is going to stay in England for several months and pick up a little easy money by beating the heavyweights over there. Burns could make as much in a fight with me in the United States as he could by beating half a dozen Englishmen. He knows that but as he is not confident that he can defeat me, Burns wants to stay and pick up the soft money floating around.

The fights Burns took were soft, too. In London he knocked out Jack Palmer, whom one writer called "an English horizontalist," in four rounds. On St. Patrick's Day in Dublin, it took him just 1:38 to knock out Jem Roche, the heavyweight champion of Ireland, so short a time that British papers seriously suggested that Burns' opponents were beaten even before the bell rang because of the champion's occult hypnotic powers.

When reporters asked Burns about Johnson, he shrugged them off. "What do I care? I am having a mighty good time and getting a lot of experience and, what is considerably more to the point, I am getting the coin. They can call me crazy for not rushing over to meet Johnson, but just put this down in your notebook. They will never have to hold any benefit for me."

That winter, while Sam Fitzpatrick tried to find a way to get Burns into the ring with his fighter, Johnson had only one bout: a three-round exhibition in New York City with Joe Jeannette, the tenth time they had met. Otherwise, he toured in vaudeville, working out the stage act from which he would derive much of his income for the next four years. He shadowboxed, sparred, danced, declaimed a few lines in a determinedly theatrical style, and ended each performance by whacking a specially rigged punching bag into the audience—a trick pioneered on the vaudeville stage by Bob Fitzsimmons. He billed himself as "Jack Johnson, Heavyweight Champion of the World. The Man who made Jim Jeffries Take to the Alfalfa."

On March 17, 1908, the day before Tommy Burns demolished Jem Roche in Dublin, Johnson's name appeared in Australian headlines once again, sparked by events that had occurred ten months earlier. A day or two after Johnson had returned from Australia, several American newspapers carried the following item:

OAKLAND, May 9—Jack Johnson, the heavyweight colored pugilist, modestly stated last night that he was to marry Miss Lola Toy, a rich Australian white woman. The rumor was called to big Jack's attention, and after much pressing, the dusky lad admitted the facts. "Yes, it is true that I am to marry Miss Toy and I expect to marry her in November. She will come from Sydney, Australia, and I expect that our wedding will take place in this country. I met her in Australia, and after my courtship she consented to accept me. I now have something to fight for aside from the honors. I want to make a name for myself that my future wife will not be ashamed of," meaning that she, a white woman, was willing and had consented to marry a negro professional pugilist.

The Sydney sporting paper *The Referee* reprinted the article. It caused a sensation, and Lola Toy dispatched an attorney to *The Referee*'s office to demand a retraction: she'd never consented to marry Johnson, his client said, had never even known him well. *The Referee* printed a qualified apology: "If the paragraph has caused Miss Troy [*sic*] any pain or annoyance we regret it." But that did not end the matter. Strangers continued to say unkind things to her on the street. Anonymous letters and postcard photographs of Johnson covered with vile accusations filled her mailbox.

And so in March of 1908 she went to the New South Wales Banco Court, claiming she'd been libeled and demanding two thousand pounds in damages from the Sunday Times Newspaper Company, which owned *The Referee*. G. H. Reid, attorney for the *Times*, sought to have the case thrown out on the ground that it was not intrinsically "libelous to say that a white woman was willing to marry a black man. That was a colour line that had never been drawn in a court of justice. . . . The noblest woman in the world could marry a colored man without the slightest imputation being made against her morality, charity or modesty."

Chief Justice Sir Frederick Darley said he could not possibly honor Reid's request to dismiss the case; only the four-man jury could decide whether libel had been committed.

Lola Toy was called to the stand. "Dressed neatly in white," she testified that she had never been "familiar" with Jack Johnson, had only said "Good evening" to him once while passing in the street, certainly had never dreamed of marrying him, and was weary of the taunts and jibes of strangers *The Referee*'s story had inspired.

In a caustic cross-examination, lawyer Reid did his best to break her down.

MR. REID: Look at this [he said, handing her a photograph]. Are you not standing next to Mr. Johnson?

MISS TOY: Yes, but I never saw this before. I was not aware that this picture had been taken.

MR. REID: Aren't you holding Johnson's walking stick?

MISS TOY: There is nothing in holding anyone's walking stick.

MR. REID: Look at his arm around your neck, with his hand resting on your shoulder. Do you want the jury to believe that you didn't know that hand was there?

MISS TOY: It was only a snap. I didn't know Johnson had his hand there.

MR. REID: And such a hand. It must have weighed a hundred-weight. Come now. Do you want the jury to believe that?

MISS TOY: The jury will have to please themselves.

MR. REID: Oh, but men only put their hands on women that they know won't object.

Toy fainted as she left the witness box and had to be helped out of the courtroom.

Reid called other witnesses to bolster the company's case. A guest at the Sir Joseph Banks Hotel remembered Miss Toy eagerly dancing with Johnson. Two constables said they'd seen Johnson and Miss Toy riding out alone together, and one remembered hearing her threaten to call him in to punch her stepfather. The trainer Stephen Hyland testified he'd seen Toy and Johnson together many times—she'd attended his public sparring shows, watched him train while he was "stripped to the buff," and come and gone from his hotel room at all hours of the day and night.

To refute their testimony, Toy's attorney, J. C. Gannon, called his client back to the stand. She denied everything again, but she knew that Hyland's testimony had been the most damaging. She had never been in a room alone with Jack Johnson, she swore. Never.

MR. GANNON: The evidence of the witness Hyland bears only one meaning to your mind?

MISS TOY: Yes.

MR. GANNON: Will you then if necessary submit yourself to the most skilled doctors in Sydney.

MISS TOY: Yes.

MR. REID: Oh, this is too bad! No imputations have been made to justify such a proposal.

The judge agreed with Reid: Miss Toy would not have to prove she remained a virgin.

Two witnesses did what they could to bolster her testimony: a hotel guest who'd attended the ball said he had not seen Miss Toy dance with Johnson, and a young woman testified that Miss Toy had been unhappy at being photographed with Johnson and had slept in her hotel room during her visits, not Johnson's.

Reid's summary for the defense lasted three hours and seemed aimed at the gallery as much as at the jury. The group photograph was incontrovertible evidence that Johnson and Miss Toy were close, he argued. If she had been uneasy having her picture made with him, her face should have shown distress, even dislike. Instead, it was "suffused with bliss and . . . beneath 'the great black towering shade' she was at perfect happiness and rest. [*Great laughter.*]"

> Johnson was the great gun of the occasion. He was the central figure. There he was like an emperor of old. . . . Those who considered themselves the most important got nearest to him. He had them to his right and to his left. Thus it was that they found Miss Toy figuring as she did in the photographs. They couldn't tell *him* that a woman didn't know when a man's arm was around her [*laughter*] particularly the arm of Johnson [*more laughter*] a champion of champions. [*Great laughter.*] Besides, she was holding his stick. [*Laughter.*] They all knew what it was. [*More laughter.*] Sometimes there was a regular fight for the stick. [*Great laughter.*]
>
> There was also that drive in the sulky from Botany to Watson's Bay. What a triumphal march was that for Miss Toy! [*Laughter.*] It was only a small sulky. [*More laughter.*] So the three of them had to sit pretty tight. [*Great laughter.*] There was no drawing of the color line there. [*Roars of laughter.*]

Toy's attorney took Reid to task for employing sarcasm to entertain and mislead the jury when there had been nothing funny about *The Referee*'s gross irresponsibility. "Pugilism was one thing," he said. "It was quite another thing to seriously publish the statement that a young white girl was going to marry a professional negro pugilist who even here in Sydney had committed an offense [by punching Alec McLean in the nose]." To believe Stephen Hyland's testimony as to his client's behavior, he said, "Miss Toy would be stamped as an abandoned strumpet."

The jury took less than two hours to render its verdict. The Sunday Times Newspaper Company was found guilty of libel and ordered to pay five hundred pounds plus court costs. Despite all the testimony, in Sydney, Australia, in 1907, the idea that a young white woman might have been romantically entangled with a black boxer, let alone have considered marrying him, was apparently unimaginable.

Johnson never commented publicly on the Lola Toy affair, but within weeks of its resolution he was on his way overseas again, to London this time, accompanied by Sam Fitzpatrick and Hattie McClay. Since Tommy Burns wouldn't come home to fight him, he said, he would "shame him out of King Edward's islands" and force him to fight in Britain.*

Negotiations with Sunny Jim Coffroth and an upstart promoter named Tex Rickard to stage a Burns-Johnson contest in San Francisco or Goldfield, Nevada, had fallen through, but Arthur Frederick "Peggy" Bettinson, manager of the National Sporting Club in London, had let it be known that the club might be interested, and within hours of reaching London, Fitzpatrick and Johnson were at its door. They were ushered inside, Bettinson remembered, and Johnson was made to wait in the foyer—"to stand on the mat until he was sent for," to use the club historian's phrase. "Johnson in those days was a normal nigger and in good hands," Bettinson remembered, still "a tractable nigger, and . . . generally acceptable."

Inside, Fitzpatrick made his pitch: "This Johnson can beat Burns or any other man; the nigger knows it; Burns knows it. If Tommy will not fight here, we will follow wherever he goes." Then a butler ushered Johnson inside as well, and he was asked to strip to his tights and put on a show of shadow-boxing. Impressed by Johnson's style and obvious strength, Bettinson offered $12,500 for the championship contest, to be held at Covent Garden, with four fifths of the purse earmarked for the winner. Fitzpatrick accepted and said he was willing to put up $5,000 of his own as a side bet. "Johnson would sooner fight in the National Sporting Club than anywhere else," he assured the press. "Money does not so much matter so long as Burns will get into the ring."

But money always mattered to Burns. The club's offer was laughably low,

---

*Later, after he and Fitzpatrick had parted ways, Johnson would allege that Hattie McClay's father had financed their passage. Boxing historian Nat Fleischer suggested a more plausible explanation: since neither Johnson nor Fitzpatrick ever had much cash—Johnson because he spent it as soon as he got it, Fitzpatrick because he was always lending it to Johnson—they borrowed five thousand dollars from George Considine, a New York hotelier, and a group of fellow sports who hoped to win big money betting on Johnson against Burns. (Jack Johnson, *In the Ring and Out*, p. 156; Fleischer, *Fighting Furies*, p. 67.)

he said. "If [Johnson] really wants to fight me he ought to be glad to accept any terms I offer. My terms are $30,000, win, lose, or draw."

No fighter in history had ever insisted on such a sum or such an arrangement. The *Police Gazette* thought the champion's demand "quite the nerviest proposition that ever was made for a fistic match."

> Surely he cannot sincerely believe that any promoter will give him such an unheard of sum. . . . Jim Jeffries, between whom and the present champion no comparison can be made, never could muster the gall to ask any club to compensate him for his services in any such sum, and when he was fighting he fought men like Sharkey, Fitzsimmons and Corbett, all of whom were better than Burns is. . . . No one wants to accuse Burns of placing insurmountable obstacles in the way of a meeting with the big negro, but unless he shifts his position quickly he will be charged with fearing to face the issue. No matter what is said of the ring career of Johnson or his personality, no one will say that he is not in earnest concerning a fight with the champion.

Johnson was more succinct: "The whole truth of the matter is that Burns does not want to fight me. It is he and not me who has a yellow streak."

To demonstrate Johnson's skills for British boxing insiders, Fitzpatrick had him spar several rounds at Hengler's Circus in Argyle Street against what the veteran referee Fred Dartnell recalled as a "very good heavyweight." "Not once," Dartnell continued, "did [Johnson's] opponent's glove get past that invincible guard." When an impatient man in the gallery shouted, "Go on, get at him!" the frustrated British boxer shouted back, "Gawd blimey! You come and have a go."

London writers were suitably impressed, though some, like John Gilbert, the novelist and literary biographer who wrote about boxing under the pseudonym of Bohun Lynch, could not get beyond his color. Johnson was "by no means unintelligent," Lynch recalled,

> and not without good reason, was regarded generally with the greatest possible dislike. With money in his pocket and physical triumph over white men in his heart, he displayed all the gross and overbearing insolence which makes what we call the buck nigger insufferable. He was one of the comparatively few men of African blood who, in a half-perceiving way, desire to make the white man pay for the undoubted ill-treatment of his forbears.

Meanwhile, Burns' noisy concern with how much he was to be paid— he saw no reason to budge from his initial demand, he said, "as I'm called a grabber anyway"—had won him few friends in British boxing circles. Nor had his overly candid assessment of British boxing talent: "I shall not return to the United States yet," he told the American press in remarks widely reprinted in Britain. "There are still some juicy lemons here that I haven't squeezed . . . altogether, there's too much easy money here for me to overlook it." His boorish behavior at the bar of the National Sporting Club didn't help, either. "Johnson strolled into the . . . Club yesterday," Burns reported to the *Police Gazette* in June, "lording it in a disgusting way, and I turned him down cold—wouldn't shake hands with the big dub."*

Burns saw himself as more generous and fair-minded than any of his predecessors: "I am the only heavyweight champion who has been ready to give a black man a chance." But his blunt personality was losing him the propaganda battle. He printed up handbills addressed to the British people defending himself and had them passed out all over London. The proposed bout with Johnson was simply a business proposition, he argued, just like any other.

> Now, let me ask you a sensible question, for I judge that most of you are business people. If you were working for three pounds a week, and you know that you could get six pounds a week for a similar job, would you take the job at six pounds? The same thing applies to the offer for Johnson and myself. Why should I accept this amount when I can get twice that amount elsewhere?

The handbills didn't help. Edward VII himself, an avid sportsman, was widely quoted as having called Burns a mere "bluffer," whose vulgar financial demands should never be met in Britain.

Johnson followed Burns to France in June. There had been talk of a title fight in Paris with Johnson's old opponent Sam McVey, who'd been there for several months and had knocked out all five men who'd faced him. Johnson, Hattie, and McVey were photographed making the rounds of Paris nightspots together, the two black fighters towering over French patrons; Johnson in a derby and a checked suit, leaning on a polished cane; Hattie, beneath a vast flowered hat, grinning from a bar stool. Johnson saw the city's sights, too: Notre Dame, the Louvre, and the tomb of Napoleon, with whose rise from obscurity to fame and power he identified.

---

*This rebuff convinced Johnson that Burns was "the most sarcastical man [I] ever met." ("Leonce," "Jack Johnson.")

When Burns' proposed fight with McVey fell through—no one could be found to put up the big money the champion insisted on—he agreed to fight Bill Squires again on June 13. It took him eight rounds to knock Squires out this time. Johnson was again at ringside. "It's downright weary work chasing a man around the world," he told a reporter. "It makes one real tired, it does indeed."

Meanwhile, the best Sam Fitzpatrick could do for his fighter was to get him a bout at Plymouth with big, slow-moving Ben Taylor, ironically labeled the "Woolwich Infant" because of his size. In Johnson's 1927 autobiography, written many years after Fitzpatrick had joined the long queue of white men who had tried and failed to tell him what to do, the fighter pretended he had been the underdog in this contest.

> This match was based upon the craziest terms under which I ever fought, and in view of the important prospects at stake, I thought Fitzpatrick had suddenly lost his senses. Taylor was in fighting trim and was much heavier than I. I was in poor shape, yet Fitzpatrick had consented to terms which provided that to win, I must knock Taylor out in ten rounds; that the rounds were to go only two minutes each; and that we should use six-ounce gloves. Had I lost this fight, and there was a chance that I might, it would have meant a sudden end to my theatrical engagements, for I would have ceased to be an attraction. Furthermore it would have placed me in a class which would have prevented serious consideration of me as a contender for the title.
>
> There was nothing for me to do but abide by Fitzpatrick's silly arrangements.

In fact, Johnson was so sure of winning that he had been drinking for the three days before the fight and appeared in the ring with bloodshot eyes, slowed reflexes, and a serious hangover. Still, as he remembered in his more candid handwritten memoir,

> it was my fight from the very beginning. I let Taylor stay just to give the spectators a run for their money. Not once during the fight did Taylor land more than a light jab on me. On the other hand, I had my man in a bad way many times during the fight but always let up on him when I saw that I had him going. However, in the 8th round I shot a terrific right hook to his jaw and he dropped like a log.

Afterward, Johnson asked his handlers to bring him a restorative of his own invention: "an egg beaten up in a bucket of stout and champagne."*

Even Johnson's innate optimism had begun to flag:

> It was just fatiguing to listen to [Burns'] miles & miles of excuses. For the last few years I had been half round the world trying to secure boxing matches but on the whole it seemed to me that I had not been successful. Like Micawber, I had changed my place of abode time after time in expectation of something turning up but it never came to pass.

Later that month, he began a two-week run at the Oxford Theater, now billed as

JACK JOHNSON
HEAVYWEIGHT CHAMPION OF THE WORLD
THE MAN THEY ALL DODGE
———————
THE GREATEST FIGHTER THE WORLD HAS EVER KNOWN
THE MAN WHOM TOMMY BURNS WON'T FIGHT
UNLESS THEY GUARANTEE HIM £6000
———————
JOHNSON IS A FIGHTER NOT A SHOWMAN

---

*Taylor's trainer, Joe Palmer, never forgot Johnson's "supreme confidence." "Talk about coolness! Johnson's was arctic in the ring. When the big fellows nowadays put down their opponents they have, too often, to be told to stand back until the fallen man rises. Johnson put Taylor down in the seventh round. Instead of trying to stand over his fallen foe, Johnson walked back, as impudent as you like, to his own corner and asked for a drink of water. . . . It was cheeky, but it betokened the supreme confidence and coolness of the man. He knew well enough he could avoid a thunderbolt by a hair's breadth if necessary." (Palmer, *Recollections*, pp. 47–48.)

CHAPTER FIVE

THE MAN WITH
THE GOLDEN SMILE

So far, neither Jack Johnson's ambition nor Tommy Burns' avarice had been enough to bring them together in the ring. That would take an unlikely combination of events far removed from the world of boxing and the bold entrepreneurship of an Australian showman.

On December 16, 1907, while Johnson was still playing five shows a day at the New Star Theater in Milwaukee and Burns was in England getting ready for "Gunner" Moir, President Theodore Roosevelt, in top hat, frock coat, and striped trousers, had stood on the bridge of the presidential yacht *Mayflower* off Hampton Roads, Virginia, and watched as sixteen gleaming American battleships steamed past him and out to sea, beginning a forty-five-thousand-mile, six-continent round-the-world voyage. Roosevelt's motives for dispatching the Great White Fleet were clear-cut. He had made the United States Navy second only to Britain's and wanted the world to see it (and Congress to continue to support it). He also wanted to impress upon the rulers of Japan—whose navy had stunned the world by humiliating Russia in 1904 and 1905—that they would not have a free hand in the Pacific.

Japan's victory over imperial Russia had alarmed Americans, but it had terrified Australians, whose fear of an imminent invasion of their mostly empty continent by Asian "hordes" had already driven one prominent daily to change its slogan from "Australia for the Australians" to "Australia for the White Man." And in March 1908, when it was announced that the American warships would call at Sydney and Melbourne that summer, many saw it as a spectacular sign of white solidarity across the seas, welcome evidence they had not been abandoned by their fellow Anglo-Saxons.

But one citizen of Sydney, a sharp-featured thirty-year-old promoter named Hugh D. McIntosh, saw something else in the arrival of the American fleet: the chance to make some really big money. He had been on the make from earliest childhood. The son of a Sydney policeman who died when Hugh was four, he left home at eight to become a jeweler's apprentice, then moved on to become a surgeon's assistant, a silver-ore picker, a farmhand, a professional milker, and a chorus boy on the Melbourne stage. He sold pies from a tray at racetracks and prizefights, too, and by the time he was twenty-one had married the boss' daughter and turned the bakery into a full-scale catering firm and a profitable restaurant chain. As president of the New South Wales League of Wheelmen, he cashed in on the worldwide enthusiasm for bicycling, promoting international six-day races at Sydney; when rumors of race-fixing undercut that sport, he abandoned it in favor of investing in holiday resorts in the Snowy Mountains.

He was, as an admirer wrote, a distinctive "blend of charlatan, genius, dreamer and bandit," and always on the prowl for bigger schemes and better profits. Twelve thousand American sailors were to come ashore at Sydney and Melbourne with the Great White Fleet, all of them looking for excitement. What could provide more of it than a pair of heavyweight title fights between the American world champion, Tommy Burns, and Australia's best, Bill Squires and Bill Lang? (Burns was actually Canadian, to be sure, and he had already twice knocked Squires cold, but those facts needn't be unduly emphasized. Australian pride in "Boshter Bill" seemed unshakable, and since Burns now lived in the United States, most Australians considered him a Yank.)

McIntosh resolved to make it happen, a decision that would make him a far richer man than he already was and earn him the nickname he would carry for the rest of his life, "Huge Deal" McIntosh. Nothing escaped his notice. When he learned that the Americans were to put in first at Auckland, New Zealand, he hurried there and bought up all the bunting he could find so that when the time came to welcome the fleet, the slower-moving city fathers would be forced to buy it back from him at a handsome profit. Then he fired off a telegram to Burns in England offering twenty thousand dollars for the two bouts. Burns was quick to accept; he had little to fear from Squires or Lang, and had run out of opponents in Britain, while no one had come up with the thirty thousand dollars he still insisted upon before he would face Johnson.

When McIntosh discovered that it would be prohibitive to rent the Sydney Exhibition Hall, he found a vacant lot at the end of the tramline on Rush-cutter's Bay, talked the gullible ironmonger who owned it into renting it to him for four pounds a week so that he could stage what he described as "a two-man show to make a few bob out of the sailors," then put up on the site an octagonal open-air stadium with seats for fifteen thousand spectators.

Everything was ready when the American warships entered Sydney Harbour on August 20. More than 250,000 people had risen before dawn to greet them. The editor of a Sydney monthly called *The Lone Hand* spoke for many of his fellow countrymen:

> As a friendly hand across the Pacific comes to Australia the Great White Fleet. In flashing white it comes, . . . a symbol of a racial ideal to be upheld, and yet of a pacific purpose. . . . "My country, right or wrong," may be questioned as a maxim of conduct, but most will confirm without a moment's doubt, "The White Race Right or Wrong."

Hugh McIntosh had assumed that most seats for the Burns-Squires bout at Rushcutter's Bay four days later would be filled with Yankee sailors, but not many actually turned up; suspicions about Burns' honesty had spread through the fleet, and few of the Americans ashore in a wide-open port that boasted so many other delights wanted to waste time watching a fixed fight. It turned out not to matter. Fifteen thousand Australians filled the stadium, and twenty-five thousand more milled about outside. Burns carried Squires for thirteen rounds this time, allowing the crowd to have its fill of chanting "Go, 'Boshter Bill'!" and the cameramen to capture enough footage to make the fight film a potentially profitable attraction—then knocked him out again.

The U.S. fleet and its badly hungover crew soon moved on to Melbourne, where just eight days later Burns fought Bill Lang in another brand-new stadium hastily built by McIntosh. Lang managed to knock the champion down for the first time since Burns had won the title—and was made to pay for it by being knocked down five times himself before he was counted out in the fifth.

It had all gone better than even Hugh McIntosh had dared hope—he personally had cleared more than fifty thousand dollars from the two fights—and he saw no reason to end things now. Ever since Burns had arrived in Australia, reporters had plagued him with questions about Johnson. To one, he claimed that Johnson had been dodging *him,* that if Johnson—who suffered from the "yellow streak" to which all blacks were prone—wouldn't fight him, he planned to retire. "All niggers are alike to me," he told another, "but I'll fight him even though he is a nigger," and he would "make it tough for Mr. Coon" when he did so—provided, of course, the money was right.

Even before the Burns-Lang bout, McIntosh had gone to work to make sure it was, by talking several wealthy sports into helping him come up with the thirty thousand dollars Burns demanded. Then he started another exchange of telegrams with England, this time with Sam Fitzpatrick. If Johnson would accept five thousand dollars and come back to Sydney, the chance at the title to which he felt he'd been entitled for more than five years would be his at last. Johnson bitterly resented having to accept one sixth of what the champion was to get, but the opportunity was too good to pass up.

Fitzpatrick had already committed Johnson to a fight with Sam Langford at London's National Sporting Club. But the club manager, Peggy Bettinson, agreed to delay it and even lent Fitzpatrick and Johnson money to help pay for their passage to Australia. In exchange, Johnson signed a letter promising to come back to London and fight Langford for five thousand dollars, whether he won or lost his fight with Tommy Burns.

The fight was on. DE BIG COON AM A-COMIN', headlined the Sydney *Truth*. It was set for twenty rounds at Rushcutter's Bay on the day after Christmas— Boxing Day in England and her colonies. John L. Sullivan, for one, was horrified to hear that Tommy Burns was going to risk his title against a black man. "Shame on the money-mad Champion!" he said. "Shame on the man who upsets good American precedents because there are Dollars, Dollars, Dollars in it."

In his book *Knuckles and Gloves*, Bohun Lynch set forth in one appalling paragraph many of the beliefs shared by whites around the world concerning Negro boxers and mixed bouts, beliefs that would now be tested as for the first time a black man prepared to fight a white one for the heavyweight championship of the world.

The history of the Nigger in boxing has yet to be fully explored. . . . Negroes . . . have fought with certain exceptions under the severe handicap of unpopularity. Without entering too deeply into the Colour question, we may say that this unpopularity comes also from tradition. The vast majority of negro boxers have been slaves or the descendants of slaves. In early days and in the popular imagination they were savages, or almost savages. Also it was recognized from the first that the African negro and his descendants in the West Indies and America were harder-headed than white men, less sensitive about the face and jaw; most black boxers can take without pain or trouble a smashing which would cause the collapse of a white man. Occasionally, this is balanced by the nigger's weakness in the stomach—but, one thing with another, the white man is at a disadvantage. But physical inequality is not the only point of difference. Niggers are usually children in temperament, with the children's bad points as well as their good ones. The black man's head is easily turned, and when his personal and physical success over a white man is manifest he generally behaves like the worst kind of spoiled child. In extreme cases, his overwhelming sense of triumph knows no bounds at all, and he turns from a primitive man into a fiend. His insolence is appalling. When the black is in this condition ignorant white men lose their heads, their betters are coldly disgusted. . . . As a rule, it is far better that negroes, if fight they must, should fight amongst themselves. No crowd is ever big-hearted enough, or "sporting enough," to regard an encounter between white and black with a purely sporting interest.

Australia would not now prove as sporting or as big-hearted toward Johnson as it had been just a little over a year earlier. In early October, he, Hattie McClay, and Sam Fitzpatrick boarded the RMS *Ortona* at Naples. At first, things went as well as they had the year before. "We have a gym fixed up on the boat," Fitzpatrick cabled to a friend in London, "and Arthur puts in a couple of hours punching the [bag] and skipping rope, now and then taking on a few husky firemen from the crew." When his party landed at Perth, Johnson showed off the handsome diamond-and-ruby scarf pin he'd won for being the best-dressed man at the captain's ball, and cheerfully boasted of what he was at last going to be able to do to Tommy Burns. "I am a larger man than Burns, and am cleverer," he said. "How does Burns want it? Does he want it fast and willing? I'm his man in that case. Does he want it flat footed? Goodness, if he does, why I'm his man again. Anything to suit; but fast or slow I'm going to win."

But the cheerful self-confidence that had charmed Australians in 1907 was now seen by many as boastful, insolent, unsporting—"flash." A Sydney reception in his honor was sparsely attended. He had often been patronized in 1907. Now he found himself hideously caricatured. In the brightly colored poster by Norman Lindsay that greeted him everywhere, his white opponent was portrayed as a handsome, sturdy little hero while Johnson loomed over him, big and black and threatening, his eyes glowing red—Bohun Lynch's Negro "fiend" incarnate.

What had happened? Newspaper stories detailing Johnson's romance with

Lola Toy probably had something to do with Australia's change of heart. (The *Bulletin,* an advocate of Australia's whites-only policy, for example, was not pleased to report that "the coloured man is accompanied by his wife, a white woman somewhat addicted to jewelry.") Then, too, the stakes were higher now than they had been in 1907, when no critical title had been on the line. But most important was the orgy of Anglo-Saxonism that had accompanied the visit of the U.S. fleet and helped reinforce Australia's sense of itself as what the poet Roderic Quinn called "the World's White Outpost."

When Burns beat Squires, Australia's best heavyweight had fallen to a foreign champion, to be sure, but at least the winner had been a white man.* Hugh McIntosh did all he could to emphasize that fact. He organized teas presided over by Mrs. Burns so that the ladies of Sydney—who would be barred from the bout itself—could get to see the title holder rattle a punching bag hung with the flags of all three countries whose champions he had defeated: England, Ireland, and the United States. And he orchestrated press interviews so that journalists could marvel in print at Burns' allegedly keen intellect and clean living, his supposed strength and skill—he was an "exquisite fighting engine," said a writer for *The Lone Hand;* no one on earth could beat him. McIntosh himself seemed to share that view: at the end of what would be "a desperate struggle," he predicted, "Burns will have the big coloured man's scalp dangling from his belt." Canada's Tommy Burns had been transformed into Australia's "Tommy Boy." And Jack Johnson had turned from the colorful curiosity he had been just a year earlier into the symbol of all the dark forces Australians seemed to fear. "Citizens who have never prayed before," said the *Illustrated Sporting and Dramatic News,* "are supplicating Providence to give the white man a strong right arm with which to belt the coon into oblivion." "This battle," according to the *Australian Star,*

---

*In *The Sportsman* on the eve of the Burns-Squires fight, a versifier named Annie Howe had made this especially plain.

> And these two men are, meeting face to face,
> A credit to the Anglo-Saxon race;
> Two men are they, beloved by British folk,
> Each with a heart as stout as English oak!
> Both have been manly in the battles fought,
> For nothing underhanded have they sought—
> Those are the warriors a world admires,
> Men of the kidney of a Burns and Squires!

Source: Wells, *Boxing Day,* p. 89.

"may in the future be looked back upon as the first great battle of an inevitable race war."*

The contest was nearly eight weeks away. Johnson used the time to do what he could to win back the Australian public. He began with an appeal to the sense of sportsmanship on which Australians always said they prided themselves. "The words I am about to speak to you, gentlemen, I speak from my heart," he told one Sydney gathering.

> Each and everyone in this room who has read the sporting papers knows that I have traveled the world over trying to get Mr. Burns. I don't believe in making a lot of noise because I believe in the old saying that a barking dog won't bite.
>
> I, myself, have picked up several papers with interviews from Mr. Burns saying that I have a yellow streak. I have traveled all over the world and nobody has yet found that yellow streak. I am a man and I say it is a thing that any man would take offence at—any man in the world would. . . . We will see who has the yellow streak. All I ask for—I don't ask any favor—is a fair field.

Based again at the Sir Joseph Banks Hotel, Johnson took part in publicity stunts amiably enough, chasing down a wallaby on the hotel lawns, then a greased pig, finally a hare—all to demonstrate his speed. He tried to show he was more than a mere athlete, as well; somewhere along the way he'd learned to play the bass viol so he and Hattie McClay played impromptu after-dinner duets for their fellow guests. He told a reporter she and he were also rehearsing for a production of *Othello*. And he put on a shadowboxing show each afternoon: while Hugh McIntosh organized no teas for Hattie to preside over, hundreds of women paid a shilling each to see Jack Johnson sweat in the sun.

But nothing he could do alleviated the apprehension the whole country seemed to feel as the day of the fight approached. And his own feelings toward Tommy Burns proved impossible to hide. He was mostly his genial self when a writer for *The Lone Hand* came to call, full of eager talk about his boyhood, his earlier bouts, his achievements inside and outside the ring. Then the reporter mentioned the champion.

---

*This notion underlay even Hugh McIntosh's advertisements for the films of the upcoming bout: "FIRST TIME IN THE WORLD'S FISTIANIC HISTORY . . . ," they read, "the Champion Representatives of the White and Black Races have met for RACIAL and INDIVIDUAL Supremacy, since cinematographic pictures became a fine art."

Johnson does not like Burns. [He] thirsts to humiliate his detractor. He hurls no charge of streak-ownership at Burns, but he says he is a grossly over-estimated battler. . . . Johnson contemns Burns for his niggardliness. He considers it beneath the white man's dignity to have but one attendant to perform the multitude of duties that are required by a world's champion. . . . * Burns is his conception of a thoroughly rude and offensive person. The colored champion has engaged in some hundreds of public contests in his time. The struggle with Burns will be the first, he claims, in which he will enter the ring with a feeling against his adversary.

Grudge matches have always sold tickets, and when two prizefighters feel no actual animus toward each other, promoters routinely do their best to manufacture some. Neither Johnson nor Burns needed any help. ("Looking back in memory," Burns wrote later, "I realize that [the fight with Johnson] was the first . . . in which I found myself hating my opponent.")

Johnson's anger intensified every time he remembered how little he was being paid in comparison to the champion. He called on McIntosh so often to make his case for a bigger cut, and did so with such vehemence, that the promoter—mindful of what had happened to Alec McLean when he had dared argue with Johnson over money—kept a lead pipe on his desk, wrapped in a roll of sheet music for the song "Rock Me to Sleep, Mother."

An early meeting between the two fighters concerning the size of the ring did not go well. Johnson arrived at McIntosh's office with a friend's seven-year-old daughter in tow. Burns told him he'd once been a good fighter but was now washed up and would have to "take your medicine." Johnson said it would be Burns who would be forced to do the swallowing. The champion countered with a string of curses, or so Johnson recalled.

When Burns started to perform I drew his attention to the presence of the child and remarked, "I would not do that if I were you." I sent the child away. Burns grabbed a chair and his language was something beautiful. He could have gotten to me had he liked. Although he had the chair & an

---

*Johnson's own sizable entourage was a revelation to Australian sportswriters. "A cloud of attendants surround him when his 'work' is done," wrote one visitor to the Sir Joseph Banks. "He has the biggest staff of helpers the writer has ever seen in waiting on any fighter. The man who rubs him down doesn't run with him; the runner doesn't put the gloves on with him; his sparring partner does nothing but spar. It resembles the state of things that prevails in a big British household, where each servitor knows his or her duties, and is prepared to drop dead or 'give notice' if an innovation is suggested." ("Leonce," "Jack Johnson.")

inkpot I said to Mr. McIntosh, "Turn him loose, Mac." Burns had cabled that he wanted a 16-foot ring, and my reply was that he could have a 10-foot one if he liked. I don't move round much, and that office would have suited me as well as anywhere.*

Then there was the matter of who would referee. McIntosh had wired Jim Jeffries, asking if he was willing. He said he'd do it for five thousand dollars plus travel expenses, but Johnson wouldn't hear of it: "I would never agree to allow that man to referee over me. He has always been very bitter against me, and would not fight me after I beat his brother." He believed McIntosh wanted Burns to win and therefore distrusted everyone the promoter suggested. Instead, he asked that two judges be appointed in addition to the referee, as they now sometimes were in America. "For every point I'm given I'll have earned two, because I'm a Negro," he said. "But I want to be sure I get my point, anyway." Burns rejected that notion, and Australian boxing authorities refused to allow it. Johnson would have to agree to let a lone referee decide who had won and who had lost.

The issue remained unresolved. With just two days to go, McIntosh called another meeting. He offered more names. Johnson rejected them all, then directed a question at Burns himself: "Before going any further with this match, I want to know if you and McIntosh are good friends."

"We are friends, the best of friends."

Did McIntosh feel the same way toward Burns?

He did.

"If you and Burns are such good friends," Johnson told McIntosh, "then you must referee the fight."

Sam Fitzpatrick tried to object.

Johnson angrily cut him off. "*I* am fighting this fight," he said, "and am going to have some part in naming the referee." He didn't much like McIntosh, but he knew the man wanted to continue as a big-time boxing promoter and therefore would presumably not dare be blatantly unfair.

In the end, McIntosh—who had never refereed a boxing match before— agreed to oversee a contest for the heavyweight championship of the world.

Given the checkered pasts of both fighters, it is not surprising that there were last-minute rumors of a fix, rumors powerful enough for Johnson to

---

*In the end, they would fight in a twenty-four-foot ring.

issue an informal denial.* In a letter said to have been written to "one of his wife's relatives in Chicago" and published in several U.S. papers on Christmas Eve, Johnson did not deny that such a deal may have been discussed but swore he would have no part of it.

> I am going to win, no matter what money they give me, and I want you to get busy. Put down all the money you can raise, and get the boys to come through with all they can gather.
>
> I don't care what Fitzpatrick and Burns may have fixed up. I don't care what I am supposed to do. They are playing hog with me anyhow, and the most money I can get out of it is almost nothing. Here's one time I can't be handled.
>
> Just remember this: they are fixing it all up to hand me the lemon, but I won't fall for the game. I'm going to double-cross all the schemers in the world and get the title. Can't I make more out of the title than I could get on all the frame-ups that ever happened?

Fans began lining up at the ticket windows at two-thirty in the morning on Boxing Day, and by the time 250 policemen got there at six-thirty, thousands of spectators were waiting for the gates to open. At midmorning, twenty thousand men were in their seats—and about thirty thousand more remained outside, some perched in trees or on telegraph poles in hope of getting a glimpse of the action.

The bout was scheduled to begin at eleven. A few minutes before Johnson was to start his walk to the ring, as McIntosh remembered it, he made one more stab at getting paid what he thought he deserved. He sent word from his dressing room that he would not fight unless he got more money—and he wanted to see the cash before he laced on his gloves. The promoter stormed into Johnson's dressing room. "So you want your money first, do you cobber? Where's my check book?" He reached into his jacket as if it were hidden there but pulled out a revolver instead. "If you're not in the ring right on time," he said, "I'll skin you alive."

---

*After the fight, the *Police Gazette* quoted an anonymous "veteran referee and matchmaker" who said he had "excellent reason for believing" that Burns had "insisted on having $30,000 . . . with only $5,000 for Johnson because he thought it would compel Fitzpatrick and Johnson to do business with him for a bunch of coin. . . . Anybody who knows Fitzpatrick will tell you that there isn't a crooked hair on his head, but I'll bet that if Burns made any such proposition, Fitzpatrick accepted it like a flash." Without it, their anonymous source said, Burns would never have climbed into the ring with Jack Johnson. (*Police Gazette,* January 23, 1909; Milwaukee *Free Press,* December 24, 1908.)

Johnson subsided and started for the ring. As soon as the crowd spotted him in his hooded robe, the old shouts of "coon" and "nigger" began. "All the hatred of twenty thousand whites for all the negroes in the world," the *Bulletin* called it. Australians had come not to see a fight, it continued, "so much as to witness a black aspirant for the championship of the world beaten to his knees and counted out." As always, Johnson appeared unconcerned, smiling and nodding as he and his seconds walked up the aisle. "He didn't get much homage," the *Bulletin* continued, "but made a lot of what he did get."

Then Burns appeared, wearing a felt cap and a rumpled blue suit, "and was nearly blown out of the Stadium by the crash of applause." The crowd stood and cheered its "Tommy Boy."

Johnson extended his hand. Burns refused it. "Hello" was all he said, and went to his corner.

Johnson betrayed no emotion, but according to one ringside reporter he did take a mouthful of water and spit it with "uncanny accuracy between the heads of one of his seconds and a pressman onto a vacant space about the size of a handkerchief." Then he leaned over the ropes and checked with one of his seconds to make sure his own sizable bet on himself had been placed.

When Burns removed his suit, folding it neatly before stuffing it into a battered suitcase, Johnson saw that he was wearing elastic bandages on both his elbows and shouted that he would have to take them off. Otherwise, he said, he wouldn't fight.

The crowd roared its disapproval. The "yellow streak" already seemed to be on display.

Hugh McIntosh—wearing a referee's costume of his own devising: gray cap, white turtleneck, white slacks, white shoes—ruled that Burns could keep the bandages on.

Johnson shook his head, sat on his stool, and folded his arms. "Don't care," he said. "I'll sit here for an hour if necessary. They must be there to do him some good, and if he don't take 'em off, there'll be no fight."

Burns settled onto his stool, too.

Unsure of what to do, McIntosh appealed to Larry Foley, the dean of Australian boxing experts, who happened to be sitting at ringside, to climb into the ring and have a look at the bandages. He did—and pronounced them illegal.

Burns angrily tore them off. The crowd rose to its feet again to cheer for the fine sportsmanship their new hero was showing.

The bell finally rang at 11:07 a.m. Burns was favored 5 to 4 to win.

"All right, Tommy. Here I am," Johnson said. A few seconds later, Burns was sitting on the canvas, a bewildered look on his face. A short right uppercut had lifted him off the canvas and put him there. "The world spun crazily," Burns recalled, "a huge red blur obscured everything." He signaled to his anxious seconds that he was all right, managed to get back to his feet at the count of eight, hurled himself at Johnson, and remained on the attack until the bell rang, doing his best to reach Johnson's body while the bigger man counterpunched and taunted him: "Poor little Tommy," he said. "Who told you you were a fighter?"

Between rounds, while Burns' anxious seconds flapped towels and sponged him down with champagne in hopes of refreshing him, Johnson took another big gulp of water—and sprayed it over the reporters nearest his corner. They ducked. Johnson laughed.

"Come right on!" he shouted at the bell, and as Burns rushed toward him, Johnson moved his head just enough to allow Burns' right hand to whistle past, then landed another uppercut on the champion's chin. Burns collapsed a second time (he would later claim his ankle had given way), rose again at eight, and held on to Johnson in the middle of the ring.

Burns called Johnson a "yellow cur." "Come on and fight, nigger!" he said. "Fight like a white man!"

Johnson just continued to smile. "Burns got through his other opponents easily by simply kidding them to death," he remembered. "He would work them up to a condition of nervous excitement." Johnson was neither excited nor nervous, and he was himself a master of mouth-fighting. "Burns started it by calling me a yellow cur," Johnson remembered, "and used other language which it would be impossible for me to report. I only kidded him in a nice way but he used the other sort of language. . . . If I had killed Burns for the language he used to me I would have been fully justified."

Instead, he slammed Burns in the body, then smashed his mouth. As Burns went back to his corner there was blood on his lips, and his left eye had begun to close. It was already clear the challenger was too much for Tommy Burns to handle. Johnson was not surprised.

I had forgotten more about boxing than Burns ever knew. Burns was a strong fellow & had a good right hand punch if he could have landed but my defenses prevented that. No crouching little man can hit a good big man. He has to straighten up to deliver and if the other chap's good & fast enough, all he has to do is get him when he is coming up. . . .

My aim in the fight at Sydney was to show Burns, after all his boasting and his talk about the yellow streak down my spine, that I could out-box him and out-slug him. I wanted to beat him in a clever way without a chance of being beaten myself. If I had knocked him out quickly, the public would have said it was a fluke. When I beat him in a long fight it gave the other side no chance to talk.

The few surviving minutes of silent film that Hugh McIntosh's camera crew made that day are an incomplete record—no footage remains of the first few rounds or the climactic moment of the last round—but they do provide the first glimpse we have of Jack Johnson in action. Standing over six feet and weighing nearly 192, with a massive, chiseled upper body and surprisingly slender legs, he is an authentic heavyweight, while Burns, at five seven and 167 pounds, looks like the overblown middleweight he was, a boy who has somehow found himself sent into the ring to do a man's work. He had made a career of beating bigger men, but even he privately doubted he could do so this time: "I don't think I can beat that nigger," he'd confided to Peggy Bettinson back in London, "but I'll give him the fight of his life."*

He tried, but as the old film shows, it was hopeless. Again and again Burns rushes at the bigger man, who hits him on the way in, then gathers him into

---

*Johnson had been so sure of victory, he remembered, that he took the time between rounds to gaze out over the crowd: "As my gaze wandered out into the surrounding territory, I saw a colored man sitting on a fence watching the fight with open mouth and bulging eyes. My glance returned to him again and again. He was one of the very few colored people present and he became a sort of landmark for me. I became more and more interested in him, and soon discovered that mentally he was fighting harder than I was. Whenever I unlimbered a blow, he, too, shot one into the air landing it on an imaginary antagonist at about the same spot where I landed on Burns. When I swayed to avert a blow from Burns, the fighter on the fence also swayed in the same direction and at a similar angle. When I ducked, he also ducked. But his battle came to an inglorious end when it was necessary for me to make an unusually low duck. He attempted to follow the movement and fell off the fence. This incident so amused me that I laughed heartily, and Burns and the spectators were at a loss to know what had so aroused my mirth."

This could not have happened precisely as described. There was no "fence" visible from the ring on which the phantom Negro could have sat. Also, the "open mouth and bulging eyes" with which he was supposed to have followed the action and the slapstick finale seem more like stock elements from a minstrel turn than real life; in 1924, in fact, Johnson would himself record a similar story as part of a vaudeville routine: "When I entered the ring with Tommy, I looked over the big crowd. Sittin' way back on the fence, behind everybody, I saw one, just one, colored man. Well sir, Burns made a swing at me. I ducked, but he swung so hard that it must have excited my colored brother, and he fell clean off the fence. He ain't got back on that fence yet! [*Crowd laughs.*]"

There was metaphoric truth in the story nonetheless. People of color around the world followed Johnson's every move that afternoon and delighted in every blow he landed. (Jack Johnson, *In the Ring and Out*, pp. 166–67; Jack Johnson 1924 recording, "Runnin' Down the Title Holder," Ajax 17024. Tim Brooks Collection.)

his long arms, rocks his head back and forth with uppercuts, and shoves him away again. And all the time Johnson keeps smiling and talking. He had set out to beat Burns "in a clever way," as he said he would, but as the rounds tick by, it is clear he has a second agenda as well: to disprove, one by one, the racist theories put forward by writers like Bohun Lynch.

Were blacks weak in the stomach?*

An American writer at ringside described how Johnson beckoned Burns inside and let him pound his body.

> "Hit me here, Tommy," he would say, exposing the right side of his unprotected stomach, and when Burns struck, Johnson would neither wince nor cover up. Instead, he would receive the blow with a happy careless smile directed at the spectators, turn the left side of his unprotected stomach and say, "Now there, Tommy," and while Burns would hit as directed, Johnson would continue to grin and chuckle and smile his golden smile.†

Did blacks betray a yellow streak when under pressure?

Johnson did not flinch from Burns' best body punches—"You punch like a woman, Tommy," he said. "Who taught you how to fight, your mother?"— and he won most of the inside exchanges at which the champion was supposed to be so good. "I was positive he would fold up under punishment," Burns admitted many years later. "How badly had I underrated his boxing skill, his tremendous strength and unquestionable cunningness! He backed slowly about the ring, employing a slow shuffling technique, coupled with superb arm blocking and head rolling."

Were black fighters less able to think on their feet than their white opponents?

"They talked of [Burns'] being a man of brains," Johnson wrote. "If I had not more brains than him I would have been sorry for it." Hugh McIntosh remembered:

---

*Peter Jackson and Sam Langford both responded to this hoary canard the same way. "They are all after my body," Jackson said. "Hit a nigger in the stomach and you'll settle him, they say, but it never occurs to them that a white man might just as quickly be beaten by a wallop in the same region." Langford is supposed to have answered it while in the ring. After a white opponent managed to land one to his belly, a spectator shouted, "The niggers don't like them down there." "No, they don't," he shouted back, "and do you know any man that does?" (Dartnell, *Seconds Out,* pp. 72–73.)

†Johnson threw almost no body punches during the fight. "Why was I afraid to hit him below the chin?" he said afterward. "Because I would most likely have been disqualified if I had. I could not take any chances where it was so earnestly desired that the white man should win." (Milwaukee *Free Press,* April 21, 1909.)

He is a funny fellow, that Johnson. He stood up before Tommy and when the latter rushed would say, "This is what is known as a left hook, Tommy," and then he'd let go. Then he'd step back and as Tommy rushed in would say, "I will now give you another little lesson on boxing, Tommy; look out for your eye!" And then he'd let go on Burns' eye. He just kidded Tommy to death.

Burns floundered after him, always game but always outfought and out-thought.

In the sixth round, Johnson turned his head to chat with the press so often, his seconds shouted that he should keep his eye on the champion. "I see him, oh yes," Johnson said, "though he is so small." Catcalls followed: "Flash nigger!" "That's flashness!" One Australian newspaperman declared Johnson's chatter "devilish gloating."

No one objected to Burns' foul language.

Johnson hit the champion with another left hand; when Burns started to sag, Johnson hauled him upright again as the bell rang, then pushed him back toward his corner.

In the seventh, he knocked Burns down for a third time. He also made a reference to Burns' wife, Jewel, that especially enraged the champion. "He said something about my wife in the ring and if the public had heard him they would have lynched him. I tell you that if he had made the same remarks about my wife in America, or about any white woman, that he did to me, he would have been lynched very quickly."*

In the tenth, the old footage shows a press photographer sliding his big camera under the ropes to get a picture. Johnson stops, smiles, and holds Burns nearly motionless, then moves him away again. "Did you get that?" he asked.

Halfway through the thirteenth round, Burns' legs buckled again. Johnson grabbed him under the arms, lifted him up, and set him straight in order to be able to punish him some more. As Burns staggered back to his corner, one eye was closed, the other closing; blood trickled steadily into both. His battered jaw had ballooned to twice its size, and his gaping mouth was bleeding.

---

*One newspaper reported that Johnson had said, "Poor little boy, Jewel won't know you when she gets you back from this fight." Given the fury his remark still evoked in Burns years later, it seems likely he said something a good deal gamier. (Quoted in Wells, *Boxing Day*, p. 175.)

Some in the crowd began to call for the fight to be stopped. Police officers, empowered to step in if they thought one or the other man was about to be injured, clambered up into Burns' corner to ask him if he'd had enough. He waved them off. He was not going to lose his title sitting on his stool.*

As the bell rang for the fourteenth round, Johnson rushed from his corner. Burns did his best to keep away, but another right hand sent him down. He got up and Johnson cocked his right hand to knock him down again when the police signaled for the fight to be halted. McIntosh shouted—"in a voice fit to wake the dead," said the *Bulletin*—"Stop, Johnson!"† McIntosh declared Johnson the winner. "As McIntosh's voice rebounded from the walls of the stadium that mighty concourse remained silent," the *Bulletin* continued. "Johnson waved his hands to the crowd that did not cheer him. A few straggling voices were raised but they were mere flecks of sound in an ocean of silence."

Burns angrily protested, and when his seconds got him back onto his stool, he began to weep. The fight should never have been stopped, he said through his torn and swollen lips. Johnson couldn't hit "worth a cent." If the police hadn't interfered, he added, "I might even have won because the big nigger was tiring fast."‡

The crowd fell silent and began to drift out of the stadium. In twelve minutes the whole place was empty. "The Australian nation, which welcomed Johnson as a challenger, had never seriously considered the possibility that he might turn into a champion," one city resident recalled.

---

*Burns would later allege that Johnson's seconds had falsely shouted that his jaw was broken in order to get the bout stopped and give the victory to their man. If they did, it's unlikely anyone could have heard them.

†The surviving footage stops abruptly with Burns halfway to the floor. Some have argued that someone ordered the cameramen to stop grinding at that precise moment, a considerable feat of long-distance coordination. But an account of the first showing of the film in Milwaukee describes clear footage of all the now-missing portions of the bout, including the final seconds. Evidently the offending footage was cut later in the editing room by someone who thought it best for moviegoers to be denied the sight of a black man pounding a white one into near-insensibility. (Milwaukee *Evening Wisconsin*, April 23, 1909.)

‡Burns' admirers would claim their man had done so much damage to Johnson's ribs that he had been briefly hospitalized after the fight. Johnson himself claimed he'd gone for a swim, "followed it up with a motor drive and that evening entertained friends at dinner." The confusion may have stemmed from a subsequent Johnson visit to a Melbourne hospital for stomach trouble. (Jack Johnson, *In the Ring and Out*, p. 168.)

The experience of a leader of the Sydney bar, who happened to have been a famous amateur boxer, was typical. He had arranged a dinner-party for twenty-four on the night of Boxing Day, to celebrate Burns' victory. The champagne was on ice. It was an occasion for the noblest brandy. When the fight ended in Johnson's victory, the host left the ringside and walked home, as unconscious of the world around him as a sleep-walker. When he got to his house he went straight to bed, like a man suffering from shock. If his friends chose to turn up and drink his champagne that was their business. They must excuse him if he kept to his bed. He need not have worried. Every guest went home too, and stayed at home, like a man suffering a bereavement.

Johnson greeted the press after the fight while lying on the rubbing table in his dressing room. There wasn't a mark on him. "Burns can't fight," he said, and then thinking better of it, "I don't want to say that. He's a game, straight fighter." But, he said, as his masseur rubbed eucalyptus oil into his shoulders, he did hope he'd disproved once and for all the myth of the yellow streak.

"I had attained my life's ambition," Johnson wrote in his 1927 autobiography:

> The little Galveston colored boy had defeated the world's champion boxer and, for the first and only time in history, a black man held one of the greatest honors which exists in the field of sports and athletics—an honor for which white men had contested many times and which they held as a dear and most desirable one. Naturally, I felt a high sense of exaltation but I kept this feeling to myself. . . . To me it was not a racial triumph, but there were those who were to take this view of the situation, and almost immediately a great hue and cry went up because a colored man was holding the championship.

That hue and cry began within hours of Johnson's victory. The Sydney *Sportsman*, which had once welcomed Johnson to Australia, denounced him after the fight as a "gloating coon" with "only the instincts of a nigger—pure nigger." "Had [Johnson's] nods, becks, wreathed smiles, etc. occurred in America," said the *Bulletin*, "a prominent citizen would inevitably have risen impressively somewhere about the close of the fourth round, and, amid encouraging cheers, have drawn a gun upon Johnson and shot that immense mass of black humanity dead." Furthermore, the paper continued, since Johnson's "insolence" had all been captured on film, any jury of white men allowed to view it would have exonerated his assassin.

Others, less outraged by the manner of Johnson's triumph than by the simple fact of it, foretold dire consequences. The poet Henry Lawson warned his fellow whites of what he feared was coming:

> It was not Burns that was beaten—for a nigger has smacked your face.
> Take heed—I am tired of writing—but O my people take heed.
> For the time may be near for the mating of the Black and the White to breed.

In the Melbourne *Herald*, Randolph Bedford—writer, would-be politician, and lyricist for "Australia My Beloved Land"—was just as agitated.

> Already the insolent black's victory causes skin troubles. . . . An hour after [the fight] I heard a lascar laying down the Marquis of Queensberry to two whites, and they listened humbly. It is a bad day for Australia and not a good day for America. The United States has 90,000 citizens of Johnson's color and would be glad to get rid of them.
>
> Blessings on the Immigration Restriction Act! I am forced to believe that much is to be said for Simon Legree and that it is a pity that the churchwardens of Liverpool and Bristol ever went into the slave trade, otherwise Johnson might still be up a tree in Africa.*

Johnson, who decided to stay on in Australia for a time and capitalize on his fame with a theatrical tour, was accustomed to abuse in the newspapers, but at least once his irritation at this kind of hysteria—and a series of stories quoting Tommy Burns as demanding a rematch and complaining he'd been robbed by the illicit intervention of the new champion's cornermen—broke through the determinedly cheerful exterior he usually reserved for the press. "As I am a descendant of Ham," he told a reporter for the *Herald,* "I must bear your reproaches because I beat a white man." But Burns had been a "mere child," he said; he could have trounced him at anything from billiards to banjo playing. Still, if the former champion really wanted a rematch,

---

*This was too much for some Australians, and *Boxing Day,* Jeff Wells' vivid book on the Burns battle, includes several letters written to the *Herald* in protest, including one from a man who said Randolph Bedford, not Jack Johnson, was "an outrage on any civilized community." (Wells, *Boxing Day,* p. 198.)

"count me in. Now that the shoe is on the other foot, I just want to hear that white man come around whining for another chance. I'll give him a real taste of my match-making genius. See how he'll relish a chance of a beating for bare expenses."*

Then, in an indirect slap at the white Australians who continued to jeer him, he went out of his way to praise the aboriginal people, whom he knew they also despised. He'd been to the Sydney museum, he said, and seen their boomerangs and stone axes: "Your central Australian natives must have been men of genius to have turned out such artistic and ideal weapons"; he envied white Australians for being able to share their continent with the descendants of such extraordinary people.

Compared to the most extreme Australian reaction, the response back home to Johnson's victory seemed almost subdued. James K. Vardaman, the fire-breathing ex-governor of Mississippi, could be counted on to say something vicious: "Personally," he said, "I took no other interest in the Johnson-Burns fight than to wish that any white man fighting a negro for money might get a knockout of sufficient proportion to cause him to continue on to eternal rest." White southern newspapers paid as little attention to Johnson's victory as possible; the Raleigh *News and Observer* devoted a single paragraph to the triumph of the man it called the "Texas Darky."

Most northern papers offered complete coverage of Johnson's achievement, however. Some editorialists were genuinely alarmed by it: "Is the Caucasian played out?" asked the Detroit *Free Press*. "Are the races we have been calling inferior about to demand of us that we must draw the color line in everything if we are to avoid being whipped individually and collectively?" Other northern papers saw little to be concerned about: "Well," said the Omaha *Bee*, "Bre'r Johnson is an American, anyway." And at least one,

---

*Humiliated by his defeat and uneasy about facing friends and family back home, Tommy Burns stayed on in Australia for fourteen months, drinking and eating too much and losing most of his thirty-thousand-dollar purse at the racetrack. In the spring of 1910, overweight and undertrained, he narrowly beat Bill Lang, to win the championship of the British Empire. He relinquished that title in 1911. When he finally went home, he sold clothing in Calgary, tried promoting, endured an acrimonious divorce, and eventually happily married again. He operated a pub in Newcastle, England, and a speakeasy in Manhattan; sold insurance in Texas; operated a saloon in Bremerton, Washington; and then turned to religion. In 1948 he became an ordained minister and began handing out business cards inscribed, "Compliments of Tommy Burns, former world's heavyweight champion, a demonstrator of Universal Love." "Looking back in memory to that great battle [with Johnson]," he wrote during the early 1950s, "I realize that . . . I actually lost that battle—through hate—before it started. How great is the power of man's thought and feeling to either build or destroy himself." He died of a heart attack in 1955. (Burns, "Tommy Burns.")

the New York *Morning Telegraph,* even saw in Johnson's win evidence of the absurdity of segregating sports.

> Now that Mr. Johnson, the Texas dinge, is the Champion face smasher in the world, the color line question is receiving an unusual amount of public attention. The color line was . . . used in the most select pugilistic circles as a subterfuge behind which a white man could hide to keep some husky colored gentleman from knocking his block off and wiping up the canvas floor of a square circle with his remains. It is a handy little invention which costs nothing and probably has saved many a white man's life. . . . Many men who are well-known in public life today owe their well-preserved appearance and success to this lifesaving compound.

The black press was exultant. A SOUTHERN NEGRO IS HEAVYWEIGHT CHAMPION OF THE WORLD, trumpeted the Richmond *Planet.* "No event in forty years has given more satisfaction to the colored people of this country than has the signal victory of Jack Johnson." The *Colored American Magazine* hailed Johnson's victory as "the zenith of Negro sport." Even the editor of the sedate Cleveland *Journal,* who disapproved of prizefighting and believed pugilists especially prone to "high-living, failure and an untimely death," couldn't conceal his pleasure:

> Johnson is a Negro. And his triumph over Burns is only another example of the old saying, "All the Negro asks is a chance . . ." Whenever this chance has been made (it is more often made than given) even though we have to chase the other fellow all over the world, literally speaking, as Johnson did Burns, the Negro makes good. . . . God knows, the sons and daughters of ebony have never been weighed in the balance and found wanting. There is light ahead, and hope and joy for such a wonderful people.

To cash in on that sort of sentiment, the lithographic firm of Brandt and Schweible began turning out an inspirational poster for sale to Negro households. Johnson stands at the center, stripped to the waist, fists cocked, beneath a victor's laurel wreath. Behind him are two ovals: one frames a drawing of a Lincolnesque log cabin labeled BIRTHPLACE OF JOHNSON; the other shows the champion gripping a steering wheel and wearing a duster and driving cap with the caption, JOHNSON IN HIS CAR. Armed only with strength and grit and quick wits, Johnson had punched his way up from poverty to wealth and success. Nothing could have been more American.

Johnson himself especially treasured a telegram from friends and family in Galveston—"the first cable ever sent to Australia by Negro citizens of the South," according to one newspaper, paid for with nickels and dimes—applauding his triumph and promising a big torchlight parade in his honor as soon as he got home.

The press solicited comments from former heavyweight titlists. Rather than concede Johnson's superior skills, they chose to denigrate the ex-champion. "Burns never was the champion prize-fighter of the world," said John L. Sullivan. Jim Corbett agreed: it was Burns' fault that "the white man has succumbed to a type which in the past was conceded to be his inferior in physical and mental prowess," and he devoutly hoped someone could quickly be found to restore the title to its rightful owners. Jim Jeffries initially declared he would not be that man. True, Burns had been a mere "newspaper champion," Jeffries said, and had no one to blame but himself for his defeat. "He took a chance on meeting the black man and got the worst of it. John L. Sullivan would never give a colored fighter a chance to win the title, and I always drew the line." Still, said Jeffries, "there will be no fight between Jack Johnson and myself. . . . I don't want the money. I am out of the game and the public might as well understand it."

No one seemed willing to take Jeffries' no for an answer. That was in large part the doing of the celebrity novelist Jack London, who had covered the bout for the New York *Herald* at twenty-five cents a word. He had been a mill worker and a hobo, a convict, a sailor, and a luckless gold miner before becoming a writer, and though he was a committed socialist, his solidarity with the working class did not extend to black people. "Personally," London wrote, "I was for Burns all the way. He was a white man and so am I. Naturally, I wanted to see the white man win."

In the widely distributed story he wrote from ringside, London used his novelist's skill to transform a prizefight into a one-sided racial drubbing that cried out for revenge. It had not been a boxing match but an "Armenian massacre," he wrote, a "hopeless slaughter" in which a playful "giant Ethiopian" had toyed with Burns as if he'd been "a naughty child." It had matched "thunderbolt blows" against "butterfly flutterings." London was disturbed not so much by the new champion's victory—"All hail to Johnson," he wrote; he had undeniably been "the best man"—as by the evident glee with which he had imposed his will on the hapless white man: "A golden smile tells the story, and that golden smile was Johnson's." He ended his overwrought account with a sentence that put into words the thoughts of millions of disappointed whites all around the globe: "But one thing remains. Jeffries must emerge from his alfalfa farm and remove that smile from Johnson's face. Jeff, it's up to you."*

Jim Jeffries had been out of the ring for five years. At first, retirement suited him. He enjoyed working his alfalfa fields near Burbank, went fishing and hunting when he liked, and made handsome profits selling scrubland to the developers who were fast turning countryside into city lots. He built himself a house in town and opened a saloon in Vernon, a few miles south of downtown Los Angeles, which featured what was purported to be the longest bar on the Pacific Coast, and put his brother Jack in charge. With several partners, he also launched the Jeffries Athletic Club, an open-air arena at Thirty-eighth Street and Santa Fe Avenue in Vernon, where he promoted fights and sometimes refereed as well.

But the saloon didn't do well. Jack Jeffries seems to have been as luckless as a business manager as he had been as a heavyweight contender, and not even the daily presence of the former champion himself could attract enough steady customers to turn things around. The arena began to lose money, too, and would have to close its doors in January of 1909, leaving Jim Jeffries saddled with some nine thousand dollars in unpaid bills.† The ex-champion badly needed to make some money.

Meanwhile, letters had begun to arrive at Jeffries' home, echoing Jack London's call for him to get himself back in shape, return to the ring, and demolish Jack Johnson. "They kept at me," he remembered. "Even in the churches they were sermonizing that I was a skunk for not defending the white race's honor." Big-money offers for the fight came in, too, some from legitimate promoters, others from dubious sources, but all of them tantalizing: clearly, a Jeffries-Johnson championship fight promised a healthy profit.

Jeffries asked his old friend DeWitt van Court, athletic director of the Los Angeles Athletic Club, what he thought he should do. Van Court gave him some hard-nosed advice. Fighting Johnson was a no-win proposition, he said; if Jeffries won, people would say Johnson had taken a dive; if he lost, they'd

---

*Curiously, Tommy Burns would later accuse Jack London of being "a strong advocate of race equality" who "belittled me in every way. London took sides with the colored man, who badly needed a boost. It was an ill-deserved criticism of my valiant efforts. . . . It was small comfort to me to have Jack London, a highly nervous man, tender me a public apology a few weeks later. When he spoke, tears streamed down his face, but the harm had been done." (Burns, "Tommy Burns.")

†In April, the club would be up for sale.

say Jeffries had been crazy to try to come back after such a long layoff. But if Jeffries really needed money, "he should get a vaudeville engagement of as long a period as possible, and . . . if the public seemed to fall for the idea, renew the engagement again and make all the money possible out of it"—and then announce he wouldn't fight anyway.

Jeffries wasn't sure about the last part—"he said that if he made a start to get in condition to fight," Van Court recalled, "he'd go through with it"—but he followed his friend's counsel nonetheless. Less than a week after Johnson beat Burns, and after vowing he'd never fight again, Jeffries invited a handful of boxing insiders to come and see him work out at Van Court's club. He looked nothing like the formidable fighting machine he had once been. Alcohol and inactivity had caused him to swell to nearly three hundred pounds; when he tried to pull on the tights he'd worn in his last fight he couldn't get them much above his knees. And chain-smoking—seven to fifteen packs of cigarettes a day, he later confessed to one reporter—had badly weakened his wind.

But to those, like H. M. "Beany" Walker of the Los Angeles *Examiner,* who were blinded by the need to see Johnson's smile erased by a white man, none of it seemed to matter. Jeffries still "stepped around as spry as a 20-year-old youngster," Walker assured his readers; he remained "the greatest big man in the world today. Give him six or eight months training and he will make Jack Johnson jump out of the ring."

A few days later, Jeffries announced plans for a thirty-week cross-country theatrical training tour. The American ticket-buying public would be able to see him spar with Sam Berger, the moon-faced heavyweight who would soon double as his manager, and judge for itself whether or not he was ready to take on the black champion.* Whichever way that decision went, his financial future seemed assured: the impresario William Morris had guaranteed him twenty-five hundred dollars a week.

Wherever he went, the crowds continued to put on the pressure. When he

---

*Berger had been the national amateur heavyweight champion until he was caught taking money for his bouts at the Olympic Club in San Francisco. In his first official match as a professional he went six no-decision rounds with Philadelphia Jack O'Brien in Philadelphia, in a contest widely suspected of being prearranged to set up a twenty-round rematch in San Francisco, where Berger's popularity would ensure a full house. That bout never came off. Instead, Berger took on young Al Kaufmann and was knocked cold. He was in the haberdashery business when there began to be talk of Jeffries returning to the ring, and he eagerly volunteered to become his trainer and sparring partner. When Jeffries' former manager, Billy Delaney, refused to have anything to do with the comeback, Berger eagerly took over those duties as well.

arrived at the Oakland dock for his first engagement—two weeks at the Wigwam Theater in San Francisco—newsboys swarmed around him, shouting,
"Say, won't you fight Johnson, Jim?" At Grand Central Station in New York
he fled through a baggage room rather than face the throng that turned out
to shake his hand and urge him back into the ring. "If I were to whip Johnson," he told reporters in Chicago,

> I realize that I would be hailed as the greatest champion in pugilism's his
> tory. I know that it would mean more fame than ever fell to any fighter's
> lot, and that it would make me a rich man. But I also realize that to lose to
> Johnson would make me a dog. . . . I simply won't fight unless I know I am
> good enough to knock out Johnson. You don't catch Jim Jeffries losing to
> a colored man.

But the idea of a title bout was clearly growing on him. He began to insist
that since he had retired undefeated, he, not Johnson, was still heavyweight
champion and would demand to be treated as champion should he decide
to return to the ring. "I want to see the championship come back to the white
race, where it belongs," he told one crowd. "I think I'll be able to make Johnson sweat if ever I do box again." It was still if, not when, but an anonymous
British versifier, who signed his work "Pink 'Un," thought he could already
discern the drift of Jeffries' thinking—and suggested what seemed to him the
inevitable outcome:

> *The shades of night were falling fast*
> *When through Los Angeles there passed*
> *A burly gent, a powerful bloke,*
> *Who shouted, "What? Me fight a smoke?*
> *NEVER!"*
>
> *His jaw was firm, his eyes were fierce,*
> *His voice was sharp enough to pierce.*
> *Each questioner he swept aside,*
> *And hissed, with each succeeding stride,*
> *"M' NO!"*
>
> *"Think of it, Jim," an old pal said,*
> *"You'll need the coin before you're dead,*
> *"Say, you can beat him. Won't you try?"*
> *To which Jim Jeffries made reply,*
> *"I'D REALLY RATHER NOT."*

"Think of it twice," another cried.
"You mustn't let a fortune slide."
The big one gave his head a scratch,
And said, "'Twould be a corking match—
I'LL THINK IT OVER!"

L'ENVOI.
One evening, 'neath a harvest moon,
The sexton tucked away a coon.
The coon was Sam Fitzpatrick's find—
It seems that Jeffries changed his mind.

On February 17, 1909, eight weeks after beating Tommy Burns and only hours before setting sail for home from Brisbane, the new heavyweight champion of the world made an unpublicized pilgrimage to the Toowong Cemetery. There, he climbed up a gentle slope and stood for a moment at the tomb of Peter Jackson, the black Australian who had never been given his chance to win the title that now, at last, belonged to Jack Johnson.

CHAPTER SIX

THE CHAMPION

IT TOOK THE CANADIAN-AUSTRALIAN liner *Makura* three weeks to steam from Brisbane to Vancouver, British Columbia, time enough for Johnson and Hattie McClay to entertain their fellow passengers several times with after-dinner music; time enough, Johnson hoped, for the world to become accustomed to the idea of a Negro champion.*

He had sought attention all his life. From earliest boyhood he had seen himself as unlike anyone else, and this should have been the moment the world saw it, too. Fourteen years of fighting in front of mostly hostile crowds had left him with few illusions about the likelihood of fair treatment, and countless encounters with newspapermen who deliberately distorted his words and cartoonists who portrayed him as less than human had only reinforced those feelings. But nothing he'd experienced had prepared him for what happened to him once he stepped onto the dock at Vancouver on March 9, 1909.

As he made his way down the gangplank, wearing a full-length fur coat, smiling and waving at the hundreds of Canadians who had come down to the waterfront to see him, a knot of derbied reporters was waiting for him on the dock. Some were sportswriters, but most had simply been assigned to cover the arrival of a Negro celebrity, a phenomenon they had never encountered before.

The questions they shouted were predictable.

How had the Australians treated him?

"I've got no kick coming," Johnson said, though "they seemed to think more of Tommy Burns after I had licked him than they did of me, and me the champion."

Would he fight Jeffries?

---

*The *Makura* stopped at Fiji on the way. According to Hugh McIntosh ("Pride of the Blacks"), "When Johnson . . . landed there . . . he was followed by almost the entire Fijian population, who, since the victory of Johnson over Burns, have displayed a keen interest in boxing."

"I am willing to meet any man in the world," he said, "and I don't think anyone can get a decision over me, much less put me out. It amuses me to hear this talk of Jeffries claiming the championship. Why, when a mayor leaves office he's an ex-mayor, isn't he? When a champion leaves the ring, he's an ex-champion. Well, that is Jeffries: he wants to try to get the championship back and I'm willing to take him on."

If Jeffries couldn't get in shape, would Johnson consider other white challengers like Al Kaufmann or the hard-hitting middleweight champion, Stanley Ketchel?

He would, if they were willing and the money was right.

When someone mentioned that Galveston was planning a big welcome, the New York *Times* reported, Johnson's "eyes sparkled and he showed his gold-tipped teeth. . . . 'Tell them I'll be there.' "

The exchange was innocuous, though some found Johnson's blithe self-assurance unseemly in a black man. But two things piqued the reporters' interest: Sam Fitzpatrick was not at his fighter's side, and a white woman was. As the champion pushed his way toward the customs shed to collect his luggage, he introduced the woman to one or two reporters as his wife, calling her "the former Nellie O'Brien of Philadelphia," and she volunteered how proud she was of her husband. Her only regret about her visit to Australia, she said, was that she had not been permitted to watch him fight, but since Mrs. Burns (and all other women) had also been barred from the stadium, she supposed she really couldn't complain.

While Johnson and his companion saw their trunks loaded into a taxicab and started downtown in search of a hotel that would accept them,* the reporters gathered around Fitzpatrick, who had come ashore separately and was more than happy to offer his explanation of why he and Johnson were no longer together. The championship had gone to Johnson's head, he said; he was "a different man before the fight. He would feed out of my hand then, but he is a hard man to handle now. Anyhow, he don't want a manager now. He has got Mrs. Johnson as his manager."†

The reporters knew that the mere existence of this woman in Johnson's

---

*They headed first for the fashionable St. Francis hotel, where the clerk politely but firmly told them all the rooms were filled. "Really, Mr. Johnson," he said, "it could not be helped." Four more hotels turned them away before they found a room for the night at the home of a black fighter named George Paris.

†Johnson would later go out of his way to denigrate Fitzpatrick for having been "too easy-going" as a negotiator and forcing him to accept a woefully one-sided contract with Burns.

company was enough to make headlines. Interracial marriage was officially outlawed in thirty of the forty-six states and discouraged by custom and the threat of violence in many of the rest. Nearly seven hundred Negroes had been lynched in the United States since 1900, some simply because someone had whispered that they had been "too familiar" with white women. The very first sentence of the Associated Press story that appeared in newspapers all over America the next morning referred to the champion's "white wife, a former Philadelphia woman who threw in her lot with him."

Over the years, Johnson's sometimes tumultuous domestic life had been a subject of interest in boxing circles, and now and again it had even sparked brief news stories—the arrest of Clara Kerr, Lola Toy's libel suit, Johnson's own occasional appearances in court—but neither the nonsporting press nor the general public had paid much attention. The private lives of heavyweight champions had never invited close scrutiny. John L. Sullivan and Jim Corbett routinely traveled with sporting women whom they pretended were their wives, just as Johnson did. (Both were also charged with drunken violence toward women, as Johnson would be one day.) Most of their bad behavior was kept out of the papers. None of it seemed to matter much to their fans. Johnson did all the things Sullivan and Corbett did—and by doing so, outraged much of the country. The difference, of course, was that he was black and the women with whom he chose to live openly were white. And now his secret was out.*

The next evening, the champion was to pick up a little easy money fighting a six-round exhibition at the Vancouver Athletic Club. Denver Ed Martin had been scheduled to go through the motions with him, but when Martin didn't turn up, a substitute was rushed in: Victor Everleigh McLaglen, a strapping British-born veteran of the Boer War, who had been fighting second-rate

---

"Repudiating is one of Arthur's long suits," his ex-manager shot back. The real reason they'd split, he said, was that the champion "could not see where he should come through with the money I loaned him some time before, which he wanted, as he said, 'to keep up appearances.' When Jack Johnson came to me two years and one half ago he had been fighting fifteen years and did not have a cent to his name. When we split up he had $10,000, the heavyweight champion[ship] of the world and [theatrical] advertising that would net him $50,000 a year for at least two years. . . . Johnson talks about me letting Burns have 'all the best of the arrangements'—that I admit. Had I not done so, the chances are [Sam] Langford would be the 'big noise' in London today and Johnson would be matched with Sam McVey, Black Bill or Joe Jeannette, and then possibly go back to Philadelphia to an obscure thoroughfare, where I found him." (Milwaukee *Evening Wisconsin,* March 31, 1909; *Police Gazette,* April 13, 1909.)

*According to the boxing historian Nat Fleischer, both George Dixon and Joe Gans also had white wives but were careful to keep them mostly out of sight, something Jack Johnson was never willing to do.

heavyweights up and down the Pacific coast for nearly two years. It was no contest. In the first round, Johnson knocked McLaglen down with a punch to the stomach, then gallantly backed away until the younger man got his wind back. "I found Johnson the most charming opponent I ever met," a grateful McLaglen remembered, "standing well back and waving me forward when I slipped into the ropes . . . chattering away blithely during the heat of a clinch." Throughout the final two rounds, he wrote,

> I tried my best to rattle him, conscious of the fistic immortality that would be mine if I were to slip him a "sleeper." But his grinning face darted in and out behind the thud of his gloves, his head bobbing up and down, taking off my blows on the side of the head, on the gloves, on the elbows, on the shoulders, anywhere, in fact, where they could do very little damage.*

Johnson's effortless win was duly reported in the sports pages. But there were other newspaper stories in the next few days as well, disturbing stories centered not on Johnson the boxer, but on Johnson the man and his supposed marriage. The Chicago *Tribune* was among the first to print them.

BEWARE MR. JACK JOHNSON
TEXAS AUTHORITIES WILL PROSECUTE THE
CHAMPION IF HE TAKES WHITE
WIFE TO THAT STATE

Galveston, Tex. March 12.—[Special.]—If Champion Jack Johnson brings his white wife to Galveston he will be prosecuted under the Texas laws forbidding whites and blacks marrying. The reports that Johnson has a negro wife living here [presumably the elusive Mary Austin] brought a reply from Johnson saying he was legally divorced from her and he would bring his white wife with him. Johnson bases his defiance of the prosecution on the grounds that his marriage to a white woman did not take place in Texas. [But] the federal Supreme Court has ruled that the state has a right to prevent the union of whites and blacks and impose penalties even if they were married in a state permitting marriages of whites and blacks.

Papers all over the country picked up the story. A telegram arrived for Johnson from the Galveston welcoming committee: it would cancel the parade in

---

*McLaglen abandoned boxing in 1915, served as a captain of the Irish Fusiliers and as provost marshal of Baghdad during World War One, and then went into the theater. In 1935, he won the Best Actor Oscar for his work in John Ford's *The Informer* and later became an important member of Ford's Hollywood stock company.

his honor if he insisted on bringing Hattie McClay with him. "The negroes in charge of the affair declare they have too many friends among the white citizens to offend them," the *Tribune* reported the following day, and if Johnson "insisted on thrusting his wife upon the friends of his boyhood and his own relatives, the celebration would be declared off."

Some Negroes, like D. A. Hart, editor of the Nashville *Globe,* were also made unhappy by Johnson's purported marriage to a white woman, their objections based on both racial pride and the impact they feared Johnson's actions might have on the safety and well-being of other black people.

It is reported that Jack Johnson has married a woman who is not a member of his people. If that report is true, then Jack Johnson is wrong, entirely wrong, and that point of order is raised and sustained by every sensible and self-respecting Negro of this country. Johnson was born and reared in the South, where his relatives still reside, and if he could not find a woman of his race suitable for a wife, then he ought to have died an anchoret.

If the persistently circulated report of his marriage is true, he has made a fatal mistake and subjected himself to the just contempt of every member of his race. If it is true, he stands before that awful and dread bar, public opinion, a defendant without defense. . . .

The Negro, be he high or lowly, who seeks to leave his race is a fawning, cringing, worthless rascal. And, without whitewashing it, no respectable Negro has the least patience with him. Out of the hundreds of thousands, yea, millions of honorable intelligent Negro womanhood any male member of the race can find a worthy and congenial companion. If he pretends that he can not, he absolutely and unequivocally lies, and deserves a fate worse than that which befell Robinson Crusoe.

The Galveston parade was canceled; the hurricane loosed by news of Johnson's purported marriage to a white woman prevented him from visiting his hometown and the now-widowed mother he hadn't seen since 1905.* He had no home of his own. For fourteen years he had drifted from fight town to fight town. After the exhibition with Victor McLaglen, Johnson sent Hattie McClay home to Milwaukee to wait out the storm, and moved on to Chicago, where a sport named William "Toots" Marshall put him up in his Dearborn Street apartment.

---

*Henry Johnson is thought to have died around 1907.

Reporters haunted the sidewalk outside, hoping for more scandal. To get rid of them, and to do what he could to restore his reputation among whites and Negroes alike, Johnson eventually called them in and offered his own wholly invented version of the facts. His wife was actually black, not white, he now said. Her name was Hattie Smith, not Nellie O'Brien. She'd been born in Mississippi, not Philadelphia, and he had married her two and a half years earlier "in a small Nevada town."

> There was nothing secret about it. The only thing is that as she has traveled with a vaudeville show we separated and it was not generally known that I was married. I wasn't in the limelight so much in those days and the public was not much interested in my affairs.
>
> I want to say one thing—that I don't see where the outside world need concern itself with a man's private affairs. If my wife were of white blood and really loved me, I can't see why we shouldn't be married. I know that I love the girl and she is fond of me, and I think that is all that is needed. I would like for people to go over my record and see if I have done anything a white man would be ashamed of doing. I wish this talk about my wife would stop. She is in Milwaukee visiting friends, and she went there to escape publicity.*

Then he tried to focus the public's attention back where he thought it belonged, on boxing. "I can lick Jim Jeffries," he said. "Jeffries never licked a young man. I am the best boxer in the world. I am not only accepting challenges, I am making them. The man I want is Jim Jeffries. I will fight him winner take all or any way he wants to split the purse."

While he waited for Jeffries to make up his mind about his ability to get back into shape, he said, he would fight Stanley Ketchel in San Francisco, in October.

---

*Johnson and Hattie McClay had failed to coordinate their stories. An enterprising reporter for the Milwaukee *Free Press* tracked her to the Martin Street home of Mr. and Mrs. George Brown and wangled a brief interview: "Mrs. Johnson gives evidence of considerable business ability. She believes herself capable of conducting her husband's business affairs and admits that hereafter she will have an important part in the arrangement of matches.

"'Mr. Johnson is a splendid fellow and I am very fond of him,' declares the woman. 'He is a big-hearted and brave man. Some people may criticize me for marrying a black man, but I am satisfied and happy and that, after all, is the best test of marriage.'

"Every effort to conceal the whereabouts of Mrs. Johnson was made by friends yesterday. They even went so far as to deny that the woman was in the city. Ed Howard of the Howard Hotel said, however, that Mrs. Johnson was a guest at the Brown home." Later, asked point-blank if she was black or white, Hattie McClay refused to answer. (Milwaukee *Free Press*, March 16, 1909.)

He also backed out of the promise he'd made to fight Sam Langford in London for five thousand dollars. "I beat Sam easy before," he explained, "and a match between us wouldn't draw." But there was more to it than that. He had not forgotten the morning he'd been made to wait in the foyer of the National Sporting Club until summoned inside by white men who thought themselves free to decide his fate without him, and he had long since developed his own version of the Golden Rule: do unto others as they have done unto you. "Being a champion," he now wrote to the club manager, Peggy Bettinson,

> I don't see that the National Sporting Club has a right to dictate to me as to how much I shall receive for my appearance and boxing ability. If they don't want to give my price, which is [thirty thousand dollars], win, lose or draw, [the precise terms Tommy Burns had insisted upon before fighting him] they can call things off. . . . I am a boxing man and can now get my price, and I don't care what the public thinks.

Two weeks after talking to the press, Johnson boarded a train for New York to begin a seven-thousand-dollar two-week engagement at Hammerstein's Victoria on Broadway. Hattie McClay was not with him. Later Johnson would say they'd parted because of her beer drinking, that he'd found bottles under their bed after she'd promised him she would stop. Whatever happened, she melted back into the sporting life she'd known before she met him, working for a Philadelphia madam until her new employer got wind of her liaison with a black man and fired her. But she remained on call, ready to become "Mrs. Johnson" again whenever another one was not available.

Johnson got a warm welcome in Manhattan. A jubilant, mostly Negro crowd filled the cavernous waiting room of Grand Central and followed him to an open automobile, shaking his hand, patting his back, shouting his name. Barron Wilkins, one of black Manhattan's leading sports and an old friend of Johnson's, had organized a parade in his honor. A brass band playing ragtime from an open car led the way. Behind it came the champion, waving and bowing, escorted by a dozen touring cars "crowded with colored 'sports.' " The procession swept down Forty-second Street past cheering crowds into the heart of the wide-open Tenderloin District and pulled up in front of Barron's Café and the attached Little Savoy Hotel at 235 West Thirty-fifth Street. It was Jack Johnson's kind of place—the basement was given over to gambling, and a horseshoe hung over the door with a sign that read

NO ONE ENTERS THESE PORTALS BUT THE TRUE IN HEART SPORTS. It became his headquarters whenever he was in town.

Black fans followed him everywhere, and blacks and curious whites alike packed Hammerstein's Victoria to see him perform five times a day. "There were no preliminaries about the act," wrote the reviewer for *Variety.*

An announcer proclaimed Johnson the undefeated champion of the world. The hisses which greeted this speech drowned the applause. The gallery held many colored people.

Johnson stepped on the stage, disregarding the disturbance, and went at the bag. On the third punch it flew into the balcony. The stage hands removed the apparatus without further ado, and Johnson proceeded to box his sparring partner, [Marty] Kid Cutler, a white man. . . . The white man, handicapped by height and reach, could not touch Johnson, who toyed with him.

The audence offered much advice. At the conclusion, [Johnson] stepped forward, and made the following speech, which turned the tide in his favor, winning him some genuine applause to close with:

"Ladies and gentlemen, kindly give me three minutes of your valuable time. Today I have deposited with the New York *American* $5,000 as a deposit on a side bet for $10,000 to fight any man in the world. If there is a fight, I hope the best man will win."

Johnson is a drawing card and seems to attract even those hostile to him through his color. His bearing while making the speech and the language proved the black champion is no novice on the stage.

Booker T. Washington had been the best-known black man in America for as long as Jack Johnson had been a professional fighter, but by the spring of 1909, his power and influence were slipping away. Segregation and the constant threat of white violence that characterized life in the South seemed to be spreading northward. A riot the previous year in Springfield, Illinois—which had seen whites storm through black neighborhoods howling, "Lincoln freed you, we'll show you where you belong," killing eight Negro citizens, and driving two thousand more from the town where Abraham Lincoln had lived (and the site of the battle-royal victory that sent Jack Johnson on to Chicago)—had provided graphic evidence that Washington's gradualism was not working. Then, when Washington called at the White House in April, hoping to go over Negro appointments to federal jobs with the new Republican president, William Howard Taft, as he had with Taft's predecessor, Theodore Roosevelt, he was turned away: Taft didn't have time to see him. Whites began replacing Negro officeholders. And a group of Washington's critics, black and white—including the Atlanta University sociologist W. E. B. Du Bois, the anti-lynching campaigner Ida Wells-Barnett, and the New York newspaper editor Oswald Garrison Villard—had recently voted to establish a new "National Association for the Advancement of Colored People" to take the kind of direct action in support of political and civil rights that Washington had always discouraged.

But Washington still saw himself as an arbiter of black behavior, and Jack Johnson's conduct frankly alarmed him: the champion seemed the antithesis of everything Washington had always said a black man should be: he was free-spending, not thrifty; brash instead of humble; defiant in the face of white laws and customs intended to hamper his movement and limit his choices. Hoping to bring the champion into line, he asked his private secretary, Emmett Jay Scott, to write a note enlisting the aid of a New York friend of Johnson's, a prominent black criminal lawyer and onetime Republican politician named J. Frank Wheaton.

Scott was writing out of personal as well as racial pride, he told Wheaton. Like Johnson, Scott was a Texan and therefore especially keen that the new champion always do "the absolutely proper and dignified thing."

> We all believe that he can defeat Jeffries, but I think it would be much better for him not to boast about what he is going to do in that particular, but simply stand on his record and on the statement that "he would fight any living man for the Heavy Weight Championship of the World."
>
> And then, too, if there is any possible way for him to again bring it about, I wish that he might again get the services of Sam Fitzpatrick as manager. I am sure he will have much to gain and practically nothing to lose from Fitzpatrick's management. I was just a bit disturbed by Fitzpatrick's statement that Johnson was hard to manage after winning a fight, simply and only because I do not like white men to feel that Negroes cannot stand a large prosperity.
>
> You can talk these matters over with Johnson in your own way.

If Wheaton did offer Johnson any advice during his New York stay, there's no evidence the champion followed any of it. He saw no need to hide his eagerness to get Jim Jeffries into the ring; wanted no part of a reunion with Sam Fitzpatrick, whose patronizing treatment of him he would neither forgive nor forget; and never had much interest in anyone else's notion of "the absolutely proper and dignified thing" to do, especially if it interfered with what he called his "pleasures."

In mid-April, Johnson returned to Chicago, still without Hattie and looking for a good time. More than forty-five thousand Negroes now lived in the city on the lake, and three out of four of them made their homes in the black belt, a narrow strip that began just south of the Loop and in 1909 already ran southward along State Street for some thirty blocks. More refugees from the Jim Crow South were arriving every day, and leadership in the neighborhood was steadily shifting from the handful of shopkeepers and professionals who had once catered to the white community, to a new generation of black entrepreneurs, editors, clergymen, and politicians whose power and profits were drawn from a fast-growing but increasingly segregated black world, with its own institutions, athletic teams, and forms of entertainment.

But there was one section of the black belt—the twenty square blocks from Eighteenth to Twenty-second streets between Federal and Halstead—where blacks and whites continued to meet and mingle, at least from dusk till dawn. It was called the Levee District, and—like Manhattan's Tenderloin and San Francisco's Barbary Coast and Beale Street in Memphis and the wide-open neighborhoods in all the other towns through which Johnson had traveled where vice was tolerated—he already knew it intimately. By one count, the Levee was home to five hundred saloons and just as many whorehouses, fifty-six poolrooms, fifteen gambling halls, six variety theaters, countless nickelodeons and peep shows, opium dens, and cocaine parlors, as well as "buffet flats"—apartments that provided food and drink, piano music and prostitutes—and "winerooms," where women sold watered drinks along with their company. There was something or someone to suit everyone's wallet and everybody's taste: on a single Armour Avenue block stood separate "resorts" offering Chinese women, Japanese women, "Mulatto girls for white gentlemen," and, for customers with catholic tastes, the "House of All Nations."

For nine years, the showpiece of the district had been a pair of attached three-story mansions at 2131–33 South Dearborn. Known as the Everleigh Club, it was run by Ada and Minna Lester, Kentucky-born sisters who had married and divorced a brace of brothers back home, spent several years on the road as actresses, and then gone into the brothel business. (They were supposed to have adopted the last name Everleigh because their grandmother had signed her letters to them "Everly Yours.") In the judgment of the Chicago Vice Commission, which yearned to close it down, their fifty-room establishment was "probably the most famous and luxurious house of prostitution in the country." Certainly, it was the highest priced and most exclusive. It cost ten dollars just to get past the door. In an era when fifty cents bought a three-course meal, dinner at the Everleigh Club cost fifty dollars. Female companionship cost a great deal more. The club had a library, an art gallery, and a dozen parlors, each with its own distinctive décor; the Gold parlor featured gold spittoons, a gold-rimmed goldfish bowl, and a miniature piano covered with gold leaf, said to be worth fifteen thousand dollars. Specially designed fountains filled the air with the scent of flowers.

"Minna and Ada Everleigh are to pleasure," said the veteran Chicago newsman Jack Lait, "what Christ was to Christianity." They were particular about the thirty young women who worked for them. No "inexperienced girls or young widows" were ever hired, Minna once explained; "we do not like amateurs." "Be polite and forget what you are here for," she told her employees. They were required to wear formal gowns, forbidden to curse, and entitled to keep half their earnings, all unheard-of anywhere else in the district. The sisters were no less choosy about their clients: "The Everleigh Club is not for the rough element, the clerk on a holiday, or a man without a check book," Minna said. Would be customers had to send in their business cards before being allowed inside; those not known personally to the sisters or without a written introduction from someone they knew were sometimes turned away.

Jack Johnson wanted in. Black customers were barred: even the "professor" who played ragtime favorites on the Everleigh Club piano was white. Not even Johnson's newfound fame could get him past the front door. But his connections could.

He had a new manager now, a sad-eyed, pear-shaped man with a mustache named George Little. He and the champion had known each other for ten years, ever since Johnson's first visit to Chicago, when, Little remembered, "ten cents was a big meal." He had run the stable at the Palmer House hotel then and allowed Johnson to come inside and sleep on its straw rather than on the lakefront. Since then, he had come up in the world and was doing so well that he could provide the champion with a fifteen-hundred-dollar diamond ring to seal their new relationship. He operated his own West Side saloon, the Here It Is; ran a combination bar and brothel called the Imperial on Armour Avenue; and helped oversee the Buxbaum Catering Company at State and Twenty-second, which billed itself as the "Acknowledged Bohemian Center of Chicago" but was actually the ground-floor restaurant of the Marlborough Hotel, which provided prostitutes and their customers with five-dollar rooms.

But more important for Johnson's purposes, Little was also now the Levee "czar," the man who collected protection money from everyone in the district each week and passed it on to "Bathhouse John" Coughlin and "Hinky Dink" Mike Kenna, the famously corrupt aldermen who made it all possible.

To stay in business, the Everleigh sisters had to pay Little one thousand dollars a month, and when he turned up at their door one April evening with the heavyweight champion of the world looming next to him, they had no choice but to let them both in. All Johnson got that evening was a chance to look around; Little had not insisted that Johnson be allowed to sleep with anyone. But he and the Everleighs alike seem to have underestimated the power of the champion's charm, wealth, and celebrity over the women working at the club. When Johnson invited five of them to go for a ride in his big touring car with him, Little, and a Chicago hustler and sometime beer salesman named Abe Ahrens, they all piled in.

One was a slender twenty-three-year-old who called herself Belle Schreiber (her real last name seems to have been Becker, though she would use at least a dozen other aliases over the next few years). She was said to be the daughter of a Milwaukee policeman who died when she was a child, and she had learned stenography and worked at the downtown Plankington Hotel for a time, taking letters for visiting businessmen. At twenty, she had come to Chicago, searching for secretarial work. Then, like many other rootless young women of her generation, she found she could do better pursuing what she called "the sporting life" instead. After answering "calls" out of a Michigan Avenue boardinghouse for a few months, she began working at the Everleigh Club in December of 1907.

Johnson showed unusual interest in her after their drive together. He pursued her with telephone calls and gifts—flowers, theater tickets, money, a framed photograph of himself signed "To my little sweetheart, Belle, from Papa Jack"—and within a few days had persuaded her to spend the night with him in his room at Toots Marshall's. The Everleighs warned her not to do so; when she disobeyed them, they let her go.* Johnson told her not to worry. He would help set her up in an apartment of her own. He also promised that when he went out on the road she could join him, with all her expenses paid plus what she remembered as "a little over to have in my pock-

---

*At least four other Everleigh Club employees were fired for the same reason that spring: Virginia Bond, Lillian St. Clair, Bessie Wallace, and Bertha Morrison, known as "Jew Bertha." All of them would travel at one time or another with Jack Johnson or members of his entourage.

etbook"; she could wear the jewels and finery Hattie McClay had worn, too, and be the new "Mrs. Jack Johnson," at least part of the time.

The arrangement seemed to suit her, at least at first. Johnson led what must have struck her as a glamorous life: constant travel, big money, big crowds. He could also be generous, and even an unsteady relationship with one generous man likely seemed better to her than congress with strangers, however well screened by her employers.

There was clearly more to their relationship than simple commerce or convenience. We can never know precisely how one person feels about another, but on the witness stand a few years later, Schreiber would be asked whether she had given herself over to Johnson "out of affection or [for] compensation." "Compensation, mostly," she answered. But when pressed as to whether she had ever been in love with Johnson, she would say only, "I don't know what love is." She did not say no.

On April 19, 1909, Jim Jeffries made it official. Standing on the stage of the American Theater on Broadway and speaking to a full house that included reporters from all the New York dailies and many out-of-town papers as well, he said he was now convinced that within eight to ten months he would be ready to wrest the title back from Jack Johnson. He planned a summer trip to Europe. The final fight details would be worked out when he got back.* The crowd stood and cheered. The Broadway song-and-dance man George M. Cohan leaped onstage waving a thousand-dollar bill and shouting that he was ready to bet it on the white man's hope.

A few days later, Jeffries drove down to the Bowery to visit an old saloon-keeper friend, "Diamond Dan" O'Rourke. No one in the neighborhood had known he was coming, but before his automobile could come to a stop, it was surrounded by passersby shouting greetings to the man they all called "the champ." He hurried inside O'Rourke's establishment and disappeared upstairs. The crowd continued to grow until all traffic was stopped; "Men and boys—and even women—were fighting for a vantage point," one newspaper reported, and reserve policemen had to be called in to clear a path for the line of waiting streetcars.

Jeffries was finally persuaded to come down and "say something to the boys."

---

*There was only one caveat: "Should Stanley [Ketchel] win [against Johnson] I would discontinue training as the title would be where it rightfully belongs"—i.e., in white hands.

"What are you going to do to Johnson?" one man shouted.

"Put him to sleep in three minutes. I want to tell you, my Bowery friends, that I am just as good a man as I ever was, and if I was to enter the ring with this so-called black champion today I think I could lick him with one hand tied behind my back."

Johnson, who had tried to get Jeffries into the ring for six years without success, was understandably skeptical. The ex-champion was still overweight and undertrained, far from fighting trim, Johnson said; the announcement was probably meant simply to boom Jeffries' vaudeville tour. "I'm faking and four-flushing am I?" Jeffries countered. "Well that fellow will eat those words when I get him in the ring."

Johnson was himself badly out of shape—"as fat as a Jap wrestler," he later admitted—and preoccupied. Clara Kerr had appeared again from out of nowhere, apparently eager for a piece of the big money the newspapers said her former lover was now making. Claiming she really had been his wife, she sued him for $406 she said he owed her. "I don't know what this woman wants," Johnson told the press. "Yes, I know her. I was never married to her."

He paid Kerr rather than battle her in court. The champion continued to spend faster than he earned; his big purses yielded only bigger debts. The Ketchel fight was likely to sell a lot of tickets, but it would not take place until October. To earn some quick money in the meantime, he agreed to a six-round bout on May 19 with Philadelphia Jack O'Brien in O'Brien's home-town.*

Johnson took considerable pleasure in forcing his white opponent to sign the papers for the fight in the back room of his friend Frank Sutton's hotel and saloon on Wiley Street in the heart of Pittsburgh's "colored district."

---

*O'Brien's most prominent booster was Anthony Joseph Drexel Biddle, an eccentric millionaire and fight enthusiast from one of Philadelphia's best-known Main Line clans. Biddle held "boxing matinees" at his home, inviting some of the best white fighters of his time to spar with him in the stable before an audience of eminent invitees and then to share a sumptuous buffet. (When Bob Fitzsimmons was asked to say grace at Biddle's home, he was so impressed by the richness of the fare he said, "May the good God 'elp us to eat all wot's on the tyble.")

Now, when the new heavyweight champion came to town, Biddle wanted to spar with him. Having a Negro at his table was out of the question, however, and so, his daughter remembered, he made his way to Johnson's training camp across the state line in Merchantville, New Jersey, gave his name as "Tim O'Biddle," and quietly took a seat on the bench from which the champion picked local youths with whom to go a round or two. When his turn came, Biddle tore out of his corner, evidently intent on showing Johnson who was boss. "Now you boy there," Johnson said. "Don't get yourself stirred up." "But Father was always stirred up," wrote Biddle's daughter, "and Johnson finally had to fetch him a smart whack on the side of the head to settle him."

Making O'Brien come to him was evidence, Johnson thought, of just who was now in charge.

But on fight night at the National Athletic Club in Philadelphia, when he left the dressing room and started toward the ring, about to defend his title for the first time, it was quickly clear to Johnson that since he'd left the United States in pursuit of Tommy Burns, nothing had changed between him and the white sporting public.

Assembled were men of all walks of life. Bankers, lawyers, doctors, businessmen and the so-called common people. In fact, it was a typical gathering of Americans. As soon as I entered the ring I was greeted with a tremendous groan of hisses and cat-calls, intermingled with but a few faint cheers of my admirers. I was there to fight as best I could and although I was credited with being crooked in my dealings, my opponent O'Brien was equally guilty by his own confession. The sole reason therefore to account for the hisses & cat-calls hurled at me was my racial difference. Why should a man who is trying to do what his audience expects him to do & pays him for, be the target of vile abuse, all on account of his color of skin? Doesn't the brute instinct of man here assert itself? Draw away the veil of civilization & you will find the human race pretty nearly equal. In science we have advanced wonderfully, but morally precious little if at all. We should all cultivate the sense of fair play.

I did not train for that battle because I knew that I could whip 6 O'Briens.

In fact, he couldn't decisively whip even one of them that night. He seemed slow as well as thick in the middle. (Some suggested he was hungover, too.) O'Brien was so much lighter than Johnson that he was forced to his knees three times when the champion leaned on him, but he also managed to dart in and out of harm's way, landing jabs and body punches that had little effect but thrilled the hometown crowd and would have scored points with ringside judges if Philadelphia's no-decision rule had permitted them.

When Johnson entered the ring against Jack O'Brien two nights later, he was startled to see Biddle working as a second in his opponent's corner. "Boy, you got yourself all mixed up," he said. "You belong in my corner."

The professionals Biddle invited to spar with him generally went easy. He was their host, after all. The sole exception was the big California heavyweight Al Kaufmann, who took one look at the onrushing amateur and knocked him cold. Biddle went on to teach hand-to-hand combat to the U.S. Marines during World War One and to FBI agents during World War Two. (Biddle, *My Philadelphia Father*, pp. 12–13.)

The newspaper consensus was that Johnson was lucky to get away with a draw. Certainly, his lackluster performance impressed no one. JACK JOHNSON WILL NEVER DO, said the May 21 Portland (Maine) *Daily Advertiser,* COLORED CHAMPION NOT A TARTAR. But he did earn five thousand dollars, and according to the *Police Gazette,* he went through most of it within forty-eight hours.

> As a two-handed spender, the big black champion has John L. Sullivan, Dixon, Gans, Young, Corbett and other pugilistic spend-thrifts tied to a mast. He pulled down $5,000 as his share of the bout with O'Brien, and in two days let $4,800 of it go for two purchases.
>
> Johnson was attracted by a fine special roadster he saw in a Philadelphia garage.
>
> "What can this machine do?" asked Johnson.
>
> "Make seventy-five miles an hour," returned the salesman.
>
> "That's my speed," replied Johnson. "You're on."
>
> Then the big negro pulled out three $1,000 bills. . . . He lost no time in getting into it and sped away from the garage, leaving the salesman astounded. . . .
>
> The day before Johnson purchased a big diamond for $1,800 and as he let a number of $20 bills go for less expensive articles the fighter virtually has none of the $5,000 left which he received from Promoter Edwards of the National A.C. on the day of the bout. That's going some.

He would go some all summer. Fast cars had become his passion. "My mind is constantly on automobiles," he once said. He loved everything about them: their power and speed, the noise they made, the sensation he caused simply by driving down a country road, the proud black owner of a vehicle that was the envy even of wealthy whites. Above all, he loved the freedom automobiles afforded him to go where he pleased when he pleased with whom he pleased—and at his own pace. There were fewer than half a million cars in the United States in 1909; by year's end, Jack Johnson would own five of them.

He drove his new Chalmers Detroit Runabout to New York, then telephoned Belle Schreiber to join him at Barron Wilkins' Little Savoy, where he introduced her for the first time as his wife. She traveled with him on an automobile trip through New England. In Boston he was fined for speeding, the first of scores of traffic arrests he would amass over the next thirty-five years, some made because he really was driving too fast and some simply because he was driving a car some policeman thought only a white man should own.

At the automobile racetrack at Readville, Massachusetts, on June 17, a friend of Johnson's—"an actress," Belle Schreiber remembered—snapped a picture of the two of them in Johnson's car that caused a stir when it later appeared in a Boston paper with the caption "Jack Johnson and his pretty white wife." One witness recalled that Mrs. Johnson had been "very much painted."

Broke again, in June Johnson fought another Pennsylvania six-rounder—in Pittsburgh's Duquesne Gardens this time, against Antonio Rossilano, a stocky Italian American who fought as Tony Ross. Ross was felled for a count of nine in the first round, and in the last deliberately fell to escape a Johnson right hand, but he was still standing at the bell. Johnson again seemed listless.

He and Belle then returned to the Midwest, where they divided their time between George Little's home on the southern edge of the vice district, and a rented cottage at Cedar Point, Indiana, a tawdry summer resort twenty-five miles from Chicago favored by residents of the Levee. His trainer, Barney Furey, and Yank Kenny, a sparring partner, went to Cedar Point with him so he could do a little desultory training, but mostly Johnson just enjoyed himself with friends. George Little came along, too, with Lillian St. Clair, who, like Belle Schreiber, had worked for the Everleigh sisters and now sometimes traveled as "Mrs. Little." Roy Jones, the Negro proprietor of a Dearborn Street café, was in residence, as well, with his white companion Victoria Shaw, one of the district's best-known madams; so were an indeterminate number of what one newspaper called "Chicago girls," including three of the other women who had left the Everleigh Club with Belle Schreiber after Johnson came to call: Virginia Bond, "Jew Bertha" Morrison, and Bessie Wallace. Late one evening, Johnson and another summer visitor named Moriaraty decided to race their cars. Several women got in with Moriaraty. The champion's forty-horsepower car was in the lead when something caused him to put on the brakes. His rival slammed into him from behind. One of Moriaraty's passengers was seriously hurt. Johnson's car was smashed; he was covered with blood but suffered no permanent injury.

A couple of weeks later, driving through Woodstock, Ontario, on his way back from an exhibition in Toronto, he was fined fifty-five dollars for leaving the scene of another accident. In Windsor two days later, he was arrested for speeding and fined again. "It's getting so they just take me now on sight," Johnson said as he forked over thirty-five dollars from a fat bankroll. "No matter what speed I may be making they just gather me in and fine me. It is far more expensive to me than traveling over railroads, but I enjoy it. And they can fine me till they're as black as I am for all I care." When a reporter told him he'd heard a rumor that he'd hit a child in Woodstock, Johnson laughed it off; the only Canadian child he ever ran over, he said, was Tommy Burns.

That year, an interviewer would ask him what would happen if something went wrong with his automobile while he was racing along the road. His answer was as close as he ever came to explaining the way he lived his life:

> "If" and "suppose"—two small words, but nobody has ever been able to explain them. . . . One man falls out of bed and is killed. Another falls from a fifty-foot scaffold and lives. One man gets shot in the leg and is killed. Another gets a bullet in his brain and lives. . . . I always take a chance on my pleasures.

By the time Jim Jeffries began a weeklong engagement at the Wonderland Amusement Park in Minneapolis in mid-July, he had been on tour for seven months, and most people who had paid to see him in action had been awed by his size and speed, his strength, and his apparent skill. But George A. Barton, a young Minnesota sportswriter hired to referee the evening sparring sessions between Jeffries and Sam Berger, privately drew a different conclusion:

> In all these appearances, Berger feigned grogginess when Jeff nailed him on the side of the head with punches which I was positive lacked power. I had also noted while dining with Jeffries and Berger . . . that Jeff indulged in a generous shot of whiskey before eating. When he ate in a public dining room, the whiskey was served in a cup so that guests at nearby tables would think the former champion was having beef consommé instead of liquor.

Still, plans for the big fight were going forward, and when Jeffries held a final press conference in New York before sailing for Europe on August 4, he seemed his old, confident self. "Someone asked Jeff if he were sore at Johnson," reported the Chicago *American*.

> Jeff has an interesting way of looking at you, wide-eyed and silent, when he is studying out the answer to a question. Just looks at you, you know. And the questioner shrivels and dries up under the long contemplation. "Well," he finally decided. "I'm not going to say, 'I'm pleased to meet you' when we get in the ring."

Everyone has read of Jeff's magnificent condition but it still comes as rather a surprise to see what a big whale of a man he has become, now that he has rid himself of that pantry. Lots of other people weigh 280 pounds—mostly cutlets. But Jeff weighs that mostly in bone and muscle right now. His wrists are as thick and hairy as a government mule's leg. His eyes are clear and bright, and his skin smooth as he moves around like a dancing master. And in the best possible humor. He laughs and talks like a big, good-natured boy until he gets down to a discussion of Jacques Johnson, Esq., the large colored gent. . . . He doesn't laugh then. He doesn't grit his teeth or roll his eyes, or do any terrifying stunts. . . . His face just hardens slowly.

"That nigger can never lick me," he said as dispassionately as though he were discussing the chances of fussing between two strangers.

"Did you ever see him fight? Well, I have—two or three times. He stands flat-footed as a washerwoman. Let me tell you no man on earth who stands flat-footed can ever lick me. They've got to get up on their toes to do that. The man who stands flat-footed in the ring is licked before he ties on a glove, if the other man is anything near his equal."

Now, that may sound like boasting. As a matter of fact, it wasn't. It was given as the calm and well-considered statement of a man who has made pugilism a business, and in that business has made a success. Jeffries seemed to weigh himself and Johnson in his mental balance and to find Johnson very much wanting. He paused and thought for a moment before he continued.

"Then, Johnson has only one punch," said he. "That is it." He illustrated by a slight movement of his hand. His big hand didn't travel half a dozen inches, but it made the idea clear. "I have 400 punches and every one of them better than his best. I can hit anywhere from anywhere. Short or long range, from the hip or the shoulder or anywhere else. I have two hands. He has one. I can send 'em in from away off, or pound 'em in with two inches play. Johnson can't."*

---

*Jack Earl, the ex-amateur heavyweight champion of Ireland, was less than impressed by Jeffries' bluster and appalled at the derisive coverage given to Jack Johnson. "I have followed the newspaper comments on these two men for the past twelve months," he wrote to the New York *Times*. "I have been offended at the gross and undeserved abuse poured over the 'nigger' by the American newspapers. . . . That the colored man, Johnson, is the superior man, physically and mentally, no intelligent person can doubt. . . . [Johnson] at least has not to keep people waiting while he takes the Carlsbad waters and otherwise patches himself up to meet championship demands." (New York *Times*, November 3, 1909.)

A week later, with Jeffries and his wife at sea, Johnson and George Little met with Sam Berger in the offices of the New York *American* to sign articles for the fight. Reporters were invited in to watch. Everyone expected Little to do most of the talking: boxers, especially black boxers, were not expected to do their own negotiating. But Little confined his remarks to an occasional whispered aside. Johnson was clearly in charge. When Berger told him he should leave business matters to the white man, Johnson shot back that since he was going do the fighting, he would attend to business matters as well. He wouldn't be dictated to by anyone; after all, he was the heavyweight champion of the world.

"How did *you* ever get the title?" Berger asked with a sneer.

"By whipping Tommy Burns," answered the black fellow. "Jeffries gave the title to Hart, and Burns whipped Hart, then I took it away from him. . . . That's how I got it."

"That's a lie," said Berger. "Jeffries never gave the title to anyone. He still is champion. Why, Hart got the decision over you and that should have eliminated you entirely."

"Everybody knows how I was robbed of that decision," said Johnson. "Sam, you ought to be ashamed of yourself as a man to even bring that fight into argument. Besides, you know that Jeffries lost his claim to the championship when he refused to fight me."

To which Berger replied: "But you were not even considered in the championship class then. . . . Why, [lightweight] Battling Nelson might as well claim the heavyweight championship if he should challenge Jeffries and Jeff refuses to fight."

Johnson then said that he had fought his way up to his present place in the fighting world, and that he did not propose to allow Jeffries to have everything his own way.

"Did you ever whip a man like Fitzsimmons, or Sharkey, or Corbett, or Ruhlin, or any of the others from whom Jeffries won and then go back and do the same thing over again?" asked Berger. "You've been fighting men like Burns [and] Hart . . ."

"Tell you what I'll do," said Johnson. "I'll bet you $1,000 that I am the recognized champion and we'll go down the street and ask the first hundred men we meet who is the heavyweight champion of the world, and the majority opinion will rule."

Berger did not take the bet, and the two men got down to business. They finally agreed that Johnson and Jeffries would fight "a certain number of rounds"—anywhere from twenty to one hundred—before the club that offered them the best "inducements."

The give-and-take between the white manager and the black champion had been remarkably evenhanded, wrote Edward Smith, the veteran referee and sporting editor of the Chicago *American*.

> There was skill on both sides, Berger perhaps being the keener in placing his thrusts, this trait being accentuated by the fact that Johnson did not speak so quickly or so often as the man with the pale skin. But what the colored man said was much to the point and pithy. . . . He really was the surprise of the meeting and several of the sports writers who were present and never got this close, first-hand view of the champion with his dander up were astonished at his wit and brightness.*

Back in Chicago on Saturday evening, August 14, Booker T. Washington was scheduled to speak at Quinn Chapel. It was the friendliest possible territory for him: the oldest African Methodist Episcopal church in the city, Quinn Chapel was a bulwark of middle-class black gradualism and, the Baltimore *Afro-American* reported, every pew was filled with well-dressed black men and women eager to hear him exhort "the men of his race to be clean and strong." As the pastor finished his fulsome introduction and Washington stepped into the pulpit to begin his address, someone spotted the heavyweight champion seated at the back. "Cries of 'Jack Johnson' were heard from all parts of the room until a delegation was sent to escort him to a front seat," the *Afro-American* continued. "He marched down the aisle amid a storm of applause, bowed to the orator from Tuskegee and was recognized with a smile, but declined to take a seat on the platform." The two men, the paper said, were the "intellectual and physical giants of the race" and "more than two thousand Negroes cheered them until they were tired." Washington's smile was broad but forced; he was not accustomed to sharing the spotlight with anyone else, especially someone like Jack Johnson, whose showy style of living he had tried without success to change. After Washington finished

---

*According to George Little, Sam Berger was so startled at having been outargued by Jack Johnson that he refused ever to deal with him directly again: "Berger did not like to talk to Johnson as he knew Johnson could best him." (George Little's 1910 "Confession.")

his remarks, the pastor called for the collection plate to be passed to help relieve the church's debt. Washington put fifteen dollars into the plate. The champion came up with ten.

In September, Johnson returned to California, the scene of his first important victories. George Little came with him on the train. So did Hattie McClay, now back in his good graces and traveling as Mrs. Johnson. But soon after he and she had settled into their rooms above Webb's saloon in the black section of Oakland, he sent money to Belle Schreiber asking her to come west as well. She rented a room at the Athens Hotel as "Mrs. Jack Leslie," and over the next few weeks Johnson moved back and forth between the two women as the mood suited.

He had signed with Sunny Jim Coffroth for two fights at Colma: the potentially big one with Stanley Ketchel in October and a sort of warm-up against Al Kaufmann on September 9. Kaufmann was a burly former blacksmith who hit hard but moved slowly. Johnson did not take him seriously, scoffing after a visit to Kaufmann's training camp that to use his uppercut against him would be "cruelty to children." More than mere self-assurance may have been in play. George Little would later claim to be in possession of a document, signed by himself, Johnson, Kaufmann, and Jim Coffroth, showing they had all agreed that the fight should go the distance in order to build the box office for the Ketchel contest: if Johnson seemed unable to defeat Al Kaufmann decisively, maybe the middleweight champion had a real chance—or so they wanted potential ticket buyers to think.

Certainly, Johnson didn't seem to try very hard on the afternoon of the fight. "Kaufmann had no more chance of blocking my left than a turtle has of running down a Bakersfield jack rabbit," Johnson recalled. "When we went into a clinch, I would playfully tap Kaufmann with my right uppercut, pin his hands, shove him away, and then wing my right and left to his jaw." Little later alleged that several times between rounds he'd had to warn his fighter to hold back for fear he'd overdo it and send Kaufmann to the canvas, and Johnson did seem unusually reluctant to close in when he had his opponent in trouble. Though most ringsiders agreed that Johnson had won all ten rounds—a writer for the San Francisco *Bulletin* counted just six punches landed by Kaufmann in the whole fight—the referee refused to declare a winner.

The crowd hissed the champion before and after the bout, but the next day he sauntered down Market Street wearing a rose in the buttonhole of his fawn-colored overcoat and without a mark on his smiling face, as if he'd won a great victory and couldn't wait to fight again. Where was Jeffries? he asked. Why couldn't they do battle right away? A passerby suggested that Jeffries would kill him. "Bring him along," he said, laughing. "I'm perfectly willing to be killed."

The *Police Gazette,* which had often championed Johnson's cause, now began to find his cockiness unsuitable.

> It wouldn't be a bad idea for Johnson, the black champion, not to forget that he is colored and to do a little catering to a tolerant white public, which is not disposed to forget the fact. . . .
>
> While conservative followers of the fight game in San Francisco feel that Jeffries must be the real Jeffries to dispose of Johnson, the greater majority of the patrons of ring events are still shouting that Jeffries will make Jack Johnson jump over the ropes. They are even saying that Stanley Ketchel will whip Johnson this month, which goes to show how deep the feeling of prejudice against the negro heavyweight is throughout the country.

To prepare for Ketchel, Johnson and his entourage took over several rooms on the second floor of the Seal Rock House, a handsome, rambling hotel overlooking Ocean Beach. "With the waning of the day the parlors blaze with electric lights," one visitor noted, "the wood leaps bright in the wide open fireplace, the entertainers play, the wine flows." Both Belle Schreiber and Hattie McClay were in residence and, if Johnson's memoir can be believed, things didn't go well between them, at least in the beginning: "Naturally, there was a state of warfare between Hattie and Belle which threatened to break out into open and disastrous hostilities at any moment. . . . I slipped in and out of the hotel in a manner that would have aroused newspaper reporters to much excited speculation . . . had they known of my maneuvers."

If there really was a turf war, Schreiber seems to have won it. McClay moved out a few days after she'd moved in, taking a room in yet another hotel. But both women were professionals, after all, and cordial relations between them seem to have quickly been restored. A lithographed postcard from Hattie addressed to "Mrs. Jack Johnson" at Seal Rock House survives. It shows a pair of naked cherubs from behind—the boy has his arm around the girl as they watch the sun rise above the sea—and bears an entirely friendly message:

"Dearest Bell Is this what you and Jack does in the A.M. . . . ? Looks good to me and their bare behind." It is signed "Lovingly Hattie."

Because Stanley Ketchel was white and Jim Coffroth was determined to sell the upcoming bout as a racial contest, the newspapers emphasized the differences between Ketchel and the heavyweight champion, not the similarities. In fact, they had a lot in common. Each was supremely self-confident: Ketchel routinely sent a wire to his father *before* his fights announcing that he had won, because, he said, he was afraid he'd forget to do it afterward. Both men loved racing cars and gambling, alcohol and the limelight: after making his New York debut, Ketchel drove up Fifth Avenue wearing a pink bathrobe and throwing peanuts to passersby just to draw a crowd. Both had what the writer John Lardner called "a dim sense of property rights in regard to women." And both men enjoyed flirting with danger: Ketchel rarely dined in public without a blue Colt revolver across his knees and once deliberately drove his roadster into a San Francisco fruit stand just to see the limes and lemons fly.

He was born Stanislaus Kaicel, the son of Polish immigrants on the rough side of Grand Rapids, Michigan. (His friends called him Steve.) He ran with a rowdy gang as a boy and was beaten frequently for it by his father. "I was a tough kid who needed walloping," he said. But at twelve he decided he'd had enough and ran away from home, just as Jack Johnson said he had done, and spent several years riding the rods in the West, stopping off from time to time to mine quartz, harvest wheat, herd livestock, and make so many friends among his fellow tramps that later, when he earned enough to ride in the chair cars, he carried a bag of money so he could toss fistfuls of coins out the window into the hobo jungles clustered here and there along the tracks. At sixteen, he got a job as a bellhop at a rough place called the Copper Queen in Butte, Montana. When the bouncer made the mistake of tripping him for laughs, Ketchel flattened him and was rewarded with his tormentor's job. It suited him: "He had the soul of a bouncer," the veteran manager Dan Morgan remembered, "a bouncer who enjoyed his work." The manager of Butte's Casino Theater then hired him to take on all comers for twenty dollars a week. "I hit 'em so hard they used to fall over the footlights and land in the people's laps," he remembered, and he began to travel the state, hammering out thirty-six knockouts in places like Butte and Lewistown, Helena and Miles City.

Amiable, even happy-go-lucky, between fights, Ketchel prepared himself for combat by inventing stories about whomever he happened to be fighting. "The sonofabitch!" he'd mutter as he waited for the bell to ring. "He insulted my mother. I'll kill the bastard!" He would then try to do just that, hurling himself at his opponent again and again, smashing with both fists, refusing to retreat until the other man could take no more. His nicknames reflected his ferocity: to his fans he was the "Wolverine," the "Michigan Wildcat," the "Michigan Assassin." "He was a savage," Dan Morgan said. "He'd pound and rip his opponent's eyes, nose and mouth in a clinch. He couldn't get *enough* blood."

Ketchel won the undisputed middleweight championship in 1908 and the following year chose as his manager Willus Britt, an alcoholic former featherweight who was both one of the game's shrewdest operators—he had guided Battling Nelson to the lightweight title—and one of its most shameless.* He was also a realist. There was no way to get around the fact that Ketchel was merely a middleweight, at least thirty pounds lighter and more than four inches shorter than the heavyweight champion. ("Why he's just a little fella," Jim Jeffries said when he learned that a Johnson-Ketchel fight was in the offing.) And, as W. W. Naughton wrote, for all Ketchel's courage and knockout power, he remained a "rusher," while Johnson was the acknowledged master of "reach and range and farawayness."

If boxing fans were going to buy tickets, they had somehow to be convinced that the fight was not a mismatch. Before the two men were photographed together, Britt had a cobbler build cowboy boots for Ketchel with four-inch heels and dressed him in a long, specially padded overcoat to disguise the difference in their sizes. Then, he invited the press to come see his man work out—and made sure all three of Ketchel's lumbering heavyweight sparring partners went down for the count in full view of gullible reporters.

But Britt was not content with that. He didn't *fix* the fight, exactly. "There is a great difference between a fix and a deal," Johnson would helpfully

---

*After the 1906 San Francisco earthquake, Britt sued the city for damage done to his property. When the city attorneys argued that the earthquake had been an act of God, Britt countered that that could not possibly be true, since several churches belonging to Him had been destroyed.

He had stolen his latest meal ticket from a less wily manager, or so boxing lore has it. Ketchel's manager Joe O'Connor had thought he'd safeguarded his prized possession by confiscating his clothes and locking him in the room of his San Francisco boardinghouse while he went out on an errand. It was a fatal error. The diminutive Britt is supposed to have shinnied up the drainpipe—or climbed the fire escape, accounts differ—talked his way through the window, and painted such a rosy picture of what he and the other members of Jim Coffroth's so-called boxing trust could do for the impressionable young man that Ketchel agreed to sign on right away. There was only one problem, he said: "I got no pants." "Think nothing of it," Britt replied. "Let's go to Coffroth's saloon. He's got spare pants." Whatever the truth of the story, Britt became Ketchel's manager, and Jim Coffroth would promote many of his biggest fights. (John Lardner, "Yesterday's Graziano," *Sport*, April 1948.)

explain, but "we did have a deal." According to him, Britt set it forth at their first meeting. "Let's be practical, Jack," he said. "We all know you can murder Ketchel. I'm not kidding myself. I wouldn't let him get into the ring with you for a million dollars unless I had your word that you wouldn't hurt him." Johnson shook hands on it, or so he later said.

But there was another more compelling reason for Johnson to agree to prolong the fight than Willus Britt's solicitude for his fighter's well-being. Johnson and Ketchel were to split 40 percent of the proceeds for the films of this fight. The longer it went—the longer the doughty little white man seemed able to hold his own against the far larger black champion—the bigger the film's box office was sure to be. And so, to "make the pictures snappy and worth seeing"—and more profitable—Johnson said, he agreed to let Ketchel "make a good showing" for at least twelve of the twenty scheduled rounds.

The two men met on the afternoon of October 16 before ten thousand fans at Jim Coffroth's arena at Colma.* Ketchel's normal demeanor just before the bell rang was grim and stoic; this was the time when he worked up hatred for his opponent. But this afternoon he was seen weeping as he waited on his stool. All sorts of explanations for this emotional display were offered later: some said he'd simply been overwhelmed by the responsibility of bearing the standard of the white race into battle; others thought he was unhappy at taking part in a contest in which he was expected to give less than his best; still others claimed he'd just been told Johnson would be fighting in earnest, not merely coasting.

For eleven rounds the bout went more or less the way the Burns fight had gone. Johnson towered over his opponent, picking off his punches, smiling and chatting with ringsiders, landing just often and just hard enough to cause Ketchel's mouth and nose to bleed but to do no more serious damage. Several times Johnson simply lifted the smaller man into the air, feet dangling like an oversized rag doll, and put him down just where he liked. One ringsider called it "a struggle between a demon and a gritty little dwarf."

Then, midway through the twelfth, Ketchel strayed from the script. He and Willus Britt, crouching below his corner, had evidently planned a double-

---

*According to one story, they had actually encountered one another earlier that day. Ketchel and Britt were on their way to the stadium in Ketchel's Thomas Flyer when Johnson pulled up beside them in his and tried to pass. Ketchel gunned his motor, and the two racers careened through the city streets at better than seventy miles an hour before Johnson pulled away, laughing. (Vernon Gravely, "Willus Britt: More Than Just a Manager," *The Ring*, June 1954.)

cross. As Johnson sent yet another long, lazy jab toward Ketchel's face, Britt shouted, "Now, Stanley, now!" and the middleweight champion lunged forward with an overhand right. It landed just behind the champion's left ear. Johnson's feet went out from under him. He caught himself with one hand, then sprang up again, a sheepish grin on his face.

The crowd was stunned. So, evidently, was Ketchel, whose gaze remained fixed on his manager. Perhaps he was waiting for further instructions. In any case, Johnson hit him in the mouth so hard with his right hand that the force of the blow sent both men to the floor.

Ketchel stayed there, flat on his back, arms outflung. Four of his teeth were strewn across the canvas. The grim-faced crowd fell silent as the referee counted him out. Johnson stood, one arm along the top rope, the other on his hip, peering down anxiously for some sign that his opponent would revive. It took several minutes.*

The photograph that appeared in most newspapers the next morning captured both the black champion, standing over his unconscious white opponent, and a lone black spectator amid the grim-faced whites at ringside, struggling to contain his glee. It only served to fuel white fervor for Jeffries' return. So did black jubilation at Johnson's triumph: at Memphis, for example, the Associated Press reported that steamboat traffic had come to a halt as "deck hands, picked exclusively from the negro race," remained onshore, first to hear the telegraph bulletins from ringside and then to celebrate the good news.

---

*George Little—soon to join the parade of Johnson's discarded managers—would later claim that everything, including the controversial climax, had been prearranged. Jim Coffroth had been in on it, too, he said, and had personally driven Johnson and himself to Willus Britt's home for a rehearsal. There they shifted the furniture, rolled back the carpets, and rehearsed the final round. Johnson had no trouble playing his part, falling again and again with a suitably agonized look, then springing back up to throw his uppercut. The problem was Ketchel: try as he might, according to Little, he couldn't seem to collapse convincingly. Finally he held up his hand. He wasn't an actor, he said; "he couldn't fake a fight and never did. It would be better to make it real as he could stand the punishment."

Denver Jack O'Keefe, one of Johnson's sparring partners, recalled the practice sessions differently. They'd taken place over ten days at Seal Rock, he said, and Ketchel hadn't been there at all. Johnson knew of Ketchel's "excitable manner when he sensed the kill and planned to take advantage of it" by feigning a knockdown, then jumping up and catching him with "the terrific right uppercut Johnson had in those days." For the record, Sunny Jim Coffroth emphatically denied that there had ever been any reason to prolong the contest for the motion picture cameras: "These pictures were contracted for by burlesque houses and would have been worth just as much money if there had been only half as many rounds." To further complicate things, Johnson would later claim he had only pretended to be knocked down. Precisely what happened in the moments leading up to the final punch will probably never be known. But there was nothing inauthentic about that final uppercut. (George Little, "Confession"; undated story from Chicago *Daily News*, 1944; Jack Johnson, *In the Ring and Out*, p. 196.)

A few days later, San Francisco began a five-day, citywide celebration meant to honor the 150th anniversary of the arrival of Don Gaspar de Portolá, the first European visitor to San Francisco Bay in 1769, and to mark San Francisco's "renaissance from ruin" after the earthquake of 1906 as well. A highlight of the festivities was to be a parade of sixteen hundred decorated automobiles down Market Street. Both sides of the street were hung with flags, bunting, and the red and yellow colors of Catalonia, Portolá's homeland. Thousands lined the sidewalks as the long line of vehicles awaited the signal to start their engines. Suddenly, a big sixty-nine-horsepower Thomas Flyer roared down the middle of the empty avenue ahead of everyone, with Jack Johnson waving from his elevated seat behind the wheel. Some cheered. Many booed. When he slowed for a crossing, a policeman leaped onto the running board and ordered him to stop. "At the police station," one paper reported, "he was flippant and gave his occupation as 'lawyer.' " It took a crisp hundred-dollar bill to get him out on bail, but it had been worth it. He had enjoyed himself.

"Jack Johnson is running wild," Beany Walker wrote in the San Francisco *Examiner,* "and the only man that figures to tame the negro is on the ocean waves battling against seasickness and homesickness. Jim Jeffries is rushing to America as fast as steam will bring him. The sooner the big boy arrives home, the better it will be for the peace of mind of the fight followers of this country."

The stakes were higher than that, the editor of the British magazine *Boxing* told his readers: Jack Johnson threatened the power and status of all white men everywhere.

With Johnson's decisive decision over Stanley Ketchel, the road is cleared for the long expected battle between the black champion and the great hero, the only man to whom we can look to wrest back the title for the dominant race. It is not so much a matter of racial pride as one of racial existence which urges us so ardently to desire the ex-boilermaker's triumph.

The coloured races outnumber the whites, and have hitherto only been kept in subjection by a recognition on their part of physical and mental inferiority.

But a great change has come over the situation of late years. The Russo-Japanese War proved that a coloured people could conquer a white nation in war even under modern conditions and ever since there have been signs of unrest among the subject nations, displaying itself in India, in the Philippine Islands, and elsewhere. Then came Jack Johnson's great triumph over Tommy Burns and White and Black stood before the world in suddenly inverted positions again.

Here we are, the hitherto dominant race, compelled to recognize that an American negro, the descendant of an emancipated slave, is the principal figure, our acknowledged master at the one great physical sport in which actual personal superiority can ever be authoritatively tested. Does anyone imagine for a moment that Johnson's success is without its political influence, an influence which has only been checked from having full vent by the personality of Jim Jeffries?

Jeff may smash Johnson when they meet . . . and by so doing restore us to something like our old position. We shall never quite regain it, because the recollection of our temporary deposition will always remain to inspire the coloured peoples with hope. While if, after all, Johnson should smash Jeffries—But the thought is too awful to contemplate.

The New York *Times* was more succinct:

Even those who have an absurdly exaggerated horror of prize fighting as a "brutal" sport should gently warm in their sensitive minds a little hope that the white man may not lose, while the rest of us will wait in open anxiety the news that he has licked the—well, since it must be in print, let us say the negro, even though it is not the first word that comes to the tongue's tip.

CHAPTER SEVEN

THE GREATEST COLORED MAN THAT EVER LIVED

ON THE AFTERNOON OF OCTOBER 29, 1909, in the banquet hall of New York's Albany Hotel on Broadway, Jack Johnson and Jim Jeffries were scheduled to meet face-to-face. They had not seen each other since the summer of 1905, when Jeffries had refereed the Jack Root–Marvin Hart bout in Reno, Nevada, and Johnson had fruitlessly challenged the winner from the ring. The ostensible reason for their getting together was to sign a second set of articles for their upcoming battle. The real reason was publicity, and a crowd of several hundred sports and sportswriters was on hand to help drum it up.

Jeffries entered promptly at three o'clock, his every move recorded by an awed reporter for *Harper's Weekly.*

> He swings through the door amid a burst of cheering and marches down the middle of the crowded room, while men hurry as close as possible to him and a few daring ones whack his big back and cry "H'lo, Jeff!" He answers no word but smiles and nods right and left. . . . [H]e stands six feet one and a half inches and in his thin serge suit weighs nearly two hundred and fifty pounds; yet his footfall is as light and brisk and sure as the step of the swiftest dancer. "Moves like a feather!" exclaims a hero-worshipper as he gazes in ecstasy. . . .
>
> The . . . connoisseurs are . . . intently staring at his waistline. They admire it. It is very brief. The man within has already worked so hard in training that he has burned away the surplus flesh. . . . The brilliance of his eyes and the glow of his clear, bronzed skin are eloquent of good physical condition. The throng press close to him, gaze, study, scrutinize, admire.

Jeffries took his seat at the head of the table on which the papers were to be signed, "like the master in his house," the *Harper's* writer thought, and when Johnson turned up fifteen minutes later, the room fell silent.

> One could not help feeling sorry for the negro. Clearly, he felt ill at ease among these hundreds of whites who if not actually hostile were certainly

not friendly. Two other black men were in the room, but they were hidden in the throng. Johnson is as tall as Jeffries but fully thirty pounds lighter. There is something of the grace and power of the panther in the long, easy swing of his walk ordinarily; but now that he encountered so many curious and unsympathetic stares, the poor fellow seemed to shrink in upon himself. His gait had lost its springy quality. He bore himself as if he expected a scolding. . . .

This black, who properly fought his way to the championship of the world, . . . advanced like an abashed servant. A vacant chair was placed for him some six feet from the chair of Jeffries.

The moment Johnson appeared . . . [Jeffries' smile] froze. . . . I have seen him in other matchmakings when he was indifferent or friendly or merely polite to the enemy, but never like this. Down came the black brows in a frown, and the eyes beneath them glared at the negro as the eyes of a stern judge glare when he tells the prisoner how sorry he is that the law won't let him impose a heavier sentence. Not a word did he utter, but kept the glare fixed on the unhappy visitor. The negro looked down at the floor, around among the crowd, but not at his adversary. Anything but that. . . .

Was he frightened? I think not. He has always shown himself a brave man in battle, and he probably will be brave when he faces Jeffries in the ring but coming suddenly against that glare in the presence of so many unfriendly strangers disconcerted for a time the present champion of the ring.

If Johnson really was disconcerted, he recovered fast. He and Jeffries were each supposed to put up $5,000 as a side bet. Jeffries slapped five-thousand-dollar bills on the table. Johnson came up with just $2,500. It was all he had in the world, he said.

Jeffries insisted that he produce the whole amount.

"I'll tell you what I'll do Mr. Jeffries. We'll throw the dice to see whether you get my money or whether I have to put up five thousand." Jeffries turned him down—and waived the requirement. "While there was no attempt at undue civility," said the Cleveland *Advocate*, "the pair showed a determination to get down to business."

Nearly everyone in the room seemed to be smoking, and after the discussion had gone on for a while, someone suggested they open a window to let out the thick blue haze. Johnson grinned. "Say," he said, "if the 'Smoke' goes out the window there will be no match made here this day."

In the end they agreed to fight for forty-five rounds on or about July 4, 1910, at a site still to be chosen. The winner was to get 75 percent of the winnings, the loser 25. (It was originally to have been winner-take-all but, as George Little later explained, he and Johnson decided that, in the unlikely event Jeffries won, "we didn't want to eat snowballs all winter"; by fight time, the split would be 60–40.) Promoters had thirty days to submit their bids.

The next morning, Johnson hurried out to Long Island for the fifth running of the Vanderbilt Cup road race. Immaculately turned out as always, and with a bottle of champagne jutting from his coat pocket, he approached the reviewing stand, assuming that he could talk his way into the exclusive box that afforded the best view of the finish line. A uniformed guard told him to go away. Blacks were barred. Not even the heavyweight champion of the world would be allowed to mingle with the wealthy automobile fanciers inside.

That rebuff alone might have made Johnson's visit to Long Island memorable, but a chance meeting that same day made it unforgettable. While he stood with the rest of the crowd waiting to see the racers roar by, someone Johnson later identified only as one of his "theatrical connections" introduced him to Mrs. Etta Terry Duryea, a twenty-eight-year-old white woman from Brooklyn. She had appeared on the stage and was currently living apart from her husband. "Famed on Long Island for her beauty," according to the New York *World,* she was elegantly dressed and slender, with dark hair, large dark eyes, and a lovely sad smile. Johnson was taken with her and she with him. They arranged to keep in touch by telephone. Jack Johnson had had numberless similar encounters. This one would turn out to be perhaps the most fateful of his life.

Meanwhile, with the Jeffries fight still nine months away, Johnson returned to the stage. In late November, he was in Pittsburgh, appearing in a revue called *The Cracker-Jacks* and living at Frank Sutton's hotel with Belle Schreiber. One afternoon, a tall, lean stranger appeared at the door and asked to see the champion. His name, he said, was Tex Rickard, and he had a proposition to make.

Johnson eagerly ushered him inside. He already knew his visitor's reputation. George Lewis Rickard was a reckless gambler and a relative newcomer to the promotion of boxing matches. He knew almost nothing about the game, but he had already proved he knew more than anyone else about turning it into big business. Born in rural Missouri in 1871 and raised in the state that afforded him his nickname, he had herded cattle as a small boy, served as a town marshal at twenty-three, and then made himself rich in the Yukon, not by mining gold but by providing miners with lavish gambling establishments in which to lose their gold to him. In 1903, he shifted his operation to Goldfield, Nevada, where he presided over a gambling palace that took in about ten thousand dollars a day. But he was always on the lookout for ways to do better.

In 1906, Rickard had heard that the managers of Joe Gans and Oscar "Battling" Nelson, rival claimants to the lightweight title, were interested in arranging a contest to decide who was the real champion. The only fights Rickard had ever seen were amateur bouts he'd staged to pull more customers into his Alaskan gambling halls. But he saw instantly that if he could attract the fight to Goldfield, he could put the little mining camp on the map and make a tidy profit for himself besides. Gans was black; Nelson was white. Rickard thought he could sell their meeting as a struggle for racial superiority, not just a boxing match. He sent off telegrams to both managers, promising a thirty-thousand-dollar purse—unheard-of for a lightweight fight—then stacked the whole sum in gold coins in his front window to show he meant business and stole the bout from established promoters elsewhere who thought they had it sewed up.

Rickard made sure the papers were filled with enthusiastic prefight stories by passing out twenty-dollar gold pieces to thirsty sportswriters. "Somehow, crude, uneducated guy though he was, he managed to do this graciously," one grateful recipient remembered. "You had the impression that it was you who were doing him the favor by accepting the money. It was always a token of friendship, never a bribe."

It all paid off. Eight thousand fans turned up for the fight on Labor Day, doubling Goldfield's population overnight. The bout went forty-two rounds before referee George Siler gave it to Gans on a foul.* The fight's savagery was remembered for years; so was a phrase from the triumphant telegram

---

*Here and there across the country, news of Gans' triumph caused trouble. In New York, a black man who shouted "Colored gentlemen can always lick poor whites" to a cluster of disappointed Nelson fans had to be rescued by the police, and in Chicago there was a fistfight between blacks and whites who had gathered around a South Side saloon to hear the telegraphed returns.

Gans sent home to his mother: BRINGING HOME THE BACON. Everybody involved made money. Gans used some of his to open the Goldfield, a handsomely fitted-out café for the sports of Baltimore, where, the pianist and composer Eubie Blake remembered, Jack Johnson was a frequent and conspicuous visitor whenever his travels took him to that town.

Now, huddled with Johnson and Belle Schreiber in their Pittsburgh hotel room, Rickard promised to make them rich, too. The Goldfield fight had been a mere dress rehearsal, he said; the coming clash between Johnson, the "Negro's Deliverer," and Jeffries, the "Hope of the White Race," would be likely to dwarf anything that had ever before happened in American sports. The films of the Johnson–Ketchel fight had earned hundreds of thousands of dollars and further whetted the white appetite for seeing Johnson bested.* The films of the upcoming fight should do far better.

Bids from promoters hoping to get in on the action were not supposed to be submitted until November 30, but Rickard saw no reason to wait. The champion didn't, either. The promoter spelled out his offer: a $101,000 purse, the largest in boxing history; two thirds of the film rights to be split between the fighters; a bonus of $5,000 more for Johnson on signing ($2,500 in cash that very afternoon and another $2,500 before he entered the ring); and, as further incentive, "the finest sealskin coat he could find" for "Mrs. Johnson."

Without even talking with George Little, Johnson signed up.† Rickard then discovered that a promoter named Jack Gleason had made a similar secret arrangement with Sam Berger, and Jeffries had already accepted a signing bonus of $10,000, twice the sum Rickard had promised Johnson. To keep his scheme afloat, Rickard agreed to become Gleason's partner and pledged a second $5,000 bonus for Johnson so that both fighters were treated equally.

With everything already settled behind the scenes, the formal opening of the bids at Myer's Hotel in Hoboken, New Jersey, on November 30 turned into a sort of dumb show, with Johnson and Berger pretending to give careful consideration to each of the offers made by the biggest promoters in boxing: Rickard; Uncle Tom McCarey and his Los Angeles rival Tuxedo Eddie

---

*Not all whites shared this view, of course. In New York, on October 29, the artist John Sloan went to see the Johnson–Ketchel films at Hammerstein's Victoria and came away dazzled by Johnson's skill: "The big black spider gobbled up the small white fly—aggressive fly—wonderful to have this event repeated." (Dan Streible, *Fight Pictures*, p. 161.)

†No such sums had ever been seen in boxing before. When the news got out, the Philadelphia *Evening Star* headlined on December 1, 1909, SEEMS HARD TO IMAGINE THAT SO MUCH REAL MONEY IS IN THE WORLD.

Graney; and Phil King, the American representative of Hugh D. McIntosh.*
The champion pretended not to understand all the details. He had only a
grade-school education, he said, and asked for twenty-four hours to look
over the offers. Tom McCarey eagerly volunteered to explain things to him.
"That's all right, Mr. McCarey," Johnson answered, "but I believe what the
good book says; I believe I'll help myself."

He already had helped himself, of course, and so had Jeffries. Tex Rickard
and Jack Gleason got the formal nod the following day, amid angry charges
of double-cross from their rivals. The site remained to be chosen. Johnson
didn't care where the fight took place, provided it was north of the Mason-
Dixon Line. "I was born and raised in the South," he said, "and I happen to
know how a colored man stands in that section." If he were to beat Jeffries
there, he continued, "I think I would be the one to be carried out of the
ring. . . . If I can't get a match where I know my life is perfectly safe whether
I win or lose, I will not fight at all."

Rickard would eventually pick San Francisco, where he and Gleason would
build a brand-new stadium at Eighth and Market Streets to seat the thirty
thousand customers they were confident would pay to see the contest they
had begun to tout as the *real* "Battle of the Century."

The Rickard publicity machine lurched into action. Even the choice of ref-
erees made headlines. The editor of the New York *Morning Telegraph* asked
the creator of Sherlock Holmes, Arthur Conan Doyle, to officiate: "I was
much inclined to accept this honorable invitation," Doyle wrote in his memoirs, "though my friends pictured me as winding up with a revolver at one
ear and a razor at the other. However, the distance and my engagements presented a final bar." Johnson thought former president Theodore Roosevelt,
himself an ardent amateur boxer, would be a good choice; he wasn't interested, either, though he did look forward to the contest.† Frederick G. Bonfils, editor of the Denver *Post,* thought the coming fight so momentous, he
wanted not one but two reporters at ringside, "the most eminent black man"

---

*Jack Gleason went through the motions of making a separate offer as well, ostensibly on behalf of
Sunny Jim Coffroth. There were evidently plots within plots. Coffroth was said by some to have thought
Gleason was acting on his behalf, to have known nothing of his secret deal with Berger, and to have
been so angered by what he saw as Gleason's betrayal that he lobbied to have the contest banished from
his city. But other stories suggest that Coffroth got half of every dollar Gleason made from the contest.

†Mindful of what had happened to him in his fight with Marvin Hart, Johnson told Jack Gleason he
wanted two judges at ringside, and that one of them should be black. In the end, no judge of either
color would be appointed.

and "the most eminent white man we can find." Booker T. Washington and William Jennings Bryan both said no.*

Despite Rickard's best efforts, rumors spread almost immediately that the fight was fixed and that Johnson had agreed to lose. The champion dismissed the idea out of hand: he'd resisted such offers when he was poor, he said; why would he entertain them when "I've got . . . money enough to live on if I never fight again?" Jeffries was indignant:

> I have never faked the public, nor am I starting now. . . . Johnson knows that I hate the ground he walks on, that I consider him an accident in the championship class, and that I propose to give him the worst beating ever given any man in the ring. There has been no frame-up—there will be none.

But the fact that the two fighters were to split two thirds of the film rights added plausibility to the rumors. "It is no exaggeration to say that the entire world will await a pictorial representation of the fight," said *Moving Picture World.*

> With good light and a battle of, say, thirty well fought rounds, and the unmistakable victory of Jeffries, these pictures should prove in the current locution, a "gold mine." This is the wish . . . of hundreds of millions of white people throughout the world.
>
> [But] . . . if Johnson wins? It is commonly believed that the pictures would then be of comparatively little value, especially among the white section of the community.

By winning, then, Johnson would actually lose money. To some, his willingness to take that gamble meant he must also have been willing to throw the fight. The rumors would persist until the day Johnson and Jeffries entered the ring.

Jim Jeffries had done so well on his first theatrical tour, he decided to undertake another before he started training in earnest, this time under the management of Jack Curley and the flamboyant Chicago impresario H. Harrison Frazee, then known as the "king of the one-night stands" for the arduous but

---

*Washington suggested that the *Post* approach T. Thomas Fortune, ex-editor of the New York *Age,* but Bonfils said Fortune was not "well enough known."

profitable vaudeville tours he organized.* Frazee and Curley guaranteed Jeffries one thousand dollars a week plus a hefty portion of the gross receipts to head an all-star "Living Wonders" troupe of boxers and wrestlers and play theaters across the country.

At first, things didn't go well. Jeffries hated the daily grind, grew tired of shaking hands and signing autographs and trying to control his appetite and his drinking. He missed his wife, too, and cursed himself for signing a contract that was earning him much less than he'd received earlier in the year from William Morris. When the show pulled into Toledo, he threatened to quit, and it took all of Curley's persuasive powers to get him to stick it out—plus the promise that he'd be pocketing ten thousand dollars a week once they left the jaded East and began to play western towns whose citizens were starved for entertainment of any kind.

Jeffries stayed on board, and when Curley left the show shortly before it came to its end in Minnesota in February, the ex-champion shook his hand. "Jack, I'm grateful to you for two things," he said. "The first is that you persuaded me to go through with the tour when I wanted to quit. The second thing is that not once on the trip have you talked 'nigger' to me."

The hourly reminders of Jeffries' responsibility as the rescuer of the white race had begun to wear on him. Scores of letters from anxious admirers arrived every day. "Jim, please, for our sakes, wallop the big Smoke good and hard," wrote a group of American sailors aboard a battleship off Okinawa. A Muncie, Indiana, man offered to show him "how to whip the nigger." The actress Ethel Barrymore said she hoped Jeffries would kill "the black bluff." The Bodega Club of Deadwood, South Dakota, assured him the whole town was pulling for him to "smash the coconut off the dinge." After a while, Jeffries ordered all letters from strangers dumped into the trash, unopened.

Only one time during the tour, Curley remembered, "was there the slightest reference to Johnson in any conversation between us." Leaving Sioux City, Iowa, one night, Curley was in the upper berth and Jeffries was reading down below when suddenly he crumpled up his newspaper and threw it to the floor, cursing.

Curley asked what was the matter.

"There's an article in there about how the skunk [his invariable term for

---

*Frazee would go on to buy the Boston Red Sox in 1917—and to earn the undying enmity of Boston fans by selling Babe Ruth to the New York Yankees three years later.

Johnson] can beat me. All I want is to get him into the ring and smash his black face."

Jim Jeffries' second tour turned out to be another financial triumph: Frazee and Curley wrote him a check for $112,500, more than two million in today's dollars.

By contrast, Jack Johnson's more or less simultaneous vaudeville tour would yield mostly chaos. After the bids for the big fight were opened, Johnson stayed on at Barron Wilkins' Little Savoy. A small-time theatrical impresario named Barney Gerard visited him there in mid-December, hoping to work out a contract for a string of vaudeville appearances—a few days as star of a touring show called the *Atlantic Athletic Carnival,* followed by seven weeks with a burlesque revue, *Follies of the Day.* The Jeffries fight was still more than seven months away, and there was no reason not to make as much money as possible in the interim.

Gerard would play only a minor role in the drama of Johnson's life, but government investigators later interviewed him at length, and his testimony offers an important backstage glimpse into the champion's troubled private world. On that first visit, Gerard was introduced to Hattie McClay as Mrs. Jack Johnson. But a week later, when he turned up again to close the deal, another white woman was introduced as the champion's wife. Gerard was baffled until a little man with a big, battered nose, who said his name was Sig Hart, took him aside and offered to explain things. Hart was a former bantamweight and flashy full-time sport from Chicago—his nickname was "the little fashion-plate"—who had known Johnson since his first visit to that town. He had a shady reputation: one sportswriter called him "a diminutive trouble-maker"; another said Hart was never happy "if not embroiled in something"; and during his boxing days at least one purse had been withheld from him for taking a too-obvious dive. But he was now a permanent part of the champion's entourage, acting as valet, fixer, court jester, and companion in nighttime adventures. Hart, Gerard remembered, warned him "not to make mention of the woman I had seen on my previous visit. This woman now present was supposed to be [Johnson's] real wife."

The woman now present was Etta Duryea, whose friendship with Johnson had clearly progressed beyond telephone calls. Like the other women with whom he lived from time to time, she kept her true identity to herself so far as possible, and very little reliable information about her survives. After her relationship with Johnson ended in tragedy, the New York *World* would run a leering account of her life, filled with gossip and half-truths. "It was notorious that Johnson had fascinated other white women," it said, although "none, to be sure, [was] of her breeding." That part, at least, was true.

Etta Terry Duryea had been raised in the midst of a kind of comfort and luxury that, until he won his title, neither Jack Johnson nor any of the women who had previously traveled with him had ever known. She was born in 1881 in her family's summer home in the fashionable Long Island community of Hempstead. Her father was the superintendent of Young, Gerard & Co., a Brooklyn firm that milled door frames and window sashes and decorative mouldings. And she had married into a family still better-off and better connected. Clarence E. Duryea was the son of a wealthy real estate man who enjoyed yachting and rode with the exclusive Meadow Brook Hunt, whose members over the years had included William K. Vanderbilt, August Belmont, and Elliott Roosevelt. She'd met him when his horse came up lame while following the pack and he'd walked the limping animal up the drive to the Terrys' door and asked her if he could water it. She said he could and brought him a glass of water for himself as well. Struck by her beauty, he'd asked if he could call again, beginning a courtship that ended with a June wedding in her family's Brooklyn parlor in 1903. Both seem to have been stagestruck. She played the piano and sang. He sang, too, well enough to have been a tenor soloist at the Garden City Episcopal Cathedral. Against the wishes of both their families, who thought show business beneath them, they tried the theater without much success. After four years or so, according to the *World,* the two drifted apart; "Mrs. Duryea began to be seen at race tracks without her husband" and was soon a favorite among what the paper called "white sporting men."

Glamorous, well-spoken, and unattached, she brought a new elegance and refinement into Johnson's life, made the hats and furs and dresses and diamonds he provided for her look as if they had been made for no one else. Many years later, his old sparring partner Gunboat Smith still couldn't get over the fact that Johnson's new companion was "a highly educated woman." And in part, perhaps, because of Etta's background and bearing, Johnson seems to have been more taken with her than he had been with any of her predecessors; he also seems to have been willing to overlook episodes of what he may have initially dismissed as moodiness but which was really early evidence of the depression that would eventually consume her.

Belle Schreiber and Hattie McClay bitterly resented Johnson's special treatment of this newcomer. Both were fearful she would displace them in the champion's affection—and cut them off from his generosity. They had quarreled with each other over Johnson in San Francisco but in the end made peace. As sporting women, they had no real reason to expect fidelity from the men who paid them for their company.

Etta felt differently. She was accustomed to better treatment than her rivals had ever known, and once she had committed herself to the champion, she saw no reason to accept his customary faithlessness without a struggle. For his part, Johnson seemed to think he would be able somehow to keep all the women in his life happy—and willing to tolerate the continuing presence of the others. But not even Jack Johnson could manage that. The result would be almost perpetual disorder.

It began right after Christmas, and again Barney Gerard would be on hand to see it. For the first time in seven years, Johnson was to be with his family for the holidays. He had a home of his own now, a handsome turreted three-story brick house at 3344 South Wabash in Chicago he had bought for his widowed mother for ten thousand dollars. Two of his sisters, Lucy and Jennie, and his young adopted brother, Charles, would eventually live there, too. "Jack Johnson was one of the two happiest persons in Chicago yesterday," the Milwaukee *Evening Wisconsin* reported afterward. "His mother was the other." A newspaper photographer caught a glimpse of this holiday idyll inside the Johnson home: George Little and a Johnson niece look on as the champion embraces his mother and his "wife" of the moment, Hattie McClay. A Christmas tree hung with tinsel occupies one corner of the room, and at its foot a bright-eyed nephew sits astride a hobbyhorse surrounded by shiny new toys.

A couple of days later, everything changed when Belle Schreiber and her younger sister turned up unexpectedly from Milwaukee. They brought still more unexpected news: Belle was pregnant, or so she said. The baby was Johnson's. According to her later testimony, he was pleased: "He wanted me to have it. He asked me to have this child and not to do anything to get rid of it."*

A little later that day, Barney Gerard happened by. He'd just come in from New York and wanted to make sure Johnson would be ready to start his vaudeville tour on New Year's Eve as scheduled. Johnson received him cor-

---

*Jack Johnson was married at least three times and had countless lovers. So far as anyone knows, he had no children. He may have seen Belle's alleged pregnancy as his opportunity to become a father.

dially, then quietly asked a favor. A young lady was coming to call, he said. Would Gerard please pretend she was *his* friend, not Johnson's? Gerard agreed to go along. But when Etta Duryea arrived moments later, the showman had no opportunity for playacting. Both Belle Schreiber and Hattie McClay recognized Etta immediately as Johnson's "girl friend from Brooklyn" and threatened to "beat her up" if she didn't leave.

Etta fled. Johnson brought her back and moved her belongings into his mother's house. He and Belle had a long private talk, after which she and her sister left again for Milwaukee, carrying what Gerard remembered being told was "a large amount of cash." Belle would bear no child. No one knows whether she aborted it or suffered a miscarriage, or if it ever existed at all. Johnson's lawyers would later speculate that her dramatic announcement had simply been a last-ditch bid to retain her position as the most important "Mrs. Jack Johnson." If it was, it failed. Johnson had, as Gerard said, "changed wives." From now on, Etta Duryea would be Mrs. Jack Johnson, and Belle would find herself relegated to the secondary role Hattie McClay had been playing when she first caught Johnson's eye.

As he started on his vaudeville tour in the dead of the midwestern winter, the champion had plenty of masculine company: Barney Gerard and George Little, Sig Hart and Abe Ahrens, all came along. But without steady female companionship he found the road intolerable. In Terre Haute, Indiana, he refused to appear onstage in tights because there was no heat in the theater. When the manager responded by calling in a constable to attach his belongings, Johnson climbed on top of his trunks and threatened to "hit the first man who touched them," backing down only when reinforcements arrived. He left George Little behind to negotiate the return of his luggage and moved on to Cleveland, where he was made to dress in the cellar; blacks were not allowed in the dressing rooms. When a taxi driver refused to carry him in Boston, he smashed the windows of the cab. In the same city he pulled a gun and threatened to shoot Sam Langford after his perennial challenger cornered him in a bar and suggested he and Johnson go down into the cellar and see who was the better man.

He eventually persuaded Belle Schreiber by telephone to join him in Boston to keep him company, but they had a violent quarrel soon after she got there—her maid, a black woman named Julia Allen, later alleged that he hit her with an automobile tool, badly bruising her side—and she left him. He gave her money for her train ticket, but she refused to say where she was going. "We were not on good terms," she remembered. A madam in Cleveland turned her away. So did one in Pittsburgh. "They didn't want me because I was Jack Johnson's white sweetheart," she remembered. "Bad as the places were, I was too bad to remain in them." She was drinking absinthe heavily now, and had begun using drugs.

Alone in New York in the early morning hours of January 20, Johnson got into more trouble. After finishing his last show at the Bowery Theater, he stopped in at Barron Wilkins' place. Sitting at a table near the bar were two sporting women and a little drunk named Norman Pinder, who boasted he'd known the champion for years. The women, eager to meet Johnson, loudly insisted that Pinder offer to buy his old friend a beer. Pinder said he'd be glad to do it.

Johnson declined. He never drank anything but wine, he said.

"Don't pull that stuff on me," Pinder shouted. "I knew you when you drank beer out of a growler and were glad to get it."

There were more words. Johnson knocked the little man down, kicked him as he lay on the floor, piled a chair and a table on top of him, and pulled a revolver halfway out of his pocket before his friends could calm him down—or so Pinder would later claim. The police arrested the champion in his dressing room the following evening and charged him with assault. When an officer asked why he'd hit the smaller man so hard, Johnson answered, "Honest to heaven, Mister, I wish I'd hit him harder. He's been casting reflections about me ever since I hit town."

The magistrate was not impressed when Johnson's lawyer argued that Pinder must have fallen downstairs, that he would have been injured far more severely had the champion actually struck him, that the whole thing was part of a plot to keep the Jeffries fight from taking place. Johnson was ordered to put up fifteen hundred dollars in bail and agree to return to face trial in a few weeks.

Pinder hired Abe Levy, one of Manhattan's ablest ambulance chasers, to lodge a twenty-thousand-dollar suit for damages. But when the case finally reached general sessions court, Johnson's accuser failed to appear. So did the two women who had been with him. The judge was convinced that Johnson's wealth and his willingness to give up some of it to get out of trouble had had something to do with their absence, a conviction reinforced by a newspaper story that quoted the champion as having offered to bet a reporter a thousand dollars the case would never come to trial. The judge issued a bench warrant for Pinder and his female companions and jailed Johnson, who spent five hours locked up with a convicted burglar before the woman who managed the Little Savoy could get to court with five thousand dollars to bail him out.

Johnson moved on. Etta Duryea joined him for the *Follies of the Day* tour—weeklong engagements at Toronto, Montreal, Buffalo, and Detroit, where it took Gerard three days to find a hotel willing to accommodate the couple. While they were in Detroit, George Little told Johnson he'd found Belle Schreiber working at Madam Rowland's sporting house on Rush Street. The champion "came and got me out of there," Belle remembered. "I did not complain about my treatment there—it was just as good there as any other place I was at." But she allowed him to pay off the madam, rent a room for her in another hotel, and visit her there daily without Etta's knowledge. They were back on good terms.

That week would set the style for Johnson's travels for months to come. He and Etta registered on the road as husband and wife and spent each night together, but with help from Sig Hart, arrangements were made for other women to be available to the champion as well, registered at other hotels and rooming houses, and subject to visits by Johnson during daylight hours. Etta was to be kept in the dark. The other women were ordered to stay away from her.

It didn't always work. Johnson was supposed to get a week off at the end of his Detroit engagement, and hoped to go home for a rest before heading out again. But he found that Gerard, without consulting him, had "loaned" him to another producer for a grueling week of one-nighters in Michigan; worse, Gerard was to collect $2,500 for the extra week and pocket the difference between that sum and Johnson's normal fee of $1,300. The champion chose to go along, at least for the time being, but he thought it best to send both women away before he set forth; the logistics of arranging separate overnight quarters for each of them seven nights in a row was too much even for him. Both wanted to go to Chicago: Etta to his mother's to wait until she could rejoin him on the road, and Belle to find herself a rooming house and resume her profession until he sent for her again. Johnson took Etta to the station himself and asked Gerard to make sure Belle got on the same train without being seen. Gerard did his best, but once on board, Etta spotted Belle, the two women confronted each other, and there was a shouting match that could be heard all over the depot.

Johnson endured the week of Michigan tank towns without further incident, but when he reached the Star Theater in Milwaukee at the end of it, and was sure Gerard had been paid his $2,500, he cornered the impresario in the manager's office and threatened to kill him if he didn't hand over all but $250 of it. No one was going to exploit Jack Johnson if he could help it. Gerard, "seeing my life in danger," handed him the money, then filed suit for breach of contract.

Etta rejoined Johnson for two final weeks in Minneapolis and St. Paul. There was trouble there, too. On the last day of the engagement, the taxi in which he and she were riding to the railroad station broke down in front of a saloon. Word spread that the champion and a white woman were inside, and a crowd of what the *Police Gazette* called "deckhands, wharf wallopers, timber jacks, mill hogs and bar flies" swarmed out to surround the cab, jeering, cursing, threatening to lynch them both. A policeman had to escort them to the depot.

Ever since Johnson's return from Australia, white sportswriters like C. E. Van Loan had routinely scolded him for his behavior.

Johnson has become reckless and foolish. If he ever knew his place he has forgotten it. An ordinary day-laboring negro charged with some of the offenses he committed would have spent a long time in jail.

Every sporting man in the country hopes that Johnson's penchant for getting himself pinched will not interfere with the big fight. It took a long time to get a white man—the only white man who has a chance to beat the black champion—out of his comfortable retirement, and having got Jeff hooked in, it would be a shame if anything should happen to call the whole thing off indefinitely.

Please be good, Johnson!

After July Fourth you can go as far as you like—get 10 years if you like—but at the present time three or four months in the Bastille would be fatal.

Some black papers had now begun to censure him, too. In the Indianapolis *Freeman*, closely allied with Booker T. Washington, a columnist who called himself "Uncle Rad Kees" compared Johnson unfavorably to his most celebrated predecessor among Negro heavyweights and charged him with doing damage to the cause of black progress.

No one ever heard of Peter Jackson creating any unusual scenes in barrooms, cafes or on public highways, neither have I ever heard of or seen

At the time this photograph was made, in 1901, Jack Johnson was twenty-three years old, had been a professional boxer for six years, and already had his eye on an apparently unreachable prize—the heavyweight championship, which had always been reserved for whites. "I had demonstrated my strength, speed and skill," he
wrote, "but still faced many obstacles, the principal one of which was the customary prejudice because of my
race."

In 1901, Johnson and the veteran heavyweight Joe Choynski were locked up together in Galveston for twenty-three days (above) for taking part in an illegal prizefight—two days longer, Johnson remembered, than a prisoner who had killed his wife. Sheriff Henry Thomas (with moustache and pistol) let them out at night, and when the time came for their release (left) made sure a photographer was on hand to capture the moment.

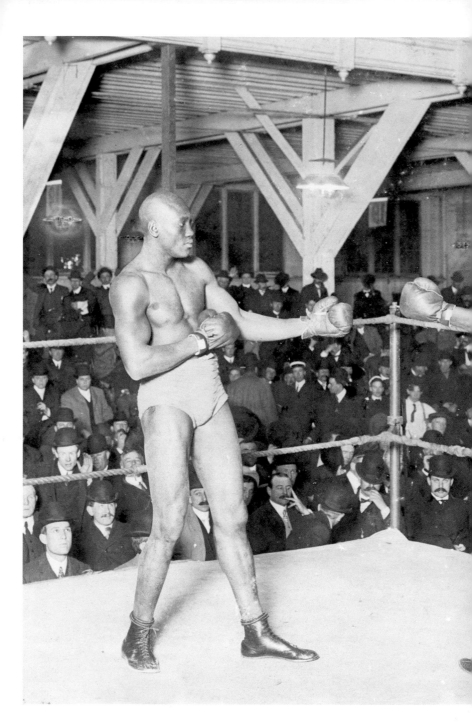

All his life, Johnson refused to conform to anyone else's expectations for him. In 1904, in defiance of local custom, he was living in a white neighborhood in Bakersfield, California, with Clara Kerr (above), a sporting woman from Philadelphia whom he introduced as "Mrs. Jack Johnson." He already held the "Colored Heavyweight Championship of the World" and had beaten Sam McVey (left) twice when they faced off in San Francisco's Mechanics Pavilion that same year. Johnson toyed with his hard-hitting but relatively unskilled challenger for nineteen rounds—enraging a good many of the derbied fans at ringside—before knocking him out in the twentieth.

Jack Johnson pursued heavyweight champion Tommy Burns for nearly two years. "I virtually had to mow my way to Burns," he remembered, following him from the United States to England to France and back again to England. The inset photograph was made in a Paris saloon in the spring of 1908; Johnson's late-night companions are Sam McVey and Hattie McClay, the new "Mrs. Jack Johnson." Johnson finally caught up with Burns at Rushcutter's Bay in Sydney, Australia, on the day after Christmas in 1908—and knocked the champion down within seconds of the opening bell (right). Fourteen rounds later (above), Burns was bruised and bloody and only moments away from losing his title to Jack Johnson. "[Burns] is the easiest fighter I ever met," Johnson said. "I could have put him away quicker, but I wanted to punish him. I had my revenge."

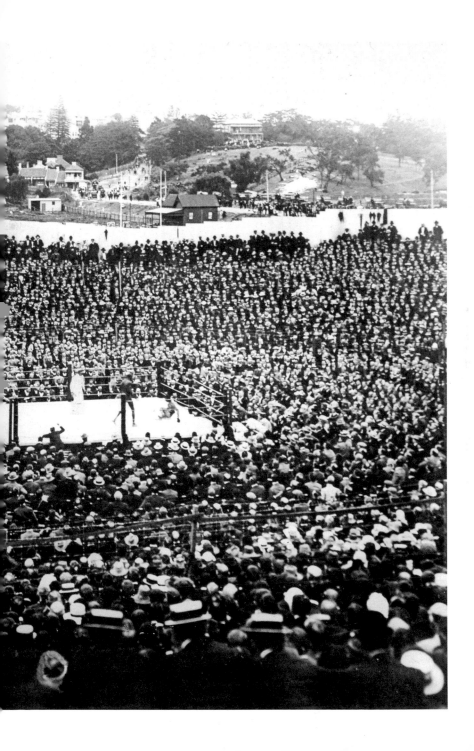

Jack Johnson, the new heavyweight champion of the world, arrives in Vancouver (top) with Hattie McClay, February 3, 1909. Reporters besieged him. When they heard him express admiration for Napoleon, whose climb to world fame from obscure beginnings he liked to compare to his own, a photographer asked Johnson and McClay to pose as Napoleon and Josephine. They happily complied.

Johnson struck this heroic attitude for a Chicago photographer not long after his return from Australia in 1909. The small boy may be his worshipful nephew, Gus Rhodes, who would grow up to become his confidant and traveling companion, sparring partner and eager publicist.

"I always take a chance on my pleasures," Jack Johnson once said. Speed and women topped his list. At the left, a Philadelphia policeman writes out a speeding ticket for the champion—one of scores issued to him over the years, sometimes because he was really going too fast, sometimes because white officers couldn't bear to see a black man behind the wheel of his own costly car. Next to him is his manager, George Little, the Chicago brothel-keeper who made it possible for him to meet Belle Schreiber (above), the prostitute who became the next "Mrs. Jack Johnson" and then his nemesis.

In October 1909, the sometimes frantic search for a "white hope," capable of winning back the heavyweight title for the white race, settled upon the middleweight champion, Stanley Ketchel, whom Johnson normally outweighed by more than twenty-five pounds. To make Ketchel seem a plausible challenger his handlers had him meet the press (left) wearing an oversized, padded coat and specially made boots. The fight itself ended predictably (above): Ketchel lay unconscious for several minutes. Among the anxious ringsiders, the lone black spectator (just above the referee's head) seems quietly pleased by the outcome.

Christmas 1909: Johnson embraces his mother, Tiny Johnson, and Hattie McClay in his South Side Chicago home. George Little is at the left; the children are the champion's niece and nephew, Ada and Gus Rhodes. This holiday idyll would end with the arrival of Etta Duryea (above). A sophisticated but troubled Long Island divorcée, she would be festooned with furs and jewelry by the champion; in this formal 1912 portrait, diamonds wink from nearly every finger.

Jack Johnson takes time out from training at the Seal Rock House in San Francisco in 1910. He had never seen his holding of the heavyweight title as "a racial triumph," he said, "but there were those who were to take this view . . . and almost immediately a great hue and cry went up because a colored man was holding the championship. The hunt for a white hope began, not only with great earnestness and intentness, but with ill-concealed bitterness. I regretted this phase of the hunt."

any one who ever knew of his being present during such a scene. Why was it not his luck to be the colored heavyweight champion? He was surely worthy. The world knows he was willing and anxious; and Corbett, Sullivan, Fitzsimmons, and all the other big attractions of that time knew Jackson was fully capable. But no. The fact of the matter . . . is that Mr. Peter Jackson was too much of a gentleman. He didn't believe in the underhand methods as adopted today, and the brazen, uncouth, notoriety attached thereto. . . .

Johnson has shown no particular liking for the colored race. . . . The cold hand of the law is reaching out for Mr. Johnson . . . and it looks to take the leading role in his future conduct. Why shouldn't it, when the lives, liberty and happiness of over nine million Negroes are being antagonized and jeopardized by his folly. If you don't believe it, holler "hurray for Jack Johnson" in the hearing of any group of white men, and see how much trouble you will have. . . .

That Jackson Johnson is a big, strong, burly, rough darkey, I'll admit, and being champion of the world he may feel that he has a perfect right to run over, beat up, ignore and otherwise make life miserable for others, but he should not forget that Samson ruled the world with all his strength, but his love for a woman got him killed.

Johnson would not be lectured by anyone, black or white. How and with whom he chose to live his life was his own business and no one else's. Back home in Chicago on March 31, he celebrated his thirty-second birthday with an all-day "barn dance" in the training quarters he'd built behind his mother's house. Taxis came and went, dropping off guests, and at some point that afternoon, he and Sig Hart were inspired to drive to Michigan Avenue and see how fast two of his racing cars could go. Johnson affixed a big hand-lettered sign to the hood of his, reading, PLEASE DON'T PINCH ME TODAY. I AM NOT SPEEDING. BELIEVE ME. It didn't work. A foot patrolman named Flynn arrested both drivers. Johnson protested that they had not been speeding; that Flynn had long been out to get him. He refused to allow the officer to get into his car for the ride to the police station. Flynn summoned a patrol wagon. A crowd gathered. "Stand back, Mr. White Officer," Johnson said, "and let the colored people have a look at me."

Automobiles had become part of his persona. Not only did he buy the latest, fastest models, but he made sure they were unmistakably his by having

them painted blue and cream or brilliant red. When in Chicago, he sometimes parked them on the sidewalk for added conspicuousness.*

He once told a traffic judge that his constant speeding was done simply
for "advertising" purposes. The court was not impressed on that occasion,
but a familiar tale told about him in black neighborhoods all over the country in those days suggests that his love of speed did help spread the word
about Jack Johnson. The story went that Johnson was roaring down the main
street of a little town in Georgia—or Virginia, or Texas, or anywhere below
the Mason-Dixon Line—when a redneck policeman pulled him over.

"What's the matter, officer," Johnson asked.

"Boy, you're going way too fast. I've got to fine you."

"How much?"

"Fifty dollars."

Johnson reached into his pocket, pulled out a roll of hundreds, and handed
one to the sheriff.

"What are you doing?" the lawman said. "I can't make change."

"Keep the change, officer. 'Cause I'm coming back just as fast as I went
through."†

In early April, Jim Jeffries began serious training at Rowardennan, California, deep in the Santa Cruz mountains. He was still short of breath, still had
a lot of weight to lose, and seemed even more unhappy with his admirers
than usual. "He growls and snarls and grumbles like an old grizzly when
strangers come around," one wrote. "He has a bear's aversion to being disturbed—particularly when he eats. He doesn't like to mingle much with the
other animals."

To keep his spirits up, Jeffries surrounded himself with familiar faces from

---

*Sugar Ray Robinson would make the same sort of symbol out of the pink Cadillac he drove around
Harlem in the 1950s. "When my car arrived it was not only exclusive, it was a symbol. When people
think they recognize a celebrity, they hesitate a moment. But when they saw me in that car, they didn't
have to hesitate. They knew. There was only one like it—Sugar Ray's pink Cadillac. Whenever my car
was parked in front of my café, the grownups liked to drop in for a drink or for some fried chicken.
They knew that if my car was out front, I was inside and they wanted to talk to me about the color
and, more than anything else, about how much it had cost. The kids stayed outside, staring at it and
reaching over to touch the pink fenders or the black leather seats. That car was the Hope Diamond of
Harlem. Everybody had to see it or touch it or both to make sure it was real. And to most of them it
literally was the *Hope* Diamond because if skinny little Walker Smith could come off the streets to own
a car like that, maybe they could, too." (Quoted in Nathan, "Sugar Ray Robinson.")

†This same story was later told about Satchel Paige and about Madame Zzaj, the comely, fast-moving
protagonist of Duke Ellington's *A Drum Is A Woman,* as well.

his glory days: Johnson's onetime mentor, Joe Choynski; former wrestling champion Martin "Farmer" Burns; and Bob Armstrong, a once-formidable black heavyweight who signed on to spar with Jeffries after he and Johnson quarreled over back wages he claimed the champion owed him. Two show business veterans were on hand, too: Walter Kelly, who played a drawling Virginia judge onstage, and Eddie Leonard, a longtime blackface minstrel. Their after-dinner performances, built around jokes about watermelon eating and chicken stealing, could be counted on to keep up the proper anti-Johnson atmosphere.

But the most prominent personality at Rowardennan besides Jeffries himself was Jim Corbett, hired to help Jeffries train, deal with the newspapermen he distrusted, and fuel the racial fires that Rickard and Gleason hoped would sell tickets. This last task came naturally to Corbett. "I dislike Johnson not so much because he is a negro," he told one reporter, "but simply because I think he is one of those fresh negroes that not alone thinks he is as good as a white man but is better."*

Sportswriters professed to be thrilled at the progress Jeffries was making. LOOKS AS FORMIDABLE AS IN CHAMPIONSHIP DAYS, said the Baltimore *American*. CALIFORNIAN GOES AT PUNCHING BAG WITH A VIM THAT THREATENED TO WRECK APPARATUS—ONLY A TRACE OF FAST FADING PAUNCH. Before long, the *Police Gazette* was reporting that "everyone" said Jeffries was now "in condition; that he is fast on his feet, that he still packs the punch, and that his eye is as good as it ever was."

Some boxing insiders were less sanguine: the former lightweight champion Jack McAuliffe worried aloud that Jeffries was not really being challenged by his veteran sparring partners, because he already knew every move

---

*No one seemed more eager to see Jack Johnson deposed than Jim Corbett. He had been retired for six years when Johnson won the title, but if Jeffries had proved unable to get himself in good enough shape to take Johnson on, he had said then, he felt it his duty to do so himself. "I am out to meet the negro purely and simply for the respect that I have for the white man," he told reporters. "Ever since Johnson squeezed the championship from 'Lemon Tommy' I have been preparing myself for a return to the ring should Jeff let the big black boy go around the country sticking out his chest."

On March 28, 1909, just a few days after Johnson's return to Chicago from Australia, Corbett and Harry Frazee had called at Toots Marshall's place with a proposition for Johnson. He and the champion would later differ over just what it had been. Corbett said he'd simply told Johnson he hoped he'd consider fighting him if Jeffries didn't. But years later, after Corbett accused him of facing only second-raters, Johnson shot back that during their visit Corbett and Frazee had offered him big money to carry the ex-champion for ten rounds. Whatever the truth about their conversation that day, there remained no love lost between Jack Johnson and the man who had been his boyhood hero. (Chicago *Tribune*, March 28 and April 4, 1909; Milwaukee *Free Press*, January 9, 1912.)

they made; if he didn't begin working out with younger men, he wouldn't be able to "regain his judgment of distance." Billy Delaney, Jeffries' former manager and longtime trainer, who had fallen out with the ex-champion when he failed to fight Bill Squires and was now eager to help Johnson defeat him, went further. Jeffries had no chance against the younger man, he said; besides, he was scared of Johnson and always had been: "The mention of Johnson's name sends cold shivers up and down Mr. Jeffries's spine. He never wanted any of Johnson's game. When I was with Jeffries merely mentioning the black man's name was like casting a pail of cold water in Jeffries's face." Some of Jeffries' followers saw such talk as something like treason to the race.

On Friday April 29, a promising young boxer named Tommy McCarthy died in San Francisco from injuries received in a fight with the British featherweight Owen Moran. The tragedy couldn't have come at a worse time for Tex Rickard. A nationwide campaign against the Johnson–Jeffries contest was already under way. Prizefighting continued to be a symbol of everything Progressive reformers deplored. It was brutal, they said, a vestige of primitive times. It was alien to small-town America; big-city immigrants dominated it, inside the ring and out. It encouraged gambling, flourished among those who frequented saloons and brothels and pool halls. And the fact that this fight would pit black against white only made matters worse. McCarthy's death now added to the furor. Bay Area ministers called for the fight to be stopped.

Johnson, Etta, and their party arrived in San Francisco the day after McCarthy's death and once again took over the Seal Rock House, where the champion had prepared for his bout with Stanley Ketchel. George Little and Lillian St. Clair had a room. So did Mr. and Mrs. Sig Hart; Johnson's sparring partners, Marty Cutler and the black journeyman George "Kid" Cotton; his trainer, Barney Furey; and his friend Frank Sutton, the Pittsburgh hotelier whom Johnson had asked to oversee the kitchens.

White reporters marveled at the luxury in which the black champion was living. JOHNSON QUARTERED LIKE A FUSSY KING, said the Milwaukee *Free Press* on June 6. John H. Washington, Jr., the nephew of Booker T. Washington, was taken aback, too. He was sent to see Johnson by his uncle's secretary, Emmett Jay Scott, who planned to come all the way from Tuskegee to attend the fight, provided Johnson would give him a free ticket. "When I sent my card up," the younger Washington reported to Scott, "his wife's maid returned and escorted me to his lovely appointed room." He shook hands with Etta, whom he called Johnson's white "two-thirds-of-a-better-half," and waited while the champion, seated in an oversized morris chair, was having his massage. "It was not long before he growled, 'Hurry up' and you should have seen his butler step." Johnson assured Washington that Scott would have a good seat for the fight if he came to California.

> With those words, the interview was closed and we three, with Mr. Little, who had just entered the room, left, Mr. Johnson and Mr. Little going in their "red devil" down the beach. I thought they meant to set this world on fire. He and his wife and their retinue of servants occupy all of that Seal Rock Hotel, and it is magnificent, too. I saw it all, from the pavilion, where he trains, the bar, even his small garage, to his suite. But, he ruined himself when he married in the other world.

Etta was not Johnson's problem at the moment. George Little was. In public, he and the champion still seemed close allies. They were both present for a publicity photograph at the Metropolitan Bank, where Tex Rickard posted thirty thousand dollars in two-dollar gold pieces. "Better take a good look at that gold," Johnson told Sam Berger, "for that's all you folks are going to see of it." And when the two camps couldn't seem to agree on a referee, it was Little who proposed that Tex Rickard do the job himself, even though he'd never so much as stepped inside a ring. Little reasoned that, like Hugh McIntosh before him, Rickard was likely to be evenhanded because he "couldn't afford to do anything wrong"; he had "an interest in the pictures, if he made a mistake the pictures wouldn't be worth a dime, but if he was on the level, they'd be worth half a million." Both sides agreed.

But behind the scenes, Johnson and Little were growing apart. Each would offer his own version of what happened between them at Seal Rock. Both cannot have been telling the truth.

Johnson's story was that Little's unreasonably suspicious nature had undermined their relationship. The trouble began, he said, in the private railroad car that carried his party west from Chicago. He and Little and Sig Hart had played poker for high stakes, he said, and when Little lost fifteen hundred dollars, he accused Hart of conspiring with Johnson to cheat him and promised to get even with them both. He then became deeply jealous of Hart, seething when Johnson took him and not Little for rides in his automobile, convinced that Hart was trying to displace him as Johnson's manager. When the two men collided at third base during a baseball game in camp, Johnson had to pull his manager off the smaller man. Little then insisted that Hart had to go. "I told Little that if anyone went, it would be he and not [Hart]," Johnson recalled. "This was like throwing kerosene on a blaze. Little became vicious."

Events growing out of an undisclosed injury to the champion further fueled Little's unease. Shortly after arriving in San Francisco, Johnson slipped and fell on the stone steps of the building in which Tex Rickard had his office, twisting his back so badly that he was unable to start serious training for two weeks—thereby offering more ammunition to those already convinced that he had no intention of making a serious fight against Jeffries.* Rickard came to call several times while Johnson was recovering, concerned about the rumors and wanting to do all he could to reassure the public that the fight was on the up-and-up. "These talks," according to Johnson, "into which Little was not invited, made him insanely jealous and he became more and more bitter. He pretended to believe that the talks between Rickard and myself concerned some crooked plan."

For his part, Little would later claim that Johnson had all along been conspiring with Rickard and others to have him throw the fight—and cut Little out of the profits. He had Johnson followed by "gumshoes," he said, fearing that he would lose the thousands of dollars he'd already bet on the champion. When Little finally asked his fighter point-blank if the fix was in, Johnson just smiled. Little took that as a signal to get some big money down on Jeffries.

Johnson never denied that pressure had been put on him to give up his crown, but he said it had come from Little himself; that his manager offered him ten thousand dollars to lie down in the eighth round. "Don't you see, Jack?" Little was supposed to have said. "The pictures will be worth $100,000 more if Jeffries wins—get wise." At first, Johnson said, he thought Little was "just feeling me out," but when he repeated the offer, the champion responded with anger. "See here, George, there isn't enough money in the world for me to throw this fight." He was sure he could beat Jeffries "on the best day he ever saw," had fought too long and too hard to give his title away. Besides, all his friends and family were betting on him. How could he let them down?

. . .

---

*According to Little, he had to spirit Johnson into Oakland after dark to keep the press from learning of his condition. There, he said, "a colored doctor" who could be trusted to keep his treatments quiet used two thirty-two-candlepower bulbs to rub mysterious oils into Johnson's torn muscles until he recovered. (George Little's "Confession.")

Despite all the distractions, by mid-May Johnson was training hard, and reporters were on hand every day in search of fresh stories.* Many were centered on the same weary stereotypes that had characterized coverage of Johnson since he first began to attract attention: his love of speed and fine clothes, his prodigious appetite and alleged fondness for chicken. And he was willing to play along if it sold tickets. "No stolen chicken ever passes the portals of my face," he said. "Chickens see the gleam in my eye and keep out of my way. Chicken and corn fritters are affinities. They are meant for each other and both are meant for me."

But occasionally newspaper readers got a glimpse of the complex, mercurial man behind the grin. One afternoon, a group of writers turned up at Seal Rock too late to see Johnson spar. "I can't box anymore today," he told them, "but if you will come upstairs I'll give you a little music, instead." The reporters trooped up the stairs after him. As a reporter for the Baltimore *American* wrote, they all expected to see something like a minstrel turn.

> [But] once in his private quarters the negro became a changed man. He ordered one of his assistants to load the phonograph, and for an hour the hotel was filled with the strains of operatic music, vocal selections rendered by Caruso, Sembrich, Nordics, Mary Garden and others. Not once did a "ragtime" piece appear, and a search of a pile of disks failed to find one in evidence. Johnson's music box is a most expensive affair and fills a corner of one of his suite of rooms. The pugilist champion tells with great pride how much it cost and can name offhand the price of any record, some of which, he explained, were worth as much as $10.
>
> In another corner there stood an immense bass viol. Somebody asked casually who played it, and Johnson said, "I do. Like to hear me?"

They said they would. He put a record on the turntable and played along, eyes closed, lost in the music.

When it was over, he took several of his visitors for a spin through Golden Gate Park in his latest automobile, a ninety-horsepower, six-cylinder machine that he said would go ninety miles an hour. Behind the wheel, the Baltimore

---

*They failed to get at least one good one. According to George Little, he and Johnson and Barney Furey were out doing roadwork one morning when "about two miles from the [hotel] we passed through a small town where colored people are not permitted to reside. There was a bunch of little girls standing at the roadside and as we trotted past they began to shout, 'Nigger, nigger, never die; black face and shiny eye.' " Johnson shouted at the children. All but one ran away. Furey rushed at her with a cane and struck her across the back. "Do you want to get us all lynched?" Little asked. Somehow they all made it back to Seal Rock without anyone else learning about the incident. (Chicago *American,* July 10, 1910.)

American man reported, "Johnson is entirely a different man, alert and almost savage."

> If there is an open stretch of road ahead of him he will cut loose at terrific speed and will not permit any car to pass him. Seated low down in the car with his powerful hands clinched on the steering wheel, he guides the machine without the slightest effort. . . .
>
> "You ain't afraid are you?" [he asked]. . . . He drove along the deserted boulevard at a speed which varied between 60 and 70 miles per hour, taking turns with a swoop that threatened to turn the car turtle any moment.
>
> All the time he was watching out of the corner of his eye the frightened passengers, who hung on like leeches, wishing that a motorcycle policeman would appear and save them from sudden death. Johnson just grinned and said, "We can't hit it up here; wait until we reach a level stretch up ahead, and then I'll show you what this car can do."

As he drove, Johnson spotted a pair of lovers strolling along the edge of the road, their arms around each other. "Oh look there," Johnson said. "Just watch me." He slid the car up behind them, then blew his horn and cut out the muffler. The terrified young lovers fled into the shrubbery "like frightened partridges." Laughing, Johnson roared back toward Seal Rock as the sun went down.

A reporter for the British magazine *Boxing* captured San Francisco's mood in late May.

> The clergy are preaching THE FIGHT, the whole fight, and nothing but the fight—and cannot stop it. The stores have statuettes of the fighters. Photos of the fighters as they were yesterday, as they are today, and as they will be tomorrow—perhaps—are in every window. Scraps of conversation in the street reach you like this: "Boxed nine rounds yesterday" — "Faster than ever" — "Can't get the Black to work hard enough" — "Had his auto out" — "Not training" — "Corbett'll do it for him" — "Too old" — "Good as ever" — "Bet you."

There continued to be plenty of talk of a rigged outcome. "You heard nothing but fake, fix, and double cross," Tad Dorgan remembered. John L. Sullivan himself told the New York *Times* the bout was likely a "frame-up," and California's governor, J. N. Gillette, agreed. "This Jeffries-Johnson fight is simply a scheme to make a lot of money out of the credulity of the public," he told a reporter.

Anybody with the least sense knows the whites of this country won't allow Johnson or any other negro to win the world's championship from Jeffries. . . . Johnson knows that. He's no fool. He knows that to win that fight he would have to whip every white man at the ringside. So he has agreed to lay down for the money.

Rickard got the governor to claim he'd been misquoted. But the whispers continued, and the national campaign against the contest intensified. A Cincinnati reformer printed up a million postcards reading "Stop the Fight. This is the Twentieth Century," meant to be signed and mailed to Gillette. The Methodist Preachers' Association of Philadelphia declared that "this fight can be regarded as nothing less than a national disgrace and a calamity to the moral life of our people" and appealed to President Taft to intervene.* Fifty preachers knelt and prayed on the capitol steps in Sacramento. Gillette stood firm: he didn't approve of boxing, he said, but California law permitted boxing "exhibitions," and no one had told him the Johnson-Jeffries fight would be anything else. He claimed to be powerless to stop the fight.

Meanwhile, to demonstrate that he was in good shape and taking the coming fight seriously, Johnson put on a three-round exhibition with Kid Cotton at the Dreamland Rink on June 3. Afterward, he addressed the crowd. "Though he was frequently interrupted by cat-calls from the gallery," a reporter noted, "the majority of fans demanded fair treatment and the negro's talk was liberally applauded."

"For the benefit of the gentlemen present," he began, "I will indulge in a few remarks regarding the heavyweight battle which will take place in San Francisco on the Fourth of July." Here, he paused for hooting in the gallery to subside. "And," he resumed, "for the benefit of the well educated gentlemen in the gallery I do hope that when the people from all parts of the world come here that they will see . . ."

---

*The Rev. Reverdy Ransom, an activist A.M.E. pastor from New York, took out after white clergymen for railing against the title fight but remaining silent about crimes against blacks: "Is a prize fight more revolting and atrocious than those lynchings and burnings which are of much too frequent occurrence?"

A. G. F. Sims, writing in the Chicago *Defender*, argued that race, not morality, was the real reason the Philadelphia clergymen were so vehement in denouncing the fight. "Just because the Negro has an equal chance, that in itself, in their opinion, is enough to constitute a national disgrace." Since that was so, he added, he hoped that when the time came, Johnson would demolish Jeffries in the ring "just to make it a good national disgrace." (Gilmore, *Bad Nigger!*, pp. 34–35.)

"A funeral," floated down a voice from upstairs.

". . . will see two men well trained," continued Johnson apparently unruffled, "both in the best condition and a fight in which the best man will win."

The close of the speech brought cheers from parts of the house.

Three days later, Johnson fired George Little. Things between them had gone from bad to worse. Someone had slipped Frank Sutton a Mickey Finn; Johnson suspected that Little had been behind it—and that it had been meant for him. Then, according to Johnson, after Little and Lillian St. Clair had an ugly public brawl during which Little broke a mandolin over his companion's head, the champion asked the manager of the hotel to throw him out. When Little refused to leave, the police were called.

Little stormed out, breathing defiance. "I am no Sam Fitzpatrick," he told the press. "He can't do this to me. I will manage Johnson, or there will be no fight." He had a contract entitling him to a quarter of the champion's earnings and demanded that he be paid back the ten thousand dollars he said he had put up as forfeit. He was also spotted stalking up and down Market Street, Johnson recalled, "showing his pistol to everybody and shouting that I'd robbed him. When I learned of this I got my car and drove there, intending to punch him in the nose." The police kept them apart.

Johnson hired the onetime Cincinnati Reds pitcher-manager Cal McVey as an armed guard to keep Little away from him and to patrol Seal Rock House at night.

Little attached Johnson's Chicago house and both his cars to keep him from disposing of his property and then pleading bankruptcy.

Johnson countered by obtaining a warrant for Little's arrest for issuing him a phony check.

Each man hired an attorney. Then, on June 22, the two announced a reconciliation. Johnson promised to pay Little $16,500 in exchange for a release from all further claims against him; for his part, Little promised to pay Johnson back $10,000 as soon as Johnson turned over to him a diamond brooch he said was worth $2,000. "I have wagered large amounts on Johnson," Little said. "I still believe he will win."

Two days later, Johnson fired Little again. The veteran trainer Tom Flanagan would see to any business matters the champion couldn't handle on his own.* He had always been his own manager, the champion explained. "You must have talent and ability to get through to the top in fighting. That's all there is to it. . . . If you keep your eyes open you . . . don't need to split up your earnings with a boss."†

By then, the fight itself seemed to be in jeopardy. On June 15, Governor Gillette reversed himself and barred the fight from his state. Money, not morality or the likelihood of a fix, had made him change his mind. A few days earlier, the president of the San Francisco Board of Trade, William R. Wheeler, received a telegram from New York Republican congressman William S. Bennett. The congressman was a delegate to the Presbyterian General Assembly and opposed to prizefighting on principle, but more important, he was an influential member of the House Foreign Affairs Committee. In the next few days, that body was to recommend either San Francisco or New Orleans as the site of the 1915 Panama Exposition, which seemed sure to bring in millions for the winning town. Bennett was quite sure, he told Wheeler, that "the moral sentiment of the House" would go against awarding the exposition to what he called "a prize-fighting city." Translation: if San Francisco gave up the fight, it stood an equal chance of being given the exposition; if it did not, the prize was sure to go to New Orleans. Wheeler went to see the governor. Millions were at stake. "Go to San Francisco," Gillette told his attorney general, "and tell Rickard to get out of my state. Tell him to take Johnson and Jeffries with him. What he is planning is a prize fight and against the law."

Rickard had less than three weeks to find a new town willing to host the fight, disassemble his brand-new stadium, ship it to the new site, and put it all together again by July Fourth. Nevada was his best hope. It prided itself on being more open-minded than its neighboring states: it encouraged gambling, made divorce so easy that unhappily married well-to-do women from

---

*According to John Lardner, Flanagan was not Johnson's first choice to take over from Little. He had first asked the boxing veteran Billy McCarney. Half an hour after McCarney said he would, Johnson telephoned him and asked for a loan of one hundred dollars. McCarney said he never advanced money to fighters. "Then I have to tell you, Mr. McCarney, that you're discharged." (Lardner, *White Hopes*, p. 36.)

†The Milwaukee *Free Press* (February 13, 1910) had already commented on the startling number of managers Johnson had discarded over the years: "There should be enough of them to give an annual parade which would take four hours to pass a given point." To find suitable seconds for the Jeffries fight, it continued, "Johnson will have to write Booker T. Washington and King Menelik [the ruler of Ethiopia]."

all over the country had begun to congregate there, and permitted anyone willing to pay a thousand-dollar license fee to put on "glove contests, or exhibitions between man and man." Best of all, its governor, Denver S. Dickerson, was said to be "prayerproof." He had only one question for Rickard. "Just tell me, man to man, it's on the level, Tex."

"It will be the squarest fight ever pulled off," Rickard promised. The contest was back on.

Two towns competed for the honor of hosting it, Goldfield and Reno. Since Rickard's gaudy career as a boxing promoter had begun in Goldfield, the city fathers believed their town the sentimental favorite. But Tex Rickard was not a sentimental man: Reno, the divorce capital of the country and the site of the Hart–Root elimination contest five years earlier, had better railroad connections than Goldfield: the Southern Pacific, capable of hauling in thousands of ticket buyers from both coasts, funneled right through the center of town.

Reno was fine with Johnson. He was sure he'd win wherever he and Jeffries fought. "I want to advise every one of you to bet on me," he told the five hundred Negroes who came to the Oakland depot to see him off for Nevada. "Just get your money down . . . and then sit back and wait until the time comes to cash in."

But Jeffries was so rattled by the change of venue that he nearly pulled out. He had signed to fight in California and nowhere else, he said; he hated to leave the congenial isolated world of Rowardennan; and he feared that all the hard training he had done would be undercut by Reno's greater heat and higher altitude. It was only his "good nature," he said, his concern that his friend Tex Rickard not be ruined, that made him agree to the move. One rumor had it that the real reason Jeffries was so upset was that the move to Nevada somehow meant Johnson was no longer willing to lie down, that he would have to face a fully engaged champion for his title. But if there had been such a deal, it is hard to see how crossing the California line would have affected it. Another tale had it that Jeffries feared the shift to Nevada because, while attending the Nelson–Gans contest in 1906, he'd lost twenty-five thousand dollars at the gambling tables and then run out on his IOUs. Rickard was said to have talked Jeffries' debtors into accepting a settlement of fifty cents on the dollar.

Until it was given its name in 1868, Reno was known as End of the Line, an obscure rail junction on the Truckee River to which the little Virginia and

Truckee line brought carloads of silver ore from Virginia City and the Comstock Lode for transfer to the transcontinental railroad. In June of 1910, it was still a small settlement surrounded by sagebrush, home to just eleven thousand people. Tex Rickard's skill at ballyhoo would soon turn it into what the novelist Rex Beach, writing for the Atlanta *Constitution,* called "the precise magnetic center of the civilized world."

More than three hundred reporters descended on the little town in the week before the fight; nearly every major American daily sent its own reporters. So did papers in Britain, Australia, and France. *Variety* sent Al Jolson. Telegraphers arrived with a boxcar full of equipment.

Rex Beach was not the only prominent literary figure to find himself in Reno. The muckraking journalist Alfred Henry Lewis was there, too, working for the San Francisco *Examiner.* So was Jack London, whose melodramatic coverage of the Johnson–Burns contest for the New York *Herald* had had so much to do with drumming up enthusiasm for this one. "I am glad I'm here," he wrote.

> No man who loves the fighting game, has the price and is within striking distance of Reno should miss the fight. . . . There has never been anything like it in the history of the ring. . . . Even if no more stringent legislation is passed against the game, even if every state threw itself wide open to prize-fighting, still there can be nothing like this fight for a generation to come.

"In a single day," Rex Beach wrote from Reno, "one hundred and fifty thousand words went out from here over the wires. The fall of Port Arthur [China, during the Russo-Japanese War] did not take one quarter that number of words to tell and every day it is the same. In other words, two novels are written every twenty-four hours, dealing entirely with the question of individual superiority."

The two individuals who would settle that question were the focus of everyone's attention from the moment they stepped down from the train at the little brick depot in the middle of town.

Jeffries turned up first. His progress from Rowardennan to Reno, Jim Corbett remembered, "was more or less of an ovation. He was cheered all the way out of his own state and far into the night we were awakened by the familiar, 'Three cheers for Jeffries,' and 'O, Jeff, come out and show yourself.' " Jeffries and Corbett had fought a series of exhibitions at Carson City in 1897, and as they ate breakfast in the dining car the following morning Jeffries was almost animated as he reminisced about Nevada's sparkling trout steams. But when the train began to slow for Reno and he saw the big crowd waiting by the tracks to greet him, he scowled. "Go on and get off first," he told the rest of his party. "All you people get off first." As Corbett remembered:

> For a few seconds, I had an idea that Jim was going to do the matinee idol thing. I thought that he was going to wait until all the other celebrities had made their bow. . . . So we all got off the train ahead of him. The members who were recognized were cheered to the echo and then there came a long wait. Men and women were fighting their way into the jam. . . . I began to think something must have happened to him, when all at once a yell from the newspaper photographer informed me what had happened. Jeffries jumped off on the other side of the train, walked around the rear car, and quietly started for the hotel.

When Jack Johnson pulled in the following day, he plunged right into the crowd, shaking hands and joking with everyone as he made his way with Etta to a waiting car. He climbed in, doffed his white hat, and bowed. "One glance at Jack's beaming face was sufficient to show that he was intensely pleased with the reception accorded him," one paper reported.

> Someone called for a speech but Jack shook his head. He compromised by removing his Panama and posing for a battery of cameras. . . . The snapshot men would have held him there till sun-down, but finally Jack became impatient. He jammed his hat over his ears, dropped into a seat, and the chauffeur, with horns tooting, made his way through a blockade of wagons, which were in turn rendered unwieldy by the jam of humanity which filled the street from curb to curb.

The fighters' camps, too, highlighted the contrast between them. Jeffries took up residence at a secluded, deeply shaded resort on the Truckee called Moana Springs. "At Jeffries' quarters you behold a vine-embowered cottage," Rex Beach wrote, "surrounded by a fence with a large readable sign 'Private, Keep Out,' and inside the cottage there is silence, peace. He has the white man's sense of privacy."

Certainly, Jeffries' own personal sense of privacy was highly developed. He may have been a "stubborn, rushing master" in the ring, Beach continued, but outside it he still had "the disposition of a tarantula," mysteriously able to detect the approach of strangers and scuttle out of reach. "There was nothing winsome about Jeffries," Arthur Ruhl wrote in *Collier's*:

he was as surly and ugly as a caged bear. He would ride past you on a country road, returning alone from a fishing trip crouched in the rear seat of his automobile, swarthy, glowering, chewing gum, and never so much as notice your greeting by the flicker of an eyelid. After the machine had stopped at the gate of his training quarters and a crowd of harmlessly demented admirers had gathered about it, he would sometimes sit there without moving for five and ten minutes, still glowering straight ahead, chewing gum and seeing only, as it seemed, the vision of his black rival coming to meet him across the ring. There was something peculiarly sinister in this static ferocity and he did not lessen the impression when he climbed down at last and walked slowly away, seeing no one, with his huge right arm partly contracted and slowly sawing the air as if aimed for a blow.

Even celebrities were discouraged from trying to see him. When Governor Dickerson arrived unannounced, Jeffries reluctantly took his hand, but then turned his back without another word to play with a terrier puppy. John L. Sullivan himself was refused entry for having earlier suggested that the fight was fixed. "I'll turn the fire hose on him," Jeffries said when he heard Sullivan had come to call. "I always hated a knocker."* And when Stanley Ketchel came to call after visiting Johnson, Jeffries ordered him out, shouting, "I don't want you here. You've been fooling around with that nigger." Ketchel was slow to leave, so Jeffries had Farmer Burns pick him up and throw him into the dusty street.

Jeffries seemed almost allergic to the hundreds of people who stood for hours outside the picket fence hoping for just a glimpse of him. By contrast, Johnson and his boisterous entourage took over a resort three miles from town called Rick's Roadhouse, where everyone seemed welcome. There, Rex Beach reported,

> You find yourself in a honky-tonk. A pair of muscular pianists and a fiddler poison the air with ragtime. There are two roulette tables going constantly, drunken men abound. The rooms, the porches, the yards, are packed with all classes and conditions of people. They elbow their way

---

*Jim Corbett, whom Sullivan had always loathed, was instructed to guard the gate against him. "What the hell do you want?" Corbett asked when Sullivan appeared. The two glared at each other. "If you're running the camp," Sullivan said, "I don't want to see him." He stalked off. Tempers cooled. Sullivan was invited back. Jeffries asked the old warrior for his advice about how best to beat Johnson. He was worried, he confessed. "I don't see why I have to be the favorite." "Jim," said Sullivan, "all I know is God Almighty hates a quitter." (Farr, *Black Champion*, p. 105.)

upstairs to the quarters of "L'il Artha." They pinch his muscles and prod him in the ribs to discover his condition. I have a mental photograph of the distorted remains of the stranger who would presume to thrust a curious finger into Jeffries' ribs.

An armed guard patrolled the grounds at night—Johnson continued to get death threats in the mail—but otherwise his doors were open to anyone.

Beneath the big trees at Moana Springs, Jeffries' afternoon workouts drew big crowds, and he dutifully went through his paces in front of them— skipping rope, grappling with Farmer Burns, going through the motions with Joe Choynski, chewing gum all the while. Reporters marveled at how the former champion had transformed his physique over the sixteen months since he'd begun to train. Rex Beach wrote:

> I saw that which I never expected to see, a man who has come back. Jeffries has renewed youth. [Ponce de León] should have gone west in his search for that fabled fountain, the waters of which he believed could roll back the years from human shoulders. . . . I believe Jeffries to be the most dangerous and most rugged fighter the world has ever seen.

The former champion's demeanor—taciturn, introspective, unsmiling—only added to that impression.

Johnson, on the other hand, constantly displayed what Beach called "the soul of a joy-rider." He loved the crowds his presence invariably drew and, as Robert Edgren reported in the New York *World,* did his best to turn even the most routine sparring session with his onetime opponent Al Kaufmann into an entertaining show.

> He has an eye for what goes on outside the ring. He kids along with the spectators and his handlers. While he was fighting with Kaufmann he managed to work around to the side of the ring where I was standing, camera in hand, and said: "Get a good one now. I'm going to punch him on the nose."
>
> Later, he began kidding Al by pretending to dictate a round by round account of the fight. "They are fighting fast," said Jack, blocking Kaufmann's left hook and slapping him on the chin with his right. "Johnson lands a right. Kaufmann staggers around the ring." Here there was some fast fighting, for Kaufmann objected to the account of the battle. He slugged as hard as he could, rushing Johnson up against the ropes, and the black champion postponed his dictation. But a moment later he was at it again.

"Johnson is beginning to feel tired," he said, and then threw his head back and chuckled, apparently paying no attention at all to the flailing blows that whizzed about his ears.

After Kaufmann came one [Walter] Monahan, an ex-amateur heavy-weight Coast champion. Monahan meant well. He rushed and jabbed, and Johnson, watching him with a wide grin, timed his jabs and beat him to it. In a moment, Monahan was bleeding freely. For all that he kept on fighting as hard as he could. He reached Johnson now and then, and Jack rushed him to the ropes and nearly knocked him out.

"Johnson wins in a walk," said Jack, beginning the dictation again, and turning to grin at me, "he let Monahan recover."

When Tex Rickard arrived at Rick's Roadhouse with Governor Dickerson in tow, the champion was effusive. Dickerson was the greatest governor in the country, Johnson said, and if he lived in Nevada he'd vote for him as often as they'd let him. Dickerson assured the champion that if he proved good enough to beat Jeffries, no race prejudice would be allowed to keep him from getting the decision he deserved. Johnson thanked the governor and put on an especially impressive display for him, urging his sparring partners to come straight at him and pull no punches. When Kid Cotton did just that, and managed to land a left hand that cut the champion's mouth, Johnson rushed him and left him dazed and helpless on the ropes. Dickerson was impressed. "I have never seen a man who can whip Jack Johnson as he stands today," he said, "and I am forced to bet on him."

When John L. Sullivan asked the champion what kind of shape he was in, Johnson answered, "Cap'n John, if I felt any better, I would be afraid of myself."

Jeffries was favored 2 to 1 a week before the fight—and since most writers believed Johnson doomed, they found his resolute cheerfulness baffling. "To all appearances," said the Baltimore *American*, "the black man is as happy and carefree as a plantation darky in Watermelon time." "The man is a puzzle," said the Chicago *Tribune*.

Physically, the greatest athlete the colored race has produced and mentally as keen as a razor in a sort of undeveloped way, he fiddles away on his bull fiddle, swaps jokes with ready wit, shoots craps, plays baseball, listens dreamily to classical love songs on the phonograph and is going to fight Jim Jeffries for the world's championship one week from tomorrow.

What on earth was wrong with him? Alfred Henry Lewis thought he knew. Johnson was "essentially African," Lewis wrote, and therefore

> feels no deeper than the moment, sees no farther than his nose [and is] incapable of anticipation. . . . The same cheerful indifference to coming events [has] marked others of the race even while standing in the very shadow of the gallows. Their stolid unconcern baffled all who beheld it. They were to be hanged; they knew it. But having no fancy, no imagination—they could not anticipate.

Arthur Ruhl of *Collier's* had another theory about the fight's inevitable outcome; while Johnson was undeniably fast and clever, he wrote, he lacked the all-important "dogged courage and intellectual initiative which is the white man's inheritance," while Jeffries, for his part, would be able to call upon "thirty centuries of traditions . . . , all the supreme efforts, the inventions and the conquests . . . Bunker Hill and Thermopylae and Hastings and Agincourt." Johnson loved to read about himself in as many newspapers as he could get his hands on, but, sadly, his opinion of this kind of solemn nonsense was never recorded.*

Reno's dusty downtown was now packed with strangers. "An army of unknowns is rapidly gathering," Rex Beach reported.

> They come tripping forth from Pullmans, day coaches and smokers; they come tumbling down from flat-topped box cars or creeping forth from between the trucks, their faces black with dust, their bodies scarred by the print of brake beams.
>
> They are coming from England and Hawaii, from Australia and Alaska, in special trains and side-door sleepers. But whether they be globe-trotters or grangers, homebodies, hobos, gentlemen or grafters, they are all red-blooded, full-fashioned men, with the age-old primitive love of fighting in their veins. There are no mollycoddles in Reno.

Reno did its best to accommodate them. "People eat at ragtime," wrote Harris Merton Lyon in *Hampton's Magazine.* "One restaurant with a seating

---

*A local judge, Lee J. Davis, offered still another race-based notion. Because of Nevada's fierce sun, he said, Johnson's color might actually give him an *advantage* over Jeffries. Davis had been to Alaska, he said, and noticed that miners who wanted to avoid snow blindness smeared lampblack beneath their eyes. Johnson's dark skin might have the same effect. The newspaper that reported Davis' theory (Chicago *Tribune,* June 29, 1910) went on to remind its readers that Johnson's possible advantage would likely be minimized by the fact that Jeffries was himself browned by the sun.

capacity of 40 served 3,600 suppers. . . . For sleeping you take anything you can get: sometimes a seven-dollar room, sometimes a private car, . . . a cot, a billiard table, a hammock or a park bench." Hundreds of Reno residents—including the mayor—offered rooms for rent. The lobbies of the better hotels were lined with cots; so were their flat graveled roofs. A fleabag called the Stick Awhile raised its overnight fee from fifteen cents to a quarter.

Black fight fans faced problems of their own. "There are few negro families in Reno," the Chicago *Tribune* explained, "and in matters of dispensing hospitality to the colored brother old mining camp ethics prevail." An enterprising real estate man rented three empty storefronts and ordered three hundred cots for black spectators who couldn't expect to find a bed anywhere else. A saloon was renamed the Johnson Club, and in the evenings Johnson's two most important black detractors, Bob Armstrong and Sam Langford, could be found there with their backs to the bar, explaining to angry Negro customers why they were sure Johnson didn't stand a chance against Jim Jeffries. "I told Johnson in Chicago I'd be at ringside when they were carrying him out," Langford said. "He ain't got no right in the ring with this man Jeffries at all."*

Pickpockets worked the crowds, lifting wallets and watches from unsuspecting fight fans—so many, one reporter noted, that "if a hand was not dipped into your pocket sooner or later it was almost a sign of disrespect." One especially skilled thief, the reporter continued, plucked the silver badge from the vest of a local policeman, then hired a boy to return it to its owner at police headquarters just "to show he was a good fellow and enjoyed a good joke." Sports thought it wise to slough off their jewelry, according to Rex Beach: "No longer does one see diamond scarf pins or jeweled watch fobs in public; neck-ties are worn with a hole in them; watches are piled in safes."

A couple of days before the fight, two movie cameramen visited both camps, collecting human-interest footage to supplement straightforward coverage of coming events in the ring. Most of the sequences featuring Jeffries were suitably serene: he punched a bag and skipped rope, played hearts on the dappled lawn while Mrs. Jeffries and four other women in vast hats looked on, and clasped the hands of well-wishers—including Sam Langford and

---

*Langford was in town because a San Francisco promoter named Sid Hester was hoping to stage a fight between him and Stanley Ketchel in Rickard's stadium on the morning of the Fourth. When Rickard refused to allow it, Hester pledged to build an arena of his own but failed to make good on his promise.

John L. Sullivan, who had by then restored himself to Jeffries' good graces. Only one scene suggested something of the bout's racial undertow: an exercise sequence ended with the ex-champion bouncing a medicine ball off the head of his black sparring partner Bob Armstrong, who was instructed to pretend to be knocked out.

At Rick's Roadhouse, the filmmakers found things much livelier. Johnson shot craps for the camera, fed chickens, and drove a sulky down a dusty road. Surrounded by a laughing, mostly white crowd of hangers-on, he also pretended to drink from a bottle belonging to a blond infant until Sig Hart snatched it from him; then Johnson shaded the baby from the sun with his big Stetson. He also staged an extraordinary tableau of his own devising, a mock trial over which he presides from a chair set up on the porch. His seconds drag a struggling white member of his entourage before him. The stern-looking champion, his arms folded across his chest, finds the man "guilty" of coming back to camp drunk after a lively night in Reno, orders him tied to a chair, and then whacks him on the backside several times with a plank. When the man has been punished, he treats another one the same way.* It was all in good humor, but the subtext seems unmistakable: Jack Johnson wanted the moviegoing public to understand who was in charge in his camp, as well as in the ring.

Newspaper editors outdid one another in talking up the fight's momentous importance. The question to be settled, said the Omaha *Daily News,* was nothing less than whether Jim Jeffries could "beat down the wonderful black and restore to the Caucasians the crown of elemental greatness as measured by strength of brow, power of heart and lung, and withal, that cunning and keenness that denotes mental as well as physical superiority." The *Afro-American Ledger* had a special message for Johnson: "Thousands of negroes have nailed your name to their masthead. Nobody has so much to win or lose as you represent."

No newspaper, black or white, seemed to have more of a stake in Jack Johnson's success than the five-year-old Chicago *Defender.* "The World's Greatest Weekly" was sensational, militant, and dedicated to the progress of

---

*"The big fellow did not know how much he hurt them," wrote a reporter for the San Francisco *Chronicle.* "The victims are now taking their meals from the nearest to a mantelpiece they can find in Reno." (Quoted in Bob Lucas, *Black Gladiator,* page 102.)

what its founder, Robert S. Abbott, insisted on calling "the Race." Some black papers did their best to play down the racial element at Reno, hoping trouble could be forestalled if people saw it simply as a contest between two heavyweight boxers who happened to be black and white. Not the *Defender*. After Johnson and Jeffries signed their contracts it had run a cartoon showing the champion surrounded by white enemies labeled "Negro Persecution," "Prejudice," and "Race Hatred," with the caption HE WILL HAVE TO BEAT THEM ALL. THE FUTURE WELFARE OF HIS PEOPLE FORMS A PART OF THE STAKES. Now, as the contest drew near, the *Defender* remained steadfast:

> On the arid plains of the Sage Brush State the white man and the negro will settle the mooted question of supremacy. . . . When the smoke of the battle clears away, and when the din of mingled cheers and groans have died away . . . , there will be deep mourning throughout the domains of Uncle Sam over Jeffries's inability to return the pugilistic scepter to the Caucasian race.

Boxers and boxing insiders were canvassed for their predictions. "If Jeff is only half as good as he used to be he will win," said Tommy Burns. "Johnson is game only against little fellows like Ketchel and myself. If Jeff ever wallops him, he'll cave in all his ribs." Johnson "doesn't have a look-in," said Bat Masterson, the gambler and onetime western lawman who now wrote a sporting column for the New York *Morning Telegraph*. Bob Fitzsimmons and Tom Sharkey and Battling Nelson all agreed. William Muldoon, the former wrestler and champion of physical culture who had once trained John L. Sullivan, concurred. "The negro won't fight," he said. "I pick Jeffries."

On July 3, the eve of the fight, Jeffries issued his own forecast: "I realize full well what depends on me. . . . That portion of the white race that has been looking to me to defend its athletic superiority may feel assured that I am fit to do my very best. . . . I will win as quickly as I can."

But privately, he did not seem convinced that he would win at all. He had been deeply wounded the day before when he learned that Billy Delaney, his longtime manager and trainer, had turned up in town, announced to the press that "Johnson will win. There can be no doubt about this point," then hurried to Rick's Roadhouse to offer the champion advice on how to beat his old friend. "To think of Delaney being with the nigger instead of me," Jeffries said.

After that, Jim Corbett recalled, the former champion seemed almost in a daze, unable or unwilling to speak with anyone. "For God's sake, Jim," Cor-

bett finally said to him that evening. "Open up and tell us what you are thinking about and what is the matter with you."

"I'll be all right once I get started" is all Jeffries would say. He went to bed
early, but his wife heard him opening and closing his window all night. He
couldn't seem to sleep.

That same evening, Johnson said he wanted to have a look at the crowds.
Some twenty thousand people were said to have come to town. He telephoned for an automobile and had himself driven to press headquarters on
Center Street, where he joked with newspapermen, bowed to the throng that
quickly gathered—then bet on himself twenty thousand dollars that had been
wired to him by Barron Wilkins. Then, he returned to camp and presided
over what one newspaperman called "a general jollification" until well past
midnight.

Before he finally went to bed, Johnson sent two wires to his family in
Chicago. The first was meant to reassure his anxious mother.

DON'T WORRY ABOUT ME. I FEEL GREAT. MY CONDITION IS FINE AND
I AM IN GOOD SPIRITS. WILL WIN SURE. RODE DOWN TOWN AND A GOT
A FINE RECEPTION FROM THE PEOPLE. I FEEL PERFECTLY AT HOME
BECAUSE I KNOW I WILL GET A SQUARE DEAL. LOVE TO ALL FROM ETTA
AND I AND REGARDS FROM ALL IN CAMP.

The other telegram was to his brother, Charles:

BET YOUR LAST COPPER ON ME.

Blue smoke hung over the Reno rail yards on the morning of July 4, 1910. It
rose from the dining cars of scores of special trains parked along a siding
three miles south of town. Twelve had pulled in since eight o'clock the night
before; seven more were due in by noon. Inside, uniformed Negro waiters
served eggs, bacon, and coffee to hundreds of boxing fans who had arrived
there from both coasts. Hundreds more had rattled their way over the Sierras in automobiles hung with signs that read RENO OR BUST!

Meanwhile, thousands of hungry men wandered the downtown streets in
search of breakfast. Reno was running out of everything. Those lucky enough
to get inside a restaurant had to settle for whatever was left in the kitchen.
When Thomas's Restaurant had no more clean cups, it served coffee in bowls;
the proprietor's wife just dropped money into a box after the cash register
overflowed. Hundreds never got fed at all.

At midmorning, Rex Beach watched the crowd begin moving toward the arena, where the fight was scheduled to start at one-thirty.*

Everything that had wheels and could be propelled or pulled was loaded to capacity. The trolley cars. . . . had people sitting on the roof every trip. The chauffeurs, who have been making tentative holdups of passengers the past week, and grew bolder every day as the traffic on their machines increased, put all pretense of decency aside this morning and refused to consider anything less than $3 per single passenger for the one and one half miles from the town's center out to the arena. At noon, they raised the ante to $5, and before one o'clock more than one $10 gold piece had been turned over for the privilege of riding on one or more flat tires from the Golden Hotel to the arena entrance.

The majority of the throng footed it. A black streak of humanity stretched from the center of the town out over the single broad road that passes the arena. It was a stream constantly augmented from side streets, pulsing, shifting with cross currents, wavering in the channel. Every manner of man under the sun was in it. Here a miner from Rhyolite with trousers tucked rakishly inside the tops of his half boots; there a Chinaman padding the dust with his felt shoes, and a clubman from Frisco with a jeweled Shriner pin in the lapel of his coat walked by the side of a flashy race-track tout from New Orleans. There were overdressed Japanese who carried insolence in their eyes and assumed the air of sports conspicuously. There were plain dips and stickup men from Seattle, Los Angeles and Chicago, mine owners, stock brokers, touts, blacklegs, politicians, bank presidents and second-story men.

Small boys with pitchers and tumblers moved through the hot crowd offering water for a nickel. Hawkers worked the periphery, selling flags, buttons, badges, shouting, "Here's your only official badge of the lineup, boys. Wear a picture of Jeffries on your coat and show him you're with him."

Carpenters were still banging together pine boards when the five gates opened and some twenty thousand people—including hundreds of women, for whom special curtained boxes had been constructed—began edging their way in past armed deputies posted by Rickard to confiscate bottles and make sure no firearms were carried inside. Fear that someone might try to harm

---

*The arena was built on the site of the stadium in which Jim Jeffries had declared Marvin Hart his successor as heavyweight champion five years and one day earlier.

the champion continued to nag at Rickard, and he had asked Jeffries himself to issue an appeal to his fans to remain calm whatever took place in the ring. "I would consider any move to intimidate Johnson as cowardly and a disgrace to the American spirit of fair play," Jeffries said. "I expect to whip [him] and then shake his hand. If Johnson should by any chance win, though, he must not be harmed. I demand this."

"The fresh pine arena was built like a funnel," Harris Merton Lyon remembered.

Right in the heart of it lay the little twenty-two-foot ring with its two strands of ropes running around and its red canvas floor. Red because white would blind the fighter's eyes. A bare, pine pit, smelling freshly, unsheltered from the sun and resembling . . . baseball bleachers. . . . The crowd came stalking in like sheep in a chute at half-past twelve. They peeled off their coats, tied handkerchiefs around their necks, bought palm-leaf fans and green eye-shades and sat down on the freshly painted number on their seats.

"The betting was now 10 to 6 on Jeffries," Arthur Ruhl reported, and as the crowd waited,

the talk about 1,000 to 1 for Jeffries, too. You couldn't hurt him—Fitzsimmons had landed enough times to kill an ordinary man in the first few rounds, and Jeffries had only shaken his head like a bull and bored in. The negro might be a clever boxer, but he has never been up against a real fighter before. He has a yellow streak, . . . and anyway, "let's hope he kills the coon."

The rest of the country was getting ready for the fight as well. At Hutchinson, Kansas, twelve hundred Negroes in a tent set up behind a Holiness church had prayed all night for a Johnson victory and planned to keep at it until word came that he had won. Students and faculty gathered in an assembly room at Tuskegee to hear the round-by-round returns when they rattled in from ringside; Booker T. Washington took a dim view of prizefighting in general and Jack Johnson in particular, but he had agreed to allow them to install a special telegraph line, provided they came up with the fifty dollars it cost.* Thirty

---

*On July 1, 1910, the Baltimore *American* ran a story claiming that the black community of Richmond, Virginia, was actually rooting for Jeffries, not Johnson. "Cornbread and water will be about the sole diet of Richmond negroes for several weeks to come if Jack Johnson whips Jim Jeffries Monday.

thousand New Yorkers streamed into Times Square, where giant bulletin boards had been set up on three sides of the New York *Times* building to provide details as soon as they started coming in from ringside. The San Francisco *Examiner* set up a ring high above the street and hired two boxers, one black and one white, to reenact the whole fight, punch by punch, for the throng gathering below.

And in Chicago, five thousand black men and women anxiously took their seats at the Pekin, the showplace of the black belt and the most elegant Negro-owned theater in the country.* Its creator, Robert T. Motts—gambler, saloon keeper, Republican political power—was to read out the bulletins as they came in. Tiny Johnson and her daughters Fannie and Lucy were seated onstage as his special guests.

Tex Rickard had provided none of the preliminary bouts that traditionally entertained fans waiting for the main event. Instead, he sent the Reno Brass Band into the ring. They began with "Just Before the Battle, Mother,"† then segued into "America" and "Dixie" while the crowd joined in. "Hats waved," Rex Beach wrote, "flags fluttered, feeling ran high—Patriotism was riot."‡

"The local blacks have a very low regard for the negro prize-fighter and they have gambled hook, line and sinker—and this is literal for the Richmond negro spends much of his time fishing—against his chances.

"And not only do the local blacks think Jeffries will win—they want him to win. They dislike Johnson, and many wish that 'dat fool niggah gets his haid busted open for bein' so smaht . . . '

"The chief reason for Johnson's unpopularity with the Southern negro probably lies in the fact that he is tryin' to 'copy the white folks.'

" 'He must tink he's bettah dan de res' of us,' said a local, ebony-hued sport. 'He am't,' he continued. 'He's black—black as I is. He ain't got no sense neithah, scootin' round in one of dem automobiles. He bettah gone and git hisself a good steady job while he got da chance. Aftah Mistah Jeffries gits through with him he won't be fit for hirin'.' "

If anyone actually said such things to a white reporter, it seems likely that it was because it was what they were sure he wanted to hear.

*The Pekin Theater was so much admired by black Americans that by 1909, 33 of the 112 black-owned theaters in the country bore its name. And the man in charge was compared by the Chicago *Broad-Ax* to Benjamin Banneker, Toussaint-Louverture, and Booker T. Washington and hailed as "the new Moses of the Negro race in the theater world." (Quoted in Kenney, *Chicago Jazz*, p. 6.)

†According to Jim Corbett, Jeffries could hear the sentimental Civil War favorite from his dressing room: "I never knew just what that tune meant before and I stole a look Jeff's way. The big fellow was bent over, fumbling at his shoe laces, and I could see the big tears pattering down on the backs of his big brawny fists. That tune, coming when it did, helped more than anything else to send Jeff into the ring in a complete state of collapse." (*Boxing*, August 13, 1910.)

‡According to Beach, plans to play the fifteen-year-old favorite "All Coons Look Alike to Me" were canceled at the last minute because "racial feeling was too high." Hugh McIntosh, who was also present, claimed it *was* played, and "received with great enthusiasm." ("Pride of the Blacks.")

The sun was hot. There was only the faintest breeze. The raw-pine seats oozed pitch. The lemonade being peddled up and down the aisles grew warm. And the band rapidly ran through its repertoire. It was not until 1:55—twenty-five minutes after the fight was supposed to start—that William Muldoon climbed into the ring to make a little speech, praising Nevada as "the only free State in the Union" because it was permitting the fight to go forward and calling upon the crowd to remain peaceful so that "no one should be able to say after it was all over that the Negro had not been given a fair deal."

There was a brief stir as Etta Duryea made her way to her sixth-row seat, accompanied by the wife of Sig Hart. Both women waved and smiled at the crowd. "By all odds," said the Los Angeles *Examiner,* "Mrs. Johnson was the prettiest woman in the place . . . apparently a white woman and becomingly gowned."

Then Billy Jordan took over. A walrus of a man with a drooping white mustache and a voice that could reach the farthest edge of any crowd, he had been a fixture at big West Coast fights for decades. One by one, he led the celebrity spectators into the center of the ring, raised his right arm above his head, and paid each a florid tribute. Tex Rickard and Jack Gleason and Big Tim Sullivan, the Tammany politician who was the stakeholder for the contest, all took their bows. So did John L. Sullivan, Bob Fitzsimmons, Tommy Burns, Tom Sharkey, Hugh McIntosh, Stanley Ketchel, Tom McCarey, Jim Coffroth, Bill Lang, Sam Langford, Battling Nelson, Philadelphia Jack O'Brien—and more, so many that when they stood in line for the cameras they stretched from one side of the ring to the other. Hugh E. Keough of the Chicago *Tribune* called it "the last roll-call of has-beens," and in the heat, the novelty of seeing so many famous men in one place faded fast. Some in the crowd began to boo. "Oh hell, pull the fight," one man shouted. "Don't introduce everyone in Reno." Billy Jordan just got louder. Even William T. Rock, in charge of the battery of movie cameras set up on a platform thirty feet from the ring, was hailed as "Rock, the moving picture man."

There was still no sign of the champion or his challenger. A rumor spread through the crowd that a physician had found Johnson near "nervous prostration" and too frightened to leave his dressing room. When he finally did climb into the ring at 2:30, wearing a black and white silk bathrobe and followed by his seconds, there were cries of "Cold feet, Johnson," and "Now you'll get it, you black coward." But there were calls for fairness, too: "Don't talk to them. Give them a square deal." And there were enough friendly voices that Johnson remembered being "amazed at the number of well-wishers I had. I heard many cheers. That's more than took place in Australia where my entry brought lusty boos and hisses."

Then the scattered shouts for the champion were drowned by a great roar—Rex Beach called it "the first blood cry of the thousands . . . the race note sounding"—as the crowd spotted the Jeffries party and rose to cheer its hero. Johnson stood, too, smiled and clapped. Jim Corbett led the way. Then came Jeffries, dressed in a gray suit and checked golf cap, his big jaw working on a wad of gum. The rest of his seconds followed, including little Abe Attell in a straw hat and big Bob Armstrong carrying a giant paper circus hoop on a stick to keep the sun off his fighter between rounds.

Jeffries seemed to pay no attention to the crowd, looked neither right nor left. And, as Arthur Ruhl noted, he spoke to no one.

> I have never seen a human being more calculated to strike terror into an opponent's heart than this brown Colossus as he came through the ropes, stomped like a bull pawing the ground before his charge, and . . . glared at the black man across the ring. If looks could have throttled, burned, and torn to pieces, Mr. Jack Arthur Johnson would have disappeared that minute into a few specks of inanimate dust. The negro had his back turned at the moment, and as he took his corner and his trainer and his seconds, crowding in front of him, concealed the white man, a sort of hoot, wolfish and rather terrible, went up from the crowd. "He daresen't look at him! *O-o-!* Don't let him see him! Don't let him see him!" And when Jeffries pulled off his clothes with a vicious jerk, and standing erect and throwing out his chest, jabbed his great arms above his head once or twice, I don't suppose that one man in a hundred in that crowd would have given two cents for the negro's chances.

Johnson, unaffected, joked with his seconds. "The man of summer temperament smiled and smiled," Jack London wrote, while the "man of iron, the grizzly giant, was grim and serious."

Jordan introduced Johnson as the "colored Heavyweight champion of the world." Jeffries got more fulsome treatment. He was "the champion of champions, the great unbeaten white champion of the world, James J. Jeffries."

Rickard, in his shirtsleeves and wearing a straw hat against the merciless sun, announced that there would be no traditional handshake, no posing together for the cameras; the white man had refused to take part.

Jeffries also wouldn't sit on his stool, perching on the ropes instead, as if he couldn't wait to get at Johnson.

At 2:46, Billy Jordan finally bellowed his familiar "Let 'er go!" and the supposed Battle of the Century was on.

Many in the crowd had expected Jeffries to rush at Johnson, seeking to intimidate and then chop down the champion, who would be undone by his inbred "yellow streak." Instead, as Johnson remembered, "Mr. Jeffries feinted a bit, and then tried the clinching game," hoping to use his greater weight to muscle his opponent around. (He weighed 227 to Johnson's 208.) As the two men shoved and shouldered each other, Johnson did most of the backing up, but he also pinioned Jeffries' arms so he couldn't punch. After a couple of minutes of this, someone shouted, "Cut out the motion pictures." The crowd laughed. Both fighters smiled, and when the round ended, Johnson reached out and gave his opponent a patronizing pat on the shoulder. "I was feeling quite fresh and going easily," the champion remembered, "able to hit him when I wanted to, and I could tell he wasn't going to beat me for strength."

George Little, sitting several rows back, thought Jeffries had won the round and bet Al Jolson four hundred dollars that he would go on to win the fight as well.

Jim Corbett's assignment that afternoon was to range up and down at ringside, shouting insults, trying to rattle Johnson, to break his concentration, make him angry—and careless. Johnson would remain as unruffled as he was when Tommy Burns insulted him in Australia, responding so politely that one writer praised him for displaying "the good sense . . . to keep the respectful, ingratiating ways of the Southern Darkey." As the second round began, Corbett shouted, "He wants to fight a little, Jim." Johnson answered, "You bet I do." And when Jeffries, his jaws still working at his gum, tried the crouch that had intimidated earlier opponents, left arm extended, Johnson just smiled, stepped away, and landed a right-hand uppercut that forced the older man to clinch. "All right Jim," Johnson said, his arms around the former champion. "I'll love you if you want me to."

"Come on now, Mr. Jeff," Johnson said at the start of the third. "Let me see what you got. *Do* something, man. This is for the championship." Jeffries was embarrassed—one reporter thought he looked "sarcastic"—and when they came together, Johnson landed four right uppercuts in a row. "He'll kill you, Jack," a man shouted. "That's what they all say," Johnson answered.

"Jeffries started out to cut me down in the fourth which was about the only round he did real well in," Johnson recalled. The older man landed a right hand to the body that could be heard all over the stadium and a left that opened the cut in Johnson's mouth Kid Cotton had given him in training.

His golden smile reddened. A ringside telegrapher tapped out "First blood for Jeff!" and when those words flashed across the continent, the crowd in Times Square cheered for half a minute, according to the New York *Times*. "Men who had never seen each other before slapped each other on the back and said, 'Jeff's getting in his work' or 'It'll soon be over.' " But back on his stool between rounds, the champion leaned down to assure John L. Sullivan at ringside that Jeffries couldn't hit hard enough to hurt him.

Johnson was in charge through rounds five and six, seven and eight. He bloodied Jeffries' mouth, reopened an old cut on his right cheek, closed his right eye. At one point, he encircled Jeffries with his arms and walked him toward Corbett's side of the ring, asking, "Where do you want me to put him, Mr. Corbett?" As the two men fought on the west side of the ring, Johnson overheard W. W. Naughton dictating to his telegrapher: "Jeffries took a left hook to the jaw." "Is that *all* he took, Mr. Naughton?" Johnson asked, and landed two more.

Jeffries was embarrassed again but unable to retaliate. All the worst fears that had gripped him in the hours before the fight were coming true. "My eyes could detect openings—or danger—as they had in other years," he said afterward. "But my muscles wouldn't respond as quickly to the dictates of the brain. . . . They were slow, slow, slow."

Between the seventh and eighth rounds, Corbett pulled Jack Jeffries aside. "Jack," he said, "your brother's whipped. What are we going to do?" The younger Jeffries had tears in his eyes. They couldn't let him lose to Johnson, he said, and suggested that Corbett try to talk his brother into deliberately losing on a foul. Neither had the heart to suggest it.

When a series of Johnson jabs forced Jeffries to crouch still lower than usual in the ninth and Johnson said, "I'll straighten him up in a minute," a fan at ringside yelled, "He'll straighten *you* up, Nigger!" Johnson ignored him and landed an uppercut that brought the older man's head back up within punching range.

Jeffries did his best to talk back through bloodied lips. "Ain't I got a hard old head?" he said to Johnson after weathering a series of blows.

"You certainly have, Mr. Jeffries," Johnson said, and pounded it again.

Etta's voice could be heard shouting, "Keep it up, Jack!"

Jeffries managed to land several hard shots to Johnson's stomach in the ninth and tenth, but Johnson countered with a left hook to the liver that made Jeffries stagger—"I didn't show you that one in Sydney," Johnson called out to Tommy Burns—and followed it up with several left hands to the head.

By the eleventh, Jeffries' "wind was going fast," Johnson recalled, "his arms were getting weak, and he couldn't put them up to block or stop my blows." In the twelfth, Johnson parried Jeffries' rushes so ably, battering his bloody face with hard lefts, that some in the crowd at last began to cheer him for his skill. Corbett seemed almost apoplectic now, shrieking and waving his arms as he ran back and forth. Johnson spoke to him over Jeffries' shoulder: "Thought you said you were going to make *me* wild."

During the fourteenth, Johnson jarred Jeffries again and again with left hands, calling out, "How you like 'em, Jim?" as the former champion's head rocked back and forth. "Do they hurt?"

"No, they don't hurt," Jeffries answered. But they did. One made him cry out, "Oh!" and his own clumsy attempts to damage Johnson's body missed their target. Corbett was frantic. "Why don't you *do* something?" he shouted at Johnson, hoping he might still somehow be made to lose his head. "So clever," Johnson shouted back. "So clever." And then, grinning, "Just like you."

At the end of that round, Jeffries' nose was broken, his eyes were swollen nearly shut, his shoulders and thighs were laced with blood, and he was desperately tired. Seated on his stool between rounds, gasping for air, he told his seconds he could hardly lift his arms. Jim Corbett, Arthur Ruhl noted, suddenly looked "grey and drawn and old. Across the ring, John L. Sullivan was half rising from his seat. . . . Behind Sullivan was Fitzsimmons, his round red face sober and anxious. No need to tell these defeated champions what was coming. They had all been there in their time."

Jeffries stalked into Johnson's corner at the beginning of the fifteenth, stoical as ever. Johnson hit him with a right hand. They clinched. Johnson shoved Jeffries back, then seemed to hurl himself at the older man, landing repeatedly with both hands. Jeffries backed into the ropes, turned, and began to stumble toward his own corner. Johnson pursued him, landing a right uppercut, then three lefts in quick succession. Jeffries sank to his haunches, one arm draped over the lower strand of the ropes. "A great silence fell," one ringsider noted, and "a guttural gust of pity came from twelve thousand chests. It was a queer, uncanny sound—'Aw-w-w-w'—from profoundly affected men." Jim Jeffries had never been off his feet before.

The timekeeper reached nine before Jeffries, shaking his massive head from side to side to clear it, managed to struggle to his feet. He spat out a mouthful of blood and tried to clinch. Johnson avoided his grasp and hit him again with his left hand. Jeffries went down a second time, sprawled over the bottom rope, dazed and confused. "Don't let the nigger knock him out!" some-one shouted. Others took up the cry. "Don't let the nigger knock him out!"

Abe Attell and Jack Jeffries jumped up onto the ring apron, hauled the beaten man to his feet, and shoved him, tottering, back toward the center of the ring.

Johnson was waiting.

Corbett waved his arms in anguish. "Oh, don't, Jack, don't hit him!"

Jack London could not bear to watch what happened next. Johnson moved in. Still cautious but sure now of victory, he slipped to the side and hit Jeffries four more times as he reeled along the ropes and collapsed once more on the opposite side of the ring. Johnson stood over him, ready to strike should he manage to rise again. Rickard shoved Johnson back and began the count. Jeffries' seconds had seen enough. Sam Berger stepped through the ropes to stop the fight. Bob Armstrong threw in a towel. Rickard clasped Johnson's shoulder as a sign that he was the winner.

Jeffries wobbled back to his corner. "I couldn't come back, boys," he said over and over again. "I couldn't come back."*

Johnson was euphoric. "I could have fought for two hours longer," he told his cornermen.

It was easy. Where is my lucky bathrobe? I'm going to give one of my gloves to Jeffries and the other to Corbett. I guess Jeff won't be so grouchy now. Somebody wire to my mother. I wish it was some longer. I was having lots of fun. Not one blow hurt me. He can't hit. He won't forget two punches I landed on him. He was only half the trouble Burns was.

Within seconds, scores of spectators clambered into the ring. Johnson's seconds formed a cordon around the champion for fear that someone might attack him. But he pushed his way past them and across the ring, hoping to offer his hand to the loser, still slumped on his stool. Jeffries' seconds wouldn't let him get close enough.

Jeffries climbed unsteadily through the ropes and out of the ring. "I could never have whipped Jack Johnson at my best," he would tell a reporter later. "I couldn't have reached him in a thousand years."

---

*Jeffries' sparring partner, Bob Armstrong, may have offered the best explanation for the ex-champion's defeat: "When a horse ain't got a race in him, he can't win a race."

A few fans cheered Johnson. Others began cutting up the ropes for souvenirs. But most of the crowd filed out of the stadium in what one reporter called "funeral gloom, grim and silent." A wealthy white woman at ringside was so overcome with grief at her hero's loss, she begged the stranger sitting next to her for help. "Please show me the way out Mister, I'm crying so I can't see." The stranger, a massive rancher and future film actor named Bull Montana, was no help. "Madame," he said, "you'll have to lead me out for I'm crying harder than you are."

Back in Chicago at the Pekin Theater, a reporter for the *Tribune* had kept his eye on the champion's mother as Bob Motts read out the round-by-round reports from Reno.

> She did not show many outward signs until the eighth round when Johnson, while in a clinch, asked Corbett how he liked it. . . . This brought Mrs. Johnson to her feet for at the Johnson home Corbett is considered one of the family's bitterest enemies. At this stage of the fight Lucy Johnson [said she] wished it was Corbett that Jack was fighting.
>
> The seventh round was the last to be announced, and at its conclusion there was a good deal of speculation as to how long the fight would go, when suddenly the instrument clicked off the words which would send the black belt into a state bordering on insanity. The operator whispered the words "Johnson wins in the fifteenth" to the champion's mother and without a moment's hesitation Mrs. Johnson burst into tears and shrieked:
>
> "I knew he would do it. I knew he would do it. . . . Oh, ain't it fine— ain't it fine for Texas. All the South and all the North never turned out a hero like him. . . . There were eighty million people against him today, but he beat them all. If his father had only lived to see it! It is certainly grand to be the mother of a real hero."

The crowd swept her onto their shoulders and carried her outside to the chauffeured car her son had arranged for her. On the sidewalk, a drunken old white man with a bandaged face begged for a handout, oblivious to the excitement all around him. "Gracious me, if there isn't poor old Jeffries now," Tiny Johnson said. "To look at him, you wouldn't think he'd refuse to shake hands with my boy." The crowd roared. The car pulled away, taking the champion's family home.

But no sooner had they made it into their house than the big crowd gathered outside began to call for Johnson's mother to come back out so they could cheer her. She finally did, stepping gingerly onto the roof of her front porch, holding a poster of her son in one hand and a victory bouquet in the other. A band struck up "There'll Be a Hot Time in the Old Town Tonight," and she and the crowd joined in. "The gritty old woman stood waving the picture and flowers," reported the *Tribune*, "and sang so long that hoarseness robbed her of her voice so she just stood and cried."

Meanwhile, people were pouring into the streets up and down Chicago's black belt, banging on pots, blowing horns, chanting "Jack, Jack, J.-A.-J.! Jack, Jack, J.-A.-J." over and over again. Hundreds pinned the front page of the Chicago *American* to their clothes, with JOHNSON WINS spelled out in big red letters above a larger-than-life-size portrait of the grinning champion. A black minister with a waxed mustache stood at the corner of Thirty-first and State shouting, "Oh that golden smile!" then knelt to offer a prayer of thanksgiving. Five blocks away, a well-dressed young black man leaped onto a broken-down float abandoned that morning by the Independence Day parade and shouted, "What's the matter with Jeffries?" "Too much Johnson!" the crowd shouted back. "Too Much Johnson!"* Hundreds of policemen were kept in reserve in case of trouble. There was none. "It's their night," said the officer in command, "Let them have their fun."

The news had spread all across the country. President William Howard Taft emerged from a Boston auditorium where he had delivered a speech on education, and asked the nearest newsboy, "Say, sonny, who won the fight?" In the mid-Atlantic a tanker steamed toward the passenger ship *Carmania* flying flags that seemed to indicate that she urgently needed help. Jack Curley was among the passengers who crowded the deck wondering what could be wrong. When she drew closer, the tanker signaled, "W-H-O W-O-N T-H-E F-I-G-H-T?"

From Lillian Paynter's whorehouse at 47 Caldwell Street in Pittsburgh, Belle Schreiber sent her maid out several times during the fight to bring her the bulletins; when she learned that Johnson had won, Belle went down to the telegraph office herself to send congratulations to the winner. Later, asked why she'd done it, she couldn't say. "There was no reason," she said. "I didn't want to bring myself to his notice again." But she had.

At Barron's Café in Manhattan, a big, well-dressed crowd had gathered around a ticker-tape machine to follow the action in Reno. "I had seen pool

---

*This was a play on the title of a perennially popular stage comedy by William Gillette, first produced on Broadway in 1894.

tables lined up and stacked with silver dollars at Mush Mouth Johnson's saloon in Chicago," the blues composer and impresario Perry Bradford remembered, "but New York sports had more green cabbage than I had ever seen before." When word came of Johnson's victory, Barron Wilkins himself jumped up onto the bar and shouted, "Everybody have some champagne on the house." Then, Bradford said, the place became a madhouse. A sport named Lovely Joe Robinson strutted in, "clinking like a knight in armor," with thirty twenty-dollar gold pieces in the pockets of his jacket. Another named Dude Foster, Bradford recalled, had also

cashed in plenty. Dude was a character widely known in the sporting world as being full of notoriety. He was walking around shaking two bottles of champagne and waving five or six one thousand dollar bills and shouting, "I am God's gift to Women. All you beat up gals and what came with you, if you need any of that little thing called money, see the Dude."

It was a Jack Johnson crowd.

In the poorest part of the southern Illinois coal mining town of Du Quoin, called the Bottom, black families celebrating the Fourth of July in their back-yards got the news from a group of running, shouting men who had been hanging around the newspaper office. "The Negroes were jubilant," a black woman who had been a little girl then remembered:

Everybody wanted to buy someone else a dinner, a glass of beer, or a shot of whiskey. Jerome Banks who had lost his leg in a mine accident came down the street waving one of his crutches. . . . The older people laughed and cried, and the children danced around and knocked each other about in good fun. Grandma Thompson stood under the grape arbor and raised her quivering voice in song. We all joined in:

"Hallelujah, hallelujah, the storm is passing over, hallelujah!"

Little Arthur had delivered. We were now a race of champions!

Later, in a poem called "My Lord What a Morning," the poet William War-ing Cuney—grandson of Norris Wright Cuney, the political strongman who had dominated Johnson's boyhood neighborhood—recalled how his family and friends had felt when they got the news:

O, My Lord
What a morning,
O My lord,
What a feeling,

When Jack Johnson
Turned Jim Jeffries'
Snow-White Face
  to the Ceiling.

That evening, Johnson and Etta and their entourage sped into Reno from Rick's Roadhouse to pick up the champion's earnings: $121,000, a sum that may have been larger than any black American had ever earned in a single day before. The streets were still filled with fight fans. Most had come to Reno hoping to see Johnson beaten into submission. Many had lost money betting on the loser. But now they applauded the winner, and a paperboy ran alongside his car till the grinning champion reached out to shake his hand.

At the depot, where they were to catch the *Overland Limited* to Chicago, they had a hard time making their way through the densely packed crowd of spectators waiting to board their own trains for home. Kid Cotton did his best to keep up, carrying a big Victrola under one arm and holding the leash of Johnson's bulldog with his other hand. Some Negroes who had come to Reno hadn't actually attended the fight, fearing that the crowd might turn on them. But they had been inside the stadium in spirit, and they now cheered Johnson loudly. One black woman was seen carefully removing her hat before stepping onto her train. Asked why, she answered, "'Cause I wants everybody to know that I'm a nigger, that's why, and I'm proud of it."

As he made his way through the crowd, Johnson spotted Tommy Burns and Hugh McIntosh. "Howdy-do, Tommy," he said. "Pretty easy wasn't it?" Burns allowed as how it had been, then asked if there was any chance of his getting a rematch. Johnson just smiled as he and his party swept into their private car.

The news of Johnson's triumph had spread along the Southern Pacific Lines, and everywhere Johnson's train paused, crowds were waiting. Most people were eager just to have a look at the champion.* At Carlin, Utah, where he got out to stretch his legs, he was asked how it felt to be the undisputed titleholder. "Same as yesterday," he said. "I'm just the same old fellow that I was before I had the pleasure of Mr. Jeffries' company for a short time." Five thousand people turned out to see him at Cheyenne, Wyoming, includ-

---

*At Ogden, Utah, three white drunks did try to get into his car, and when they were barred, began to curse him. One called him "Nigger" and, according to the Los Angeles *Times* (July 6, 1910), got spattered with tobacco juice and slapped "in a rather vigorous fashion for his trouble" by members of the champion's entourage. Two railroad detectives then climbed aboard to protect Johnson as far as Omaha.

ing a thousand men from the all-Negro 9th Cavalry, the "buffalo soldiers" who had fought Indians in the West and the Spanish in Cuba. The troopers surrounded the champion's car, waving their hats and cheering. Johnson got down to shake their hands, answer their questions, sign autographs, and bow to the ladies, including a shy young woman with an infant she said she'd named for him. The champion carefully shook the baby's tiny hand.

Ed Smith of the Chicago *American,* also traveling back to Chicago aboard the train, marveled at the way Johnson handled himself.

> The black man, were he of white skin, doubtless would be the most pop-
> ular champion we ever had. He has all the manners to make him such, and
> is so accommodating and polite all the time that people who know him
> well get to like him immediately. No matter what the request Johnson is
> willing to go out of his way to grant it. Especially is he willing to pose for
> amateur photographers along the way and laughs and jokes continuously
> during the process. . . . He is naturally that sort of way. He is sunny Jack,
> for sure.

But that same morning, the Los Angeles *Times,* the newspaper that had been the first to portray Jack Johnson as more than merely another Negro boxer, issued a chilling warning to his black admirers. "A word to the Black Man," it began:

> Do not point your nose too high. Do not swell your chest too much. Do
> not boast too loudly. Do not be puffed up. Let not your ambition be inor-
> dinate or take a wrong direction. . . . Remember you have done nothing at
> all. You are just the same member of society you were last week. . . . You
> are on no higher plane, deserve no new consideration, and will get
> none. . . . No man will think a bit higher of you because your complexion
> is the same as that of the victor at Reno.

And as the train rattled its way eastward, Johnson began to get word of trouble erupting everywhere. "Rioting broke out like prickly heat all over the country," the New York *Tribune* reported, "between whites sore and angry that Jeffries had lost the big fight at Reno and negroes jubilant that Johnson had won." The Fourth of July had always been greeted with drunken violence, but nothing like this had ever been seen before. There were confrontations in Chattanooga and Columbus; in Los Angeles and Norfolk, Pueblo and Philadelphia, Roanoke and Washington, D.C.

On Canal Street in New Orleans, a ten-year-old paperboy named Louis Armstrong was told to run for his life. "Jack Johnson has knocked out Jim Jeffries," one of his friends shouted. "The white boys are sore about it and they're going to take it out on us." Nearby, members of a black marching band struck up a joyous tune when news of Johnson's victory flashed—and had to flee for their lives from a shower of bricks. In Clarksburg, West Virginia, a mob of more than one thousand whites stormed through black neighborhoods, driving everyone off the streets. White sailors from the Norfolk Navy Yard roamed the town, attacking Negroes "wherever they met them." In Pittsburgh, when more than one hundred black men and women rounded up for rioting seized the courtroom and demanded that their cases be heard by a black judge, the police locked the doors and "clubbed them unmercifully." In Manhattan's San Juan Hill neighborhood—a warren of densely packed tenements in the West 60's—a mob set on fire a building occupied by blacks, then tried to block the doors and windows so no one could get out. A white passenger on a Houston streetcar slit a black man's throat because he had dared to cheer for Johnson. When whites in Wheeling, West Virginia, came upon a Negro driving a handsome automobile, as Jack Johnson was now famous for doing, they dragged him out from behind the steering wheel and hanged him. Near Uvalda, Georgia, white riflemen opened fire on a black construction camp, killing three and wounding five.

At least eleven and perhaps as many as twenty-six people would die before it was over. Hundreds more were hurt, almost all of them black. No event since emancipation forty-five years earlier seemed to mean so much to Negro America as Johnson's victory. And no event yielded such widespread racial violence until the assassination of Dr. Martin Luther King, Jr., fifty-eight years later. To some, like William Pickens, president of the all-black Talladega College in Talladega, Alabama, all of it had been worthwhile.

> It was a good deal better for Johnson to win and a few Negroes be killed in body for it, than for Johnson to have lost and Negroes to have been killed in spirit by the preachments of inferiority from the combined white press. . . . [White writers had been] ready to preach insulting homilies to us about our inferiority. Many . . . editors had already composed and pigeonholed their editorials of mockery and spite—and we shall not conceal . . . our satisfaction at having these homilies and editorials all knocked into the wastebasket by the big fists of Jack Johnson.

At every stop more news of unrest was brought aboard Johnson's train and, one reporter noted, by the time the train reached Milwaukee the champion's mood had changed.

> His black tilted brow puckered in deep frowning thought as he read of white men fighting black ones all over the country.
>
> "And just because my black fists happened to be too many for a pair of white fists," he said sadly. "If both colors knew the real Jack Johnson they'd behave themselves, like he does."
>
> "And what is your idea of the psychology of these outbursts?" I asked. . . .
>
> "The psychology of it is the American small boy," he replied promptly. "It is the little kid of 12 or 14 who knows he is immune from physical punishment who starts most of these riots. He makes a nasty remark or two and gives the idea to the grown-ups in the crowd. They do the rest."
>
> Johnson's point was illustrated at the next stop. The crowd grew impatient when Johnson did not appear on the platform. The ever-present small boy blurted out, "Ah, bring out the damned coon; we won't hurt him."
>
> In a moment the men had taken up the small boy's attitude and became abusive because their curiosity was denied.
>
> "There is good and bad in each color," Johnson went on, deeply serious on a subject he has always before refused to discuss.
>
> "The fellows that are making trouble over my victory at Reno ain't got no class. They're only scum. The black ones that swell up and cut a swath because I've got a hard fist are without education. If they had any manhood they wouldn't fight. The whites are supposed to know better on general principles."

Chicago planned a big South Side welcome for the champion on July 7. Bob Motts organized everything, even printing up handbills meant to guarantee a peaceful celebration:

> Don't talk to white strangers.
> Don't drink any gin.
> Don't tote a gun.
> But be there.

They were. The mayor had refused to issue an official parade permit in Johnson's honor, fearing the kind of racial violence that had convulsed other cities, but even he admitted that there was no way to keep people from coming out to cheer their fellow Chicagoan. Thousands mobbed the Dearborn Street Station, including large numbers of whites. Thousands more lined State Street from Twelfth all the way south to Thirty-fifth. It was as if there had been no victory celebration in Chicago three days earlier.

Eighty policemen with clubs struggled to keep order on the platform as Johnson's train hissed to a stop nearly four hours late. A reporter noticed an old black man holding his granddaughter high above the crowd. "Now watch close there, honey," he said, "'cause you're going to see the greatest colored man that ever lived."

When Johnson emerged from the train, the crowd surged so strongly and seemed so intimidating to the outnumbered police that they rushed him out of the depot, pushed him into a hansom cab, and ordered the driver to whip up his horses. The champion shifted to a taxi as soon as he could, but in the general jubilation it took half an hour for the parade organizers to locate him again. During the scramble, "colored men stood in automobiles which forced their way through the crowd and looked in every direction for the missing pugilist." The Chicago *Daily News* sheepishly reported that one of its reporters was fooled

> when he saw the burly figure of "Rube" Foster [now managing as well as pitching for Chicago's Leland Giants], a Negro whose complexion, stature and smile are almost identical to Johnson's, standing in a big red automobile as the car rounded the corner from the station into Wells Street. The reporter told in vivid fashion his story of how Johnson smiled at the plaudits of the crowd, when the smiling one was Foster.

Johnson finally got seated in the right car, and the parade began the slow ride through the dense crowds along State Street. At nearly every corner, the same white traffic policemen who had arrested and harassed him so many times before now reached out to grasp his hand.

The brass band that belonged to the all-black 8th National Guard Regiment had been forbidden to escort Johnson from the railroad station, so it had set up on his mother's lawn instead and was playing "Hail the Conquering Hero Comes" when he swung into view. A big portrait of the champion framed by the American and Texas flags hung over the front door. Thirty little black girls in blue dresses with blue ribbons in their hair formed a sort of honor guard up the porch steps and waited for their hero.

The car inched its way through the throng. There were so many people so eager to clasp Johnson's hand and pat his back that he could not open the car door. He had to climb over it, then muscle his way up the sidewalk and onto the porch, where his sister Fannie and Tiny Johnson were waiting. "Oh, Jackie," his mother shouted as she took him in her arms, "you kept your promise."

Johnson disappeared inside. The crowd called for a speech. He stepped out onto the porch roof twice to give one but couldn't make himself heard above the cheering and had to be content with waving the big white handkerchief with which he wiped the perspiration from his brow. The last revelers did not leave Johnson's trampled lawn till 5 a.m.

The next morning, Johnson deposited more than $100,000 in the First Trust and Savings Bank. "There's plenty more where that came from," he told the teller. Then he bought a $3,000 car for his mother's "exclusive use" and wired a total of $4,000 to eight friends in Galveston. Four had been members of his old Eleventh Street and Avenue K gang; $750 went to Ed Harrison, according to the Los Angeles *Examiner,*

> an old-timer who taught Johnson how to fight on the docks. He used to tell the young darkey that one day he would be a great fighter and Johnson often promised the old man that if he ever got to be champion he would buy him two suits and a red necktie. Sure enough he kept his promise and sent word to order two suits of clothes and not to be stingy with the price.

The climax of the two-day celebration was to come that evening at Bob Motts' Pekin Café, a black-tie banquet in the champion's honor, attended by fifty of the most prominent black Chicagoans. Johnson was getting dressed for it when he happened to look out the window and saw a white man with a rifle walking up Wabash Avenue. The police were called. The man was arrested. He turned out to be a drunken Canadian-born mechanic from St. Louis named Richard McGuirk, who had lost his savings betting on Jim Jeffries. His weapon was unloaded when he was seized, but the police believed he'd come to town to kill Johnson. The champion did not press charges.

Etta was said to be ill that evening—perhaps she had been unnerved by the rifleman or undone by the frenzied crowds—so Johnson drove off alone to the Pekin for an evening of music, dancing, and champagne. He bathed in the attention and needed little urging when his host asked him to say a few words. He planned to stay out of the ring for at least a year, he said, and he might retire altogether; there was no one else to fight, and he now had enough money in the bank so that "I never will be broke."

He was proud that he had resisted the temptation to increase his take by lying down to Jeffries. "Not alone has Jack Johnson shown the world that there are honest men in the black race," he said, "but I also have shown the world that there is one black man who loves honor more than money."

He would be off the next morning for New York and a return to the vaudeville stage, he continued, but he would always remember this outpouring of affection. Chicago's love for him seemed so overwhelming, he wanted one day to be buried here "among my friends." But his study of history had also taught him to be wary. "I only hope the colored people of the world will not be like the French," he told the crowd. "History tells us that when Napoleon was winning all his victories the French were with him, but when he lost, the people turned against him. When Jack Johnson meets defeat, I want the colored people to like and love me the same as when I was the champion."

BOOK TWO

THE FALL

CHAPTER EIGHT

THE BRUNETTE
IN A BLOND TOWN

T HE MORNING AFTER THE FIGHT in Reno, Major P. M. Ashburn, a white
surgeon in the Army Medical Corps who professed to have "the highest
esteem for the Negro," sat down and wrote what he evidently believed would
be a helpful letter to his friend Emmett Jay Scott, Booker T. Washington's secretary at Tuskegee. He was delighted at the champion's victory, Ashburn said,
but deeply concerned about his behavior. Johnson, he said,

> will now for some years be the most talked of and in some respects the
> most eminent black man in the world. It seems to us a matter of great
> importance whether his eminence is to be that of the purely sporting, loud,
> dislike-exciting nigger, or that of a sober, sane, wise and admirable Negro.
>
> With his youth, health, wealth, international reputation and fair edu-
> cation (I think you said he went to school with your wife) almost anything
> is possible for him, and a sane bearing that will excite sympathy and admi-
> ration rather than antipathy and distrust is not too much to ask. Conduct
> that was condoned in John L. Sullivan will be cursed in Jack Johnson and
> if his success should lead him into similar courses it will be a misfortune
> for his cause.

The condescending tone of Major Ashburn's letter aside, the concerns he
expressed were now shared by a good many people of both races. And the
violence that followed in the wake of the Jeffries fight had only intensified
their anxiety. Johnson knew that, and sometimes did his best to try to put
their fears to rest. But the private life he'd created for himself, the enemies
he'd made along the way, and his own unwillingness to let anything or anyone interfere with his pleasures all had begun to work against him.

There was something else at work as well. No black man—and very few
Americans of any color—had ever drawn the unrelenting fire that Jack Johnson had attracted over the past two years. Damning editorials and death
threats had been directed at him almost daily. It was not Johnson's race alone
that inspired such hatred; it is hard to know how the white public would have

reacted if, say, Sam Langford or Joe Jeannette or some other more acquies-
cent black fighter had won the title. Johnson had proved not only that he
could beat white men—but that he could take the women who they believed
were theirs alone, as well. It was this lack of deference toward white men and
the power they wielded, his refusal ever to remain in the "place" to which
they insisted his color had permanently assigned him, that so inflamed their
passions.

Johnson was incapable of living any other way, but the relentless pressure
had begun to take its toll. "I was not myself for a year after the Jeffries fight,"
he would later concede, and he sometimes claimed to have suffered from
what he called "brain fever." Whatever may have been wrong with him, he
exacerbated it with alcohol. He had always been a heavy drinker, settling for
beer at first, then demanding wine and finally fine champagne. He was said
to have been badly hungover for at least two of his fights—against England's
Ben Taylor and Philadelphia Jack O'Brien—and it seems unlikely a sober
man would have bothered to do as much damage to the diminutive Norman
Pinder as he had done earlier in the year. Now, he seems to have become more
and more dependent on alcohol, and more and more erratic.

New York Negroes had joined in the nationwide black celebration of the
champion's victory. "I have never seen so many colored people reading newspapers as since the fight," Lester A. Walton wrote in the New York *Age*.

> I saw one enthusiastic citizen of color with every New York daily paper of
> July 5, including a German and a Hebrew paper he could not read. He told
> me that he wanted to cut out the pictures of the two fighters. That the
> Negro race should feel highly elated over the fact that a member of their
> race is champion of champions is to be expected. All other races feel proud
> of their members who achieve name and fame; then, why not we?

And black Manhattan's reception for Johnson on July 10, organized by his
old friend Barron Wilkins, came close to matching black Chicago's. Hundreds of handbills had been passed out in Negro neighborhoods.

> TO EVERY COLORED MAN, WOMAN OR CHILD IN GREATER NEW YORK,
> BE AT GRAND CENTRAL STATION AT 9:30 O'CLOCK MONDAY MORNING,
> AND LET US ALL SHAKE THE HAND OF THE STALWART ATHLETE, THE
> GREATEST OF THE TWENTIETH CENTURY. COME ANY WAY YOU CAN.
> COME IN VEHICLES OR ON FOOT. ALL BE THERE.

Thousands mobbed Grand Central and lined Johnson's route. And as in Chicago, there were also a fair number of whites in the throng. The *Twentieth Century Limited* had arrived five hours late, the Washington *Post* reported, so there was no time to stop at the Little Savoy before Johnson performed for the matinee audience at Hammerstein's Victoria.

> The Victoria was jammed alow and aloft. No negroes sat in the auditorium but the balcony and gallery [were] solid with them. . . . Up went the curtain and showed nothing but a punching bag swinging gently. A short thick-necked person waddled to the footlights and announced that the audience was to have the pleasure of seeing "the champeen of all champeens, Mr. Jack Johnson."
>
> Out danced Johnson from the wings in a blue low-necked and sleeveless jersey with a silk American flag for a belt. He flashed a smile and went about his business. The more you looked the more you saw what Jeffries was up against. Johnson moved his great bulk with a cat's quickness. He tapped the bag until he had it hammering the oak. . . . Finally, the rope broke and the bag went spinning. The spectators clapped enthusiastically. Johnson grinned and ran off the stage.

He returned, sparred three decorous rounds with Walter Monahan, and then made a short speech, extolling Jim Jeffries as "the gamest man I ever fought" and promising to hold on to the title as long as he could, defending it against "all comers . . . fair and square." "There was applause all over the house," the *Post* continued. "Not a man . . . hissed him or showed sign of disapproval."

The crowd outside the theater was so big that the police allowed him to drive through an alley to get to the Little Savoy.* There, as soon as he and Etta were settled in their suite, the champion invited Nat Fleischer up for an interview. The future boxing historian and founding editor of *The Ring* was then a young reporter for the New York *Sun-Press*. Johnson was still brooding about the violence triggered by his latest victory:

> Nat, why should they bring in the black race against the white race? I licked Tommy Burns fairly. I did the same in my fight with Jeffries. My battle with

---

*Neither the police nor New York bystanders were always so friendly. A week later, Johnson was arrested for speeding away from the theater. He tried to explain in court: "I have to go up Seventh Avenue and through Forty-third Street to dodge the hoodlums who call at me 'nigger' and 'coon' and throw stones at me. The police told me to go fast and get away as soon as I could to prevent congestion of traffic. I have never run down or injured anyone, but I don't want to be struck by stones." The judge fined him fifteen dollars. (New York *Times*, July 21, 1910.)

Jeffries was not a contest between a black man and a white man. But between two boxers. . . . I beat him and now the matter is settled. Let's avoid any talk that is likely to antagonize my people or yours.

The champion's statesmanlike summary of the fight and its meaning ran in the next morning's *Sun-Press*. What happened next did not. As the two men wound up their interview, Etta emerged unexpectedly from the bathroom. "She had been preparing for the evening's celebration," Fleischer remembered, "and, having no idea that Jack was entertaining a guest in the living room, was completely nude." Embarrassed and furious at Johnson for failing to warn her that he was not alone, she began to shout at him. "Jack tried to explain," Fleischer remembered, "but was cut short when his wife, her eyes blazing menacingly, raised a chair. Discretion being the better part of valor, this seemed to both of us the propitious moment to leave. The chair caught Jack in the center of the back as we raced down the stairs with her curses flooding after us."

Stories like this one were thought off-limits by newspaper editors in those days. Fleischer wouldn't commit his memory of Etta's fury to paper for more than four decades. But other tales were now circulating about the champion. Hattie McClay called on Bat Masterson at the New York *Telegraph*, hoping to embarrass her former lover into letting her in on his financial success. "According to her story," Masterson reported,

> she has been pushed aside for another woman whom Johnson took with him from this city when he went out to San Francisco. . . . The original Mrs. Johnson asserts that she pawned what jewelry she had to defray the expenses of her and her husband's trip to England at a time when Johnson was unable to procure the funds necessary to make the trip.

Meanwhile, back in Chicago, George Little called reporters in to have a drink with him at the Workingmen's Exchange, the cavernous saloon from which Hinky Dink Kenna ran the First Ward.* Johnson's quarrels with his earlier managers had only occasionally made the papers. But big money was

---

*The Exchange was Kenna's headquarters for thirty years. "Politics is business," he once told a European visitor. "This is where we make voters. They drink 12,000 glasses of beer a week in my place." To make sure they kept up that brisk pace, the bartender had instructions never to turn off the water tap. "The sound of running water," Kenna explained, "makes 'em thirsty." (Lindberg, *Chicago by Gaslight*, p. 116.)

at issue now. Newspapers all over the country had carried Johnson's charge that his ex-manager had offered him $100,000 to throw the Jeffries bout, and Little was determined to strike back. Furious at having been fired and having lost thousands betting on Jeffries, the ex-bagman and brothel keeper assumed an air of injured piety and attacked his former fighter's character. Johnson, he charged, suffered from the universal Negro trait of "prevarication." It was "a downright lie" that Little had ever proposed to fix any fight. It had all been Johnson's idea. The "real reason" for their split had been the champion's refusal to honor the tradition that "women are barred" from training camp. "Johnson's wife insisted on being with Jack most of the time"; she also wore "a whole lot of diamonds that Jack borrowed from me and I got sore and demanded their return." As proof that he could have provided such baubles, he displayed a ring the Chicago *Tribune* said outshone all the electric lights in the Exchange.

Five days later in New York, halfway through Johnson's act at Hammerstein's Victoria, Little rose from the audience and tried to storm the stage. The ushers stopped him. As they wrestled him out the door, Johnson shouted, "I'll see him in my dressing room." The two men spent an angry hour and a half behind closed doors, but nothing was resolved. Little went off to write a four-page self-serving "confession," typed up for use by his lawyers, in which he alleged that Johnson's recent fights in the West—against Al Kaufmann, Stanley Ketchel, and Jim Jeffries—had all been fixed. Then he filed suit against Johnson to recover the cost of a diamond ring he said he'd loaned the champion after his return from Australia. Johnson didn't deny that he'd borrowed the ring but said he'd more than made up for it with gifts for Little over their time together—a $125 pair of eyeglasses, a $500 trunk, and much more. It was clear that Johnson and his former manager now detested each other.

On the morning of July 13, Johnson drove Etta and Sig Hart from Manhattan over the East River to Vitagraph Village, the moviemaking complex in Flatbush where the films of the Reno fight were being duplicated for release to theaters. Johnson no longer had any financial interest in them. Like his opponent, he had sold his share before ever entering the ring—he'd said then that he'd rather have fifty thousand dollars than risk being cheated by middlemen—but he still wanted to see for himself just how he had beaten Jim Jeffries.

As the first images flickered on the screen, Johnson leaned forward, fascinated at seeing himself in action, and started a running blow-by-blow commentary that kept Etta laughing through all fifteen rounds. He seemed to remember everything Jim Corbett had shouted at him and everything he'd said in response. "That's where he got me good," he said when Jeffries landed to his stomach in the fourth round. He pointed out punches that looked powerful on-screen but had had no actual effect and others that looked like what he called "love taps" but had done serious damage. At the end, the Vitagraph workers watching from the back broke into applause.

Most Americans would never get a chance to see the films at all. Within twenty-four hours of the Reno fight, a nationwide crusade had been launched to stop theater owners from showing them. The United Society of Christian Endeavor, four million strong, started it, sending a wire to every governor.

> RACE RIOTS AND MURDER IN MANY PLACES FOLLOWING ANNOUNCE-
> MENT OF JOHNSON'S VICTORY.... THESE RESULTS WILL BE MULTIPLIED
> MANY FOLD BY MOVING PICTURE EXHIBITIONS. WILL YOU JOIN OTHER
> GOVERNORS IN RECOMMENDING PROHIBITION OF THESE DEMORAL-
> IZING SHOWS? SAVE OUR YOUNG PEOPLE. WIRE ANSWER.

Many southern governors wired yes. So did the chief executives of several northern and western states. The Woman's Christian Temperance Union seconded the call. The Hearst papers, which had devoted yards of column space to promoting the fight, now gave over their front pages day after day to trying to prevent anyone from seeing what had actually happened in the ring. Former president Theodore Roosevelt, who had told friends how much he looked forward to the fight, also now called for the films to be banned.

There had always been those who believed prizefighting wicked and dangerous to public morals. But race gave this campaign its special urgency. It was simply wrong, said the San Francisco *Examiner*, to make it possible for white women and children to see "members of their own race beaten into physical disability by a gigantic negro." Boss Ed Crump of Memphis issued a ban on fight films—and Negro boxers—in the town he ran. "Labor on the cotton plantations is needed badly," he explained. "Negroes may make an honest living there. The South has been through one bloody war on account of the negro. It is not ready to repeat."

Mrs. James Crawford, vice president of the California Women's Club, claimed that her opposition to exhibiting the films was based on the best interests of black people:

> The negroes are to some extent a childish race, needing guidance, school-ing and encouragement. We deny them this by encouraging them [through the showing of these films] to believe that they have gained anything by having one of their race as a champion fighter. Race riots are inevitable when we, a superior people, allow these people to be deluded and degraded by such false ideals.

Black editors were quick to point out the hypocrisy in all this. No one interfered with the staging of melodramas like Thomas Dixon's *The Clans-man*, which preached race hatred, and the same newspapers that now edito-rialized against the fight films willingly carried advertising for them. Clergymen who denounced boxing films did nothing to stop parishioners from sending picture postcards of lynchings through the mails. "Had Jeffries won," said Lester A. Walton,

> there would have been no opposition . . . , but as Johnson came out vic-torious the cry "Don't show the fight pictures" was set up which now extends as far as India. . . . The attitude of the anti-fight picture clan reminds me of the reluctance of some mothers to put long trousers on their overgrown sons—fearing that the young men will become too fresh and mannish.*

---

*In the midst of the controversy, Hugh McIntosh reported to the readers of *Boxing* on the impact the Johnson–Burns films had had on nonwhite British subjects throughout the empire the year before. In South Africa, he said, the "Kaffirs" had cheered every blow struck by Johnson and after each showing "congregated together in great numbers around the streets, discussing with great energy and excite-ment the various points of the contest they had seen." This "unrest" so alarmed the authorities that McIntosh had thought it best to stop showing the films altogether. When he heard that similar enthu-siasm for Johnson had been shown by Indians and Ceylonese, McIntosh said, he consulted an "author-ity on Anglo-Indian affairs," who told him not to be concerned. "Physically," he said, "the Hindus and Cinghalese are small and weak, by reason of their enervating climate, and while a section of them are active in treachery, matters physical do not disturb them much."

McIntosh offered no opinion on whether or not the Johnson–Jeffries films should be shown in the United States. "The coloured mind is very susceptible to influence," he assured his readers, "and only time will tell whether the pictures will influence them for good or evil."

In the end, the British found the Johnson–Jeffries films far more inflammatory than those of Johnson–Burns, and they were barred from large parts of the empire, this time including India and Ceylon. The American occupiers of the Philippines followed suit: the Municipal Board of Manila banned the films "in fear of the effect on the Filipinos." (McIntosh, "Pride of the Blacks.")

"What folly!" said the Washington *Bee*. "There are separate moving picture theatres among the whites and blacks in this country. . . . Let the pictures be shown, and if the whites get mad with themselves and fight themselves, they are to blame. The blacks on the other hand will shout among themselves only."*

In the end, the films were shown without incident in several large cities, including Kansas City, Missouri, Detroit, Philadelphia, New York, and Hoboken, New Jersey. Johnson never publicly commented on the issue, but it must have seemed to him that whites were once again intent on keeping him from showing the world what he could do.†

Milton W. Blumenberg, president of the American Cinephone Company, offered him a way to get around them. Commercially viable sound films were still seventeen years away, but Blumenberg's firm was one of several already trying to create talking pictures by showing silent footage simultaneously with specially recorded disks that provided a kind of primitive soundtrack. He paid Johnson to stand before the silent camera in his street clothes and describe the action in the ring—even though nothing he said could actually be heard. Then, eleven days after his visit to the Vitagraph Studios, Blumenberg took Johnson to the New York studio of the fledgling Columbia Phonograph Company, where the champion stood in front of a big funnel-shaped sheet-metal horn to record his version of the fight. Footage of the bout might be forbidden, but no one was going to stop Jack Johnson from telling about it himself. And he would deliver it in the distinctive staccato style he used onstage that made everything he declaimed sound almost like free verse.

> *Ladies and gentlemen,*
> *with your kind indulgence*
> *I will endeavor*
> *to say a few words*
> *in regards*
> *of the great*

---

*On September 30, according to the Chicago *Defender* (October 1, 1910), "Professor Page," principal of the black public school in Moundsville, Virginia, "shortened by one hour the afternoon of school . . . for the purpose of taking his pupils to witness the Jeffries–Johnson fight pictures. The white people are threatening to tar and feather Prof. Page. Great excitement is now prevailing among the lower class whites and better elements of both classes are doing all in their power to avert a clash."

†Some well-to-do whites made their own arrangements to see the films. The millionaire sportsman Joseph E. Widener invited one hundred guests to dinner at his Newport mansion, then showed the Reno film, accompanied by a live appearance by McClellan's Colored Singers.

heavyweight battle
which took place
Fourth of July of this year
between myself
and one of the gamest
and greatest
heavyweights
that ever laced on
a boxing glove.
And the name:
Mr.
James
J.
Jeffries . . .

Johnson went on to offer the highlights of each round with special emphasis on the one-sided finale.

Round fifteen
was the round
that Jeffries met his Waterloo.
And a great round it was.
I fought with all the courage,
all the science
and gameness combined
that I had in me.
And then a left
to the jaw
that staggered Jeffries,
and a right hand uppercut
which knocked him down.
And then he was assisted to his feet
by a few of his seconds . . .
and Jeffries went down,
and I was declared
the winner.
And the sports at the ringside
considered me
one of the greatest

of modern times.
And they all wished me well,
and the battle was fought
strictly on the level
and the best man won.

Like a good many schemes that piqued Johnson's interest over the years, this one does not seem to have paid off. The challenge of synchronizing the footage of the champion speaking with his recorded voice must have been too great for most theater managers, and the result, according to *Moving Picture World*, was not very compelling: "Orally, Mr. Johnson was a success; photographically, and histrionically, Mr. Johnson was not. . . . He just stood there on the screen, unaccompanied by the fistic gestures we naturally look for." But the champion presumably received his check, and was glad to get it.* There seemed to be no big-money fights on the horizon. He'd beaten everybody. Even Jim Corbett had to admit it: "The worst of it is we have no white man in view able to defeat Johnson and two colored fighters won't draw training expenses."

The champion could not help but laugh at the implausible challengers the newspapers came up with. Major-league ballplayers said they'd be willing to take him on in the interest of restoring the white race to its rightful place. So did Earl M. V. Long, the center on Harvard's varsity football team. Corbett himself suggested that wrestling champion Frank Gotch might be prevailed upon to undergo emergency boxing training. A big black former convict was said to be on his way north from Mississippi, his passage paid by planters, who said that if a black man had to hold the title, at least he should be one who knew his place. (Their candidate doesn't appear to have turned up; maybe he was just looking for a one-way trip north.) When former feather-weight titleholder Young Corbett II appeared outside the Little Savoy late one night, spectacularly drunk, shouting that *he* was the "natural defender of the supremacy of the White Race" and daring Johnson to step outside so he could prove it, no one even bothered to wake the champion.†

---

*In an advertisement in the New York *Age*, the American Cinephone Company also sold the record-ing of "the unconquerable Jack Johnson" separately from the film. With each pair of disks came "a let-ter from Johnson in facsimile, certifying to the authenticity of the record and commending it to his friends. . . . You hear Jack Johnson's own voice telling how he won the big fight. Price $2.50." (Brooks, *Lost Sounds*, p. 244.)

†There was even sporadic talk of a rematch with Jim Jeffries. Tex Rickard, always eager for another big payday, mused aloud that Jeffries might do better the second time around because he would feel less "pressure." When a reporter was sent out to Jeffries' home to get a response, the former champion wouldn't even come to the door.

Friends urged Johnson to invest in real estate and build his fortune that way. He briefly scandalized the wealthy white residents of Brooklyn Heights by offering sixty-two thousand dollars for a big ivy-covered mansion at 82 Pierrepont Street (His offer was not accepted.)* Later he paid sixty thousand dollars for Chicago's Turner Hall, a South Side complex of theaters and dance halls at State Street and Thirty-first Street. The previous owners were German immigrant societies, which had barred Negroes from renting the facilities; he planned to turn part of it into a black-and-tan club, catering to blacks and whites alike, to be called the Café de Champion.†

Outside the few big northern cities where the Johnson–Jeffries films were shown, black Americans had little opportunity to see their champion in action. It didn't seem to matter. His impact was everywhere, among all kinds of people. In the all-American *Ziegfeld Follies of* 1910, the master comic Bert Williams played Johnson in a burlesque version of the Reno battle, sandwiched between Fanny Brice singing a song called "Goodbye Becky Cohen" and a chorus of dancers costumed as southern colonels. In the Richmond *Pilot*, a black poet named Lucille Watkins expressed her pleasure in the champion's triumphs in formal verse.

> *Jack Johnson, we have waited long for you*
> *To grow our prayers in this single blow.*
> *Today we place upon your wreath the dew of tears—the*
> *   wordless gratitude we owe.*
> *We kiss the perspiration from your face.*

In North Carolina, others used simpler words to sing the same sentiment.

> *Amaze an' Grace, how sweet it sounds,*
> *Jack Johnson knocked Jim Jeffries down,*

---

*In an uncharacteristically deferential moment, Johnson later claimed he'd never made any offer. "I know my place as a colored man," he told the Chicago *Tribune* on August 6, 1910, "and I do not intend to make enemies among the white people by doing anything as foolish as buying a house at Brooklyn Heights." Besides, he said, he was too "patriotic" to want to live anywhere but Chicago.

†The prospect of Jack Johnson's occupying a home in Brooklyn Heights had been seen by local whites as a threat to neighborhood property values. The black-owned Chicago *Defender* (December 3, 1910) saw neighborhood improvement in his purchase of Turner Hall from allegedly lawless whites: "Although numerous cutting scrapes, murders, etc., have been committed there by whites, the way the place is run has become obnoxious to the neighborhood; the hallways and alleyways have been abused by the patrons of this hall to such an extent that complaints have been made time and again. We are glad that Mr. Johnson contemplates securing the building and thereby putting a better class of citizens in it in future."

Jim Jeffries jumped up an' hit Jack on the chin,
An' then Jack knocked him down again.

The Yankees hold the play,
The white man pulls the trigger;
But it make no difference what the white man say,
The world's champion's still a nigger.

Along a street in Monroe, North Carolina, an old blind beggar was heard rattling his cup and chanting, "Jack Johnson be the champion of the worl'," over and over again. When a white passerby demanded to know what he was singing, he quickly switched to "Oh, blessed be the name of the Lord." In small southern towns, black men who refused to follow white law and custom—often called "bad niggers" by people of both races but with very different emphasis and meaning—now sometimes became "Jack Johnsons." When ordering breakfast in a Negro restaurant, a diner was likely to get a laugh out of the waitress by ordering his coffee as strong and black as Jack Johnson and his scrambled eggs as beat up as Jim Jeffries.*

Word of mouth may have accounted for most of what southern Negroes knew—or thought they knew—of Johnson. But the growth of his legend was also immeasurably aided by the Chicago *Defender*. By the mid-teens, it would be the most widely read Negro newspaper in the nation. Pullman porters carried bundles of papers into the deepest south, where the *Defender* was quietly distributed from churches and barbershops. Its arresting headlines, often printed in crimson—

WHITE GENTLEMAN RAPES COLORED GIRL;
SOUTHERN WHITE GENTLEMEN BURN RACE BOY AT STAKE;
WHEN THE MOB COMES AND YOU MUST DIE
TAKE AT LEAST ONE WITH YOU

—were meant to stir blacks to action, to encourage them to leave Jim Crow behind and come north. The *Defender*'s publisher, Robert S. Abbott, considered Johnson both a personal friend and a hero of the race. In his eyes, nothing Johnson ever did was wrong. When the champion was arrested for driving too fast, the paper asked, "Why not arrest the man who built the auto

---

*According to the writer Larry Neal, the morning after Joe Louis beat former heavyweight champion Primo Carnera in 1935, an exultant black man entered an Evansville, Indiana, diner, ordered his breakfast using this ancient formula, and was slapped and then shot to death by the white man behind the counter. (Neal, "Uncle Rufus.")

for speed violation instead of the innocent purchaser? Then Jack would go free." The Champion Statuary Company of Chicago was speaking for the *Defender* as well as for itself when it assured readers that for just $2.50 they could possess their own eighteen-inch statue of Johnson: "AN ORNAMENT for the home of every negro for he is the first negro to be admitted the best man in the world."

By the end of July, the champion had been training or performing onstage for twelve straight weeks and wanted a few days' vacation before returning to the road. He and Etta, Sig Hart, and Barney Furey drove to Atlantic City, where he rented rooms on the stretch of Boardwalk around Missouri Street reserved for blacks called Chicken Bone Beach. It was the kind of neighborhood Jack Johnson liked best, a garish jumble of hotels and boardinghouses and clubs and cafés that never closed, and he was determined to have the best possible time.

He hadn't seen Belle Schreiber since March—she was still working in Lillian Paynter's Pittsburgh whorehouse—but she'd written him from time to time while he was out west and congratulated him after his victory at Reno. As soon as he got to Atlantic City he wired her money to come and join him. She said she would, she was eager to return to Johnson's fast-moving world. Telling her employer she had a family emergency and would need some time off, she and her maid, Julia Allen, hurried aboard a train for Atlantic City on August 1. Hart and Furey met them at the depot and took them to Young's Hotel, where Belle registered as "Mrs. Jack Allen."

The champion was out strolling the next morning when he happened upon Charles Horner, a former sparring partner who was now working as a chair-pusher, wheeling tourists up and down the Boardwalk. Johnson hired him to bring a woman he identified only as "my girl" from Young's to Ben Allen's, a café with upstairs rooms, where he said he would be waiting for her. "Fully expecting to see a colored girl," Horner said, he did as he was told, and was astonished when a white woman emerged from the hotel and took her seat in his chair. As he rolled her along the Boardwalk, he remembered, Belle "talked very loud and considerable" about her closeness to the champion. After an hour or so upstairs, Belle came down again and Horner took her back to where she was staying. Johnson gave him $1.75 for his trouble.

By mid-August, Johnson and his entourage were back on the road for another six-week theatrical tour with a burlesque revue called *The Rollickers*. They traveled in two big cars. Johnson drove one, with Etta at his side. A second car, with a chauffeur named Jack Mervin at the wheel, carried Barney Furey, Sig Hart and his wife, and Johnson's onstage sparring partner Walter Monahan. Belle Schreiber went, too, but separately, moving from town to town by train—Cleveland, Detroit, Buffalo, Toronto, Montreal, Boston—staying in different hotels as she had the previous spring, and visiting Johnson at the theater for an hour or so before or after most of his matinee performances. One Cleveland hotel employee remembered seeing Belle "on the stage and about the dressing rooms . . . carrying on and kidding with Johnson" in what he called "a disgusting manner."

During the week they spent in Buffalo, Etta seems to have discovered Belle's presence and to have bitterly protested. The landlady at the Munroe Hotel, where she and the champion stayed, remembered her steadily drinking champagne and "grieving" over being "married" to an unfaithful husband. For her part, Belle, still resentful that she was no longer first in Johnson's affections, still searching for a way to pry him away from his new lover, told him Etta was being unfaithful to him. He took the accusation seriously, confronted Etta, and forced her to spend a humiliating day sending telegrams to old friends, asking them to vouch for her character.

Johnson fired Sig Hart that week, perhaps because Etta had insisted she couldn't bear to see every day the little man who made the secret arrangements that kept her rival always available. But as soon as his party reached Canada, Belle turned up there as well.

In Montreal, Johnson tried to cheer Etta by buying her a whole new wardrobe. While he bought his way up and down the aisles of a St. James Street department store, the Montreal *Daily Herald* reported on September 19, a crowd gathered outside.

> One of Jack's retainers came out of the store entrance, staggering under the weight of an armful of parcels, but he couldn't get through the crowd. So a shower of parcels was sent flying out into the hands of a colored gent in the auto.
>
> Then Jack in all his glory emerged. He lifted his big grey felt hat in response to the cheers, beamed his golden smile, and the car rolled off.

The tour went on. In Boston, Johnson and Etta stayed at the Upton, "a colored hotel" near Back Bay Station. Belle had a room at the Brewster; she took all her meals in her room, a bellboy remembered, but she had eagerly shown him a magnificent fur and a silver manicure set and said they were gifts from the heavyweight champion of the world. There, Julia Allen remembered, Belle and Johnson had another fierce quarrel. This time he tore off most of her clothes, perhaps to demonstrate that everything she wore belonged to him, that if she was not willing to accept her subordinate position she would have to move on. She did—and he gave her money to get back to Pittsburgh and resume her life as an inmate in Lillian Paynter's whorehouse.

The tour continued without her, a series of grueling one-nighters in Albany, Granville, and Binghamton, New York; Rutland, Vermont; Wilkes-Barre and Scranton, Pennsylvania. In Scranton Johnson heard from Belle again. She needed help, she said. She had no one else to turn to. Lillian Paynter had been ill when Belle went back to work. Her sister, Estelle, had been in charge. Somehow, Estelle learned Belle had been sleeping with Johnson and instantly ordered her off the premises. Desperate, again without a home or a place to work because of her relationship with the champion, she had moved into her maid's house, then talked Johnson's old friend Frank Sutton into helping her track him down by telephone.* He heard her out and, on October 15, wired her seventy-five dollars. Later she said he also told her to go to Chicago, get a room at Mrs. Graham's boardinghouse on Indiana Avenue, and wait for him. She boarded the train that evening.

He wasn't able to come to Chicago himself right away because he had an appointment at the Sheepshead Bay dirt track in Brooklyn. Having conquered the boxing world, he had now convinced himself that he had the makings of a champion race-car driver as well. "I have the car, the money and the skill," he said, and he was about to test all three against the man who billed himself as the "World's Champion Automobilist," Barney Oldfield.

Once again, color had presented a big stumbling block, and, once again, Johnson had acted as if it did not exist. The American Automobile Association Contest Board, which governed sanctioned races, barred Negroes from the track. The previous December, Jim Jeffries had been given the honor of riding in the first car ever to circle the new brickyard track at Indianapolis. But when Johnson asked to be allowed to take part in a race there on Labor Day, he was told he could not. Might he simply take a turn around the track before the race, then, so his fellow automobile enthusiasts could see him as they had seen Jeffries the year before? No, he couldn't do that, either.

---

*It was not the first time she'd asked Sutton for help. The previous year she'd hidden in his hotel for several days after a customer accused her of stealing his wallet.

Johnson knew the board would never license him to race professionally, so he sent a surrogate to the board's New York office, a white member of his retinue, who filled out the necessary paperwork, paid a dollar, and was issued license number 669 in the name of "John Arthur Johnson." Then the champion issued a five-thousand-dollar challenge to the three most prominent drivers of the day: George Robertson, Ralph Da Palma, and the legendary Barney Oldfield.

Oldfield and Jack Johnson were both sports pioneers. Johnson had shown how well a black man could do in what had been a white man's game. Oldfield had proved that a poor boy could succeed in what had been a rich man's sport. Born on an Ohio farm in 1878, just a few weeks before Johnson's birth, he left school at twelve or thirteen and worked at odd jobs, just as Johnson had, while looking for something exciting to do. Like a good many American boys of his era, he became obsessed with speed. He did well as a bicyclist, leading his Racycle Racing Team in contests all over the Midwest, and he toyed with motorcycles as soon as they were introduced. Then, in 1902, in his very first automobile race, and at the tiller of young Henry Ford's "999"— nothing more than an engine and frame with exposed crankshafts that bathed the driver in oil—he careened past the American automotive champion Alexander Winton to win. Up to that point, American auto racing had largely been the cozy preserve of wealthy sportsmen like Winton and William K. Vanderbilt, for whom racing was an avocation. Oldfield dismissed them as the "Eastern Millionaires." In 1903, he became the first man in America to drive a gas-powered automobile a mile a minute. "Men were white-faced and breathless," said *The Automobile* magazine, "while women covered their eyes." From then on, he was a legend. Automobile-mad schoolboys learned the names of the cars in which he smashed records and overtook rivals: "999," "Bullet #2," "Golden Submarine," "Green Dragon," "Old Glory," the "Blitzen Benz." They worried over his frequent crashes: he was badly injured several times and responsible for the deaths of three people when he hurtled through fences. And they pinned up his photograph: gloved hands gripping the wheel, goggles splattered with mud, a dead cigar clamped between his teeth. Thirty years after he left the track, policemen would still be pulling over speeders and asking, "Who the hell do you think you are, Barney Oldfield?"

There were other similarities between Oldfield and Johnson. Oldfield, like Johnson, was fond of sealskin coats and diamond rings. He was married four times but rarely faithful. "He's a devil with the ladies," his forbearing second (and fourth) wife once told a reporter. He drank too much and brawled too

often. "I've done more fighting getting old Barney out of scrapes," his friend
Jim Jeffries once said, "than I ever did in the ring." And Oldfield once turned
up for a race so badly hungover that he spun off the track on his first practice run. He spent too much, too, ordering two thousand cigars at a time,
handing out five-dollar tips to startled busboys, running up an $845 bill buy-
ing drinks and dinner for all sixty-five members of a marching band that had
greeted him at the depot in San Francisco. Above all, Oldfield shared Johnson's willingness to run big risks, provided that the potential rewards were
still bigger. "I'd rather be dead than dead broke," he liked to say.

Oldfield had jumped at Johnson's challenge. "Automobile racing is my
business," he said, "and if Johnson or any other man in the world has $5,000
to bet he can beat me I am ready to meet him. . . . I will race Johnson for the
same reason Jeffries fought him—for the money it will bring."

Most sportswriters thought the whole thing absurd. It would probably
have been better if Oldfield had refused to race the champion, said a writer
for the Milwaukee *Herald,* because it would have dealt Johnson "the snub he
richly deserves"; on the other hand, he wrote, there was the hope that the
race would permanently remove the champion from the scene, that there
would be "a sprint, a crash and a funeral."

The British editor of *Boxing* saw it differently:

> It is impossible to withhold a certain meed of admiration for the heavy-
> weight champion's quixotic effort. It may, of course, be held that his action
> is only an effort to air his overweening vanity. Admit that much if you will;
> it is patent, if he succeeds in forcing the white automobilists of America to
> accept him amongst them as a competitor on equal terms, that he will have
> done something towards weakening the rigidity of the colour line, and to
> that extent will have been instrumental in making life socially fuller, if not
> for the great bulk of the coloured population at least for those amongst
> them who stand possessed of this world's wealth.

That was precisely what the members of the AAA Contest Board feared most,
and when they figured out who "John Arthur Johnson" really was, they
rescinded his license, mailed him back his dollar, and accused him of having
obtained the permit under false pretenses. Johnson sent the dollar right back,
along with a stiff letter of his own.

> I return herewith the $1 which you returned to me, same being in payment
> of license fee. I conformed to all conditions named on the application blank

furnished me by your office, and will not accept cancellation of my license. You are in error when you state that I obtained the license by trickery or misrepresentation. You cannot blame me for your lack of office system. I will go to the courts if necessary to secure my rights and privileges.

The AAA went further. Since Johnson had no legitimate license, it said, Barney Oldfield must not race with him. If he insisted on doing so, *his* license would be canceled, as well. Oldfield didn't believe they'd do it. "Barney Oldfield is bigger than the AA Contest Board," his promoter, Bill "Soft" Pickens, said. "They don't dare outlaw him." A crew was hired to film the contest. Johnson and Oldfield would split the profits.

In the end, the buildup to the race didn't get the kind of coverage either man had hoped for. Automobile racing itself had received a blow earlier in the month when six onlookers were killed and twenty more were injured during the Vanderbilt Cup race on Long Island. And on October 15, the day before fifteen automobiles filled with "colored sports" welcomed Johnson to Sheepshead Bay, the sports pages were filled with stories about the murder of Stanley Ketchel.*

Public interest was further undercut when several days of cold rain turned the track to mud and forced two postponements. On the morning of October 25, fewer than five thousand people were in the grandstand built for ten thousand. "I am going to win," Johnson said, "or run through the fence trying." Moments before the race began, he spotted a second, unauthorized film crew prepared to record the race. He ordered them to put their camera away; when they wouldn't, he kicked the tripod out from under it, then stomped it to pieces. It might have been better for his reputation had he smashed the contract cameraman's equipment as well.

---

*Ketchel's manager, Willus Britt, had died unexpectedly just twelve days after Ketchel's fight with Johnson. The fighter was devastated, and Britt's successor, the sometime playwright and full-time alcoholic Wilson Mizner, was unable or unwilling to control him. "Steve, my boy," he is supposed to have told his charge, "all I can do for you is improve your mind. Your morals are the same as mine already."

Soon, newspapers were running stories about Ketchel's "dissipating"—drinking, dancing, driving too fast, and spending too much time in the company of what one newspaper called the "almond-eyed celestials" of San Francisco's Chinatown. He fought five more times, including a newspaper decision over the great Sam Langford, but not long after visiting Reno for the Johnson–Jeffries fight, even he began to realize that he was slipping and left the ring to get himself back into shape on a friend's Missouri ranch. There, under murky circumstances never fully explained, he was shot to death by a ranch hand named Walter Dipley. Dipley and his companion, Goldie Smith, were jailed for the crime. Ketchel was just twenty-four. Told he had died, Wilson Mizner said it wasn't possible. "Start counting over the dear boy," he said, "and he'll get up." (Milwaukee *Free Press*, November 19, 1909; Gilmore, "An Ozarks Melodrama"; Edward Dean Sullivan, *The Fabulous Wilson Mizner*, p. 216.)

As the champion drove his long, six-cylinder seventy-horsepower Thomas to the starting line and pulled alongside his rival, he leaned out and said, "Mr. Oldfield, which heat am I going to win? Mr. Pickens said I was going to win one heat." It was a perfectly reasonable question; Oldfield's barnstorming races were often rigged to add excitement. Not this one.

"He did, did he?" Oldfield shouted back, jamming his frayed cigar into his mouth and impatiently revving the engine of his sixty-horsepower Knox. "Well, let me tell you something. If you win a heat in this race, it'll be the one Pickens drives."

When Tim Sullivan, the Tammany stalwart who had been the stakeholder at Reno, waved the starter's flag, Oldfield roared away, spattering Johnson with mud and finishing the five-mile course in 4:44, more than half a mile ahead of the heavyweight champion. Oldfield slowed down a bit in the second heat, perhaps to make sure the cameras could get footage of both cars in the same shot, but he still finished far in front of his rival. There was no need for a third.*

"A sorrier lot of spectators were never seen," one writer noted. "The whites were sore Johnson had no accident, and the blacks were down in the mouth because Oldfield not only romped away with the event, but made joy-riding Jack look like a dead one."

The AAA made good on its threat. Oldfield was indefinitely suspended for "conduct injurious to the welfare of the sport," and for two years would be forced to make his living working county fairs. But Oldfield believed his easy victory over Johnson had been worth it, because it had forestalled the sort of blow to white pride that had been struck by Jeffries' defeat.

> I raced Jack Johnson for neither money nor glory, but to eliminate from my profession an invader who would have had to be reckoned with sooner or later. If Jeffries had fought Johnson five years ago, the white man would have won, and after Jeffries retired he would never have had to fight him again.
>
> If I had ignored Johnson for a year or so, he would probably have gained much experience on the tracks and bought high-powered cars, while I am not getting better from day to day.

---

*According to the special correspondent for *Boxing* (November 12, 1910), Johnson and Oldfield had quietly driven the track together several days earlier in order to be sure they got some compelling if inauthentic footage, "going through the motions of an automobile race behind a touring car that had a moving-picture machine mounted in its tonneau."

> I am glad if my victory over Johnson today will have any effect on the "white man's hope" situation.

"No more of that automobile racing for Jack Johnson," the champion said. "I may be able to drive a car fast on a straight road, but I never will take any chances on the turns like Oldfield does. . . . He has had so much experience in that sort of work that he made a monkey out of me."

The editor of the Chicago *Defender* took in stride Johnson's defeat on the racetrack: after Reno, he wrote, white people probably needed some harmless "consolation." But the editor of the accommodationist Indianapolis *Freeman* believed that Johnson's defeat had been an embarrassment to the Negro race.

> Jack Johnson just had to keep on monkeying until he got what he wasn't looking for. . . . The *Freeman* tried to argue with Mr. Jack, fairly prayed to him, virtually saying, please don't make a fool of yourself. O, please don't Mr. Jack. . . . Well, Barney put him out and nobody is sorry. We are all chagrined, however, . . . to think Johnson insisted on this display. We hope he is cured, and that he stays cured.

Johnson was cured. But he had never seen the contest in racial terms. Like the one-sided battle at Reno, it had simply been a case of the best man winning. The manner in which Oldfield had outdriven him, he said, "convinced me that I was not meant for that sport." He did not, however, promise to slow down on country roads or city streets.*

Back in Chicago in late October, Belle Schreiber was waiting for Johnson, still without a home or a job. Her sister, Gladys, had come with her from Pittsburgh. She, too, was homeless—and pregnant. He met both women at the Hotel Vendome on South State Street. He was sorry Belle's relationship with him had caused still another madam to turn her out. But why depend on madams? he asked her. She should go into business for herself. "He said to me to get my furniture and open a flat," she remembered, "and

---

*Oldfield remained close to Jim Jeffries, and upon returning from a hunting trip with him in the Sierras in June of 1911, he announced to the world that the ex-champion now believed he'd been poisoned before the fight in Reno. Johnson hadn't really beaten him after all. Jeffries himself would make the same charge in *Two-Fisted Jeff*, his as-told-to autobiography, published in 1929, also claiming he was *still* feeling the effects of the mysterious potion seventeen years after it was administered. Almost no one believed him.

I might as well make the money as to give half of what I was making to someone else, and for me to keep a couple of girls . . . and make money in that way."

He volunteered to help get her started. She picked out a flat in the Ridgewood Apartments at Twenty-eighth and Wabash. There were sixty-eight flats in the building. Some were brothels, others were home to call girls; as Bertha Morrison later testified, "I don't think [a man] could make a mistake by ringing a bell." Morrison and Lillian St. Clair, both old friends from the Everleigh Club, became Belle's first employees. Johnson paid the first month's rent—there were no leases at the Ridgewood; no one wanted anything incriminating in writing. Then he escorted Belle to the Marshall Ventilated Mattress Company, where they picked out furnishings—four beds and mattresses, tables, linens, pillows, commodes, rugs, curtains, even framed pictures for the walls—for which he paid $1,196.53. He also made arrangements with the Heileman Brewing Company to supply beer off the books and gave her an additional five hundred dollars for incidental expenses. For these acts of generosity he would one day be made to pay a heavy price.

On Sunday evening, November 7, two days before Election Day, Johnson was in Manhattan, where Tammany Hall had contracted with him to make a whirlwind tour of black churches in support of Alderman Tom McManus—known as The McManus—and Thomas G. Patten, the Democratic candidate for Congress.

Johnson was still at least nominally a Republican and had recently campaigned on behalf of Edward H. Wright, the first black candidate for alderman in Chicago, at some risk to his reputation. Advisers had told him to stay out of politics in the months leading up to the Jeffries contest: things were tense enough, and he didn't need new enemies. But he had refused to keep silent. "I was told not to come here," he'd told one black Chicago crowd.

I was told I was a man before the public. I replied I was a man fighting against the world. I'll be surrounded by 30,000 or 40,000 people on July 4, and some will holler "good" and some will holler "bad," but the most will holler "bad," and the more they holler "bad" the braver I'll be. That's Jack Johnson's motto. That's what this man Wright's going to do in local politics—lick 'em. You can put it down, Johnson and Wright will win.

Johnson did. Wright did not, though he remained a behind-the-scenes power in the GOP—and a prominent attorney whose services Johnson would one day need.*

But the champion was not averse to switching parties if the Democrats in one place or another seemed more likely to act on behalf of black people than the Republicans—especially if there was a little something in it for him as well. And, like many black Republicans, he had been genuinely angered by the way Theodore Roosevelt had handled an incident in his native Texas in 1906. Three companies of the 25th Infantry (Colored) that had fought alongside Roosevelt's Rough Riders in Cuba had been assigned to Fort Brown, Texas, that year. Resentful of their presence, the white citizens of nearby Brownsville barred the troops from saloons, shoved them off sidewalks, beat them when they resisted. One summer night, shots were fired in town, killing one white man and wounding another. The mayor blamed the black troops. So did Roosevelt. When none would confess to knowing anything about the shooting, he ordered every single soldier—167 men—dishonorably discharged without so much as a hearing. Until that moment, T.R. had been a hero to most black voters, in part because he had invited Booker T. Washington to dine with him at the White House five years earlier. But afterward, many felt betrayed, and some northern Democratic bosses were still working hard to exploit that feeling.

The one-day canvass of black churches did not go as smoothly as Johnson's Democratic handlers would have liked. Four black ministers refused to turn over their pulpits to the champion because of his well-publicized private life. When he and his party swept into the Bethel A.M.E. Church at 336 West Sixty-second Street, they found three hundred men and women on hand for a prayer meeting. The pastor blanched, but before he could object, the Montreal *Daily Herald* reported, a local Democratic leader named Lee raced up the aisle, and launched into an introduction of the champion.

---

*Johnson made a still more impassioned appeal to a group of black churchwomen gathered in Quinn Chapel during the same campaign. "The black race is the greatest race ever," he said, according to the Chicago *Tribune* on April 1, 1910. "In every walk of life there is a black man coming out winner— black ministers, black school teachers and black bicycle riders. Yes, and other people. We want to stick together like that other great race, the Jews. They've all flocked together and stuck. . . . If we stick together as a race we can elect Mr. Wright. . . . Every other race, east or west, is against you and me. The odds are against us, but we can win if we stick together. Now ladies, go home to your sweethearts and husbands as a personal favor to me, and see they find out what it means to elect a man like Mr. Wright—what an honor to the race."

Johnson so enjoyed campaigning that he seriously considered running for alderman himself.

"Sisters and brothers," said Lee. "The church must do its part in this campaign. Let us not become excited, but I am here to introduce a man who came thousands of miles to tell you folks what to do at this next election. He is the greatest man that ever lived."

Then, with a sweep of both arms, Chief Lee called Johnson to the reading desk. Behind the speaker sat Jimmy Hagan, leader of the district, and "The" McManus.

"Mr. Roosevelt, he travels on one thing," roared Johnson. "He ate dinner with Booker T. Washington." A thump of the fist imperiled the Bible stand. "It's one of the greatest honors for a colored man to sit with a white family, but it's an insult for a white man to take a colored man in a private room to meals. Let Roosevelt be sincere from the heart and say, 'Booker, come dine with my wife and family.' But when he dines 'alone,' he is not a man.*

"When Roosevelt was in Cuba, our great black army saved him. After that he comes home and hears one man was killed in Brownsville and expels the whole army. I don't want no favors but only fair play for the race. Ladies, remember your meat bill. I am here to fight for you and your men, just as I was on the Fourth of July."

Meanwhile, word had spread that Johnson was in the neighborhood, and hundreds of men, women, and children had streamed out of the surrounding tenements to see him. Someone broke a window. People began climbing inside. Others tore the door off its hinges and rushed up the aisle, cheering for "Our Arthur." The McManus could not make himself heard. The champion thought it best to leave. "As the taxi in which Johnson had been carried swiftly from prayer meeting to prayer meeting rolled up San Juan Hill into Tenth Avenue," the newspaper continued, "a horde of negroes followed."

In public, Jack Johnson remained a hero to his admirers. But in private, his behavior seemed more and more unpredictable, its legal ramifications steadily more threatening. The lawsuit lodged against him by Norman Pinder had just been dropped: neither Pinder nor any of his witnesses turned up in court in October, perhaps because Johnson or people working for him had paid them off. But George Little's suit still hung over his head. So did the

---

*This was rhetorical overkill. Theodore Roosevelt's wife and daughter were both present when Washington dined with the president.

one lodged by the impresario Barney Gerard. A New York sculptor named Cartaino Sciarrino had recently gone to court as well, seeking four thousand dollars for a full-size statue of the fighter Johnson had commissioned and then refused to pay for.

In November, Johnson, Etta, and Walter Monahan began yet another arduous series of one-night stands through New England. An eighteen-year-old French "automobile mechanician" named Gaston Le Fort had been hired to do the driving. His presence would soon trigger a near-tragedy.

It is impossible to know precisely what happened over the next few weeks. Only scattered hints appeared in the newspapers, but clearly, events were spinning out of control. The trouble seems to have begun at Lawrence, Massachusetts, on November 12. The champion went onstage as usual, punched the bag, and sparred—then could not remember a single line from the speech he'd been delivering nearly every day since July. "I couldn't seem to understand what was going on," he said afterwards. He ran offstage, frightened and agitated; poured cold water on his head to cool down; and gave his revolver to Etta, telling her to keep it away from him "as something told me I might do harm with it." A doctor who was called told him he badly needed a rest.

Two days later, at Haverhill, he forgot his lines again. At Lowell on the seventeenth, after drinking from a bottle of beer, he became violently ill and convinced himself that someone was trying to poison him, just as he had been sure George Little had sought to poison him at Seal Rock before the Jeffries fight. He was committed to a sanitarium for at least one night.

Friends "fear he has fought his last battle," the New York *Times* reported; while Johnson looked well enough, his constitution had been undercut "by the rapid pace at which he has been living." He tried to be reassuring after he was released. "I'm all right," he said, "except that sometimes I don't know what is going on around me."

But he wasn't all right. In Portland, Maine, on the nineteenth, he broke down again, refused to go onstage at all this time, threatened suicide. If Etta hadn't been with him, he said, and willing to nurse him day and night, he would have hanged himself or leaped from the window of his room. The hotel doctor was called. He diagnosed Johnson to be suffering from "aggravated nerve exhaustion" and told him he must not drive the hundred frigid miles to his next engagement at Rumford Falls, Vermont. Instead, the New York *Times* reported, "to the astonishment of the natives the big fellow nonchalantly ordered a special train, and the party of three whirled over the Maine central to Rumford Falls, with tracks ordered 'clear ahead.' "

The next day, the Milwaukee *Free Press* ran a stern editorial.

JOHNSON SUFFERS FROM SERVILE FLATTERY

Traveling burlesquers have passed the word along and their stories of the capers of the negro reflect no credit to him. Johnson, with his easy-going ways, love of adulation, and hankering for white trash company, has been living it up almost continuously since his Reno victory.

It is the old, old story, with only the scenario and characters changed. Pugilistic champions by the score have gone the same route that Johnson is traveling. . . . Black fighters especially are prone to fall for the servile flattery of that class which delights to fawn upon successful gladiators. . . .

The champion says, though, that he has seen the light and will switch before it is too late. He will have to, or else the black bugaboo of the prize ring will be removed without the necessity of developing another white man's hope.

That light was still only dimly seen. On November 25, Johnson and Etta were in New York, on the way home to Chicago, when the police came for him again, this time with a month-old charge of disorderly conduct. At the Gaiety Theater back in October, a few days before he addressed the New York prayer meetings on Tammany's behalf, he had asked Miss Henrietta Cooper, "a white woman appearing in a burlesque chorus," to join his traveling show. When she said no, he grabbed her wrists, she told the police, and only her loud protests made him let her go. Johnson claimed it was a frame-up, and, according to the New York *Times*, "drew from his pocket a roll of bills as round as a teacup, peeled off a $1,000 bill and tossed it on the desk, remarking as he did so: 'I guess that'll hold me for a while.' "*

Etta Duryea, who had spent the last week nursing her increasingly disturbed lover, cannot have been pleased, either at learning that he had made a clumsy pass at a chorus girl or by the humiliating newspaper stories it inspired. Still, she returned to Chicago at his side.

There, Johnson did his best to appear as if all was well again. He had a doctor pronounce him in tip-top shape. "The only thing that worries me is my health," he assured a reporter. "It's getting so good I'm afraid *it* will challenge me." He planned to spend at least one thousand dollars on Christmas gifts for friends and family, he said. On December 15, he learned that his Chicago

---

*Like so many of the cases lodged against him, this one does not seem ever to have reached the courts.

lawyer, Gustav Beerly, had obtained a divorce for Etta. She and Johnson were now free to marry.

But all was not well. Again, the details are sketchy and sometimes contradictory. But it seems clear that a friendship of some kind had grown up between Etta and Gaston Le Fort, the young Frenchman who now drove her around town each day. It would have been understandable. Etta was a handsome woman, often lonely, resentful of the champion's serial infidelities, perhaps even angry enough about them to want to show him that she, too, was attractive to others. Certainly she would have been happy to have a sympathetic ear.

Johnson grew suspicious. Chronically unfaithful to the women with whom he lived, he was bitterly resentful of anyone who even hinted at disloyalty to him. When Clara Kerr had run away from him in Los Angeles the first time, he'd tracked her all the way to Tucson, and when she left him again in Chicago, he'd spent weeks drinking heavily and scouring Pittsburgh and New York for her, looking for revenge. When Belle Schreiber had suggested that Etta was two-timing him the previous summer, he had believed it and forced her to prove her innocence.

Now, when he had to go to Pittsburgh on business for a couple of days, he hired a detective to follow Etta and the chauffeur while he was gone.

He left on December 19. The next day, he got a bit of good news. Part of Barney Gerard's suit had been thrown out of court. Sig Hart, not Johnson, had signed the original contract with Gerard, and the champion's attorney was able to make the case that Hart had merely been a "messenger boy," unauthorized to represent Johnson.* That evening, he was at ringside at Pittsburgh's Labor Temple, where he had arranged a six-round fight for Walter Monahan. He had taken it into his head to turn his young sparring partner into his own personal "white hope." Monahan needed schooling, Johnson admitted, but he hit as hard as anyone in the division. Any challenger who wanted to fight Johnson would have to beat Monahan first, the champion said, and as Monahan's manager, he would be entitled to a piece of the action. To make sure his protégé looked impressive in his first East Coast outing, Johnson had hired for his opponent his own former sparring partner, Kid Cotton. But things didn't go as planned. Cotton was a journeyman at best—

---

*Gerard would eventually win, however, and Johnson would be fined $3,489. He was in exile overseas when the judgment came down, and it is unclear whether he ever paid it. (Washington *Post,* January 31, 1915.)

he had a career record of nineteen fights with just one win—but he was abler than Walter Monahan and may have resented his former employer's attempt to build up Monahan's reputation merely because he happened to be white. In any case, Cotton had his opponent reeling from the first round, and only Johnson's shouted advice to clinch and hold on kept Monahan upright until the final bell. Johnson and Cotton cursed each other all through the fight.

Meanwhile, a man named Brooks Buffington was trying to get into the arena, a drunken white southerner later said by the New York *Times* to have been "hostile to the colored race." He had a revolver in his pocket and had hoped to shoot the champion the moment he climbed into the ring to introduce his fighter. The ticket taker turned him away: he was too drunk to be let in. After the fight, Buffington went to Frank Sutton's hotel and café, where a reception for Johnson was under way, but couldn't get in there, either, because of the big crowd of the champion's friends. Frustrated and angry, he'd staggered into a nearby saloon and loudly cursed Johnson. When a black patron named Robert Mitchell objected, Buffington shot and killed him. This genuine attempt on Johnson's life can only have intensified his fear that people were plotting against him.

The Christmas holidays in 1909 had been marked by chaos, as Hattie McClay, Belle Schreiber, and Etta Duryea all found themselves at Tiny Johnson's home at the same time. Christmas Eve 1910 would be far worse.

Back in Chicago that afternoon, Johnson drove to Lippman's jewelers, where he purchased something, perhaps an engagement ring. He may have been planning to ask Etta to marry him. But then he got a telephone call at home from the detective he'd hired. Etta and the Frenchman had been seen together at several South Side cafés.

Here the stories diverge. According to the version Johnson later gave to the Chicago *Tribune,* he got a second call moments later, this time from Etta, who was at the Pekin Café and in what the *Tribune* called a "hysterical condition." He rushed there, found her badly beaten—presumably by Gaston Le Fort—and sent her in his car to the Washington Park Hospital. Later that night, he charged, the Frenchman had tried several times to break into his Wabash Avenue home. Johnson's mother and sisters, he said, had scared the driver off.

Federal prosecutors would later insist that Johnson himself had beaten Etta while drunk, and the preponderance of evidence suggests that they were right. According to his friend Roy Jones, the champion turned up at his door in the Levee District late that night, clearly frightened that Etta would file a complaint against him. Johnson told him he and Etta had had "a disagreement . . . a fight," and implored Jones to visit her in the hospital as soon as he could, "to intercede and bring [us] together again." Later, asked in court why he had been entrusted with these delicate tasks, Jones simply said that Etta "always had a lot of confidence in me." But like Johnson, Jones was a black man who lived with a white woman; he was also a brothel keeper and therefore presumably expert at talking abused women out of going to the law. (In the end, he was never allowed into the hospital to see Etta.)

Meanwhile, Johnson got out of town. At eight o'clock the next morning, he picked up Belle Schreiber at her new apartment and, with Barney Furey, set out for Milwaukee, where he was scheduled to appear onstage that afternoon. A new chauffeur named Charles Lumpkin was behind the wheel. It was bitterly cold, and Johnson was ill as well as hungover. He thought a drink might steady him. They stopped in Libertyville, Illinois, long enough to get him some brandy. It made him feel worse. He asked Lumpkin to pull over on a bridge. Johnson urinated blood. They continued on to the St. Charles Hotel, where he and Belle registered once again as husband and wife. The champion was too ill to spar that afternoon or evening. The next day, the Milwaukee *Free Press* played Johnson's illness for laughs and he went along, grateful that the press hadn't yet caught wind of what had really happened.

SNORT OF SQUIRREL WHISKEY PUTS
JACK JOHNSON DOWN FOR THE COUNT
SMALL TOWN BOOZE SCORES CLEAN CUT VICTORY
OVER THE BLACK DEMON AND CAUSES HIM MORE TROUBLE
THAN JEFFRIES OR BURNS EVER DID

On his arrival here at 1 o'clock he was forced to take to bed. He was routed out at 5 o'clock just long enough to allow him to appear at the Star Theatre and make a short speech, and after that he took to the hay again. He expects to be in good shape today.

"Mercy me, that sure was some red-eye they handed me. . . . You see it was pretty chilly drivin' that buzz wagon up here so I thought I'd take a little swing of ol' corn to warm me up a bit. We stopped at some small town along the way and I asked the barkeep for a drink of his best whiskey. He handed out a black bottle and remarked that it was guaranteed to be the best in the land. Well, all I got to say is if it was his best, I'd hate to tackle the rest of the stock. Any drink of that stuff will kill an ordinary man at ten paces."

The whiskey must have been unusually bad because it was plainly evident that Johnson felt the effects. Beads of sweat stood out on his close cropped head and it was with difficulty that he was able to move around in the afternoon.

Early the following morning, Johnson took the train back to Chicago and was at his home shortly after noon when Gaston Le Fort appeared suddenly on the front porch, waving a pearl-handled pistol and shouting that he was going to "wipe out the whole goddamned Johnson family." Johnson yelled for him to go away, then telephoned the police. The chauffeur left. Two officers turned up. Johnson told them he thought Le Fort had also tried to poison him in Massachusetts. While the policemen were talking to Johnson, the Frenchman reappeared. They seized him, took his weapon, searched his pockets. He had a note from Etta at the hospital asking him to bring her some things from her trunk, and a letter from him to her, written in French.

Why did the champion think this man wanted to kill him? the police asked. Johnson said he didn't know.

"Sure he does," said the Frenchman as they led him away. "Sure he does."

Le Fort told the police he had fallen in love with Etta. He had visited her in the hospital, where she had asked him to pawn a diamond ring and bring her at least a hundred dollars in cash. She had also given him money to spend from time to time. Johnson's sister Jennie told reporters she had seen her do it.

Johnson followed the police to the central police station and visited the prisoner in his cell. No one knows what they said to each other, but four days later Le Fort was released after paying a fifty-dollar fine for threatening the champion.

Etta, her eyes blackened and her face badly swollen, blamed no one for her condition. She told the admitting physician that she had hurt herself falling from a streetcar, and she never deviated from that story. All week Johnson commuted back and forth between Chicago and Milwaukee by train, but no one knows whether he tried to visit Etta. A nurse at the hospital recalled that there had been a long-distance call for her from Milwaukee one evening. She had been reluctant to leave her bed to take it at first, saying it must be her mother, with whom she did not care to speak. But Mrs. Terry lived in Brooklyn, not Milwaukee, so it seems likely it was Johnson or someone calling on his behalf. In the end, she took the call. On the twenty-eighth Johnson called the Chicago *Tribune* and claimed that the whole thing had been "a misunderstanding." But in a Washington *Post* story headlined "CASTS JOHNSON ASIDE: Former Companion Prefers the Black Man's Chauffeur," he was said to have declared himself "through" with "the white woman whom he introduces as his wife."

On New Year's Day, the champion paid Etta's bill and checked her out of the hospital, nonetheless. A nurse remembered that her face still showed the marks of her beating.

According to the Washington *Post,* Johnson had planned to bring Etta home to Wabash Avenue that morning, but Tiny Johnson had refused to have the woman the paper called "the Duray person" in her house. Her son would have to choose between his mother and his white companion. Johnson chose Etta, staying only long enough to gather a few things, then storming out to join her somewhere else in the city.

He surfaced briefly three days later in a Chicago courtroom. George Little's suit had come to trial. Johnson testified that he and his ex-manager had once been so close Little had called him "Little Jackie," and when times were hard, had sometimes shared a room with him.

"I never slept with a nigger in my life!" Little shouted.

Johnson jumped up from the witness chair at that, fist cocked, and had to be ordered to sit down. The jury failed to reach a verdict. Little would eventually drop the suit, but the charge that Johnson was ungrateful to those who helped him would persist.*

Several newspapers ran articles that week hinting at Johnson's personal troubles. "Daily dalliance with the grape and its attendant evils combined with the wearisome grind of stage work . . . are having a serious effect on the giant black," said the Milwaukee *Free Press* on January 6. "Erratic events are developing fast in Jackey Johnson's life," the Pittsburgh *Press* reported the same day. "They sound ominous. Old sports can well shake their heads. They will tell you, if asked, that a run of domestic and other escapades usually prefaces the beginning of the end of a star's fistic existence."

No one knows how Johnson and Etta were reconciled, but on Wednesday

---

*George Little never regained his status in the First Ward after his fifteen months at Jack Johnson's side. By 1912, he had been banished from Chicago and was running a workingman's saloon in Lancaster, Ohio.

afternoon, January 18, 1911, they walked into the office of the marriage clerk in Pittsburgh's City Hall and applied for a license to marry. She was divorced, she said. He said he had always been single. They were married that evening in the parlor of Frank Sutton's hotel. Alderman John Pugasi officiated, and was said to have been paid five hundred dollars for performing the ceremony and promising to keep it quiet.

Tiny Johnson and her daughters were bitter. They believed that Etta was after Jack's money; that she was liable again to be unfaithful to him, as they believed she had been with the French chauffeur; that Johnson's marriage to a white woman could only result in more trouble for him and his family.

Etta's people were horrified at the news. In its lurid posthumous profile of her, the New York *World* probably overstated its impact on them, but not by much. Etta's folly in falling under Johnson's spell, it said, had been the cause of it all:

> She must have known . . . that her act had ruined her younger sister's romance, that this spirited and estimable girl had insisted upon releasing her fiancé from his given word, that her brother was suffering a self-imposed ostracism from his social comrades and young women friends. She knew, too, that she was taboo with every relative she had. Not even her cousin, Florette Whaley—who had eloped with the Rev. Jerre Cooke, the Long Island clergyman who deserted his wife in running away with the young choir girl—had sent her a word of condolence.

Etta's father was said to have refused to speak to his daughter again and, already ill, to have taken to his bed out of mortification. Only her mother kept in touch, and when relatives asked how her daughter could have done such a thing, she told them an injury to Etta's spine in childhood had destroyed Etta's ability to think clearly and made her "not altogether accountable."

The marriage—and the identity of the bride—were to remain a secret to spare further damage to the feelings of both families.

For a few days, at least, back in Chicago, Johnson seemed determined to get his life under control. Thanks to him, Belle Schreiber was now in business for herself. He contacted Hattie McClay and amicably settled his affairs with her as well, handing her a check for five hundred dollars (more than nine thousand dollars today) in exchange for all the letters and photographs he'd sent her over the years—plus a promise never again to go to the press to complain about him.

He seemed clear about business matters as well. When Hugh McIntosh offered him 60 percent of thirty thousand dollars to fight Sam Langford overseas, he indignantly turned him down. "I don't understand McIntosh," Johnson said.

I informed [him] some time ago that I would require as much as Burns received. . . . Surely, if he could afford to give Burns $30,000, he can offer me an equal amount to box in a big city like Paris or London. . . . On my way up I made up my mind that when I was on top of the ladder I would treat others just as I had been treated. I am on top now and I am not asking a cent more than was asked by the champion who won before me. . . . Let Langford take a share, same as I did.

If his demands weren't met, he'd leave the ring. "And when I retire, I'll stay retired. There will be no getting me to come back to regain the supremacy for the black race."

Then he announced he was going west for two months, back to San Francisco and a rented eight-room cottage at Forty-eighth Avenue and K Street. There, just a block from the ocean, he and Etta, his brother, Charles, Walter Monahan, and Monahan's new bride all planned to rest away from the Midwest's bitter cold. All three of his cars were going with him: two racers and a big "pleasure machine."

But if he really had resolved to straighten up, that resolution did not last long enough for him to get aboard the train. He continued to pull up in front of the Ridgewood Apartments in his conspicuous car so often, honking his horn for Belle Schreiber to come down and join him, that the other tenants complained to the buildings' owner, John Worthington, who was finally "compelled to see Jack Johnson and have him take the girl out of the apartment." Belle had lost yet another home because of her relationship with the champion. What was she to do now? Johnson tried to talk her into joining him in California. She refused, she later explained, because when she confronted him with the rumor that he and Etta were legally married, he had denied it, but his mother had told her it was true. Instead, she vanished into a whorehouse at 1229 D Street in Washington, D.C., run by a woman named Grace Sinclair. It must have seemed to both of them as if Belle Schreiber and Jack Johnson were finally finished with each other.

Johnson got little rest on the West Coast. As soon as he reached San Francisco and had seen to the unloading of his automobiles, a local car dealer had one of them seized for nonpayment of an old bill for twenty-five dollars. When the champion tried to take it back by force, a policeman threatened to shoot him. "All right, white man," he said. "I'll be good." He paid the bill and reclaimed his car. A week later, he was arrested for speeding and for refusing to stop when told to do so by a policeman. When he protested the stiff five-hundred-dollar bail imposed on him, the judge would not reduce it, and the chief of police warned him to "watch your speedometer and keep out of trouble."

Three weeks later, he was driving through Golden Gate Park in his Thomas Flyer when he came upon two men in a gleaming new Simplex. The man behind the wheel was a Simplex demonstrator named Johnny Burge. His companion was a potential customer from the South. Johnson pulled alongside and asked Burge if he'd like to race. The customer bristled. "If you beat that nigger," he told the salesman, "I'll buy the car." The two roared off and were clocked side by side at sixty-two miles per hour by a traffic policeman, who arrested both drivers.

Johnson failed to turn up in court to answer the charge the next day. Two days after that, on March 25, Acting Peace Judge A. B. Treadwell, citing the fact that Johnson had now been arrested at least fourteen times on similar charges, sentenced him to twenty-five days in the county jail at Ingleside. The champion refused to ride in the prison van like an ordinary prisoner and hired a car to drive him to jail instead. Most newspapers were gleeful. The *Police Gazette*, which had once championed Johnson's cause, now praised the judge for the way he'd dealt with "the big, black swaggering bully." The sheriff put him to work whitewashing cells, currying horses, and cleaning out the stables. An enterprising movie cameraman turned up one day, convinced that white filmgoers would flock to see exclusive footage of Jack Johnson behind bars, maybe even shoveling horse manure. The champion refused to cooperate. "You all get away with your picture machine," he shouted, "and don't mind coming around again."

Johnson pleaded with the judge to be allowed out early. Etta was ill, he said. So was Charles. He had been a model prisoner. He promised never to exceed the speed limit again. The judge agreed to cut his sentence to eighteen days. When he was released, on Easter morning, a Los Angeles *Times* reporter asked if he was going to be good from then on. No, he said. "I think I will drive as fast as ever." All he wanted now, he added, was to get out of California and then never to return.

. . .

On May 15, he was in Manhattan, where police arrested him for having Illinois, not New York, license plates on his car and for going too *slowly* around Columbus Circle. "Pinched again," he said. "If I go fast they arrest me, and now it seems like if I go too slow they do the same. Next thing, somebody'll arrest me for being a brunette in a blonde town." This time, the magistrate agreed with Johnson: he'd been unfairly treated by policemen out to get him because he was black and famous. The charges were dismissed.

Johnson was in town that week for a special event at the New York Athletic Club, where a promoter named Tom O'Rourke had organized a round-robin tournament to name a "World's White Champion." The hunt for some white man—*any* white man—who could conceivably take back Johnson's title had been going on ever since he'd won it from Tommy Burns. Jeffries' failure had only intensified the effort.

"In the heat of the search," John Lardner wrote, "well-muscled white boys more than six feet two inches tall were not safe out of their mothers' sight." Jim Corbett spotted Oscar W. Stuckey, a twenty-year-old Floridian who stood six foot nine and declared that beating the black champion was his "sacred duty." The Los Angles *Times* on March 26 called him the "Florida Hercules" and with no evidence at all alleged he had SLEEP WALLOP IN BOTH MITTS. He didn't, however, and soon returned to his father's turpentine business. Joe Choynski came up with an overgrown seventeen-year old Missouri farmboy named Miles McLeod, whom he took on a vaudeville tour, sparring gently with his discovery onstage, then listening with a suitably grave expression as the youngster told respectful audiences what he planned to do to Johnson once he got him in the ring. At the end of the tour, student and mentor split the proceeds; Choynski returned to retirement; and McLeod went back to Missouri without ever having fought a single authentic round.

Twenty-three hopefuls had answered Tom O'Rourke's invitation to the New York tournament, weighing from 105 pounds all the way up to 280, but on the evening of May 26, only eleven actually turned up to fight. Johnson sat in a special ringside box, trying to keep from laughing as the big, poorly trained white challengers pounded away at one another. The winner was a big New Yorker named Al Palzer.* It was an entertaining evening but, as the

---

*According to the veteran trainer-manager Dan Morgan, the most promising entrant seemed to be a young Englishman named Fred McKay. He was big, and in the first round of his bout with a club fighter named Sailor White, he looked good and moved fast as well. Every manager and trainer in the

New York *Times* reported, "there was nothing uncovered that will cause John A. Johnson to lose any sleep." There was no money to be made in fighting anyone he'd seen, the champion said. "Nobody wants to see me win." He needed new fields to conquer. A trip overseas would provide them, and maybe, away from America and its pressures, he and Etta would have a chance to start over.

---

club edged toward his corner, dreaming of the big money they could make matching him against Johnson. In the second round Sailor White hit him on the jaw and knocked him cold. "You should have seen the boys melt away," Morgan remembered. "He had to carry his own bucket to the dressing room when he came to." (Lardner, *White Hopes*, pp. 32–33.)

CHAPTER NINE

THE BLACK MAN
GARBED IN BLACK

O N JUNE 5, 1911, Mr. and Mrs. Jack Johnson set sail for England. With them went a Negro chauffeur named Charles Brown and two sparring partners, Monte Cutler and Walter Monahan, as well as a pair of racing cars, twenty trunks, and a small safe containing Johnson's cash and his wife's jewels.

"There was consternation at the offices of the North German Lloyd Steamship company," the New York *Times* reported, "when it was discovered that the chief engineer's room on the *Kronprinz Wilhelm* . . . had been booked by an outside agency for 'Mr. John Johnson and wife.' "

"Is it the colored pugilist?" an officer was asked.

"We are afraid it is" was the reply.

"What are you going to do about it?"

"Do? We can't do anything, the passage is booked and the money is paid."

Barron Wilkins came to see the Johnsons off. So did many other friends and several reporters, including one working for the Washington *Post*. The Johnsons' cabin was filled with flowers.

Mrs. Johnson was not visible at first. Over in the corner was a well-equipped jewelry establishment. Mr. Johnson moved it and this revealed the background of the store as his white wife. On her left hand reclined a small carload of diamonds. Her shirt waist front was littered with similar decorations, but the fingers of her right hand were almost bare. Even to be liberal one could hardly say she had more than $8,000 there. While her protector exuded conversation she daintily picked at $8 worth of toast and coffee. She was not feeling chipper.

"If you had paid a large sum of money for a nice stateroom on the upper deck of the *Kronprinz Wilhelm*," the Milwaukee *Evening Wisconsin* asked on June 6:

and then had figured on having a nice neighborly party in the large cabin that you did not feel you could afford and suddenly were confronted with

Jack Johnson and his wife beating it to the dining room when the gong sounded for dinner, wouldn't it make you wish some white hope was on board to make him eat in his stateroom?

What the New York *Times* called "the delicate question" as to whether the Johnsons—who had paid $750 for their first-class passage—would be permitted to dine alongside their fellow passengers was finally resolved by the chief steward, who set up a small table for them in the dining saloon at the foot of the companionway leading from the promenade.

In the end, stormy seas kept the Johnsons in their stateroom at most mealtimes. But they did take arm-in-arm walks on deck, and Johnson was amiable even when asked the most intrusive questions.

Why did he wear a ruby on one hand and an emerald on the other?

"I always dress port and starboard when at sea," he explained with a grin. "Because in the night when I'm out on deck and it's dark, people can see the lights and tell whether I'm coming or going."

Scores of passengers turned out each morning to watch him spar in the ship's gymnasium: "No race prejudice came to hinder the curious from watching him at work," wrote one shipboard correspondent. "All of those on board took a chance on losing caste and race supremacy by taking in the show." And the champion generously bought drinks for everyone who would drink with him. "I wish we'd seen more of him," said one man described as a "Canadian millionaire." "He is unobtrusive and his intelligent conversations are worth listening to."*

Johnson met the British press at Plymouth wearing a crisply cut brown suit, brown gloves, and gleaming patent leather boots, one of twenty new outfits he'd had specially tailored in Chicago at a cost of $3,480—roughly $64,000 in today's terms—so that he could look his best in London during the festivities surrounding the coronation of King George V.

He looked forward to the kind of mostly warm British reception he had received during the days when he was pursuing Tommy Burns. Everything he and Etta did in London made news. Reporters followed them to their fashionable rented flat near Shaftesbury Avenue, and pursued the champion's car

---

*Memories of the newspaper fuss made over Johnson's traveling first class on an ocean liner would become confused with reports of the sinking of the *Titanic* the following spring, and the legend grew that Johnson had been refused passage on the fatal voyage. Blind Lemon Jefferson performed a song about it that was later recorded by Huddie Ledbetter—Leadbelly. In it, Johnson is refused passage by the *Titanic*'s captain, who says, "I ain't hauling no coal." When Johnson hears that the ship has gone down, he dances on the dock with glee.

to "Messrs Hamilton, the well-known jewelers in the Strand," where Johnson startled the clerk by stripping off all his jewels, flinging them on the counter "like so many lumps of coal," so that they could be cleaned and polished, then hurrying off again without even waiting for a receipt.

Throngs gathered outside the Johnsons' flat every day. British boxing writer Trevor Wignall called on Johnson there and never forgot two things about his visit: the "crowds of women obstructing the passage-way" in hopes of getting inside, and his remarkable conversation with the champion once he'd pushed his way through them.

> It ranged from politics to astronomy and it ended with Johnson requesting me to strike him with all my might in the stomach. This came about as the result of a paragraph he had read in one of the newspapers [alluding] to an alleged weakness in his mid-section. . . . He requested me to judge for myself by punching him. I did so: striking his stomach was like hitting a piece of corrugated iron.

A writer for *Boxing* came away impressed as well. Although Johnson was "a big slate-coloured mass of humanity," he was otherwise very different from the man portrayed by "negro-haters," a "merry, unaffected, shrewd and likeable man" who offered his "views on life in a carefully reasoned, philosophic fashion which affords instant proof that there is not only plenty of brain inside that shaven skull of his but that that brain has also undergone careful cultivation." Johnson was a fine swimmer, an expert driver, and a skilled musician who played classical duets with his wife, a "most excellent pianist"; *Il Trovatore* was his favorite opera, and he never let a day go by without listening to the Miserere on the gramophone that went with him everywhere.

And when the Johnson's took their special sixty-dollar grandstand seats in Piccadilly for the coronation procession on June 23, cheering Londoners gathered around to gawk and cheer. "It got me, it was so grand," Johnson told a reporter after the royal procession had passed. His only regret, he said, was that the king hadn't fought for his crown "instead of just happening to be born in a palace."

A few days later, one newspaper reported, the Johnsons strolled into the Trocadero restaurant for lunch and found Jim Jeffries and his wife, also in London for the coronation, already seated there.

> The fighters saw each other, but Jeffries glared stonily in the other direction and refused to recognize Johnson. The noise of the gay restaurant

immediately ceased. Johnson avoided a scene. His wife scintillating with diamonds, he passed Jeffries and took a table at the farther end of the room. Jeffries appeared highly uncomfortable and hurriedly finished his meal and departed, leaving Johnson laughing over his wine.

On the afternoon of July 4, the British press was invited to the Oxford Music Hall to see the champion spar onstage. He had just signed with a British promoter named James White to fight Britain's best heavyweight, an Indian Army veteran named "Bombardier" Billy Wells, whom the *Police Gazette* accurately described as "a good second-rater." The bout was scheduled for October 2 at the Empress Theater at Earl's Court. Once Johnson had beaten Wells, he said, he planned to undertake a tour of British overseas outposts—India, the Straits Settlements, Australia—organized by his old associate Hugh McIntosh. While he was about it, he added, he would "polish off all the white trash and niggers . . . lying around loose," including Sam McVey and Sam Langford. Then, with no further worlds to conquer, he would retire.

The idea behind the performance before the press, according to the London *Times,* was "to break [in] Johnson lightly, so as not to frighten the enormous numbers of 'the Fancy' who had assembled to inspect the terror of their profession." First, an orchestra played while films of the champion's training camp at Reno flickered on a vast screen, "swift, beguiling, pictures of Johnson, in various stages of domesticity, feeding chickens and playing with a baby." Then the screen was rolled up to reveal Johnson in the flesh, sparring with Monte Cutler against a sylvan backdrop. The *Times* continued:

[Johnson] was about five or six stone heavier than the well-trained pugilist of the films. [I]n a year or so, if he does not take better care of himself, he will become too "streaky" (to use Jem Mace's phrase) ever to get back into hard condition and will degenerate into a vast, human punching bag. For all that, he gave an engaging display of artistry in the three short easy rounds with his sparring partner, who thumped away to the best of his ability. All the great gifts of the great boxer born and made were there, the panther-like glide in and out of distance, the straight infallible left, and the power of timing an antagonist to the third place of decimals. He does not withdraw into himself like the average American boxer . . . but stands up . . . and makes the most of his height and reach. It was pretty to see how, in every little mix up, he contrived to be inside the unhappy Cutler who could never get away without taking both body blows and hooks to the head. . . .

On the other side of the Atlantic Johnson passes for a "flash nigger," a type not to be encouraged by those who have kept ten millions of black men in subjection to the dominant race. In private life, however, the conqueror of Jeffries is an amiable person with a fund of quaint humour and a sportsmanlike trust in human nature (as long as it is not a question of dollars) which reconciles one to his golden teeth and the multitude of diamonds which cause him to resemble a starry night. It is to his credit that he feels at home in England, which he believes, not without reason, to be inhabited by a race of sportsmen.

Afterward, a reporter asked the champion if, when he entered the ring overseas, he saw himself as fighting for his country.

"Fight for America?" Johnson answered. "Well, I should say not. What has America ever done for me or my race? Here I am treated like a human being."

"Are you going back to America?"

"Not until I have to, and then as soon as I get through I am coming right back here."*

The following day, July 5, Johnson rented a flat at Luxborough House, an apartment-hotel in Paddington, just off Regent's Park. Etta was to spend the next few weeks there while Johnson toured provincial music halls. To keep her happy in his absence, he ordered an $18,000 royal blue limousine with $2,500 worth of interior fittings, including "a solid gold arrangement" of flasks and cigarette boxes. Brown, the chauffeur, stood ready to drive her anywhere in the city she wanted to go.

It didn't work. Left alone to brood, Etta retreated into depression. There were angry arguments whenever Johnson came home. Neighbors complained. On July 22, the landlady ordered the Johnsons to vacate the premises, weary of what she called the champion's "lively conduct." They told her they would go, but when she returned to clean the flat on August 5 she found Etta still inside, pleading that she was too ill to move. The flat was "filthy," the landlady said, and she would later collect thirty-seven pounds from Johnson for smashing her crockery.

---

*On August 25, Johnson made a second appearance at the Empress Theater to drum up interest in the bout. Among those who came up afterward to shake his hand was twenty-year-old Manuel II of Portugal, who had just lost his crown when the cities of Lisbon and Porto voted to establish a republic. Someone asked Johnson how it had felt to meet an ex-king. "Sir," he answered, "I tried to put him at his ease. . . . I've never been hard on a guy just because he's fallen."

The couple shifted to a hotel near Piccadilly the next day. Two weeks later, Johnson suddenly canceled his theatrical tour, telling the press his wife was suffering such "great nervous prostration that the attending physicians fear for her life."* They would proceed to Paris instead, he said, where he would train while staying close to her bedside.

It was actually Johnson who feared for her life, and with good reason. She had tried—or threatened—to hurl herself from the window of their hotel room. And, if a later interview with her mother is to be believed, it was Johnson's insistence on shifting to Paris that had helped drive her to it. Etta had bitterly opposed the move, perhaps because she feared that her husband would prove unable to resist the city's pleasures. "Before she left for Paris," Mrs. Terry said, "she told me she would rather die than go." They went anyway, but from that moment on, Johnson would live with the constant fear that his wife might harm herself.

Johnson knew that Negro boxers had been big attractions in Paris since his old rival Sam McVey had begun fighting exhibitions there in 1907. And the French fascination with them had only intensified after McVey and Joe Jeannette staged a grueling "finish fight" in which they knocked one another down a total of thirty-eight times before the battered McVey, no longer able to see his opponent, was forced to quit after the forty-ninth round. Sam Langford's arrival to fight McVey in the spring of 1911 further excited Parisians: one sporting magazine headlined its coverage LE CHOC DES DEUX SAMS (The Clash of the Two Sams), and the French press was filled with overwrought stories about black American heavyweights—their power and dark skin and supposed exoticism.†

Now the French press welcomed the heavyweight champion back to Paris as the greatest of them all. He made the most of it. After checking into the Grand Hotel, he invited the French reporters—over whom he towered—up to his suite to watch him bathe and dress before making his first appearance onstage at Magic City in Montmartre. They were suitably awed. One pronounced him "as handsome as a Congolese Apollo." Because he was naked,

---

*This last-minute decision would cost him $7,500 for breach of contract.

†When the San Francisco promoter Sunny Jim Coffroth visited Paris in 1911, a French reporter asked him why battles between superb fighters like these drew such big crowds in France and such small ones back home. "For one simple reason," Coffroth said: "blacks are detested in America." McVey spent almost four years fighting in France, then three more in Australia, where Langford also spent the best part of two years. (Claude Meunier, *Ring Noir*, p. 37.)

wrote another, one could admire his chiseled arms and shoulders, and his legs, so "beautiful and slender." A third, watching as two valets helped him into evening dress and carefully put all his diamonds in place, compared him to an African king. This private display made the champion two hours late for his performance at Magic City, but the crowd in evening dress cheered him anyway as he sparred gracefully with the handsome young French favorite, welterweight Georges Carpentier.

For the next few weeks Johnson continued his nightly exhibitions at Magic City and worked out each afternoon in front of paying crowds at the Pelican Boxing Club on the Rue des Acacias as well. All his appearances were well attended, but it was clear to boxing insiders that Johnson wasn't working very hard. The reason was simple: Bombardier Wells was genial and good-looking and much loved by his British fans, but he was also inexperienced, fatally unenthusiastic about finishing his opponents, and the frequent victim of a sort of stage fright that made him dangerously vulnerable in the early rounds.* Johnson did what he could to build up the gate, praising the Bombardier's courage to any British reporter who would listen, talking with a straight face of his opponent's youth and speed and science, pretending always that he faced a serious challenge. But he was fooling almost no one. And when an American writer took him aside and asked about his lax training, Johnson let his guard slip a little.

"How about your training?"

"For Wells?" he smiled. "I don't have to do much trainin'. I never did have to train much. I didn't train but a month for Jeffries . . . "

"How about Wells?"

"I'll beat him easy."

Photographs published in the French papers that month show the Johnsons having what looked like a wonderful time: watching the balloon races at Saint-Cloud, Johnson in a handsome suit and straw boater, Etta in furs and a vast hat set off with a white egret feather at least a foot and a half long; seated in their new ninety-horsepower Thomas Flyer racing car somewhere in the French countryside; laughing together as they help clear a herd of sheep from their path in the Bois de Boulogne.

---

*American observers differed as to his skills. Jim Corbett, ever hopeful that Johnson would be defeated, said he believed Wells was the white man who could "dangle the scalp of the illustrious darky." The American heavyweight Frank Moran, on the other hand, called Wells "all chin from the waist upwards" and would prove it by knocking him cold in 1915. (Dartnell, *Seconds Out*, p. 21.)

But behind closed doors, things remained tense and troubled. Etta's gloom had not lifted. Women waited for Johnson at the Grand Hotel, just as they had haunted the sidewalk outside their first London flat, just as she had feared they would, and she knew that Magic City was surrounded by all the temptations of Pigalle. Hattie McClay, Johnson's companion on his first visit to the City of Light, had never felt that she could interfere with his nighttime adventuring. Etta was determined to do so. She was his *wife* and so insisted that they move out of town and that her husband come home to her every night, to a furnished house in the quiet suburb of Neuilly. Johnson did so, but reluctantly. Soon a newspaper story quoted unidentified sources close to the champion as saying that Etta's "watchfulness" was keeping him from "seeing 'the sights' and spoiling his good time. They hint that he is somewhat peevish with Mrs. Johnson, too. . . . Jack is giving up Paris rather than fall out with her."*

On September 23, Johnson and his wife headed back across the Channel. They were on their way to a new training camp in Epping Forest on London's northern edge to make final preparations for the big fight, now just nine days away. Every one of the ten thousand seats in the Empress Theater had been sold. But as the Johnsons settled into their new quarters, there was growing reason to believe the bout would never take place.

The heavyweight championship had been caught up in the intricate world of British ecclesiastical politics. The Reverend F. B. Meyer—the charismatic young Baptist secretary of the Free Church Council, a coalition of churches that did not conform to the doctrines of the Church of England—had been looking for a national issue around which its members could rally. A recent campaign to ban the works of Karl Marx and the American economic reformer Henry George had failed. Meyer hoped a crusade against the evils of prizefighting in general and the Johnson-Wells contest in particular might be just the thing.

On Sunday, September 15, he signed a letter calling on all Nonconformist clergymen to devote the following Sunday's sermon to arousing the public's conscience against a spectacle that was sure to be bloody and degrading, sullied by gambling and high stakes and meant only to "gratify that craving for

---

*She did not entirely cramp his style, apparently. "Paris!" he told a reporter on his return to the United States. "There's the place that makes an old man young and a young man old. Only Cook County, Chicago, has it beaten." One evening at the Café de l'Opéra, he said, he "danced the Turkey Trot and the grizzly bear from midnight until dawn." Both dances were officially illegal in Chicago. (*Police Gazette,* January 13, 1912.)

the sensational and the brutal which is inconsistent with the manhood that makes a great nation."

Clergymen all over Britain followed Meyer's suggestion and called for the fight to be stopped. So did the fifth Earl of Lonsdale, president of the National Sporting Club, though for a different reason. The bout would be a mismatch, he said; sending Bombardier Wells into the ring against Jack Johnson would be like matching a two-year-old against a three-year-old.

Still, the editor of *Boxing* was confident that what he called the "Sackcloth and Ashes Brigade" would fail in the end to stop the bout. Boxing remained the best possible test of British manhood, he argued; it would be a sign of weakness to ban it.

Then race was injected into the debate. George Swinton, a London County councillor, started it. A fight between "a white soldier and a black champion," he said, was likely to spark "quite unnecessary trouble," and he urged Winston Churchill, the home secretary, to keep it from taking place. The Rev. J. H. Shakespeare, secretary of the British Baptist Union, raised the stakes still further. If the fight went forward, he wrote to the London *Times*, "white and black will be pitted against each other in anger, revenge and murder, especially in those lands like America in which the negro is the gravest of all problems. . . .

> There can be no greater disservice to the negro race than to encourage it to seek glory in physical force and in beating the white man. Booker Washington is incessant in the cry to his people, "Educate, educate." Slowly, they are climbing the steep path but every voice which exalts animal passion in them is that of an enemy. It matters not to us if an Englishman is beaten, for we have proved our place in the realm of courage, endurance, service, art, and learning. But to a race which has not as yet achieved glory it is a crime to turn its ambitions to such glory as can be found in the prize ring.

The Rev. Meyer now felt free to include race in his bill of particulars as well. "When white opposes black it is not a game of skill," he told the press, "for the black nature has more fire in the blood than the white and has more passion. . . . It introduces the element of animalism."

Still others now saw the proposed contest as a threat to the empire itself. R. W. Rose-Innes, a South Africa–born Briton, explained the problem as he saw it to readers of the *Times:*

> We have hitherto . . . attempted with success . . . to maintain the supremacy of the ruling caste—viz, the European element. To affect this by weight of

numbers is, of course, impossible, but there are other means. Surrounded, as we are, by natives in all stages of civilization, from the sea to the Zambesi, we seek to establish our supremacy, by force of character and by codes of conduct . . . based upon principles that we can stand up for and defend.

To attempt to do this by precept, if not backed by example would be futile and worse than futile, for we should be held up to scorn and derision by the natives who think—and there are many such—and who draw conclusions and comparisons.

How can we look them in the face when such a fight is permitted to take place in the heart of the Empire? . . .

Why pit black against white at all, and why do so with all the odds in favour of the black man? And why permit the contest to take place in London before a European audience and with official sanction? The baneful effects will be felt far beyond the spectators who witness the fight. It will make the position of the white man more difficult still in distant parts of the Empire.

Johnson was disgusted. English preachers knew nothing about boxing, he said, and even less about black people. Boxing simply pitted one individual against another. It had nothing to do with race. But still more Nonconformist clergymen had rallied to Meyer's cause, and many of their Anglican counterparts now felt called upon to join them. On September 20, the archbishop of Canterbury himself wrote to Churchill, urging him to halt the fight. The bishops of London, Oxford, Ripon, Durham, and Truro echoed his call. They were joined by Sir Robert Baden-Powell, the founder of the Boy Scouts, as well as the Lord Mayor of London, and the headmasters of Rugby, Dulwich, Mill Hill, and Taunton schools.

On September 24, Churchill gave in. "I have made up my mind to try to stop the Wells-Johnson contest," he told his wife. "The terms are utterly unsporting and unfair." The director of public prosecutions promptly took out summonses against Johnson and Wells, their managers, and promoter James White. All five were ordered to appear at the Bow Street Court of Summary Jurisdiction to answer the home secretary's charge that they planned a "breach of the peace."

The following morning, Johnson was getting a rubdown after his first morning's workout at the Royal Forest Hotel in Chingford when a detective-sergeant from Scotland Yard knocked on the door. "Come right in," the champion called out. "You've got a summons for me. I know who you are or you might have had a rough time."

The detective advised Johnson to hire a solicitor. The champion thanked him for his advice but said he'd prefer to speak for himself.

So many people gathered outside the court on the morning of September 28, eager to have a look at the champion and his challenger, that traffic in Bow Street came to a halt. Johnson's automobile had to inch its way to the curb. Etta sat beside him, one newspaper reported the next day, dressed in "a Paris costume of dark brown, with a long ermine fur and many diamonds."

The *Daily Mail* reported every detail of the morning's proceedings.

From the moment when Jack Johnson, with his retinue of secretaries, sparring partners, and massage men behind him, shouldered his way through the multitude and entered the court he was the dominant figure of the proceedings. All the interest concentrated on this huge coloured boxer with his golden smile, which shone round on everybody, including the Rev. Meyer. It was apparent that even Mr. Marsham, the magistrate, behind his official bearing was amused by the . . . champion.

Johnson, Wells, their handlers, and James White stood shoulder to shoulder before the bench. When they were told to be seated, Johnson alone remained on his feet.

During the opening statement by the Solicitor General [Sir John Simon], Johnson leaned easily against the rails of the dock behind him, letting his eyes wander in search of acquaintances, and when he caught a familiar face his upper row of gold teeth flashed out in his capacious smile. When he had occasion to speak he leaned toward the magistrate. His words were clear; his sentences as straight to the point as one of his "left-hand leads."

When the solicitor general misspoke, saying that "Jackson" held the heavyweight title, the champion interrupted, " '*Johnson,*' if you please."

Sir John bowed to acknowledge his error, then went on to argue that the proposed fight was a financial matter rather than a sporting venture; a violent contest, not a scientific exhibition, meant "so [to] reduce the other [man] that when he was knocked to the ground he could not rise."

The first witness for the government was Superintendent McIntyre, the police officer in charge of the Earl's Court area, whose testimony was to be based on his reading of newspaper accounts of prizefights. The magistrate asked Johnson if he objected. He did.

Yes, I object because these papers printed in England are no authority upon contests in America. In these records, which the honourable solicitor holds in his hand, it is said Jack Johnson fought Jim Scanlon 14 rounds. The contest only lasted eight rounds; the records are wrong.* From these records the witness is simply refreshing his mind. Reading a paper refreshes his memory of things he has perhaps never known.

The objection was overruled, and the officer was allowed to testify as to his belief that the upcoming match would constitute a breach of the peace.

"I want to cross-examine him now," Johnson said as soon as the policeman had finished. The magistrate—whom Johnson carefully called "His worship"—again advised him to leave that work to the better-qualified "legal gentlemen" present.

The champion thanked the "honorable solicitors" but went ahead on his own.

"Are you familiar with Queensberry rules?"

"No I am not."

"Did you say I knocked Tommy Burns out in the fourteenth round?"

The officer turned pages in his bound volume of newspapers.

"I object to your looking at that book every time I ask you a question," Johnson said sharply. "You are simply refreshing your memory."

The officer apologized, saying he'd meant to say only that the fight *ended* in fourteen rounds. There had been no actual knockout.

"He admits he made a mistake," said the magistrate.

Johnson went right on: "Why do you say that when Jack Johnson and Mr. Wells box on October 2 there will be a breach of the peace?"

"I said I feared there might be."

"Did Sam Langford and Bill Lang [when they fought at the National Sporting Club in London] cause a breach of the peace?"

"I do not know."

"Did you see that fight?"

"No."

"Have you ever seen any championship contest?"

"No."

"Then you have no idea what they are like."

"No."

---

*The record was wrong, as Johnson said, but the actual number seems to have been seven.

With a dismissive wave, Johnson turned to the magistrate and said, "The witness can go now."

His cross examination had been "a sharp, swift attack, very skillful for one not experienced in courts," according to the *Daily Mail,* but in the end it made no difference. While the magistrate's court had been in session, the London Metropolitan Railroad, which owned the land on which the Empress Theater stood, had persuaded the High Court to issue an injunction against the promoters of the contest.

There would now be no championship purse, no return to Australia, no victory tour of imperial outposts.* Instead, Johnson and his wife would live out of trunks for nearly three more months, moving around the Continent and back and forth across the Channel while he performed in theaters and cabarets for smaller and smaller fees. Rumors began to spread that Johnson was penniless, that he had had to pawn his wife's jewels to pay their passage back from Paris to London and had been forced to travel third class. Back in the United States, Tex Rickard told the press he thought the champion had gone through more than $100,000 since Reno.

Johnson bravely denied it all in an open letter to his old friend Tad Dorgan. "Does this appear like a man who is broke?" he asked. "I can write a check any day in the week for $100,000. Besides this, I have property in the way of automobiles and jewelry. I value my cars at $25,000 and jewelry at $60,000, and I have a few thousands in my pocket. Outside of that, I'm kind of shy."

The champion's indiscreet remarks about how much better he was treated overseas than at home, unwisely delivered in London on America's Independence Day, had been reprinted widely in the States. So had subsequent stories about the Bombardier Wells debacle and the Johnsons' domestic difficulties. And in December, when the Chicago *Tribune*'s H. E. Keough learned

---

*Back in the summer of 1910, one of Jack Curley's London promotions had nearly suffered the same fate. He had brought the American wrestler, Dr. B. F. Roller, across the Atlantic to take on an Indian grappler, the Great Gama, at the Alhambra Theater. On the eve of the match, Curley remembered, he received a summons from the Foreign Office. There, a pleasant young man told him he'd allow the match to go on since it had already been announced, but henceforth "there must be no more matches between Indians and Caucasians in England. The danger that the Indian might triumph was inimical to the security of Great Britain's hold on the subject races. It would not do to get it into the heads of these races that one of their numbers could humble a white man at anything. Did I understand? I did."

Several "Indian potentates in . . . huge and colorful turbans looked on from boxes" at the theater the next evening, Curley wrote, but "the match, sad to relate, did not last long. Gama, having completed what apparently was a prayer ritual in his corner, grunted once or twice and, with a cry, leaped at Roller, hurled him to the mat, flattened him . . . , and broke three of his ribs." (Curley, "Memoirs.")

that the champion was finally setting sail for home, he typed out some dog-gerel aimed at putting Johnson in his place.

And so you're coming home, Jack, to settle down for life,
Resolved forever to eschew the pugilistic strife.
Your title, we suppose, Jack, you mean to let it lapse,
Or pass it on to Langford, or to Fireman Flynn, perhaps,
O, well, you're twenty-one, Jack, and free—and though not white,
We're not inclined to interfere—do what you think is right.

You'll find that when you return, Jack, no prejudice obtains
Against the colored person with a normal set of brains,
Who picks his line of going, understanding all the while
That a stingy inch of license does not contemplate a mile.
If you will cut the pace, Jack, below the second speed,
We'll try to get ourselves to think your presence here we need.

But if you come in strong, Jack, the way you used to come,
You'll find you'll be as welcome as a crutch or a bum.
If you will flaunt again, Jack, the garish and bizarre
As if you do not realize just who and what you are;
If ever you repeat, Jack, the things you used to do,
We'll try to make it plain, Jack; this is no place for you.

The Johnsons landed at New York three days before Christmas, bringing with them an English valet and sometime secretary named Joseph Levy; Charles Brown, their American chauffeur; plus a Pomeranian named Baby, three cars, fourteen trunks—and a mountain of debt. The European journey, meant to add to the champion's fortune, had depleted it. Jack Johnson needed to make some money.

Once again, Jack Curley turned up to help provide it. Like Johnson, he had recently had his ups and downs. His hopes for a lucrative victory tour by Jim Jeffries had been dashed by Johnson's victory at Reno. In September of 1911, he'd put on a hugely successful wrestling show at Comiskey Park in Chicago, a two-out-of-three fall grudge match between George Hackenschmidt, the "Russian Lion," and America's favorite, Frank Gotch. Curley sold ninety thou-sand dollars' worth of tickets and took home fifteen thousand dollars as his share. "The American won," Curley recalled, "the championship remained in this country—and all was right with the world." Then rumors began to fly:

Hackenschmidt had wrenched his knee in training; Curley had insisted that the bout go on anyway because he'd already spent his share of the advance sale; the match had been a fake. No arrests were ever made, and Curley indignantly dismissed all the complaints as "synthetic squawk." But the Illinois legislature banned professional wrestling in the match's aftermath, and Curley found himself back in the fight game.

He was still the manager of record for Jim Flynn, whom Johnson had knocked out five years earlier. Curley had largely lost interest in Flynn after that fight. But while Johnson was overseas, the hard-hitting "Pueblo Fireman" had banged out four knockouts. Curley reassessed his man's money-making potential and got him a fight with young Carl Morris, whom the papers were hailing as the first serious white heavyweight challenger to come along since what some writers called the "tragedy" at Reno.

The hunt for a "white hope" hadn't been going well. Size now seemed to be everything. If a white fighter with sufficient skills couldn't be dredged up from somewhere, the argument went, surely one could be found who was simply big enough to make victory inevitable.

The veteran Ohio sportswriter William A. Phelon, who had been at ringside since the end of the bare-knuckle era, explained the folly of their reasoning:

> Nowadays every manager who has unearthed a white hope brags mainly of his enormous size. "My man is 6 feet 4, and weighs 245 pounds," is the one and only argument they seem to use when proclaiming the virtues of a new protégé. They seem to think that a champion must be a mastodon— that he must be at least as large as Jim Jeffries, last of the great white champions—and any boxer around the 170-pound mark is regarded with pity and derision by these impresarios. It is the Reign of Fat—not even the Reign of Beef and Brawn—and these elephants are a sight to look upon. They are immense, bovine, amiable-faced young men, clumsy and shambling, falling over their own feet—the sort of monsters whom the old-time football coaches used to play guard positions. The strength is there, of course, but they don't know what to do with it. They can hit a dreadful blow, but they don't know how, when, or where to hit. What earthly good are they, excepting to wallop one another.

There had been some genuinely freakish entries in the white-hope sweepstakes. An eight-foot-tall vaudeville attraction named George Suger made headlines briefly, one writer likening him to a "playful skyscraper"; and Fermin Arrudi, Suger's counterpart from Spain, who weighed four hundred pounds, was briefly considered a possible challenger, though his sole qualification seemed to be that he'd once eaten eleven dozen eggs at a sitting.

Carl Morris appeared to be the most plausible contender. He was a big, amiable twenty-four-year-old railroad engineer from Sapulpa, Oklahoma, who had supposedly jumped down from his cab on the day Jeffries lost to Johnson, vowing, "I'm going to quit this job right here. I'm going to be a fighter and whip the Negro sure." He stood six foot four, weighed 240, and was billed variously as the "Sapulpa Giant" and the "Original White Hope" (though he was only an honorary Anglo-Saxon, since he had some Cherokee ancestors). He scored seven early-round knockouts in a row in his native state. Two of his victims—Marvin Hart and the man who handed Tommy Burns his first defeat, Mike Schreck—were celebrated if long past their prime. When Curley and Flynn challenged him to fight at Madison Square Garden in September of 1912, the Oklahoma oilmen who backed him eagerly accepted.

A few writers worried that Morris might be being moved along too fast, but the New York *Evening Sun* was rapturous when he arrived.

A WHITE HOPE IN THE MAKING
CARL MORRIS AND HOW HE TRAINS AT ALLENHURST
AN UNUSUAL MAN
HE IS MIGHTY OF BODY AND PLEASANT OF FACE
HAS A WISE MODESTY
SAYS HE IS NOT ABLE TO BEAT JACK JOHNSON TODAY

He wasn't able to beat Jim Flynn, either. Morris was big and he hit hard, but he was slow and clumsy, too, and utterly unprepared for the kind of onslaught an old pro like Flynn could still mount on a good night. In what the Los Angeles *Times* called "the bloodiest fight ever seen in this city"—so bloody the referee had to change his shirt after the fifth round—Carl Morris' career as a serious contender ended and Jim Flynn's was reborn.*

On the strength of this much-headlined victory, Curley recalled, "I immediately launched a boom for Flynn as the logical contender for Johnson and took him on tour at the head of a troupe of fighters and wrestlers." The tour

---

*Morris stayed in the game for thirteen years, derided sometimes as the "Sapulpa Bleeder." He won more fights than he lost—even beating Jim Flynn twice in 1914—but he also served as a hapless name "opponent" for up-and-coming youngsters like Jack Dempsey, who took just fourteen seconds to knock him out in 1918.

opened—and closed—in Oklahoma; even in Choctaw and Muskogee few proved willing to pay good money to see the conqueror of Carl Morris shadowbox. An easy win over a California journeyman named Charlie Miller added nothing to Flynn's luster. And when he went to Salt Lake City for a December 27 bout with Tony Caponi—another second-rater he'd already beaten—and Curley's old friend Billy Porter, sporting editor of the *Herald-Republican,* refused to help publicize the mismatch, even Curley did not put up much of an argument.

But then his luck changed again. Flynn knocked out the hapless Caponi early, just as Porter had scornfully predicted he would, but Porter wasn't there to see it. He'd started drinking in a bar across the street early in the evening, and by the time the main event began was too drunk to leave his stool. His job was now in peril. Curley, convinced that he could still snatch a public-relations triumph from an otherwise meaningless evening, hurried to the newspaper office, told the night watchman that Porter had sent him, commandeered a typewriter, and banged out a blistering assault on everyone involved in the one-sided fight, including himself. Then he signed Porter's name to the story and handed it to the compositor.

When it appeared in the next morning's paper, Billy Porter was badly hungover but deeply grateful for Curley's apparently selfless act. "What a friend!" he kept saying, "What a friend!" How could he ever repay him? By interviewing him for the paper, Curley said. "Gladly," Porter answered. "That's the least I can do." Porter's interview with Curley was reprinted all over the country. In it, the promoter issued still another challenge to the champion. Flynn was so sure he could beat Johnson, Curley said, that he would fight him for free.

Curley got back to Chicago three days later and was attending a New Year's Eve party at the College Inn when he got a call from the champion just before midnight. "Come right out to my house to a real party," Johnson said. "There are a lot of your friends here who want to see you."

The promoter hailed a cab. When it pulled up in front of 3344 South Wabash, the champion was waiting in the doorway. He embraced Curley and ushered him inside. "Gentlemen!" he said to the other guests, black and white. "Meet your old friend Jack Curley! I have just accepted his offer to defend the heavyweight championship . . . against Jim Flynn!"

"Accepted my offer!" Curley wrote later. "I hadn't *made* an offer!" He did so right away: thirty thousand dollars (again, the sum Tommy Burns had insisted on for fighting Johnson) plus eleven hundred dollars for travel and training expenses and one third of the film rights for a forty-five-round contest to be held on July 4, 1912, two years to the day after Reno.

Johnson eagerly accepted. His troubles were multiplying. Most were trivial annoyances of the kind to which he'd long since grown accustomed: his sister Lucy's landlord was suing him for $110 in back rent; the Elite Laundry Company won a judgment against him for three months' worth of unpaid bills; a young woman named Ruth Mehl filed suit for damages, claiming he had permanently injured her when he swatted his specially rigged punching ball out into the audience at Chicago's Plaza Theater.

But then in mid-January, Etta's fifty-eight-year-old father, David Terry, died after a long illness in Brooklyn. He had not spoken or written to his daughter since learning of her secret marriage to Jack Johnson. Etta was devastated. She thought it best not to attend his funeral, but she had once been close to him, and after his burial in Hempstead, on Long Island, she made a private visit to Brooklyn to see her mother. "I begged her to stay with me," Mrs. Terry remembered.

> But even as I begged her I could not give her assurance that all her old associates would forgive her [for marrying Johnson]. I begged her not to go back to the life she was living. I begged her to stay—just with me. But she just kissed me, and said she was afraid that would not do—could not be thought of. And she went away.

Three weeks later, on February 10, the Terry family's hometown paper, the Brooklyn *Eagle*, carried a story headlined CHAMPION JOHNSON WED FORMER MRS. DURYEA, WELL-KNOWN IN HEMPSTEAD. The Johnsons had been married more than a year and had managed to keep Etta's identity a secret all that time. But someone in the clerk's office in Pittsburgh had got hold of their marriage license application and gone to the authorities and then the press with it, suggesting that Johnson had lied when he said he'd never been married previously. If not, who were all those women he'd introduced as "Mrs. Jack Johnson" over the years?

Similar stories appeared in papers all over the country in the next few days. The Washington *Post* reported that Etta had once been "one of the popular society girls" of Hempstead, "a pronounced brunette, particularly attractive. It is generally understood that she would have inherited a portion of the estate of her grandmother, Mrs. James P. Whaley. She probably will now be ignored."

Reporters badgered the champion for further details. When a writer for the New York *Herald* called him at home in Chicago, Johnson refused to say anything about Etta's family or previous life. "Who she was before I married her concerns nobody but me," he said, "and I'm not bothering my head about it." He also refused to answer any questions about what the *Tribune* called his "alleged previous marriage . . . to a negress" except to say that "in the presence of my wife, my mother and my sister, who are all sitting here, I want to say I never was married until I married this woman."

Four days after that, Secret Service agents knocked on Johnson's front door. They had a warrant for a diamond necklace. Since his hoboing days, Johnson had often been at odds with local law enforcement. Now, for the first time, the federal government was interesting itself in him. Sometime soon after their return from Europe, he and Etta had attended a party at which she showed off her husband's latest gift, a necklace of fifty-five white diamonds. He boasted to the other guests that he had paid nearly two thousand dollars for it in London and had managed to get it past the customs inspectors unseen. Word got around. Someone alerted the Treasury Department. The Johnsons now faced smuggling charges. He offered to pay four thousand dollars—twice the purchase price—to have the charges dropped. The Treasury Department refused. Arraignment before the U.S. Customs commissioner was set for July.

Reeling from all these blows, Johnson returned to the vaudeville circuit, traveling with Etta through the Midwest this time: Omaha first, then St. Louis and Kansas City, Missouri. There, when no hotel would house them, the manager of the Century Theater and his wife moved out of their upstairs apartment so the Johnsons could have somewhere to sleep. But on opening night, a long line of would-be ticket buyers was kept waiting in the cold along Twelfth Street long after showtime. Etta had tried to kill herself again, this time by swallowing carbolic acid. A doctor was called. Her stomach was pumped. Johnson refused to go on until he was sure she would recover.

The Johnsons struggled on—to Indianapolis, then Louisville, and Cincinnati, where a 128-pound housepainter named Joe Clark ran out into the street and punched the champion in the head as he drove past. A reporter asked Clark why. "Just did it because I don't like him," he said. He was not arrested. In Pittsburgh, on April 24, Johnson was leaning out of his car to shake hands with black admirers when a truck sideswiped him. It may have been deliberate; the truck kept going. Johnson's car was smashed. He was thrown to the ground, pulled tendons in his back, and, on doctor's orders, had to postpone the start of his training for Jim Flynn.

Meanwhile, Jack Curley looked for a site for the fight. He had hoped to hold it at Madison Square Garden, but Frank O'Neill, the New York state boxing commissioner, vowed that Johnson would never fight in his state so long as he was in charge. "I guess that's discrimination for you," the champion said. "As an American citizen why have I not the same right to box in New York as anyone else?" He was particularly incensed that other black fighters like Joe Jeannette and Sam Langford remained free to fight there. Clearly, the commissioner's ban was purely personal.

Eventually, Curley settled on Las Vegas, in the brand-new state of New Mexico. Once a thriving trading center on the Santa Fe Trail, then a haven for tuberculosis patients, Las Vegas had recently been eclipsed by nearby Albuquerque. Town boosters believed that a title fight would help restore some of its former glory and were willing to put up a $100,000 guarantee to make it happen. "Las Vegas will be the cynosure of the world's eye on July 4," said the Las Vegas *Optic and Livestock Grower*.

> If Flynn should . . . redeem the glory of the white race, Las Vegas will be regarded as having performed a patriotic service indeed, which the entire Caucasian people cannot fail to appreciate and reward. Sooner or later, some American state and town would have to do it, and why should not Las Vegas, New Mexico, accept the chance to become the most popular city in the civilized world?

By the time Johnson, Etta, and their entourage got to Las Vegas on May 26, Jim Flynn had been in residence for nearly three weeks, and the white citizens of the town had taken him to their hearts. He was invited to use the handsome Montezuma Castle Hotel as his headquarters, asked to lead the grand march at a dance held in the armory and to throw out the first ball at the local baseball team's opening game.

To train Flynn, Curley had hired Tommy Ryan, the former middleweight and welterweight champion, and then had spread the story that Flynn was battering his sparring partners so badly that they regularly had to be replaced. Flynn assured the press that he would fight Johnson differently this time— outbox him, force the champion to come to him. Once he'd restored the title to the white race, he added, he'd be "a bigger man than Taft, and running neck and neck with T.R."

Johnson just smiled. Flynn would touch him only twice, he promised: once when they shook hands and again when he tried "to hold on to keep from being knocked out." The original plan had called for the champion to live and train at the Forsyth Ranch, six miles from town. He lasted just two days there. Coyotes interrupted his sleep, he said, and there weren't even any trees. Instead, he shifted into town, "where I can see people and where they can see me"; that way, "there will be no stories told of me fooling away my time."

The Johnsons moved into a two-story house in the Mexican-American neighborhood called Old Town. Crude bleachers and a thirty-foot training platform were banged together in the yard so their new neighbors could see the champion spar every afternoon at a dime a head.*

After an anonymous note signed "K.K.K" arrived, telling Johnson to LIE DOWN OR WE'LL STRING YOU UP, he tucked a revolver into his pants and hired an armed guard to patrol the yard at night, just as he had at Reno.

Otherwise, the life the Johnsons led in Las Vegas was comparatively tranquil. Their legal troubles seemed far away. So did the temptations of the big city. Etta had her husband to herself at least part of every day. A cameraman caught the Johnsons breakfasting together on the porch of their rented home, Johnson absorbed in the sporting section of the newspaper, Etta gazing warily into the lens.

After at least sixteen years of it, Johnson was weary of training—he would enter the ring against Flynn twenty-five pounds heavier than he was when he faced Jeffries—and he was rarely content to stay on his porch for long. "He may be seen at any time of the day driving around in his big touring car," reported the *Optic,* "his rah-rah hat turned up in front and down in the back and his diamonds glittering like headlights on the California Limited." He drove out of town to shoot prairie dogs, mired his car in mud one day, and tried to race a train the next, terrifying Curley, who feared that the champion—and his own potential profits—would end up at the bottom of a canyon. Johnson went along with publicity stunts, eating the better part of two watermelons sent to his camp by a Florida admirer as the press looked

---

*One of those who worked with him during the hot afternoon sparring sessions was a very young Harry Wills. "I was still growing," Wills remembered, "but I already had a right hand to the body that I thought I could hit anybody with. I was working with Johnson one day and sure enough, I nailed him. . . . I got cocky and in the next round I tried the same thing again. Old Jack reached down and caught my fist like you catch a ball and grinned at his wife who was sitting at the ringside."

on, and picking up an extra six hundred dollars for sparring onstage at the Elks Theater in Santa Fe.* And he delighted in the attention his clothes drew in the dusty little town: "Johnson continues to dress up in his dandy togs," the *Optic* reported. "He looks like a Rah! Rah! Kid from some Ethiopian College with his fancy duds and loud hosiery." When the national press began turning up a few days before the fight, he and his trainer Tom Flanagan had a good time roaming through town with scissors, snipping off the ends of sportswriters' ties.

Curley's outdoor stadium—built at the town's expense and never completely paid for—was made to hold 17,950 fans. But Las Vegas, New Mexico, was a long way to go to see a fight that seemed sure to be one-sided, and when the afternoon of the fight arrived, fewer than four thousand turned up.

Both men were to drive to the arena. Johnson refused to get into his car until Curley handed him his promised $31,100 in cash and he had a chance to count it.

When the two men were finally in the ring, Flynn spotted Etta seated in the crowd. He broke away from his handlers, leaned over the ropes, and said in a loud voice that since she was a white woman she really ought to cheer for him. She didn't answer, but her husband was not amused. When the referee, Ed Smith, sporting editor of the Chicago *American* and one of the few writers willing to give Johnson a fair shake in print, brought the boxers together for their final instructions, Johnson refused to take Flynn's hand.

At the opening bell, Flynn returned to his old ways, rushing at Johnson, trying to bull his way inside. Johnson alternately jabbed him and tied him up. By the middle of the second round, there were cuts over both of Flynn's eyes and he was gulping blood. "Time and again," one ringsider recalled, Johnson would "stick out his big black stomach that looked like an inflated bass drum and invite Flynn to punch at it. But every time the white man was foolishly lured into this trap he was peppered with a series of stinging lefts and rights to the face which . . . continued to disfigure his already awesome countenance."

Johnson smiled and laughed and kept up a running conversation with Etta. A spectator shouted for Johnson to end it. "Wait a minute!" he shouted back, and brought more blood from Flynn's nose. By the sixth round, the challenger had grown so frustrated by Johnson's ability to smother him that

---

*He canceled a similar engagement in Albuquerque when no hotel in that town would give him a room.

he began employing what he apparently considered his secret weapon—his skull—trying repeatedly to slam his head into the point of the taller man's chin. When Ed Smith warned him that he would be disqualified if he kept it up, Flynn shouted back: "The nigger's holding me. He's holding me all the time," and went right back to butting. "Flynn's feet were both off the floor time and again with the energy he put into his bounces," noted the New York *Times.* "Sometimes he seemed to leap two feet into the air in frantic plunges at the elusive jaw above him."

Johnson continued to evade Flynn's angry leaps—and to punish him mercilessly—until Captain Fred Fornoff of the New Mexico Mounted Police, a revolver strapped to his side, stepped in and stopped the bout in the ninth. He said it had turned into "a slaughter and a merely brutal exhibition." Smith then awarded Johnson the fight because of the challenger's repeated fouling. Afterward, Johnson told reporters he would have knocked Flynn out a second time had he stuck to fair fighting and not acted "like a billy goat."*

Cynics—and there were a lot of them—once again suggested that Johnson had simply carried Flynn in order to make the fight films more lucrative. The champion, said his old rival Joe Jeannette, was now just a "motion picture fighter." Johnson didn't care what anyone thought. Within moments of his victory, he, Etta, and their party crowded into his touring car and roared off toward Albuquerque to catch the train for Chicago. With them went the $31,100 Jack Curley had handed over, plus $5,000 more the champion had won betting on himself.

Somewhere along the way, distressed perhaps by the idea of returning to Chicago and the distractions that were sure to consume her husband when he got there, Etta tried to jump to her death from the window of their sleeping car. Johnson dragged her back inside. As soon as they got home, he hired two maids to be with his wife day and night to keep her from harming herself.

In San Francisco a few days later, Sunny Jim Coffroth, who had bought the western distribution rights to the fight films, held a private screening for

---

*A few days before the bout, Tommy Ryan had suddenly walked out of the Flynn camp, telling the press only that the challenger was overweight and sure to lose. Curley had then explained the embarrassment away by saying that Flynn had found Ryan too dictatorial. But after the fight, Ryan offered a fuller explanation: "If ever a man deliberately trained to fight a foul fight . . . , Jim Flynn was that man. You have heard the stories about Flynn's partners being disabled? Well, they were disabled through the same sort of thing as Flynn attempted to pull on Johnson. He practiced butting and fouling, and it was a surprise to me that he did not bite Johnson when he got into the ring." (*Boxing* August 3, 1912.)

sportswriters and boxing insiders at the Miles Brothers motion picture establishment on Mission Street. When the lights came up again, most of the invitees had been struck by the same thing that had impressed ringsiders: the contemptuous ease with which Johnson had handled his smaller, bullheaded challenger. But two of the shrewdest among them thought they'd seen something else. W. W. Naughton of the San Francisco *Examiner* had been writing about Johnson for at least eight years, while the trainer Spider Kelly's memories of the fighter went all the way back to the summer of 1901, when they'd barnstormed together through the mining towns of Colorado. Naughton conceded that the champion had deserved the decision, but Flynn, he wrote, had been the better trained and more energetic of the two—"full of fight and ginger at all times"—while Johnson had seemed to tire after the sixth, content to stall for half of every round, clinging to the "under-sized fireman like a creeper to a fence" and hoping to win on a foul. Kelly was still more blunt: "When Johnson boxes again, no matter where it is, I will be at the ringside to bet against him. He has had his day."*

Johnson may privately have agreed. He'd been talking of retirement for months, had even mused that he might oversee a tournament among the least implausible white hopes and then hand his title over to the winner without a fight, just as Jim Jeffries had done, to Johnson's disgust, seven years before. "I've got sense enough to know that Old Dame Nature is going to take the speed and strength away from Jack Johnson the same as she did to Sullivan, Jeffries and the rest of them," he told a visitor not long after he got back to Chicago. "When a man gets to my age the training grind gets to be too much of a strain." "No sir," he told another visitor, "this pitcher is through going to the well."†

---

*In the end, no one would make money from the motion pictures Naughten and Kelly watched that day. On July 31, Congress passed a law barring the interstate shipment of it and all other prizefight films. The bill, sparked by films of the Johnson-Jeffries bout, had languished on the Hill for two years until the prospect of the Johnson-Flynn contest breathed new life into it. The notion that the American public was about to see yet another film of a black man battering a white one was more than most congressmen could endure. "No man descended from the old Saxon race can look upon that kind of contest without abhorrence and disgust," Congressman S. A. Roddenberry of Georgia said on the House floor. "I call attention to the fact that the recent prize-fight which was had in New Mexico presented, perhaps, the grossest instance of base fraud and bogus effort at a fair fight between a Caucasian brute and an African biped beast that has ever taken place."

†Following the Flynn bout, Johnson was reported to have asked his old friend Rube Foster, now managing the Chicago American Giants, if he could try out for first base. Foster invited him to take morning batting practice to see what he could do. No one knows whether Johnson ever turned up. (James A. Riley, *The Biographical Encyclopedia of the Negro Baseball Leagues*. New York, 1994, p. 436.)

Besides, he now believed he'd found a way to support himself and his wife in something like the manner to which both had become accustomed. There was nothing new in his plan to go into the saloon business: John L. Sullivan and Jim Corbett, Jim Jeffries and Tom Sharkey and Spider Kelly and Joe Gans had all tried their hands at it.

But Johnson's Café de Champion at 241 West Thirty-first Street, between Armour Avenue and Dearborn Street and just south of the wide-open Levee, was going to be something else again. With help from several silent partners, including the Heilman Brewing Company, which supplied the café's beer, he had transformed the old Palace Theater into a three-story showcase for himself, a glowing backdrop against which he could present himself as the man he had always wished he could become: elegant, sophisticated, surrounded by friends and admirers, whatever their race.

Every newspaper in town, white and black, covered the grand opening on the evening of July 10. To the Chicago *Tribune,* Johnson was "the white man's despair," and the overwhelmingly black crowd that began gathering at noon and eventually grew so large it halted streetcar traffic reminded its reporter of "the coal bin of the wise purchaser in midsummer." Street vendors peddled novelties. The best-selling item, the Chicago *Defender* reported, was "a miniature frying pan with a piece of bacon in it," symbolizing the "bacon" Johnson had brought home with him from Reno.

The doors were scheduled to open at nine. As the sun went down, workmen were still laboring frantically to finish up the interior. The wine and liquor arrived late, and Johnson himself lent a hand, unloading the trucks and carrying cartons inside. Then, he had rushed home to dress.

Meanwhile, the doors opened and the crowd began to push its way inside. There were "three drink-dispensing parlors," according to the July 11 *Examiner:* the grillroom on the main floor, with a gleaming mahogany bar, mosaic-tile floor, gilt-rimmed silver spittoons said to have cost sixty dollars each, and walls hung with oversize portraits of the champion and Etta; the Pompeiian Room, in which singers, dancers, and an orchestra offered a nonstop show; and a private second-floor room for more intimate dining. Johnson and his wife were to live in a large, richly furnished third-floor apartment, which would offer Etta shelter from the continuing hostility of her mother- and sisters-in-law.

No nightspot quite like it had ever been seen in Chicago, certainly none that welcomed black patrons as well as white ones. It was always Johnson's intention, he said, that "in my cabaret the races [would have] an opportunity to come in contact."

Each opening-night customer received a handsome green-and-gilt-covered, thirty-two-page souvenir program that explained what it called the "Why and Wherefore" of his establishment. The Café de Champion was meant to be a headquarters for Johnson's "many acquaintances and friends throughout the civilized world," it explained. A lengthy tribute to his "Many Sides" attested to the champion's wit and musicianship, his skills as swimmer and horseman, wrestler and automobile driver. A separate section proclaimed his devotion to his mother "an inspiration to every race in every clime." There were advertisements for Johnson-related products—"The Johnson-Flynn Feature Film Co.," "Jack Johnson Drives a Chalmers," "Our Champion Jack Johnson Clear Havana Cigars"—alongside notices for Levee establishments run by Johnson's sporting friends, including the Marquette Club, a "Swell Café with Private Dining Rooms for Private People," and Roy Jones' Casino at Wabash and Twenty-first.

At nine forty-five a great cheer went up as Johnson and his mother pulled up in his red limousine. Policemen ran interference as they made their way inside. Two minutes later, the grinning champion raised his hand and shouted to the orchestra leader, "Let 'Er Go!" just as Billy Jordan had shouted at him and Jim Jeffries to begin the big fight at Reno. "La Paloma" was the first selection, followed by the "Barcarole" from *Tales of Hoffmann*. But according to the *Examiner*, things soon heated up:

> Owing to the audience cabareting down the aisles the promised cabaret show was abandoned. Lena Leanor, the "Southern Oriole," made the audience stand on the chairs when she sang "All Night Long," accompanied by a "modified" turkey trot (modified being placed in quotation marks so the police won't recognize the dance).

"Although many of the daily [white] newspapers delighted in quoting the champion in 'dis and dat,' " said the *Defender*, even they had been forced by the crowds attending the opening of his café to concede that "Mr. Johnson [is] the most popular man in the city of Chicago."

Ada Smith certainly felt that way. As "Bricktop," she would one day run a cabaret of her own in Paris that was a magnet for black and white celebrities, but in 1912 she was still just a nervous light-skinned, red-haired teenager from West Virginia, new to the Chicago black belt and working her first cabaret job as a singer and dancer in the back room of Roy Jones's Casino. One evening Johnson dropped in to see Jones and stayed on to watch the show. He was "surrounded as always by friends, fans and hangers-on," Bricktop remembered, and "you could feel the electricity in the air. The entertainers put a little extra into their performances, and whatever I sang must have pleased him. The 'no entertainers at the tables' rule was suspended for me when Roy Jones said, 'Ada, the Champ wants you to join his party.'" Johnson was kind, attentive, and encouraging. "There were reasons why his smile was so famous," she remembered. "It reflected the real champion, the warm, generous, impulsive, wonderful, loveable man. That smile gave him a handsomeness his looks didn't really deserve."

When he offered her a job at his new café, she jumped at the chance. There were eight pieces in the orchestra that played in his Pompeiian Room, she remembered, and six or seven singers took turns performing with them.

> You began your song from the platform, then started down and went from table to table. At each table—there were about forty—you stopped and sang a half a chorus. . . . You carried a little skillet—the "kitty"—and the customers would drop money into it. It was nice to hear the tinkling sound of coins, but even nicer when the money was a bill and made no sound at all. Any time you got to the table where the Champ was sitting, you knew you were going to get a lot of that silent green money in your skillet. Big bills, too. People naturally showed off for the Champ.

So did the entertainers. Each performer had his or her own special tribute to the boss. Bricktop's was a ragtime tune the Whitman Sisters had introduced on the black vaudeville circuit:

> *You do the Teddy,*
> *and you do the Bear,*
> *but when you do the Jack Johnson [fists up in a winsome boxer's pose]*
> *kid you're there!*

Whenever she sang it for him, Johnson was good for a fiver.

> He was a wonderful man [said Bricktop]. I never saw him once being ordinary or vulgar. When he hit the door of the place at night, the millionaires from Lake Shore Drive and everybody else would all be screaming, "Jack come over here!" He would just stand there with his big, wonderful self

and say he'd be right over. Sooner or later he'd hit all the tables, having a drink at each. He never drank anything but champagne. He cleverly covered up for his lack of education by letting other people do the talking. There was always a twinkle in his eye, as though he was saying, "This is all a funny game, isn't it?" He wasn't a bowing man.

Nor was he a faithful one. His old acquaintance Tad Dorgan once dropped in from San Francisco to spend the day and watched as a series of women made their way up to the private dining room where Johnson often held court. "I made it seven in twelve hours," Dorgan told the sportswriter Al Stump, "not counting repeaters."*

Johnson's attention lingered longest on two women at the café. One was Ada Banks, the club's "star songstress," a classically trained soprano from Texas who had toured for three seasons with the vaudeville team of Williams and Walker. "She was a good-looking, brown-skinned girl with a lovely . . . voice," Bricktop remembered. "The rumors [of a romance] must have been true because she was a haughty big-timey girl who . . . paraded around like she was too good for us." (The rumors were true; Banks' husband, a dining car waiter for the Pennsylvania Railroad, would eventually sue Johnson for twenty-five thousand dollars for alienation of his wife's affections.)

The other woman was Lucille Cameron, a pretty, blond eighteen-year-old from Minneapolis who caught Johnson's eye when she visited the Café de Champion with a friend shortly after it opened. He put her on his payroll at one hundred dollars a week, and took her for automobile rides from which they didn't get back till morning. He would one day claim she'd simply been his "stenographer" and "a companion to his wife," but few believed it.

Two days after the grand opening, Johnson and his wife were arraigned before U.S. Commissioner Charles Buell for smuggling Etta's diamond necklace into the country. "The pugilist regarded the proceedings as a joke," reported the Chicago *Examiner*. "When arraigned he chewed on the end of a big black cigar and kept his straw hat on and raised his left hand to be sworn. The bailiff rushed to his side, pulled down his arm, snatched the cigar from his mouth and his hat from his head." Johnson stopped smiling and raised his right hand. Etta looked frightened. The Johnsons were each released on a

---

*Also according to Stump, a reporter once asked Johnson for the secret of his staying power. "Eat jellied eels," the champion answered with as straight a face as he could manage, "and think distant thoughts." (Stump, "The Rowdy Reign of the Black Avenger.")

five-hundred-dollar bond. If found guilty, they faced up to two years in federal prison.

Later that evening, their ex-chauffeur Charles Brown dropped by the café. He had been called to testify before the federal grand jury as to what he knew about the smuggled necklace. When Johnson demanded to know exactly what he'd said, Brown refused to answer. He'd been sworn to secrecy, he said. The champion slapped him, and members of Johnson's entourage kicked Brown into the street. He pressed assault charges. Johnson was arrested and bailed out again, for five thousand dollars this time.

He was still not unduly worried. The line between lawbreaking and law enforcement in Chicago was always hard to discern, and he was used to paying his way out of trouble. Every city official who had anything to do with the Levee District was on the take, and Johnson had always been willing to shoulder his share of the cost of doing business—one thousand dollars a week in his case just to keep his club open. And even though his break with George Little had damaged his relations with the political machine that ran the First Ward, he seems to have feared no one. When several thugs called on him to pass the word that their bosses thought the presence of white women in his establishment was bad for the neighborhood, he threw them down the stairs. He paid his protection money; he didn't have to listen to anyone's advice.

Why should he assume that federal officials would be immune to the same enticements that made city and state officials cooperative? Johnson believed that his personal charm and the power of his celebrity could win over anyone. All they had to do was to get to know him. And so one evening that summer, he arranged for a friend of his, a bail bondsman and sometime courthouse fixer named Sol Lewinsohn, to shepherd a party of six into his café. They included Assistant U.S. District Attorney Harry A. Parkin; Charles F. DeWoody, chief of the Justice Department's Chicago office; and DeWoody's younger brother, Wade, who happened to be in town and was eager to "see the sights" of the Levee. Johnson greeted them all warmly and, after several rounds of drinks on the house, led them upstairs to his private dining room, where a chicken dinner had been prepared by his chefs. Johnson seated himself between Parkin and Charles DeWoody. "I am going to get fixed for life now," he said as he raised his glass to his new friends. "I surely feel as safe now as though I was home and in bed." Lucille Cameron, not Etta, acted as his hostess that evening, and at three or so in the morning, she joined Johnson and his guests as they piled into two of his cars, headed for the lakefront, and raced each other up and down Michigan Avenue until dawn.

Johnson had not exaggerated the power of his personality, but he had underestimated the complexity of the challenge he faced from the federal government. Treasury as well as Justice handled smuggling cases like his. And while Parkin and DeWoody may have had a good time in his company, their first allegiance remained to their superiors in Washington.

The Café de Champion continued to flourish. One evening in early September a reporter for the Chicago *Defender* accompanied a band of five black big spenders as they wove their increasingly cheerful way down State Street, moving from one bar to the next. Their host was a prominent South Side attorney, Beauregard F. Moseley. The climax of their tour was Jack Johnson's black-and-tan.

> The Café de Champion, both on the main and second floors, was crowded to its fullest capacity with men and women of both races mixed in together and all seemed to be having the time of their lives. . . .
>
> Champion Jack Johnson, in an easy quiet manner, and with a mild voice, walked around . . . and cordially shook hands with all of his white and colored guests and before sitting down he eased up in the corner of the café reserved for the entertainers, reached for his "Bull Fiddle," the very same fiddle he practiced on at Reno, Nev., prior to putting James J. Jeffries to sleep in that city, July 4th, 1910, and assisted the orchestra to play several lively and catchy selections, much to the great delight of his many patrons.
>
> Jack Johnson, without any question about it, is smooth goods or a smooth article; and he knows how to get the money, or the "bacon," as he calls it, and he is doing his part in his own way in helping to solve the "Race Problem."
>
> Many very beautiful pictures hang on the walls . . . including the life-sized picture of Mr. and Mrs. Johnson, which is encased in a fine and very heavy gold frame.

Etta Johnson's portrait gazing up in apparent adoration at her husband was an important part of the club's décor, but she herself remained a sort of prisoner, confined to the apartment on the top floor, aware of her husband's pursuit of other women but unable to do much about it, constantly watched as well as waited on by the two maids, Helen Simmons and Mabel Bolden, he had hired to keep her from harming herself. The death of her father had added to her sense of isolation, and she may have in part blamed herself for it.

A neighbor remembered hearing her complain that she had become a recluse and a social outcast. Her family felt itself disgraced by her. Most whites scorned her. She had grown used to that. But "even the Negroes don't respect me," she said. "They hate me." She could see no way out.

On August 12, sitting alone in her room, Etta Johnson wrote a note to her mother in Brooklyn.

My dear Mother:

I am writing this and am going to have Jack put it in his safe, so if anything should happen to me there will be no hard feelings left behind me. I would send this letter to you only I know much you worry and I do not want you to know how sick I really am.

Jack has done all in his power to cure me but it is no use. Since papa's death I have worried myself in[to] my grave. I haven't been worrying about papa's loss, only over some horrible dread—I don't know what.

I want to be buried here in Chicago. Never try to take my body to Hempstead only to be a mark for curiosity-seekers—let me rest for once.

With love and always the sweetest to you,

I am your loving daughter,

Etta

She slipped the letter into an envelope, sealed it up, and locked it away.

Nearly a month later, on the morning of September 11, a furrier called at the café to say that the new winter furs Etta had ordered were ready to be tried on—five thousand dollars' worth, including a twenty-five-hundred-dollar sealskin coat. Mrs. Johnson seemed strangely "disinterested," her visitor remembered; she said she might come to the shop that afternoon but never turned up.

Depression had enveloped her again. Seeking to raise her spirits, her husband bought her a train ticket for a trip out west. Ed Smith's wife was heading back to Las Vegas, New Mexico, on the evening of the twelfth to be with her tubercular daughter, who was undergoing treatment at a local sanitarium. Johnson urged Etta to go along. She had been relatively content there, away from the turmoil that always seemed to surround him. Perhaps she could be happy there again. A rest in the sunshine would do her good.

But that evening Etta suffered another attack of "nervous prostration" and said she wasn't well enough to go. Johnson drove to the railroad station to change the tickets. When he got back to the café about ten thirty, police vans were parked at the curb and people were milling around the entrance. As he pushed his way through the crowd, someone told him something had happened to his wife.

He vaulted up the stairs.

Etta was lying on their bedroom floor in her nightdress, a revolver by her side. Her "horrible dread" had evidently overwhelmed her. There was a bullet hole in her temple. She was still breathing. Her eyes were fixed and staring, but her lips were moving soundlessly.

The distraught maids took turns telling Johnson what had happened. As soon as he had left, they said, Etta had telephoned her sister-in-law Lucy and asked her to come over. It had struck them as odd, since she and her husband's family rarely spoke. They had helped her dress for bed. She asked them to pray with her. All three women knelt. The maids left the room. She closed and locked the door.

Bricktop was performing in the private dining room on the second floor that evening. "I was singing Sheldon Brooks's 'All Night Long' when a shot rang out," she recalled. "Everything came to a standstill in the private dining room. No one heard it on the first floor and the orchestra kept playing."

A bartender broke down the door. Someone called the police.

Johnson followed along behind as Etta was lifted onto a stretcher. He held a big white handkerchief to his eyes. "That woman has been troubled with nervousness for two years," he told a newspaperman as he climbed into the ambulance. "Ain't got no more to say. I'm going to the hospital."

Etta died at Provident Hospital at about three in the morning.

A coroner's inquest was held at a mortuary on South State Street that afternoon. Johnson was the most important witness. He testified that he had himself sometimes felt suicidal since winning the title. He had broken down after beating Jeffries, he said—"although it has not been known generally"—and only Etta's selfless nursing had kept him from being institutionalized. He was afraid it was that ceaseless devotion that had finally destroyed her will to live. She had tried to kill herself several times before, her father's death had added to her unhappiness, and Johnson had hired two maids "just to prevent her from doing what she did." Reports of trouble between him and his wife did him an injustice, he added. "I thought the world of her and she thought the world of me."

The jury ruled Etta's death a suicide.

. . .

Later that afternoon, a reporter for the Chicago *Examiner* joined the throng gathered outside Johnson's home.

> Wabash Avenue [he wrote] was crowded with people, black and white, rich and poor, who were neither the friends of the living nor mourners for the dead. They were sightseers. "Well, I guess Jack's lost his lucky horseshoe," said a Negro, and that was typical of the sympathy he could get from his own race. Fashionable people in their automobiles switched over from Michigan Avenue, millionaires who have seen Johnson fight and now wanted to see his "knockout."

The champion stood in an open first-floor window, gazing out at the crowd. The newspaperman made his way across the lawn to speak to him. A friend of Johnson's had remarked that, for all her finery and jewels, Etta had been profoundly lonely. The reporter asked Johnson about it. "Yes, she was lonesome," he answered. "We were both a little lonesome, I guess. But God, how we loved each other—and how lonesome I am now."

"Never had Johnson looked so dark," the reporter wrote. "He was a black man garbed in black."

"There's one thing I'll never get over," said Johnson as he stared down into the street. "She had a message for me—and I couldn't get it. Understand that? Can't you see how I feel? When my head was right down close to hers and I begged her to speak to me—then to see her lips tremble and twitch a little—but no message—Oh, for God's sake go away and leave me alone."

Motives for suicide rarely make sense to anyone but the desperate people driven to it. Even those left behind who loved and thought they knew them best never fully understand. The circumstances of Etta's life had undoubtedly been hard. She was often betrayed and sometimes abused by her husband. She was lonely, scorned by whites and blacks alike. Everybody stared. But what else may have been at work beneath the surface—what emotional wounds and chemical disturbance helped deepen her despair and strengthen her resolve to end it all—is unknowable now.

At the time, however, a host of strangers were quite sure they understood and only too eager to offer explanations. The New York *World*'s account was gaudier than most, but the argument it made was echoed on editorial pages all over the country. Etta's death had been the preordained outcome of a union between a white "girl of gentle breeding" and a "negro with . . . shining gold teeth and diamond-bedecked fingers." At first, it said, she had "seemed actually unconscious of all this."

> She even publicly flaunted herself with the big, notorious negro. When she did not remain impassive before the sneers of even the painted women she encountered at cafés and racetracks and notorious motorcar roadhouses, she spiritedly returned them.
>
> This was at first. But gradually the stings sunk to the woman's heart. She was a woman without a race. She was on occasion even ostracized by the women in the cheap burlesque shows in which her husband punched a bag.
>
> And the negro women were as pitiless. They were jealous of her possession of the negro hero and Croesus; they were even honestly contemptuous of her superior race. . . .
>
> Ostracism was the inevitable penalty of this ill-assorted marriage, as it is of marriages between white men and negro women. Political equality under the Constitution is one thing, but a degree of social equality admitting of the intermarriage of the races is impossible.

The New York *Times* was no friendlier to miscegenation than was the *World*, but Johnson's obvious grief did elicit at least a modicum of pity from its editors.

> While it cannot be said that [Johnson] will have anything like general public sympathy because his venture in miscegenation has come to an end [only] a little more dreadful than was confidently to be expected from such a violation of the social proprieties, still his apparently sincere grief over the suicide of the white woman who married him will have its effect in mitigating judgment of him. It at least shows that he is not the entirely callous animal that a Negro prize-fighter is supposed by most to be. . . . His display of emotion may be racial rather than personal [but] animal or not, he is not callous.

Etta's funeral was set for noon on Saturday, September 14, at St. Marks A.M.E. church at Fifteenth Street and Wabash Avenue. Jack Curley had stepped in to make the arrangements. Thousands of curiosity seekers again surrounded the Johnson home that morning, and police had to clear a path from the front porch to the waiting hearse. The onlookers fell silent as the front door opened and six pallbearers, picked from among Johnson's closest friends both black and white, carried the gray casket down the front steps. The champion was right behind it, his arm linked with that of Etta's widowed mother, so distraught that she had difficulty walking on her own. Mrs. Terry, with her younger daughter, Eileen, had come in from Brooklyn the night before. "My daughter," she explained to a reporter, "begged me not to put her out of my heart and I did not."

Why her daughter had married Jack Johnson was a "mystery" to her, she would tell another newsman, "although Etta was never right in her mind, and I have attributed many things to that fact. And I believe her suicide came at a period, not of temporary madness, but of ultra-lucidness. I believe that for one brief moment the mental fog lifted from her, revealing the position to her in all its hideousness. In the revolt which followed, she shot herself." She had asked Johnson to allow her to take Etta's body home to be buried with her father, but he had refused. Etta had been his wife, he said. They had loved each other, and someday he wanted to be buried next to her.*

Scores of cars fell in line behind the hearse, including a big touring car filled with reporters from all the Chicago dailies, and another from which a movie cameraman ground away.†

The church was small and stifling, the scent of flowers overpowering. Johnson's sister Jennie fainted. Jack Curley had to carry her outside. The choir sang "Nearer My God to Thee" and Etta's own favorite anthem, "Take the Name of Jesus with You." Ada Banks, the entertainer whose relationship with Johnson was common gossip at the Café de Champion, sang a hymn. The pastor, Reverend John H. Robinson, gently chided those among his parishioners who had questioned Etta's devotion to her husband. "Is there anyone in this church who can be so cruel as to deny the star of hope to the weary one?" he asked. "Is there anyone who cannot let the great mantle of charity cover the call of a disquieted heart?" The black-owned Chicago *Broad Ax* was harsher:

---

*It was a decision for which Mrs. Terry would never forgive him. Nor would she ever understand what Etta had seen in him.

†Within hours of Etta's death, the Pekin Theater had begun promising to show exclusive film of her funeral. Johnson's friend Bob Motts had died, and the new white owners of the Pekin thought they would make a killing. Their crew captured seven thousand feet of film of the cortège. Johnson was furious. "This exhibition," he said, "which is unauthorized by me, may cause the impression to go abroad that I am profiting financially from the pictures. I am going to fight hard against anyone who tries to show the pictures." Before the film could be processed, Johnson obtained a restraining order against showing it, then personally called on the chief of police to make sure nothing got onto the screen. (Chicago *Defender,* September 21, 1912.)

Many colored women who in the past had bitterly denounced Jack Johnson for his marriage were dead anxious to occupy the seats of honor in the church . . . and to be ahead of everyone else during the progress of the funeral. . . . If these women [had] extended the hand of love, friendship and sympathy to Mrs. Johnson in her lifetime instead of belching forth indiscriminately loud slurring remarks in relating to her marriage, she might be living today.

At the end of the service the casket was opened once more so that Johnson and his mother-in-law could kiss Etta's brow. Then it was closed and blanketed with flowers for the journey to the cemetery. HUSBAND TO ETTA, read Johnson's floral tribute, GONE BUT NOT FORGOTTEN.

The cortège moved away from the black belt toward the North Side and Graceland Cemetery, the beautifully landscaped final resting place of Chicago's elite. Governors of Illinois and mayors of Chicago were buried there; so were many of the city's leading merchants and industrialists: Philip Armour, Marshall Field, Potter Palmer, George Pullman. Johnson had purchased plots for himself and his wife. It was the sort of company he thought they should keep. And he had already commissioned a $3,500 stone monument to mark the spot.

As the mourners filed back to their cars from the gravesite he spoke to a reporter. "It's over," he said. "That's all I can do."

CHAPTER TEN

THE ACCUSED

JACK JOHNSON WAS A MASTER of timing in the ring, seemed always to know just when to strike, when to lie back and wait. Outside the ropes, that mastery often deserted him. One evening in the first week of October 1912, Bricktop remembered, the champion turned up at the Café de Champion with Lucille Cameron on his arm. It had been just over two weeks since he had buried his wife.

Before the tragedy, Lucille had possessed just one outfit, as far as we could tell—a checked suit that she wore all the time—but that night, when she and Jack walked in after seeing Thomas Shea in *The Bells*, Lucille was wearing a black broadcloth suit, a big hat covered with white egrets and diamonds all over her hands. Whether these things had belonged to Mrs. Johnson, I don't know, but we knew Lucille had never worn a diamond before. Naturally, our eyes went from Lucille to Ada Banks. We giggled among ourselves, because Ada had been so nasty and mean to us because she was Jack's girl. . . .

We all went over to do our songs. I did my song with the prizefighter stance. Jack's favorite song for Ada to sing was "My Hero," and when her turn came she started to sing it. She went along fine until she got to one of the high notes, then her voice cracked and she broke into tears. She ran through the café. With me behind her. Trailing me were two or three other girls telling me to leave her alone—she deserved to cry, the way she had treated everybody.

A few nights later Ada and Lucille met in the ladies' room. Ada said, "We'll see who's going to be the next Mrs. Jack Johnson!" The white girl didn't open her mouth. She *knew* who the next Mrs. Johnson was going to be.

Johnson could not have picked a worse moment to return to the public eye— or a companion better suited to draw the lightning.

. . .

Reform had come to Chicago. It had been on its way for several years, though Johnson seems to have been too preoccupied to notice. In his early years in the ring every large city to which he traveled had a "segregated" district like Chicago's Levee, a carefully delineated area in which vice was tolerated even if technically illegal. He knew them all intimately. And every city he visited had also been home to men and women determined to close them down, often the same men and women who were determined to ban his profession as well. Like most sports, he was scornful of them all.

But on the evening of October 18, 1909, two days after Johnson knocked out Stanley Ketchel in California, a British-born evangelist named Gipsy Smith had led thousands of Chicagoans through the vice district, pausing to pray and sing hymns in front of its most notorious resorts. After the parade broke up, the district was said to have had the busiest night in its history. ("We were certainly glad to get all this business," Minna Everleigh said, "but I was sorry to see so many nice young men down here for the first time.") Gipsy Smith was not discouraged. "Time will show that great good has been done," he said.

He knew segregated districts like the Levee were now being attacked from many directions. Clergymen had always opposed them on moral grounds. But now the Social Hygiene movement demanded they be put out of business for reasons of public health. Muckraking journalists were laying bare the nexus between corrupt politicians and saloon- and brothel-keepers. And middle-class Americans everywhere fretted that more and more young single women were moving away from home and into the cities where degradation seemed to lurk around every corner. Millions were convinced that young white women were in constant danger from organized bands of cruel and wily men—immigrants mostly—intent on coercing them into becoming prostitutes, or "white slaves." As one crusader wrote, "We know that no innocent young girl would or ever could go [into prostitution] of her own free will—those who are there are enticed—those who employ these artifices are men—devils in the guise of men."

No one was a more zealous believer in the existence of this underground traffic than the U.S. district attorney in Chicago, Edwin W. Sims. He claimed to know to "a moral certainty" that there was a nationwide network of white slavers run by a mysterious "Big Chief." Their agents lurked everywhere, he said; even "the ordinary ice cream parlor is very likely to be a spider's web for . . . entanglement"—especially if run by a "foreigner." (Eastern European Jews and Frenchmen were particularly suspect.)

There never was any evidence of such a network, and the best estimate seems to be that nine out of ten prostitutes were not coerced, but facts did not matter in the midst of what by 1909 had become a national frenzy. Lurid best sellers were built around white slavery. Movie screens showed white girls menaced by swarthy white villains.

"The white slave traffic . . . is much more horrible than any black-slave traffic ever was in the history of the world," said Republican Congressman James Robert Mann of Illinois. And in 1909, with District Attorney Sims' help, he drafted the White Slave Traffic Act, which came to be known as the Mann Act. It barred the transportation of women in interstate or foreign commerce "for the purpose of prostitution or debauchery, or for any other immoral purposes." It had gone into effect on June 1, 1910, when Johnson was busy training for his fight with Jim Jeffries, but the first arrest under its provisions was not made until July 8, the day he thanked Chicago's black elite for their big welcome after he'd retained his title. Deputy U.S. marshals had arrested a madam named Jenkin as she was about to board a train at Chicago's Union Station that morning; she had just bought tickets for herself and five women she had hired for her resort in Houghton, Michigan, which catered to the copper miners who worked the Upper Peninsula.

That was the sort of straightforward arrest most of the act's supporters had had in mind. Their intent had been to suppress the interstate traffic in prostitution. But the language of the act was loosely drawn, and both within and without the Justice Department's Bureau of Investigation (forerunner of the F.B.I.), there were those who believed that "debauchery" and "other immoral purposes" might be more broadly defined to include what the newspapers called "escapades," sexual relations between consenting adults.

On September 28, 1912—fourteen days after Etta Johnson's funeral—more than five thousand people marched through the Levee District despite a steady downpour, demanding that John E. W. Wayman, the state's attorney of Cook County, close it down.

Six days later, he did. On the evening of October 4, a fleet of patrol wagons pulled into the Levee. Scores of policemen went from door to door, handing out summonses, evicting the inmates. Johnson's friend Roy Jones and his wife, Victoria Shaw, were among the brothel keepers taken to jail. "Electric pianos stopped as if paralyzed," said the Chicago *Record-Herald*.

> Bright lights went glimmering. Into the streets poured a crowd of half-dressed women, some with treasures tied in tablecloths. Others were pack-

ing suitcases as they moved, and most of them were running, a majority not knowing where they were going, but anywhere to get out of the district. In front of a few of the more pretentious establishments automobiles suddenly appeared. Women soon loaded them down, and they raced away.

More than one hundred resorts were shuttered. Hundreds of prostitutes found themselves without a base of operations. Ike Bloom, the district's most powerful vice lord, tried to strike back by sending the women who worked for him and several others into respectable neighborhoods with orders to walk the streets wearing daring outfits and smoking cigarettes to shock the citizenry into calling for the Levee to be reopened. It didn't work.

The raids continued on the fifth, sixth, seventh, and eighth.

It was during that week, against that background, that Jack Johnson decided to end his brief mourning period and introduce the world to Lucille Cameron.

On Friday, October 11, a short, determined woman in a very large hat arrived in Chicago. She was Mrs. F. Cameron-Falconet, Lucille Cameron's mother, and she was looking for her daughter. A Chicago reporter had called her at home in Milwaukee, she said, and asked if she knew that Lucille was "under the influence of Jack Johnson." She had not known, and she was horrified, or so she said. She caught the first train to Chicago and hurried to the last address she had for Lucille, a boardinghouse on Grand Avenue. The landlady told her her daughter hadn't been there for at least three weeks. She had no idea where she had gone.

Mrs. Cameron-Falconet got herself a room at the Brevoort Hotel and spent a sleepless night. The next morning, she called Jack Johnson and demanded to see her daughter. It was Saturday. Johnson said he knew where Lucille was and would take her there. He picked Lucille's mother up in his car and drove her to the Sheridan Road home of Jack Curley and his wife. Lucille greeted her mother. Mrs. Cameron-Falconet urged her to come away with her. Lucille refused. Johnson took mother and daughter back to the Brevoort, where they talked some more. Lucille wouldn't budge. Then she told her mother she had to make a phone call, went downstairs, and disappeared.

The next morning, the Chicago papers happened to carry interviews with Johnson. He was in an expansive mood. He'd signed for three fights overseas, he said. First, he planned to go to Australia, where Hugh McIntosh had guaranteed him fifty-five thousand dollars to fight Sam Langford in Sydney on Boxing Day, the fourth anniversary of his victory over Tommy Burns. Then he would take on Sam McVey in an Australian city to be chosen on a date to be decided. Once he'd disposed of those two, he thought he'd go to Paris, where Jack Curley wanted him to face Fireman Jim Flynn for a third time. Following that, he'd come back to the States and take on the likeliest of the latest white hopes, Luther McCarty. Curley would promote that contest, too; Curley was his friend, Johnson said, and since he had lost money promoting the second Flynn contest, in New Mexico, it was only fair to give him "a chance to get it back." The champion was eager to get away from Chicago and "forget my troubles" for a while, he added, and while he didn't say so publicly, it seemed likely that when he sailed for Australia on October 25, Lucille Cameron would go along to help with his forgetting.

Her mother determined to stop her. To help, she hired one of Chicago's most colorful and controversial criminal lawyers. Charles E. Erbstein specialized in murder and divorce—he took part in 1,772 divorce trials—and he gloried in the publicity that went with many of the cases he handled. He represented more than one hundred accused murderers during his long and lucrative career and liked to boast he never lost one to the executioner. Because of his divorce work and because every one of the twenty-two women he'd represented in murder cases had been found not guilty, he liked to portray himself as the gallant defender of innocent women. He also had a statewide reputation for cutting corners in and out of the courtroom, and had been brought up before the Illinois legal grievance commission at least twenty-seven times by the time Mrs. Cameron-Falconet signed on with him; a former state's attorney denounced him as "an unconscionable crook, a trickster, a jury fixer and suborner of perjury."

Together, the angry mother and the shrewd but unscrupulous lawyer set out to ruin Jack Johnson.

On Thursday, they went to the police, claiming that the champion had kidnapped Lucille. When the police pointed out to them that the young woman was over eighteen and there was therefore no way they could force her to leave the champion if she didn't want to, the two went straight to the newspapers.

With a good deal of prompting from Erbstein, Lucille's mother offered a lurid, teary account of her encounter with the champion, calculated to wring sympathy from whites and destroy what was left of his reputation. The front page headline of the Chicago *Daily News* was typical:

"JACK" JOHNSON DEAF TO PLEA OF A MOTHER

MRS. F. CAMERON-FALCONET,
BETWEEN SOBS, TELLS HOW
NEGRO HOLDS DAUGHTER

INSULTED HER SHE SAYS

She said her innocent daughter had attended business college after high school and had come to Chicago with her mother's blessing "to take up a business position. I had reason to believe she was under the best of influences." Instead, she had come under the influence of the heavyweight champion. "Jack Johnson has hypnotic powers," she said, "and he has exercised them on my little girl." When she had confronted her daughter's captor and begged him to give her up, she claimed he had cruelly taunted her as well.

When his automobile arrived [to pick Mrs. Cameron-Falconet up,] he was in it himself, although he had said he would send an empty car for me. When I entered the car I drew down the shades of the limousine so as not to be seen. This nettled Johnson.

"Oh, some of the best white women in Chicago ride in this car," is what he said to me.

I told him he must give up my daughter. I begged him to give her up. He said he wouldn't. Then he leered in my face.

They brought her in [at Jack Curley's home], but the Negro hung around all the time and did not let me see her for long at a time. She wept and told me she had gone too far to go back. She said she did not know what to do or which way to turn, that her mind was in the balance.

Every little while the Negro would walk into the room, and once or twice she went out and talked with him away from me. I told her I should stick to her through thick and thin and would do anything in my power to save her.

Johnson has told me he will give every dollar he has to hold her. When he said that I told him I could not understand how she could be attracted by such as he, and he said he could "get" any woman he wanted. "I could get you, too, if I wanted you."

Jack Johnson was not a humble man. Nor would he have sat still for individual insults of the sort Mrs. Cameron-Falconet had leveled at him. But it seems inconceivable that even he would have said anything so instantly inflammatory as this. Charles Erbstein was a master manipulator of the press, and it seems most likely that this was an embellishment he urged his client to "remember" for maximum effect.*

"I am appealing to all of Chicago to help me," Mrs. Cameron-Falconet said in conclusion. "It does not seem possible that such things could happen in Chicago or that white men would see their civilization so outraged."

Her story seemed to affect every white man who heard it. The assistant chief of police telephoned Captain Max Nootbar, in charge of the Thirty-fifth Street station house. "Get a warrant out for Johnson," he shouted. "If there is anything he can be arrested for in connection with this case bring him into court." "There is nothing I would like better than to punish this man," he told the papers. "My blood boiled when I heard the story told by the mother."

The white public's blood was soon boiling, too. The story had everything: a grieving mother; a presumably innocent white girl from out of town; a notorious black man who pursued white women and seemed almost to enjoy the havoc he caused.

Within hours, the police had Mrs. Cameron-Falconet sign a complaint against her daughter for disorderly conduct, the only way the police could think of to get her away from Johnson. "I am doing this for humanity's sake," said Captain Nootbar. "Legally, I have no right to hold the girl . . . but I believe the case warrants my action."

At about 5 p.m., the champion himself brought Lucille in a taxi to the Harrison Street Annex of the city jail. In the captain's office, Frank H. Hilliard, a Minneapolis businessman and friend of Lucille's mother, stood alongside her. Johnson smiled, stuck out his hand, and said, "Howdy."

Hilliard turned away, his hands in his pockets. "I won't shake hands with scum of the earth like you," he said.

"What!" the champion said and stepped forward, fist cocked. "You call yourself a gentleman? Why you dog, what do you mean?"

Captain Nootbar separated the two men.

"When Miss Cameron appeared," the Milwaukee *Evening Wisconsin* reported,

she was stylishly dressed in black silk and a black velvet picture hat with yellow feathers, and wore a haughty mien. However, she began to cry when

---

*According to a sworn deposition by Johnson's sister Jennie Rhodes, her brother's British valet, Joseph Levy, was present at the station house when Mrs. Cameron-Falconet told her woeful tale to the press and heard Erbstein prompt his client to add this incendiary detail. (Undated Rhodes Grand Jury deposition, DOJ File.)

she entered the captain's office. For several minutes she lay sobbing on a couch. Then, she collected herself . . . [and told] Nootbar she loved Jack Johnson, and that while the negro champion had not made her a proposal of marriage, she expected to become his wife in the near future.

At that, Mrs. Cameron-Falconet collapsed in tears. "I would rather see you spend all your life in jail," she sobbed, "than one day in the company of that nigger." Lucille was led away to a cell. Jane Addams of Hull-House came to see her there. So did a social worker from New York and Mrs. Alice Phillips Aldrich, president of the Law and Order League. Lucille insisted to each of them that she was not a victim, nobody's white slave.

Meanwhile, Johnson seemed sure that this would all blow over. "How can I help it if the girl is crazy about me?" Johnson said as he left the police station. "I'm going to pick my own girls." He vowed that he'd bail Lucille out right away.

To keep that from happening, Erbstein quickly persuaded another judge to order Lucille's detention until her sanity could be examined. Only a deranged white girl, he argued, could believe herself in love with Jack Johnson. The judge agreed.

When Johnson got back to his café that evening, he found Ada Banks waiting for him upstairs. Like Hattie McClay and Belle Schreiber and Etta Duryea and others before her, she had hoped to emerge as Johnson's favorite. She had left her husband for him, had even sung at his wife's funeral. But the newspapers had now made clear what her fellow entertainers at the café already knew: Johnson's first choice was Lucille Cameron, younger than she, and white. Banks had a pistol. There was a confrontation. She may have pointed the weapon at Johnson, even fired and missed. Then she fled. A rumor spread that the champion had been shot. (A white Mississippian immediately sent a congratulatory wire to the Chicago chief of police: "The undersigned and 100 others will back the woman or man $50,000.") When Banks was tracked down several days later and asked by a newspaperman if she really had shot Johnson, she would only say, "I didn't do quite that."*

. . .

---

*Some papers reported that Johnson had been wounded in the foot, and at least one reported that he had been seen limping, but a prison physician who later catalogued Johnson's scars and distinguishing marks noted no such injury. Banks herself later said the whole notion that she had fired at him was "ridiculous." (Jack Johnson File, Inmate Case Files, United States Penitentiary–Leavenworth; Records of the Federal Bureau of Prisons; Record Group 129; National Archives–Central Plains region; Chicago *Defender*, November 2, 1912.)

Public furor had forced the Chicago police to act, even when they weren't quite sure they had the authority to do so. It now influenced the federal government to do the same. The Justice Department had targeted Johnson for possible violation of the Mann Act almost from the moment it came into effect,* but when U.S. Attorney General George W. Wickersham first heard about Johnson and Lucille Cameron, he'd sent a cautionary wire to James H. Wilkerson, the U.S. district attorney in Chicago: "Suggest great care . . . so as not to involve federal authorities in mere question of abduction or anything not within the general scope of evils sought to be reached by the white slave act."

But Wilkerson and others in the Chicago office were convinced that there was a city "clearing house for the procuring of white girls for well-to-do negroes." This case might be the one that led to its exposure. Wilkerson dispatched special agents Bert Meyer and Martin J. Lins to see what they could find out. "[Miss Cameron] denies that she has been intimate with Jack Johnson or any other person," Lins reported. "Her appearance, however, belies that statement, as she dresses in the height of fashion, wearing a hat said to cost $150; and it is known she has deposited six or seven hundred dollars in a local bank since she came to Chicago." Further investigation showed that her mother had either not known much about the life her daughter had been leading, or had hoped it could be concealed. Lucille Cameron had been in Chicago since April, months before she met Johnson. She'd spent the first two weeks of her stay at the Brevoort, where her bills had been paid by a "friend" she refused to identify. Her claim to have been a "cloak model" in a downtown store was false. And she continued to insist that she had fallen in love with Jack Johnson the first time she saw him, didn't "care whether he was black or white," and hoped someday to marry him. It was hard to see how a federal case against Johnson could be constructed around Lucille Cameron.

Special Agent Meyer was more hopeful. There was at least a possibility that a woman named Catherine Dorsey had introduced Lucille to the champion and might therefore be guilty of "procuring girls for immoral purposes," though the all-important "transportation feature," without which no federal charge could be made to stick, still seemed to be lacking. It was a start. Wilkerson filed a case against Dorsey for violating the Mann Act, and had Lucille

---

*In the summer of 1910, according to federal agent F. Pigniuolo, he had interviewed Belle Schreiber in Pittsburgh after hearing a rumor that she had traveled with the champion from Washington to Chicago, "but she denied ever having had anything to do with Johnson." (Report by F. Pigniuolo, November 18, 1912, DOJ File.)

confined to the Winnebago County Jail at Rockford as a material witness. "Public sentiment was aroused to such an extent," he said, that he could do no less. Lucille's bond was set at twenty-five thousand dollars. No one other than her mother or a federal agent was to be allowed to communicate with her in any way for fear that Johnson or his agents might influence her testimony.

The next morning, Thursday the 17th, Lucille's mother and Charles Erbstein appeared before a municipal judge and persuaded him to sign a warrant for Jack Johnson's arrest on a charge of abduction. He was arrested at home at one o'clock. Bail was set at eight hundred dollars, and he was released to find a judge to approve his bond. He had nothing to worry about, he told a reporter. "They can't get me. I've got money. You can keep on knocking me all you want to."

Johnson was to be arraigned on Friday morning. When he drove up to the Municipal Court Building at South Dearborn and West Monroe, a knot of angry white people shook their fists and shouted at him. Johnson acted as if he hadn't a care in the world. He "strolled into the courthouse half an hour late," the *Daily News* reported, "carrying a long black cigar in his mouth and smiling at every step."

Entering the courtroom, he glared at Lucille's mother.

She would not even glance at him.

Erbstein asked the judge to raise Johnson's bail because of the gravity of the alleged offense.

"I don't think it is necessary to increase the bond," Johnson said. "I am a responsible citizen. I have a business [the Café de Champion] worth $60,000."

"It may be worth that to you," Erbstein said. "But it's illegal and you ought to be put out of business."

"All right, Mr. Mayor," Johnson said with a laugh.

"If I was mayor," Erbstein snapped back, "you would not be in business three days."

The judge raised Johnson's bond to fifteen hundred dollars and continued the case until October 29.

Johnson offered a check for seven hundred dollars to make up the difference.

"No checks go with me," said Erbstein.

The champion said he'd make it cash and brought in a professional bondsman to post bail. "I'm going to marry Lucille," he said, "no matter what they do. They can put her in jail or try to put her in the asylum but I'll marry her in time, anyway." And he had powerful allies of both races that would help him. "Just to show how I stand, my café was crowded with white folks last night. I've got plenty of friends sticking to me."

He drove to the First National Bank. As he walked toward the door, some-one hurled an inkstand from a tenth-floor window. It missed, spattering the sidewalk with ink. He stepped inside and withdrew several thousand dollars. A big angry crowd gathered outside. When he came back out and started for his car, someone shouted, "There he comes! Get him now!" The crowd pressed forward, but no one quite dared throw a punch. The champion found himself with his back to the wall. He edged back inside, then hurried out the rear entrance, hailed a cab, and disappeared into the sanctuary of his own café. The mob hung around the bank until it closed. "Popular indignation over the numerous outrages on public morals perpetrated by the negro prize fighter," reported the Chicago *Examiner,* "has reached such a stage that it is dangerous for him to walk in the public streets." When Johnson tried to hire detectives from the Burns and Pinkerton agencies to protect him, he was told neither one wanted his business.

Threatening letters now arrived daily in the mail. Strangers telephoned day and night to curse him. Hugh McIntosh canceled plans for the Langford and McVey fights Down Under; Australians wouldn't stand for them now, he said. W. W. Naughton thought Johnson's behavior had "eliminated [him] "as thoroughly from the pugilistic outlook as though he had been signally defeated by some rival heavyweight." The *Police Gazette* denounced him as the "vilest, most despicable creature that lives. . . . He has disgusted the American public by flaunting in their faces an alliance as bold as it [is] offensive." Sam Sparks, former state treasurer of the Lone Star State, called for one hundred Texans to follow him north to Chicago to "attend to Jack Johnson."*

A reporter for the New York *World* looked up Mrs. David Terry, Etta Duryea Johnson's mother, to see if she might have anything to say about her ex-son-in-law's latest troubles. She did. It was her "Christian duty," she said,

---

*The black-owned Chicago *Broad Ax* advised the "red-eyed, shallow-pated Texan" not to try invading Chicago's black belt without a force many times that size.

to do all she could to aid Mrs. Cameron-Falconet: "If the suicide of my daughter might be taken as a warning by other white girls; if I thought it might save someone else from a similar fate, my own crushing burden of sorrow would be easier to bear and I would feel that her death has not been in vain."

What should be done with Johnson?

It would be wrong for me to tell you what ought to be done. It is not for me to judge. God will do that, but every night a prayer goes up from my pillow asking God to send upon this man the punishment he deserves. Two weeks ago I had a vision of Jack Johnson and I believe that vision was God's promise of its fulfillment.

In a vision as plain as day, I saw a boat on a beautiful stream. In that boat was my daughter, dressed in white, talking to my dead husband.

Suddenly, out of the water rose a giant, glistening black man. It was Jack Johnson. With both hands he grabbed for the boat as if he would crush it. But he missed it. My daughter rowed away and disappeared with a ripple of happy laughter on her lips. Then the water turned black as ink and swallowed the black man up. It was all so real that it frightened me, though I am a practical woman and not given to visions.

The interview was widely syndicated. When it ran in the Los Angeles *Times* the headline was, HOW JACK JOHNSON TORTURED HIS WHITE WIFE. THE STORY OF A BEAST. WHY DIDN'T JEFF KILL 'IM?

More and more Negroes were now edging away from Johnson, too. The black Philadelphia *Tribune* headlined one story JACK JOHNSON DANGEROUSLY ILL, VICTIM OF WHITE FEVER. A Negro mass meeting at the Cosmopolitan Baptist church in Washington asked "all self-respecting black men and women" to repudiate Johnson. "How silly!" said the black Nashville *Globe*.

Negroes can be depended upon to go to extremes on such occasions. . . . Negroes who have common sense have never been affected by the victories of Jack Johnson to the extent to make them forget themselves; and when he married a white woman right-thinking Negroes lost all respect for him. In the present trouble Johnson is not receiving any sympathy from Negroes. They have turned him over to his white friends. . . . There is nothing in common between the champion and the race to which he belongs.

He has placed a great gulf between himself and his people. He has no respect for black women and black people despise his name.*

On Sunday, October 20, before the Detroit Y.M.C.A., the Wizard of Tuskegee made his feelings known. Booker T. Washington had never approved of Johnson or the life he led. Now he formally disowned him—as if he'd ever owned him in the first place.

It is unfortunate that a man with money should use it in a way to injure his own people in the eyes of those who are seeking to uplift his race and improve its conditions. Chicago is now witnessing a good example of the result of educating a man to earn money without due attention having been given his mental and spiritual development.

In misrepresenting the colored people of this country this man is harming himself the least. I wish to say emphatically that his actions do not meet my personal approval, and I am sure they do not meet with the approval of the colored race.

Johnson, fortunate or rather unfortunate, it seems, in the possession of money, is doing a grave injustice to his race. It only goes to prove my contention that all men should be educated along mental and spiritual lines in connection with their physical education.

A man with muscle, minus brains, is a useless creature. Education, in addition to fitting a man for earning money, should prepare him for the attainment of some of life's higher ideals.

Asked for a response, Johnson would say only, "I never got caught in the wrong flat. I never got beat up because I looked in the wrong keyhole."†

---

*G.B. Aldrich, a black attorney from Tacoma, Washington, writing in the November 23 Indianapolis *Freeman*, urged a more charitable attitude toward the champion. Negroes were too prone to criticize other Negroes if they fell from favor with whites. "The fact that [Johnson] likes white women is no reflection on the race." After all, he continued, "most men like fair women; if you don't believe it just go into the best Negro homes amid the blackest of the most prosperous Negro families and you will find a yellow or almost white woman occupying the leading place of wife."

†Johnson was referring to a humiliation his accuser had suffered the previous March. Washington had entered the foyer of an apartment building on Manhattan's Upper West Side that was home exclusively to whites. There, a white man attacked him with his fists and then chased him down the street beating him with a cane. Sixteen stitches were required to heal the wounds in his scalp. Later, his attacker accused Washington of being a burglar, then of peering at a white woman through the keyhole in her apartment door. Precisely what happened remains unclear: both Washington and his assailant told unconvincing stories. But to Washington's Negro critics, the incident was the most vivid possible proof that despite a lifetime of accommodationism, when it came down to it, whites would treat even Booker T. Washington as just another black man.

Public pressure and the lure of big money eventually persuaded former champion James J. Jeffries to emerge from retirement and try to restore the title to the white race. Johnson signed for their fight at the Albany Hotel in New York City in December 1909 (top), surrounded by boxing insiders (including Jeffries, to his left, with fingers spread) who were nearly unanimous in their desire to see him beaten. The fight was scheduled for Reno, Nevada, where the relaxed picture above was taken. Etta Duryea nestles in the arms of her lover; at left is the champion's sometime trainer, Sig Hart.

Showdown at Reno, July 4, 1910: Billy Jordan introduces Jim Jeffries to the crowd (top) while Johnson waits in his corner (above). The novelist Jack London called them "the man of iron" and the "man of summer temperament." Tens of millions waited anxiously for news of the Battle of the Century, but the fight itself was anticlimactic. Jeffries was unable to catch the younger champion and collapsed in the fifteenth round. "And, as of old," London wrote, "it was play for Johnson."

"Not since the gladiatorial days of Rome," wrote the *Indianapolis Freeman*, "has there been a scene enacted as that which greeted Johnson's return from Reno." Johnson shakes hands with admirers from his private railroad car (above) somewhere en route to Chicago; next to him is his longtime trainer, Barney Furey. Johnson's jubilant Chicago neighbors (right) welcome the champion back to his mother's home; Johnson is somewhere in the crowd beneath the American flag. F. Fox's cartoon (inset) appeared in the *Chicago Evening News*.

Everywhere they went, Jack Johnson and Etta Duryea drew crowds. Here, in two never-before-published photographs taken in Ballston Spa, New York, on October 12, 1910, a local cameraman caught them as they set out together for the champion's next theatrical engagement at Binghamton. "I felt that in Etta," Johnson wrote, "I had found a love that would continue uninterrupted." They were legally married the following February.

KIRBY BANK FAILURE A STEAL, SAYS LANDIS

THE WEATHER.
FORECAST—Fair to-day: Sunday, increasing cloudiness and warmer; moderate west to southwest winds.

CHICAGO AMERICAN

2ND EDITION

VOL. XIII, NO. 111.—P. M.   SATURDAY.   CHICAGO, NOVEMBER 9, 1912.   SATURDAY.   PRICE ONE CENT

JOHNSON LOCKED UP IN 4½ By 8 Ft. CELL

CALL FOR HOLY WAR ISSUED

All Turks Summoned to Kill Christians at Constantinople Is Threatened.

BULGARIAN ARMY RESTS

Maroon-Purple Lineup.

MAROONS SEE CLOSE FIGHT WITH PURPLE

Purple If's for Play.

U.S. COURT HUNTS WIFE OF KIRBY

Judge Landis Wants Woman Under Arrest in City Court to Explain Loss of $75,000.

DECLARES DOCTOR SANE

5 BILLION IN CROPS THIS YEAR

$1,850,000,000 Value of Corn Alone—Yield is $41,721,000 Above Greatest in Past.

MEANS CHEAPER FOOD

U.S. Officers Seek Missing Rich Wife Here
FEAR KIDNAPING PLOT

NEGRO IN RAGE AS HE IS JAILED

Knocks a Photographer Down; Curses and Fumes When He Is Handcuffed

PUGILIST SEES GALLOWS

What Johnson Asked For in Cell.
Champagne.
Box of Cigars.
Dozen Candles
And a Soft Bed

What He Got.
Bottle of Milk.
One Small Candle
And a Wooden Bench!

The champion's marriage to nineteen-year-old Lucille Cameron (left) on December 3, 1912, just weeks after Etta Johnson committed suicide, enraged much of the white public—and alienated many blacks, as well. He was already under federal indictment for having violated the Mann Act (above). After he was found guilty the following spring and sentenced to a year in prison, he and his new bride fled the country for France, where they were photographed (below) in a Paris park.

On April 5, 1915, Johnson faced the biggest of the white hopes, Jess Willard (top), in Havana, Cuba. For the first twenty rounds Johnson more than held his own against his bigger, younger challenger. But in round 26, heat, age, and exhaustion—and a hard right hand by Willard—combined to knock him out. The photograph at the right, in which Johnson appears to be shading his eyes from the sun, helped foster the myth he had thrown the fight.

PLAZA DE TOROS MONUMENTAL
DOMINGO 23 ABRIL DE 1916
A las 3 de la tarde
GRAN FIESTA DE BOXEO
en la cual tendrán lugar
6 interesantes combates entre notables luchadores, 6

JACK JOHNSON = ARTHUR CRAVAN

Finalizará el espectáculo con el sensacional encuentro
entre el campeón del mundo

Jack Johnson
Negro de 110 kilos
y el campeón europeo

Arthur Cravan
Blanco de 105 kilos

En este match se disputará una bolsa de **50.000** ptas.
para el vencedor.

Véanse programas

PRECIOS (incluidos los impuestos)

SOMBRA Y SOL Y SOMBRA. Palco con entradas, 20 pesetas.—Silla de ring 1ª fila con entrada, 35 ptas.—Silla de ring 2ª fila con entrada, 25 ptas.—Silla de ring 3ª y 4ª filas con entrada, 16 ptas.—Sillas de ring 5ª, 6ª, 7ª y 8ª filas con entrada, 12 ptas.—Barrera con entrada, 10 ptas.—Contrabarrera con entrada, 6'50 ptas.—Sillón delantero de Palco con entrada, 8 ptas.—Sillón tendido de Presidencia con entrada, 8 ptas.—ENTRADA GENERAL, 3'50 ptas.—Entrada de tertulia (numerada) 9'60 ptas.

SOL. Silla de ring 1ª fila con entrada, 18 ptas.—Silla de ring 2ª fila con entrada, 12 ptas.—Sillas de ring 3ª y 4ª filas con entrada, 8 ptas.—Silla de ring restantes con entrada 6 ptas.—ENTRADA GENERAL, 2 ptas.

Sobs. de López Robert y Cª, impresores. Asalto, 63

After Jack Johnson lost his championship to Jess Willard in 1915, his reputation declined abroad just as it had back home. His 1916 fight in Barcelona with the Dadaist poet Arthur Cravan was advertised (above) as if it were the real thing, but it was really a one-sided farce. By 1920 he was reduced to running a saloon in Tijuana, Mexico, and (right, top and bottom) putting on strongman shows and exhibitions against nonentities for small crowds in Mexican border towns.

Johnson ended seven years of exile on July 20, 1920, when he shook hands with sheriff John H. Cline of Los Angeles County, stepped across the Mexican border onto U.S. soil, and surrendered to federal officers. He served his sentence in Leavenworth where, at a "boxfest" on May 28, 1921, he entertained his fellow inmates by easily outfighting a journeyman named Joe Boykin.

In December 1932, Jack Johnson and his third wife, Irene Pineau Johnson, take a turn around the deck of the liner taking them to France. A divorcée from Peoria, Illinois, Irene Pineau Johnson would remain loyal to her second husband through the last nineteen years of his life. "As a husband," she wrote, "Mr. Johnson is everything that he could possibly be."

Early on Monday morning, a mob of some one thousand white Chicagoans gathered at the corner of Clark Street and Montrose Boulevard, slung a rope over a tree limb, and hauled up a dummy with a blackened face. Somebody called the police and the crowd was hustled off the corner. But the dummy was left dangling from the tree so that men and women riding the streetcars to work could see it. A placard pinned to its breast read, THIS IS WHAT WE WILL DO TO JACK JOHNSON.

That same morning, Charles Erbstein and several deputy U.S. marshals banged loudly at the door of Johnson's café, armed with subpoenas for women the Justice Department thought might know something about his relationship with Lucille Cameron and demanding that they be allowed to come in and look around. No women were present. When Johnson spotted Erbstein, his friends had to hold him back. "Throw that lawyer out of the place," he shouted, "or I'll kill him."

Chicago politicians who had once sought Johnson's company now hurried to disentangle themselves from him. "I hope Johnson gets his block knocked off in Australia," said Mayor Carter Harrison, Jr. "That's the quickest way to get rid of him." Alderman A. R. Tearny of the Third Ward, stakeholder for the second Jim Flynn fight, now refused to help Johnson raise bail for Lucille. "I will never have relations, even of a business nature, with Johnson again," he told the press. Alderman Ellis Geiger of the Twenty-first Ward said that Johnson had "brought burning shame to the fair name of Chicago" and vowed to push a resolution through that evening's city council meeting calling on the mayor to close down the Café de Champion as a "disorderly resort."

As the aldermen took turns denouncing him at City Hall Johnson was defending himself before one hundred well-to-do black businessmen and professionals gathered at the Appomattox Club at 3441 Wabash Avenue. He'd been invited to appear there by Beauregard F. Moseley, the attorney who'd been happy enough a few weeks earlier to take out-of-town associates to Johnson's café for an evening of champagne and entertainment but who had now helped draft a formal resolution beseeching white citizens not to "hold the race guilty or responsible for the charges made against an individual of said race." Many of those present had stood and cheered Johnson at the late Bob Motts' black-tie testimonial dinner after the Jeffries fight. He had said then that he feared "the colored people of the world" would one day desert him. It now seemed to be happening. Moseley asked him if he'd like to say a word or two in his own defense before the resolution was officially adopted. "Yes," he said, "I should like to do that."

There was only scattered applause as he rose to speak. Johnson's customary smile was missing. He spoke slowly and with great earnestness.

First I want to say that nothing ever is said of the white man who waylays the little colored girl when she goes to market. Nobody has anything to say about that. But when the Negro does something that is not nearly so serious there is a great hue and cry.

I want to say that I never made any statement attributed to me to the effect that I could get any white woman I wanted. I can lay my hand upon the Bible and swear that I never made such a statement. My father was a Christian and my mother is a Christian, and I know what it means to swear by the Bible. I want to say that I never said anything of the sort about any woman of any color.

I have been quoted falsely. The newspapers and the public have taken advantage of me because of my color. If I were a white man not a line of this would have reached the newspaper.

But I do want to say that I am not a slave and that I have the right to choose who my mate shall be without the dictation of any man. I have eyes and I have a heart and when they fail to tell me who I shall have as mine I want to be put away in a lunatic asylum.

So long as I do not interfere with any other man's wife, I shall claim the right to select the woman of my own choice. Nobody else can do that for me. That is where the trouble lies.

On Tuesday afternoon, October 22, Lucille Cameron was brought to the Federal Building under armed guard to appear before the grand jury. "Tell all you know," her mother said as they passed each other in the corridor. "There still is a chance for you if you only give up the nigger."

Mrs. Cameron-Falconet and the government still hoped that Lucille would turn on the man she continued to insist she loved. She would not. She admitted that she had been a prostitute before she left Milwaukee. It had been her idea to come to the city and pursue her profession, no one else's. Neither Johnson nor any one else had had anything to do with it. After about an hour on the stand, she collapsed in tears and had to be carried out of the grand jury room. A physician was called.

After she was back on her feet, federal agents escorted her back to Rockford. They would keep her behind bars, hoping further reflection might lead her to change her mind. But the attempt to build a Mann Act case around

Lucille Cameron had collapsed. "It has been established beyond doubt that the Cameron girl was in the city of Chicago for at least three months prior to the time she met Johnson," agent Lins admitted to his superiors, "and the possibility that he aided in any way in her transportation from Minneapolis to Chicago is very remote."

Harry A. Parkin, the Assistant U.S. District Attorney in Chicago, was not satisfied. He was determined to get Jack Johnson, one way or another. There were plenty of people prepared to testify that the champion frequented prostitutes; despite Johnson's frantic effort to pay them off and send them out of town, the Bureau of Investigation had twenty-two such witnesses on call. The problem was, there was as yet no proof he'd taken any of his women across state lines. Parkin was sure such proof could be found and asked the bureau to mount an all-out effort to "secure evidence [of] illegal transportation by Johnson of any other women for an immoral purpose." U.S. Attorney General Wickersham and A. Bruce Bielaski, the acting chief of the Bureau of Investigation in Washington, both pledged their full cooperation. They, too, now felt that the public would never be satisfied until Jack Johnson was behind bars.

On October 28, Mayor Harrison ordered Johnson to halt all music and entertainment at his café. The champion pleaded with the chief of police to have him reconsider. Without entertainment, he would have to close the business that was the center of his life outside the ring. "He cried," the chief said afterward, "whined like a baby, when I told him there was nothing doing." That same day, according to the Chicago *Tribune*, a deranged man turned up with a pistol at the Federal Building, threatening to "blow the nigger's brains out." The police told him Johnson wasn't there. No one bothered even to take his name.

Two days later, the authorities put Johnson out of business altogether by refusing to renew his liquor license. To get it back, he would be required to prove he was of good moral character, "and *that*," the mayor said, "he'll have a deuce of a time doing if half the reports about him are true." That night, the police refused to allow any customers through the doors. Hundreds stood outside, listening to the orchestra play one last time for the champion and his valet. The next morning, November 1, men from the Heilman Brewing Company seized the chairs and tables and gold-rimmed spittoons of which Johnson had been so proud. Then the police moved in, hauling out the liquor that was left and nailing shut the doors and windows.

"There are plenty of white gentlemen running saloons right now in this city," the *Broad Ax* protested, who are ten thousand times worse in every way than Jack Johnson. Their places are the headquarters for thieves, murderers, . . . and every other kind of violators of the laws of deceny and morality. . . . Some of [these white gentlemen] who have never been accused of conducting Sunday saloons . . . are warm political associates of Mayor Harrison.

The champion tried to appear unruffled at the closing. He thought he might take a vacation, he said. "I'll take my car and go traveling somewhere until the trial comes up, but I don't think there ever will be a trial." He was doing all he could to make sure there wasn't one, focusing his charm on the federal agents assigned to his case to find out what they were up to, hiring detectives to track down potential witnesses and offer them money to leave town until things died down.

In the midst of Johnson's troubles, a flamboyant promoter came to call. Richard Klegin was just twenty-three years old and barely five feet tall, but by taking Sam McVey and four other black boxers to Paris in 1911 he'd begun to build a reputation for himself as an international impresario.* He was now acting as the American representative of George Thomas, an expatriate American living in St. Petersburg. Thomas was a black onetime valet and waiter from Georgia who had saved his money, moved overseas in 1890, opened a restaurant in Berlin, and then made himself rich as a showman in Russia, running a chain of theaters as well as a glass-enclosed amusement park called the Aquarium. Thomas had sent along a check for five thousand dollars plus three round-trip tickets to Russia that could be Johnson's if he agreed to fight McVey there in January. The champion's friends urged him to accept the offer and leave right away, before he faced more legal difficulties. He told the press he couldn't do it while Lucille was behind bars for no fault of her own. But he had also been warned by District Attorney Wilkerson that he could not leave the country until his smuggling case came to court.

Then the Chicago office of the Bureau of Investigation got the tip it had been looking for. An anonymous letter, written by a man whose motive, he said, was to "send this nigger to jail for the balance of his life," urged the govern-

---

*Klegin tried to make a career of taking American sports to the Old World. He accompanied baseball teams to France and England, introduced "motor polo" to the Continent, and got a lot of publicity in 1915 by claiming to be close to a deal with the Italian government to stage ancient Roman games in the Colosseum or the Baths of Caracalla. Proposed events included a procession of "vestal virgins," boxing with the cestus, chariot races, and "a sea fight with Carthage in a flooded arena." The Italian government evidently thought better of it.

ment to look for a former inmate of the Everleigh Club who had traveled all over the country with Johnson and called herself "Belle Gifford" and "Mrs. Jacques Allen." Agents turned to their contacts in the Chicago underworld. James Duffy, an "ex-post office safe-cracker and all around crook," pointed them toward Johnson's still-angry ex-manager, George Little, and a small-time vaudevillian named Mortie Heyman, from whom he said Johnson had stolen the woman in question. A brothel keeper named Ollie Davis said he'd heard she was working out of a whorehouse in the nation's capital.

Martin Lins immediately wired Washington:

BELLE BAKER, ALIAS BELLE GIFFORD, ALIAS BELLE ALLEN, FORMERLY INMATE EVERLEIGH CLUB, CHICAGO, SAID TO HAVE BEEN ILLEGALLY TRANSPORTED BY JACK JOHNSON, NOW SAID TO BE INMATE SOME SPORTING HOUSE WASHINGTON, D.C. DURING ONE TRIP WAS PHOTOGRAPHED WITH JOHNSON IN BOSTON. PICTURE APPEARED PAPERS THERE ENTITLED JACK JOHNSON AND HIS PRETTY WHITE WIFE.

Agents tracked Belle Schreiber to Grace Sinclair's "resort" at 1229 D Street in Washington. She proved eager to talk. She hadn't seen the champion since early 1911, when he had lied to her about his marriage and her relationship with him had forced her onto the street for the last time, and she remained bitter. Her memory of where and when they'd gone together seemed encyclopedic—and she had bills and receipts to back up much of what she said. Most of their travels had taken place before the Mann Act went into effect in June of 1910, but prosecutors thought a case could be built around events in mid-October of that year, when Johnson had paid Belle's rail fare from Pittsburgh to Chicago and then set her up as a madam at the Ridgewood Apartments. Lins told Bielaski that everyone in the Chicago office was "very much pleased with the prospects of making a case against Johnson with the evidence you have furnished us."

To corroborate and amplify Belle's version of events, federal agents quietly fanned out across the country, interviewing prostitutes, chauffeurs, waiters, bellhops, Pullman porters, ex-managers, former sparring partners, looking for something—*anything*—that could be used to bolster their case that the champion had broken federal law with Belle Schreiber.

Meanwhile, on the afternoon of November 7, agents brought Belle to Chicago to tell her story to the federal grand jury. Everything was cloaked in secrecy, Lins explained, "in view of the fact that Johnson is possessed of large means and will leave no stone unturned in his efforts to make away with any possible witness." Lucille Cameron was paraded along one corridor to confuse the reporters who haunted the Federal Building and to throw off the track any informants who might be working for Johnson, while Belle Schreiber was hustled down another and slipped unseen into the grand jury room.

There, for four hours, she poured out her memories of couplings and beatings and constant travel with the champion. When she was finished, she was hurried back out of the building, then escorted into a taxi and onto a night train to Manhattan, where she was to be hidden away inside the Waverley Home, an institution run by the New York Probation Association. No one had recognized her.

Even before she'd boarded her train, the grand jury voted to issue seven Mann Act indictments against Jack Johnson, charging him with transporting her on October 15, 1910, from Pittsburgh to Chicago for the purpose of prostitution and debauchery and in violation of the "peace and dignity of the . . . United States." Within minutes, federal Judge Kenesaw Mountain Landis issued a bench warrant for the champion's immediate arrest. Bail was set at an unprecedented thirty thousand dollars.

Special Agent Meyer and a party of U.S. marshals and city detectives found the champion with several friends in room 21 of the Hotel Vendome, the same hotel where he had agreed to help Belle Schreiber find the flat that was now at the heart of the case against him. They broke down the door, prepared for a struggle. There was none. Johnson had been expecting them, though he had not known who would be testifying against him or what they'd say he'd done.

He went along willingly enough to the Federal Building. But once he got to Assistant District Attorney Harry Parkin's office, he was indignant. "I think you ought to give me a fair and square deal," he told Parkin. "Why didn't you arrest me earlier, so I could get a bondsman? I can give $50,000 cash if necessary. I'm easy to find."

"We'll give you a square deal, Jack," Parkin answered. "You'll get all the chance you are entitled to. No more and no less—just the same as anybody else."

But he wasn't being treated as anybody else would have been—had they been white. And he had expected better from Parkin. He and Charles DeWoody had been his guests for dinner at the Café de Champion, after all; he had even raced automobiles with them on Michigan Avenue in the early morning hours. Clearly, his attempts to win friends—and influence—among federal officials had failed.

Parkin permitted Johnson to place calls to a lawyer, Edwin Day, and to Sol Lewinsohn, the shady bondsman who had brought Parkin and DeWoody and their party to his café just a few months earlier. But when they were slow to turn up, Parkin ordered the champion handcuffed for the trip to jail.

Johnson's eyes filled with tears. "You don't have to do this," he said. "I won't run away." They did it anyway. The first set of cuffs they tried was too small. A second pair fit. But before he and his escorts left for the lockup, the lawyer and bondsman appeared, further phone calls were made, and Judge Landis permitted Tiny Johnson to sign a temporary bond against her house so the champion could go home for the night. "I knew the Schreiber girl well," Johnson told the reporters waiting outside. "But I never transported her anywhere." He still believed the government had no case, and at his home he handed Lewinsohn thirty thousand dollars in cash to protect him against loss in negotiating an acceptable bond.

The next morning, Johnson appeared before Judge Landis for a bail hearing. Landis was only in his mid-forties, but already had the white mane and the flair for self-promotion that would one day characterize him as the first commissioner of baseball. He was no respecter of persons—he had won fame for hauling John D. Rockefeller himself into court to testify, then levying a huge fine against Standard Oil that was swiftly overturned by a higher court—and he had no time at all for a black man accused of dallying with white women. When he learned that neither of the men Lewinsohn had arranged to underwrite Johnson's bond actually owned the property they said they owned, he was enraged. The whole thing, he bellowed, had been "a brazen attempt to put over a dirty deal on the court that would have degraded the old police courts of Chicago in their worst days." He dressed down Lewinsohn, threw one of the would-be guarantors out of his courtroom and threatened to have him arrested if he came anywhere near it again, then had the other jailed for contempt for lying to him.

Johnson was accompanied to court by a well-respected Chicago trial attorney, Benjamin Bachrach.* Bachrach offered to put up $65,000—$50,000 in real estate and $15,000 in cash—and Johnson could be heard whispering in his new lawyer's ear to "tell the judge I'll give more if he wants to take it." The government said cash wouldn't do. Johnson was rumored to be on his way to Russia. Landis agreed. "I will not accept a cash bond," he said. "There is a

---

*Twelve years later, Bachrach would be Clarence Darrow's codefense counsel in the celebrated murder-kidnapping case of Leopold and Loeb.

human cry in this case." Nor would he accept surety from anyone who was indemnified against loss if the prisoner fled. Johnson would have to go to jail.

Reporters and photographers were waiting on the sidewalk in front of the Cook County Jail that evening as Johnson and his escorts pulled up. When the champion got down from the car, they could see that he was handcuffed to Deputy Marshal Edward Northrup. A photographer named Edwin A. Wiegel stepped forward to get a flash picture. Johnson cursed, raised his cane with his free hand, and brought it smashing down on Wiegel's camera. "Please don't, Jack," pleaded Northrup, who was being pulled along "like a palm leaf fan." "Please be a gentleman."

Johnson calmed down. Two diamond watch charms and a jeweled Swiss watch were taken from him for safekeeping. Someone stole a watch fob with his jeweled initials on it. He was stripped and searched. The county jail was strictly segregated, but it amused Johnson's jailers to lead him to cell number 508, in the middle of the white section. There were some 530 white prisoners in the lockup. Many cursed him as soon as he was spotted. Then they began to chant in unison, "Hang Johnson! Hang Johnson!"

When there was a brief pause, and someone called him a black bastard, Johnson shot back, "I'll give $50 for the chance to slug that one."

He took it as long as he could, then called for a doctor, saying he felt ill. Guards took him to the infirmary for the night. The physician looked him over and pronounced him in perfect health. "The only thing wrong with Johnson is cold feet," he said. The jailers had evidently had their fun. When morning came, they locked him in a new cell in the Negro tier. His cell mate was a cook named John Brown, accused of stabbing a friend to death aboard a lake steamer.

Johnson called for candles, cigars, and a case of champagne to make his stay more pleasant.

He was given only a bar of soap.

"When I was in jail in San Francisco," he said, "those gentlemen treated me like a prince. And I am a prince, ain't I?"

His mother and sisters came to see him. So did Sig Hart, a part of his inner circle once again and bearing a box of cigars.

Meanwhile, Benjamin Bachrach petitioned the federal court for a writ of habeas corpus. The thirty-thousand-dollar bail Judge Landis had set was excessive and "on terms onerous and prohibitive," he argued, and the Mann Act itself was unconstitutional. When federal judge George A. Carpenter denied his petition, he took it straight to the United States Supreme Court for review. There, without ever mentioning Johnson's name for fear of prejudicing the justices against him, he tried to argue that his client be admitted to bail pending a hearing. But the government objected. Solicitor General William Marshall Bullitt interrupted to say, "That's the Jack Johnson case." The Court did not order Johnson's release, but it did agree to hear arguments on January 6, 1913, along with several other cases challenging the legitimacy of the Mann Act. Until Johnson's case was heard by the Court and a decision was rendered, no date for the trial could be set.

While Benjamin Bachrach saw to Johnson's federal appeal, two prominent black Chicago attorneys went to work to get him out on bail: W. G. Anderson, who specialized in habeas corpus cases, and Johnson's old friend Edward H. Wright, the only black man ever to serve as president of the Cook County Board of Commissioners and still a force in the Republican Party. It took them a week to come up with thirty thousand dollars in surety acceptable to the government. Half was provided by property owned by a real estate agent named Matthew S. Baldwin, the other half by the Wabash Avenue home Johnson had bought for his mother. The champion celebrated hard the evening he came home, sending out three of his cars to ferry guests to and from the party. He still was assuring everyone that there would never be a trial. He was a rich man, and rich men didn't go to jail.

Mrs. Cameron-Falconet had been overjoyed when Johnson was locked up. Now that "the negro has been indicted for bringing another woman from one state to another," she'd said then, she wanted her daughter released. Judge Landis wouldn't hear of it. If he let her out, she might elope with Jack Johnson, he said; she would have to stay where she was. But as the weeks went by, it became more and more clear that Lucille was unjustly confined, that the government's case against the champion had nothing to do with her. Finally, on November 25, Judge Carpenter allowed Mrs. Cameron-Falconet to pay a reduced bond of one thousand dollars and take her daughter back to her Chicago hotel.

Meanwhile, Belle Schreiber was causing trouble for the government. Striking back at Johnson had appealed to her at first, and she enjoyed being taken seriously by the agents who questioned her and escorted her everywhere. But she hated being confined to the Waverley Home. Occasional walks and car rides, accompanied always by one agent and shadowed by another, did not lift her spirits. Neither did dinners out or visits to the movies. The home was "a regular prison," she wrote to a friend. "Bars on the windows—no papers to read—no fire and cold indoors—this is a place for wayward girls—girls in the family way and witnesses for the government—food awful—retire at 9 p.m. and get up at 6:30 a.m.—what a life! I am almost crazy and so unhappy."

Her unhappiness was due in part to enforced withdrawal from the absinthe and narcotics upon which she had come to depend. A physician was finally called and dosed her with what an agent called "special medicine for such persons." It didn't help. She wanted to move to a hotel, she said. She was a witness, not a criminal; they had no right to keep her locked up this way. She asked to be taken to visit an old friend named Mrs. Vickers. Vickers turned out to be a madam, and when Belle arrived, she applied for a job once she was free to take it. Her embarrassed escort hurried her back to the Waverley Home. Forbidden to contact any more madams about future work, she talked a fellow inmate into writing a letter doing so on her behalf; the letter was discovered, and the woman who wrote it and had been on probation at the home was sent back to prison for a year.

Then Belle learned that Lucille Cameron had been released from jail. She was still more upset. She wrote to Raymond S. Horn, a Bureau of Investigation official in Washington, demanding to know why the Cameron girl was free to move about while she remained confined. Horn tried to pacify her. Miss Cameron was unimportant—"All that she knows worthwhile to the Government could be bottled up in a thimble"—while Belle should be proud that she was essential to the government's case and needed round-the-clock protection from the defendant's agents. Since her "surroundings were so utterly different from those to which you have been accustomed," he sympathized with her loneliness, but surely it was "consoling to know you will soon render your country a service such as few are ever fortunate enough to duplicate and one that will go a long way toward wiping out those acts of your past which I know you are not particularly desirous of reflecting upon." He couldn't tell when the trial would take place—that was up to the federal courts—but he hoped it would be soon. In the meantime, he urged her to "continue to be the good little girl that you have been."

On November 30, in Chicago, Llewellyn Smith, a black messenger working in the U.S. district attorney's office, was asked to take a fresh subpoena for Belle to the office of the Bureau of Investigation. The subpoena was marked for the Manhattan office, whose task it would be to serve it on her. Smith did as he was told, then made straight for the champion's house. He would later say he'd gone there to call on one of Johnson's sisters, but his superiors insisted that his real purpose was to tell the champion Belle

Schreiber was somewhere in New York. He was fired two days later, and the restrictions on Belle Schreiber's movements were tightened still further. It made her "peevish," according to her guards. Three days later, her peevishness would turn to fury.

Lucille Cameron had moved into her mother's hotel room after her release from prison, but she didn't stay there long. It is impossible to be sure precisely what went on over the next few days. In his autobiography, Johnson said she came to him and begged him to marry her. She was "ruined in the eyes of the world," she knew, but "her mother was making her the object of abuse and nagging which she could not bear." He said it was the wrong moment to marry, and she agreed to go to Toronto to think things over. But she returned within a day or two, "again begging me to marry her." He said yes.

There may have been more to it than that. Johnson's sister Jennie Rhodes would later allege that in order to be able to marry Lucille without fear of further harassment from the state, her brother met with State's Attorney Wayman at the Pekin Café on Sunday evening, December 1, and handed him an envelope containing ten thousand dollars. And Tiny Johnson claimed that her son had also had to pay five thousand dollars to Mrs. Cameron-Falconet—of which Charles Erbstein, "her brave defender and protector of all women," kept five hundred dollars—in order to keep them from making any more trouble for the couple. The whole thing, she insisted, had been a shakedown.

Whatever happened behind the scenes, Johnson and Lucille drove up to City Hall on Tuesday morning, December 3. She stayed in the car while he strode inside to the marriage clerk's office and applied for a license. "They ought to refuse him on general principles," one woman shouted. But there were no grounds on which to turn him down, and he emerged a few minutes later with the all-important piece of paper.

"I had a long talk with Miss Cameron yesterday, and we decided to be married tonight," he told the City Hall reporters who quickly gathered around him.

I explained that I had been blamed for ill-treating her and that we might as well be married right away. She is alone in the world now. Her mother has left her and her step-father is quoted as saying he wants to have nothing more to do with her. We love each other and I see no reason why we should not be married. We will spend our honeymoon near Chicago, but will not leave the state.

319

They were married in Tiny Johnson's parlor that afternoon. The Reverend John Robinson, who had officiated at Etta Johnson's funeral less than three months earlier, performed the ceremony. Fred Daniel, a white saloon keeper, was best man. Johnson's brother Henry hurled the first fistful of rice. Deputy Marshal Edward C. Marsales, who had grown fond of Lucille while in charge of her incarceration at Rockford, joined in the champagne toasts that followed.

"I am so happy," the bride told the press. When a reporter asked where her mother was, she said, "I don't know and I don't care."

Asked what she thought of the marriage, Tiny Johnson kept her own counsel. "Sometimes I say things Jack doesn't like, so I'll keep my thoughts to myself."

As the reporters filed out the door, one looked back and saw Johnson remove his bride's new twenty-five-hundred-dollar wedding ring and slip it into his own pocket.

As always, the front page of the Chicago *Defender* offered Johnson its unqualified support.

THE WEDDING CEREMONY WAS HELD AT THE HOME OF THE
JOHNSONS, 3344 WABASH AVENUE, AND WHITE AND COLORED
FOLKS FREELY MINGLED WITH EACH OTHER WHILE SHOWERING
CONGRATULATIONS AND KISSES ON THE NEW BRIDE

THE GROOM PRESENTED HIS BRIDE WITH A $2,500 DIAMOND RING
A $5,000 NEW MOTOR CAR AND TOSSED THE COLORED PREACHER
A NEW HUNDRED DOLLAR BILL FOR MARRYING THEM

MRS. CAMERON-FALCONET HAS WASHED HER HANDS CLEAN OF
THE WHOLE WHITE AND BLACK MESS AND HAS RETURNED TO HER
HOME IN MINNEAPOLIS, MINN. IN UTTER DISGUST

"I never will believe that [Johnson] married his white women just to spite white people," his friend Bricktop wrote. "I just think he did what he wanted to because he wanted to do it." That was pretty much why he did everything. But his second marriage had all sorts of repercussions for all kinds of people, close to home as well as far away.

Deputy Marshal Marsales, an eight-year veteran of the Justice Department, lost his job for attending the wedding. News of the marriage further infuriated Belle Schreiber. It was bad enough that she had to remain isolated and confined, but to learn that Johnson, whom she blamed for all her troubles, was still out on bail and free to celebrate yet another wedding was more than she could bear. She vowed to run away if she was still locked up at New Year's. On the evening of December 14, agents tried to cheer her up by taking her along to a series of cafés to search for one of her friends from the old days, Lillian St. Clair. They didn't find St. Clair, and when, after midnight, it was time to take her back to her room at the Waverley Home, she refused to go. Standing on 125th Street outside what one agent called "a nigger joint," she began shrieking that she could not stand being a prisoner anymore. A crowd gathered. The agents got her into a cab and checked her into the Prince George Hotel for the night. Then they wired Washington for instructions.

They were told to bring her back to the capital the next morning. "During the trip from New York," one of her escorts reported, "Belle acted in a manner which caused some embarrassment. She also accosted one Jerry Moore, a passenger on the train, whom she remembered as a former patron of hers when she was an inmate of the Sinclair house of prostitution in Washington." Belle was transferred to Baltimore and placed in a new institution, the Florence Crittenton Home. She lasted only a few days before the matron in charge asked that she be removed. Agents found her a room in a boardinghouse at 926 North Calvert and made sure the door was guarded day and night so she wouldn't run away and Jack Johnson's agents couldn't contact her if they managed to track her down.

Whites who had denounced Johnson for marrying one white woman were enraged to learn he'd married another. An Oklahoma woman expressed her anger to an Ohio paper: "Down in this part of the country, he would never have lived to marry the second white girl." In Shreveport Louisiana, funds were collected in a saloon to pay a posse currently pursuing a Negro offender in the area to turn its attention to Johnson. At the National Governors' Conference at Richmond, Virginia, Governor Cole Blease called for the champion to be lynched: "There is but one punishment, and that must be speedy, when the negro lays his hand upon the person of a white woman." Northern governors used less inflammatory language, but they, too, deplored what had happened. "That Johnson wedding," said Governor John Dix of New York, "is a blot on our civilization."

Congressman Seaborn A. Roddenberry of Georgia, who had campaigned in 1910 against the interstate shipment of films showing Johnson beating a white man in the ring, took the floor to introduce an amendment to the U.S.

Constitution banning marriage between whites and "any and all persons of African descent or having any trace of African blood."

> No brutality [said Roddenberry,] no infamy, no degradation in all the years of southern slavery possessed such villainous character and such atrocious qualities as the provision of the laws of Illinois which allows the marriage of the Negro, Jack Johnson, to a woman of Caucasian strain. . . . Inter-marriage between whites and blacks is repulsive and averse to every senti-ment of pure American spirit. . . . It is destructive of moral supremacy, and ultimately this slavery of white women to black beasts will bring this nation a conflict as fatal and as bloody as ever reddened the soil of Virginia or crimsoned the mountain paths of Pennsylvania. . . . Let us uproot and exterminate now this debasing, ultra-demoralizing, un-American and inhuman leprosy.*

On the evening of December 14, Lucille Cameron Johnson and three friends—two women and a man, all of them white—swept into the elegant Pompeiian Room at the Congress Hotel on Michigan Avenue and asked for a table. They were quickly seated by the maître d'. "Bedecked with diamonds and clothed in white furs, [Lucille] attracted the attention of several hun-dred guests," the Los Angeles *Times* reported the next morning. "It was whis-pered she was some famous actress. No one knew them."

Two young men came in. One murmured to the other. They laughed and sat down at a table near Lucille's party. Then, "in a voice that could be heard all over the great dining-room one of them said, 'Harry, that's Lucille Cameron, wife of Jack Johnson.' Immediately, there was confusion. Women and men pushed their chairs from their tables and walked out. Orders were cancelled by those who had not been served."

Several guests stormed into the manager's office to protest Lucille's presence.

> Detectives were ordered to eject the Johnson woman. The man with her objected. She said, "Why, you have no right to put us out. We are orderly. They serve us elsewhere."

---

*"Representative Roddenberry . . . had a surplus of hot air Wednesday, and had to let it out," said the black-owned Washington *Bee* on December 13. "Roddenberry is from Georgia, sah! And he doesn't want a Negro to marry a white woman, and yet many of the Southern crackers still pursue the high yellows whenever they get an opportunity. The colored people of this country are not responsible for the acts of Jack Johnson. Roddenberry's next move will be to keep Negroes from breathing."

The detective placed his hand on the man's shoulder and said: "You will have to get out. We do not want your money here. The other guests object, and you will have to get out now."

Apparently unabashed, Johnson's wife rose and stared at the shocked diners who were standing in the halls. She attempted to go down the corridor toward the main entrance but was prevented by the detective who showed her to the side door. The other two women in the party did not say a word. They hung their heads and followed. As they walked toward the door accompanied by the detective, women guests . . . standing in the hall caught their skirts and shrank back. The men only glared angrily at the retreating party, but said nothing.

As soon as the news of Johnson's marriage to a second white woman broke, his two black attorneys, Edward H. Wright and W. G. Anderson, went to court to have their names stricken from the records. They were so appalled, they assured the New York *Times,* that they no longer wished to be associated with him. Politics may have played a part in Wright's abandonment of his client. Defeated during his campaign for alderman in 1910— when Johnson had taken considerable risks to campaign for him—he may have calculated that continuing to be linked to the champion might damage future opportunities.

Anderson's break with Johnson was more symbolic than real. He continued to work with him on a scheme that promised to profit both men by exploiting the fears of well-to-do bigots. The story surfaced just before Christmas. Johnson had anonymously obtained an option to buy the big lakeside home of the late Helen M. Sherman in the heart of one of Chicago's most exclusive summer colonies, Lake Geneva, Wisconsin. It was to be a thirty-five-thousand-dollar Christmas gift for his new bride, Johnson told the press, and he was also buying a farm just down the road on which he planned to raise cattle and a herd of buffalo. The house was surrounded by the vacation homes of some of Chicago's wealthiest families. Henry J. Evans, director of the National Biscuit Company, lived next door. John G. Mitchell, president of the Illinois Trust and Savings Bank, lived a few doors away. When a reporter called Mitchell to see how he'd taken the news, the banker tried a joke: Johnson's purchase, he said, constituted a case of "black male." Mrs. Mitchell was not amused. "It is an outrage," she said. "I am astounded that Mr. Sherman should have sold his property to a negro."

The seller, the late Mrs. Sherman's seventy-year-old son, was unrepentant: he needed to sell, he said, and no one other than Johnson had made him a decent offer.

From the point of view of the colony's residents worse was to come. Johnson and Lucille did not plan to be alone at their new address. According to lawyer Anderson, the champion was just one of ten black investors, who planned to transform part of the Sherman mansion into the "Lincoln Social and Athletic Club." Then he offered the Chicago *Tribune* a description of what would go on there, carefully calibrated to further alarm the colony—and eventually loosen its purse strings:

> We intend to make a clubhouse of the place [but] the social amenities are to be given their proper place. In view of the fact that Mr. Johnson is one of the chief investors and is himself a leading athlete, it is to be expected that more or less attention will be paid to calisthenics. But the merely physical is not to be allowed to predominate. There will be dances and soirées, receptions and carnivals. The best people in Chicago from the district of the south side . . . will participate.
>
> Mrs. Jack Johnson probably will be the chief patroness of these affairs. Other white wives of negroes also will participate. No matter what the attitude of the Lake Geneva people may be, *we* do not intend to draw the color line.

South Side real estate agent W. H. Harris, another member of the syndicate, said the Lake Geneva purchase was only the beginning. He and his associates hoped to buy up property in exclusive white communities all over the country, he said—Florida, Alabama, California, anywhere "it can be shown that we will make money out of it."

On Christmas Eve, the elite of Lake Geneva held an emergency meeting to see what they could do to stop what the next day the New York *Times* called a "NEGRO INVASION."

The situation put one Chicago *Tribune* writer in mind of Bert Williams and William Walker's 1909 musical hit, *Bandana Land:*

> In its original form, "Bandana Land" . . . told how a group of negroes purchased a plot of land in the heart of a fashionable settlement, and how the negroes sold out to the white folks who didn't care for their proximity, at fabulous prices. There was a laugh in every line. As the play will open today

for the benefit of Lake Geneva it assumes the aspect of a tragedy. Reduced to stern reality, with the Judson G. Sherman house . . . as the headquarters of the negro Lincoln Social and Athletic Club and with Jack Johnson . . . as the star actor, the laughs evaporate.

More pertinent perhaps was a similar move by several Negro investors who had quietly purchased a big house in the Chicago suburb of Wheaton a few years earlier, then told the newspapers a prominent Levee sport named "Honey" Moore planned to make it his home. Wealthy Wheaton residents pooled their money and bought back the house, providing the investors a handsome profit.

In the end, the Lake Geneva colonists proved cannier. They agreed that none of them would make an offer on the Sherman house, the Los Angeles *Times* reported on December 26, "but would allow the sale to go by default. Then, they say, if the negroes purchase the property and actually occupy it, steps will be taken to oust them." Anderson, Johnson, and their friends let the option lapse and backed off.

On New Year's Eve, Johnson and Lucille turned up unannounced for the 8th National Guard Regiment ball, organized each year by the all-black outfit that had twice sent its band to welcome the champion home to Chicago. When the Johnsons made their entrance, he in evening dress, she glittering with the diamonds Etta had been wearing only three months earlier, some women hissed, and an officer took Johnson aside and told him that since he had no invitation, he would have to leave.

A few days later, Johnson and several friends drove up to Bill O'Connell's Chicago Gym. He'd been training there off and on for years, but this time O'Connell met him at the door. He was embarrassed, he said, but the rest of his regulars had told him they'd go elsewhere if he allowed the heavyweight champion of the world on the premises. Johnson got back in his car and drove away. When other arenas were closed to Jack Johnson, the sporting world had always welcomed him. Now that door, too, seemed to be closing.

At 2 a.m. on January 14, the telephone rang at the home of Bureau of Investigation Chief Charles DeWoody. A reporter was on the line. He'd heard that Johnson had jumped his bond and was already aboard a train on his way to Canada; Lucille was said to be with him; so was his valet, Joe Levy. DeWoody called the Johnson home. "Jack is upstairs sleeping," his mother said. "I can't wake him now. He will get up later and then you can talk with him yourself. . . . My boy would never run away."

DeWoody sent a man to check, but he also placed calls to the chiefs of police in the three most important stops on the train's route: Detroit, Port Huron, and Battle Creek, Michigan. The train had already passed through the first two. It was due in Battle Creek at 3:25 a.m.

As soon as the train hissed to a stop there, two officers boarded the champion's car and banged on the door of his stateroom. He was under arrest, they said. The train was held for nearly half an hour in the cold while the Johnsons' luggage was located and unloaded from the baggage car. A black policeman named John Patterson, with whom the champion happened to have grown up in Galveston, escorted the Johnsons and Levy to the home of Will Cook, a black barber. They spent most of the day there waiting for Special Agent Meyer, who was coming by train to escort Johnson back to Chicago.

Johnson insisted that he and his wife hadn't been running away but were just planning to spend a few days in Toronto enjoying themselves and talking over with Tom Flanagan final arrangements for a spring fight in Paris with the "Iowa Giant," Al Palzer. "If I had known I was to stay here I'd have got off early and showed at a theater," he told a reporter. "If pulling a fellow out of bed in the middle of the night when he is on a pleasure trip, mixed with a little business, wouldn't make me mad, I'm a pretty good sort, ain't I?" He'd cleared his trip with his bondsmen, he said, and hadn't realized he'd also needed to get permission to travel from the district attorney's office.

Charles DeWoody didn't believe a word of it. He reported to Washington:

> Personally, I have not the slightest doubt but that Johnson, knowing the Supreme Court would pass within a few days upon the constitutionality of the [Mann] act, intended [to place] himself in advance in a nonextraditable jurisdiction, [from] where he could proceed to France and Russia to carry out his plans for future fights, forfeiting the bonds for his appearance in this country; and I may add that this is [the] general and unanimous impression.

That impression was not shared by the one person who mattered most. Judge Carpenter found Johnson's explanation plausible. He told him he should have informed the authorities of his plans, but he refused to do more than that, and he scolded Chief DeWoody and Special Agent Meyer for excessive zeal in halting Johnson's train and bringing him back to Chicago. Under the terms of his bond, he said, they really had no power to insist that Johnson remain in the city so long as he was on hand for his trial.

On Tuesday February 3, the U.S. Supreme Court dismissed Johnson's habeas corpus petition. Judge Carpenter was now free to set a trial date. The smuggling case would be decided first, on February 28. "The impudent air of Jack Johnson has departed," said the Milwaukee *Free Press,* "and the former boastful negro is now a humble, pleading coon, according to advices from Chicago. Your Uncle Samuel has swung about twenty adverse court decisions on the champion and Lil' Artha is decidedly groggy."

Everything was going badly for him now. Sig Hart was spying on the Johnsons for the government and filing reports on what his old employer was up to. When Johnson bought an old car and sent an agent north to map out the safest possible escape route to Canada by road, Hart made sure his new employers knew about it. Charlie Johnson went to the authorities, claiming that someone had threatened to "bump him off" if he went through with plans to testify against his brother in the smuggling case; he was afraid to go home, he said, and was handed a dollar for a night's lodging.* Even Tiny Johnson was worrying aloud that if her boy ran away again and forfeited his bond, she would lose her home.

Meanwhile, though Johnson had paid out hundreds of dollars for detectives and even privately offered a ten-thousand-dollar reward to anyone who could tell him where Belle Schreiber was hidden, her whereabouts remained a mystery.

On February 17, Lucille informed the government that Johnson was confined to his bedroom and gravely ill with pneumonia. DeWoody now took nothing for granted. A week later, he sent Agent Lins with Benjamin Bachrach to verify the champion's presence as well as the state of his health. Johnson's longtime trainer, Barney Furey, let them in. They told Tiny Johnson they just wanted to see that Johnson really was ill and in bed and promised not to say a word to him if she'd just let them have a look. His mother said they'd have to speak to her daughter-in-law. Lucille would not let them go upstairs.

---

*Charles Johnson remains something of a mystery. Adopted by Tiny and Henry Johnson before the age of two, he was smaller and frailer than his siblings, often in ill health and forced to wear thick spectacles to see. The champion paid for surgery on his eyes, put him through undertaking school, called him "son." But relations between them were evidently complicated, and shortly before Johnson's arrest for kidnapping Lucille Cameron, he'd had Charles arrested for forgery and embezzlement. The younger man's eagerness to testify against the champion may have been payback.

Bachrach suggested they call the attending physician. Dr. R. W. Carter— "(white)" according to Lins' official report and therefore presumably reliable—who came right away. He said Johnson was very ill, but they could certainly stick their heads in the door without doing him any harm. "But Mrs. Lucille Johnson would listen to no argument," Lins reported, "stating that the Government was the cause of all of her and Jack's troubles and she berated every one connected with the Government, saying she did not care who came to the house, no one should be allowed to see Jack." Johnson's nurses—also "(white)"—attested to the high fevers Johnson had been running. That was enough for the judge to grant a continuance on the smuggling trial until the champion was back on his feet.

On March 3 and again on the fourth, Johnson called DeWoody and asked if he would come and see him in his sickroom. It would "advantage and interest the government," he said. The Bureau's chief said he would wait until Johnson was able to come and see him at the Federal Building. He did so, on the tenth, walking "very feebly," DeWoody noted, "with the assistance of convenient tables and chairs." The champion said he was well enough for the smuggling trial to go ahead. (DeWoody would duly notify the judge, who set the date for April.) But it was the Mann Act trial Johnson wanted to talk about. He saw no need for the government to go to the trouble and expense of gathering witnesses from all around the country. He was happy to plead guilty and pay a "substantial" fine provided that the judge promised not to send him to prison. He had consorted with prostitutes, but he was no pimp, and the government would never be able to show he had ever earned a penny from any of the women he'd known. More important, "on account of his color it would be impossible for him to secure a fair trial." The Chief told him there was no point in discussing this with him. Johnson could of course submit such a plea to the court, but there would be no guarantee of leniency; he would have to be prepared for the government to lay out its case and then request suitable punishment. "The defendant left in a downcast mood," DeWoody reported, "and with a promise (or threat) to appear tomorrow with a list of cases where defendants had pled guilty to a violation of the White Slave Traffic Act and the cases involved pandering for profit, following which plea sentences consisting of fines only were imposed."

March 31, 1913, was Johnson's thirty-fifth birthday. Not even the coming trials were allowed to mute his family's celebration. At least a hundred guests filed through Tiny Johnson's house that evening to have dinner and pay tribute to her embattled son. "The table was a dream," the *Defender* reported, covered in fine lace with a huge centerpiece basket of bridesmaid roses and lilies of the valley. Lucille headed the receiving line in a gown of "Copenhagen blue, décolleté, with a bodice beaded with jet and cut-steel buttons. She carried a huge bouquet of sweet peas and lilies of the valley. The champion looked immaculate in the conventional tuxedo." One hundred choice filets mignons were served, along with 150 spring chickens, one hundred portions of French peas, three hundred loaves of bread, and a huge birthday cake—"thirty-five biscuits in circumference"—baked and decorated by William Ingram, the "Johnson major domo."

The Elite Café, one of the best-known nightspots on the South Side, provided an orchestra. Johnson played along on his bass viol. "The champion enjoyed himself immensely . . . and discussed poetry," the *Defender* concluded. "He spoke of the poem written by Miss Bettieloo Forton in 1910 predicting his victory. He lauded Paul Laurence Dunbar, and recited 'If,' his favorite poem by Kipling."

> *If you can keep your head when all about you*
> *Are losing theirs and blaming it on you;*
> *If you can trust yourself when all men doubt you,*
> *But make allowance for their doubting, too;*
> *If you can wait and not be tired by waiting,*
> *Or, being lied about, don't deal in lies,*
> *Or, being hated, don't give way to hating,*
> *And yet don't look too good, nor talk too wise:*
>
> *If you can dream—and not make dreams your master;*
> *If you can think—and not make thoughts your aim;*
> *If you can meet with Triumph and Disaster*
> *And treat those two imposters just the same;*
> *If you can bear to hear the truth you've spoken*
> *Twisted by knaves to make a trap for fools,*
> *Or watch the things you gave your life to, broken,*
> *And stoop and build 'em up with worn-out tools;*
>
> *If you can make one heap of all your winnings*
> *And risk it on one turn of pitch-and-toss,*
> *And lose, and start again at your beginnings*
> *And never breathe a word about your loss;*

If you can force your heart and nerve and sinew
To serve your turn long after they are gone,
And so hold on when there is nothing in you
Except the Will which says to them: "Hold on!"

If you can talk with crowds and keep your virtue,
Or walk with kings—nor lose the common touch,
If neither foes nor loving friends can hurt you,
If all men count with you, but none too much;
If you can fill the unforgiving minute
With sixty seconds' worth of distance run—
Yours is the Earth and everything that's in it,
And—which is more—you'll be a Man, my son!

Johnson's own time of testing was coming closer. Sol Lewinsohn, his supposedly influential friend, had done nothing for him. His deviousness in arranging Johnson's bond had caused the champion to spend a week in jail. Since then, he had resisted repeated requests to hand back the thirty thousand dollars Johnson had advanced him on the night he was arrested, promising instead to use it to influence federal officials who owed him favors, including Harry Parkin and the U.S. commissioner who had set Lucille Cameron's bond. When no such influence was detected, Johnson demanded repayment. Lewinsohn then confessed that he no longer had the money. He'd invested it with a friend, who'd turned out to be a crook. The money was gone. Johnson said he wasn't interested in excuses. He could do little about it himself without attracting more unwanted attention from the law. Instead, he dispatched Lucille to Lewinsohn's office with a pistol. He had twenty minutes to arrange payment in full, she told him. Lewinsohn came up with twenty-five thousand dollars of it by looting his own fledgling Trader's Bank of Chicago, and soon had to skip town himself to escape prosecution.

On the afternoon of April 22, U.S. Marshal H. B. Coy called at the Johnson home. He'd been delivering subpoenas all day—to Sig Hart, Charles Johnson, even Walter Mueller, the salesman who supplied Belle Schreiber's flat at the Ridgewood with beer. He had two to go—Joe Levy and Barney Furey—and both were thought to be at the house on Wabash Avenue. Levy was sitting on the porch. When Coy handed him the subpoena, the Englishman sighed. "I've got so many," he said, "if I keep on getting cards my pockets won't hold them."

"You're going to have a full deck," Coy said. Levy said he already had one. Johnson came onto the porch, asking, "What's up?"

Coy asked for Barney Furey. Johnson said he'd call him. "Come on in."

"How are all the boys and how do they feel about me?" he asked. Coy said he hadn't heard much one way or the other. A servant brought a decanter and glass, and the marshal poured himself a drink.

Lucille greeted Coy warmly. She, too, wanted to know about the boys in the office. What had happened to their friend Deputy Marsales? Coy didn't answer.

Furey was out, but Johnson took his subpoena and promised that his trainer would be present for the trial. Then he asked if he could see the list of other witnesses. Coy showed it to him. The champion's face fell as he read the names of people he'd never dreamed would appear against him—old friends and lovers, former employees, his own adopted brother.

He thanked Coy and handed the list back. "Goodby and good luck to both of you," Coy said as he left. "I'm sure Judge Carpenter will give both you and the Government a square deal."*

The following day, Johnson was allowed to plead nolo contendere to having concealed Etta's necklace from the government, and to pay a one-thousand-dollar fine. The smuggling case was dropped, perhaps because the champion now claimed that his late wife had hidden the jewels without his knowledge. The Mann Act trial was set for May 5.

Meanwhile, the government went back to the grand jury and asked for four new indictments against Johnson, this time for "crimes against nature." It was Harry Parkin's idea, but Carpenter warned against it. He disliked having matters usually confined to the municipal courts take up time in a federal courtroom, and he thought "unnatural and perverted practices" beyond the purview of the Mann Act, which he believed pertained only to prostitution. DeWoody was also opposed at first. The only "evidence" they'd collected came from Yank Kenny, an alcoholic ex-sparring partner with a grudge against Johnson (who had fired him) and a patchy legal history of his own.†

---

*For showing Johnson the witness list—and for having a drink at his home—Coy was reprimanded by his superiors but not dismissed. He had been "thoughtless" but not guilty of "wrongdoing." (Charles DeWoody to A. Bruce Bielaski, May 15, 1913, DOJ File.)

†Kenny, whose real name was Anthony Xenny, had been jailed at least twice, for beating up two newspapermen in 1897 and for stealing a wallet in 1905. He was not an overly cooperative witness. Days before the trial was set to begin, he vanished in Kansas City, Missouri DeWoody frantically wired the Justice Department office there to "arrest and hold [him]" if found. . . . Keep him good-natured.

Kenny claimed that in the middle of one night at Cedar Lake in 1909 he'd overheard Belle Schreiber say, "Don't beat me any more and I will do it or I will do anything." Precisely what "it" was, no one could say, and once Schreiber was on the stand, DeWoody wrote, he feared that "an effort to open the door upon this subject will only increase her embarrassment." But he soon changed his mind. When agents gingerly raised the subject with Schreiber, he told his boss in a coded telegram, she had been quite prepared to add it to her bill of particulars against the champion.

> PRINCIPAL WITNESS DOES TESTIFY CONTINUOUS ATTEMPTS BY JOHN-SON FORCE HER COMMIT PERVERTED PRACTICES. SAYS ATTEMPTS WERE ACCOMPANIED BY VICIOUS BEATINGS. IS CORROBORATED BY AT LEAST ONE WITNESS WHO OVERHEARD THESE EFFORTS [KENNY]. . . . WHILE I WAS NOT INCLINED TO AGREE UNITED STATES ATTORNEY'S OFFICE AS TO ADVISABILITY RETURNING INDICTMENT I NOW BELIEVE IN VIEW OF DEVELOPMENT EVIDENCE IT IS BEST. SEEMS TO ME THESE ACTS OF PERVERSION CONSTITUTE THE MOST VICIOUS ELEMENT IN THE CASE OVERCOMING DEFENDANT'S CONTENTION HIS VIOLATION IS TECHNICAL AND INVOLVING NO GREAT DEGREE IMMORALITY. COM-PLAINING WITNESS IS IN EXCELLENT SPIRITS, ENTIRELY FRIENDLY WITH US, FREE FROM NERVOUSNESS AND APPARENTLY WILLING TESTIFY FOREGOING CHEERFULLY.

On May 1, Johnson had to go to court again and plead not guilty to the new indictments still more invasive of his private life than the earlier ones had been. "If the attitude of the Grand Jury can be taken as any criterion of the jury trial," Charles DeWoody boasted to his bosses in Washington, "there will be no difficulty in convicting Johnson. That evening, an anonymous federal informant found the champion at home, suffering from what he called "a fit of the blues." He said he was weary of being watched and followed. Men and women he had thought his friends were lining up to testify against him. He'd never been able to find Belle Schreiber. There now seemed to be no hope.

Four days later, on the morning of May 5, 1913, the case of the *United States v. John Arthur Johnson,* finally got under way in Chicago's Federal Building.

Suggest [you] try saloons across from Santa Fe Station—Dugan's or Bill O'Leary's." He was found and brought to Chicago in time for Johnson's trial, but in the end he never testified. (*Police Gazette*, February 13, 1897; Los Angeles *Times*, August 23, 1905.)

Judge Carpenter closed the courtroom to everyone but newspapermen, and a small group of Johnson's friends and family. Those whom the judge called "scandal-seekers" crowded the halls of the courthouse to see Johnson arrive, but then had to wander off when the bailiff closed the door.

At Bachrach's instruction, Johnson wore a conservative suit in the courtroom and not a single diamond. Tiny Johnson sat at his side. Lucille stayed away: his lawyer feared that her presence would further inflame the jury. It took two long days to pick twelve jurors in part because Bachrach sought to bar from it anyone who admitted having "convictions" against blacks' marrying whites. Several men were excused, the Washington *Post* reported, "because they said they had decided opinions about Johnson's guilt and strong convictions as to the punishment they would mete out to him." Bachrach eventually ran out of challenges, and twelve jurors were seated, some of them, as one government agent noted happily, "strongly prejudiced against negroes."

On the morning of May 7, Assistant District Attorney Parkin began to lay out the government's case. There was nothing complicated about it, he said. "The charge is simply and solely that the defendant, on the date mentioned in the indictment [October 15, 1910], aided, assisted, caused and induced this girl to go from Pittsburgh, Pennsylvania, to Chicago, Illinois." After they had heard all the evidence, the gentlemen of the jury would need to ask themselves just two questions: Did he do it? And, if he did, did he do so for "an immoral purpose"? Parkin promised to prove beyond a moral certainty that Johnson had had not one but *three* such purposes: prostitution, "the giving up of a woman's body to indiscriminate intercourse"; debauchery, by which he meant traveling (and sleeping with) two and sometimes three women; and a third purpose—almost "too obscene to mention"—which was "to compel these women to commit the crime against nature upon his body." He would demonstrate how Johnson "controlled" the three women with whom he most often traveled, and show that he had ordered Belle to come to Chicago from Pittsburgh, had sent her seventy-five dollars for her ticket, then spent an additional one thousand two hundred dollars setting her up as a madam. And he would show that Johnson was himself "one of the men who practiced immoral purposes and conduct in that flat."

"Now, the defendant is a prize fighter," he continued;

and in that connection it will be interesting, as the evidence develops, to see upon what victims he practiced the manly art of self defense. It will appear these women whom he carried about the country with him were very, very many times, when he had a fit of anger, or when the girls refused to do some of the obscene things which he demanded of them, that he practiced the art of manly self-defense upon them, blacking their eyes and sending them to the hospitals.

When Parkin sat down, all twelve jurors were glaring at the defendant.

Benjamin Bachrach began his case for the defense by begging them to maintain open minds. If the "horrible story" Parkin had told were true, he said, "there is hardly any punishment great enough for the defendant." But it was not true. When Johnson came into prominence as a pugilist, he said, "as is customary with a certain class of women, sporting women, they are attracted by an exhibition of physical prowess and throw themselves in the way of a pugilist." The evidence would show that Belle Schreiber was "an ordinary prostitute" when she first met Johnson, that she often moved from sporting house to sporting house for reasons having nothing to do with the champion. He reminded them that nothing Johnson did before July 1, 1910—the date the Mann Act went into force—was relevant to the case.

Prior to that time, however much you might deprecate the idea of a . . . bachelor having intercourse with a woman not his wife, it was no crime against the laws of the United States to do it, and it was no crime for a man, if he saw fit, to take a prostitute with him when he took a trip, to take her along and have intercourse with her on the train in the stateroom.

Johnson had never taken Belle Schreiber anywhere after July 1, 1910, Bachrach declared. He had never sent her money to move from Pittsburgh to Chicago; and he'd given her money to rent and furnish an apartment only because he'd wanted to help her establish a home for her pregnant sister and aged mother. "He did not get her to engage in any prostitution. She was a prostitute, and had always been, so far as he knew; and there was not anything that he did in any way that violated any federal law."

The government called six witnesses to set the stage for the main accuser and supposed victim, Belle Schreiber.

Jack Mervin, Johnson's chauffeur for much of 1910 and 1911, described driving Belle Schreiber to and from hotels to see Johnson in several cities.

Lillian Paynter, who ran the Pittsburgh whorehouse in which Belle had worked in 1910, testified that Belle had been fired as soon as it was learned that she was "mixed up with a colored man." Her sister, Estelle, took the stand to say she was the one who had actually "ordered her out."

John T. Lewis, the building manager at the Ridgewood, remembered renting an apartment to Schreiber, though he claimed he hadn't known anything about her "occupation" or what went on in any of the building's sixty-seven other apartments. "How can I, except I seen it?" he asked.

Bertha Morrison—"Jew Bertha"—said she'd also worked out of a sporting flat at the Ridgewood and had noticed Johnson there two or three times, though under cross-examination she admitted that she'd never actually seen him inside Schreiber's apartment.

John O'Halloran, a Chicago patrolman, testified that until the preceding March, the Ridgewood Apartments had been wholly occupied by prostitutes, either entertaining customers on the premises or going out on call. He'd made many arrests there over the years.

Finally, Leopold Moss of the Marshall Ventilated Mattress Company offered a detailed receipt listing all the furnishings—including four mattresses—he'd sold to the champion for Schreiber's flat.

Belle Schreiber was called to the stand on the morning of Thursday, May 8. She was modestly dressed and without the vivid makeup people had often remarked upon when she had been the champion's companion. She spoke in "a low voice," according to the Chicago *Daily News* the next day, "haltingly and seemingly embarrassed." Parkin led her through a numbing chronicle of her life with the champion, from the moment they met at the Everleigh Club in the spring of 1909 until her last sight of him in March of 1911, after his marriage to Etta Duryea and before he headed for California. To prove that the champion had borne all the costs, Parkin offered into evidence a clutch of receipts signed by his agents George Little and Sig Hart. And to show how close Belle and Johnson once had been, he introduced the photograph the champion had given her early in their relationship, inscribed "To my little sweetheart Belle from Papa Jack."

In October of 1910, she said, she'd been desperate after losing her job with the Paynter sisters and would have gone anywhere, done anything. It had been entirely Johnson's idea, not hers, that she come to Chicago and set herself up in business. She testified that he had been a frequent visitor to her sporting flat at the Ridgewood, that he had had sex with her there, and that she had once paid him twenty dollars out of her earnings as a prostitute. And every day during the week after Christmas in 1910, while Etta Duryea lay in the hospital, she said, she had ridden back and forth with Johnson aboard the train between Chicago and Milwaukee—crossing still another state line for immoral purposes.

In his cross-examination, Benjamin Bachrach did everything he could to shake Belle's story and cast doubt on her character. He showed her the inscribed photograph again and asked, "Were you his 'little sweetheart'?"

SCHREIBER: I suppose I was.

BACHRACH: Were you in love with him?

SCHREIBER: I don't know.

BACHRACH: Don't you know now? Did you think you were then?

SCHREIBER: I don't know what love is.

BACHRACH: The favors that you extended to him, were they extended simply for money?

SCHREIBER: I don't know. . . .

BACHRACH: You cannot say now whether you were in love with the defendant or not?

SCHREIBER: No.

BACHRACH: At this time?

SCHREIBER: I don't believe I ever was in love. . . .

BACHRACH: Isn't it a fact that from the time you first met Johnson you determined to get out of him all the money you could.

SCHREIBER: No. It is not a fact. . . .

Then why had she kept all those hotel bills? Bachrach asked.

SCHREIBER: I don't know why I saved the hotel bills and didn't save anything else. It is not a fact that I saved those bills so that at some future time I might be able to testify that I was at those places with him. . . . I probably did it because I feared he might not believe me when I said my hotel bill was a stipulated amount.

Hadn't she once told Sig Hart that she planned to get all the money she could from the champion? She had not. Then why had she kept asking him for more money?

She'd only gone to Johnson after she was let go in Pittsburgh because "I didn't have any more friends. I lost all my friends, and he was the only one I could turn to. I suppose I regarded him as my friend, too. I thought it was due for him to see me through my trouble."

BACHRACH: And did you love him then?

SCHREIBER: I told you I did not know what love was.

BACHRACH: Well, did you think you loved him then?

SCHREIBER: I don't remember what I thought. My memory is good on all the other portions of the testimony, but about this one question—whether I was in love with him or not—my memory is poor. . . .

Bachrach took Belle through a catalog of all the trips on which she'd accompanied the champion.

BACHRACH: You were not forced to go on any one of these trips?

SCHREIBER: No, not forced.

BACHRACH: You were not coerced?

SCHREIBER: I was asked to go, that was all.

BACHRACH: And you acceded to the request, did you?

SCHREIBER: Yes.

BACHRACH: You were willing, were you not?

SCHREIBER: I suppose I was. . . .

If she'd kept her hotel bills, why hadn't she kept a copy of Johnson's telegram that supposedly promised to send her seventy-five dollars? She couldn't say.

Belle had testified that she'd been "on the outs" with Johnson at the time of the Jeffries fight in Reno and therefore hadn't traveled there with him. If that was so, Bachrach asked, why had she sent him a congratulatory telegram?

She didn't remember why. "I did not want to bring myself to his notice again." She never called him, she said, "unless it was absolutely necessary."

"To get money?"

"Yes, when I was put out."

What did she mean by "put out"?

When she was recognized as Jack Johnson's companion, and therefore "not admitted into a house."

"Oh," Bachrach said, his voice heavy with sarcasm, "did you *apply* to houses of prostitution and try to get in?

"Yes."

"And you were refused admittance?"

"Yes."

"And then you would call up Johnson for some money?"

"Yes, when I could find him."

How often had she got money out of him this way? Fifty times? Twenty-five times? Ten times?

"Three or four," she said.

The flat had all been Johnson's idea, she insisted. She'd never wanted an apartment of her own, "because I never knew how to take care of any."

Hadn't she told him he owed her help since he was about to marry Etta Duryea? Never, she said. She hadn't known anything about his coming marriage. Nor had she ever told him she wanted a place for her pregnant sister or her mother to live.

But hadn't she used Johnson's money to pay for her sister's fare from Pittsburgh as well as her own?

"Yes."

And didn't her sister live with her in her flat?

"Yes."

Three more government witnesses followed Schreiber. None was on the stand more than a minute or two. Her former maid, Julia Allen, said she recalled seeing the seventy-five-dollar postal telegraph from the champion; Hattie McClay began an account of her relationship with Johnson, which Bachrach cut short by successfully objecting that since they had been together long before July 1, 1910, her testimony was irrelevant. James Stilwell, an attorney for the Pennsylvania Railroad, attested that at the time of the alleged offense it had been a common carrier in interstate traffic and therefore covered under the Mann Act.

The government rested its case.

When Johnson finally took the stand on the morning of May 13, "he spoke in a low voice and at times hesitatingly," one reporter noted. "Sweat stood out on his forehead and trickled down his face."

He denied everything. He had never beaten anyone, had taken only one train trip with Belle, well before the Mann Act went into effect; had given her money only because she said she'd lost her job and needed help. He had never told Belle she should go into business for herself, had never even meant for her to come to Chicago. "She said she was sick," that was all. And when he met her at the Hotel Vendome, he added, she had claimed that her sister was pregnant and needed a place where she, her mother, and her sister could all live. "I said, 'Certainly, I will do anything to make you happy.'" He'd had no foreknowledge that she was planning to open a brothel and had never taken a penny of her earnings.

How much money did he think he'd given Belle Schreiber over the years?

"As near as I could guess, it would be between nine and ten thousand dollars [roughly $179,000 in today's terms]; that includes all that I spent on her, everything—expenses and everything."

His voice was growing stronger, his manner more confident. Even here, Jack Johnson seemed to enjoy the spotlight.

He said he had not traveled back and forth between Chicago and Milwaukee with Belle during Christmas week of 1911. Nor had she stayed with him in Milwaukee all week. They'd had a disagreement, he said; she'd been "a little angry" because he "was not paying the proper attention to her. . . . I had a reason for not being attentive to Belle Schreiber up to that time; it was because I was going to be married—and I told her and explained everything to her."

It was the government's turn to cross-examine. Harry Parkin leaped to the attack.

PARKIN: Why was Etta Duryea hospitalized?

JOHNSON: She was sick, that is all I know.

PARKIN: That is all you know about it?

JOHNSON: That is all I know.

PARKIN: What was the cause of her sickness?

JOHNSON: I don't know.

PARKIN: As a matter of fact that was a sickness caused by blows from your hands, wasn't it?

Bachrach objected to this as irrelevant. The judge overruled him and directed Johnson to answer.

JOHNSON: No.

PARKIN: Well, was it caused by a blow or blows from your hand?

JOHNSON: No, no.

PARKIN: Was it not caused by blows received by Etta Duryea in the Pekin Theater here in Chicago at your hands?

JOHNSON: No.

PARKIN: Did you not carry her out or have her carried out and put in the automobile and taken to the Washington Park Hospital after you had beaten her up?

JOHNSON: No, no, and I will take the oath on it. No.

Belle had given him a share of her earnings, had she not?

"How could she give me money, [when I was] making $2,500 a week? . . . I say I never took any money from Belle Schreiber, not a newspaper." Nor had he had any idea what kind of business she and the other women living at the Ridgewood flats were doing.

"You knew it was full of fast women, didn't you?"

"I did not."

Parkin pointed out that Johnson had lived less than a mile from the Ridgewood for several years. Surely he knew what went on there.

JOHNSON: I can look the jury right in the face and as a man tell them I didn't know that the Ridgewood was a sporting house, and look at them and swear to it. . . . I didn't know anything about the fast women. I was not keeping up with them. . . .

PARKIN: Now, you say you were not keeping up with the fast women. You had as many as three at a time in your travels, didn't you?

JOHNSON: No, sir.

PARKIN: Didn't you [sometimes] have Hattie and Etta and Belle there at the same time?

JOHNSON: No. . . .

PARKIN: Now, why did you have Belle come to Atlantic City?

JOHNSON: I never had her come to Atlantic City.

PARKIN: You entertained her there?

JOHNSON: I wasn't there long enough to entertain myself.

PARKIN: What did you do there with her?

JOHNSON: Nothing.

PARKIN: Did you buy her meals or pay her hotel bills or give her any money?

JOHNSON: I never gave her nothing that trip at all.

PARKIN: Did you buy her meals?

JOHNSON: Never—nothing.

PARKIN: Pay her hotel bill?

JOHNSON: Nothing. Never even bought her a drink.

PARKIN: So she spent her own money at that time?

JOHNSON: She must have, she didn't spend mine.

PARKIN: Well, did you have sexual relations in Atlantic City?

JOHNSON: Belle and I were very friendly. . . .

PARKIN: Just answer the question. Did you have sexual relations with her in Atlantic City?

JOHNSON: I did not.

PARKIN: In August, 1910?

JOHNSON: I did not.

PARKIN: [But] you did in every town where you and she were together?

JOHNSON: I don't remember. I never kept tab.

PARKIN: Well, did you skip any?

JOHNSON: Oh certainly, everybody skips.

Some in the courtroom laughed. Parkin bore down. Did Johnson have more than one woman with him when he visited Philadelphia?

JOHNSON: They may have been there; I did not have them. There is a lot of women in that town; that doesn't signify that I have them. I have told you I never kept tab of those things. I am here today and gone tomorrow. I never kept any tabs. I was too busy. I had too much to think of.

Parkin pressed him. Didn't he have both Belle and Hattie with him in California at the time of his fight with Stanley Ketchel?

"Lots of people came to see me. . . . " They may have been there. He hadn't paid their way.

"Did you not, on December 9, 1909, the date of the Kaufmann fight, have sexual intercourse with the girl Anna, 'Mac' [Hattie McClay]?"

"I did not. After a man has a fight, he is not feeling like it."

Bachrach objected again and again that these events were irrelevant since they allegedly took place before the Mann Act went into effect. Judge Carpenter overruled him each time and insisted that Johnson answer.

PARKIN: The Ketchel fight was after the Kaufmann fight, wasn't it?

JOHNSON: Yes.

PARKIN: Did you win the Ketchel fight?

JOHNSON: Did I win it?

PARKIN: Yes.

JOHNSON: It is in the book, doesn't the book say so?

PARKIN: Just answer my question. . . .

JOHNSON: I suppose I did. Somebody might say I did not.

PARKIN: You knew you were going to win it before you went into it, didn't you?

Bachrach objected that this line of questioning was also irrelevant; Parkin was trying to attack his client's character by suggesting that he took part in "crooked fights."

"They are all crooked," Johnson muttered as the lawyers argued.

Over Bachrach's repeated protest, Parkin once again tried to get Johnson to admit that he'd beaten the women with whom he'd traveled.

Hadn't Hattie once been hospitalized after he'd mistreated her?

JOHNSON: No.

PARKIN: Did you have any similar difficulty with Belle—fisticuff difficulty?

JOHNSON: I don't understand the definition of the word. . . .

PARKIN: You had struck Belle on various occasions?

JOHNSON: Never in my life.

PARKIN: Do you remember using an automobile tool on her?

JOHNSON: Never in my life.

PARKIN: You never did that?

JOHNSON: Never.

PARKIN: You say you did not?

JOHNSON: I say no; emphatically no.

PARKIN: And bruised her side until it was black and blue?

The judge objected. Johnson had said he'd never beaten anyone. Next question.

Parkin wound up his cross-examination by attacking Johnson's account of the time he and Belle Schreiber had spent together in Milwaukee. The champion said again that he had told Belle of his marriage plans while they were there.

But after he told her, Parkin asked, hadn't they continued to live together in their hotel room in Milwaukee?

"Some of the time."

"Yes?"

"Yes, sure."

Johnson stepped down from the stand. Seven defense witnesses did their best to bolster different parts of his case. They included chauffeurs, trainers, hangers-on, some of them still on Johnson's payroll, as well as his old Pittsburgh friend Frank Sutton, who had overheard Belle's half of her money-seeking telephone call to the champion. Several of the witnesses denied that Belle had ever accompanied the champion on the trains he took back and forth daily between Chicago and Milwaukee during Christmas week.

As a final rebuttal witness, the prosecutor called Johnson's old friend Roy

Jones. He confirmed that the champion had told him he'd had "a fight" with Etta Duryea on Christmas Eve and feared being prosecuted for it. He also claimed to have seen Belle get off the train from Milwaukee at least once in Johnson's company. In cross-examining him, Bachrach did his best to imply that Jones' testimony had been heavily influenced by the predicament in which he found himself. Like Johnson, Jones had lost his saloon license; unlike Johnson, he hoped to get it back again. Helping to fortify the government's case would make the licensing authorities feel more warmly toward him.*

With that, the trial ended.

Bachrach immediately moved that since the government had failed to produce any evidence of "debauchery" or "crimes against nature," four of the eleven indictments should be thrown out. Judge Carpenter agreed. All four were dismissed.

Few in the courtroom had any doubt of what the jury's verdict on the remaining seven counts would be. "If you should find the defendant not guilty," the prosecutor said in his summation, "I do not see how you could ever look squarely in the faces of your mothers, wives, and daughters."

The case went to the jury at ten in the evening. In less than two hours Johnson was found guilty on all counts.

Sentencing was set for June 4.

For once, the champion refused to talk to the press. "I have nothing to say, not a thing. My attorneys will speak for me."† Benjamin Bachrach said only that it had been "a hard case" and that he would file an immediate appeal.

Harry Parkin was not so reticent. "This verdict will go around the world," he told reporters on the courthouse steps.

It is the forerunner of laws to be passed in these United States which we may live to see—laws forbidding miscegenation. This Negro, in the eyes of many, has been persecuted. Perhaps as an individual he was. But it was his misfortune to be the foremost example of the evil in permitting the intermarriage of whites and blacks.

Five years ago he was obscure, penniless and happy. He beat down a

---

*Jones was back in business within weeks.

†He found another way to make his feelings known, however. He attached an especially noisy "cut-out muffler" to one of his cars and roared through the city streets until he was fined again—for "creating a public nuisance."

man and became famous with a blow. He beat down another and riches poured into his pockets.

Money and fame, such as it was, brought white women. One is a suicide, the others are pariahs. He has violated the law. Now, it is his function to teach others the law must be respected.

Parkin was right that the Johnson case would inspire calls for laws against miscegenation. During 1913, such statutes were introduced in the legislatures of half the twenty states that did not already have them. Five were proposed in Illinois alone. In the end, neither Congressman Roddenberry's antimiscegenation amendment nor any of the state statutes would be enacted.*

The day after the verdict was handed down, Frank Sutton was to return to Pittsburgh by rail. The champion drove him to the Union Depot and walked him to the train. As it began to pull out, Johnson looked up into the eyes of Belle Schreiber, peering at him through the Pullman window. She, too, was headed back to Pittsburgh, where so much trouble for both of them had begun. They did not try to speak, or even make the smallest gesture of recognition. But they stared at each other until the train disappeared from sight.

Johnson was desperate now. At the very least, he expected a large fine, and he now had very little money left with which to pay it. He swallowed his pride, set aside the tradition that required champions to wait for others to challenge them, and called on Luther McCarty, who had beaten Al Palzer on New Year's Day to win the dubious "white heavyweight championship of the world," to face him for the real title.† Born on a Nebraska ranch, McCarty was just twenty-one, but he could box well and hit hard enough with both hands to have beaten Carl Morris, Al Kaufmann, and Jim Flynn. DeWitt van Court thought him "unquestionably the greatest young heavyweight since the days of John L. Sullivan," and a fight between him and Johnson was thought likely to draw a big gate. Jack Curley hoped to be the one to stage it, back in Las Vegas, New Mexico, on July 4. But on May 24, before the details could be worked out, McCarty stepped into the ring at Calgary against Arthur Pelkey. During a clinch in the first round, Pelkey landed to McCarty's head. McCarty winked at his cornermen to show he hadn't been hurt. The referee

---

*Fifty-four years later, the U.S. Supreme Court would declare all such laws unconstitutional.

†Since McCarty's father was a medicine-show peddler who billed himself as "White Eagle, the Indian Doctor," his eligibility for his title did not bear close examination.

separated the fighters. McCarty collapsed. He was dead of a cerebral hemorrhage within eight minutes. There would be no big-money fight that summer for Jack Johnson.

On the afternoon of June 4, the day of his sentencing, Johnson clung to two hopes. First, that Judge Carpenter might agree to Benjamin Bachrach's motion for a new trial based on alleged errors made in the first one. If that failed, the judge might still simply impose a large fine and let it go at that. The champion was to be disappointed on both counts. There would be no new trial, and he would have to serve time in the penitentiary as an example to other Negroes.

"The crime of which this defendant stands convicted is an aggravating one," Carpenter explained. "The life of the defendant, by his own admissions, has been such as to merit condemnation."

> We have had a number of cases where violations of the Mann Act have been punished by fines only. We have had a number of defendants found guilty in this court of violating the Mann Act who have been sentenced to severe punishment, from one to two years in the penitentiary.
>
> This defendant is one of the best known men of his race, and his example has been far reaching and the court is bound to consider the position he occupied among his people. In view of these facts, this is a case that calls for more than a fine. Considering all circumstances in this case, therefore, the sentence of the court is that the defendant, Johnson, be confined to the penitentiary for one year and one day and be fined $1,000.

Johnson's lawyers had two weeks to file an appeal. "Oh well," Johnson said afterward. "They crucified Christ, why not me?"

On Tuesday evening, June 24, the heavyweight champion of the world disappeared. He'd seemed to be everywhere in Chicago that day, buzzing through the streets in his unmistakable red racer, and when he returned to his home in the evening, the informants who were paid to watch him evidently assumed that he was there to stay. They were wrong.

At about four o'clock Thursday afternoon, someone reported to Charles DeWoody that Johnson had been spotted in Montreal. DeWoody called the house on Wabash Avenue. Joseph Levy answered, sounding so nervous that DeWoody concluded the rumor must be true. He asked to speak to Jennie Rhodes. She said her brother and her son, Gus Rhodes, had left town for Johnson's old haunts at Cedar Lake, where they planned to fish for a few days;

they'd be back by the weekend. But when DeWoody called Bob Russell, the Cedar Lake resort keeper who'd rented the champion a cottage several times in the past, Russell said he hadn't seen him for at least three weeks.

At three the following morning, acting Bureau of Investigation Chief Bielaski wired DeWoody from Washington that the Associated Press confirmed Johnson's presence in Montreal. He seemed to be on his way to Europe.

This time, Johnson's escape had been meticulously planned. Benjamin Bachrach had persuaded Judge Carpenter to halve the thirty-thousand-dollar bond, thus making Matthew Baldwin the sole bondsman and guaranteeing that Johnson's mother could hold on to her house while he was gone. Violation of the Mann Act was not an extraditable offense north of the border, but as a convicted criminal he might still have been deported back to the United States as an "undesirable alien." To get around that, Johnson had quietly purchased tickets from Chicago to Le Havre via Montreal, thus making himself an alien in transit through Canada—and untouchable. Lucille had slipped out of town and reached Canada on her own before her husband vanished. Two of Johnson's cars had been sent ahead as well.

Preparations for flight were one thing. But how had Johnson and his nephew managed to slip out of town unseen—particularly when the authorities had been given so many hints that he might try to do so? The story to which Charles DeWoody and his colleagues always clung doesn't seem entirely plausible: uncle and nephew had set out on what seemed to be a fishing trip, they said, and then, somehow, the most celebrated—and notorious—black man in America had managed to drive himself over the border without being recognized by anyone along the way. So far as Justice Department files reveal, their superiors never seriously questioned their story.

Part of the reason for the apparent laxity may have been the nature of the bond on which Johnson remained free. So long as he was on hand for his court appearances it was unclear whether or not he could leave the country, and federal agents remained angry that Judge Carpenter had criticized them for halting his first flight back in January: "If Johnson had told me he was going to step aboard a train and leave the jurisdiction," Charles DeWoody said long after the champion made good his escape, "I would have made no effort to detain him."*

---

*"Johnson would be foolish to run away," Benjamin Bachrach told a reporter after hearing that his client was missing. "If, however, it is true that he has left he has a perfect right to do so. The bond he is under does not prevent him from leaving the States or the country. The only condition imposed is that Johnson shall appear in the United States Court of Appeals at the time his case is called there."

But Johnson couldn't have been certain DeWoody felt that way. He offered two other, very different versions of how he got away. In one—which would make headlines early the following year—he claimed to have paid thousands of dollars to federal and state officials to look the other way while he left town.

He first told the other tale to a British reporter about two weeks after it allegedly happened. He and Gus had indeed dressed in old clothes as if they were going fishing, he said, but instead of driving into the countryside, they'd had someone take them to Englewood Station. There, Johnson had arranged to meet his friend Rube Foster and his Giants baseball team, who were waiting for a train to Canada. As soon as the train pulled in, Johnson and Gus, their arms full of bats and gloves, climbed aboard with the ballplayers. White policemen patrolled the station, but, unable to distinguish one big athletic black man from another, they failed to recognize the champion. The train pulled out. Johnson stepped into the drawing room he'd reserved for himself and locked the door. "I am not a coward, gentlemen," he told his British listeners, "but I can assure you I trembled every time the car stopped."

Some writers doubt the Rube Foster story. One biographer states flatly, "It never happened." But two bits of evidence suggest that it could have. First, according to the Chicago *Defender,* Foster and his Giants really did leave Chicago for "Detroit, Buffalo and Canada" on the evening of Tuesday, June 24, just when Johnson said they did. Then, too, Johnson and Foster had been mistaken for each other before: hundreds of white Chicagoans—and many black ones as well—who turned out to welcome Johnson home from Reno in 1910 had cheered Rube Foster as he drove down State Street in an open automobile, convinced he was the champion.

At Hamilton, Ontario, Johnson and Gus hopped off the train. They were arrested and taken before a justice of the peace. But someone had provided them with the telephone numbers of two local solicitors. With their help, Johnson and his nephew were released on the ground that there was no official demand for their return to the United States. (There was no such demand in part because the U.S. authorities still had no idea Johnson had left the

---

On April 14, 1914, the Circuit Court of Appeals, Seventh Circuit, would make its ruling. While it refused to overturn the "immoral conduct" counts, it did call for a new trial on the prostitution indictments, citing improper cross-examination, the admission of irrelevant material "regarding whether the defendant exercised his fighting abilities upon women," and "an overall atmosphere of prejudice." Johnson was not present to hear this good news, and his absence made him for the first time officially a fugitive from justice.

country.) "That j.p. never had a chance," Johnson said afterward. "Those lawyers just talked me loose."

Tom Flanagan drove the fugitives to his hotel in Toronto, where he served them beer and cheese sandwiches and Lucille joined them. Then the trio moved on to Montreal.

On June 28, Charles DeWoody got a telegram from the champion.

AM SAILING SUNDAY MORNING . . . YOU DON'T NEED TO WORRY. WILL BE BACK FOR TRIAL. ANSWER STEAMER CORINTHIAN.

JACK JOHNSON

There was a mix of frustration and relief among federal officials back in Chicago. "This may solve the whole problem," said one assistant U.S. attorney. "The passengers may mutiny and heave [Johnson] away on an iceberg."

The *Defender* offered its own front-page bon voyage.

JACK JOHNSON IS CRUCIFIED FOR HIS RACE
FAMOUS FISTIC GLADIATOR SAILS FOR FRANCE AFTER
BEING PERSECUTED IN THE UNITED STATES.
WHAT HAS HE DONE? IF HE CHOSE A WOMAN OF
A DIFFERENT COLOR FOR HIS COMPANION
AND LEGALLY MARRIED HER, WHOSE BUSINESS IS IT?
WHAT HAS THE WHITE MAN DONE?

JACK JOHNSON HAS DONE NO DIFFERENT
FROM ANY OTHER BIG SPORT

FOR NO OTHER REASON THAN WHIPPING JEFFRIES
AND BEING A NEGRO IS JACK JOHNSON PERSECUTED.
CONSORTING WITH WHITE WOMEN IS NO CAUSE.
JACK IS ONE OF THAT HOST THAT
JOHN COULDN'T NUMBER.

CHAPTER ELEVEN

THE FUGITIVE

WHEN JACK JOHNSON ARRIVED IN Paris in 1911, the French press had greeted him as a conquering hero. Eager reporters stood around his steamy hotel bathroom while he bathed, comparing notes on his physique. This time, they piled into a string of taxis and followed him, his wife, and Gus Rhodes as they drove from hotel to hotel in search of a place willing to rent them rooms. The Grand Hotel turned them away. So did the Ritz and the Elysée Palace, the Excelsior and the Hotel Neuilly. They finally got rooms at the St. Lazare Terminus hotel. Johnson was still a celebrity, but he was also a fugitive.

He did his best to minimize that fact. He had big plans, he said. He and his wife planned to build themselves a cottage in Neuilly that would be headquarters for their new lives in the Old World. He had the recipe for an elixir drawn up by his mother that he hoped to market all over Europe. He also wanted to build a sanitarium for "neurasthenic" people, for whom he had developed a special empathy after his wife's tragic death. But first, he said, "I must complete my library of all books written about Napoleon. I visit his tomb at least twice a week and on August second I am going to see Waterloo. I am also going often to the opera. I should like to see something by Alexandre Dumas played, as I have read all his works." He planned to apply to become a naturalized citizen of France. "My ambition has always been to live in France, but I am very melancholy in my mind, for I shall never again see the land of my birth." Meanwhile, he was going to appear for twelve evenings at the Folies-Bergère and use the daylight hours to star in a motion picture called *Jack Johnson's Adventures in Paris*. (Its provocative title promised more than the film would deliver, but it did give the champion a chance to show how well he and Lucille could dance the Grizzly Bear.)

In London, where he began a music hall tour in August, crowds still followed him everywhere—and to insure that they did, one eyewitness noted, he sometimes stood on "prominent street corners" until enough people had gathered around him to start his stroll. But the executive committee of the

Variety Artists' Federation urged that no member of the federation appear onstage with him because, as the editors of the London *Times* put it, "Johnson's engagements in the existing circumstances are a question of public decency." Even the normally friendly *Mirror of Life and Boxing World* couldn't resist asking, "Isn't it rather remarkable that in his three visits to England, Jack has brought a different Mrs. Johnson every time?"

He rented a furnished flat in the West End and, wearing "a gay frock coat" and "giving full display to his diamonds," invited reporters in for tea to see if he couldn't calm things down. "Take anybody educated with a brain, properly developed—those who know Jack Johnson—they know he isn't the fellow they read about," he said.

The people in Paris—the select people—know Jack is a loyal, true fellow. As for the music hall people they will soon come around and will be the first to lend a pal a hand. And as to that conviction in the United States, why, when the jury was selected I leaned across to my lawyer, and said, "My boy, eleven of those men are for life conviction and the other is for hanging before hearing the evidence." If you could only have seen those jurymen! They were the sort of people to give you two years for drinking cider.

Did he plan to fight Sam Langford?

"No, I am going to draw the color line like some other actors."

The reporters laughed.

The music hall audiences gave him a mixed reception. At the Euston Theatre of Varieties, for example, two actresses known to have opposed Johnson's appearance were booed off the stage, but as soon as he himself appeared men seated in the boxes who had been silent until that moment hissed and jeered so loudly he gave up trying to speak and retreated behind the curtain.

The next day, the tenth marquess of Queensberry, son of the Scottish peer who lent his name to the rules of modern boxing, wrote an open letter to the London *Daily Express* offering a carefully qualified defense of the American visitor. Johnson was not actually at fault, he said. The real issue was the inexplicable lack of laws to keep black and white boxers from facing each other in the ring.

As regards Johnson's domestic affairs, again we get back to exactly where we started, the problem of black and white. Why is not a law passed in all civilized countries forbidding these marriages? Until this is done what reason was there that Johnson should not marry [Lucille Cameron]? Perhaps if the truth were known it is in all the circumstances the most decent thing he has ever done.

We pride ourselves in this country on fair play. Give the man fair play and take on yourselves, you the great public, the lawmakers, the blame for the present state of affairs.

Give the devil his due. Johnson is not the principal sinner. It is the people who with both hands have held the cup to his mouth—the cup which bore wine which begets vanity, greed, and passion—and who now despise him because he is drunk with the wine they themselves concocted for him and gave him.

By fall, Johnson was back on the Continent. Gus Rhodes was now his uncle's road manager, sometime trainer, and full-time press agent, assigned to provide reassuring reports to the readers of the Chicago *Defender* that all was well with their hero. His first story, datelined Vienna, appeared in October. "Besides giving boxing exhibitions," Rhodes reported, "[the champion] and Mrs. Johnson do the tango and the audience goes wild. They are called back again and again." Johnson was being paid five thousand dollars a week, Rhodes wrote, and was "rumored" to be worth two million. "He is being shown the greatest courtesy and especially entertained by aristocracy. All eyes are on him when he and his wife are out driving along the boulevards."

Six weeks later, Rhodes reported, the Johnsons were packing the Orpheum Theater in Budapest. A boxing tournament was staged in the champion's honor at Budapest University, "which is six times larger than the Chicago University." Wherever Johnson traveled, Rhodes continued,

> his headquarters are where the noblemen and lords are seen daily and they treat him as they do their fellowmen. . . . There is no discrimination against the colored man [in Europe]. When one sees how like a man he is treated here, he wonders why he remains in America to be treated as serfs. Johnson is in Europe to enjoy his freedom. Who can blame him?*

Johnson always did enjoy his freedom wherever he happened to be, but in reality he was now scuffling. Rhodes had grossly exaggerated how much

---

*Europeans did flock to see Jack Johnson, though they were sometimes less than clear as to just who he was. When he appeared in Bulgaria, for example, he was billed as "the man who received $1,000,000 for beating Jim Jeffries . . . and was directly responsible for the civil war in the United States between the blacks and the whites."

money he was being paid and how much he still had in the bank. His flight had forced him to forfeit his bond. Belgium had banned him. His show now included strongman feats: spinning audience volunteers round and round while they hung from his neck; allowing three at a time to stand on his belly; stopping two horses with chains clamped to his biceps. In November, back in Paris, he took part in staged wrestling matches at a Montmartre music hall called the Nouveau Cirque. His opponents—the "Great Uhrbach" from Germany; André Sproul, the "Savage Siberian"; and a Scot named Jemmy Esson—didn't matter much. Crowds came to see Jack Johnson lose his temper at their wicked tactics and lay them out with a choreographed roundhouse swing. By the third match, some people had seen through the theatrics and began pelting the ring with vegetables.

Johnson's personal reputation was already badly tarnished. Now his reputation as a fighter had begun to crumble as well. That month, the French Boxing Federation declared the world's heavyweight title vacant. There were two reasons, its director, the Paris promoter Theodore Vienne explained: Johnson had been sentenced to prison in his own country, and more important, he seemed unwilling to face serious challengers, "notably Sam Langford." To reassert his ownership of the title—and to make some money—Johnson hastily agreed to face "Battling" Jim Johnson, a black journeyman, in Paris in December, and to take on Frank Moran, a white hope from Pittsburgh, in the same city the following month.

The champion's bout with Jim Johnson was to be the first-ever heavyweight title contest between black boxers—it would also be the last for more than a quarter of a century—but it did not turn out to be much of a fight. Because Jim Johnson shared the champion's last name and was also said to come from Galveston, some British reporters suggested that the two men must be related. They weren't, but in the weeks before the fight, the challenger—who was tall and dark and, like the champion, shaved his scalp—had a fine time signing "Jack Johnson" in autograph books proffered by worshipful but confused Parisians. If Jack Johnson really did want to remain history's sole black heavyweight titleholder, as some papers insisted he did, a fight with Jim Johnson was a pretty safe bet. Joe Jeannette and Sam Langford might conceivably have beaten the champion: Jeannette had at least held his own with Johnson over their ten matches, and Langford had grown in size, skill, and punching power over the seven years since their first encounters in Massachusetts. But Jim Johnson wasn't in their class: he'd lost almost half of his thirty-three fights. Fireman Jim Flynn and Joe Jeannette had beaten him; Al Kaufmann and Sam McVey had knocked him out.

When the two men met at the Nouveau Cirque on December 19, nothing much happened for two rounds. Both were counterpunchers, and Battling Jim seemed especially wary. In the third, the champion launched an attack that sent the younger man reeling. Then, for no apparent reason, he pulled back. There were cries of "Fake!" Some customers called for their money back. In fact, the champion had fractured his left forearm slamming the challenger's head and had to fight the next seven rounds with just one hand, clinching whenever he could. At the end, it was the younger man who was breathing hard. The referee declared the bout a draw. The crowd, unaware of Johnson's injury, hissed both men. "A terrific hubbub marked the conclusion of a wholly unsatisfactory encounter," the London *Times* reported. "The audience dispersed, continuing to express its disapproval of the whole proceedings." Johnson walked away with just a little over one thousand dollars. His contest with Frank Moran would have to be postponed until spring.

On January 22, 1914, he was at ringside in Paris, watching two Frenchmen go at each other, when an American named C. F. Bertelli tapped him on the shoulder and asked if he could have a word with him between rounds. Johnson agreed. Bertelli explained that he was a stringer for the Chicago *Examiner*. The paper had run a series of sensational stories over the past few days suggesting that Johnson had paid twenty-five thousand dollars in bribes to federal officials in order to be allowed to flee the country. He'd been sent to ask Johnson whether or not these tales were true. Johnson grinned. They were indeed, he said, and dictated a statement for the paper.

I am delighted that some people in Chicago are beginning to be awake to the fact that I have been shamefully treated and am the victim of blackmailing officials in that city.

Just before I got away I handed $20,000 to Roy Jones, who said he was sent to me by a man named DeWoody, who represented Harry Parkin, Assistant District Attorney.

DeWoody and Parkin used to frequent my saloon during the early part of my trouble in Chicago. They were accommodated in a private room back of my saloon.

In various sums I paid out this way a total of $25,000. I am going back to see the thing through when the time is ripe (and I think that will be soon) and prove the case was a put-up job against me.

The truth was finally out, he said. He could hardly wait to get home and tell his wife.

The story had broken in the *Examiner* on January 18. Mrs. Sol Lewinsohn, the wife of the shady South Side bondsman and fixer who, Johnson claimed, had acted as his go-between and then disappeared, had gone to U.S. District Attorney James H. Wilkerson and demanded that he launch a grand jury investigation. She had check stubs, she said, proving that her husband had paid money to federal officials, including Assistant District Attorney Parkin, Bureau of Investigation chief DeWoody, and U.S. Commissioner Mark Foote before whom defendants in need of bondsmen appeared, and the man who had set bail for Lucille Cameron. Wilkerson agreed to a hearing. Most of the case had no bearing on Jack Johnson. Mrs. Lewinsohn's real object was to bloody the federal officials most likely to prosecute her husband for embezzling from his bank. And everyone she and Johnson charged with wrongdoing denied it categorically. DeWoody called the charges "absurd." Parkin said he'd never taken a dollar. Roy Jones said Johnson was just out to get even with him for having testified about the beating of Etta Duryea—though he also thought his old friend had "got a dirty deal somewhere." Stung by the champion's new charges, an angry Department of Justice now threatened to have him extradited on a charge of "conspiracy to defeat the ends of justice."

A grand jury investigation began. Johnson's mother, his sister Jennie, and a former woman detective were all deposed. Each yielded potentially explosive evidence against the authorities. Tiny Johnson told of the five thousand dollars her son had been forced to pay to Mrs. Cameron-Falconet and claimed twenty thousand more had been handed along to state and federal officials through Lewinsohn. Jennie Rhodes said that her brother had paid ten thousand dollars to State's Attorney Wayman to the same end; she also insisted she'd been present when Lewinsohn and her brother gave Parkin five thousand dollars and then had watched him count it out. Mrs. M. Evalyn Knitzinger, who had once worked for Wayman as a private investigator, said she'd personally carried bribe money from Wayman to DeWoody, and that afterward her boss had ordered her a drink in a restaurant, saying, "Have one on Jack Johnson." In addition, she swore she'd overheard Johnson's own attorney, Benjamin Bachrach, say, "We'll fleece that nigger before we get through with him."

In the end, the grand jury did not believe the two black women or their white friend. No one was indicted.*

Meanwhile, Johnson's prospects overseas seemed more and more bleak. When he tried returning to the stage in England, the town councils of Hanley, Wolverhampton, and Swansea all called for his appearances to be canceled. And when the National Sporting Club once again asked him to fight Sam Langford for three thousand pounds—the same sum he'd rejected five years before—his contemptuous turndown further antagonized British boxing fans:

> I must say that the offer which you have made me is absolutely ridiculous to my thinking. I have defeated Langford, and not only that, Langford has been beaten four times in the last two years. He was beaten by Sam McVey in Australia; he was also defeated by Joe Jeannette on two different occasions in New York City, and not so long ago he was defeated by Gunboat Smith in his own home-town, Boston, and the only thing I can get out of the fight is money, because there will be no glory in defeating Langford as I have already done the trick. . . .
>
> I am very proud that I have made all my matches—I myself—and being a true champion I do not see where the NSC has a right to dictate to me how much I shall receive for my appearance and boxing ability. If they do not want to give my price, which is [thirty thousand dollars]—win, lose, or draw—they can call things off on receipt of this letter. I won my title on those conditions, and any time that I shall do battle it will be under those conditions and none other.
>
> I am boxing a man now, and I am getting my price. I don't care what the public thinks.

"The tone which Jack Johnson has taken in communicating with the National Sporting Club," said the London *Times,* "is such as to preclude the possibility of his making a public reappearance in England."

---

*Charles DeWoody was removed from white-slave cases for a time but was subsequently made chief of agents of the Department of Justice in New York City, where he pursued shadowy spy plots and rounded up draft resisters during the Great War. (New York *Times,* March 12 and 19, April 14, September 4, 1918.)

In late February, he wrote a very different sort of letter to the sporting editor of the Chicago *Defender*. His arm had healed, and he was eager to make good on his promise to face Frank Moran.

Paris
Dear Sir:

Permit me to inform the public once and for all time that my match with Frank Moran is on and will take place the last week in June as now scheduled.

The whole world wants to see a white man champion. I have signed to fight a white man, and because I refused a ridiculously small price to meet Langford the proposed promoters and Langford's manager tried to create the impression that I would never fight again. Langford or his agent never would induce anyone with real money to back him against me. That's the reason for his soreness.

I am the same John Arthur Johnson, undisputed champion of the world, and after Moran I will fight the white man who stands out, be he "Gunboat" Smith, "Battling" Levinsky, Jess Willard or Georges Carpentier.

I refuse no one when I get my price. Moran's backers met my terms, and all the others have the same chance as Moran. I understand that "Gunboat" Smith defeated Langford. Here's the gunner's chance to get a crack at my title.*

The public wants a white man to be my successor. I am ready to fight 'em all and bar no one, at $30,000 apiece.

Yours truly,
JACK JOHNSON
World's Heavyweight Champion

It was a brave letter but misleading. Johnson was fighting Frank Moran for a percentage of the purse, not the thirty thousand dollars his pride always

---

*Gunboat Smith had become the "White Heavyweight Champion of the World" by knocking out Arthur Pelkey on New Year's Day, 1914. He was proud of that accomplishment, he remembered, "but still, I knew in my heart that I wasn't the champion of the world. White, yes—but there was Jack Johnson." And Smith, who had once been one of Johnson's sparring partners, wanted no part of a serious fight with him. That summer, Smith was in England preparing for a fight with Georges Carpentier, when Fred Dartnell asked him "if he thought of meeting the big black." The fighter pretended not to hear the question. Dartnell asked again, he remembered, and "Smith became suddenly busy with some gymnastic apparatus." Dartnell tried a third time. "Mr. Smith gazed at me with a rather set expression and a ruminative look in his eyes. After a few seconds' silence he replied: 'Oh, Johnson will wait . . . ' Then, suddenly, as if struck by an afterthought, he continued: 'And the longer he waits, the better.'" (Peter Heller, *In This Corner . . . !*, p. 42; Fred Dartnell, *Seconds Out*, p. 181.)

dictated he demand. He and Moran's manager, Dan McKetrick, had spent a week wrangling about it back in January. "Stop your kidding, Jack," McKetrick told him. "You ought to be glad to get a chance to fight a white man for the best purse you can get." No one was willing to put up that kind of money any longer. If he didn't defend his title soon, it would surely be stripped from him. Johnson gave in, but he didn't want anyone to know he had backed down, so cameras were set up at the Restaurant Dauphine in the Bois de Boulogne to film McKetrick handing Johnson a check for thirty thousand dollars, plus five thousand for expenses. The money was said to have been provided by "three American millionaires" who happened to be in Paris. The worthless check was torn up afterward. Johnson himself had to borrow thirty-five hundred dollars to help promote the bout.

According to Henri Wolf, a Frenchman whom Johnson hired as his secretary, the champion was now living "like a rajah" at Asnières, surrounded by retainers and falling more and more deeply into debt each day. Advertising the bout was proving far more costly than he'd expected, and the French Boxing Federation refused to declare the upcoming bout in Paris a title contest until a new, clandestine contract was drawn up awarding one third of the proceeds to Theodore Vienne, its none-too-scrupulous director. (Johnson and Moran were to divide the rest, 90–10.)*

If Moran managed to land a knockout blow, said the Washington *Post* on February 25, it would be worth a million dollars to him, would "lift the white man's burden, would cause as big a stir as the blows Admiral Dewey delivered in Manila Bay, which won for Uncle Sam the Philippine Islands." Rhetoric like that bewildered the French and amused Jack Johnson. "Basi-

---

*No sooner had Johnson agreed to fight Moran in February than he signed for a wrestling match on a German brewer's private estate outside Hamburg. McKetrick was furious. Johnson's arm had just healed. Suppose he reinjured it? Johnson was adamant. "I'm needy!" he said. McKetrick decided he'd better go along as an escort. When he turned up at Johnson's home to pick him up, he found Lucille pointing a revolver at her husband. She, too, wanted him to stay in Paris. Johnson promised that he would, left the house with McKetrick—and then raced to the station to catch the train for Hamburg. As it pulled out, McKetrick remembered, Lucille came running along the platform in her bathrobe and jumped aboard. Johnson entertained the brewer and his guests and afterward, McKetrick said, "he was paid off in cash and the merchandise of the house."

In March, when he traveled to Sweden for what was evidently a fixed wrestling match, Swedish officials escorted him back to the border and warned him not to try to return. "Tryin' to pick a quarrel with a wrestler," wrote the sportswriter Sandy Griswold in the Omaha *Herald*. "Now waddya know about that? We could almost pity the poor old crooked coon." (Lardner, *White Hopes*, pp. 42–43; Omaha *Herald*, March 21, 1914.)

cally," he told a reporter, "the Americans are already dancing around my scalp. They think I'm finished, used-up. Don't worry, they won't get my scalp yet."

Johnson had reason to be confident. Frank Moran was a brash, red-haired Irish-American who had studied dentistry in his hometown and so was sometimes billed as the "Pittsburgh Dentist." He'd served four years in the Navy—part of the time aboard the presidential yacht *Mayflower*—and learned his brawling style battling other sailors. He was big and had a powerful right hand he called his "Mary Ann," but he threw it on what a British writer called the principle of "I-don't-know-where-you're-going-to-land-but-I'm-hoping-for-the-best." Johnson always enjoyed beating and bewildering that kind of opponent. "If it is true that American children are praying for Moran's victory," said the London *Times*, "they had better pray very hard."

Johnson barely bothered to train. He slept late, and when the press asked why they hadn't seen him out doing roadwork in the early mornings, he explained that he'd done it all before dawn. When some began to doubt that story, he had himself driven to a spot near a café where he knew sportswriters liked to drink and raced past it on foot, with Gus Rhodes panting along behind, pretending to have exhausted himself trying to keep up with the tireless champion.

Johnson was sure he would retain his title in a fair fight, but as the contest grew closer he began to worry that the title might be stolen from him. He didn't like it that McKetrick was both the promoter for the fight and his opponent's manager; he was also concerned that Georges Carpentier was to referee under French rules that barred hitting on the break. That was the moment when Johnson's uppercuts traditionally did some of their most damaging work. He went to McKetrick with what he believed was a nonnegotiable demand: he would go through with the fight, he said, only if Moran would promise to go down in the eighth round. In exchange, he'd give the challenger 40 percent, not 10.

McKetrick appeared to agree but refused to sign anything. Henri Wolf got wind of Johnson's scheme and asked McKetrick how he could even consider such a thing. Moran's manager told him the end justified the means; if it took a false promise of surrender for his man to get at Jack Johnson, he was happy to make the gesture.

But Johnson wasn't to be put off with winks and nods. He wanted to be certain that Moran was on board. McKetrick did his best to duck him, but on the morning of the fight, the champion cornered him at Tod Sloan's bar.

Johnson was waving a document he'd had typed up on official fight stationery.

MATCH JOHNSON-MORAN POUR LE CHAMPIONNAT DU MONDE

June 27th, 1914

I hereby agree to divide receipts of my contest with Frank Moran on June 27th on a basis of forty percent to Moran and sixty percent to me provided that Frank Moran loses inside of eight rounds.

The champion signed it with a flourish, then added, "After fight must return this receipt!" and handed it to McKetrick as evidence of his good faith. The two men shook hands as if they'd made a deal. That evening, McKetrick and Vienne, still anxious that Johnson might not fight, had policemen posted outside his dressing room with instructions to seize him and take him to the French border should he balk. They weren't needed. Johnson thought he had a sure thing.

Meanwhile, a big, fashionable crowd was filing into the vast covered Parisian cycle track called the Vélodrome d'Hiver. The sixteen-foot ring was roofed with a canopy of purple silk, hung to disguise row upon row of electrical tubes. Meant to provide proper lighting for the movie cameras, the London *Times* reported, they also "threw a greenish tint over everything . . . and made everything and everybody look ghastly." The *Times* continued: "Here—but for the presence of an occasional tweed suit and the preponderance of men in the audience—one might have fancied that it was the first night of a new play instead of a boxing match. There were scores of women, almost all in evening dress in many vivid hues and much bejeweled." Colette was there. So was Mistinguette, the music hall performer who was thought by some to have had more than a purely aesthetic interest in Johnson. "It might have been a night at the opera," wrote the British boxing writer Fred Dartnell.

Boxing had become something more than a sport or an entertainment. It was La Mode. One's brain registered strange impressions. Some were agreeable, some otherwise. Nearby was an Eastern prince, a coffee-coloured elegant, with wonderful pearls. On either side of him sat a radiant white woman with her hair dyed a kind of emerald gold. Next to me was a handsome middle-aged American lady with her two daughters. All three were painfully anxious that Moran should win.

As Johnson prepared to answer the opening bell, he whispered to McKetrick, "Everything O.K, Dan?" meaning was Moran going to live up to his part of the bargain and collapse on schedule in the eighth?

All Moran's manager would say was "Get on with the fight."

In the first round, one writer noted that Johnson seemed "awfully serious" and "unusually aggressive." By the end of the second, the champion realized he'd been had. "Those are pretty wise guys," he told one of his seconds. "That boy is trying some."

His red-haired challenger was trying. But he was only rarely able to land. A big-time sport named George Considine was assigned the hopeless task of getting Johnson's goat. "Come on! Come on!" Considine shouted. "You don't know how to lead. Never did."

"Hush now, Jim Corbett," Johnson said, remembering how Corbett had tried to rattle him in Reno.

"Poor old man!" Considine yelled back. Johnson smiled and thumped Moran three times.

Lucille shouted encouragement: "Hit him, Daddy! Come along Papa!" Johnson talked to Moran, too. "You don't know anything about fighting," he told his opponent, drawing blood from his nose, then shifting smoothly out of range.

As Carpentier separated the two men in the tenth, Johnson seemed to forget the French rules and threw a stiff left jab that staggered Moran and opened an old cut over his eye. Blood began to trickle down Moran's face. The crowd roared its disapproval. A ringside judge shouted through a megaphone that Johnson had fouled Moran. A second transgression would mean disqualification. Johnson was not apologetic. "How do you feel now, Frank?" he asked.

Two rounds later, the challenger managed to land a left hand on Johnson's neck. Johnson stepped back, grinning and pounding his gloves together. "My sincere congratulations, Frank," he said. In the fifteenth, he stood in the middle of the ring for nearly a minute, pivoting slowly while Moran circled him without daring to throw a punch. Both men seemed tired at the end of the twentieth and final round, but Johnson was the clear winner.

The correspondent for the New York *Times* called it "positively the poorest bout ever staged as a championship contest." But in his story for the *Defender* the ever-loyal Gus Rhodes declared it "the finest fistic encounter ever witnessed since glove fighting was inaugurated in 1892." And the newspaper's headlines echoed Rhodes' enthusiasm.

WORLD ACCLAIMS
JACK JOHNSON
KING OF PRIZE FIGHTERS
CHAMPION'S VICTORY OVER FRANK MORAN OF PITTSBURGH
IN PARIS, FRANCE, FOREVER SETS AT REST ANY DOUBT
AS TO HIS ABILITY—SPEED AND POWER OF JOHNSON
ASTONISHES FIGHT FOLLOWERS AND OUTCOME OF 20-ROUND
BATTLE NEVER IN DOUBT—IN A CLASS OF HIS OWN—
PICTURES MAY NOT BE SHOWN IN UNITED STATES

MORAN WAS GAME, DID HIS BEST BUT WAS NO
MATCH FOR JOHNSON

BOASTED "WHITE HOPE" IS PUNCHED AT WILL AND
ANGLO-SAXON SUPREMACY IN HEAVYWEIGHT CLASS RECEIVES
CRUSHING BLOW AS CRAFTY CHAMPION
PLAYS WITH HIM LIKE A CAT WITH A MOUSE—IN FINE
CONDITION—ALL SORTS OF EXCUSES OFFERED
MORAN DROWNS IN BLACK SEA

When the news reached Chicago's South Side, Johnson fans celebrated in the streets. Tiny Johnson sent her son a congratulatory telegram and invited the neighbors in for Sunday dinner.

After the fight, Johnson had to content himself with secondhand accounts of the celebrations back home. Neither he nor Frank Moran would collect a sou for their efforts in the ring. A vengeful Dan McKetrick was responsible. "I'm as bitter a man as there is in the world," he told the writer John Lardner many years later, and it was his own fighter, not Jack Johnson, who was the target of his wrath. Between the time Moran signed for his fight with Johnson in January and the June fight itself, he'd undertaken a vaudeville tour in the United States, just as Jim Jeffries had done before the Reno battle. When he got back to Paris, he had a new manager with him, Ike Dorgan, brother of the cartoonist, Tad. McKetrick, fearing that his potential champion was about to be stolen from him, demanded that Moran sign an exclusive contract. He refused. After serving in the Navy, he had taken a vow never to sign another legal document. Instead, he said, he would put his trust in the good faith of those with whom he dealt. McKetrick, who put his trust in no one, was furious and took a bizarre revenge. Claiming that Moran owed him $1,462 in monies advanced him for training, he hired Lucien Cerf, a French attorney, and had him impound all the profits the moment the fight was over, not to be distributed until he and Moran and Johnson had all signed a release—and McKetrick vowed not to sign until he and Moran had a contract. The attorney deposited the money—some $34,000, of which Johnson was supposed to get $14,400—in the Bank of France. Then, disaster: Lucien Cerf, who had joined the French army, was killed early in World War One. The paperwork was lost. The bank said it had no record of the deposit. No one ever collected.*

Johnson's creditors moved in. Not for the first time, he and his party hastily packed up and moved on, this time all the way to St. Petersburg. He had been invited there again by the expatriate black American impresario, George Thomas, to be his headliner for the season.

Johnson, Lucille, and Gus Rhodes arrived in the Russian capital on July 1, 1914. They enjoyed themselves among the czarist officers and courtiers who dined and drank at Thomas' glass-roofed Aquarium. But once again Johnson's timing was off, and this time it was not his fault. Germany declared war on Russia on August 1. The Great War had begun. The police told Johnson and his party to leave the country right away. "They invoked the five-and-ten law," Johnson remembered. "That means five minutes to pack, and ten minutes to get out of town."

We have only Johnson's extravagant memories of their flight across Europe. They lost most of their fourteen trunks while changing trains at War-

---

*McKetrick's vendetta against Frank Moran was unrelenting. In October of 1915, Moran was in his dressing room at Madison Square Garden, getting ready to fight Jim Coffey of Dublin, when a process server handed him a paper attaching $2,800 from his share of the gate receipts. McKetrick still wanted those training expenses, plus interest. "I won't take my pants off till I get some cash!" Moran shouted. The promoter gave him enough to motivate him to climb into the ring—where he demolished the Irish Giant in three rounds.

A few months later, according to John Lardner, Moran got a kind of revenge. McKetrick's suit was dismissed on the ground that the money should have been collected from "the famous purse that McKetrick had paralyzed in Paris." Moran and his lawyer went to a chophouse to celebrate. McKetrick and his attorney turned up a few minutes later. Moran's lawyer said something to McKetrick. McKetrick punched him. Soon, he and both lawyers were rolling on the floor, punching and cursing, as Frank Moran looked on. "The rarest bliss that can befall a pugilist," Lardner wrote, "is the sight of managers and lawyers punching each other, for nothing."

In 1927, McKetrick enlisted the mayor of New York, James J. Walker, who was on his way to France for a vacation, to try to talk the Bank of France into coming up with the cash. It refused, Walker told McKetrick when he got home: "The French think you're running some kind of a con game, Dan." (Lardner, *White Hopes*, pp. 48–49; New York *Times*, October 20, 1915.)

saw, he said. Soldiers and refugees were everywhere. In Berlin, Gus Rhodes managed to bribe their way onto a train crowded with refugees bound for the Belgian border. From there, they carried their remaining baggage three miles on foot to catch a train for Paris. The French capital was "in chaos," Johnson recalled, filled with Americans and Britons desperate to get to the English Channel and escape to England.

"I met Jack Johnson on the boulevard," one of them remembered. "His face was wreathed in smiles. Crowds surrounded him urging him to fight for France." He sometimes said he would. He had applied to become a French citizen, after all, and Gus Rhodes wired the *Defender* that Johnson had actually accepted a colonelcy in the French army. Lester A. Walton, the editor of the New York *Age,* was thrilled to hear it. The French were about to send black troops against the Germans, he wrote, "the first time such a thing has been done since the Moors of Northern Africa were driven out of Spain after ruling it quite eight hundred years. If it should do so we shall expect none of them to fight more bravely under the Tri-Color than JOHN ARTHUR JOHNSON, the Champion Prize-Fighter of the World."

But Johnson did not see himself on the front lines. General Sherman was right about war, he told an American reporter he met outside the American Express office in Rue Scribe. He wanted no part of it. "The only thing left for me is to pose as the statue of Hard Luck," he said with a sigh. "But all the sculptors are at the front."

The next day, he got one of his cars out of storage and set out for Boulogne with Lucille and Gus. They could hear the thump of German guns as they drove, and the roads were choked with French troops and military vehicles. Trying to get around them, he drove over an embankment and had to ask for help to get on his way again. Waiting at the pier at Boulogne, he watched English and Scottish troops come ashore singing, "It's a long way to Tipperary."

The Johnsons made it across the channel and settled into another London flat.

The champion was in real trouble now. His money was running out. War kept him off the Continent and preoccupied the British.* He couldn't go

---

*In an effort to recoup his losses, he returned to the recording studio—the Edison Bell Company in London's West End this time—and delivered a booming monologue on physical culture. He encouraged everyone to "strut and walk and run," but his most important recommendation was to drink prodigious amounts of cold water, "the most strengthening thing that we can possibly use." (Tim Brooks, *Lost Sounds,* p. 248.)

home. He made plans to sail to Buenos Aires and try his luck in South America. "I've been told it's a good place for a spade," he told a friend. Then a telegram arrived: his old friend Jack Curley was coming to England with a proposition for him.

One day that summer, Curley and Harry Frazee had lunched together at the Astor Hotel in Manhattan. Curley hadn't really been able to afford it. "Times were slack with me," he remembered. "I was practically broke. I was getting meager returns from two or three obscure fighters . . . but I needed more than that." He was thousands of dollars in debt, in fact, and had hoped to borrow the money from his former partner. But Frazee, who had moved from small-time vaudeville to big-time Broadway since he and Curley had sent Jim Jeffries around the country before the battle at Reno, was also low on cash. His partner, L. Lawrence Weber, could provide the money. But Frazee had another idea.

"Why don't you get somebody to beat the nigger?"

"I've got somebody," Curley said. "Or at least I know somebody, Jess Willard."

Why Willard?

"Because Johnson is ready to be taken," he answered, "and Willard, big, strong and punch-proof, is the man to do it."

If the current crop of white hopes was "an awful herd of harmless elephants," as the sportswriter William A. Phelon insisted it was, Jess Willard was the biggest bull in the herd. The "Pottawatomie Giant" stood six feet six and a half inches tall, weighed 230 pounds when in fighting trim, and had a fingertip-to-fingertip reach of eighty-four inches. "God made me a giant," he once told a friend. "I never received an education, never had any money. I knew that I was a big fellow and powerful strong. I just sat down and figured that a man as big as me ought to be able to cash in on the road to boxing."

Born in 1881 on a farm in Pottawatomie County, Kansas, he left school early rather than allow the teacher to whip him, broke horses for a living, then traded them. He ran a livery stable in the little town of Emmett, married his childhood sweetheart (with whom he eventually had four children), then moved to Elk City, Oklahoma. There, he went into business selling mules and driving freight wagons, only to have his partners swindle him out of his savings. In 1911, bitter, broke, and distrustful, he thought he'd try the ring. He was twenty-nine years old the first time he laced on a glove as a professional—and he promptly lost on a disqualification to an otherwise unremembered tank-town fighter named Louis Fink. His wife said he'd been beaten up so badly he'd barely been recognizable when he came home. But Willard got paid and decided to stick with it. "I never liked [boxing]," he remembered. "I hated it as I never hated a thing previously, but there was money in it. I needed the money and decided to go after it."

He won his next seven fights, including a three-round knockout of Fink, and briefly attracted the attention of the veteran manager Billy McCarney, who matched him with another western newcomer, Joe Cox. Cox came for him with such fervor that Willard grabbed the referee and hid behind him, then jumped out of the ring altogether in the fourth. "I quit the big dog on the spot," McCarney recalled.

But another manager soon took him on: Tom Jones, a sharp-tongued one-time barber from Illinois who had already shepherded Ad Wolgast to the lightweight title and Billy Papke to the middleweight championship. Jones accepted no excuses from his fighters, but even with his ceaseless exhortations to bear down, the big Kansan remained an inconsistent performer. He did better than insiders expected in no-decision bouts with Arthur Pelkey and Luther McCarty, but looked so lethargic losing to Gunboat Smith that some writers suggested he should quit the ring. "I never really knew how to fight," Willard later admitted. "I never could do anything to the other fellow in the way of damage. I simply couldn't do it. Harming the other fellow seemed to be cruel, and so long as the other fellow didn't harm me much I didn't see any reason why I should hurt him." But if the other fellow *did* hurt him, he also said, "I got real mad and just swung on them."

In August of 1913, he was matched in San Francisco with a big, fearsome-looking victim of pituitary gigantism from Wyoming named John "Bull" Young. In the eleventh round, Willard landed a right uppercut. Young went over backward, his head slamming into the canvas. He suffered a concussion and died the next day of a cerebral hemorrhage. Willard, Jones, the fight's promoter, Tom McCarey, and several others were arrested and charged with second-degree murder.

The case was later dropped, but Willard was unnerved. His next opponent was George "Boer" Rodel, a handsome South African. He had been brought to America by James J. Johnston, a Briton who billed him as a hero of the Boer War Siege of Ladysmith until a cynical sportswriter did the math and pointed out that Rodel had been twelve years old at the time. Rodel was a foot shorter and fifty pounds lighter than Willard and had already lost to Jim Coffey and Gunboat Smith. If his import was to continue to sell tickets in

America, Johnston needed to do something dramatic. He visited Willard in his dressing room moments before the fight was scheduled to begin. "Jess," he said, "here's something I think you ought to know for your own good. My Boer has got a weak heart. A doctor told him a really good punch might kill him. You do what you like about it." Willard turned pale. For ten pacific rounds he kept his powerful right hand safely at his side and used his long left to keep the smaller man from doing him any harm. "His behavior in the fight was a model of tenderness," John Lardner wrote. "He might have been Rodel's mother." Later, when Willard figured out that Johnston had tricked him, he took pleasure in twice knocking the Boer senseless.*

Willard won more fights than he lost after that, but he was neither fast nor aggressive nor popular. When he and Carl Morris lumbered through ten no-decision rounds at Madison Square Garden, the Los Angeles *Times* headlined its story GEE! WHAT A ROTTEN FIGHT. Willard showed initiative only once, the *Times* added, when he attempted "an annihilating right hand swing and nearly fell out into Twenty-third Street when he missed by a couple of yards."

By the summer of 1914, Willard's career seemed to have stalled, and he was considering changing his line of work again. Still, Curley knew, Johnson himself had said he'd like to fight him, "just to show Tom Jones he can't pick a champion." Willard was big, he was strong, and, most important, he was white.

Curley went to work right away. He went around Tom Jones and wired Willard in Los Angeles directly, saying only that he wanted to talk. Willard agreed to meet him halfway across the continent in Kansas City. There, they sat together on a baggage truck on the railroad platform while Curley made his pitch.

"Jess," he said, "I want to put you into a ring with Johnson. If you string along with me, I'll do it."

Willard was happy to string along. He'd always wanted to fight Johnson, he said. "I'm sure if I get the chance I'll beat him. And I'll never forget you for giving it to me."

Curley took Willard back to New York with him. Together they got Tom Jones' agreement. Then Curley set out for England to see Jack Johnson.

He found the champion walking his dog on the sidewalk outside his rented flat in St. Mary's Mansions, Paddington.

---

*This happened so often to the good-looking but weak-chinned Rodel that some sportswriters began to call him the "Diving Venus."

Johnson greeted Curley warmly. They'd known each other for sixteen years, ever since the battle royal in Springfield, Illinois, that first brought the future champion to the attention of boxing insiders in Chicago. "We had been close friends and had met in previously mutually satisfactory business deals," Johnson wrote later. "At one time in my life, when I was in serious trouble [after Etta Johnson's suicide and during the Lucille Cameron crisis], "he had stood loyally by me. As a result of this, I had the utmost confidence in him."

"Come on up," Johnson said, "we've waited dinner for you. And I know you'll like it because it's a real American dinner—chicken, corn, biscuits I mixed myself and everything." Upstairs, Curley chatted with Lucille while Johnson put on his apron and bustled around the kitchen. At dinner, according to Curley, Johnson at first said he had no wish ever to return to the United States. But "[a] moment later, his eager questions about friends and scenes back home belied his declaration that he did not ever want to go back. I told him as much as I could in reply to the innumerable questions." Then Johnson brought the conversation around to the possibility of a fight against the newest white hope whose name he pretended not to be able to pronounce. "And who is this WeeLARD you want me to fight?"

"Don't pull that Parisian accent on me you mug—plain American 'Willard,' " Curley said. "He's a big mule-skinner from Kansas. He's six-feet-seven-inches tall, weighs 260 pounds, has dynamite in either hand, and can't be hurt." The champion chuckled. Other guests arrived. The fight talk ended. But, Curley remembered, "I knew I had landed Johnson."

After dinner, the champion had his car brought around and offered to show Curley the town. It was late. The promoter begged off, so the champion drove him back to his hotel, instead. On the way, he pulled over beneath a streetlight and handed Curley a sheaf of telegrams to look through. "They were from fight managers and promoters in New York," Curley recalled, "some of them men I had reason to think were friends of mine—that is, until I saw the messages they had sent to Johnson in an effort to get him to refuse to sign with me."

"I don't pay any attention to that stuff," Johnson said, starting up the car again. "I'm ready to go along with you, Jack."

How far he was willing to go along with Jack Curley would later become the subject of bitter contention between them—and still stirs controversy among boxing historians. The basic outline of the deal they worked out together over the next few days was clear enough: Johnson was to get the thirty thousand dollars plus the training expenses his pride demanded—the same sum Tommy Burns had received to risk his title against Johnson in Sydney—for a forty-five-round title contest with Willard in Mexico at a site as close as possible to the U.S. border, so American fans could get there. And he was to get one third of the foreign-film rights, as well (there were no U.S. rights, since a new federal law forbade the shipment of such films across state lines).

But, according to Johnson, there was more to their negotiations than that. "Curley was a cunning fellow," he wrote. One evening, Johnson began sadly to list the wrongs he believed had been done him.

Curley cut him off. "Don't you know if you weren't champion you would not have all this trouble?"

Johnson agreed. White America could never forgive him so long as he held the title. But what could he do about it?

Again, according to Johnson, Curley had a ready answer. If Johnson would lie down to Willard and give up his championship, he could have a sizable off-the-record payment, in addition to which Curley promised to use his personal connections to see to it that he was allowed to go home again without fear of prison. "He frankly told me that if I lost the fight to Willard," Johnson wrote, "I could return to the United States without being molested [by the government]. These hints were inducements, of course, but the greatest inducement of all was the opportunity it offered me to see my mother, for all who know me and who have read about me know that whatever other failings I may have had, the love I had for my mother was so deep and sincere that I would have done anything to end the separation between us. . . . After that . . . conversation . . . I did not care anymore for the title of world's champion than a child does for the stick from which the lollypop has vanished."

It is impossible now to know precisely what arrangement Jack Curley and Jack Johnson may have made with each other in London. Johnson did want to go home, and really was eager to see his mother, but he was not naïve. It's hard to imagine he could ever really have believed Curley was capable of arranging such a deal with the federal government—or that Curley, even at his most expansive, could have pretended to have the power to pull it off. (When Johnson later charged the promoter with having double-crossed him, Curley shot back, "Did he think I was mayor of the United States?") Neither Jack Johnson nor Jack Curley was above a little mutually beneficial prearrangement, but despite all Johnson said about his fight with Willard in later years, there is no evidence that he ever did anything but try his best against Jess Willard once the two men climbed into the ring.

Curley apparently did promise to do his best to persuade the government to go easy on the champion, and there is documentary evidence that he followed through on that pledge. He may have further impressed the champion with talk of a potential ace in the hole: Secretary of State William Jennings Bryan was an old friend and former client; Curley had handled Bryan's lecture tour one season and had even persuaded him to attend a prize fight, which the pious prairie orator admitted he'd enjoyed.

In any case, the promoter sailed home to get things organized, while Johnson and Lucille sailed for South America and waited for further word from their friend, Jack Curley. Curley and Frazee scheduled the fight for March 6, 1915, at the race track at Juárez. A big cattlemen's convention was to take place then just across the border at El Paso and the promoters hoped to attract plenty of American ticket buyers. But Mexico was in chaos. Francisco "Pancho" Villa, who controlled most of the northern part of the country, was delighted at the prospect of a heavyweight title contest in his region, especially when Curley offered him a cut of the proceeds. But to get there from South America, Johnson would have to land on the Caribbean coast at either Tampico or Veracruz, then travel overland to Juárez. Both ports were in the hands of General Venustiano Carranza, who wished to do nothing to strengthen Villa's hand or to antagonize Washington. Carranza let it be known that if Johnson set foot in his territory, he would arrest him and turn him over to the Americans.

Meanwhile, Johnson and his party sailed north from Montevideo aboard the British steamer *Highland Harris*. Johnson ate four meals a day, the captain remembered, and filled the long hours at sea playing shuffleboard and shooting at sharks. They spent several days at Barbados, where Johnson earned a few dollars showing the film of his fight with Frank Moran and sparring at the Electric Theater with a Trinidadian so frightened he kept running into the wings. Then he chartered a boat for Cuba, arriving on February 15. From there, he was expected to sail for Tampico aboard the steamer *Morro Castle*. Two days later, on February 17, Jack Curley sent two trusted emissaries to call upon federal officials in Chicago with instructions to see what they could do to make Johnson's homecoming after the fight as easy as possible. Robert Cantwell, a former federal agent who had briefly been employed by Johnson as a private investigator during the months leading up to his Mann Act trial, asked to see U.S. Attorney Charles Clyne. At the same time, Ed Smith of the Chicago *American*, got an appointment with federal agent L. C. Wheeler. Smith was Johnson's closest friend among sportswriters—he had written friendly pieces about him after Reno and refereed the fight at Las Vegas with Jim Flynn; his wife was supposed to have accompanied Etta Johnson to New Mexico on the evening she killed herself.

Both men told the same story. Johnson was "about broke" and eager to come home, provided "matters could be adjusted satisfactorily with the government"—by which he meant if he were allowed to pay a substantial fine and not have to serve any time. It was also "well-known in sporting circles," they said, that the upcoming fight was "a frame up," "that it has already been decided as to who is to win and for this agreement on Johnson's part to permit Willard to win he will be paid a considerable [sum] of money other than the stipulated percentage of the gate receipts."

Clyne was opposed to what Agent Wheeler called any kind of "dicker": he told Cantwell no such agreement could be made in advance. But Hinton G. Clabaugh, now superintendent of the Justice Department office in Chicago, took a different view. He proposed he be allowed to go to Juárez personally to try to talk Johnson into surrendering once the fight was over. Cantwell was "close to the sporting and the underworld," while he had "the utmost confidence" in Ed Smith. With the help of these two men, he said, "I believe somehow I can on one pretext or another get Johnson back on American soil and into custody."

His boss, A. Bruce Bielaski, would have none of it. "I personally would be very much opposed to entering into agreement with this defendant"; Jack Johnson should be treated like any other fugitive. Curley's connections had not moved the Justice Department. Nor did his supposed closeness to the secretary of state turn out to mean anything: instead of showing sympathy for the fugitive, Bryan personally interested himself in finding a way to seize Johnson from the ship that was to take him from Cuba to Mexico, and he would later wire Havana to make sure Johnson was refused a new passport.

On the evening of February 18, 1915, the day after Curley's agents made their pitch for leniency to federal officials in Chicago, President Woodrow Wilson, and his cabinet gathered in the East Room of the White House in Washington to see D. W. Griffith's epic film *The Birth of a Nation*.

The Birth of a Nation was based on Thomas Dixon Jr.'s 1905 best seller, *The Clansman*, and offered an upside-down version of Reconstruction in which the terrorist night riders of the Ku Klux Klan were portrayed as heroes while, as W. E. B. Du Bois wrote, the freedman was "represented either as an ignorant fool, a vicious rapist, a venal or unscrupulous politician or a faithful but doddering idiot." The main black characters were portrayed by white actors in blackface.

The distinguished audience loved it. "It teaches history by lightning," President Wilson told the director when the lights came on again.

Chief Justice Edward White agreed after he, his fellow judges, and eighty-eight senators and congressmen attended another special screening at a downtown hotel the next night. He had himself ridden with the Klan and believed it had been a fully justified "uprising of outraged manhood." Millions of white Americans already shared their view.

The National Association for the Advancement of Colored People mounted a national campaign to ban the film—and succeeded only in further publicizing it. *The Birth of a Nation* opened at the Liberty Theater on Broadway in March, beginning a record run of forty-four weeks. It would become the most-seen movie of its time. Miscegenation was the supposed evil at the heart of its story—and its moral was that every self-respecting white man had a duty to avenge it if he could.

With Jess Willard matched to fight Jack Johnson, white Americans would finally get their chance at vengeance—in the ring.

Preparations for the fight moved forward at Juárez. Willard went into training at El Paso. Then, on February 22, Curley got a telegram from Johnson at Havana. He wasn't coming to Mexico.

SHIPS HERE REFUSED CLEARANCE FOR TAMPICO OR OTHER MEXICAN PORTS BECAUSE OF TROUBLE IN THAT COUNTRY. BRING THE FIGHT HERE. THIS IS AN IDEAL SPOT FOR IT.

With less than two weeks to go, Curley hurried to New Orleans, boarded what he remembered as "a vermin barge" bound for Cuba, and went to see the champion. Carranza's ultimatum had had something to do with Johnson's change of heart, but there was more to it than that. He now feared that if he made it to Juárez, federal officials might somehow snatch him across the border. And, Curley wired a friend at the New York *Morning World,* he also "didn't want to take a chance on having some hot-headed Texan pop him off while he was punching Willard around the ring, a feat he feels absolutely sure he can accomplish."

Curley would have to move the fight to Havana and set a new date.* Curley went right to the top. He called on the Cuban president, General Mario García Menocal, offered him a suitable "gift," and received the go-ahead. H. D. "Curly" Brown, the American sport who owned the Orient Race Track at Mariano, six miles from town, said he'd be happy to have the fight take place there. It was rescheduled for the day after Easter, Monday, April 5.

The upcoming bout was not likely to be a real title fight, said the New York *Times*, but, rather, a "contest between Champion Johnson and another ambitious heavyweight." The boxing world had seen it all before. Johnson had faced seven white hopes in the six years since winning the title. None had come close to beating him. And there was little to suggest that Jess Willard would be different. Asked who would win, Bob Fitzsimmons said, "Why, Johnson, of course. Willard hasn't a chance in the world. He is a big raw novice. The 'Smoke' will cut him to ribbons." John L. Sullivan reluctantly agreed; so did Gunboat Smith and Joe Choynski. Tommy Burns and Jim Jeffries confessed that, while they would of course be rooting for the white man, they really didn't know much about him. A newspaper columnist named Walt Mason spoke for most insiders.

> *Jess Willard would restore the wreath that Johnson wrested from the whites;*
> *With warlike zeal he grinds his teeth, this hero of at least two fights.*
> *Alas, our bosoms are not warmed when such a hero gambols in.*
> *Unless black Jack is chloroformed, we do not see how Jess can win.*
> *The chances are he'll come to grief before they're fairly down to biz;*
> *For, while he's surely long on beef, the spark of genius isn't his. . . .*
>
> *He has the lard, his heart is game, he has the height, he has the reach;*
> *But, oh, he lacks that deathless flame which makes the pugilistic peach.*
> *With confidence he goes to meet the greatest fighter on this sphere,*

---

*Some influential American expatriates in Cuba were dead set against the fight's coming off there. "I and the other ranch owners are unalterably opposed to having [Johnson] beat up a white man," Captain Cushman A. Rice told the Philadelphia *Evening Bulletin*. "The colored champion can fight any of his own race if he desires, but there must be no inter-racial feeling engendered if it can be prevented." Johnson was so angered by Rice's attitude that on the afternoon of the fight, when Miss Cecilia Wright Keith, the rancher's "protégée" and a stringer for the United Press, showed up in a ringside seat, he insisted that she be made to sit farther back. As she left, she waved her seat number—13—at him, hoping he'd be "hoodooed." (Philadelphia *Evening Bulletin*, February 26, 1915; Chicago *Evening American*, April 6, 1915.)

But he will tumble o'er his feet and cork himself and interfere.
They'll bear him helpless from the ring while drearily the White Face groans,
And Johnsing, he will dance and sing, and draw his thirty thousand bones.

Reporters still flocked to Havana, and there were the predictable personality profiles meant to point up the differences between the two men. Johnson met "witty remarks with rapier-like answers," the New York *Herald* noted,

> while Willard simply stares at the facetious one, slowly assimilates the point of the jest and more slowly allows a boyish, bashful smile to shyly illuminate his face. He is . . . a slow thinker, a plodder, but one who knows what he is seeking and one with a dogged courage. He is trained to the minute and looks the part. His skin is dazzling in its pureness.

Their training camps, too, were examined in search of telling contrasts. A writer for the same newspaper visited both camps.

> Veteran sports in Havana today are marveling at the great changes in the conduct of prize fighting since the days of the early championship contests. . . . The crude and rigorous regime of former days has been abandoned in favor of an up-to-date and pleasant diet.
>
> For example, Willard's camp is in the most expensive hotel in Havana, where he has a large suite of rooms with windows and a balcony overlooking a broad boulevard. There is a striking view of the ocean. Willard eats his meals in a palm garden, among the other guests. . . .
>
> Jack Johnson lives a little further out of Havana on the same shore road. He has rented a large private apartment, breezy and with a good view, beautifully furnished and with service supplied. His meals are prepared by the Cuban cook, except when the champion desires to do this himself. Johnson takes great pride in his culinary ability, and claims to be almost as good a chef as he is a pugilist.

Willard worked hard to get in shape, hammering away at his sparring partners, including Johnson's former protégé, Walter Monahan. Tom Jones and his fighter were said to be so confident of victory, another paper reported, that they spent their idle hours planning "a triumphal entry into the United States . . . [with] back-platform speeches in every town and hamlet between Key West and New York."

By contrast, Johnson seemed to be coasting. He clowned during sparring sessions with Bob Armstrong and Sam McVey, swam in the Caribbean rather than do roadwork. He was "fat to the point of a paunch," wrote the New York *Herald*'s man, and "appears to breathe heavily and with difficulty after even light exercise. . . .

One of his coworkers said that after the camp is escaped by the visitors Johnson discards his smile, forgets his wit and enters upon a tirade against the forces that command him to get into condition. The champion, this man says, is a different man entirely when he is not showing off to the crowds, the followers, the curious, the hero worshippers who create an atmosphere which when absent almost seems to leave the negro much in the same condition as a lamp would be if the oil was taken therefrom. Johnson lives on applause. Without it he fades away to nothingness.

Johnson was seen often at the Orient Race Track, leaning on a silver-headed black cane and wearing a blinding white head-to-toe ensemble. One morning he bet on a black gelding at 8-to-1 odds. "I know that baby can't lose," he said. "He's got the winning name. They got him billed here as *negro*." When the horse came in first, he laughed and said it was a sign he'd knock Willard out in eight rounds. He was scheduled to spar in public that afternoon, but when it began to rain, he decided not to bother; disappointed fans threw chairs and pillows and had to be subdued by the police.

Johnson's casual attitude toward training further fueled rumors of a fix. The champion professed to be indignant. "There is not enough money in Cuba to make me forfeit my title to Willard or any one else. I like the honor of being heavyweight champion of the world and when I lose it there will be a knockout administered by a better man. And that won't be Willard."*

Johnson was cocky in private, too, and apparently still optimistic that Jack Curley would influence the government on his behalf. "I AM GETTING TIRED

---

*Most newspaper stories about this fight were virtually interchangeable with those banged out from Sydney or Reno or Las Vegas, New Mexico. But a few were unique to Cuba. On March 26, for example, the Milwaukee *Free Press* reported a racial incident involving both the champion and Lucille:

"HAVANA. Fear is felt that race trouble may arise here following an altercation between the white wife of Jack Johnson . . . and a pretty manicurist. . . . Johnson has threatened legal proceedings against the manicurist. The police . . . are endeavoring to hush the matter up.

"The altercation arose . . . when the manicurist refused to serve a white woman 'who had married a negro.' Heated words followed and the manicurist seized the other woman by the hair, jerking it completely down, and violently pummeled her in her face with her fists. Other girls working in the establishment called the police who came in and parted the scrapping women.

"Afterward, Johnson demanded an apology, which was immediately forthcoming from the proprietor but flatly refused by the manicurist. She flung a wet towel in the proprietor's face, told the champion what she thought of him, and left the place."

OF KNOCKING AROUND," he wired his mother on March 15. "AS SOON AS I HAVE WHIPPED WILLARD I WILL COME BACK TO CHICAGO AND TAKE MY MEDICINE, AS THE GOVERNMENT HAS FIXED IT UP FOR ME."

On Easter morning, Curley dropped by the champion's headquarters with the final installment of his purse—$28,500 in cash. Johnson immediately sought to multiply his money.

Betting was unusually light for a heavyweight championship contest. Newspapers reported that sports in San Francisco, Los Angeles, Denver, Chicago, and New York all seemed reluctant to risk their money. Trying to stir things up, Johnson stalked into the lobby of Willard's hotel, loudly offering to bet ten thousand dollars on himself at 10 to 8, but he could only place twenty-five hundred. He was chatting there with Jack Welch, an old San Francisco friend who was to referee the fight the next day, when the big challenger happened to saunter in with his manager.

"Here's your cute little friend," Welch said.

Johnson grinned. "Yes, he's so small I'm going to take advantage of him Monday."

Willard smiled, too. "You'd better get a ladder, Jack."

"Everybody tells me I'll need a Gatling gun."

Tom Jones led Willard away.

That afternoon, both men went to the bullfights. A torero panicked when his bull got too close, and jumped behind the barricade to avoid its horns. The crowd jeered. "Hey *señor*," Johnson shouted. "What are you afraid of that little bull for? You should see Willard!"

That evening, with the fight just hours away, Damon Runyon wired the Baltimore *American* that a "fistic frenzy has now completely enveloped the Cubans. Nothing is discussed in the clubs and cafés but this fight. On every corner brown-skinned small boys are seen squaring off at one another by way of illustrating the American amusement." Havana hotels were overbooked. Some fans were quartered in private homes. Hundreds more were still fighting to get onto ships at Key West for the ninety-mile voyage to Cuba. The Cuban Congress was suspended so that its members could be at ringside. And at the race track crews would work all night to construct a ring and set up wooden benches where horses had raced that afternoon.

The sun was already hot and a band was playing ragtime from the covered grandstand as the first ticket buyers began looking for their seats at ten thirty on the morning of the fight. By one o'clock, when the contest was scheduled to begin, the ringside temperature would be nearing 105 degrees, Runyon reported:

> From the stands the scene unrolled like a panorama. Groups of soldiers and barefooted natives dotted the distant green landscape beyond the pagoda-like judge's stand, while in the immediate foreground was a maze of bobbing straw hats, dotted here and there with black derbies and felt hats from the States.

Herbert Bayard Swope wrote in the Chicago *Tribune:*

> Never in the history of the ring was there such a wild, hysterical, shrieking, enthusiastic crowd [as] the 20,000 men and women who begged Willard to wipe out the stigma that they and hundreds of thousands of others, especially in the south, believe rested on the white race through the negro holding the championship. Nowhere was the feeling stronger than in Cuba, whose race hatred is near the surface, although the negro is ostensibly received on a parity with the white.

Hundreds clutched miniature white flags meant to symbolize their solidarity with the white challenger. Mounted cavalry and soldiers with carbines were on hand in case of trouble.

At about twelve thirty, Johnson's chief trainer, Tom Flanagan, escorted Lucille to her box seat. She wore a light summer dress and a white hat with a long feather. "There was a mad craning of necks," the Los Angeles *Examiner* reported, "and someone yelled at Fred Mace, director of the motion pictures, but he only grinned and made no attempt to take the picture. 'Where would I show it?' he asked. Someone asked Lucille how she thought the fight would go. "I am absolutely confident that Jack will win. I don't know in what round, but Jack told me he would knock out Willard before the twentieth and he keeps his word."

The buildup had seemed all too familiar to the sporting world. So did the first few rounds. Johnson had said he planned to take the heart out of the challenger from the opening bell, to show him he was just a beginner, and then put him out early. Everything seemed to go just as Johnson predicted it would. He befuddled and punished his big, awkward opponent in the first round, wanting to show him who was boss. "I can hit him any place at any time I want to," he told his seconds after the bell. The second and third were more of the same. In the fourth, when Willard missed with a big clumsy right, Johnson laughed, slamming a right hand into Willard's body. "You got to do better than that. Here's the spot," he said, tapping his own chin with his glove.

In the fifth and sixth, Willard still looked "puzzled," according to the New York *Times*. Johnson flew out of his corner in the seventh, apparently determined to end things. He drove the taller man back to the ropes and pinned him there, reaching up to rock his head back and forth again and again. Willard was beginning to show the evidence of his pummeling. His lip was bleeding. So was his cheek. The whiteness of his torso was blotched with red where Johnson's fists had landed. But he was still standing when the bell rang, and Johnson was breathing hard.

Willard took the initiative in the eighth and ninth, and for the first time backed the champion up. Johnson continued to land, but Willard was unaffected and he had begun to land as well, including a right hand to the body in the eighth that momentarily slowed the champion down. Toward the end of the tenth, ringsiders noticed that the champion's mouth was bloody.

"Johnson," an American bellowed, "you'll get yours today."

"Well," Johnson shouted back. "There's good money in it, isn't there?"

Cubans began to chant, "Kill the black bear!"

Johnson took the tenth and easily won the eleventh, twelfth, thirteenth, and fourteenth. He ended the fifteenth with five hard rights in a row to Willard's head. "What a grand old man!" he said after landing the last one.

Willard was being outfought, but he was not being overwhelmed. And slowly, as the rounds stretched on in the fierce heat, his size and Johnson's age began to tell. The champion was no longer smiling, no longer talking. It was harder and harder simply to reach his big opponent. Willard leaned his great weight on Johnson in the clinches and began to block more of his punches. By the twentieth, the pace had slowed so much that some in the crowd began to shout, "Get busy!"

Johnson was still doing the most damage in the twenty-first, but Willard kept coming. As the champion stalked back to his corner he looked grim, and for the first time in his career his legs seemed unsteady. He slumped on his stool and asked Harry Frazee to bring Jack Curley to him. It was important, he said. Curley was still at the box office tallying the proceeds, but Frazee agreed to go get him.

Johnson struggled through the next three rounds. The challenger was now often beating him to the punch. In the twenty-fifth, Willard landed a right hand above Johnson's heart that made him grunt with pain and gasp for breath. When he tried to hold on, Willard shoved him back, working to wear him down, to keep him from getting any rest.

By the end of the twenty-fifth, Jack Curley had made it to ringside. Johnson leaned down and whispered to him, "Jack, go take my wife away. . . . Tell her I'm awful weak and that I want her to leave." Curley sent Johnson's old acquaintance, the international sports promoter Richard Kegin, to Lucille's box. She was already on her feet. "Johnson looked pitifully toward his wife," the New York *Herald* reporter wrote. "His expression was a hopeless one of despair and helplessness that those who saw it will never forget. It was as though Johnson had called aloud to his wife—'The end has come. They've been clamoring for it this last five years. Now they've got me.' "

Someone called out that Johnson had quit laughing. Johnson turned and winked. But he did not smile.

The bell rang. He was slow getting off his stool. An eager Willard met him two thirds of the way across the ring and landed a long left to the face, then a hard right to the stomach. Johnson held on. Jack Welch separated the two men. Willard muscled Johnson toward his corner and slammed a left into his body that made the champion's legs quiver. Then he feinted as if to hit him there again, and when Johnson lowered his hand to block it, Willard hurled an overhand right to his jaw. Johnson fell forward and clutched at Willard's legs to keep from collapsing completely. The challenger kicked himself free. Johnson sprawled on his back.

"Oh my God," Lucille screamed.

Johnson lay motionless, his right arm over his face.

The crowd was on its feet. Welch began the count. Johnson did not move. Welch reached ten, and raised Willard's hand in victory. Hundreds of spectators waved white handkerchiefs and flags in honor of the white man's triumph. Some hurled their hats as high as they could. Others took off their coats, ripped them up the back, and tossed the pieces into the air.

As Willard's admirers climbed into the ring in celebration, Johnson's seconds helped him to his feet. He seemed confused at first. "What's the matter?" he asked, and made as if to go back at Willard. Sam McVey stopped him, patted him on the back, draped a towel over his head.

It was all over.

"Something approaching a race riot followed," Damon Runyon wrote. "Thousands paraded the race track, chanting, '*Viva El Bianco!*' " while "blacks drew off in little groups."

Johnson stood a moment, gazing out at the crowd from beneath the towel, listening to the chants. He was glad he'd lost, he told Tom Flanagan. "Now all my troubles will be over. Maybe they'll let me alone."

Later he issued an official statement. His hat was off to Willard, he said; he'd been beaten fairly by "youth and condition." Then he added, "I have no complaint to make excepting this. While I was champion . . . I made a great many enemies most of whom hated me for no other reason than that I am a Negro. These persons have gotten vindication in my defeat and I hope they obtain full enjoyment out of it."

Mounted cavalry with drawn sabers escorted Jess Willard's automobile back to Havana. Hundreds of people lined the road into town. Thousands crowded the streets of the city. They, too, waved white flags and handkerchiefs tied to sticks. "At one point," the New York *Times* reported, "a group of negro children who evidently had heard that Johnson was the victor waved black flags at the white champion, who was much amused." A huge crowd waited in front of his hotel. They pelted him with flowers, patted his back, chanted his name. As darkness fell, much of the city was illuminated in his honor.

At nine o'clock that evening, Curley and Frazee were still in the ticket office at the racetrack counting the proceeds when there was a knock on the door. It was Johnson, all alone. They invited him in for a drink.

Curley asked him how he felt. "Pretty blue," he said. "I haven't any kick coming. I met a young big boy and he wore me down. I didn't dream there was a man alive who could go fifteen rounds with me once I started after them." He thought Willard would be champion for a long time; he was just too big for ordinary heavyweights to hurt. "And here's something you didn't know," he said. "Jess ruined my golden smile." He moved nearer to the light, parted his bruised lips, and showed the gap where two of his gold-capped teeth had been knocked out. "It was a left crack . . . that did it. I felt them drop down on my tongue and my pride wouldn't let me spit them out. I knew what a howl would go up if they saw them in the sunlight, so I did the next best thing, I swallowed them."

Tiny Johnson refused to believe that her son had lost. "It can't be true," she said. "My son licked, knocked out? No, siree." The Chicago *American* printed a lurid pink special edition with the headline WILLARD CHAMPION! Whites who waved it along South State Street found themselves in trouble: three were hospitalized; twenty-five Negroes were taken to the station house. "Every

white man should be happy," the evangelist Billy Sunday said; his wife attributed Johnson's defeat to "too much booze and too much Paris."

Newspaper reaction fell along predictable lines. Johnson's old friend James
Weldon Johnson paid tribute to the loser in the New York *Age:*

> Johnson fought a great fight, and it must be remembered that it was the
> fight of one lone black man against the world. . . . The white race, in spite
> of its vaunted civilization, pays more respect to the argument of force than
> any other race in the world. As soon as Japan showed that it could fight, it
> immediately gained the respect and admiration of the white race. Jack
> Johnson compelled some of the same sort of respect and admiration in an
> individual way.

Some other black editors were less charitable. "For some years past," said the
Chicago *Broad Ax,* at least temporarily tired of defending its hometown
favorite, "Jack Johnson has been a great menace to the colored race, greatly
assisting to retard their progress along many lines of honest endeavor, and
no doubt that there was great rejoicing among sober and industrious colored people over his defeat." The Kansas City *Sun* hoped that Johnson, the
"extravagant reveler and maker of race hated," would simply disappear, while
the Washington *Sun* blamed his downfall on his unwise "connubial connections" with white women, his failure to seek "some worthy colored woman"
with whom to share his life.

Most white papers expressed their pleasure at Willard's victory. "The
Ethiopian has been eliminated," said the Detroit *News.* "There will never be
a black heavyweight champion . . . at least as long as the present generation
endures." Willard seemed to agree: within hours of winning the title, he said
that just as he had never fought a black man before he faced Johnson, he
would never do so again.*

---

*Later, he or someone working for him laid out the reasoning that allegedly lay behind this decision in
a document that was published by a number of black newspapers, including the June 19, 1915, Chicago
Defender: "A championship fight between a black man and a white man makes bad blood between the
races. Jack Johnson did more to hurt his people than Booker T. Washington did to help them. I am not
saying this in a mean way. I'm not excusing white men for feeling that way. I think it shows ignorance.
But lots of white men did feel that way. Who doesn't remember all the sickening 'white hope' business?
And just as ignorant white men thought their race disgraced, so did a lot of ignorant colored men think
that their race had been proved the better by Johnson's victory. That's why I'm going to draw the color
line. I say this because I don't want anybody to think that I'm doing it from any mean, dirty little prejudice. It isn't race or color that counts: it's brains. A sober decent Chinaman looks better to me than a
drunken bum of an American. A Negro who uses his intelligence is a finer man than a white man who
soaks his mind in a whisky glass. Some of the greatest fighters in history have been black men. And I
want to say that they have always showed up as game . . . as white fighters."

"It is a point of pride with the ascendant race," said the Chicago *Tribune*, "not to concede supremacy in anything, not even to a gorilla. The fact that Mr. Willard made it possible for many millions of his fellow citizens to sit down to their dinners last night with renewed confidence in their eight inch biceps, flexed, and their twenty-eight inch chests, expanded, is his peculiar triumph."

On April 7, most of the fight principals, including the new champion, his entourage, Jack Curley, Harry Frazee, and Johnson's own seconds and sparring partners, boarded the steamer *Governor Cobb* headed for Key West and home. Jack Johnson came aboard to say goodbye. He seemed cheerful enough shaking hands and joking with the fight crowd he knew so well. He took Willard aside and told him he hoped good luck would follow him all of his life and urged him to take care of himself and his money. But when the all-ashore warning sounded and he had to walk back down the gangplank, there were tears in his eyes. "I wish I was going back to the States," he said to a friend. "It's hard to be exiled this way." Jack Curley called it "the saddest thing I ever saw in my life. Beaten and a fugitive from his own country, it broke him all up to see our happy crowd headed for the land of the free."

The return of the new champion to the United States inspired an orgy of white self-satisfaction. Every vessel at Key West was decked with flags when the *Governor Cobb* steamed into the harbor. Navy vessels blew their whistles. So many cheering, pushing whites crowded the wharf that rope barriers and wooden barricades fell as the new champion made his way down the gangplank. "If he had saved the country," wrote Robert Edgren, "he could hardly have received more frantic applause from the white citizens of Key West."

A reporter for the Baltimore *American* rode along on the special train that carried Willard north toward Manhattan, where he was to appear on Broadway at Hammerstein's Victoria for ten thousand dollars a week—twice as much as Jack Johnson had been paid at the same theater after he won the title.

Not a station along the East Coast Railroad line is there that was not crowded to meet the big train. Even stations that are passed without notice have their crowds, who [hope] for a fleeting glimpse of big Jess. Small boys and girls, boys and girls a little bigger, youths and maidens, young men and older girls, fathers and mothers, even grandfathers and grandmothers, rushed to the station in all sorts of vehicles to shake the hand that shook the laurels off the brow of Jack Johnson.

The elation of the Southern people at Willard's victory is emphasized here and there. One old woman at Folkston, Ga., pushed in a box of strawberries surmounted by a bunch of violets. Another had a suckling pig which she wanted to present. Jess had to pass up the pig but [his sparring partner] Jim Savage grabbed it for his Jersey farm and stuck it in the baggage car.

Jack Curley was aboard as well, trying to manage relations between the new champion and his public. It wasn't easy. Only Jim Jeffries seems to have been less enthusiastic about his fame.

Men, women and children besieged the train, clamored for a sight of Willard, roared with his praises, swept police lines aside in an almost hysterical effort to get close to him.

And Willard? Willard sulked in his sleeping compartment in a private car and was deaf to every plea that he show himself!

"But Jess," I begged of him, "you must come out. This is a wonderful tribute to you. I've never seen anything like it. These people want to see you. If you don't come out, they're likely to tear the car apart to get at you."

"Let 'em tear it apart, then. If I had got beaten they wouldn't want to see me."

"No, and if you had got beaten you wouldn't be signed up for a tour at $10,000 a week, either. Think that one over."

"I have. But that's different. I'll take their money but I don't want any part of them."

At every stop from Key West to New York I had to face the multitudes and explain to them, as best I could, why their hero could not oblige them to the extent of stepping out onto the observation platform and waving his hand at them.

"The champion is resting."

"The champion doesn't sleep well on trains and had a bad night. He's just fallen asleep."

Meanwhile, Walt Mason, the versifier who had lampooned Willard's skills before Havana, now ridiculed the loser.

Alas, poor Johnson, badly whipped,
And of his wreaths and honors stripped;

When he appeared in yonder ring
He was that ring's unconquered king;
And when he left it, sick and sore,
He was a has-been, nothing more,
And all the country felt relief
When Brother Johnsing came to grief;
No words encouraging he heard;
No breasts with sympathy were stirred,
But all were glad to see him slump
Before Jess Willard's cultured thump,
And e'en the men of his own race
Exulted in his loss of place.
'Twas not because his skin was brown
That men rejoiced when he came down.
But Johnsing, since he gained his fame,
Seemed destitute of sense of shame,
And laughed with foul, unholy glee,
At all the claims of decency.
An outcast from his native land,
And by most other countries banned,
He'll skulk, since from the height he's hurled
Along the edges of the world,
A blot on every decent scene,
A leper with the sign, "Unclean."
A man all morals can't defy
And with that sort of thing get by;
And when he falls as fall he must,
Rejoicing follows long disgust.

Jack and Lucille Johnson would wander along the edges of the world for the next five years, turning up here and there in newspaper stories, most of which were either slanted to demonstrate that the ex-champion was enduring the proper punishment for his alleged misdeeds, or fostered by Gus Rhodes and Johnson himself to make their sometimes desperate scramble seem like a sort of royal progress.

From Havana they sailed to Spain, then made their way to Paris, where a reporter asked Johnson if he'd returned to France in order to enlist. "Man, for me war is over," he responded. "I am at peace for the first time in years."

Another newsman reminded him that the French called the shell hurled by a big German siege gun the "Jack Johnson" because it caused so much damage and yielded so much black smoke. That alone, the reporter said, would ensure him a place in history. Johnson shot back, "Wasn't I in history before the war?"

In late May, Johnson moved on to London where he expected to begin a tour of British theaters, narrating films of his fight in Cuba. But when he and Lucille got there, there was no film to show. Jack Curley had failed to send it to him. Their relationship had gone sour after they'd said goodbye to each other on the wharf at Havana.

Curley claimed it was all Johnson's fault. The trouble began, he said, moments before the Willard fight, when Johnson had produced a last-minute surprise for him and Harry Frazee. A lawyer hired by Johnson had stepped into the ring, Curley said, with a contract demanding the champion be given 51 percent of the fight film proceeds, not the one third he'd agreed to beforehand. If Curley and Frazee wouldn't sign, Johnson explained with a grin, he wouldn't fight. " 'Oh, hell,' " Curley remembered Frazee saying, "but he took the contract and using my back for a writing desk, signed it."

The promoters were furious. "It was very irregular of Johnson to insist on this new division," Curley continued; "so I was greatly amused and thought the ends of justice had been served when Mr. Frazee and Mr. Fred Mace, the moving picture man, loaded Johnson's trunk with old films and sent him away to London where he called in a distinguished audience of theater people who wished to book the film for their houses and showed them a lot of views of the Havana fire department and comedy policemen chasing pickpockets through revolving doors."

Johnson's account was very different. He had carried no cans of film to London, he said. Instead, before he left Cuba, Curley told him they hadn't been developed yet and promised to send copies to him as soon as they were ready. When they didn't turn up, he cabled Curley asking where they were. "He replied they were on their way," Johnson wrote. "I watched eagerly for their arrival, and when they did arrive, I was astounded to find they were blank—that they had never been on a spool." He cabled Curley again. The promoter said Fred Mace was to blame; the real film was its way. Again, it did not arrive.

Johnson began haunting the American Express office in London, convinced he was being "flim-flammed," that Curley and Frazee were likely to send the film to someone else in an effort to rob him of his rightful share in the proceeds. Sure enough, he wrote, a round-faced hustler named E. A. Weil, who had served as Curley's "treasurer" in Cuba, turned up one day to claim two cans of film. The ex-champion strong-armed Weil, commandeered the film, and began exhibiting an eight-minute, carefully edited version.

But he was bitter. The title he'd fought so hard to win and hold was gone, and he was still an exile; Curley's efforts to persuade the government to relent and allow him to come home without fear of imprisonment had come to nothing, and he had convinced himself his old friend had never even tried.

Johnson now began to blame Curley for everything that had gone wrong, to plot a way to get back at him—and maybe even get some more money for himself at the same time.

On June 9, he fired off a cable to Curley and Frazee.

YOU SIGNED CONTRACT TO PAY ME $50,000 TO LAY DOWN TO WILLARD WHICH I DID. YOU NEVER KEPT YOUR PROMISE. I DID. NOW YOU MUST PAY ACCORDING TO CONTRACT. LITIGATE ALL YOU LIKE. I WILL PUT MY CASE BEFORE ANY COURT AND PRESS IN THE WORLD.

JACK JOHNSON

There was no such signed contract, of course. Curley and Frazee shot back that if he were to make such false charges public, they would sue him for libel and attempted blackmail.

Johnson answered on the eleventh.

BLACK MAIL PROPOSITION RIDICULOUS. WANT PAYMENT FIRST MONEY WAS TAKEN.* WILLARD, AS FIGHTER, A JOKE. IF YOU [HAVE] CONFI- DENCE HIS ABILITY TO BEAT ME WILL BET $25,000. WINNER TAKE ALL AND PURSE MONEY.

JOHNSON

When the editor of *John Bull,* the British magazine that had exposed the machinations behind the 1914 fight with Frank Moran, got hold of the telegrams and reprinted them, Curley and Frazee claimed they were phony. "To say that Johnson has wired for his lay-down money is a lie of the worst kind," Frazee told the press. "Why, he'd be insane to do anything of the kind. He owns an interest in the moving pictures, and they are doing a big busi- ness in England. Johnson has sense enough to know that any such action

---

*This was a reference not to his phantom contract to take a dive but to his legitimate share of the first proceeds from showing the fight films in Canada, a sum Curley and Frazee had evidently delayed.

would be a confession of wrongdoing that would kill the pictures." Curley said if the former champion really wanted a rematch with Willard he could have one—but only if the referee declared all wagers off before the bell rang, so Johnson couldn't make any money betting against himself. Johnson did not respond.

From Jack Johnson's point of view, the Great War, like everything else that stood in his way, was a personal affront. Not long after he moved on to England, in late May, to exhibit the films of the Willard fight and undertake another tour of music halls, German zeppelins began bombing London. The South London Theater at Elephant and Castle, where he was appearing, "became a favorite target for air-raiders," he wrote. One evening after the show, he and Lucille climbed into his car and started off across the city for their rented home at Haverstock Hill. It was a tortuous drive, he remembered, because the streets were littered with rubble and shattered glass. Then the bombing began again.

> Between blasts of bombs which were falling all around us, we could hear the whir and swish of a Zeppelin overhead. I speeded the car up in an effort to get outside its bombing radius, but was surprised to learn that no matter how fast I traveled or in what direction I turned, the bombs were close upon us. It was then I learned with considerable alarm that the Zeppelin was following us. My car was a white Benz, and must have loomed up conspicuously to the raiders, who found it a tempting target. They persisted in the chase until I reached home, and I scrambled under shelter with all the haste I could summon. It was a miracle that we were not blown to bits. How we escaped I do not know. When we were under shelter, the Zeppelin did not desist, but remained over that section of the city for a long time, dropping countless bombs.

Lucky for Haverstock Hill, perhaps, Johnson and Lucille soon left town to play provincial towns with a new revue called *Seconds Out.* Johnson sparred and performed feats of strength, as he always had. But he also exchanged comic patter with a diminutive British straight man. Lucille appeared onstage now, too, performing a ragtime "oyster-shell dance" while her husband played the bass viol. And he made occasional gestures toward the Allied cause: leading the audience in choruses of "It's a Long Way to Tipperary"; sending three footballs and half a dozen pairs of boxing gloves to Tommies on the Western Front; exhorting a crowd of four thousand in front of the Royal Exchange in Glasgow to join the British army.*

But he sold fewer and fewer tickets and began once again to act erratically. At the Hippodrome in Preston in October business was so bad that Jack du Maurier, the company's road manager and Johnson's onstage sparring partner, quit and demanded his back pay and train fare back to London. Instead, the ex-champion punched him in the eye. In a pub, undercover agents overheard Johnson make drunken remarks they considered pro-German. He was arrested for cursing a London bobby who had told him he had to move his car. A printer sued him for failure to pay for theatrical posters, which he claimed had failed to do him justice. And there was talk that he'd made advances to chorus girls during an appearance at Northampton.

In January 1916, the Home Office ordered Jack Johnson to leave the country under the Aliens Restriction Act. He did his best to stay. He called upon Sir Hiram Maxim, the American-born inventor of the Maxim machine gun, who was now a British citizen, hoping he would help. Maxim passed him along to Lord Lonsdale, founding president of the National Sporting Club and Britain's preeminent sportsman. Lonsdale received him at his home in Carlton House Terrace and said something polite about doing what he could. When a footman appeared with the ex-champion's coat, Lonsdale held it for him. "Let me help you, Johnson," he said. The former champion never forgot Lonsdale's aristocratic courtesy but neither Lonsdale nor Maxim nor anyone else could alter the decision of the Home Office.

On March 2, 1916, the Johnsons and Gus Rhodes left England for neutral Spain, where they would spend the next three years. He first staged a series of exhibitions against unknowns in Madrid and Barcelona, for which he continued to bill himself as "Champion of the World." One of his opponents was an old friend, the British expatriate Dadaist poet, Arthur Cravan, whom he fought in the bullring in Barcelona on April 29. An eccentric alcoholic and sometime thief, he had caroused with Johnson in Paris and had boxed a little in France—where he claimed the light heavyweight title after his opponent failed to turn up—but he had never faced anyone remotely as skilled as the former champion, and he was terrified. His solution was to crouch and cover up, making himself as tiny a target as possible. Since a movie camera

---

*German propagandists seized upon his war work to ridicule the British: "To this, proud England has come," said the *Prager Tagblatt,* "that they are obliged to use the efforts of a colored boxer to obtain recruits for the war. And this man is an exile from America!" (Washington *Post,* January 2, 1916.)

was filming the proceedings and there was hope at least a little money might be made by exhibiting it, Johnson toyed with him until the start of the sixth and final round.

The poet Blaise Cendrars left an account of what happened then:

[Cravan] contented himself with turning round and round trembling visibly. The Negro prowled around him like a big black rat around a Holland cheese, tried three times in a row to call him [to] order by three kicks to the rump, and then in an effort to loosen [him] up, the Negro thumped him in the ribs, cuffed him a bit while laughing, encouraged him, swore at him, and at last, all of a sudden furious, Jack Johnson stretched him out cold with a formidable punch to the left ear, a blow worthy of a slaughterhouse.

It was soon clear exhibitions alone wouldn't pay the Johnsons' bills. They opened a Barcelona café and costarred in a Spanish film, a seven-reel costume melodrama called *False Nobility*. The former champion played a mysterious strongman who helps a deposed princess regain her mythical kingdom. Lucille played the heroine. The film itself has long vanished, but a surviving still shows Johnson in evening clothes, cheerfully hoisting a villain high above his head.*

Johnson tried bullfighting, too, with the help of the great matador Joselito, though it is not clear whether his appearances were burlesque performances or the real thing.

He also lent his name to a Barcelona advertising agency which, according to a *Defender* story by Gus Rhodes, sent him on an extraordinary journey in early 1917.

JACK JOHNSON CAPTURED BY AUSTRIAN SUBMARINE
FIGHTS CAPTAIN SINGLE HANDED; U-BOAT BLOWN UP
PUGILIST IS RESCUED AFTER THREE DAYS

Gibraltar, by way of London, Feb. 22—Jack Johnson, America's world champion pugilist, passed through Gibraltar, en route to Barcelona, Spain, aboard the *Aguinaldo Alfonso*.

---

*Retitled *The Black Thunderbolt*, the film would play Harlem's New Douglas Theater and other black movie houses across the country in 1922. Later, a Barcelona chocolate-maker would include a photograph of Lucille in a series of giveaway cards devoted to "famous movie stars of the world." She posed in a dressing gown with the Johnsons' two Pomeranians. "Fragile and beautiful," the caption said, "her figure contrasts with that of her husband, the formidable black man whose fists of iron broke down so many adversaries."

Jack Johnson, Jan. 15, with passports signed by King George of England, left Barcelona, by way of France and England, arrived at Archangel, Feb. 3, crossed through Russia and into Roumania and secured signatures for his World's Advertising Corporation. Crossing through Italy, he embarked for the return journey and was captured by an Austrian submarine. Jack, single-handed, subdued the Austrian captain and blew up the submarine and was rescued after drifting three days, by the Spanish freighter *Aguinaldo Alfonso*, and was landed at a Spanish port. Johnson has returned safely to Barcelona, Spain, having secured all rights from Allied capitals for his World's Advertising Corporation. He has cornered all important hotel, railroad, steamboat and street car advertising rights, and has secured all English, French, Spanish, Portuguese and Roumanian rights. He has also secured rights from Buenos Aires. Jack Johnson is now located at 30–32 Rambla Del Centro, Barcelona, Spain.

How much of Rhodes's report was true it is impossible now to say, and it may be significant that Johnson himself makes none of these claims in his own highly colored 1927 autobiography. In any case, advertising did not hold him long; he blamed what he called Barcelona's "ancient ways of doing business" for the fact that his "undertaking was not a very flourishing one."

Through it all, one friend remembered, Johnson remained almost lordly. If a reporter turned up asking for an interview, he would mutter, "One of those bloody pressmen" and make him wait, and whenever a bill was presented, he waved it away, saying, "*Mañana, mañana,*" and then would add contemptuously, "Asking money from the champion of the world!"

On April 6, 1917, the United States entered the war. Johnson's first impulse was to flee Europe for Mexico, where several wealthy men seemed willing to underwrite a series of boxing matches. When that didn't pan out—he was using the notoriously unreliable Arthur Cravan, who had now moved there, as his middleman—he and his companions shifted to Madrid, where he approached Major John W. Lang, the American military attaché, with a proposition. The Allies suspected German submarines were secretly being fueled and supplied along the Spanish coast. Since Johnson was traveling from town to town, performing his strongman act and staging exhibitions against his nephew, he said he was ideally equipped to gather reliable information about their comings and goings. Lang took the gamble and agreed to pay some of Johnson's expenses.

Johnson would later make much of his wartime adventures as an under-cover agent. He had taken "numerous risks," he wrote, "including the tra-versing of rough water into dangerous and out-of-the-way places . . . , infested not only by possible war enemies but by smugglers and others engaged in outlaw practices. Then, too, there was the danger of capture by the enemy and of death by promiscuous shooting which frequently took place between the furtive craft in those waters. . . . For my work and the infor-mation I obtained I received due recognition from the officials under whose instructions I operated, and I had the great satisfaction of being of service to my native country, even though I was in exile."

In fact, Johnson's career in espionage lasted only a few weeks. It ended when Major Lang accused him of padding his expense accounts and John-son quit.

On March 17, 1918, Tiny Johnson died in Chicago. She was seventy-four and hadn't seen her favorite child for almost five years. "For a brief time in the heyday of the career of her son," wrote the Washington *Post* on the nine-teenth, "Mrs. Johnson knew a prosperity and notoriety such as seldom comes to a colored 'mammy,' but the curious who gazed at the house on Wabash Avenue today saw the mute testimony of fallen grandeur, a sign reading, 'Boarders Wanted.' " Johnson sent what he could to his sister to help pay for the funeral, but he was unable to be there himself.

His mother's death seems to have made him more anxious than ever to go home. That spring, he wrote to the friends and acquaintances he thought might have influence in Washington. Emmett J. Scott, Booker T. Washing-ton's former second-in-command, was now special assistant to the secretary of war in nominal control of "Negro matters" in the military. Frank S. Armand, a mutual friend and fellow Texan, wrote Scott on Johnson's behalf to say the former champion was now "very anxious to wipe out his past record" and "win back the good opinion of the American people that he lost by reason of indiscretions" by serving in the U.S. Army in France. In exchange, Armand hoped Johnson could be "pardoned of the crime that is charged against him." If Scott could help Johnson, Armand said, "you will be doing a service for the entire race everywhere." Scott sent the letter along to the Justice Department for its comments. Meanwhile, Johnson himself wrote to former New York congressman Fiorello La Guardia, now an army officer in Europe, volunteering to serve. "I am as good an American as anyone liv-ing," he said, "and naturally I want to do my bit. I fairly believe I wasn't fairly treated at home. All I ask now is a chance to show my sincerity. America is my own country. There's no position you could get for me that I would consider too rough or too dangerous." All La Guardia needed to do was guarantee him a pardon when the war was over. La Guardia could make no such promise, and the Justice Department told Emmett Scott it saw no reason to "do anything for a man who is a fugitive from justice until he gives himself up."

His country continued to reject him. His finances had collapsed. He was reduced to barnstorming Spanish theaters and bullrings with reliably nonviolent opponents like Gus Rhodes and "Blink" McCloskey—a weary veteran so-named because, before the bell rang, he carefully removed his glass eye and handed it to his cornermen for safekeeping.

One day that spring, the U.S. consul in Málaga wrote the American ambassador in Madrid that Johnson had dropped in to see him, asking that "the Hotel Regina where he is staying" be notified that "he would meet his bill for board. In this connection, he informed me confidentially that he was employed by Major Lang and that he expected money from him." The consul told the former champion he was not aware of any such underground activity, and in any case "this consulate [is] unwilling to make guarantees for anyone."

American undercover operatives and informants now ghosted after Johnson wherever he went, reporting to Major Lang what he was doing and saying. The ex-champion spent most of his time with "down-and-outs, cheap gamblers, pimps and prostitutes," one said. "There are in Madrid a crowd of so-called Americans, Spaniards, and shady characters of other nations who, having no visible means of support, most of whom appear to have a resentment against the English, French, and U.S. Officials for not providing them with passports so they can leave the country. . . . Johnson is surrounded by a set of cheap admirers and parasites, principal among whom are a Spaniard named Sanchez (locally called 'Spex'), who claims Norfolk, Va. as his home, and one Veleau (George Velois) who hails from Toledo, Ohio, and various other young sports of the type which can be found any night in Chelito's 'Cabaret del Amor' at 31 Calle Teutan. They are all hand in glove with the German element." In January of 1919, the same operative dined at Johnson's home with Lucille, Gus Rhodes, a Spanish woman named Sánchez, and Otto, a German wrestler. There, he plumbed the depths of the ex-champion's rancor. Johnson claimed Britain, not Germany, had started the war; that the Allies had been the first to use poisoned gas; that he knew firsthand who in Madrid was helping to supply German submarines and where off the coast of Málaga it was being done. The agent asked him why he hadn't reported what he knew to the embassy. "Report? Hell, I offered them my services and they gave me a little job and kicked about my expense accounts, so I stopped dealing with them. . . . " But if he'd done so, surely the government would have allowed him to return home "in honor." "To hell with them," Johnson said. "I would not believe any promises they would have made me. The Germans treat me as a man and my wife as a lady."

On February 17, 1919, in a story headlined JACK JOHNSON BROKE IN SPAIN, Henry Wales of the Chicago *Tribune* reported how the former champion was doing. His main source was the American jockey Guy Garner, who said he'd found

the Negro . . . looking pretty seedy, wearing a shabby old fur coat, which he boasts cost five thousand dollars but he does not say how long ago. Every little while one of Mrs. Johnson's diamonds disappears, presumably going to the pawnshop.

A few days ago, Johnson fought an interned German U-boat sailor, whom he nicknamed Bill Flint of Brooklyn, at Madrid. In the first round the sailor poked Jack in the fat stomach, worrying the Negro, but in the second round the German walked straight into Jack's stiff arm, turned around three times, and dropped like a dead man for the count. Jack said afterward he would not take on another tough guy like that. . . .

The Spaniards don't like prize fighting or horse racing much, preferring a gory spectacle like a bullfight. Even when [King] Alfonso attends the races there are only a handful of spectators and at none of the Johnson fights are there more than a couple of hundred fans.

Johnson announces he has got the recipe for a wonderful patent medicine that will remake his fortune, but at the same time tries to borrow money, explaining that his agents in America are holding up his money and says he still owns Chicago tenements. . . .

The hotel at Barcelona where Johnson stayed during the time he was running bullfights there is holding his personal property, including much of his wife's clothing. Johnson formerly lived at the Ritz and Palace hotels in Madrid but now he is barred owing to the nonpayment of bills. When he enters the Palace grillroom or bar, where the biggest cabaret and dancing ballroom are continually going full blast, the head-waiters frequently approach him with folded bills on plates asking payment of old accounts. Johnson merely waves them aside or kids them if they speak English.

Two days after that article appeared, Johnson did what he so often did when his debts caught up with him—he fled, this time to Havana. There, he upset the boxing world again. Jack Curley had paid eloquent tribute to Johnson the last time he'd been in Cuba. "I found [him] a man before, during and after the fight," he'd said then. "It doesn't make any difference what he's done outside the ring, he was a brave, game, generous warrior inside of it. He is the first man defeated since John L. Sullivan who has been man enough to acknowledge defeat without a hue and cry of being tricked and doped out of his title." Curley already knew he had spoken too soon.

On March 13, 1919, Johnson released a signed statement to the Associated Press' man in Havana. In it, he claimed again that his fight with Jess Willard four years before had been a put-up job, and that he'd been the victim of a double-cross, planned and carried out by Jack Curley and Harry Frazee. Lucille had advised him against surrendering his title to Jess Willard, but Johnson had overruled her. He felt he'd had no choice:

> Everyone knows how anxious I was to straighten out the little Chicago difference. I would have done almost anything in reason to be able to visit my mother, who was old and feeble. . . .
>
> Then [he and the promoters] figured on the best round to lose in, and agreed upon the tenth. They were to give the word in the first three or four rounds if Willard could make a good showing.
>
> [But at] the end of the tenth round Willard's showing had been so poor it was necessary to continue the fight further. The signal agreed upon was given in the twentieth round [when Lucille was supposed to have gone and collected Johnson's final payment, then returned and signaled that the money was in her hands], but I considered Willard's showing so poor I was forced to wait until the twenty-sixth before carrying out the agreement. . . .

He signed the letter "Jack Johnson, Champion." He'd been paid well for lying down, he said now, but Curley and Frazee had failed to keep the part of the bargain that had mattered most to him. He had not seen his mother again before she died, was still an exile, still open to arrest the moment he tried to go home.

For those who'd never understood how a big, clumsy, comparative beginner like Jess Willard could have beaten a master boxer like Johnson, two factors lent his story additional plausibility. First, some at ringside had always believed an exhausted Johnson had simply given up rather than endure further punishment. Johnson himself had frequently said that boxing was a business; that if he ever felt he was going to lose he would find a way to make a graceful exit rather than endure unnecessary punishment. ("I'll quit before I take a beating," he once told Gunboat Smith.) Then, too, the federal ban had kept Americans from seeing the film of the fight in which it is clear that Johnson had tried hard to beat his challenger, that he was hit hard by Willard, and that he had tried just as hard not to fall down, clutching at the younger man as he slid to the canvas. Instead, they'd become familiar with the single iconic photograph that hung in saloons and barbershops and other places where white men gathered. It seemed to show Johnson taking his ease on the canvas, his arm raised as if he were shading his eyes from the Cuban sun. To them, the knockout had always *looked* like a fake, and now Johnson's "confession" provided a kind of confirmation.

Curley and Frazee once again denied the charges. Tom Jones, Willard's former manager, reminded people that Johnson had tried to bet ten thousand dollars on himself the day before the fight he supposedly knew he was going to lose. But Jess Willard himself may have provided the best argument for the 1915 bout's authenticity: "If Johnson throwed that fight, I wish he'd throwed it sooner. It was hotter than hell down there."

The Cuban government evidently believed Johnson, and a warrant was issued for his arrest for fraud. He quickly moved on to Mexico, his party's passage paid by Mexican businessmen interested in promoting boxing there. It was new territory for him and for the fight game, and when he reached Mexico City on March 26, 1919, it seemed like old times. Some two thousand people greeted him, shouting, "Bravo, Jack!" and "Viva Johnson!"; a mariachi band blared its welcome, and an awed newspaperman compared his luggage to that carried by operatic tenors: eighteen trunks that "contained 90 suits, 50 pairs of shoes, and the entire output of a necktie factory."

Johnson would make Mexico City his base of operations for the next eleven months. It was an armed camp. The country where he had chosen to light was no less turbulent than it had been when he was barred from reaching Juárez four years earlier. General Carranza was president, but much of the countryside was still held by others—Pancho Villa, Emiliano Zapata, and Carranza's former ally, General Álvaro Obregón, who was now determined to overthrow him and institute reforms promised under the Constitution of 1917.

Gus Rhodes assured the readers of the *Defender* that the life he and the Johnsons led there was splendid: Johnson is "a constant companion of the most prominent military dignitaries and political leaders," he wrote.

He is training at the home of Gen. Alfredo Brecceda. . . . Despite all reports of his indolence, Mr. Johnson is in fine physical condition. He weighs 215 pounds and his wind is almost perfect. . . . His home, of the sort that one might find in the 1000 block on Lake Shore Drive, has become a social center. Already, Mrs. Johnson's social secretary has been kept busy answering invitations for the Johnsons to accept dinner parties and theatrical engagements.

At least at first, Mexicans did treat him as a celebrity, even as an honored guest. Some expatriate Americans did not. One hot afternoon in April, he and Lucille strolled into the House of Tiles, a fashionable restaurant run by a Californian named Walter Sanborn. The American waitress refused to take their order. The Johnsons stalked out and entered a restaurant down the street, where one of Johnson's friends among the ruling generals happened to be dining. Johnson told him what had happened. Three hours later, the couple returned to Sanborn's, accompanied by three generals in uniform. Everyone ordered ice cream. The generals and Lucille got theirs. The former champion did not. The soldiers berated Sanborn. He argued that Americans would no longer come to his restaurant if it were known that a Negro had been served there. The generals threatened to close him down. An angry crowd gathered. A lawyer raised his cane to strike the restaurant owner. Lucille stopped him. The police came. Sanborn gave in, shook Johnson's hand—and personally brought him a dish of ice cream.

Four days later, the Johnsons were having a late supper in another restaurant when a noisy delegation of businessmen from New Orleans stumbled in after a night on the town. One of them, a man named D. H. Moore, said loudly that no nigger could eat with white people where *he* came from. Gus Rhodes reported:

Unfortunately for him, Jack overheard the remark and without further preliminary landed an uppercut on his chin. No arrests were made, as the champion was in a country where the color of a man's skin is no bar to him receiving justice. Although D. H. Moore attempted to have Johnson arrested, he was only laughed at by the police and was told that any man would resent such an insult.

Johnson had several fine-sounding schemes to make money in Mexico. He announced plans for two motion pictures, *For the Love of the Flag* and *The Call of the Heart*, in which he was to play a "Mexican adventurer in the old days on the Mexican border." And he allowed a syndicate of real estate men to form the Jack Johnson Land Company and signed his name to a handbill addressed to "the Colored People of the United States," promising a bright future as farmers in Mexico.

> You, who are lynched, tortured, mobbed, persecuted and discriminated against in the boasted land of liberty. . . . Own a home in Mexico. Here, one man is as good as another, and it is not your nationality that counts, but simply you.
>
> Rich, fertile land only a few miles from Mexico City . . . is now on sale for $5 an acre and up. The soil is very productive and capable of raising four crops a year. The climate is the best in the world, neither too warm nor too cold. Beautiful scenery enhances the lover of nature.
>
> Best of all, there is no race prejudice in Mexico, and severe punishment is meted out to those who discriminate against a man because of his color or race.*

But as always, Johnson had to fall back on boxing to pay the bills. Also as always, trouble seemed to follow. He sold tickets to those who wanted to see him train—the old flying punching bag trick played well with Mexican fans who had never seen it before—and the promoters of his first exhibition on June 22 hoped it would spark interest in boxing all over the country. They even persuaded *El Democrata* to print the Marquess of Queensberry Rules to help people understand what was happening in the ring. But, nothing much did. Johnson's opponent was an ex-soldier named William Hamilton,

---

*The presence of Jack Johnson and other black Americans south of the Texas border troubled both state and federal officials. "Many negroes are going into Mexico," Captain W. Hanson of the Texas Rangers reported to the Justice Department. "Twenty were counted at the theatre in Mexico City one night. They are publicly in favor of riots in the United States and are conferring with many Carranzista generals in Mexico City, with a view, supposedly, of assisting the Carranzistas in case of trouble with the United States. It is an open secret in Mexico City that Carranza is working with labor organizations through [Samuel] Gompers and others, and with the protestant churches, to further propaganda in the United States. The above information was given me very confidentially, by Don Pablo Recandon, just from Mexico City. . . . In this connection, I will state that Jack Johnson gave a boxing exhibition in Nuevo Laredo a short time ago and something like 20 negroes from the United States [met] and conferred with Johnson, and it is suspicioned by well posted Americans, that this meeting was held in Nuevo Laredo for the purpose of giving Johnson [a] chance to have an understanding with his visitors, and to further Carranza propaganda in the United States. At this time there are three negro musicians, and a small, well-educated yellow negro in Nuevo Laredo, and several Americans have informed me that they have seen [Johnson] in close consultation with the Carranzistas there. It is rumored that Johnson has a commission under the Carranza government." (DOJ File.)

who fought as Captain Bob Roper and had had just one fight since leaving the army. Johnson toyed with him for ten rounds without throwing a single serious punch. Lucille was at ringside, *El Democrata* reported, and "don Jack, whenever he could in the clinches, cast loving and tender glances at his beautiful wife." The crowd grew restless, then angry. They'd expected a knockout. Some became so vociferous the police had to be called in.

A week or so later, Johnson made headlines again outside the ring. The businessmen who had paid his way to Mexico were now suing him for failing either to pay them back or to agree to engage in the serious contests they'd hoped to put on. The judge ruled in their favor and sent three officials to the Johnson home with instructions to seize the champion's car as partial payment. Lucille saw them coming. She refused to hand over the keys to the car, ordered her servants to lock the doors and windows, and telephoned her husband. The officials called the police. Five officers turned up just as Johnson arrived with five friends. The police took a look at them and put in a call for armed reinforcements. Johnson tried to drive away. The police blocked him. Then, wrote a reporter for *El Universal*, "in the grand tradition of Hernán Cortés burning his ships on the beach at Veracruz 400 years earlier, he proceeded to rip out some essential parts of the motor, so the police would not be able to drive his car. They had to hire some laborers to drag it away."

Johnson was soon reduced to burlesque bullfights and meaningless exhibitions. Only one fight made news, and this time Johnson had nothing to do with it. On September 28, three thousand people paid their way into Mexico City's bullfight arena to see him go six rounds with one of his old sparring partners, Kid Cutler. During one of the preliminaries a novice referee made a controversial call that inspired jeers from the crowd and a dressing-down by one of the ringside judges. As the opening bell of the main event rang and Johnson and Cutler advanced toward each other, two shots were fired at ringside. The humiliated and hot-tempered referee had borrowed a pistol from a friend and returned to shoot the judge who had dared criticize him. Police overpowered him. The exhibition went on.

Meanwhile, back home, the heavyweight picture had changed. Jess Willard's popularity had not lasted long past Havana. He continued to dislike boxing and to recoil from boxing fans. Money remained his sole motivator. He fired his manager, Tom Jones, rather than share profits with him, severed his connection with Curley and Frazee rather than pay them their commissions, and defended his title just once in four years, winning a newspaper decision against Frank Moran. He much preferred to earn his living touring the country in his own private Pullman with the 101 Ranch Wild West Show. But he had wanted one more big payday before he retired, and Jack Johnson must have been envious when he read that Tex Rickard had guaranteed Willard a record one hundred thousand dollars to fight young Jack Dempsey.

The fight was scheduled for July 4, 1919, at Toledo, Ohio. Willard's inactivity had left him overweight and out of shape. His opinion of his own skills was inflated, too. "There isn't a man living who can hurt me, no matter where he hits me or how often he lands," he said. "I am better today than when I restored the championship to the white race." Willard supervised his own training to save money, had himself driven to and from his sparring sessions in a chauffeured town car, and remained so sure of victory he asked Rickard to provide him legal immunity in case he killed Dempsey, who stood several inches shorter and weighed some forty pounds less than he did. Even Dempsey's father feared that his son would get hurt.

He should have known better. He had once advised his boy to think of obstacles as stepping-stones; if he couldn't get around them, "goddamit go through them," and that was how he fought. Born in a log cabin near Manassa, Colorado, in 1895, the ninth of thirteen children, Dempsey had just one toy as a child: a wooden top whittled by his father. His mother hoped he'd be a boxer like her hero, John L. Sullivan. His oldest brother, Bernie—also a fighter, but cursed with a glass chin—was his trainer; he made the youngster chew pine pitch to strengthen his jaw and, to toughen his fists and face, had him soak them in buckets of beef brine hauled home from the butcher shop. Dempsey began fighting professionally at sixteen as "Kid Blackie," flattening bullies and barflies in saloons for a hatful of change. His real first name was William, but when he graduated to small-town smokers in 1915 he renamed himself Jack Dempsey after a legendary Irish middleweight nicknamed "the Nonpareil." Most boxers hope to demolish their opponents; Dempsey seemed bent on obliterating his. He fought from a crouch that made him look smaller than he was, but he came at his adversaries in furious rushes, teeth bared. He could hit hard with either hand and from any angle (including from behind, whenever he could get away with it). Such niceties as retreating to a neutral corner after knocking your opponent down were still years away, and Dempsey was especially effective at standing over his opponents and hitting them on the rise.

Even he was intimidated at first by Willard's size—"God, he was big!" Dempsey remembered thinking before the bell rang at Toledo—but size turned out not to matter. Dempsey tore Willard's title from him. He knocked the champion down seven times; cracked four of his ribs; knocked out six teeth; splintered his jaw in seven places. Willard quit on his stool rather than answer the bell for the fourth round. As he stumbled out of the ring he was heard muttering to himself over and over again, "I have a hundred thousand dollars and a farm in Kansas."

Jack Dempsey now occupied the stage Jack Johnson had once had all to himself. In a January 1920 interview with the New York *Times,* Johnson argued that since Willard had not really defeated him in Havana, Dempsey's victory at Toledo had meant nothing; he would never be the *real* champion until he beat Jack Johnson. Dempsey and his manager, Doc Kearns, both insisted that he would never fight a black challenger. But Johnson had heard that before. He knew time was against him, but he was now eager, he said, to find some way to go home, serve his time, and then shame Dempsey into getting into the ring with him before he fought anyone else. Friends approached Charles F. Clyne, now the United States district attorney in Chicago, with a message from Johnson: he was willing to come home if he could have thirty-six hours to arrange bail and confer with his attorneys before he was arrested. Clyne answered that the only basis on which he could proceed was "unconditional surrender"; Johnson would have to submit to arrest the moment he stepped onto American soil.

Johnson was coming closer to taking that step. In late February, he and his party left Mexico City and headed north, toward the border town of Tijuana, where the son-in-law of the governor of Baja California hoped to make some money in the fight game. According to Johnson's own account, Yaqui Indians held up his train in Sonora—and allowed it to move on unmolested once they realized who was aboard. At the Pacific port of Mazatlán, they bought passage on a gasoline-driven launch being used to smuggle fifty Chinese into the United States. It skirted the coast for nearly a thousand miles, buffeted by storms. Johnson and Rhodes feared for their lives. Lucille remained stoical. "I never knew such gameness in man or woman," Johnson wrote. They finally entered the mouth of the Colorado and made their way upriver to an unmarked landing. The Chinese left the ship and set out on foot for the Texas border. Johnson and his companions got off, too, only to suffer what he called a "regrettable accident": somehow, his revolver discharged, badly wounding his nephew in the arm. They managed to telephone Tijuana for a car and got Rhodes to a hospital before he bled to death.

On January 16, the Eighteenth Amendment had gone into effect in the United States, and transformed the dusty little border town of Tijuana into a pleasure resort to rival Chicago's Levee District or any of the other segregated vice zones with which Jack Johnson had once been familiar. Five hundred to a thousand cars rattled across the wooden International Bridge into Tijuana every day, filled with thirsty American sports looking for a drink and a good time. "Imagine a wide main street after the old Western style, or the Spanish plaza of colonial pueblos," wrote a reporter for the Los Angeles *Times*.

On either side is a succession of saloons, dance halls, moving picture barns and gambling dens. In other places, not so largely advertised, one may cook a pill or otherwise dally through the lotus hours. The air reeks of dust, warm humanity, toilet perfume, stale tobacco and that curious congenial aroma which makes the camel twitch its nostrils afar. And also the welkin rings and vibrates with the laughter and chatter of abnormal good spirits, the notes of an occasional fracas, the whirl of the roulette wheels, the clatter of the little ball seeking its owner's salvation, the musically liquid swickety-swish-swish of the Great American cocktail, the tap-tap-tap of hammers where new joy palaces are being shot up overnight to accommodate the business of this prohibition boomtown, and, above all, a continuous jangle of jazz—the smiting of cymbals, the raucous clatter of cowbells, the frenzied runs and trills of the automatic piano, and the voice of the saxophone.

Tijuana seemed made for Jack Johnson. He haunted the racetrack, knocked over carefully selected opponents in the bullring, and presided over a ramshackle saloon and gambling palace—he was either a greeter or a part-owner, sources differ—called the Main Event. "He struts about like a chanticleer in his own barnyard," the *Times* continued,

expecting homage from all strangers and bestowing his famous smile on all who come up to shake hands. A large revolver slung beneath his sweater in front of his left hip is one of his proudest possessions, and although he insists he is no bad man, he likes to create that atmosphere.

Old friends came to see him, including a flamboyant onetime Chicago alderman named Tom Carey, who had represented the stockyards district for many years. After making millions as a banker, brick manufacturer, and owner of the Hawthorne Race Track, he had retired with his wife to Los

Angeles, but he remained a dedicated sport and was a frequent visitor to the Main Event. Johnson badly wanted to go home to Chicago, he told Carey, but he didn't have any way of raising money for his bond. Carey was reassuring and expansive. Johnson was welcome to borrow up to fifty thousand dollars to get himself out of trouble. Money had always talked in Chicago. He knew a good lawyer, too. Johnson took Carey up on his offer and began negotiating his surrender by telephone with federal and state officials in California. He wanted to go straight to Chicago, he said; he wanted a Negro deputy sheriff to escort him; and he wanted no "indignities," no handcuffs, no strong-arm stuff. No one made him any promises.

Johnson was ready to take his chances, but he insisted surrendering at a time of his own choosing, no one else's. On June 5, a Tijuana judge ordered him to leave Mexican territory within thirty days. He said he'd cross on July the fifth, then the ninth, then the fifteenth. He didn't leave then, either. A newspaperman asked him why he'd delayed his departure so many times.

"Well," he said, "the word was passed out that I had to leave Mexico by July 5 and I want to show them all that I don't have to leave until I get ready."

He was ready at last on the morning of July 20. Lucille and Gus Rhodes had gone ahead and were waiting for him in Los Angeles. Sheriff John Cline of Los Angeles picked him up at the battered desert cottage in which he and Lucille had been living and started walking with him toward the customshouse at the border. Johnson asked to stop at the Main Event for one last drink. "Several white women there drank with him at the bar," the Los Angeles *Times* noted, "wishing him much good luck and regretting that he was leaving. The only time Johnson lost his famous L'il Arthur smile was when he started away from the crowd there. He applied his handkerchief vigorously to his eyes, saying it was hard to leave friends."

Crowds were waiting on both sides of the border. Johnson hesitated until he was sure all the motion picture cameras were trained on him, then stepped across the line and shook hands with the federal agents who were waiting for him. "The center of the stage or none for him," the *Times* wrote.

Deputy U.S. Marshal George Cooley read out the warrant for his arrest. Johnson listened, asked to read it himself, then handed it back and walked to one of several waiting automobiles. There were no handcuffs. "I'm back home," Johnson said, "and it sure feels mighty good. It is home sweet home for me and no one who has never been away can know how good it feels to get back again, whatever is in the future."

Cline and Cooley drove him first to San Diego, where he was arraigned and bond was set at ten thousand dollars, then on to Los Angeles, where he was to spend the night in the county jail before leaving the next morning for Chicago. He was hungry when he got there, and two accommodating deputies walked him down the street to a restaurant, where he ordered two plates of pork and beans, downed his first glass of near-beer with a shudder, and asked after old L.A. friends.

A big crowd gathered outside, then followed along as, juggling two bars of toilet soap, he strolled back to jail. There, his belongings were taken from him—$463 in cash and a pair of red dice—and he was told to have a seat in the general waiting room until he got his cell assignment. "Johnson sprawled down in a seat," a reporter noted, "pulling the cuffs of his shirt so that the stripes would show, balanced his . . . straw hat on his head, gave his kid gloves an extra twist, and took his ease."

When the deputies finally ushered him out of the room toward his cell, the *Times* noted, "the colored visitors crowded around him, everybody wanting to take the hand that had put the kibosh on Jim Jeffries." So many people stood around outside to peer through his cell window that he finally called for the blinds to be drawn.*

He boarded a train with two federal agents the next morning. Initial plans had called for him to take the southern route through Texas. He had protested, fearing that someone might board the train and attack him, and the government had agreed. Crowds waited to cheer him at every stop—"It was a memorable journey," he remembered—and thousands gathered in Chicago to welcome him home to the South Side. He never got there. Deputy marshals, fearing trouble, flagged down the *California Limited* at Joliet, Illinois, and locked him up in the Will County Jail on July 22.

"I'm damn glad to get back, even as far as this," he told newsmen. "The reason I decided to give myself up and come back was to show the world I'm still champion. As soon as I get out of this mixup with the Federal Government, I am going to start training and clean up this Dempsey fellow. Nothing to it."

He'd confidently told reporters in Los Angeles that Tom Carey and his influential friends had "everything arranged" in Chicago. They didn't. He'd

---

*Mrs. Josephine B. Blanchard, a white woman wrongly arrested for car theft, happened to be in the waiting room while Johnson was there. Later, she sued for false arrest and asked for additional aggravated damages because members of the big crowd outside, peering through the barred windows, had "pointed her out as 'Mrs. Jack Johnson.' " (Los Angeles *Times*, July 21, 1921.)

been assured that Judge Samuel L. Aschuler of the United States District Court would let him out on bail. But Aschuler refused, citing Johnson's previous flight from the law. Tom Carey's fifty thousand dollars was worthless to him. Federal Judge George Carpenter, who had presided over his case, was recovering from surgery and wouldn't be able to hear arguments from the attorneys Carey had hired for Johnson for thirty days.

He would have to spend at least a month behind bars. Johnson seems to have made the best of it. The New York *Times* reported that he had persuaded the sheriff to let him out of Joliet for "ice cream sprees and automobile trips." Federal agents then moved him to the Kane County Jail at Geneva, which was said to be run with more rigor.

On September 14, Judge Carpenter finally heard Johnson's request for bail—and rejected it. Johnson had defied the court and held the laws of the land in open contempt, he said. "This man deserves no clemency." Jack Johnson would have to serve his year and a day in the federal penitentiary at Leavenworth and pay his thousand-dollar fine.

Five days later, federal agents escorted the ex-champion to prison. At the Leavenworth depot a Negro cabdriver named Jim Crawford offered to take him and his escorts to the penitentiary. Johnson agreed, provided that Crawford got out from behind the wheel. Jack Johnson would drive himself to prison.

CHAPTER TWELVE

THE STEPPER

O N SUNDAY MORNING, SEPTEMBER 19, 1920, Jack Johnson became Federal Prisoner No. 15461. He gave his occupation as "pugilist-chauffeur." Asked for a "full history" of his crime, he answered only, "It is alleged that I violated the Mann Act to which charge I entered a plea of not guilty." And when led before the camera so that full-face and side-view identification photographs could be made, he smiled into the lens with the relaxed ease of a celebrity accustomed to admiring attention. Clearly, he was not going to be an ordinary prisoner.

Nor was Leavenworth an ordinary prison. Known to its inmates as the "big L," or the "Big Top" because of the dome above its administration building, it was established in 1895 for punishment, not rehabilitation. It was a city unto itself, with its own power station and farm and factories, and its own cemetery called Peckerwood Hill. Some seventeen hundred men lived within its forty-foot-high redbrick walls. More than four hundred of them had been convicted of violent crimes.

At first, Johnson's family and friends must have worried about his safety. He still received death threats. Violence was commonplace in prison. There were madmen among his fellow inmates. The all-white guard staff routinely imposed its will with clubs, and Johnson's lifelong refusal to defer to anyone's authority seemed designed to set them off. But Johnson turned out to have a powerful ally. Former Nevada governor Denver S. Dickerson, the man who had made the battle at Reno possible—and, according to Johnson, had also made "several thousand dollars" betting on the outcome—was now superintendent of federal prisons and president of the parole board as well.*

Dickerson may or may not have let it be known that he was taking a personal interest in how the former champion was treated, but the morning Johnson

---

*"Throughout my prison term," Johnson wrote in his autobiography, Dickerson remained "a staunch friend and adviser . . . and one of the greatest things in the world is friendship." More than mere friend

arrived, Warden A. V. Anderson announced that his new prisoner would not be laying bricks or plowing the prison field, laboring on the road gang or breaking rocks in the quarry. Instead, he would become the "baseball park orderly," in charge of making sure the field was kept "spick and span for the Saturday afternoon games." When the season ended, Anderson continued, he planned to put the ex-champion in charge of an exercise program for the men. As soon as Johnson could be fitted out with the prison uniform, a hickory shirt and dungarees, he was hustled out onto the field to umpire a game between two prison teams, the Kitchens and the Twilights.

"In all," Johnson wrote, "my imprisonment was in no wise as severe as I had anticipated. There was virtually no one over me and there was no one to whom I was answerable in the performance of my duties in the prison except the executives." That was how Jack Johnson liked things. But it did not please the men in charge of day-to-day life on the cell blocks, and they made their feelings plain in a sheaf of written complaints addressed to their superiors. An indignant officer reported that on October 4 Johnson "did use the guard's toilet . . . in the brick yard." Two months later, the ex-champion loudly questioned another guard's judgment in changing a friend's work assignment, employing what the complaining officer called "rude language." When the guard asked "what business he had to talk about me, [Johnson] replied in a very insolent manner that he had as much right to talk that way to me as I had to ride him, and I could not stop him." A few days later, another officer came upon Johnson in the bakery, asking for extra bread; when he was ordered to move on, he took his own sweet time. "This prisoner does not get up for the A.M. count," another officer reported in January. "This is a daily occurrence and he seems to think the guard's orders as to this do not apply to him." A month later, he was reported again, this time for "loafing in main hall and offices. He comes in hall when ready. . . . All by hisself. Goes where he pleases. Asks nobody no permission."

Most of Johnson's transgressions—which would likely have been pun-

---

ship may possibly have been involved in the relatively gentle treatment Johnson received at Leavenworth. The murderer Robert Stroud, who would one day be known as the "Birdman of Alcatraz," had been a prisoner at Leavenworth for several years when Johnson arrived; he claimed that the champion had paid someone seven thousand dollars to exempt him from hard labor. Stroud was a conscienceless liar when it came to his own crimes but would not seem to have had any motive for fabricating this story. It is impossible now to know whether he was merely reporting prison scuttlebutt or repeating what Johnson himself told him—and if it was the latter, whether Johnson was telling the truth or just boasting of his wealth and influence. (Thomas E. Gaddis, *Birdman of Alcatraz*, p. 74.)

ished summarily had he been any other prisoner, let alone a black one—were routinely minimized by the guards' superiors. The "loafing" charge, for example, did lose Johnson his yard privileges for two weeks, but Deputy Warden L. J. Fletcher remained sympathetic to him: "This prisoner is an orderly in Isolation and is supposed to go anyplace inside the walls if he has business. . . . He no doubt stops and visits places he should not, but on account of the unusual number of necessary trips and the fact that he is more conspicuous than ordinary prisoners, some allowance should be made."*

In prison, Johnson wrote in his 1927 memoir, he "found little cause for complaint . . . and outside the fact that I chafed under the ordeal of restriction from the outside world, my life was pleasant and comfortable." Only once, he said, did he get really angry. With permission from the warden, he had arranged for a hunter to shoot a possum for him. The man "was unable to find one, and rather than lose the dollar which I had promised him, killed and dressed a cat, being careful to remove all parts of the animal which would reveal its identity." The cook, unfamiliar with possum anatomy, duly served it

> with all the approved . . . trimmings. I had invited two or three friends to dine with me, but before we had partaken of the delicacy which we had anticipated with watering mouths, the deception was discovered. . . . Had I been able to lay my hands on the hunter at that moment, I fear that I would have treated him rather roughly.

This story sounds like the crudest kind of minstrel turn. But like so many of Johnson's apparently tall tales, it turns out to have been true. A blind item in the prison newspaper, the Leavenworth *New Era*, provides corroboration:

---

*Johnson served as an Isolation orderly for three months. It was a euphemistic title for an often ugly job. Orderlies were expected to act as strong-arm men, helping guards impose brutal discipline on uncooperative prisoners already enduring solitary confinement. Isolation was a separate two-tiered facility, a prison within a prison. Men caught fighting or smuggling or flouting prison rules who were expected eventually to rejoin the prison population were housed downstairs. Upstairs were the hard cases who had no hope of ever leaving their dark cells: rapists, escape artists, men like Robert Stroud who had murdered guards. During Johnson's time there was also a third category of inmate in Isolation: conscientious objectors who had refused to fight in the Great War and members of the Industrial Workers of the World (Wobblies), whose unwillingness to obey the orders of federal officials was met with regular beatings administered by orderlies, sometimes with baseball bats. According to Stroud, Johnson was a relatively benign presence in Isolation—his size and reputation alone may have discouraged defiance—but some prisoners, at least, never warmed to him: "It pays to be a celebrity," a bitter I.W.W. member named Ralph Chaplin wrote after spotting him returning from lunch at the warden's house, "all duded up" in a starched trusty's "snitch jacket." (Babyak, *Bird Man*, pp. 84–86; Gaddis, *Birdman of Alcatraz*, p. 74; Ralph Chaplin, *Wobbly*, p. 267.)

"Wonder why 'Meow! Meow!' has a strange sound to the ears of Jack Johnson? Can it be that he is suspicious about that kind of music?"

Not long after Johnson got to Leavenworth, he welcomed an old acquaintance to the prison. Melville Butler was a jug-eared stickup man and former cheese salesman from Indiana who, like the ex-champion, was beginning a one-year sentence for white slavery.* The two men had met somewhere in Mexico, where Johnson had told so many gaudy stories about himself that Butler asked why he hadn't published an autobiography for American readers. Never had the time, the ex-champion had answered then. They had nothing but time now, Butler said. Why didn't they try to produce a book together? Johnson liked the idea and began jotting down in pencil in his big self-confident scrawl what he remembered best about his boyhood and early ring career. Butler corrected his sometimes wayward grammar and spelling but was careful not to alter Johnson's distinctive voice. "I have used his expressions," Butler wrote. "The prize ring is not an elocution contest. . . . My story is [meant] for the virile, the red-blooded." The little heap of pages in Butler's cell grew slowly, but Johnson lost interest once he had described in loving detail just how he'd beaten Tommy Burns, and the manuscript was never finished.†

Johnson had plenty of other things to do to fill the time. Over the years, nothing had amused skeptical white reporters more than his occasional claims that he was an inventor as well as an athlete; the idea of a negro inventor—especially one who was also a prizefighter—struck white newspapermen and a good many of their readers as inherently ludicrous. At various times, he said he'd been working on a new kind of coupler for railroad cars, a flying machine, even a treatment for tuberculosis. Johnson was not above exaggerating his accomplishments, and no evidence survives for any of those claims, but in the spring of 1921 "JOHN ARTHUR JOHNSON, a citizen of the United States, and a resident of Leavenworth, in the county of Leavenworth and State of Kansas," applied for two patents—for an improved auto-

---

*The woman he'd been caught taking across a state line for allegedly immoral purposes was now his wife—and was herself in prison in Arizona for prostitution.

†When Butler left prison in the summer of 1921, he unaccountably left the manuscript in the care of a thief named Bernard A. Muckerman. When he wrote to the warden, asking that he be allowed to contact Muckerman to tell him where to send it, the warden refused to help: ex-convicts were not allowed to communicate with one another, and no one had given either him or Jack Johnson permission to write anything for publication while in prison. The fragmentary manuscript languished, unread, in the Leavenworth files for some eighty years. Excerpts from it appear throughout the first half of this book, attributed as "Prison Memoir."

mobile wrench and a "theft-preventing device for vehicles"—and was awarded them: Nos. 1,413,121 and 1,438,709.*

He also seemed to have plenty of time to get to know other prisoners, both black and white. Perhaps his closest friend was a black Kentuckian named Roy Tyler with whom he sparred, worked out, and played countless hours of dominoes. Tyler was one of sixty-eight soldiers sentenced to life for taking part in the Houston Riot, a 1917 shoot-out between black troops of the 24th U.S. Infantry, angered by their treatment at the hands of white policemen, and white citizens of the city. He also played baseball so well with Leavenworth's black team, the Booker T. Washingtons, that in 1925 he was paroled to the care of Rube Foster, for whom he played parts of three seasons. Since Johnson was a friend of both men, it seems likely that it was he who suggested that Foster take responsibility for the younger man.

Certainly it would have been like him. "He was a good friend to have," a white inmate remembered, "regardless of creed or color. While in prison he expended hundreds of dollars in charitable acts. Many a black boy, and many a white boy, would have left Leavenworth friendless and penniless had it not been for the philanthropy of this gladiator of the dusk."

"Nothing seemed to trouble him," an inmate who arrived after Johnson had left remembered being told by others who had known him. "He would get as many as six and seven letters daily from as many woman friends and many more from sharpies, promoters, and leeches. He'd read them intently. Then, with the air of a man tearing up an advertisement, he pulled them to pieces and threw the scraps away, always grinning to himself."

He didn't throw them all away. Every couple of days, Johnson visited the record clerk's office, where a forger named Ray Perry acted as his typist in exchange for handfuls of the fat cigars Johnson asked his friends to send him, fifty at a time. Johnson's Leavenworth file is thick with correspondence.

He had three main agendas while in prison: to make sure his wife and family were cared for in his absence; to see if he could find some legal way to get out of prison; and to rekindle public interest in his career so that he could return to the ring and start making big money again the moment he got out.

After Tiny Johnson died, the handsome Wabash Avenue home her son had bought for her with his winnings was sold. Lucille, Jack's sister Jennie, and

---

*A fellow inmate named James Pearl Thompson shared the second patent with Johnson. He worked in the prison automobile repair shop and was a member of the Industrial Workers of the World from Chicago, imprisoned for "conspiracy." Johnson had quietly obtained still another patent—for a "hydraulic lift"—back in 1910. (Chicago *Tribune,* December 10, 1910.)

her son, Gus Rhodes, all now lived in far humbler rented quarters at 3642 Grand Boulevard. Johnson's first task was to find some way to keep them all afloat. On November 1, 1920, he signed a two-year contract with a new manager, a Kansas City, Missouri, lawyer and entrepreneur named Lawrence K. Goldman, who was so pleased with the terms of their agreement, he spelled them out in *Billboard*. He would represent Johnson in "every field," he said. "Johnson will work for no one else." Goldman planned to organize a "great athletic carnival and, with Jack as the chief attraction, tour the country as the first step of Johnson's coming back." Then he would try to arrange a fight with Dempsey. When Johnson was not on the road, he was to manage Goldman's Lincoln Theater in Kansas City, "said to be the largest colored motion picture theater in the United States." Johnson didn't argue. All he cared about for the moment was that Goldman was willing to advance him a weekly check to send home to Chicago.

Then he set about trying to get himself either paroled or pardoned. With his friend Denver Dickerson heading the Federal Parole Board, Johnson was optimistic about his chances. He asked Gus Rhodes to see if he could enlist Clarence Darrow in his cause. When that didn't work out, Goldman armed a black lawyer from Topeka named Elisha J. Scott with copies of Johnson's trial transcript and sent him to Washington to speak with Federal Pardon Attorney Robert H. Turner.* The attorney was authorized to say that if Johnson was pardoned, he would willingly pay his thousand-dollar fine. "Scott will win sure," Johnson wrote to a friend; the attorney general himself, A. Mitchell Palmer, had agreed to see him.

Meanwhile, Johnson set about seeing what he could do from inside prison walls to restore his reputation as a fighter. Within days of his arrival he sent a wire to Lucille asking Gus to send him "boxing gloves, punching bag and arm bracelets to pull against horses. Need them very bad." He worked out with Roy Tyler, and on October 21 entertained inmates, prison officials, and a delegation of visiting Shriners by boxing three two-minute rounds with fellow inmates. He toyed with his two black opponents—a brash youngster named Malcolm Brockenbrough, who had challenged the ex-champion the day he arrived at the penitentiary, and Henry "Overseas" Jackson, a left-

---

*Scott was one of the most prominent black attorneys in Kansas: mail addressed simply to "Colored Lawyer, Topeka" was routinely delivered to him. He was also instrumental in establishing the Negro National League. In 1951 two of his sons, John and Charles Scott, would help file the landmark *Brown v. Board of Education of Topeka* case.

handed pitcher for the Booker T. Washingtons who, Johnson said, was a good enough boxer to beat Georges Carpentier—but he knocked out the white one, an Irish-born army deserter named Thomas Scullion, serving a life sentence for killing two Frenchmen.

The Shriners were thrilled. So was the warden, who asked Johnson to organize another "boxfest" for Thanksgiving Day. Prisoners would fight one another in the preliminaries, but in the main event this time, Johnson would face two professionals in front of a big crowd that would include sportswriters for midwestern dailies as well as inmates.

That was just what Johnson wanted. He was forty-two years old. American writers hadn't seen him perform in the ring since his loss to Jess Willard in 1915, and reports of his barnstorming through Europe and Mexico had only further damaged his standing. This was his opportunity to begin to restore it, to show the world he was still capable of taking on the best of the current crop of heavyweights. To help get him into shape, he hired Billy McClain, an old friend, minstrel star, and sometime trainer.

But as always, Johnson saw no reason to take unnecessary chances. It had been left to him to pick his two opponents. He did so carefully. One would be "Topeka Jack" Johnson, a slender ex-sparring partner and professional baseball player, with whom he planned to go through the motions to show off his old defensive skills. But he needed to seem powerful as well as scientific, capable of not just avoiding trouble but dealing out real punishment. To be sure that he made just the right impression, he needed a cooperative opponent. Frank Owens was his choice, a formidable-looking but minimally talented black heavyweight from Chicago. Owens seemed to offer no serious opposition—a few weeks after facing Johnson he would be savaged by an obscure second-rater named Rough House Wilson. But just to be sure there would be no embarrassment on his big day, Johnson sent his wife a coded message: "Tell Gus to . . . locate [Owens] immediately and find out if everything is O.K." By "everything is O.K." he meant that he wanted his nephew to ask Owens if, for a price, he would be willing to look good but lie down, just as he had wanted to be sure that everything was O.K. with Frank Moran before their bout in Paris.

Owens was agreeable. Everything was O.K.

A day or two before Thanksgiving, Lucille had a dream in which her husband hadn't managed to get back in shape and got hurt. She wrote to him about it. "Nothing wrong with me," he wrote back. "Feeling fine. Sorry you had bad dreams. . . . Everything is fine for Thursday. Sorry you can't come to see me, but you will understand—no ladies admitted. . . . I'm going to try and make this the greatest fight and exhibition that I've ever had."

The inmates enjoyed a big Thanksgiving dinner on November 25. Then more than a thousand of them filed into the prison yard, where they found three hundred outsiders, including a row of reporters, already in their seats. They enjoyed the preliminaries. The prison band played between bouts. But, as Joseph A. Kerwin, the editor of the prison paper, wrote, everyone was there to see Jack Johnson in action. At the first sight of him, Kerwin noted, a big cheer went up from his fellow inmates; for perhaps the only time in his life, the fans at ringside that afternoon saw Jack Johnson as one of them.

There comes Jack now. He looks mighty good in that flowing bathrobe and skullcap. He has conditioned himself as best he could. . . . He weighs two hundred and fifteen after three weeks' training.

Take this INSIDE tip from us. . . . Jack Johnson is not all in.

Following Jack is that Grand Old Man, Frank Owens, who has come all the way from Chicago to give our lads a show. . . . He's going to try to stay six rounds with Jack. Frank weighs two hundred twenty-seven.

Into the ring they get and the timekeeper pulls the gong. . . .

Man what a scrap! Every time Frank would make a lead, Jack would stop him with one of these famous counters and uppercut. Jack kept his glove in Frank's face—oh, CONSTANTLY! In the second round, Frank let one go and caught Jack on the portside of the jaw. Things got all mixed up right then! Jack don't like to get walloped on the jaw. Frank tried to hunt cover, but the great, great sky was all around him. . . . He had to take Jack's comeback. The canvas was the closest cover—and Frank took that—for the count of eight. Getting back perpendicular seemed easy for the big fellow, for he got right into the way of another haymaker a moment after, went down, came back quickly—and then tried the whole thing over again, for fear that some of us missed seeing the first two. Jack was fighting a cautious battle the while, never letting Frank get settled for another stinger. But the more that Jack let Frank have, the more Frank came back for more. Talk about your scrappers taking punishment—well, Frank Owens deserves a special medal. Johnson's uppercuts in the clinches sounded as though he had broken all Frank's jawbones, but Owens just grinned and came back for the same dose in the same way. He went down for the count twelve times in the five rounds of fighting, and every time you could read, "For heaven's sake, are you back again?" on Johnson's face. A body blow and a cross to the jaw finally put Frank out of the running for the big count. But in his defeat he became a popular hero with the fight fans here. They admire him for the sacrifice he made for our entertainment.

The four-round exhibition with "Topeka" Jack Johnson, one of Arthur's old training camp warhorses, showed what Jack knew about the scientific side of the boxing game. He toyed with "Topeka" almost at will, and showed us all the probable openings a fighter exposes for the final dreamland touch. "Topeka" weighed two hundred ten and showed speed and the powers of assimilation. He proved himself a good receiver-general.

Are we thankful? YOU HEAR US. WE ARE!

Johnson was thankful, too. It had all gone perfectly. "Hello dear," he wrote to Lucille. "Everything went lovely . . . , had a fine show. Was sorry that you weren't there. . . . Lovely crowd, sport writers and papers were here. Sending you clippings." The clippings were proof that his ploy had worked: "It was the opinion of newspaper men and boxing critics at the ringside," the New York *Times* reported, "that Johnson is in very good condition and still retains much of his punching power. . . . At the finish of the bouts he seemed as fresh as when he started."

That was precisely what Johnson wanted the boxing world to believe. "I am filled with power and strength, not dope," he would declare in an open letter to the manager and promoter Alfred Lippe. "If I get any stronger I'm liable to bust. I am just like T.N.T. and ready for the time to put the fuse to it and let the public see what I can do. I cannot see Jack Dempsey as champion. I can beat all the Dempseys that ever put on the gloves."*

Then, more good news. Elisha Scott's trip to Washington appeared to have paid off. The Federal Pardon Attorney had ruled that Johnson could not officially apply for a pardon until late January, when he had served half his sentence, but Scott believed clemency was possible if he could prove his client's claim that providing Belle Schreiber with rail fare to Chicago from Pittsburgh had been a "purely philanthropic act." Meanwhile, the Leavenworth parole board was meeting in early January. Johnson would have a chance to make

---

*The day's festivities were filmed for use in an official motion picture "to be exhibited generally over the country to show what the prison system of the Government is doing." But the U.S. attorney general ordered the boxing sequence cut after Kansas Governor Henry J. Allen objected to the showing of films of Johnson anywhere in the country. The footage seems to have disappeared. (New York *Times*, December 16, 1920.)

his case in person. He wrote Lucille on New Year's Eve that he hoped to be reunited with her soon, "and then we will continue our happiness." Johnson was at his most charming and persuasive at the hearing. The board unanimously recommended parole. Warden Anderson and Deputy Warden Fletcher sent telegrams to the attorney general urging that the ex-champion be placed on the New Year's list of parolees. Denver Dickerson agreed. Only A. Mitchell Palmer's approval was needed.

But functionaries at the Justice Department, still smarting at Johnson's charges of bribery and still outraged that he had slept with white women, determined to sabotage him. Asked for a straightforward outline of the case to accompany the parole petition when it went to the attorney general, they produced instead a shrill document filled with fresh and wholly unsubstantiated charges. Johnson had "abducted" Lucille Cameron, its authors said, knowing that he hadn't. They charged him with kidnapping another woman in June 1911, at a time when they should have known he was on his way to England with his wife. Without offering a scrap of evidence, they claimed that because of his "mania," there were "30 or 40 young white girls who fell victim to his vicious practices without the interstate feature." And as an afterthought, they alleged that while in Mexico he had sought to incite "riots among Negroes" in Texas and Louisiana, a false allegation carefully calculated to prejudice Palmer, whose obsession with supposed radicals and revolutionaries had brought about the arrest of some four thousand men and women, most of them innocent of any crime other than political dissent.

The Bureau of Investigation's report carried the day. On January 21, 1921, Palmer overruled the board's recommendation. Parole was denied. Johnson would have to serve out his sentence.

Two months later, his hopes rose again. The Wilson administration left office in March and Palmer went with it, replaced by the new Republican attorney general, Harry M. Daugherty. Republicans were still thought more likely to be sympathetic to Negro grievances than were Democrats. If Daugherty could be persuaded to review the case, Johnson wrote to a friend, it would be obvious to him "what an unfair trial they gave me. I am sure our Attorney General will be fair." The problem was to get him to look at the evidence. An old friend and Harlem casino owner named Dick Ellis assured Johnson that two "influential friends" close to the new Warren Harding administration would be happy to lobby Daugherty on his behalf—provided the money was right. Johnson agreed to provide it—and fired Lawrence Goldman and Elisha Scott.

Ellis' friends took the money but got nowhere. Then Denver Dickerson lost his job, replaced by Vice President Calvin Coolidge's brother-in-law, the Reverend Heber Votaw. Johnson was now without any strings to pull, and when the Chicago sport Bill Bottoms wired Johnson in late April saying *he* had a friend who could arrange his release in ten days for just $250, Johnson wearily turned him down: "Cannot see my way clear. Too many have failed."

The former champion was disappointed at his failure to win a parole or pardon, but he couldn't help but be pleased that his impressive Thanksgiving showing had let loose a flood of proposals from old friends and eager strangers, all hoping to cash in on his comeback once he was free. "From Jack Johnson's correspondence," the *New Era* reported, "you can bank on it that he will have all the mitt business he can care for when he's released."

There were offers from would-be promoters in El Paso, Philadelphia, Omaha, Havana. The Committee of American Woodmen of St. Louis wanted him to lecture on his travels overseas. The most promising offer came from Elmer Tenley in New York, a guarantee of thirty thousand dollars plus 35 percent of the gross for a Jersey City fight with Johnson's former sparring partner Harry Wills, who was now the leading black challenger for Jack Dempsey's title. Johnson eagerly agreed.

But that did not prevent him from simultaneously signing up with others, including Bill Bottoms, who advanced him $2,000 with a promise of $1,500 more for a series of Chicago exhibitions in the basement of his Dreamland Café. He also accepted a $1,000 advance against $7,500 from W. A. Andlauer, a Kansas City, Missouri photographer, to star in a motion picture, *The Heart of Jack Johnson*. Andlauer's attorney explained what his client had in mind to Warden Anderson:

> The idea is that a young man who is rather a physical weakling goes to Johnson, who has a gymnasium as a physical trainer, to be coached in boxing so that he can "lick" a rival in his love affairs, who it seems is, through "bullying" the boy, taking his sweetheart away from him. He later succeeds in "licking" his rival, through Johnson's training, and later marries the girl, at which time Johnson returns him the check he gave in payment for the training as a wedding present.

The lawyer had contacted the warden to ask whether the filming could be quietly done inside the prison; since Johnson had already been paid some of his money, the lawyer and his client both feared that Johnson might skip town after his release. The warden said that Andlauer would have to take his chances; there would be no moviemaking inside Leavenworth. To keep Johnson happy and more likely to fulfill his obligations after his release, Andlauer ordered him a blue serge suit from the best men's tailor in Kansas City and had it delivered to his cell. Johnson liked it so much he asked for two more.

As spring inched along, the ex-champion worked hard to stay in shape. "Jack Johnson and his punching ball are inseparable," the *New Era* reported in April. Warden Anderson was leaving Leavenworth in June. As a farewell to the men, he organized another "boxfest" on May 28. Johnson was again the feature attraction: he demolished Fred Allen, a fat white journeyman from St. Louis, in two rounds, and then—after allowing Joe Boykin, a black fighter from Philadelphia, to slam away at his stomach for two minutes to demonstrate that Johnson was in tip-top condition—he knocked him out, too.

Johnson was growing impatient. His sentence did not officially end until September 20, 1921, but with time off for good behavior he could expect to get out on July 9. That wasn't good enough. On July 2 at Boyle's Thirty Acres in Jersey City, Jack Dempsey was to defend his title against Georges Carpentier, Johnson's old Paris sparring partner, who was now the light heavyweight champion of the world. Tex Rickard was the promoter. Just as he had at Goldfield and Reno, he'd seen the commercial possibilities in turning a simple prizefight into a contest between good and evil, light and darkness, that no sports fan would want to miss. The handsome blond Carpentier had served with distinction in the French army during the Great War. The dark, scowling champion had not served at all, and many believed he had dodged the draft—though Dempsey had been found innocent of that charge in court. Even though the challenger was a foreigner, American boxing fans seemed eager to see the supposed "slacker" toppled. Rickard was confident that this would be boxing's first million-dollar gate. More than ninety thousand spectators were expected. Everyone was going to be there: Vincent Astor, Henry Ford, John D. Rockefeller, Jr., Franklin D. Roosevelt, three of Theodore Roosevelt's children, William H. Vanderbilt, Harry Payne Whitney.

Jack Johnson wanted to be there, too, to appear suddenly at ringside, leap into the ring to announce his coming fight with Harry Wills, and perhaps to challenge Dempsey as well, just as he had challenged other white titleholders in the past. What better way to begin his comeback? He enlisted the aid of Kansas Congressman Daniel Read Anthony, Jr., and former Illinois congressman James T. McDermott to try to get him an early release. At first, it seemed to work: on June 24, Attorney General Daugherty said he'd be willing now to consider a pardon in light of Johnson's record as a model prisoner. But Justice Department prosecutors again protested, and Daughterty, like A. Mitchell before him, changed his mind. He would not issue a pardon, he said, "considering the crime." Johnson would have to wait until July 9.*

The last few days seemed to crawl past, brightened only by the arrival of two more beautifully tailored suits courtesy of the nervous filmmaker, W. A. Andlauer. On July 3, Johnson sent Lucille a poem and two affectionate letters. She was thrilled: "DADDY," she wired back, "TWO SPECIALS TODAY AND THE POEM OUR LAST SUNDAY AND OUR FUN BEGINS." Gus Rhodes told his uncle to be ready for a warm welcome home. Chicago's two most important Negro politicians, former alderman Oscar de Priest and Alderman Louis B. Anderson, would be there to greet him. So would Bill Bottoms and the black belt's leading banker, Jesse Binga, as well as large groups of black Elks and Masons. "EXPECT A GOOD TIME," Rhodes said. "GET IN GOOD CONDITION WANT YOU TO STEP."

At a little before ten o'clock on the morning of July 9, 1921, Jack Johnson walked through the front gate of Leavenworth penitentiary a free man. Six motion picture cameramen were on hand to capture the moment. Johnson was dressed as only he could dress: straw hat, exquisitely tailored gray suit, blinding-white soft-collared shirt, bright polka-dot tie, gleaming patent leather shoes. Lucille was there. She had paid his thousand-dollar fine with cash advanced from Bill Bottoms. Gus Rhodes and his sister, Ada, were on hand to greet their uncle, too. "Many close friends came to meet me at the gates," he recalled. "There was a sort of general celebration, the extent and nature of which surprised and disconcerted me. There were four bands. Hundreds of people. . . . If I had ever felt that my life had been a failure I changed my opinion and found myself rejoicing, eager and confident."

He was chatty with the reporters who were waiting for him, optimistic, expansive, happy to be the center of attention again. He was forty-three years old—and "proud of it," he said. The first thing he planned to do was order up a dozen more suits from his Kansas City tailor. Then he wanted a fight with Jack Dempsey. "It doesn't make any difference what Dempsey says about

---

*On July 2, Dempsey faced the most hostile American crowd any heavyweight champion had faced since Jack Johnson made his way into the ring at Reno. But public sentiment did not help Carpentier any more than it had helped Jim Jeffries. Dempsey knocked him out in four rounds.

drawing the color line, the public wants Dempsey whipped. And the public knows I am the one to do it." Wouldn't Dempsey's youth and ferocity now simply be too much for Johnson? No, he said. Bullfighting had taught him everything he'd need to come out on top: "Many boxers are of the bull type. When they rush you four or five times and by deft footwork you have avoided them and jabbed them a few times as they pass by, you have them whipped—man or bull. I can use *this*," he added, tapping his forehead, "to win from the best ones now boxing."

With that, he shook hands with the new warden, W. I. Biddle, and Deputy Warden Fletcher, climbed with Lucille into his gleaming Haynes touring car, and led a cavalcade of a dozen automobiles roaring off toward Kansas City.

"What a relief," said the warden.

"Amen," said the deputy.

Johnson stayed in Kansas City for a few days, boarding with Kid Martin, an old friend from Galveston who had helped arrange his first professional fight against John "Must Have It" Lee back when he was a boy. He delivered a lecture at the Bethel Methodist Church, put on a sparring show for three thousand ticket buyers at Billion Bubble Park, an amusement park run by the Peet Brothers soap company. Proceeds went to the local post of the American Legion; unlike Jack Dempsey, he told the press, "Jack Johnson never was a slacker and never will be." Then, to W. A. Andlauer's intense relief, Johnson "posed" for the seven-reeler for which he'd already been paid his thousand-dollar advance.*

But he was eager to get back to his old life. He returned to Chicago on the

---

*In the end, the film was retitled *As the World Rolls On,* and its melodramatic plot was supplemented by a grab bag of footage Andlauer thought would be sure to draw black patrons: Rube Foster and the Chicago Giants were in it; so were Sam Crawford and the Kansas City Monarchs, and Bruce Petway of the Detroit Stars, plus "scenes of Elks Celebration, Odd Fellows encampment (St. Joseph) and Knights of Pythias National Conclave (Topeka)." In one scene, Johnson routed a band of bullies, and audiences were promised "close-ups of his great masculine body of steel responding instantaneously to perfect control of mind over action." Andlauer ordered two thousand dollars' worth of handbills:

THRILLING FAST MOVING. INTERSPERSED WITH EVENTS OF
UNUSUAL INTEREST. THIS PICTURE WAS MADE AND PRODUCED
IN AMERICA BY AN ALL STAR AMERICAN COLORED CAST.
DO NOT CONFUSE WITH FOREIGN MADE PRODUCTIONS
A REVELATION IN RACE PHOTOPLAYS
DON'T MISS IT!

The film opened at Love's Theater at Twenty-fourth and Vine in Kansas City on September 18, then played four days at King's. It netted $213. The film evidently no longer exists. (Exhibitor's file card, George P. Johnson Collection, University of California at Los Angeles.)

morning of July 13. The editor of the *Broad Ax* spoke for a good many residents of the South Side.

> Jack Johnson is out, and to tell the truth, he should never have been in. . . .
> The great crime Jack committed was to knock the crown off Jim Jeffries'
> head. Stealing a lot of worn out old hens of course had to supply public
> sentiment some . . . excuse for imprisonment. . . .
>
> He is a great fellow, after all, and here and there can be found men with
> eloquent words in praise of his courage. He is not an object of anybody's
> pity. He has stood the test and shown himself a man with all of the odds
> of white man hatred concentrated against him. . . .
>
> The *Broad Ax* wishes his after moments jeweled with the joys of a noble
> life and if he does not turn preacher, study law, or go into the undertaking
> business it appears he has done enough to make him honored and re-
> spected by his race. Success to you, Jack, and may you have luck in all the
> big things you contemplate for the future.
>
> You are suffering because of your black skin. You whipped the white
> man's hope. That was your undoing and we are proud of you.

The city refused his friends a parade permit, just as it had when he came home from Reno eleven years before, and there was no band to greet him at the station. Johnson professed not to care. "Chicago and my friends look mighty good to me," he said, "with or without music." When he pulled up in front of his sister Jennie's apartment there were two thousand men and women on hand to shake his hand. "The reception and the feasting and the drinking of real wine," reported the *Broad Ax*, "lasted until 3 o'clock, at which time Johnson wended his way to the Dreamland Café, 3250 South State Street."

Bill Bottoms' Dreamland was an opulent, mirror-hung black-and-tan, the closest thing to the Café de Champion left in the city: pimps and prostitutes and the "fixers" who found black women for white men in more disreputable places were barred at the door; the New Orleans cornetist King Oliver had played there two years earlier; Louis and Lil Hardin Armstrong would occupy its bandstand in 1925. "There," the *Broad Ax* continued, Johnson "received a great ovation from all of the leading white and colored sports, both men and women, in this great city." For the next few days, the ex-champion made the Dreamland his headquarters, and to pay back the money Bottoms had advanced him while in prison, he staged several exhibitions in the cellar.

Then it was on to New York. There was no crowd to cheer him when he stepped off the *Twentieth Century Limited* at Grand Central on July 22. During the nine years since he'd last visited the city, the center of its black life had moved north from the Tenderloin and San Juan Hill districts to Harlem. His friend Barron Wilkins had moved north, too, and was now running Barron's, a club for sports that was still more richly appointed and exclusive than his downtown café had been. Wilkins and Dick Ellis helped organize a hero's welcome along 125th Street, hosted a reception and dance in Johnson's honor at the Manhattan Casino, too, and paid him one thousand dollars just for turning up.

At first, then, it seemed like old times, as if the years of exile and incarceration had never happened. But reality quickly set in. Jack Dempsey would not fight him. "Johnson is through, through with his own people," explained Doc Kearns, Dempsey's manager. "He stands discredited in the eyes of the civilized world." There was no sum of money large enough, he said, to persuade Dempsey "to dignify the Negro with a fight."* The chairman of the New Jersey boxing commission wouldn't allow the Jersey City fight with Harry Wills to go forward: "The commissioners are in office to promote and protect the boxing game in the state," he said, "and we believe the appearance of Johnson in a contest there would be derogatory to the sport." Then, William Muldoon, John L. Sullivan's onetime trainer and now the chairman of the New York Boxing Board, refused to grant Johnson a license to fight in his state either: he was simply too old; New York boxing law barred anyone over thirty-seven from getting into the ring.

And once again, he was without a permanent place to live. His sister's home was now off-limits to him: he and Bill Bottoms had disagreed on whether he had put on enough exhibitions in the Dreamland cellar to repay the money advanced to him in prison, and Bottoms said he'd sue Johnson the moment he set foot in Chicago. Johnson's life after prison, like his life before he won the championship and during the years he and Lucille were wandering overseas, would be lived largely on the run.

Black Manhattan had changed since Johnson had last seen it. He had not: he still seemed to be one person one day, another the next. On Friday evening August 1, he spoke at the Baptist Tabernacle at 125th and Madison. His old

---

*Dempsey wouldn't "dignify" any Negro with a fight. He had no personal objection to taking on a black challenger. He'd fought and beaten Negro boxers on the way up. But his manager and big promoters like Tex Rickard were against it, and so, like his predecessor, he drew the color line and never had to face Johnson or Harry Wills.

friend, the Harlem attorney Frank Wheaton, introduced him as "the victim of unfair treatment." "Denied a square deal," Wheaton said, "this man has declared, 'If society feels wronged I have paid the penalty.' Should not a Christian community receive with open arms he who comes out into the world with clean hands and a clean heart?" The one hundred members present, almost all of them women, certainly thought so. They cheered the ex-champion as he stepped to the pulpit, and they punctuated everything he said with cries of "Yes!" "Yes!"

Pointing to the Bible, Johnson said,

This book teaches you to be fair-minded and sympathetic to others in their trouble. I have always tried to live by the Bible's teaching, as my mother told me to do. Is there anyone here who has done more, anyone who has really lived up to the Golden Rule? If there is one without sin here, let him rise.

The Bible teaches us to go into the bottomless pit, if need be, and get out the one who is sinking there. All the dirt that has been done me was done by those cowards with prejudiced minds, those hypocrites who kneel and pray on Sunday and commit slander the rest of the week. Cut me open, and you will find written upon my heart that I have never done wrong to my fellow men.

The Bible says, "Thou shalt take unto thyself a wife." It doesn't say what kind of wife. Chinese or white or green or black, or any other kind. I took unto myself a wife, just as the Bible told me to, and just because she was a college woman people were down on me. If I had married some woman of the streets it would have been all right. I'm sure I've lived up to all the rules any husband should live up to.

For Johnson, of course, those rules were always made to be broken. A few weeks later, he was back onstage, headlining at a Philadelphia theater with an "Extra Added Attraction—Ethel Waters and Fletcher Henderson's Jazz Masters." The twenty-five-year-old Waters had begun her career as a tent-show shimmy dancer billed as "Sweet Mama Stringbean," but she had recently become a headliner on the strength of two sly blues recorded for the brand-new, Negro-owned Black Swan Company. Johnson fascinated her. She had heard about him since childhood, and now never missed a chance to watch from the wings as he sparred and shadowboxed. But she also knew enough about his reputation to keep her distance—which only served to whet the ex-champion's interest, Waters remembered.

I was in my dressing room between shows one day when Jack's valet came in and said, "Mr. Johnson wants to see you."

"All right," I told him, "it is exactly the same number of steps from his dressing room to mine as it is from mine to his. So tell him to drop over."

The valet got an odd look on his face. I guess no colored person had ever responded like that before to an invitation from his boss. When Jack Johnson said, "Come!" they all came running. Especially the girls. But in a few minutes Jack himself knocked on my door and asked very politely if he could come in. He said, "May I ask you something?"

When I nodded he asked why I was so unfriendly and standoffish with him.

"I always speak to you, Mr. Jack, don't I?"

He invited me to have dinner with him that night. He was surprised because, unlike other colored girls, I didn't get blown over when he spoke to me. I thanked him and shook my head.

"But why not?" he asked. "Why won't you have dinner with me?"

I told him I wanted to make myself clear. "That white girl I see hanging around the theater, Mr. Jack—isn't she your wife?"

"No, she's just a friend."*

"But I never see you with any colored girls."

"I have nothing against colored girls," he said. "And I'd be proud to be seen out with you, Ethel."

But I wouldn't have dinner with him. . . . I don't think he had met one other colored girl since becoming famous who didn't try to track him down.

Johnson and Waters remained friends over the years. "He regarded me as one of his buddies," she remembered, and once she said to him, "It's universally known, Jack, that you have the white fever." Johnson replied:

I like colored women. I could love a colored woman. But they never give me anything. Colored women just won't play up to a man the way white girls do. Look at you. What do you tell me? You fluff me off. No matter how colored women feel toward a man, they don't spoil him and pamper him and build up his ego. They don't try to make him feel like he's somebody.

Johnson's desire to be "somebody," to enjoy "the distinction," as he himself wrote in his American autobiography, "of being a celebrity pointed out

---

*She *was* his wife, of course.

above all others," burned as brightly within him as it ever had. After most boxers' careers ended they had to be content with the nostalgic applause their names evoked when they were introduced from the ring before a big fight. Not Jack Johnson. He would spend the rest of his life struggling to stay within the spotlight that gave his life meaning. With time, that struggle would become more and more difficult. The newspapers chronicled some of what he did. But increasingly, Jack Johnson was old news, and he would only occasionally turn up in their pages, just as he had in the years when he was struggling toward the championship.

Johnson's love of speed had not diminished while he was in prison. While playing Philadelphia that fall, he was also commuting daily to a small-time studio in Cliffside, New Jersey, where he was starring in another movie, a melodrama called *For His Mother's Sake*. A sleet storm settled in one morning as he and the director, R. E. Wortham, set out for Cliffside in Johnson's Franklin racer. Johnson just went faster, Wortham remembered, splashing along at eighty miles an hour:

> I just held my breath and it was hard enough holding on to that, for Johnson forgot all about traffic regulations and the driving sleet. That machine must have had invisible wings. . . . My hair stood on end . . . and I for one want it emphatically understood that while I like Jack Johnson, he will never again entice me to take an auto ride with him.

The film opened at the New Douglas Theater at Lexington and 142nd—advertised to the people of Harlem as "Your Theater"—in January of 1922. It was billed as "a super production of mother love. . . . A story of pathos, home and filial devotion. A blending of sobs and laughter, the love of a son who shouldered hardship and misfortune for love of his mother." The film didn't do well—and there was evidently only a single print; the owners of the studio in which it was made seized the negative because the producers failed to pay their bills.

That February, Johnson's old friend Nat Fleischer published the first issue of a new boxing magazine called *The Ring*. Not long afterward, Johnson came to call at Fleischer's New York office. He wanted advice, he said. He'd written a detailed account of how he had thrown the Willard fight in order to get home to see his ailing mother. The New York *Mirror* had offered him two hundred dollars for it, but he wasn't sure he wanted to sell it so cheap. What did Fleischer think he should do? Actually, Johnson had written nothing, may never have even spoken to the *Mirror;* he was just looking for some quick money. Fleischer offered him $250—fifty more than the *Mirror* had allegedly promised—and Johnson returned a week later with an eighteen-hundred-word "confession." The editor put it in his desk drawer and declined to publish it during Johnson's lifetime because he didn't want to further damage the ex-champion's reputation.

That reputation needed help. The American Burlesque Association canceled its twenty-week contract with him because he refused to appear in some of the theaters it had booked. In May, when he returned to Chicago for the first time since his release from prison to play the Avenue Theater with a new All-Star Vaudeville Company—"in which all the performers except myself were white," he wrote—Bill Bottoms made good on his threat to sue him for the money he'd advanced him while in Leavenworth. The police department forced the cancellation of an engagement in Passaic, New Jersey, when they learned he was to appear onstage "surrounded by 30 white women." The troupe disbanded, and when Johnson earned four hundred dollars fighting an exhibition with a second-rater named James "Tut" Jackson in Washington Court House, Ohio, he had to turn over most of the money to his angry ex-employees. Someone then set him up in a brokerage office at Forty-ninth and Broadway in New York City. Perhaps understandably, it did not stay open long.

In February of 1923, he was working in New York as a $250-a-day sparring partner for Luis Angel Firpo, a cocky young heavyweight from Argentina with fourteen early-round knockouts behind him, whom the Broadway columnist Damon Runyon had already dubbed "the Wild Bull of the Pampas." Firpo was preparing for a fight with "KO" Bill Brennan, who had almost taken Jack Dempsey's title two years earlier, and Tex Rickard was already thinking that big money might be made someday from a Dempsey-Firpo fight. But when the fight crowd was invited down to McLevy's gymnasium on Twenty-sixth Street to see the newcomer go through his paces with the ex-champion, the temptation to show up his opponent proved more than Johnson could resist, just as it had when he'd worked with Kid Carter twenty-two years earlier. Firpo rushed at Johnson, only to find himself punching thin air or trapped within the grinning forty-four-year-old's encircling arms as he bowed to the ringsiders—who broke into applause. As the bell rang ending the first round, he patted the youngster on the rear end. Firpo was furious. So was Rickard, who saw to it that Johnson was fired and refused entry to the gym so long as the Argentinian hopeful was training there.

A few weeks later, Johnson sailed to Havana, where he puffed his way to victory over two nonentities and then was fined for having failed to train. He was still wistful for the ring, he told the press. "I am forty-five years old. But them are 45 mighty light years. I would like to box Mr. Dempsey for about six rounds to no decision. My, how I could show what kind of a champion he is! And Firpo, what I wouldn't do to Firpo. But I guess Jack ain't never going to get them chances. I'm a business man now."

A year earlier, the owners of the New Douglas Theater in Harlem, where Johnson's ill-fated five-reeler *For His Mother's Sake* had flickered into brief life, had announced that they were going into partnership with him to turn an old second-floor dance hall into a glittering new cabaret. The renovations had been completed by the spring of 1923, and the thousand-square-foot Café de Luxe had been fitted out with what a handout called ten thousand dollars' worth of "beautiful decorations *à la Parisienne*." Johnson's "partner" in this enterprise—actually, his employer—was Budd Levy, the mob-connected proprietor of a chain of New York billiard parlors and bowling alleys. According to a handbill that advertised the café, more than one thousand "bowlers and sporting men" attended its opening. Twenty performers and two jazz bands entertained nonstop, and Johnson acted as master of ceremonies. He was a conspicuous presence at the club, greeting the customers, moving from table to table, sometimes playing his bass with the band, just as he had a dozen years earlier in his own Café de Champion.

The Café de Luxe was a hit—so much of a hit that representatives of the British-born gangster Owney Madden decided to take it over as the ideal spot to peddle his "Number One" beer to white customers thirsty for a taste of Harlem good times. By the end of the year, Madden's men were in charge, the club's décor had been altered once again to suit its new name, the Cotton Club, and Johnson soon found himself back on the road, sparring, performing feats of strength, and telling bad jokes in stage dialect that had little to do with the way he really talked: "As a prize-fighter, I'm a runnin' fool. I started running after Tommy Burns, and run from one end of the world to the other. Oh, boy! I was runnin'. And before you could tell, I had done run clear over here."

In February 1924, Lucille Cameron Johnson sued her husband for divorce, citing "evidence involving Johnson and other white women," according to the New York *Times*. He did not contest her suit. Johnson's own account of what happened between him and the wife who had endured exile with him was characteristically opaque:

> Echoes of the old wrath which my mother-in-law, Mrs. Cameron nursed for me, came out of the past, and Lucille, after twelve years of a marriage that had been a happy and successful one, obtained a divorce in New York City. . . . Our love, after the many years of trials and tests through which it endured, was destined to fade. She had been in my life longer than any other woman and . . . was always loyal and steadfast.

Lucille's departure may have had more of an impact than his ghosted words suggest. He began drinking heavily again and turned over his car four times during the year, walking away from one accident near Elgin, Illinois, with a scalp wound that required twenty stitches.

He was not alone long. That autumn, he attended the races at Aurora, Illinois, and was introduced to two middle-aged white women from nearby Waukegan, Irene Marie Pineau, and her friend Helen Matthews. Both were impressed by what Pineau recalled as Johnson's "gentlemanly and courteous manner of speaking. He was a great deal more courtly than most men one meets." The following February, she sued her husband for divorce, and she and her friend began seeing Johnson together. "Miss Matthews and I became quite friendly with Mr. Johnson," Pineau continued, "and our friendship progressed rapidly, until it became an issue as to which one of us he liked best. It so happened that I was the favorite one. . . . The day came when I would have defied the world, and anybody in it, to separate us."

In June, Johnson was hospitalized with appendicitis. She nursed him day and night. They were married in Waukegan in August of 1925. "There could not be a man of any race," his bride said, "more worthy of being loved and honored than is my husband."

For one afternoon in a bullring at Nogales, Mexico, in May of 1926, it seemed that Johnson might somehow still revive his ring career. His opponent was Pat Lester, an Arizona-born twenty-four-year-old hopeful who was being brought along by Johnson's old acquaintance Spider Kelly. Lester had banged out seventeen wins in and around San Francisco over small-time fighters with names like Truck Hannah, Bombo Chevalier, and Frenchy the Coal Man, but the ringside reporter for the Universal Press Service was probably laying it on a little when he called Lester "the best heavyweight in the West."

Certainly, he had never faced anyone like Jack Johnson. Many years later, a sportswriter named David Beardsley remembered what he'd seen from ringside that afternoon: "Lester had youth, some finesse and a lot of bulk. He was half Johnson's age and before the fight he . . . seemed concerned about his elderly rival's health." Johnson seemed unconcerned about anything. He sat serenely in the shade of an umbrella until the referee began his instructions, then leaned forward, winked at the crowd, and held his glove to his ear as if too old to hear what was being said. Lester kept up furious shadowboxing while waiting for the bell. Johnson stood with his hands on his hips and his back to his opponent, surveying the steep tiers of spectators that rose to the top of the bullring wall.

At the bell, Lester rushed at the ex-champion as so many had before him. Johnson sidestepped, hit him three times, and tied him up. Johnson's stance, Beardsley remembered,

> was identical with [that] of the old London prize ring, lead foot just touching the scratch on the turf between the two fighters, body tilted as far back out of danger as waist muscles allowed, hands advanced, of course, in the prevailing style. Swaying straight back from an opponent's head shots is supposed to be a cardinal sin. I have known only two fighters to get away with it—Jack Johnson and Muhammad Ali.

"Archaic as this stance was," wrote Beardsley, it made Johnson seem impregnable.

> Although Lester threw a lot of punches, and with good steam, Johnson's forearms, elbows, shoulders were always a split second ahead, or Jack's open gloves would fall with feather touch on Pat's biceps and rob his chugging hooks of all power.
>
> Johnson would let his front foot slide forward until it was inside his opponent's lead foot. Then a sudden lunge and the old boy was on target. He had a trick that all but decapitated the bulging-jawed Lester about three times. He would rest his right forearm, glove up on Pat's chest, then drive upward with a thrust that began all the way back in his right buttock. . . .
>
> Lester was doubly frustrated. He couldn't cope with this senior citizen either in science or strength. Photographers called out "Bring him over here, Jack." This was when Johnson was holding aloft the struggling and almost tearful Lester, his body one vast blush.
>
> Between rounds, Johnson would stay on his stool until the rushing

Lester was standing over him, then he would rise [and render] futile everything Lester threw. Johnson was hit just three times in the whole fight—
body blows that h-u-u-r-t. But aside from that the old gentleman had a
good time.

The fight went fifteen rounds. According to Beardsley, Johnson won every
one of them. After the referee raised his hand, Johnson asked the ringside
reporter from Universal Press to be sure to say that he was "back on the
boards" and eager to fight Dempsey "or any other heavyweight."*

But Johnson was now forty-eight years old. Three weeks after beating Pat
Lester, he faced Bob "the Alabama Bearcat" Lawson in the bullring at Juárez.
This time, he was knocked down in the seventh and refused to come out for
the eighth, claiming he'd been fouled. The referee disagreed and gave the
decision to his young opponent on a technical knockout. In July, Johnson
lost a ten-round decision to Battling Norfolk. In September, he lost again, to
Brad Simmons at Ponca City, Oklahoma. "Johnson used his old-time tactics
of twitting his adversary in an effort to make him mad," Simmons' manager
remembered, "but this had no effect. Johnson did not have the wind."†

In October of 1926, Paul Robeson opened at the Comedy Theater on Broadway in a play based loosely on Johnson's career. Called *Black Boy*, it was written by Frank Dazey and Jim Tully, himself a former hobo and onetime club
fighter. It was not a flattering portrait. In the first act, Black Boy wanders into
a training camp a self-styled "peaceable nigger," who turns out to have a terrific wallop. A promoter who calls himself "Square Deal"—clearly a reference to Hugh "Huge Deal" McIntosh—turns him into a champion. In act 2,
the critic Brooks Atkinson wrote in the New York *Times*, the protagonist is
shown surrounded by " 'white buzzard' hangers-on at his Harlem apartment
and with Irene whom he worships as a white woman." (So as not to offend
the sensibilities of white theatergoers, Irene was played by the light-skinned
but safely Negro Fredi Washington.) In the third act, Atkinson continued,
the playwrights chronicled the collapse of their protagonist's "tinsel paradise,"

---

*In later years, Johnson would declare this victory his last "official" fight, conveniently rendering all
the less impressive ring appearances that followed mere "exhibitions."

†The previous month, in his own hometown of Drumright, Oklahoma, Simmons had ended the career
of forty-six-year-old Sam Langford. Langford was blind in the left eye by then—he'd fought at least
190 times—and very nearly so in the other. A first-round punch by Simmons destroyed what little
remained of Langford's vision, forcing him finally to leave the fight game.

but not before "they devote one scene to a drunken jollification on the eve of Black Boy's last bout, Negro musicians whoop up the jazz, Irene dances a Charleston, Black Boy sings, every one drinks, and dissipation flows like a tidal wave."

Paul Robeson got good notices, but the play lasted just a few weeks. The Pittsburgh *Courier* expressed regret that Broadway audiences had been treated to yet another portrayal of the Negro as an "ignorant, perverse child . . . [by whites] who evidently know . . . extraordinarily little of the psychology of Aframericans."*

The Johnsons agreed. The following April, Jim Tully wrote a once-over-very-lightly history of blacks in boxing for *Vanity Fair*. In it, Tully lauded his old friend Joe Gans for what he called his "humility and spirituality." But he dismissed Johnson as a "primitive" who, because his "capacity for affection was still that of a levee negro," had been unmoved by his first wife's suicide. Johnson had silently endured similar assaults in the past. But this was too much, and his new wife rose to his defense in a letter to the editor that eventually served as a preface to Johnson's autobiography:

Must a man, because of his color, be disparaged and ridiculed by every white man who takes pen in hand to scribble a story for the already over-prejudiced people? . . . You writers from whom words and stories flow so glibly, most times do not look beneath the surface to see the facts . . .

Have you any idea of the hours of misery and sorrow that Jack Johnson spent over this tragedy? Must he wear his heart on his sleeve for all the world to see? Is not accepting misery stoically a form of bravery? I think so. . . .

Black Boy was not the only play to be inspired by Johnson's struggles. Howard Sackler's *The Great White Hope* opened on Broadway in 1968. Its hero, "Jack Jefferson," was, as Randy Roberts has written, "Jack Johnson as he wished to be remembered." With James Earl Jones' magisterial performance as the embattled champion and Jane Alexander's sensitive portrayal of his tragic lover, it won the Tony, the Pulitzer Prize, and the New York Drama Critics Award.

It also profoundly affected Muhammad Ali, who saw, in the way the government pursued the protagonist because of the way he chose to conduct his private life, the precursor of the way it was pursuing him because of his refusal to register for the draft during the Vietnam War. "When Ali came to see the play and came backstage," Jones remembered, "he said, 'That's my story. You take out the issue of the white women and replace that with the issue of religion. That's my story.' He kept coming back. He kept bringing people back to see the play."

Drew "Bundini" Brown, Ali's confidant and cornerman, took up the cry, the late George Plimpton remembered, and in the midst of several of the champion's biggest fights Bundini was heard to shout, "Ghost in the house. Ghost in the house. Jack Johnson's here. Ghost in the house." Johnson "sort of overrides boxing," Plimpton said, "and the whole culture that surrounds it like some sort of a ghost. 'Ghost in the house.' " (Roberts, *Papa Jack*, p. 228; Ken Burns' film *Unforgivable Blackness*.)

He is quiet and gentle-spoken, contrary to your statement of his being "primitive." And in his head is more knowledge than most men can boast of.

Tully claimed that because Etta Johnson had married a black man, she had "seldom appeared [in public] without a shamed expression." Jack Johnson now had a wife, Irene Johnson continued, "who goes about with . . . a look of happy confidence and love in her eyes."

Two months later, Nat Fleischer, who had seen them all from Jim Corbett to Gene Tunney (who had taken Dempsey's title the previous summer), wrote that Jack Johnson had been the best counterpuncher and the best defensive fighter, the most crafty boxer and the possessor of the best uppercut in his division—and was therefore the "best all-around heavyweight in history." It was a view that Johnson devoutly shared and that Fleischer never saw any reason to change.

In July 1927, Johnson published his American autobiography, *Jack Johnson—In the Ring and Out,* in which, with the help of a ghostwriter named Bill Sims, he sought to redeem his reputation and recast himself as the man his most ardent admirers had wanted him to be. His Jack Johnson never told a lie and rarely lost a fight unless he'd wanted to; he had treated all women with respect and thought it best that young ladies not be permitted to go to nightclubs; he preferred "the splendid compositions of the old masters" to the "clever syncopation" of jazz—and urged his readers to eat more fruits and vegetables.

The book did not sell, and in Chicago in October, he was evicted from his apartment, and forced to file for bankruptcy. Among his outstanding bills, he said, was the $2,500 balance on $11,000 worth of jewelry he'd bought five years earlier, trying to keep Lucille from divorcing him. "I would have been able to pay my debts by receipts from a barnstorming trip," he explained, "but we hit a row of rainy days and nights, and had to call our exhibitions off."

He was in Winston-Salem, North Carolina, in September of 1928 when an Associated Press reporter asked him if he was going to continue boxing. "My next fight will be in politics," he said. "I am going to enter the ring on behalf of Al Smith, Democratic Presidential candidate." The Democrats were not pleased. The Catholic governor of New York was already viewed with suspicion by a good many of the white Protestant southerners without whom the Democrats could not win; an endorsement by Jack Johnson would do nothing to help bring them around. Senator Carter Glass of Virginia dashed off a letter to the Democratic National Committee chairman, John J. Raskob, asking if anyone had spoken to Johnson about organizing the Negro vote in the South. Raskob was quick to respond. "The story of Jack Johnson being authorized to speak on behalf of the Democratic National Committee," he said, "is cheap Republican propaganda. Johnson has no connection with this committee in any capacity." Johnson professed to be deeply wounded and came out for Herbert Hoover. "If the Democrats are so opposed to my working for them," he told a black reporter, "what can we expect if they win?"*

In the spring of 1929, a young reporter named James Thurber came to call on Johnson, on assignment for the "Talk of the Town" section of the *New Yorker*. As he always had, Johnson cooperated with the press—and, as nearly always happened, the final result was a condescending blend of truths, half-truths, and stereotypical distortion. Its title was "Big Boy."

> The tall, somewhat paunchy, but still erect figure of Jack Johnson may be seen about Broadway these days. He walks proudly. He never forgets his gloves. His step is a little less springy, and his face no longer gleams in the ebony and gold splendor which admiring Londoners compared to a "starry night" almost twenty years ago when he was the rage over there. He might pass for thirty-five. He was fifty-one on his last birthday. People turn to look at him as he walks majestically about the town, but most of them probably do not recognize the man many experts call the greatest heavyweight of them all. It is different from the day in 1911 when he sailed into New York on the *Kronprinzess Cecile* with a white valet, a white secretary, a limousine, a touring car, two racers, boasting of the prodigious amounts of his weekly hotel bills abroad. Crowds followed him around in the years of glory, but the once famous champion and notorious *bon vivant* has

---

*At Madison Square Garden the following year, Johnson happened to encounter New York Democratic Party chairman James A. Farley at ringside. "In this diplomatic crisis a strange expression overspread Mr. Farley's features," wrote Westbrook Pegler, who happened to be sitting nearby. "It was a far-away expression, such as cartoonists generally ascribe to a gentleman who has stooped to pick up a lady's glove and heard his trousers rip." But in the end, Farley offered his hand and Johnson took it, smiling with pleasure. Johnson and the Democrats eventually made peace, and after FDR's election in 1932, he was sometimes called upon by the party to explain to Negro voters the advantages of abandoning their traditional Republican loyalties and rallying to the New Deal. "Franklin Roosevelt is champion now," he said in his stock speech, "and he is wearing the belt. Abraham Lincoln was a good fighter in his prime but he can't help us now. Always string along with the champion." The reason Jim Jeffries lost at Reno, he sometimes added, was that Jeffries was a Republican. (Washington *Post*, November 2, 1934.)

fallen on less glamorous days. He is not broke, but he is not affluent. Wealth he never hoarded. The fifty-one hundred dollars he got for boxing Philadelphia Jack O'Brien before the war, for instance, he spent in four days, on dinners, a ring, and an auto. Now, he is eager to sell stories of his life for money. Unlike the ordinary celebrity, he has not one but three autobiographies in mind, the story of his fights, the story of his loves and the story of his travels. If you are interested in buying these works, you can get the lot of them for one hundred thousand dollars. Jack Johnson lives in Harlem, gets around to the prize-fights, takes in the shows, some of which he sternly criticizes as immoral.

We called on the old champion at the offices of his agents in a building way over in the West Forties. He sat in a swivel chair behind a desk, gesturing every now and then with a big, banded cigar, closing his eyes to listen, opening them wide when he talked. His plans are uncertain, but he may go into vaudeville as he did some years back, or he may fight some more obscure fights as he has been doing off and on for several years, for small profits in the West and Southwest. He won a match in 1926 but was knocked out the following year by an unknown colored boxer named Bearcat Wright of Omaha, tasting the bitter cup that he himself handed to Fitzsimmons in 1907 and the groggy Jeffries in 1910. He still thinks he could lick Tunney, and that Dempsey would be easy. ("Dempsey is one o' dem slashin' boys, and de slashin' boys is mah meat.") Corbett is the only white heavyweight for whom he has any real respect and the only one he calls "Mistah." It saddens him to recall that Mistah Corbett picked Jeffries to win on that Fourth of July nearly twenty years ago.

Some people have the notion that Johnson is still legally banned from America. He gave himself up in 1920, however, and served ten months in Leavenworth for violation of the Mann Act, after evading sentence for seven years, living abroad. He is free to come and go. The churches and the women's clubs, which made his heyday miserable, have forgotten him. The death of his first white wife, and his subsequent marriage to another white woman, are vague memories. Proof of this was given, not long ago, when Johnson was cheered by the clergy at a general conference of the Methodist Church in Kansas City at which he denounced liquor saying, "To serve God you must train the mind as well as the soul." His Café de Champion in Chicago was padlocked some years ago.

Johnson enjoys recalling the old times. He loves to talk of his favorite city, Budapest, and of the time at the start of the war when the Germans did not molest several trunks containing all his wife's sables. During the war, he says, he did secret-service work in Spain, at the request of a Major Lang, U.S.A. Of his "deeper life" he is proud and sensitive. "Ah am," he says, "a very tendah man." He likes to display his hands and face to show how unscarred they are by battle. There is no mark on his head. His skull was X-rayed in San Francisco eighteen years ago. It took five and a half minutes for the rays to go through, as against the customary five to fifteen seconds. The bone was found to be from a half to three-quarters of an inch thick, which is thicker than the skull of an ox. Surgeons said that a blow which would fell a steer would simply jar Mr. Johnson.*

We were going to ask him about the time Ketchel knocked him down but thought better of it. Anyway, the old boy probably remembers only that a few seconds later he knocked the gallant middleweight into the next county. We inquired about Mr. Johnson's literary tastes, and he said that he enjoys the books of Richard Harding Davis. Apparently he has never heard Paul Robeson sing. At any rate, he told us he had never met him. We found ourselves on dangerous ground when we brought up the name of [master tap dancer] Bill Robinson. Jack's eyes had been closed, but they opened quickly and shone like the headlights of a Pierce Arrow. "Nevah mention Bill Robinson in the same breath with Jack Johnson," he warned us. "When he takes off his dancin' shoes he is through, whereas Ah am a deep an' culluhful personality."

Jack Johnson is living up on 148th Street now, no longer in the magnificent style of the years of his grandeur. He once had an apartment in New York that you reached by walking over an expensive, deep and colorful crimson plush carpet. Legend has it that the day Johnson took up residence there, the carpet was stretched all the way out to the curb. But those were the great days of the dimming past, the days when Li'l Arthuh owned a white Mercedes racing car, hired white people to serve him, and was feared by every white heavyweight prize-fighter in the world.

In December, Johnson was filmed leading an orchestra at a place called the Checkers Club in Harlem. He is in evening clothes, wearing patent leather shoes with velvet bows. He speaks directly to the camera, declaiming in his now-familiar short phrases.

---

*Thurber dug up this vintage bit of racist nonsense from a newspaper morgue. Since few opponents ever managed to hit Johnson in the head, it's hard to see how this alleged anomaly helped his career.

Ladies and gentlemen,
I have been requested by many
To tell you just how
I knocked out
So many of my oh-pponents.
As far as I am concerned that day is past.
I have a new way of knocking them out
And I will show you.

Then the eleven-piece band breaks into "Tiger Rag" and Johnson pretends to lead it, baton in hand. The musicians seem amiably disposed toward him but pay little actual attention as he begins a lumbering soft-shoe and manages to end with an uppercut more or less at the same moment they reach the tune's climax. The band and the club lasted just long enough for Johnson to give his profession as "orchestra leader" when the police pulled him over in January 1931 for racing down Central Park West at forty-four miles an hour.

Two months later, he was back barnstorming the Midwest with Brad Simmons, who had beaten him the previous year. In Tulsa, Simmons outpointed him again in a ten-round contest that left Johnson gasping for air. That evidently didn't go down well with the former champion, who must have spoken sharply to his overeager employee; according to *The Ring*, six days later in Wichita, Kansas, "Jack Johnson made a few voodoo passes at Brad Simmons in the second round . . . and Brad swooned and passed out." The Wichita *Eagle* agreed: "Nothing of the great master of other days was apparent in the quick fiasco which ended when Brad Simmons . . . curled up in the second round. . . . Johnson was puffing with exertion. . . . Someone said afterwards that Simmons didn't feel well and quit. No one gave much credence to the Johnson knockout punch." Two days later, the pair were barred from ever fighting again in Topeka.

Summer 1932 found him living in Los Angeles, running a place called the Club Alabam, next to the Dunbar Hotel on Central Avenue. He got a few days' work in Hollywood as a bit player alongside Tom Sharkey and the wrestler Stanislaus Zbyszko in a Jack Oakie comedy, *Madison Square Garden*. In its climactic brawl, in which Sharkey, Zbyszko, and other former ring stars polish off gangsters trying to take over the fight game, Johnson alone never throws a punch. A quarter of a century after Reno, Hollywood evidently still thought it best not to let Jack Johnson be seen hitting a white man onscreen.

He continued to fight occasional exhibitions up and down the West Coast.

He went three rounds at the Olympic Auditorium in Los Angeles with Ernest Bendy, a promising young black heavyweight who called himself Dynamite Jackson; toyed with Chief White Horse at Oakland; outclassed Bob Frazie in Seattle. But when he signed to face a more serious-seeming opponent, the six-foot-eight-inch "Portuguese Giant," Joe Santa, the California boxing commission refused to sanction the bout. Letting Johnson fight someone like Santa, its chairman said, would be "a crying shame. We gave Johnson an exhibition permit on the understanding that he was to go in with the right kind of sparring partners. We won't let him be matched with young men who might like to make a reputation by knocking him out. The title he once held should protect him against that." Johnson demanded a hearing in Sacramento, only to be told that his age alone made him "physically unfit" to fight seriously in California. "Physically unfit!" he said. "Why man alive there isn't a man on the board nor in this city of Sacramento who is in better shape physically than I. I may be a little round around the belly, but I'm hard as a rock." The commission was unmoved.

The Club Alabam soon went under—Johnson's fondness for locking the doors in the early morning hours and letting everyone inside be his guest hadn't helped receipts—and when the staff sued him for back wages, he fled the state rather than appear in court to answer the charges.

In December of 1932, Johnson and Irene set sail for Europe. He planned to appear in a series of exhibitions in Paris, he told the press, then head for Berlin, where he said he had had an offer to open a boxing school.

On January 2, he sparred one round each with two young European heavyweights, Maurice Griselle and Ernst Guehring in the French capital, and was given "a tremendous ovation as he left the ring." Afterward, the Johnsons headed for Bricktop's, the elegant cabaret run by the entertainer Ada Smith, who'd received her first big break at his Café de Champion in Chicago. "You had to come up a flight of stairs to get into Bricktop's," she remembered, "but you still weren't inside once you got there.

First, the big patent-leather curtains had to be parted. Whenever they [were,] everyone in the room would turn around to see who it was. On the night that they parted and Jack Johnson stood there with his last wife . . . the room went into an uproar. There was no mistaking those broad shoulders and that big wonderful smile of the Champ. I flew over to him and threw my arms around him . . .

He came in night after night. No one ever created the commotion Jack Johnson did when the curtains parted and he stood there. His prestige in the world at large may have dropped, but Jack the Champ still stopped traffic out on the street and up in Bricktop's. People like Josephine Baker, Maurice Chevalier and Mistinguette would come into my place asking if Jack Johnson was coming in. . . . Even Cole Porter, who never got excited over nothing or no one, watched those curtains . . . to see if Jack Johnson was coming through them. . . .

Jack and his wife came to my house nearly every night for dinner. . . . One night . . . my butler called me aside and said, "Madame Bricktop, Monsieur Johnson is on his fourth or fifth chicken." I told him to tell the cook to give the Champ fourteen chickens if he wanted them. . . .

If anybody ever made me feel proud of who and what I am, it was Jack. He bowed to no one, yet everything was "yes," "no," "please," and "thank you." His behavior only made stronger my belief that you're either born with "it," or you're not. Greatness comes from knowing who he is, being satisfied with nothing but the best, and still behaving like a warm, gracious human being.

The Johnsons evidently never got much beyond Paris. Adolf Hitler was within weeks of winning power in Germany, and even Jack Johnson may have viewed the prospects for a black-run boxing enterprise in Berlin under the Nazis less than bright.

Johnson was back in Chicago in the summer of 1934, appearing in Dave Barry's Garden of Champions, a sort of sideshow at the Century of Progress International Exposition organized by a veteran referee to compete with such attractions as the Midget Village, Sally Rand's Balloon Dance, and the Aunt Jemima Cabin. For a dollar, children could throw punches at Jack Johnson while he ducked and laughed and popped his eyes. One evening, he fought an exhibition there against Tom Sharkey, whose sparring partner he had briefly been back in 1901. It was supposed to be a nonviolent sparring session, but the old brawler was incapable of pretending. He rushed at Johnson, murder in his eyes. Nothing much had changed in thirty-three years. Sharkey still couldn't hit him. Johnson tied him up, and winked at the audience. "What you aim to do to me, Tom?" he asked, grinning and pinioning Sharkey's arms. "What you tryin' to do?"

Johnson took off the evening of July 4. A twenty-year-old Negro named

Joe Louis from Detroit was making his professional debut at Bacon's Casino, and Johnson didn't want to miss it. Even he now knew that his ring career was over. The novelty of seeing him onstage had long since worn off, and vaudeville was dying, in any case. None of his other moneymaking enterprises had paid off. He needed a meal ticket, and if this young Golden Gloves winner from Detroit was as good as people said he was, he might be just what Johnson had been looking for.

Born Joseph Louis Barrow on May 13, 1914, almost a year after Jack Johnson's flight to Canada, Louis was an Alabama sharecropper's son raised by his mother in a Detroit neighborhood called Black Bottom. His managers were two Negro real estate men: John Roxborough and Julian Black. Both were streetwise—Roxborough was also a successful numbers operator; Black ran a casino—but neither knew much about the fight game. For boxing expertise, they'd turned to a veteran Chicago-based trainer, Jack Blackburn.

Jack Johnson hated Blackburn. Blackburn, a wiry, hot-tempered, hard-drinking man with a razor scar across one cheek, hated Johnson. Blackburn said it all began in early 1908 when Johnson had swaggered into a Philadelphia gym with several admiring women and called for someone to spar with him. Blackburn stepped forward, though he was only a lightweight, and, as he told it, managed to bewilder Johnson with his skill and speed, bloodying his nose and parrying everything the increasingly embarrassed heavyweight threw back at him.* Johnson left the gym in a rage. The following year, Blackburn found himself behind bars for manslaughter—he had killed a former friend and wounded the man's mistress in a street fight—and asked Johnson to come see him in jail and help raise money to mount a legal appeal. Johnson took pleasure in turning him down. "Let the son of a bitch stay in jail," he said.

Blackburn was pardoned in 1914, but while he kept fighting and mostly winning for nine more years, he never managed to reestablish himself as a serious contender. As a trainer, he worked almost exclusively with white fighters and was reluctant at first to take on a Negro novice, even one as promising as Louis. Colored heavyweights were a dime a dozen, he said. Just as in Johnson's day, there was nowhere for them to go. And, Blackburn believed, Johnson himself was to blame. He might have opened the door when he beat Tommy Burns, but the way he behaved once the title was his had slammed

---

*Blackburn was a remarkable fighter, so remarkable that men like Stanley Ketchel, Billy Papke, and Battling Nelson thought it wise to avoid him. He fought at least 163 times and lost only 10.

it shut again. Blackburn made that clear to Louis during one of their first meetings:

> You know, boy, the heavyweight division for a Negro is hardly likely. The white man ain't too keen on it. You have to be something to go anywhere. If you really ain't gonna be another Jack Johnson, you got some hope. White man hasn't forgotten that fool nigger with his white women, acting like he owned the world.*

Blackburn carefully chose Louis' first professional opponent, a sturdy white journeyman named Jack Kracken, whom Louis felled in less than two minutes. Afterward, Johnson was invited up into the ring to say a few words. The mostly black crowd expected to hear some encouragement for the newcomer from the sport's black elder statesman. They didn't get it. The young man *might* make a good fighter someday, Johnson said. But a big punch wasn't enough. Louis needed better training: his stance was all wrong; he didn't move his feet correctly. The crowd began to get restless. One or two began to boo. Johnson kept right on. He was used to hostile audiences, though until now they'd always been white. Above all, he said, Louis needed a new trainer. Jack Blackburn would never do.

Johnson loathed Blackburn, but he couldn't deny that the man's protégé was impressive. In his first eleven months as a professional Louis thumped out twenty-two straight victories (with eighteen knockouts). In June of 1935, he reached the big time, a fight with the ex-heavyweight champion Primo Carnera at Yankee Stadium. He had earned $750 from his last fight; the Carnera bout promised more than $60,000. Jack Johnson, reduced for the moment to peddling "Old Champ L'il Arthur Gin—The Gin That'll Make You Smile," wanted a piece of the action. He drove up to Louis' training camp at Pompton Lakes, New Jersey, and introduced himself to the newcomer.

"It was thrilling to meet Johnson," Louis remembered. He'd heard stories about him since boyhood. "I liked him. He never mentioned the problems he was having. . . . He was an impressive-looking guy and a good talker. He

---

*Johnson must have found Blackburn's piety on this point especially galling. The razor scar on his cheek had been put there in 1908 by his brother Fred after an argument over Blackburn's alleged fondness for white women, and the common-law wife in whose defense Jack Blackburn said he had shot two people in 1908 had been white as well. Nor did the prosperity Joe Louis' success brought Blackburn do much for his behavior. After a drunken brawl in 1935, he staggered home to get his pistol, returned, and opened fire, hitting two bystanders: an elderly man, who died, and a nine-year-old girl, who was badly wounded. Mysteriously, no charges against him were ever filed.

told me I was going to run into every kind of situation possible, and he warned me to keep my head at all times." After Johnson left, a newspaperman asked Louis what he thought about the way the older man had lived his life. "Every man's got a right to his own mistakes," Louis said. "Ain't no man that ain't made any."

Johnson took to hanging out at the Renaissance Restaurant, Louis' Harlem headquarters on Seventh Avenue, where, a writer for the *Amsterdam News* noted, he "imbibed with joy the looks of respect and wonder" the hangers-on gave him. He was back at the center of things and full of praise for Louis, who most experts predicted would lose. Carnera, a former circus strong man who stood six and a half feet tall and weighed 275 pounds, was simply too big. Johnson begged to differ. "Louis has the stuff," he said. "He oughta win. I reckon he'll win."

Louis did win, knocking the oversized Carnera down three times. ("He went down slowly," wrote John Kieran, in the New York *Times* the next day "like a great chimney that had been dynamited.") Afterwards, Johnson elbowed his way into the victor's dressing room, pounded him on the back, and shouted, "Boy, you're the greatest fighter in the last twenty-five years!" Much of Harlem celebrated that night, its pleasure amplified by the triumph of a black man over an Italian just as fascist Italy was about to march into Ethiopia. And Johnson celebrated with it, leading the crowds in cheers for Joe Louis.

A day or two later, Johnson made his move. He called on John Roxborough with a business proposition. "I can make a champion out of that boy if you turn him over to me," he said. Blackburn, of course, would have to go. Roxborough turned on him. "He cursed Johnson out," Louis recalled, "told him how he had held up the progress of the Negro people for years with his attitude, how he was a low-down, no-good nigger and told him he wasn't welcome in my camp anymore."

Stung, Johnson took his case to the newspapers. Louis was just a "flash in the pan," he said now. Even at fifty-seven he could beat him—and Carnera, too. The younger man read the story and couldn't believe it. "I respected this man; he had come to my training camp and all. It really disappointed me." A few weeks later, Johnson turned up again at Pompton Lakes, where Louis was getting ready to fight a second ex-champion, Max Baer. Louis spotted him in the bleachers and refused to enter the ring to spar until he left. "Get that black cat out of here," he muttered to his handlers. "I don't want him in my camp." Johnson returned to his car and drove back to the city. A few weeks later, he turned up again. *Life* magazine wanted a photograph of Johnson and Louis together. This time, Julian Black ordered Johnson away; no such picture would be taken. From then on, Jack Johnson would remain a relentless critic of the rising star.

As Joe Louis punched his way through the heavyweights, hoping to win a chance at the title, two Jack Johnsons haunted him. One was the real man—middle-aged, down on his luck, envious of anyone getting attention he insisted should be his, an irritant but not a real obstacle. The other was the grinning specter of the gaudy figure he once had been. *That* Jack Johnson threatened to bar him and all other Negro heavyweights from the championship.

The treatment Louis received from the white press was more respectful than that which Johnson had had to endure, but not by much. Cartoonists portrayed him as a stereotypical "darkey," precisely as they had Johnson. His race remained a central element of nearly every story. He was the "Brown Bomber," the "Dark Destroyer," the "Sepia Slugger." Everything he said was translated into Uncle Remus dialect. Paul Gallico of the New York *Daily News*, one of the more sympathetic sportswriters, nonetheless felt free to say that Louis "lives like an animal, fights like an animal, has all the cruelty and ferocity of a wild thing."

If he were to get a shot at the title, Louis' handlers told him, he had to be made to seem as different from Johnson as possible. He was forbidden to smile in the ring, or to say anything unkind about an opponent, or to exult in victory. And he was never to be photographed with white women.* Louis liked cars, just as Johnson had; to be sure there would be no headlines about speeding tickets, Roxborough and Black hired him a chauffeur. "One time," he remembered, "we were talking about these little black toy dolls they used to make of fighters. Those dolls always had the wide grin with thick red lips. They looked foolish. I got the message—don't look like a fool nigger doll. Look like a black man with dignity." Louis wouldn't eat watermelon or fried chicken for the cameras, refused to pretend to shoot craps.

---

*"They never told me not to go out with white women," Louis remembered, "they said don't ever get your picture taken with one—that would be the end of my career." This was an important distinction for him. Like Johnson, he was a magnet for women of every color. Among those with whom he had discreet but intimate relationships were said to have been the film star Lana Turner and the Norwegian skater and actress Sonja Henie.

Louis demolished Max Baer on September 24, 1935. That same day, he married Marva Trotter. She was lovely and slender—and reassuringly black. Afterward, he promised a Negro reporter that he would "never disgrace the Race." Even Louis' mother joined the chorus. "If Joe becomes champion," she told a reporter, "he's going to make Jack Johnson ashamed of himself all over again."

It is little wonder, then, that Johnson came to see every Joe Louis victory, every sports-page paean to the young boxer's alleged humility and exemplary private life, as a personal slap at him. Every time Louis was called "a credit to his race," the implication was that Jack Johnson had been a discredit to it.

On June 19, 1936, Louis was to face his third former heavyweight champion, Max Schmeling of Germany. Schmeling was considered over-the-hill and more or less an easy mark for Louis, who entered the ring at Yankee Stadium a 10-to-1 favorite. But Johnson disagreed. "Louis holds his left too low," he told everyone who would listen, "and the first fellow who makes him step back and then throws a right at his chin will knock him out." He was right, and Johnson was at ringside to see it. Schmeling hit Louis with overhand rights all evening, and in the twelfth round, groggy and bewildered, he was knocked out. His steady march toward a title shot had been halted by the German veteran, just as Johnson's had been by Marvin Hart twenty-seven years earlier.

Johnson couldn't have been more pleased. He'd bet heavily on Schmeling, and after collecting his winnings he headed uptown with a fat roll, which he insisted on waving around as he walked along 125th Street. Black fans who had already taken out their disappointment on several whites who had happened to stray into Harlem—five had been sent to the hospital—were not amused by Johnson's noisy celebrating. An angry crowd surrounded him. Punches were thrown. Policemen had to be called to rescue Jack Johnson from the people who had once lined the same street to cheer him.

Louis fans were unforgiving. Months later, when Johnson was introduced from the ring at a charity boxing show in Harlem, the crowd rose to its feet to jeer him. "Once the hero of his race, he is now the most despised man in it," the Pittsburgh *Courier* reported. "Jack Johnson felt the full brunt of his own people's disapproval of him. Johnson attempted to make a speech, but such a salvo of boos greeted him, he stood in embarrassment for five minutes, while the crowd refused to give him a chance to talk." The *Amsterdam News* headlined its story JACK JOHNSON RAZZED—AGAIN.

Johnson was unrepentant. White people had never been able to make him change his mind or alter his behavior. Black people couldn't, either. When James J. Braddock unexpectedly granted Joe Louis a shot at his championship—the first time a white champion had given a Negro challenger a chance to fight for the title since Tommy Burns faced Jack Johnson twenty-nine years earlier—Johnson not only continued to denigrate the black challenger but volunteered to help train the white champion. "Jack Johnson was still running his mouth," Louis recalled. "He was telling anybody and any paper who'd listen to him that Braddock had everything in his favor, and what he lacked, Johnson'd bone him up on it. He'd advise Braddock from his corner [just as Corbett had counseled Jeffries at Reno], and this would unnerve me. With all his talking and such, Braddock never hired him. Nobody likes a poor, sore-ass loser."

The champion could have used the help. On June 22, 1937, at Comiskey Park in the heart of the Chicago black belt that had once hailed Jack Johnson as its hero, Joe Louis battered Braddock for seven rounds and knocked him out in the eighth to become heavyweight champion of the world. A big crowd was waiting outside when the champion and his wife got home. One black man shouted his thanks to God that "we got another chance!" Another called out, "Don't be another Jack Johnson."*

As Joe Louis reached the pinnacle that year, Jack Johnson slid further toward the bottom. A small-time promoter named Morris Botwen sued him for $360.90 for failing to promote "Old Champ Liniment" as he had promised. "I figured out the formula years ago," Johnson told the judge. "I have given it away to friends for years, and they all say it will cure toothaches, headaches, or any other kind of ache. I just refused to make personal appearances for Botwen because I didn't think the stuff he was making was the same as my product." Then a man named Alex Sachs sued him to get back his $619 deposit for a coat-room and cigar-stand concession in a new Fifty-second Street nightclub that never materialized.

That same year, Johnson began what would be an annual thirty-five-

---

*The integration of heavyweight championship boxing took an unconscionably long time, but it took less time than did the integration of other big-time sports. The first black football players did not take the field for the old All-America Football Conference until 1946. Jack Robinson did not play for the Brooklyn Dodgers until 1947. And it was not until 1962 that Charlie Sifford was allowed to join the Professional Golfers' Association.

dollar-a-week run at Hubert's Museum and Flea Circus, a cellar sideshow just off Times Square.* Brooks Atkinson wrote:

> When the culture quotient of 42nd Street began to decline during the thirties the Flea Circus was blamed. It was rated as one step lower than the burlesque houses, which in turn were the poor farm of the theater. . . . By the time 42nd Street had become the most depraved corner of the Broadway district, patrolled day and night by male and female prostitutes, Hubert's Museum was the ranking cultural institution.

There were pool tables and pinball machines on the first floor, and punching bags young men could batter for a dime. For ten cents more, they could peer into a movie machine and see Jack Dempsey beat Luis Firpo or lose to Gene Tunney. There were no films of Jack Johnson, winning or losing.

To see Johnson in person, visitors had to pay a quarter, a writer named Linton Baldwin remembered. Yellowing newspaper clippings from Johnson's career were taped to a booth in which a bored hawker sat making change without looking up from his *Daily Mirror*. Visitors pushed through a little turnstile, made their way down a flight of stairs, and took their seats in the dank, dimly lit cellar. One dreary act followed another—a sword-swallower, a trick dog, a half-man-half-woman, Congo the Wild Man, Sealo the Seal-Finned Boy. Finally, a paunchy little man in shirtsleeves stepped in front of the curtain. "Ladies and gentlemen," he said, "here to answer your questions about boxing, training and the world of sports is the former heavyweight champion of the world—Jack Johnson."

Johnson stepped smoothly onstage, wearing a blue beret, a blue tie, and a worn but sharply cut suit. He held a glass of red wine with a straw in it. He smiled and asked his visitors what they would like to know.

An elderly man asked who had given him his toughest fight.

"Sam Langford could step around right well."

He grinned when his questioner said he'd been there in Chelsea, Massachusetts, in 1906 to see it happen.

"How do you think you would have done against Joe Louis?"

"I'd have done okay." He sucked on the straw. "On the whole I don't think modern fighters are as good as the old boys were."

---

*It was owned and operated by "Professor" Roy Heckler, the son of William Heckler, whom the magic historian Ricky Jay calls "the doyen of the American flea world." (Jay, *Anomalies*, p. 41.)

Had hard-living and dissipation undercut his career?
He didn't much like the question.

I made a million and a half dollars in the ring. I've still got some of it left.
I have one of the nicest Bugattis you've ever seen in the parking lot down
the street. As for dissipation, I fought my last official fight when I was forty-
eight . . . and won it. I can honestly say that I never overindulged in overeat-
ing, overdrinking or in any other way.

He'd always exercised, he said, taken long walks, gotten plenty of sleep and
eaten plenty of the bananas that he believed gave him strength.

Someone asked about alcohol. When not taken in excess he said, "it is beneficial. . . . It's heat producing and invigorating. A glass of wine—not too
cold—is an excellent aid to weak stomachs and I believe good beer, in mod-
eration, is health building. Does that answer your question, sir?"

It did. A smirking man asked, "How about the Willard fight?"

Johnson's face betrayed nothing. "The Willard fight?"

"Yeah, you know. Did you dump it?"

"You saw the picture didn't you?" Johnson said. Then, "Thank you for your
attention," and he was gone.

Joe Louis continued to win—and Johnson continued to scoff at his skills. "It
didn't do him much good," Louis recalled. He was working at Hubert's
Museum, "and by my standards that ain't shit. And the black people who were
rallying around me put him down for talking against me."

When the champion signed to fight Max Schmeling again in the spring of
1938, Johnson was the only one of ten living ex-champions to predict that
the German would win again. "Everybody thinks I'm jealous of Joe Louis,"
he told Nat Fleischer, "but it ain't so. Louis, to me, is the hardest hitter that
ever fought, but I still think his stance is all wrong."

After Louis demolished Schmeling in two minutes and four seconds of
the first round, Johnson tried to get right with the Negro public. "I want to
say here," he told a reporter after the fight, "that I think Joe's victory has done
the race a lot of good and has improved race relations in every field of
endeavor." But in an article about Louis' victory for the Pittsburgh *Courier*,
he did his best to redirect the focus back where he was always sure it
belonged—on himself. In his day, he wrote,

intense race hatred burned everywhere. White people were inclined to
think that the victory of a black man over a white man was indicative of

the racial superiority of the Negro race, but today they think differently and more sanely. We might call this a development of mental processes. But I think the sociologists of the future will be able to trace this change to my fight with Jeffries. They finally decided that my fight with Jeffries was merely a fight between two men and had nothing to do with racial superiority. As soon as this point was driven home, the road was paved for Joe Louis to come along and fight for the heavyweight championship. . . . If you want to know the truth, these thoughts were on my mind when I met Jess Willard in Havana. I was thinking of the Joe Louises who were to come along in my wake. I didn't want to make the road harder for them.

Johnson continued privately to try to make the road as hard as possible for Joe Louis. He helped train a six-foot-five white hope named Abe Simon, only to see him toppled by the champion in thirteen rounds in one fight and six in the rematch, and he later took the veteran Jersey Joe Walcott aside to volunteer his services if and when Louis gave Walcott a chance. "Johnson's background wasn't savory," Walcott remembered. "I knew that whatever fame I might win would be in his shadow. I did not want to march arm in arm to success with him." He turned Johnson down.*

In June of 1943, billed as THE CHAMPION OF ALL CHAMPIONS, THE IMMORTAL JACK JOHNSON, he appeared every evening for a week at Fred Irvin's Gymnasium on 116th Street in New York, sparring three rounds with young heavyweights. "Johnson has stated," reported the *Amsterdam News*, "that he does not want any of the men he will meet to have respect for his age. If they want to slug, he says that he will slug; if they want to box, he'll meet them on their ground."

In March of the following year, he and Jess Willard sparred genially for servicemen in Los Angeles. Current heavyweights "got plenty of nothin'," he said afterward, and he talked of organizing an old-fashioned medicine show to tour the country and sell a line of liniments and salves with his initials on the containers. He also appeared on a West Coast radio interview show with Tor Johnson, a bald, three-hundred-pound wrestler who billed himself as the

---

*As later as 1963, some black boxers were still blaming Johnson for the difficulties they faced getting big-money fights. "We're still paying for him," light heavyweight champion Archie Moore told the sportswriter Al Stump that year. "The man was a disaster to anyone who came near him." (Stump, "Black Avenger.")

"Super Swedish Angel." The host, sportswriter Al Stump, asked each guest how he'd lost his hair.

"The Angel said he'd lost his slipping headlocks," Stump recalled.

"And you, Jack?"

"Lost mine makin' babies."

In 1945, Clem Boddington, a small-time Manhattan promoter, arranged for Johnson and his old friend Joe Jeannette to put on the gloves one more time in the ballroom of the Henry Hudson Hotel to raise money for Liberty Bonds. Johnson was sixty-seven and Jeannette sixty-four. Harry Wills was to act as referee.

The night before, Jeannette called Boddington to say he couldn't come. He was running a limousine service in Jersey City. There had been an accident involving one of his cars, and he was required to appear in court. The promoter called Mayor Frank Hague and got the court date postponed. Then Johnson called. He, too, had to go court, he said. A car dealer was suing him.

How'd it happen?

"It was like this," Johnson said. "I bought a car in California and made the first payment. After I drove it here, the finance company got hot under the collar and wanted me to fork over a second payment."

What was wrong with that?

"I told them that since deterioration had set in since the first payment there would have to be some adjustment made."

Boddington somehow got Johnson's Manhattan court date set aside as well, and the old masters put on a good show for three rounds. Afterward, Johnson made an impassioned speech calling on the crowd to buy bonds. They did—nearly $15,000 worth. When the crowd had filed out of the ballroom, Johnson asked Boddington for twenty-five dollars and a dozen bottles of gin. He got his money plus two bottles and an invitation to Boddington's home for dinner. Two former bantamweights, Terry Young and Packey O'Gatty, came, too, and after the table had been cleared they asked the old champion if he thought he could keep them from hitting him. Johnson just grinned. They moved the furniture, Boddington remembered; Johnson took off his jacket, then picked off every punch while he "conversed with my wife as if he had nothing else to consider."

On Monday June 3, 1946, Johnson dropped by Nat Fleischer's office at *The Ring*. He had a big check and was waving it around. "This," he told the editor, "is the beginning of a new era for your pal, Jack Johnson." Fleischer was glad to see him, even if he'd heard it all before. Johnson was on his way south by car, back to his native Texas, where he was to perform for a few days with a traveling tent show—punching a bag, telling his stories, and passing out signed photographs to old fans and well-wishers.

His opinion of his own skills had not lessened with time. Nor had his assessment of Joe Louis' skills risen. "In my humble opinion," he told Fleischer in an interview that appeared in the issue of *The Ring* on the newsstands just as he started south, "not only could I have whipped Joe when I was at my best, but I'll name Sam Langford, Jeffries, Corbett, Choynski, Tom Sharkey, Fitz and Tommy Ryan among some of the old timers who would have taken Joe into camp." Louis was to meet light heavyweight champion Billy Conn for a second time at Yankee Stadium on June 19. Conn had outboxed Louis in their first fight in 1941 and might have won, had apparent success not gone to his head; in the thirteenth round he'd made the fatal error of mixing it up with Louis and been knocked cold. "I still think [Louis's] fighting stance is all wrong," Johnson said. "He must knock Conn out in six rounds or that sour stance will get him so tired that Conn will come out the winner." Johnson wanted to be back in town to see it, and Fleischer promised him a ringside seat as his guest.

He was on his way back from Texas on the evening of June 9 when he pulled into a diner just outside Raleigh, North Carolina. With him was a young man named Fred L. Cook whom he had hired to relieve him at the wheel when he got tired. "They told us we could eat in the back or not at all," Cook remembered. "We were hungry and the food had already been served, so we ate. But back in the car, Jack really got angry."

Johnson took the wheel of his latest high-powered automobile, a Lincoln Zephyr, and roared north along Highway One at better than seventy miles an hour. Hurtling around a sharp curve near the little town of Franklinton, he didn't see the truck rushing toward him until it was too late. He lost control. The car swerved across the white line, left the road, and slammed into a telephone pole.

Fred Cook was thrown clear and survived.

Jack Johnson died in the hospital some three hours later.

His funeral was held in Chicago at the Pilgrim Baptist Church on South Indiana Avenue, just a couple of blocks from the home he'd bought for his mother thirty-seven years before. He would have liked the venue, a big, richly ornamented former synagogue designed by Louis Sullivan and celebrated for its gospel choir. The turnout was impressive, too: twenty-five hundred people were seated inside, and thousands more stood outside to say goodbye. But he would not have relished the Reverend Junius Caesar Austin's funeral sermon. It paid tribute to Johnson's fearlessness, but it also placed him in a supporting role. "He struck the first blow as the heavyweight champion," Austin said, "and had it not been for a fighter like Jack, there might not have been a fighter like Joe."

Afterward, a gleaming hearse bore Johnson's casket slowly northward. Behind it, heavily veiled in black, Irene Pineau Johnson rode alone. A long line of automobiles filled with old friends followed her. The cortège moved slowly along Lake Shore Drive to the gates of Graceland Cemetery, then wound its way past the tombs and mausoleums of some of Chicago's most prominent citizens, toward the stone obelisk where the champion would be buried next to Etta Duryea Johnson.

The press had never hung back when it came to Jack Johnson, and at the graveside, a reporter dared ask his widow just what it was she had loved about her husband. "I loved him because of his courage," she answered. "He faced the world unafraid. There wasn't anybody or anything he feared."

ACKNOWLEDGMENTS

Those who write about boxing often work too hard to find high-minded reasons for the visceral pleasure they take in watching two total strangers try to batter one another senseless. Even A. J. Liebling, the undefeated heavyweight champion among boxing essayists, could be uncharacteristically portentous about it. A boxer, "like a writer," he once intoned, "must stand alone."

In writing this book I was never alone for a moment. The idea for the documentary from which it grew came from my friend and fellow fight-fan, Dave Schaye, more than a decade ago; his enthusiasm for Jack Johnson and his story has never flagged over the years. Ken Burns' decision to make the film got me started; more than twenty years of working with him have only made me more glad to know him.

Boxing is a tough, unforgiving game, but I have found boxing fans—at least those who share my fascination with the sport's history—generous and welcoming. Six of them were central to writing this book:

Ben Hawes allowed me to consult Jack Johnson's early autobiographical writings published in French, provided never-before-seen images of Johnson and his world, and let me spend an unforgettable day rummaging through his family collection.

Hap Navarro and Charles Johnston shared with me their encyclopedic knowledge of early boxing in Los Angeles, where Johnson got his start in the big-time.

Clay Moyle not only allowed me to consult his extraordinary boxing library but continued over the course of my research to send me care packages filled with copies of obscure items he thought I shouldn't pass up.

Harry Schaffer made available to me thousands of pages of newspaper clippings from the Archives of Antiquities of the Prize Ring (antekprizering.com) on everyone from Bob Armstrong and Abe Attell to Joe Walcott and Harry Wills.

And Kevin Smith, omniscient about early black boxing, spent hours on the phone with me, patiently answering questions to which only he has the answers. (If you want to know how "Scaldy Bill" Quinn got his nickname, Kevin's your man.)

I am grateful to Stanley Crouch, who helped me thread my way through several potential briar patches over the course of this project, and to Gerald Early, who was kind enough to look over a partial early draft and ease at least some of my anxieties about the finished product.

I also owe a debt to Arly Allen, Ellen Beaseley (who helped me make sense of the geography of turn-of-the-twentieth-century Galveston), Dave Bergin (who let me ask for help on his Web site pugilistica.com), Tim Brooks (who let me hear rare recordings of Jack Johnson's voice), Lee Brumbaugh of the Nevada Historical Society, Tracy Callis of the International Boxing Research Association, Kate Egan, Alan Governar, Douglas Hales, Jim Johnston (who shared copies of hard-to-find items from his collection), Jim Kroll and Bruce Hanson at the Western History Collection of the Denver Public Library (who confirmed Johnson's presence in the Rockies during the summer of 1901), Bill Loughman (who let me pore over precious original newspapers), Bradshaw Mathews, Mike Musick of the National Archives (who took on the task of solving the puzzle of Henry Johnson's Civil War service), Kelly Nichols, Rick Nott, Lynn Novick (for her friendship and forbearance), Rich Pagano, Gary Phillips, Randy Roberts, Phil Schaap, Dan Streible, Tracy Thibeau, Andrew Ward, Casey Ward, Jacob Ward, Nathan Ward, Jeff Wells, and Jason Wesco.

My old friend Mike Hill, the biographer's secret weapon, provided me with a wealth of new material patiently gleaned from scores of sources. A new friend, Timothy Rives, Archives Specialist at the National Archives—Central Plains Region office in Kansas City, went far beyond the call of duty to hunt down answers to esoteric queries ranging from the crimes for which Johnson's fellow inmates at Leavenworth were locked up to the playing schedule of Rube Foster's Chicago Giants.

Other researchers were essential, too: Jeannine Baker scoured Australian newspapers to help me reconstruct the story of Johnson's relationship with Lola Toy; Elizabeth Hoover helped me breathe at least a little life into the elusive Etta Duryea; Shana Johnson explored Johnson's little-known movie career in the George P. Johnson Film Collection at UCLA; Elizabeth Patterson heroically made transcripts of stories from Chicago newspapers too delicate to copy; Paul J. Patterson found important material on Johnson's adventures in Britain and Europe at the University of Notre Dame; Patricia Perry consulted early Galveston newspapers in the Southwest Collection at Texas Tech University in Lubbock; Damon Wright at the Dallas Historical Society confirmed Johnson's youthful visits to that city.

Susanna Steisel gathered the photographs in this book, several never previously published. (Thanks to her, there are plenty more where these came from.) Once again, Wendy Byrne brought her taste, skill, and professionalism to the book's design.

I'd like to thank everyone at Florentine Films, but especially Paul Barnes, for his patented calm, creative determination to do justice to whatever subject he tackles; Erik Ewers, who helped make Johnson come alive onscreen; Brenda Heath, who continues to take my quarterly calls without complaint; Dan White, who at key moments made it possible for me to see footage of my subject, inside and outside the ring. I'm also grateful to Gerald McCauley and Carl Brandt, as well as the team at Alfred A. Knopf: Ashbel Green, Sonny Mehta, Kathy Hourigan, Kevin Bourke, Luba Oshtashevsky, and especially Candice Gianetti, who did a heroic job of copyediting.

Above all—and as always—I want to thank my wife, Diane, without whom I could never have written this or done much else over the past twenty-four years. "We have faith in and love for each other," Jack Johnson wrote about himself and the woman he married in 1924, "and we look to the future with keen anticipation of the happiness it holds." Given Johnson's track record, it's impossible to tell if he really meant it. I do.

NOTES

NOTE: So far as possible this book is built from contemporaneous sources, and as often as possible, Jack Johnson is allowed to speak for himself. No modern biographer is quoted anywhere in its pages, but two pioneering studies were nonetheless essential to telling Johnson's story: Al-Tony Gilmore's *Bad Nigger!* remains an indispensable survey of black and white newspaper reaction to Johnson's rise and fall; and Randy Roberts' biography, *Papa Jack*, the first serious scholarly look at Johnson's life, was an invaluable resource all along the way. I owe a special debt to both of them.

CHAPTER ONE:
THE PURE-BLOODED AMERICAN

3 Halley's comet: The May 18, 1910, events inspired by the comet come from newspaper clippings cited in Etter and Schneider, *Halley's Comet*.
"But there ain't gonna be": Quoted in Rickard, *Everything Happened to Him*, pp. 234–35.

4 "When a white man writes his memoirs": Jack Johnson, *Ma Vie et Mes Combats*.

6 "Those devilish brooms": Jack Johnson, *Ma Vie et Mes Combats*.

7 "Jack was readin'": Galveston *Daily News*, January 3, 1909.
"keep your mother's image before you": Milwaukee *Evening Wisconsin*, March 11, 1910.
"grew up with the thought": Jack Johnson, "Mason-Dixon Line." No specific date or newspaper name is found in the clipping of this article in the Alexander Gumby Collection, Folder 50, Special Collections Division, Columbia University—hereafter called Gumby Collection.

8 "You had all walks of life": Galveston native Bill Millican, quoted in Beasley, *Alleys and Back Buildings of Galveston*, p. 12.
"From the time I was old enough": Jack Johnson, "Mason-Dixon Line."

9 "It was in that year": Unpublished manuscript memoir found in the Jack Johnson File; Inmate Case Files; United States Penitentiary-Leavenworth; Records of the Federal Bureau of Prisons, Record Group 129; National Archives and Record Administration–Central Plains Region (Kansas City)—hereafter called Prison Memoir.

10 "as luck would have it": Prison Memoir.

11 "I didn't have a nickel": Chicago *Tribune*, July 5, 1910.
"I got there just as fast": Ibid.

12 "I went to Boston": Ibid.
"Sonny, [boxing's] a great game": New York *Evening Graphic*, April 5, 1929.

13 "He could predict every blow": Farr, *Black Champion*, p. 8.
"grown and toughened": Prison Memoir.
"people went around asking": Ibid.
"It was arranged for us to fight": Ibid.
"Why, Jack's going to fight": Galveston *Daily News*, January 3, 1909.

14 "we were stripped ready for battle": Prison Memoir.
"nothin' at all for me to drop": Galveston *Daily News*, January 3, 1909.
"it was the hardest earned money": Prison Memoir.
"We are in the midst of a growing menace": New York *Sun*, December 15, 1895.

15 John L. Sullivan: My portrait of Sullivan draws heavily on Michael T. Isenberg's *John L. Sullivan and His America*, which I reviewed altogether too critically when it first appeared in 1988. (Had I known then how hard it is to separate fact from fiction in boxing history, I'd have been more admiring.)
"all . . . fighters": Ibid., p. 301.
"the clapper of some great bell": Ibid., p. 242.

16 "Mr. Sullivan was quite as good": Ibid., p. 289.
"I done him up": Ibid., p. 33.
"I go in to win": Ibid., p. 219.
"the most phenomenal production": Ibid.
"Sullivan is as fierce": Gorn, *Manly Art*, p. 207.

17 "I have never felt a man's blow": Isenberg, *John L. Sullivan*, p. 219.
"I thought a telegraph pole": Gorn, *Manly Art*, p. 109.
"never been angry": Isenberg, *John L. Sullivan*, p. 185.
"a son-of-a-bitch": Ibid., p. 227.
"full but never drunk": Ibid., p. 186.

18 "Peter is doing a great deal": James Weldon Johnson, *Along This Way*, p. 208.
"humiliation of being defeated": David K. Wiggins, "Peter Jackson."

19 "It was a mistake": New Orleans *Daily Picayune,* September 8, 1892.

20 "Gentlemen . . . All I have to say": Isenberg, *John L. Sullivan,* p. 318.
"the most beautiful boxer": Stockton (CA) *Independent,* May 6, 1936.
"had no objection to fighting Peter Jackson": David K. Wiggins, "Peter Jackson."

21 "He was 'Black Prince Peter' ": Langley, *Life of Peter Jackson,* p. 78.
"all the big fellows": Prison Memoir.
"I was nothing but a poor Negro": Jack Johnson, "Mes Débuts dans le noble art."
"For the love of God": Ibid.
"There have been countless women": Jack Johnson, *In the Ring and Out,* p. 70.

22 "My fortune in those days": Ibid., p. 71.
"There was nothing more for me to do": Prison Memoir.

23 "I waited until dark": Ibid.
"All the managers": Ibid.

24 "Two very clever": Curley, *Memoirs.*
"an enlightened form": Heinz, *What a Time It Was,* p. 212.

25 "In those days most all Battle Royals": Prison Memoir.
"like he was praying": Ibid.

26 "the glamour of the streets": Curley, *Memoirs,* May 1930.
"Did you see that battle royal": Ibid., July 1930.

27 "the big coon": Ibid.
"thimbleful of victuals": Siler, *Inside Facts, on Pugilism,* pp. 112–14.
"Hogan bellowed, 'One!' ": Curley, *Memoirs,* July 1930.

29 "Frank . . . disliked me": Jack Johnson, "Mes Débuts dans le noble art."
"it seemed to me": Ibid.

30 "Oh, what a pleasant week": Ibid.
"brimming full of dollars": Ibid.
New Haven: Johnson's time here is described in a clipping from the Milwaukee *Free Press,* July 27, 1910.

31 "I was digging": Jack Johnson, *Ma Vie et Mes Combats.*
"In those days there were very few carriages": Prison Memoir.

32 "the managers, trainers and fighters": Prison Memoir.

CHAPTER TWO: THE GOOD MAN

33 "one of the few residents": Jack Johnson, *In the Ring and Out,* pp. 240–41.
"saved many lives": Ibid.

34 "I am my own manager": Chicago *Tribune,* June 25, 1910.

35 "had progressed rapidly": Curley, *Memoirs,* July 1930.
"Oh, say, what a lacing": Prison Memoir.
"No, I don't want any more": Cleveland *Advocate,* March 1, 1919.
"no white boxer should meet a negro": Milwaukee *Evening Wisconsin,* February 1, 1901.
"We've got a big, fresh Negro": Curley, *Memoirs,* July 1930.
Joe Choynski: My sketch of him draws on contemporaneous newspaper accounts, as well as his own "I Fought 'Em All" and Kramer and Stern, "San Francisco's Fighting Jew."

36 "Little Joe was the hardest hitter": Ibid.
"He lives right out here": Curley, *Memoirs,* July 1930.
"I had whipped a big fellow": Fleischer, *Fighting Furies,* pp. 26–27.
"two colored boys": Galveston *Daily News,* February 26, 1901.

37 "we both did a lot of dancing": Fleischer, *Fighting Furies,* p. 27.
"I never asked anyone": Prison Memoir.
"a pugilistic encounter": Galveston *Daily News,* February 27, 1901.
"Joe went to his hotel": Prison Memoir.
"A lot of us": "Old sports reporter," quoted in undated clipping from *Police Gazette,* archives of the Antiquities of the Prize Ring.

38 "A man who can move like you": Prison Memoir.
"very tame draw": *Rocky Mountain News,* April 27, 1901.
Colorado summer: Randy Roberts suggests in *Papa Jack* that the events Johnson describes as having taken place in the Rockies in the summer of 1900 are imaginary, since he could find no independent evidence of them. But there is ample evidence that they happened the following summer. Events were important to Jack Johnson only in that they affected him; *when* they occurred and in whose company never mattered to him much.
"Sharkey could not hit me": Prison Memoir.
"a dispute of minor origin": Jack Johnson, *In the Ring and Out,* p. 72.

39 "it appeared as if his stomach": Los Angeles *Times* (hereafter LAT), November 22, 1903.
"imperious manner": Ibid.
Frank Carillo: My description is drawn largely from Stump, "Rowdy Reign."

40 "The wisest among my race": Harlan, *The Making of a Black Leader, 1856–1901,* p. 219.
"Today, two classes of Negroes": Reverdy

Cassius Ransom, quoted in Lewis, *W. E. B. Du Bois*, p. 329.

40 "White people often point": Jack Johnson, *In the Ring and Out*, p. 329.

41 "The fight was one of the cleanest": Bakersfield *Daily Californian*, November 5, 1901.

"Oh mister officer": New York *Journal*, July 4, 1910. This same story is told with somewhat different details in the Philadelphia *Tribune*, December 6, 1913, and in Hietala, *Fight of the Century*, p. 129.

42 "Akron" and "Cleveland": Nicholson, *A Man Among Men*, pp. 35–36.

"I could lick that fellow myself": Philadelphia *Tribune*, December 6, 1913.

43 "The first time he really hit me": Nicholson, *A Man Among Men*, p. 44.

"Nobody can ever hurt him": Ibid., p. 143.

"as silent as General Grant": Inglis, *Champions Off Guard*, p. 211.

"No mortal ever born": Nicholson, *A Man Among Men*, p. 110.

"Jeff! Why, Jeff's the fellow": Inglis, *Champions Off Guard*, p. 206.

44 "I never will fight a negro": LAT, November 19, 1904.

"Johnson, at that time": Preface to Jack Johnson, *In the Ring and Out*, p. 13.

45 "That was the first time": Johnson, "Mes Premier Combats."

"nigger club": LAT, May 16, 1903.

47 "The great crowd": Ibid., May 17, 1902.

"For four rounds": *Knockout Weekly*, April 12, 1929.

48 "I can lick you, too": New York *Times*, July 5, 1910.

PINK FURIES: LAT, April 17, 1902.

"invisible something": Jack Johnson, *In the Ring and Out*, p. 72.

"Mary was a splendid woman": Ibid.

49 "a big, gobby coon": LAT, October 20, 1902.

"Johnson was punching him": Ibid.

"Candor compels me": Curley, *Memoirs*, September 1930.

"I still hate to think": Ibid.

50 Frank Carillo and the revolver: The Los Angeles *Times* for January 2, 1903, tells this story.

"tugged and hauled": Curley, *Memoirs*, September 1930.

51 "to turn his opponent": Stanley Crouch interview, Ken Burns' film *Unforgivable Blackness*.

"A lot of fellows": Prison Memoir.

52 "I was *always* attacking": quoted in Farr, "Black Hamlet of the Heavyweights."

"Johnson was a fellow": Gunboat Smith, quoted in Heller, *In This Corner*, p. 44.

"Johnson makes you do all the work": Sam McVey, quoted in unsourced newspaper clipping dated April 2, 1915, Jim Johnston Collection.

"It was his easy-going manner": Preface to Jack Johnson, *In the Ring and Out*, p. 13.

"while they were fighting": LAT, December 5, 1902.

53 "It is said that Jack": Quoted in Randy Roberts, *Papa Jack*, p. 28.

54 "the magnificent footwork": San Francisco *Examiner*, February 4, 1903.

CHAPTER THREE: THE SPORT

56 "a good showman": "Sports Mirror: The Heavyweight Parade from John L. Sullivan to Louis of the Present," undated clipping from the San Francisco *Chronicle*, Jim Johnston Collection.

"towering figure clad": LAT, February 11, 1903.

57 "Well, I've got": Ibid.

58 "tasty" "ready for occupancy": LAT, October 6, 1903.

"diamond rings with matching stickpins": Bricktop and Haskins, *Bricktop*, p. 29.

"very mosey walk": Lomax, *Mister Jelly Roll*, p. 19.

59 "There ain't much money": LAT, February 11, 1903.

"you never know what that nigger": LAT, February 15, 1903.

60 "short and merry mix-up": *Police Gazette*, March 1903.

"the worst-acting gang": LAT, June 10, 1903.

61 "speckled" bouts: LAT, June 12, 1903.

"Both were colored girls": Jack Johnson, *In the Ring and Out*, p. 72.

"A great attachment grew": Ibid.

62 the rabbit story: The story of Johnson, Walcott, and the unfortunate rabbit is from the LAT, July 16, 1903.

"That Ferguson stayed the six rounds": Philadelphia *Inquirer*, August 1, 1903.

63 TEXAS WATERMELON PICKANINNY: LAT, October 4, 1903.

"the dance was never given": LAT, October 27, 1903.

64 "Sam McVey was hammered": LAT, October 28, 1903.

"Johnson . . . has to fight wherever": LAT, October 30, 1903.

"Aren't you having a pretty good thing": LAT, October 30, 1903.

65 "The color line gag": Ibid.

66 "I waive the color line myself": Quoted in Randy Roberts, *Papa Jack*, p. 32.

66 "Johnson improved to some extent": San Francisco *Examiner*, April 23, 1904.

67 "Kill that nigger!": Al Stump described the near riot and Johnson's flight from the arena in "The Rowdy Reign of the Black Avenger." He places it in 1905. I have moved it back to where logic suggests it happened.
"By beating Sam McVey again": *Police Gazette*, April 19, 1904.
"piebald match": Milwaukee *Free Press*, April 10, 1904.
"too much on the brotherly love order": Chicago *Tribune*, June 1, 1904.
"the big black boy": Ibid.

68 "I want Mr. Jeffries next": Unsourced clipping, archives of the Antiquities of the Prize Ring.
"fast as an electric spark": *Police Gazette*, July 1904.

69 "I ain't a cellar fighter": Jeffries, *My Life and Battles*, p. 123.
"Jack . . . boxed with me": James Weldon Johnson, *Along This Way*, p. 208.

70 "I am a Southerner": Undated *Police Gazette* clipping, archives of the Antiquities of the Prize Ring.
"I tell you right here": San Francisco *Chronicle*, March 28, 1905.
"I have notified Johnson": San Francisco *Chronicle*, March 29, 1905.

71 "Please hit him!": San Francisco *Examiner*, March 29, 1905.
"Though [Hart's] face": San Francisco *Chronicle*, March 29, 1905.
"the opinion of all fair-minded witnesses": *Police Gazette*, July 3, 1905.
"After fighting until I reached the top": Milwaukee *Evening Wisconsin*, May 9, 1905.
"That coon has enough yellow": Ibid.

72 "I've got all the money I want": Inglis, *Champions Off Guard*, pp. 229–30.
"I will never go back": Nicholson, *A Man Among Men*, p. 119.
"Hart may win": Milwaukee *Free Press*, July 3, 1905.

73 "any man in the world": Ibid., October 14, 1905.
"What right has Hart": *Police Gazette*, August 1905.

74 "It was a wonderful fight": Ibid.
"He ain't human": Ibid.

75 "I hailed him": Jack Johnson, *In the Ring and Out*, pp. 72–75.
"Unknown to me": Ibid.

76 "I'd have liked to show you": Baltimore *Sun*, December 2, 1905.

"Our money was low": Jack Johnson, *In the Ring and Out*, pp. 72–75.
"Of this dollar": Ibid.
pickup fight in Topeka: Johnson's brief but disinterested appearance is detailed in the Topeka *Daily Capital*, January 27, 1906.

77 "his championship stock": Chicago *Tribune*, December 12, 1905.
visit to Jeffries' farm: Curley, *Memoirs*, February 1932.

78 "Why Mr. Hart": Burns, "Tommy Burns."
"a hugger and a wrestler": Milwaukee *Free Press*, March 4, 1906.
"I will defend my title": Quoted in Rutter, *White Hopes*, p. 49.

79 "give the white boys a chance": Broome, "Australian Reaction to Jack Johnson," p. 346.

80 "I gave Langford": Prison Memoir.
"Woodman's startling fiction": Fleischer, *Fighting Furies*, pp. 55–56.

83 "why Jeffries had taken so much trouble": *Police Gazette*, October 1906.
"the yellowest pack": *Police Gazette*, November 1906.
"easily beat any fighter": McLean, "Next Heavyweight Champion."

84 "Po' Artemis Johnsing": Milwaukee *Free Press*, January 6, 1907.

CHAPTER FOUR:
THE MAN THEY ALL DODGE

85 "Johnson is a big coon": Sydney *Truth*, January 30, 1907.
"it wasn't an Australian's": *The Referee*, January 30, 1907.
"Jeffries has stated": *Australian Star*, January 28, 1907.

86 Sir Joseph Banks Hotel: My description is based on Jervis and Flack, *Jubilee History of Botany*, pp. 87–96, 301–3.
"Now, Jack, I think you've done enough": *The Referee*, February 6, 1907.
"Jack's 'enough' ": Ibid.

88 "He's a beautiful man": *The Referee*, March 18, 1908.

89 "Felix suddenly found himself": Sydney *Bulletin*, February 28, 1907.
"Johnson, laughing": Newcastle *Herald and Miner's Advocate*, February 20, 1907.
"staggered to his feet": Sydney *Bulletin*, February 28, 1907.

90 GRAND INTERNATIONAL BATTLE: Melbourne *Argus*, March 2, 1907.
"chintz or cretonne": *Australian Star*, March 6, 1907.

90 "We don't want to see *Mrs.* Johnson!": Ibid.
"They're all squabbling": Ibid.
"This is a joke": Ibid.

91 "He began to decide": McLean, "Next Heavyweight Champion."
"How much more is coming to you?": Ibid.

92 "big black bastard": *Australian Star,* March 19, 1907.
"MR. LEVIEN: Your Worship": Ibid.

93 "I expect to get married": Sydney *Sunday Sun,* March 24, 1907.
"This was the first": McLean, "Next Heavyweight Champion."
"When he got within ten feet": Ibid.

96 "Worry your opponents": Quoted in McCaffrey, *Tommy Burns,* pp. 146–47.

97 "I had $700": Prison Memoir.
"In my fight with Fitzsimmons": Ibid.

98 "poor old Bob Fitzsimmons": Ibid.
"The scene after the game": New York *Times* (hereafter NYT), April 25, 1907.

99 "A wicked right hand": Prison Memoir.
"How'd you like that": Quoted in Farr, *Black Champion,* p. 48.
"I don't see where": *Police Gazette,* May 1908.
"living at what they called a 'Call House' ": Testimony of Hattie McClay, *US v. Johnson,* General Records of the Department of Justice, File Number 16421, Record Group 60 (hereafter DOJ File).
"a splendid pal": Jack Johnson, *In the Ring and Out,* p. 76.
"The heartaches which Mary Austin": Ibid.

100 "The affair could hardly be called": Prison Memoir.
"There was a dearth": Curley, *Memoirs,* July 1931.

101 "My advice to a young fighter": Quoted in Kammer, "TKO in Las Vegas."
"Time was called": Prison Memoir.
"The best man won": Unsourced clipping from a San Francisco newspaper, archives of the Antiquities of the Prize Ring.
"I knew I had him": Ibid.

102 "Jack Johnson is a colored man": Quoted in Fleischer, *Fighting Furies,* pp. 66–67.
"He rather rubbed us": Corri, *Gloves and the Man,* p. 217.

103 "What do I care?": Milwaukee *Free Press,* February 23, 1908.
"Jack Johnson, Heavyweight Champion of the World": Milwaukee *Free Press,* November 16, 1907.

104 "If the paragraph has caused Miss Toy": *The Referee,* March 18, 1908.
"libelous to say that a white woman": Ibid.

"Dressed neatly in white": Ibid.
"MR. REID: Look at this": Sydney *Truth,* March 22, 1908.

105 "stripped to the buff": Ibid.
"MR. GANNON: The evidence": Ibid.

106 "suffused with bliss": Ibid.
"Pugilism was one thing": Ibid.

107 "shame him out of King Edward's islands": Milwaukee *Free Press,* February 27, 1908.
"to stand on the mat": Deghy, *Noble and Manly,* pp. 165–66.
"Johnson in those days": Bettinson and Bennison, *Home of Boxing,* p. 95.
"This Johnson can beat Burns": Ibid.
"Johnson would sooner fight": Ibid., p. 96.

108 "quite the nerviest proposition": *Police Gazette,* April 25, 1908.
"The whole truth": Ibid.
"very good heavyweight": Dartnell, *Seconds Out!,* p. 171.
"by no means unintelligent": Lynch, *Knuckles and Gloves,* p. 149.
"as I'm called a grabber anyway": Milwaukee *Evening Wisconsin,* March 7, 1908.

109 "Johnson strolled into the . . . Club": *Police Gazette,* June 1908.
"Now, let me ask you": McCaffery, *Tommy Burns,* p. 175.
"bluffer": *Police Gazette,* May 30, 1908.

110 "It's downright weary work": Quoted in Wells, *Boxing Day,* p. 113.
"This match was based": Jack Johnson, *In the Ring and Out,* pp. 156–57.
"it was my fight": Prison Memoir.

111 "an egg beaten up": Quoted in Farr, *Black Champion,* p. 56.
"It was just fatiguing": Prison Memoir.
Oxford Theater bill: *Police Gazette,* July 1908.

CHAPTER FIVE:
THE MAN WITH THE GOLDEN SMILE

113 "blend of charlatan": Hetherington, *Australians: Nine Profiles,* p. 48.
"a two-man show": Ibid., p. 49.

114 "As a friendly hand": Quoted in Wells, *Boxing Day,* p. 94.
"All niggers are alike": Ibid., p. 85.

115 DE BIG COON AM A-COMIN': Ibid., p. 120.
"Shame on the money-mad Champion!": Quoted in Al-Tony Gilmore, *Bad Nigger!,* p. 27.
"The history of the Nigger": Lynch, *Knuckles and Gloves,* pp. 44–45.

116 "We have a gym fixed up": *Police Gazette,* November 1908.

116 "I am a larger man": *The Referee,* October 28, 1908.

117 "the coloured man is accompanied": Sydney *Bulletin,* November 5, 1908.
"exquisite fighting engine": Wells, *Boxing Day,* p. 107.
"a desperate struggle": Ibid., p. 110.
"Citizens who have never prayed": *Illustrated Sporting and Dramatic News,* November 15, 1908.

118 "The words I am about to speak": Quoted in Wells, *Boxing Day,* pp. 128–29.

119 "Johnson does not like Burns": "Leonce," "Colored Champion of the World."
"Looking back in memory": Burns, "Tommy Burns."
"Rock Me to Sleep, Mother": Lindsay, *Comedy of Life,* p. 237.
"take your medicine" . . . "When Burns stared to perform": Prison Memoir.

120 "For every point I'm given": Wells, *Boxing Day,* pp. 145–46.

121 "I am going to win": Unsourced newspaper clipping, December 25, 1908, Alexander Gumby Collection.
"So you want your money first": Quoted in Wells, *Boxing Day,* pp. 153–54.

122 "All the hatred": Sydney *Bulletin,* December 27, 1908.
"uncanny accuracy": Ibid.
"Don't care": Quoted in Wells, *Boxing Day,* p. 155.

123 "All right, Tommy": Sydney *Bulletin,* December 31, 1908.
"The world spun crazily": Burns, "Tommy Burns."
"Poor little Tommy": Broome, "Australian Reaction to Jack Johnson."
"Come right on!": Wells, *Boxing Day,* p. 58.
"Come on and fight, nigger!": Randy Roberts, *Papa Jack,* p. 64.
"Burns got through his earlier opponents": Prison Memoir.
"Burns started it": Ibid.
"I had forgotten more": Ibid.

124 "I don't think I can beat that nigger": Deghy, *Noble and Manly,* p. 165.

125 " 'Hit me here, Tommy,' ": London, *Stories of Boxing,* p. 150.
"You punch like a woman, Tommy": Quoted in Randy Roberts, *Papa Jack,* p. 63.
"I was positive he would fold up": Burns, "Tommy Burns."
"They talked of [Burns'] being a man": Prison Memoir.

126 "He is a funny fellow": *Police Gazette,* May 8, 1909.

"I see him, oh yes": Quoted in Broome, "Australian Reaction to Jack Johnson."
"Flash nigger!": Ibid.
"devilish gloating": Ibid.
"He said something about my wife": Quoted in Wells, *Boxing Day,* p. 175.
"Did you get that?": Sydney *Sportsman,* December 27, 1908.

127 "in a voice fit to wake the dead": Sydney *Bulletin,* December 27, 1908.
"I might even have won": Quoted in Wells, *Boxing Day,* p. 174.
"The Australian nation": Unsourced clipping from a British book, Jim Johnston Collection.

128 "Burns can't fight": Quoted in Wells, *Boxing Day,* p. 173.
"I had attained my life's ambition": Jack Johnson, *In the Ring and Out,* p. 58.
"gloating coon": Sydney *Sportsman,* December 27, 1908.

129 "It was not Burns that was beaten": Broome, "Australian Reaction to Jack Johnson."
"Already the insolent black's victory": Sydney *Herald,* December 31, 1908.
"As I am a descendant of Ham": Quoted in Wells, *Boxing Day,* pp. 178–79.

130 "Your central Australian natives": Ibid.
"Personally, I took no other interest": Baltimore *American,* December 27, 1908.
"Texas Darky": Quoted in Al-Tony Gilmore, *Bad Nigger!,* p. 28.
"Is the Caucasian played out?" Detroit *Free Press,* January 1, 1909.
"Well, Bre'r Johnson": Quoted in Randy Roberts, "Heavyweight Champion Jack Johnson."

131 "Now that Mr. Johnson": Quoted in Al-Tony Gilmore, *Bad Nigger!,* p. 31.
"No event in forty years": Ibid., p. 32.
"the zenith of Negro sport": Ibid., p. 31.
"high-living, failure": Cleveland *Journal,* January 2, 1909.

132 "the first cable ever sent": Buffalo *Express,* December 28, 1908.
"Burns never was the champion": Ibid., December 27, 1908.
"the white man has succumbed": Chicago *Tribune,* December 27, 1908.
"newspaper champion": Buffalo *Express,* December 28, 1908.
"Personally, I was for Burns": London, *Boxing Stories,* pp. 142–50.
"Armenian massacre": Ibid.

133 "They kept at me": Quoted in Nicholson, *A Man Among Men,* p. 186.

134 "he should get a vaudeville engagement": Van Court, *Making of Champions,* p. 99.

134 "he said that if he made a start": Ibid.
"stepped around as spry": Los Angeles *Examiner*, January 9, 1909.

135 "Say, won't you fight Johnson": Milwaukee *Free Press*, January 17, 1909.
"If I were to whip Johnson": Ibid., March 4, 1909.
"I want to see the championship": Hietala, *Fight of the Century*, p. 34.
"The shades of night": Police Gazette, February 1909.

136 Johnson's visit to Jackson's grave: Noted in Broome, "Australian Reaction to Jack Johnson."

CHAPTER SIX: THE CHAMPION

137 "I've got no kick coming": Associated Press, March 10, 1909.

138 "I am willing to meet": Ibid.
"eyes sparkled": NYT, March 10, 1909.
"the former Nellie O'Brien": Associated Press, March 10, 1909.
"a different man": NYT, March 10, 1909.

140 "I found Johnson the most charming opponent": McLaglen, *Express to Hollywood*, p. 151.

141 "The negroes in charge": Chicago *Tribune*, March 14, 1909.
"It is reported that Jack Johnson": Nashville *Globe*, March 12, 1909.

142 "in a small Nevada town": Chicago *Tribune*, March 16, 1909.
"There was nothing secret": Ibid.
"I can lick Jim Jeffries": Milwaukee *Free Press*, March 16, 1909.

143 "I beat Sam easy before": *Police Gazette*, April 10, 1909.
"Being a champion": Bettinson and Bennison, *Home of Boxing*, p. 98.

144 NO ONE ENTERS THESE PORTALS: Bradford, *Born with the Blues*, p. 171.
"There were no preliminaries": *Variety*, April 3, 1909.

145 "the absolutely proper and dignified thing": Emmett Jay Scott to J. Frank Wheaton, March 23, 1909. Booker T. Washington Papers, Library of Congress.

147 "Minna and Ada Everleigh are to pleasure": Quoted in Washburn, *Come into My Parlor*, p. 28.
"inexperienced girls or young widows": Ibid., p. 46.
"Be polite": Ibid., p. 24.
"The Everleigh Club is not for the rough element": Ibid.
"ten cents was a big meal": In August of 1910, George Little got into a legal dispute

with Jack Johnson and prepared a lengthy document offering his version of events. Several collectors have typed copies of it; mine (hereafter called George Little "Confession") was supplied to me by Benjamin Hawes.

148 "the sporting life": Belle Schreiber testimony, DOJ File.
"a little over": Ibid.

149 "out of affection": Ibid.
"Men and boys": NYT, April 22, 1909.

150 "I'm faking and four-flushing": Milwaukee *Evening Wisconsin*, August 24, 1909.
"as fat as a Jap wrestler": San Francisco *Examiner*, October 16, 1909.

151 "Assembled were men": Prison Memoir.

152 "As a two-handed spender": *Police Gazette*, June 1909.
"My mind is constantly": Jack Johnson testimony, DOJ File.

153 "very much painted": Agent W. P. Schmid report of interview with Frederick C. Gale, March 13, 1913, DOJ File.
"It's getting so they just take me": NYT, August 7, 1909.

154 " 'If' and 'suppose' ": Quoted in Randy Roberts, *Papa Jack*, p. 81.
"In all these appearances": Darton, *My Lifetime in Sports*, p. 41.
"Someone asked Jeff": Chicago *American*, August 5, 1909.

156 "How did *you* ever get the title?" *Police Gazette*, August 11, 1909.

157 "There was skill on both sides": Chicago *American*, August 12, 1909.
"the men of his race": Baltimore *Afro-American*, August 21, 1909.

158 "Kaufmann had no more chance": Prison Memoir.

159 "Bring him along": LAT, September 20, 1909.
"It wouldn't be a bad idea": *Police Gazette*, October 2, 1909.
"With the waning of the day": Quoted in Randy Roberts, *Papa Jack*, p. 80.
"Naturally, there was a state of warfare": Jack Johnson, *In the Ring and Out*, p. 77.
lithographed postcard: DOJ File.

160 "a dim sense of property rights": John Lardner, "Yesterday's Graziano."
"I was a tough kid": Fleischer, *Michigan Assassin*, p. 7.
"He had the soul of a bouncer": Quoted in John Lardner, "Yesterday's Graziano."
"I hit 'em so hard": Ibid.
"The sonofabitch!": John Burke, *Rogue's Progress*, p. 133.

161 "He was a savage": McCallum, *Encyclopedia of World Boxing Champions*, p. 128.
"Why he's just a little fella": NYT, March 10, 1909.
"rusher," "reach and range": San Francisco *Examiner*, October 10, 1909.
"There is a great difference": Jack Johnson, "How Ketchel Tried to Double Cross Me."

162 "Let's be practical, Jack": Ibid.
"make the pictures snappy": Jack Johnson, *In the Ring and Out*, p. 195.

163 "deck hands, picked exclusively": Milwaukee *Evening Wisconsin*, October 18, 1909.

164 "At the police station": Ibid., October 21, 1909.
"Jack Johnson is running wild": San Francisco *Examiner*, October 18, 1909.
"With Johnson's decisive decision": *Boxing*, October 23, 1909.

165 "Even those who have an absurdly exaggerated horror": NYT, November 1, 1909.

CHAPTER SEVEN: THE GREATEST COLORED MAN THAT EVER LIVED

166 "He swings through the door": *Harper's Weekly*, December 20, 1909.

167 "I'll tell you what I'll do": Cleveland *Advocate*, March 8, 1910.
"Say, if the 'Smoke' goes out the window": Ibid.

168 "we didn't want to eat snowballs": George Little "Confession."
"theatrical connections": Jack Johnson, *In the Ring and Out*, p. 78.
"Famed on Long Island": New York *World*, September 13, 1912.

169 "Somehow, crude, uneducated guy": Samuels, *Magnificent Rube*, p. 113.

171 "That's all right": NYT, December 2, 1909.
"I was born and raised in the South": Milwaukee *Evening Wisconsin*, March 21, 1909.
"I was much inclined": Quoted in Farr, *Black Champion*, p. 78.
"the most eminent black man": Frederick G. Bonfils to Booker T. Washington, April 25, 1910, Booker T. Washington Papers, Library of Congress.

172 "I've got . . . money enough to live on": Chicago *Tribune*, March 25, 1909.
"It is no exaggeration": Streible, *Fight Pictures*, p. 149.

173 "Jack, I'm grateful to you": Curley, *Memoirs*, February 1932.
"Jim, please, for our sakes": Milwaukee *Evening Wisconsin*, April 5, 1910.
"how to whip the nigger": Ibid.
"the black bluff": Ibid., March 23, 1910.

"smash the coconut": Ibid., April 5, 1910.
"was there the slightest reference": Curley, *Memoirs*, February 1932.
"There's an article in there": Ibid.

174 "not to make mention": Barney Gerard to Raymond E. Horn, March 11, 1913, DOJ File.

175 "It was notorious": New York *World*, September 13, 1912.
"Mrs. Duryea began to be seen": Ibid.
"a highly educated woman": Heller, *In This Corner*, p. 42.

176 "Jack Johnson was one of the two": Milwaukee *Evening Wisconsin*, December 27, 1909.
"He wanted me to have it": Belle Schreiber trial testimony, April 1913, DOJ File.

177 "girl friend from Brooklyn": Barney Gerard to Raymond E. Horn, March 11, 1913, DOJ File.
"hit the first man": Milwaukee *Free Press*, January 3, 1910.
"We were not on good terms": Belle Schreiber testimony, April 1913, DOJ File.

178 "They didn't want me": Quoted in Farr, *Black Champion*, p. 170.
"Don't pull that stuff on me": Philadelphia *Evening Telegraph*, January 20, 1910.
"Honest to heaven, Mister": NYT, January 20, 1910.

179 "came and got me out of there": Belle Schreiber testimony, April 1913, DOJ File.

180 "seeing my life in danger": Barney Gerard to Raymond E. Horn, March 11, 1913, DOJ File.
"deckhands, wharf wallopers": *Police Gazette*, April 16, 1910.
"Johnson has become reckless": Baltimore *American*, February 27, 1910.
"No one ever heard of Peter Jackson": Indianapolis *Freeman*, March 15, 1910.

181 "Stand back, Mr. White Officer": Quoted in Farr, *Black Champion*, p. 81.

182 "He growls and snarls and grumbles": Randy Roberts, *Papa Jack*, p. 92.

183 "I dislike Johnson": Chicago *Tribune*, June 19, 1910.
LOOKS AS FORMIDABLE: Baltimore *American*, May 15, 1920.
"in condition; that he is fast": *Police Gazette*, June 1910.

184 "regain his judgment": Chicago *Tribune*, May 2, 1910.
"When I sent my card up": John H. Washington, Jr., to Emmett Jay Scott, May 24, 1910, Booker T. Washington Papers, Library of Congress.

186 "I told Little that if anyone went": LAT, May 30, 1910.

"These talks, into which Little": Ibid.

"Don't you see, Jack?" Los Angeles *Examiner*, July 8, 1910.

"See here, George": Ibid.

187 "No stolen chicken ever passes": Quoted in Farr, *Black Champion*, p. 104.

"I can't box anymore today": Baltimore *American*, June 26, 1910.

188 "The clergy are preaching THE FIGHT": *Boxing*, June 18, 1910.

"This Jeffries-Johnson fight": Quoted in Randy Roberts, "Heavyweight Champion Jack Johnson."

189 "Stop the Fight": NYT, June 6, 1910.

"this fight can be regarded": Chicago *Tribune*, May 4, 1910.

"Though he was frequently interrupted": San Francisco *Examiner*, June 4, 1910.

190 "I am no Sam Fitzpatrick": LAT, June 18, 1910.

"showing his pistol to everybody": Jack Johnson, "Mes Premiers Combats."

"I have wagered large amounts": Chicago *Tribune*, June 22, 1910.

191 "You must have talent": Chicago *Tribune*, June 25, 1910.

"Go to San Francisco": Quoted in Farr, *Black Champion*, p. 81.

192 "prayerproof": Chicago *Tribune*, June 23, 1910.

"Just tell me, man to man": Quoted in Farr, *Black Champion*, p. 90.

193 "the precise magnetic center": Beach, *Jeffries-Johnson Fight*.

"I am glad I'm here": London, *Stories of Boxing*.

"In a single day": Beach, *Jeffries-Johnson Fight*.

"was more or less of an ovation": Chicago *Tribune*, June 23, 1910.

194 "One glance at Jack's beaming face": Milwaukee *Free Press*, June 25, 1910.

"At Jeffries' quarters": Beach, *Jeffries-Johnson Fight*.

"There was nothing winsome": Ruhl, "Fight in the Desert."

195 "I'll turn the fire hose on him": Randy Roberts, *Papa Jack*, p. 101.

"I don't want you here": Chicago *Tribune*, July 4, 1910.

"You find yourself in a honky-tonk": Beach, *Jeffries-Johnson Fight*.

196 "I saw that which I never expected": Ibid.

"He has an eye for what goes on": New York *World*, June 27, 1910.

197 "I have never seen a man": Quoted in Lucas, *Black Gladiator*, p. 97.

"Cap'n John, if I felt any better": Chicago *Tribune*, July 4, 1910.

"To all appearances": Baltimore *American*, July 2, 1910.

"The man is a puzzle": Chicago *Tribune*, June 27, 1910.

198 "essentially African": San Francisco *Examiner*, July 3, 1910.

"dogged courage": Ruhl, "Fight in the Desert."

"An army of unknowns": Beach, *Jeffries-Johnson Fight*.

"People eat at ragtime": Lyon, "In Reno Riotous."

199 "There are few negro families": Chicago *Tribune*, June 28, 1910.

"I told Johnson in Chicago": Los Angeles *Examiner*, July 3, 1910.

"if a hand was not dipped into your pocket": Lyon, "In Reno Riotous."

200 "beat down the wonderful black": Quoted in Randy Roberts, "Heavyweight Champion Jack Johnson."

"Thousands of negroes": *Afro-American Ledger*, April 30, 1910.

201 HE WILL HAVE TO BEAT THEM ALL: Chicago *Defender*, February 5, 1910.

"On the arid plains": Ibid., June 16, 1910.

"If Jeff is only half as good": Chicago *Tribune*, June 29, 1910.

"doesn't have a look-in": Ibid., June 25, 1910.

"I realize full well": Baltimore *American*, July 4, 1910.

"Johnson will win": NYT, July 3, 1910.

"For God's sake, Jim": San Francisco *Examiner*, July 6, 1910.

202 DON'T WORRY ABOUT ME: Ibid.

BET YOUR LAST COPPER ON ME: Chicago *Tribune*, July 3, 1910.

203 "Everything that had wheels": Beach, *Jeffries-Johnson Fight*.

204 "I would consider any move": Milwaukee *Free Press*, July 4, 1910.

"The fresh pine arena": Lyon, "In Reno Riotous."

"The betting was now 10 to 6": Ruhl, "Fight in the Desert."

205 "Hats waved, flags fluttered": Beach, *Jeffries-Johnson Fight*.

206 "the only free State": Ibid.

"By all odds": Los Angeles *Examiner*, July 5, 1910.

"the last roll-call of has-beens": Chicago *Tribune*, July 5, 1910.

"Oh hell, pull the fight": Ibid.

461

206 "nervous prostration": *Boxing,* July 9, 1910.
"Cold feet, Johnson": New York *American,* July 5, 1910.
"Don't talk to them": Ibid.
"amazed at the number": Jack Johnson, "A Champ Recalls."

207 "the first blood cry": Beach, *Jeffries-Johnson Fight.*
"I have never seen a human being": Ruhl, "Fight in the Desert."
"The man of summer temperament": London, *Stories of Boxing.*

208 "Mr. Jeffries feinted a bit": Jack Johnson, "Johnson's Story of His Victory."
"Cut out the motion pictures": NYT, July 5, 1910.
"I was feeling quite fresh": Jack Johnson, "Johnson's Story of His Victory."
"the good sense": Ruhl, "Fight in the Desert."
"He wants to fight a little": Fields, *James J. Corbett,* p. 67.
"All right Jim": NYT, July 5, 1910.
"Come on now, Mr. Jeff": Ibid.
"He'll kill you, Jack": Chicago *Tribune,* July 5, 1910.

209 "First blood for Jeff!": NYT, July 5, 1910.
"Where do you want me to put him": Fields, *James J. Corbett,* p. 167.
"Jeffries took a left hook": New York *American,* July 5, 1910.
"My eyes could detect openings": Ibid.
"Jack, your brother's whipped": *Boxing,* August 13, 1913.
"I'll straighten him up": NYT, July 5, 1910.
"Ain't I got a hard old head?": Ibid.
"Keep it up, Jack!": New York *American,* July 5, 1910.
"I didn't show you that one": *Boxing,* July 9, 1910.

210 "wind was going fast": Jack Johnson, "Johnson's Story of His Victory."
"Thought you said you were going to make *me* wild": Chicago *Tribune,* July 5, 1910.
"How you like 'em, Jim?": NYT, July 5, 1910.
"Why don't you *do* something?": New York *American,* July 5, 1910.
"A great silence fell": Ruhl, "Fight in the Desert."

211 "Don't let the nigger knock him out!" London, *Stories of Boxing,* p. 173. (London used a more polite term; I've restored the one ringsiders surely used.)
"I couldn't come back, boys": London *Daily Telegraph,* July 5, 1910.
"I could have fought": NYT, July 5, 1910.
"I could never have whipped Jack Johnson":

Quoted in Farr, "Black Hamlet of the Heavyweights."

212 "Please show me the way out": Beach, *Jeffries-Johnson Fight.*
"She did not show many outward signs": Chicago *Tribune,* July 5, 1910.

213 "It's their night": Ibid.
"Say, sonny, who won the fight?": Denver *Post,* July 5, 1910.
"There was no reason": Belle Schreiber testimony, April 1913, DOJ File.
"I had seen pool tables": Bradford, *Born with the Blues,* p. 171.

214 "The Negroes were jubilant": Ruby Berkley Goodwin, *It's Good to Be Black,* pp. 78–79.

215 "'Cause I wants everybody to know": Story by A. B. Simpson, unsourced clipping, July 5, 1910, Nevada Historical Society.
"Howdy-do, Tommy": Ibid.
"Same as yesterday": San Francisco *Examiner,* July 5, 1910.

216 "The black man, were he of white skin": Chicago *American,* July 5, 1910, ibid.
"A word to the Black Man": Los Angeles *Times,* July 6, 1910.
"Rioting broke out": New York *Tribune,* July 5, 1910.

217 "Jack Johnson has knocked out": Armstrong, *Satchmo,* p. 36.
"clubbed them unmercifully": Milwaukee *Free Press,* July 6, 1910.
"It was a good deal better": Quoted in Al-Tony Gilmore, *Bad Nigger!,* p. 71.

218 "His black tilted brow": Milwaukee *Free Press,* July 7, 1910.
"Don't talk to white strangers": Chicago *Tribune,* July 7, 1910.

219 "Now watch close there, honey": Quoted in Farr, *Black Champion,* pp. 122–23.
"Even a reporter for the *Daily News*": Chicago *Daily News,* July 7, 1910.

220 "Oh, Jackie": Ibid.
"There's plenty more": Chicago *Tribune,* July 9, 1910.
"an old-timer who taught Johnson": Los Angeles *Examiner,* July 8, 1910.

221 "I never will be broke": Ibid.
"Not alone has Jack Johnson": Ibid.
"I only hope the colored people": Ibid.

CHAPTER EIGHT: THE BRUNETTE IN A BLOND TOWN

225 "the highest esteem for the Negro": Major P. M. Ashburn to Emmett Jay Scott, July 5, 1910, Booker T. Washington Papers, Library of Congress.

226 "I was not myself": NYT, September 15, 1912.
"I have never seen": New York *Age*, July 7, 1910.
TO EVERY COLORED MAN: Farr, *Black Champion*, p. 131.

227 "The Victoria was jammed": Washington *Post*, July 10, 1910.
"Nat, why should they bring in": Fleischer, *50 Years at Ringside*, pp. 76–77.

228 "According to her story": New York *Age*, July 28, 1910 (reprinted from New York *Morning Telegraph*).

229 "prevarication": Chicago *Tribune*, July 10, 1910.
"I'll see him": Milwaukee *Free Press*, July 13, 1910.

230 "That's where he got me good": Chicago *Tribune*, July 14, 1910.
RACE RIOTS AND MURDER: Quoted in Al-Tony Gilmore, *Bad Nigger!*, p. 76.
"members of their own race": Quoted in Streible, *Fight Films*, p. 365.
"Labor on the cotton plantations": Chicago *Tribune*, July 11, 1910.

231 "The negroes are to some extent": Quoted in Randy Roberts, *Papa Jack*, p. 112.
"Had Jeffries won": Quoted in Streible, *Fight Films*, p. 359.

232 "What folly!": Washington *Bee*, July 9, 1910.
"Ladies and gentlemen": Tim Brooks Collection, transcribed by Brooks.

234 "Orally, Mr. Johnson": Quoted in Brooks, *Lost Sounds*, p. 245.
"The worst of it is": *Police Gazette*, November 5, 1910.

235 *"Jack Johnson, we have waited"*: Quoted in Al-Tony Gilmore, *Bad Nigger!*, p. 48.
"Amaze an' Grace": Ibid.

236 WHITE GENTLEMAN RAPES COLORED GIRL: Quoted in Ottley, *Lonely Warrior*, p. 106.
"Why not arrest the man": Ibid., p. 110.

237 "Fully expecting to see a colored girl": Federal Agent Carbarino report, March 24, 1913, DOJ File.

238 "on the stage and about the dressing rooms": Sworn statement by Prince Hunley, February 21, 1913, DOJ File.
"One of Jack's retainers": Montreal *Daily Herald*, September 19, 1910.

239 "I have the car": *Boxing*, September 3, 1910.

240 "Men were white-faced": Quoted in Oldfield, "Wide Open All the Way."
"He's a devil": Nolan, *Barney Oldfield*, p. 88.

241 "I've done more fighting": Ibid., p. 47.
"I'd rather be dead": Oldfield, "Wide Open All the Way."
"the snub he richly deserves": Milwaukee *Herald*, October 10, 1910.
"It is impossible to withhold": *Boxing*, September 3, 1910.
"I return herewith the $1": NYT, October 12, 1910.

242 "Barney Oldfield is bigger": New York *Herald*, October 11, 1910.
"I am going to win": Ehrman, "White Hope."

243 "Mr. Oldfield, which heat": Bill Corum column, unsourced newspaper clipping.
"A sorrier lot of spectators": NYT, October 26, 1910.
"conduct injurious to the welfare": Nolan, *Barney Oldfield*, p. 110.
"I raced Jack Johnson": *Police Gazette*, November 5, 1910.

244 "No more of that automobile racing": NYT, October 26, 1910.
"Jack Johnson just had to keep on": Indianapolis *Freeman*, November 1, 1910.
"convinced me that I was not meant": Jack Johnson, *In the Ring and Out*, p. 152.
"He said to me to get my furniture": Belle Schreiber testimony, April, 1913 DOJ File.

245 "I don't think [a man] could make a mistake": Bertha Morrison testimony April, 1913, DOJ File.

247 "Sisters and brothers": Montreal *Daily Herald*, November 8, 1910.

248 "I couldn't seem to understand": Washington *Post*, November 18, 1910.
"as something told me": Ibid.
"I'm all right": NYT, November 18, 1910.
"aggravated nerve exhaustion": Quoted in Randy Roberts, *Papa Jack*, p. 120.
"to the astonishment of the natives": NYT, November 18, 1910.

249 JOHNSON SUFFERS FROM SERVILE FLATTERY: Milwaukee *Free Press*, November 20, 1910.
"a white woman": NYT, November 26, 1910.
"The only thing that worries me": *Police Gazette*, December 24, 1910.

251 "hostile to the colored race": NYT, December 21, 1910.
"hysterical condition": Chicago *Tribune*, December 26, 1910.

252 "a disagreement . . . a fight": Roy Jones testimony, April 1913, DOJ File.
SNORT OF SQUIRREL WHISKEY: Milwaukee *Free Press*, December 25, 1910.

253 "wipe out the whole goddamned Johnson

family": Washington *Post*, December 28, 1910.

253 "Sure he does": Ibid.

254 "a misunderstanding": Chicago *Tribune*, December 29, 1910.
"I never slept with a nigger": NYT, January 3, 1911.

255 "She must have known": New York *World*, September 13, 1912.

256 "I don't understand McIntosh": Chicago *American*, March 25, 1911.
"compelled to see Jack Johnson": Agent Charles L. Sterling report, March 5, 1913, DOJ File.

257 "All right, white man": NYT, March 25, 1911.
"If you beat that nigger": LAT, April 2, 1911.
"the big, black swaggering bully": *Police Gazette*, April 15, 1911.
"You all get away": Milwaukee *Evening Wisconsin*, April 20, 1911.

258 "Pinched again": NYT, May 16, 1911.
"In the heat of the search": John Lardner, *White Hopes*, p. 27.

259 "there was nothing uncovered": NYT, May 27, 1911.
"Nobody wants to see me win": Chicago *Tribune*, May 27, 1911.

CHAPTER NINE: THE BLACK MAN GARBED IN BLACK

260 "There was consternation": NYT, June 7, 1911.
"Mrs. Johnson was not visible": Washington *Post*, June 8, 1911.

261 "the delicate question": NYT, June 7, 1911.
"I always dress port and starboard": Milwaukee *Free Press*, June 6, 1911.
"No race prejudice came": NYT, June 10, 1911.
"I wish we'd seen more of him": Ibid.

262 "Messrs Hamilton, the well-known jewelers": *Boxing*, June 24, 1911.
"crowds of women": Wignall, *Story of Boxing*, p. 257.
"a big slate-coloured mass": *Boxing*, June 24, 1911.
"It got me, it was so grand": Washington *Post*, June 23, 1911.
"The fighters saw each other": NYT, June 25, 1911.

263 "polish off all the white trash": *Police Gazette*, May, 1911.
"to break [in] Johnson lightly": London *Times*, August 7, 1911.

264 "Fight for America?": Ibid.
"lively conduct": Milwaukee *Free Press*, October 24, 1911.

265 "great nervous prostration": Milwaukee *Evening Wisconsin*, August 29, 1911.
"Before she left for Paris": Ibid., October 25, 1912.
"as handsome as a Congolese Apollo": *Boxeurs*, September 14, 1911.

267 "watchfulness": Milwaukee *Evening Wisconsin*, September 14, 1911.
"gratify that craving": London *Times*, September 16, 1911.

268 "a white soldier": Quoted in Mews, "Puritanicalism, Sport and Race."
"white and black will be pitted against each other": London *Times*, September 19, 1911.
"When white opposes black": Mews, "Puritanicalism, Sport and Race."
"We have hitherto": London *Daily Mail*, September 23, 1911.

269 "I have made up my mind": Mews, "Puritanicalism, Sport and Race."
"Come right in": London *Times*, September 26, 1911.

270 "From the moment when Jack Johnson": London *Daily Mail*, September 28, 1911.

272 "Does this appear": *Boxing*, November 18, 1911.

273 *"And so you're coming home"*: Chicago *Tribune*, December 22, 1911.
"The American won": Curley, *Memoirs*, June 1931.

274 "Nowadays every manager": Phelon, "Fitzsimmons and the White Hopes."

275 "I'm going to quit this job": Quoted in Lardner, *White Hopes*, p. 26.
"A WHITE HOPE IN THE MAKING": Ibid. p. 26.
"the bloodiest fight ever seen": LAT, September 16, 1911.
"I immediately launched a boom for Flynn": Curley, *Memoirs*, July 1931.

276 "What a friend!": Ibid.
"Come right out to my house": Ibid.

277 "I begged her to stay with me": Milwaukee *Evening Wisconsin*, October 25, 1912.
"one of the popular society girls": Washington *Post*, February 11, 1912.

278 "Who she was before": New York *Herald Tribune*, February 10, 1912.
"Just did it because I don't like him": Milwaukee *Evening Wisconsin*, March 6, 1912.

279 "I guess that's discrimination": NYT, January 12, 1912.
"Las Vegas will be the cynosure": Quoted in Kammer, "TKO in Las Vegas."

280 "to hold on": Wilson, "Another White Hope."

280 "where I can see people": Albuquerque *Morning Journal*, May 28, 1912.

"He may be seen": Quoted in Wilson, "Another White Hope."

281 "Time and again": Unsourced clipping signed "An Old Fan," Jim Johnston Collection.

"Wait a minute!": NYT, July 5, 1912.

282 "The nigger's holding me": Quoted in Roberts, *Papa Jack*, p. 135.

"Flynn's feet were both off the floor": NYT, July 5, 1912.

"like a billy goat": Milwaukee *Free Press*, July 5, 1912.

283 "full of fight and ginger": San Francisco *Examiner*, July 5, 1912.

"I've got sense enough": Chicago *Daily News*, July 11, 1912.

"No sir, this pitcher is through": Ibid.

284 "the coal bin of the wise purchaser": Chicago *Tribune*, July 11, 1912.

"a miniature frying pan": Chicago *Defender*, July 13, 1912.

"three drink-dispensing parlors": Chicago *Examiner*, July 12, 1912.

285 "in my cabaret": Jack Johnson, *In the Ring and Out*, p. 68.

"Owing to the audience": Chicago *Examiner*, July 12, 1912.

"Although many of the daily": Chicago *Defender*, July 13, 1912.

286 "surrounded as always by friends": Bricktop and Haskins, *Bricktop*, pp. 42–48.

287 "I made it seven in twelve hours": Quoted in Stump, "Rowdy Reign."

"She was a good-looking": Bricktop and Haskins, *Bricktop*, p. 47.

"The pugilist regarded the proceedings": Chicago *Examiner*, July 12, 1912.

288 "I am going to get fixed for life now": Ibid., January 24, 1914.

289 "The Café de Champion, both on the main and second floors": Chicago *Defender*, September 22, 1912. (Covers events of September 8, before Etta Johnson's suicide.)

290 "even the Negroes don't respect me": NYT, September 12, 1912.

"My dear Mother": Chicago *Examiner*, September 17, 1912.

291 "I was singing": Bricktop and Haskins, *Bricktop*, p. 47.

"That woman has been troubled": Chicago *Tribune*, September 12, 1912.

"just to prevent her": Ibid.

292 "Wabash Avenue was crowded": Chicago *Examiner*, September 12, 1912.

"girl of gentle breeding": New York *World*, September 12, 1912.

293 "While it cannot be said": NYT, September 14, 1912.

294 "My daughter begged me": Cleveland *Gazette*, September 21, 1912.

"Is there anyone in this church": Chicago *Defender*, September 21, 1912.

295 "Many colored women": Chicago *Broad Ax*, September 21, 1912.

"It's over": Ibid.

CHAPTER TEN: THE ACCUSED

296 "Before the tragedy": Bricktop and Haskins, *Bricktop*, pp. 47–48.

297 "We were certainly glad": Quoted in Asbury, *Gem of the Prairie*, p. 283.

"Time will show": Ibid.

"We know that no innocent young girl": Quoted in Rosen, *Lost Sisterhood*, p. 133.

"a moral certainty": Quoted in Langum, *Crossing over the Line*, p. 30.

298 "The white slave traffic": Quoted in ibid., p. 43.

"for the purpose of prostitution": Ibid., pp. 45–46.

"Electric pianos stopped": Quoted in Asbury, *Gem of the Prairie*, p. 299.

299 "under the influence": Chicago *Daily News*, October 17, 1912.

300 "a chance to get it back": Chicago *Tribune*, October 15, 1912.

301 "JACK" JOHNSON DEAF: Chicago *Daily News*, October 17, 1912.

302 "Get a warrant out for Johnson": Ibid.

"I am doing this": Ibid.

"I won't shake hands": Milwaukee *Evening Wisconsin*, October 18, 1912.

"When Miss Cameron appeared": Ibid.

303 "The undersigned and 100 others": Quoted in Al-Tony Gilmore, *Bad Nigger!*, p. 96.

304 "Suggest great care": George W. Wickersham to James H. Wilkerson, October 19, 1912, DOJ File.

"clearing house for the procuring": Chicago *Tribune*, October 19, 1912.

"[Miss Cameron] denies": M. J. Lins report, October 21, 1912, DOJ File.

"care whether he was black or white": Chicago *Tribune*, October 19, 1912.

"procuring girls for immoral purposes": Agent B. J. Meyer Report, October 18, 1912, DOJ File.

305 "Public sentiment was aroused": Agent B. J. Meyer, October 18, 1912, DOJ File.

"They can't get me": Chicago *Tribune*, October 19, 1912.

"strolled into the courthouse": Chicago *Daily News*, October 18, 1912.

305 "I don't think it is necessary": Ibid.
306 "I'm going to marry Lucille": Chicago *Daily News,* October 19, 1912.
"Popular indignation": Quoted in Farr, *Black Champion,* p. 50.
"eliminated" [him] "as thoroughly": Quoted in Al-Tony Gilmore, *Bad Nigger!,* p. 98.
"Christian duty": LAT, October 25, 1912.
307 JACK JOHNSON DANGEROUSLY ILL: Quoted in Randy Roberts, *Papa Jack,* p. 146.
"all self-respecting black men": Milwaukee *Evening News,* October 23, 1912.
"How silly!": Nashville *Globe,* October 24, 1912.
308 "It is unfortunate": Baltimore *Afro American,* October 25, 1912.
"I never got caught": Chicago *Tribune,* October 24, 1912.
309 "Throw that lawyer out": Ibid., October 21, 1912.
"I hope Johnson gets his block knocked off": Washington *Post,* October 2, 1912.
"I will never have relations": Ibid.
"brought burning shame": Chicago *Tribune,* October 2, 1912.
"hold the race guilty": Chicago *Defender,* October 26, 1912.
"Yes, I should like to do that": Ibid.
310 "Tell all you know": Milwaukee *Evening Wisconsin,* October 22, 1912.
311 "It has been established": Agent M. J. Lins Report, October 26, 1912, DOJ File.
"secure evidence": Quoted in Randy Roberts, *Papa Jack,* p. 148.
"He cried, whined like a baby": Chicago *Tribune,* October 30, 1912.
"and *that* he'll have a deuce of a time": Ibid.
"There are plenty of white gentlemen": Chicago *Broad Ax,* October 23, 1912.
312 "I'll take my car": Washington *Post,* October 30, 1912.
"send this nigger to jail": "A Chicagoan" to United States District Attorney, Chicago, October 28, 1912, DOJ File.
313 "ex-post office safe-cracker": Agent B. J. Meyer Report, October 26, 1912, DOJ File.
"BELLE BAKER, ALIAS BELLE GIFFORD": M. J. Lins Report, November 4, 1912, DOJ File.
"in view of the fact": M. J. Lins, November 4, 1912, DOJ File.
314 "peace and dignity": Quoted in Roberts, *Papa Jack,* p. 153.
"I think you ought": Chicago *Tribune,* November 8, 1912.
315 "You don't have to do this": Ibid.

"I knew the Schreiber girl": Ibid.
"a brazen attempt": Washington *Post,* November 9, 1912.
"tell the judge": Ibid.
"I will not accept a cash bond": Ibid.
316 "Please don't, Jack": Quoted in Randy Roberts, *Papa Jack,* p. 156.
"I'll give $50": Chicago *Tribune,* November 10, 1912.
"The only thing wrong": Ibid.
"When I was in jail": Quoted in Randy Roberts, *Papa Jack,* p. 156.
317 "That's the Jack Johnson case": Washington *Post,* November 14, 1912.
"the negro has been indicted": Chicago *Tribune,* November 9, 1912.
"a regular prison": Attachment to memo from William M. Offley to A. Bruce Bielaski, November 19, 1912, DOJ File.
318 "special medicine": William M. Offley to A. Bruce Bielaski, November 21, 1912, DOJ File.
"All that she knows": Raymond S. Horn to Belle Schreiber, December 2, 1912, DOJ File.
319 "ruined in the eyes of the world": Jack Johnson, *In the Ring and Out,* p. 83.
"her brave defender": Tiny Johnson, grand jury deposition, 1914, DOJ File.
"They ought to refuse him": Chicago *Daily News,* December 3, 1912.
"I had a long talk": Chicago *Daily News,* December 4, 1912.
320 "I am so happy": Chicago *Tribune,* December 4, 1912.
"Sometimes I say things": Quoted in Farr, "Black Hamlet of the Heavyweights."
THE WEDDING CEREMONY: Chicago *Defender,* December 7, 1912.
321 "During the trip": J. A. Poulin Report, December 14, 1912, DOJ File.
"Down in this part of the country": Quoted in Al-Tony Gilmore, *Bad Nigger!,* p. 106.
"There is but one punishment": Ibid., p. 107.
"That Johnson wedding": Ibid., p. 108.
322 "No brutality": Ibid.
323 "black male": NYT, December 24, 1912.
324 "We intend to make a clubhouse": Chicago *Tribune,* December 24, 1912.
"Negro invasion": NYT, December 25, 1912.
"In its original form": Chicago *Tribune,* December 24, 1912.
326 "Jack is upstairs sleeping": Charles DeWoody Report, January 14, 1913, DOJ File.
"If I had known": Chicago *Daily News,* January 14, 1913.
"Personally, I have not the slightest doubt":

B. J. Meyer Report, January 14, 1913, DOJ File.

327 "The impudent air of Jack Johnson": Milwaukee *Free Press*, January 15, 1913.

328 "But Mrs. Lucille Johnson": M. J. Lins Report, February 25, 1913, DOJ File.
"advantage and interest": Charles DeWoody Report, March 10, 1913, DOJ File.
"very feebly": Ibid.
"The defendant left": Ibid.

329 "The table was a dream": Chicago *Defender*, April 6, 1913.

330 "I've got so many": H. B. Coy report, April 22, 1913, DOJ File.

331 "unnatural and perverted practices": Charles DeWoody to A. Bruce Bielaski, April 20, 1913, DOJ File.

332 "Don't beat me any more": Ibid.
"an effort to open the door": Charles DeWoody Report, May 1, 1913, DOJ File.
"PRINCIPAL WITNESS": Charles DeWoody Report, May 5, 1913, DOJ File.
"If the attitude of the Grand Jury": Ibid. p. 169.
"a fit of the blues": Charles DeWoody, May 1, 1913, DOJ File.

333 "because they said": Quoted in Randy Roberts, *Papa Jack*, p. 153.
"strongly prejudiced": Quoted in Ibid., p. 170.
U.S. v. John Arthur Johnson court proceedings: My account, from the opening statements to the verdict, is drawn entirely from the trial transcript in the DOJ File.

344 "I have nothing to say": Chicago *Tribune*, May 14, 1913.
"This verdict will go around the world": Ibid.

345 encounter between Johnson and Schreiber at the depot: Noted by Agent M. L. Lins Report, May 14, 1913, DOJ.
"unquestionably the greatest": Van Court, *Making of Champions*, p. 86.

346 "The crime of which this defendant stands convicted": Chicago *Tribune*, June 5, 1913.
"Oh well": Ibid.

347 "If Johnson had told me": Chicago *Examiner*, January 24, 1913.

348 "I am not a coward, gentlemen": *Mirror of Life and Boxing World*, July 19, 1913.
"It never happened": Quoted in Randy Roberts, *Papa Jack*, p. 181.

349 "That j.p. never had a chance": Quoted in Farr, *Black Champion*, p. 176.
AM SAILING SUNDAY: Charles DeWoody Report, June 28, 1913, DOJ File.

"This may solve the whole problem": Quoted in Farr, *Black Champion*, p. 177.
"We're the three musketeers!" Ibid., p. 176.

CHAPTER ELEVEN: THE FUGITIVE

350 "I must complete my library": NYT, July 18, 1913.
"prominent street corners": London *Times*, August 27, 1913.

351 "Johnson's engagements": Ibid., July 22, 1913.
"a gay frock coat": Ibid., August 25, 1913.
"Take anybody educated": Ibid.
"As regards Johnson's domestic affairs": London *Daily Express*, August 26, 1913.

352 "Besides giving boxing exhibitions": Chicago *Defender*, October 4, 1913.
"which is six times larger": Ibid., December 15, 1913.

353 "notably Sam Langford": LAT, November 6, 1913.

354 "A terrific hubbub": London *Times*, December 20, 1913.
"I am delighted": Chicago *Examiner*, January 22, 1914.

355 "absurd": Ibid., January 24, 1914.
"got a dirty deal somewhere": Ibid.
"Have one on Jack Johnson": Undated deposition of M. Evalyn Knitzinger, DOJ File.

356 "I must say": LAT, February 9, 1914.
"The tone which Jack Johnson has taken": Quoted in Farr, *Black Champion*, p. 186.

357 "Permit me to inform the public": Chicago *Defender*, March 14, 1914.

358 "Stop your kidding, Jack": LAT, July 30, 1914.
"like a rajah": Ibid.
"Basically, the Americans": Washington *Post*, June 27, 1914.

359 "I-don't-know-where": *Mirror of Life and Boxing World*, September 27, 1913.
"If it is true": Quoted in Randy Roberts, *Papa Jack*, p. 92.

360 MATCH JOHNSON-MORAN: Reproduced in *John Bull*, July 18, 1914.
"threw a greenish tint": London *Times*, June 29, 1914.
"It might have been": Dartnell, *Seconds Out!*, pp. 123–24.

361 "Everything O.K., Dan?": LAT, July 30, 1914.
"Those are pretty wise guys": Ibid.
"Come on! Come on!": NYT, June 28, 1914.
"Hit him, Daddy!": Ibid.
"How do you feel now": London *Daily Mail*, June 29, 1914.
"My sincere congratulations": Quoted in Farr, *Black Champion*, p. 44.

361 "positively the poorest bout ever staged": NYT, June 28, 1914.
"the finest fistic encounter": Chicago Defender, July 4, 1914.

362 "I'm as bitter a man": John Lardner, White Hopes, p. 44.

363 "They invoked the five-and-ten law": Quoted in Farr, Black Champion, p. 193.

364 "I met Jack Johnson": Washington Post, August 26, 1914.
"the first time such a thing": New York Age, August 13, 1914.
"The only thing left for me": Washington Post, August 26, 1914.

365 "I've been told": Curley, Memoirs, August 1931.
"Times were slack with me": Ibid.
"an awful herd": Phelon, "Where Boxing Stands Today."
"God made me a giant": Rex Lardner, Legendary Champions, p. 188.

366 "I never liked [boxing]": Ibid.
"I quit the big dog": Quoted in John Lardner, White Hopes, p. 36.
"I never really knew how": Rex Lardner, Legendary Champions, p. 188.

367 "Jess, here's something": Quoted in John Lardner, White Hopes, p. 39.
"His behavior in the fight": Ibid.
"just to show Tom Jones": LAT, July 15, 1914.
"Jess, I want to put you into a ring": Curley, Memoirs, August 1931.

368 "Come on up": Ibid.
"[a] moment later": Ibid.

369 "He frankly told me": Ibid.
"Did he think": Washington Post, August 12, 1927.

371 "about broke": Agent L. C. Wheeler Report, February 17, 1915, DOJ File.
"that it has already been decided": Hinton G. Clabaugh to A. Bruce Bielaski, February 19, 1915, DOJ File.
"It teaches by lighning": Quoted in Lennigg, "Myth and Fact."
"uprising of outraged manhood": Ibid.
"close to the sporting": Ibid.
"I personally would": A. Bruce Bielaski to Hinton G. Clabaugh, February 23, 1915, DOJ File.

372 SHIPS HERE REFUSED: Curley, Memoirs, August 1931.

373 "contest between Champion Johnson": NYT, March 15, 1915.
"Why, Johnson, of course": New York Herald, April 4, 1915.
"Jess Willard would restore": LAT, March 6, 1915.

374 "witty remarks": New York Herald, April 1, 1915.
"a triumphal entry": Ibid.

375 "fat to the point of a paunch": Ibid.
"I know that baby can't lose": Ibid., April 2, 1915.
"There is not enough money": Ibid., April 3, 1915.
"I AM GETTING TIRED": Chicago Tribune, March 16, 1915.

376 "Here's your cute little friend": Ibid., April 4, 1915.
"Hey señor": Ibid.
"fistic frenzy": Baltimore American, April 5, 1915.

377 "From the stands": Ibid.
"Never in the history": Chicago Tribune, April 6, 1915.
"There was a mad craning": Los Angeles Examiner, April 6, 1915.
"I am absolutely confident": Chicago Evening American, April 5, 1915.
"I can hit him": Los Angeles Examiner, April 6, 1915.

378 "You got to do better": Ibid.
"Johnson, you'll get yours today": Ibid.

379 "Jack, go take my wife away": Washington Post, April 12, 1915.
"Johnson looked pitifully": New York Herald, April 6, 1915.
"Oh my God": Los Angeles Examiner, April 6, 1915.
"What's the matter?": Chicago Evening American, April 6, 1915.
"Something approaching a race riot": Los Angeles Examiner, April 6, 1915.

380 "Now all my troubles will be over": Ibid.
"youth and condition": Washington Post, April 6, 1915.
"At one point": NYT, April 6, 1915.
"Pretty blue": Washington Post, April 6, 1915.
"It can't be true": NYT, April 7, 1915.
"Every white man": Ibid., April 6, 1915.

381 "Johnson fought a great fight": Quoted in Al-Tony Gilmore, Bad Nigger!, p. 140.
"For some years past": Chicago Broad Ax, Quoted in ibid.
"extravagant reveler": Al-Tony Gilmore, Bad Nigger!, p. 141.
"connubial connections": Ibid.
"The Ethiopian has been eliminated": Detroit News, April 18, 1915.

382 "It is a point of pride": Chicago Tribune, April 8, 1915.
"I wish I was going back": Washington Post, April 8, 1915.

382 "the saddest thing I ever saw": Ibid., April 12, 1915.
"If he had saved the country": LAT, April 8, 1915.
"Not a station": Baltimore *American,* April 9, 1915.

383 "men, women and children": Curley, *Memoirs,* October 1931.
"Alas, poor Johnson": LAT, May 14, 1915.

384 "Man, for me war is over": NYT, May 15, 1915.

385 "Wasn't I in history": Ibid.
" 'Oh hell' ": Washington *Post,* August 12, 1927.
"It was very irregular": Ibid.
"He replied": Johnson, *In the Ring and Out,* pp. 200–1.

386 "BLACK MAIL PROPOSITION": Washington *Post,* July 23, 1915.
"became a favorite target": Jack Johnson, *Inside the Ring and Out,* p. 145.

387 "Between blasts of bombs": Ibid.

388 "Let me help you, Johnson": Farr, *Black Champion,* p. 210.

389 "[Cravan] contented himself": Quoted in Randy Roberts, *Papa Jack,* p. 207.
JACK JOHNSON CAPTURED: Milwaukee *Free Press,* April 22, 1916.

390 "ancient ways of doing business": Johnson, *In the Ring and Out,* p. 105.
"One of those bloody pressmen": Anonymous, "Arthur Cravan vs Jack Johnson."

391 "numerous risks": Johnson, *In the Ring and Out,* p. 109.
"For a brief time": Washington *Post,* March 19, 1918.
"very anxious": Frank S. Armand to Emmett J. Scott, June 29, 1918, Record Group 165, National Archives.
"I am as good an American": Pittsburgh *Courier,* June 14, 1918.

392 "do anything": Unsigned letter to Emmett J. Scott, August 20, 1918, Group 165 National Archives.
"the Hotel Regina": Quoted in Farr, *Black Champion,* p. 217.
"down-and-outs, cheap gamblers": Major John W. Lang to Director, Military Intelligence Division, December 9, 1918, Group 165, National Archives.

393 "Report, hell": Ibid., January 18, 1919.

394 "I found [him] a man": Washington *Post,* April 12, 1915.

395 "If Johnson throwed that fight": Quoted in Farr, *Black Champion,* p. 206.
"a constant companion": Chicago *Tribune,* April 17, 1919.

396 "Unfortunately for him": Chicago *Defender,* July 11, 1919.
"Mexican adventurer": Undated clipping, Gumby Collection.

397 "You, who are lynched": Quoted in Randy Roberts, *Papa Jack,* p. 212.

398 "don Jack, whenever he could": McGehee, "Dandy and the Mauler."
"in the grand tradition": Ibid.

399 "goddamit go through them": Quoted in Ward, *American Originals,* p. 52.
"God, he was big!": Ibid.

400 "unconditional surrender": NYT, January 30, 1920.
"I never knew such gameness": Jack Johnson, *In the Ring and Out,* p. 119.
"regrettable accident": Ibid., p. 120.

401 "Imagine a wide main street": LAT, June 6, 1920.
"He struts about": Ibid., July 15, 1920.

402 "Well, the word was passed": Ibid., July 16, 1920.
"Several white women there": Ibid., July 21, 1920.
"The center of the stage": Ibid.

403 "Johnson sprawled down in a seat": Ibid.
"the colored visitors": Ibid.
"It was a memorable journey". Jack Johnson, *Inside the Ring and Out,* p. 123.
"I'm damn glad": NYT, July 19, 1920.
"everything arranged": LAT, July 20, 1920.

404 "ice cream sprees": NYT, July 27, 1920.
"This man deserves": Ibid., September 15, 1920.

CHAPTER TWELVE: THE STEPPER

405 "It is alleged": Trusty Prisoner's Agreement, Jack Johnson File, Inmate Case Files—United States Penitentiary–Leavenworth; Records of the Federal Bureau of Prisons, Record Group 129, National Archives—Central Plains Region (hereafter, JJ File).
"several thousand dollars": Jack Johnson, *In the Ring and Out,* p. 128.

406 "baseball park orderly": Leavenworth *Post,* September 20, 1920.
"In all, my imprisonment": Jack Johnson, *In the Ring and Out,* p. 129.
"did use the guard's toilet": Report, November 3, 1920, JJ File.
"rude language": Report, November 29, 1920, JJ File.
"This prisoner does not get up": Report, January 21, 1921, JJ File.
"loafing in main hall": Ibid.

407 "This prisoner is an orderly": Undated report, JJ File.

407 "found little cause for complaint": Jack Johnson, *In the Ring and Out*, p. 132.
"was unable to find one": Ibid.

408 "Wonder why 'Meow! Meow!' ": Leavenworth *New Era*, May 6, 1921.
"I have used his expressions": Melville Butler File, Inmate Case Files—United States Penitentiary–Leavenworth; Records of the Federal Bureau of Prisons, Record Group 129, National Archives—Central Plains Region.

409 "He was a good friend": O'Dare, *Philosophy of the Dusk*, p. 131.
"Nothing seemed to trouble him": Rudensky, *The Gonif*, p. 210.

410 "every field": *Billboard*, November 27, 1920.
"Scott will win sure": Jack Johnson to Billy McLean [*sic*] (MicClain), November 18, 1920, JJ File.
"boxing gloves, punching bag": Jack Johnson to Lucille Johnson, November 20, 1920, JJ File.

411 "Tell Gus to . . . locate [Owens]": Jack Johnson to Lucille Johnson, November 8, 1920, JJ File.
"Nothing wrong with me": Ibid., November 11, 1920.

412 "There comes Jack now": Leavenworth *New Era*, November 26, 1920.

413 "Hello dear": Jack Johnson to Lucille Johnson, November 26, 1920, JJ File.
"It was the opinion": NYT, November 26, 1920.
"I am filled with power": Beloit (WI) *Daily News*, February 21, 1921.

414 "and then we will continue": Jack Johnson to Lucille Johnson, December 31, 1920, JJ File.
"30 or 40 young white girls": Lewis J. Baley to D. S. Dickerson, January 20, 1921, JJ File.
"what an unfair trial": Jack Johnson to Ben Allen, March 30, 1921, JJ File.
"influential friends": Dick Ellis to Jack Johnson, March 29, 1921, JJ File.

415 "Cannot see my way clear": Jack Johnson to William Bottoms, undated, JJ File.
"From Jack Johnson's correspondence": Leavenworth *New Era*, February 25, 1921.
"The idea is that a young man": M. D. Waltner to August V. Anderson, March 31, 1921, JJ File.

417 "EXPECT A GOOD TIME": Gus Rhodes to Jack Johnson, June 20, 1921, JJ File.
"Many close friends": Jack Johnson, *In the Ring and Out*, p. 134.
"It doesn't make any difference": NYT, July 10, 1921.

418 "What a relief": Leavenworth *New Era*, July 15, 1921.
"Jack Johnson never was a slacker": NYT, July 10, 1921.

419 "Jack Johnson is out": Chicago *Broad Ax*, July 14, 1921.
"Chicago and my friends": Chicago *Tribune*, July 14, 1921.
"The reception and the feasting": Chicago *Broad Ax*, July 14, 1921.

420 "Johnson is through": Quoted in Hietala, *Fight of the Century*, p. 142.
"The commissioners are in office": NYT August 1, 1921.

422 "I was in my dressing room": Ethel Waters, *His Eye Is on the Sparrow*, p. 133.

423 "I just held my breath": Chicago *Defender*, March 11, 1921.
"a super production": Advertisement for New Douglas Theater in New York, January 8, 1922, Hawes Collection.

424 "in which all the performers": Jack Johnson, *In the Ring and Out*, p. 135.

425 "I am forty-five years old.": Undated 1923 clipping, archives of Antiquities of the Prize Ring.
"beautiful decorations": Undated handbill from Hawes Collection.
"As a prize-fighter": Jack Johnson 1924 recording, "Runnin' Down the Title Holder," Tim Brooks Collection.
"evidence involving Johnson": NYT, February 17, 1924.

426 "Echoes of the old wrath": Jack Johnson, *In the Ring and Out*, p. 138.
"gentlemanly and courteous manner": Irene Johnson, "My Husband," preface to Jack Johnson, *In the Ring and Out*, p. 16.
"There could not be a man": Ibid.

427 "Lester had youth": David Beardsley, undated article, *Boxing Report*, Jim Johnston Collection.

428 "back on the boards": Jack Johnson, *In the Ring and Out*, p. 249.
"Johnson used his old-time tactics": Drumright (OK) *Evening Derrick*, September 7, 1926.
" 'white buzzard' hangers-on": NYT, October 7, 1926.

429 "ignorant, perverse child": Quoted in Duberman, *Paul Robeson*, p. 104.
"Must a man, because of his color": Irene Johnson, "My Husband," preface to Jack Johnson, *In the Ring and Out*, p. 16.

430 "the best all-around heavyweight in history": *The Ring*, June 1927.

430 "I would have been able to pay my debts":
Beloit (WI) *Daily News*, October 4, 1928.
"My next fight": NYT, September 16, 1928.

431 "The story of Jack Johnson": NYT, September 14, 1928.
"If the Democrats": NYT, September 19, 1928.
"The tall, somewhat paunchy": Thurber, "Big Boy."

434 "orchestra leader": NYT, January 24, 1929.
"Jack Johnson made a few voodoo passes":
Undated 1931 clipping from *The Ring*, Jim Johnston Collection.
"Nothing of the great master": Milwaukee *Eagle*, April 29, 1931.

435 "a crying shame": LAT, June 12, 1931.
"Physically unfit!": Undated clipping from *The Ring*, Jim Johnston Collection.
"a tremendous ovation": London *Times*, January 3, 1932.
"You had to come up": Bricktop and Haskins, *Bricktop*, p. 185.

436 "What you aim to do": Quoted in Farr, *Black Champion*, p. 234.

437 "Let the son of a bitch": Quoted in Dan Parker, "Johnson-Louis Feud Traces Back to Blackburn," New York *Daily Mirror*, June 12, 1946.

438 "You know, boy": Louis, *My Life*, p. 36.
"It was thrilling": Ibid., p. 57.

439 "Every man's got a right": quoted in Horn, "Two Champions."
"imbibed with joy": quoted in ibid.
"Louis has the stuff": Ibid.
"Boy, you're the greatest fighter": Louis, *My Life*, p. 69.
"I can make a champion": Ibid.
"flash in the pan": Ibid.
"I respected this man": Ibid.
"Get that black cat": Horn, "Two Champions."

440 "lives like an animal": Mead, *Champion*, p. 68.
"One time we were talking": Louis, *My Life*, p. 39.

441 "never disgrace the Race": Quoted in Hietala, *Fight of the Century*, p. 159.

"If Joe becomes champion": Quoted in Horn, "Two Champions."
"Louis holds his left too low": Richmond *Afro-American*, June 15, 1936.
"Once the hero of his race": Quoted in Horn, "Two Champions."
JACK JOHNSON RAZZED: New York *Amsterdam News*, March 13, 1937.

442 "Jack Johnson was still running": Louis, *My Life*, p. 111.
"we got another chance!": Ibid., p. 119.
"I figured out the formula": quoted in Farr, *Black Champion*, p. 232.

443 "When the culture quotient": Jay, *Anomalies*, p. 41.
"Ladies and gentlemen": Undated unsourced article by Linton Baldwin, Jim Johnston Collection.

444 "It didn't do him much good": Louis, *My Life*, p. 69.
"Everybody thinks I'm jealous": quoted in Fleischer, "Johnson, Craftiest Boxer."
"I want to say here": Quoted in Hietala, *Fight of the Century*, p. 185.
"intense race hatred": Pittsburgh *Courier*, June 21, 1938.

445 "Johnson's background": Quoted in Hietala, *Fight of the Century*, p. 146.
"Johnson has stated": New York *Amsterdam News*, undated clipping, Gumby Collection.
"got plenty of nothin'": Associated Press in undated 1944 clipping, Gumby Collection.

446 "The Angel said": Stump, "Rowdy Reign."
"It was like this": Clem Boddington, "$15,000 Windfall."
"conversed with my wife": Ibid.
"This is the beginning": Fleischer, "Johnson, Craftiest Boxer."

447 "In my humble opinion": Ibid.
"They told us we could eat": Lucas, *Black Gladiator*, p. 186.

448 "He struck the first blow": Richmond, *Afro-American*, June 22, 1946.
"I loved him because of his courage": Ibid.

BIBLIOGRAPHY

ARCHIVES

Antiquities of the Prize Ring

Tim Brooks Collection

Hawes Collection

Jim Johnston Collection

Alexander Gumby Collection, Special Collections Division, Columbia University

Inmate Case Files; United States Penitentiary–Leavenworth; Records of the Federal Bureau of Prisons, Record Group 129 National Archives and Record Administration—Central Plains Region (Kansas City)

George P. Johnson Film Collection, University of Southern California (Los Angeles)

Jack Johnson Vertical Files Folder, Schomburg Collections, New York Public Library

Bill Loughman Collection

Gary Phillips Collection

Booker T. Washington Papers, Library of Congress

Records of the War Department, Group 165, National Archives

U.S. v. Johnson, General Records of the Department of Justice, File Number 16421, Record Group 60.

BOOKS AND ARTICLES

"Amateur, The" (W. F. Corbett). *Burns & Johnson in Australia.* Sydney, 1909.

Anderson, Jervis. "Black Heavies." *American Scholar,* Summer 1978.

Anonymous. "Arthur Cravan vs. Jack Johnson." *The Soil,* April 1917.

Armstrong, Louis. *Satchmo: My Life in New Orleans.* New York, 1968.

Asbury, Herbert. *The Gangs of New York.* New York, 1998.

———. *Gem of the Prairie: An Informal History of the Chicago Underworld.* De Kalb, Ill., 1986.

Ashe, Arthur R., Jr. *A Hard Road to Glory: A History of the African-American Athlete, 1619–1918.* New York, 1998.

Astor, Gerald. *. . . And a Credit to His Race: The Hard Life and Times of Joseph Louis Barrow a.k.a. Joe Louis.* New York, 1974.

Babyak, Jolene. *Birdman: The Many Faces of Robert Stroud.* Berkeley, Calif., 1994.

Barr, Alwyn. *Black Texans: A History of African Americans, 1528–1995.* Norman, Okla., 1973.

Barton, George A. *My Lifetime in Sports.* Minneapolis, 1957.

Batchelor, Denzil. *Gods with Gloves On.* London, 1946.

———. *Jack Johnson and His Times.* London, 1956.

Beach, Rex. *The Jeffries-Johnson Fight.* Chicago, 1910.

Beardsley, Dave. "I Saw Jack Johnson Fight." *Boxing Report,* undated clipping, Jim Johnston Collection.

Beasley, Ellen. *The Alleys and Back Buildings of Galveston.* Houston, 1996.

Beasley, Ellen, and Stanley Fox. *Galveston Architectural Guidebook.* Houston, 1996.

Bederman, Gail. *Manliness & Civilization: A Cultural History of Gender and Race in the United States, 1880–1917.* Chicago, 1995.

Bell, Frank. *Gladiators of the Glittering Churches.* Helena, Mont., 1985.

Bell, Leslie. *Inside the Fight Game.* London, 1952.

Bennison, Ben. *Famous Fights and Fighters.* London, 1938.

Bercovici, Konrad. *Around the World in New York.* New York, 1924.

Berlin, Edward A. *King of Ragtime: Scott Joplin and His Era.* New York, 1994.

Bettinson, A. F., and Ben Bennison, *The Home of Boxing.* London, 1923.

Blight, David. "The Birth of a Genre: Slavery on Film." *Common-Place* 1, no. 4 (July 2001).

Biddle, Cordelia Drexel, as told to Kyle Crichton. *My Philadelphia Father.* New York, 1967.

Boddington, Clem. "$15,000 Windfall." Unsourced clipping, Jim Johnston Collection.

Booth, J. B. *Boxers and Others.* London, 1933.

Borràs, Maria Lluïsa. *Arthur Cravan: Une stratégie du scandale.* Paris, 1997.

Bradford, Perry. *Born with the Blues.* New York, 1965.

Brearley, H. C. "Ba-ad Nigger." *South Atlantic Quarterly* 38 (1939).

Bricktop, with James Haskins. *Bricktop.* New York, 1983.

Brooks, Tim. *Lost Sounds: Blacks and the Birth of the Recording Industry.* Chicago, 2004.

Broome, Richard. "The Australian Reaction to Jack Johnson, American Pugilist, 1907–9." In Richard Cashman and Michael McKernan, eds., *Sport in History.* St. Lucia, Queensland, 1979.

Buchan, Don. "I Promoted Jack Johnson's Last Fight." *Boxing Illustrated,* undated clipping.

Burke, Carolyn. *Becoming Modern: The Life of Mina Loy.* Berkeley, Calif., 1996.

Burke, John. *Rogue's Progress: The Fabulous Adventures of Wilson Mizner.* New York, 1975.

Burns, Tommy. "Tommy Burns: The Rise and Fall of Our Almost Forgotten Champion." *Toronto Globe and Mail,* July 3, 1971.

Butters, Gerald R., Jr. *Black Manhood on the Silent Screen.* Lawrence, Kans., 2002.

Callis, Tracy. "Jack Johnson . . . 'Bad Nigger.' " *Wail! . . . The CBZ Journal,* November 2000.

———. "Jeffries and Other Heavyweights." *Wail! . . . The CBZ Journal,* April 2003.

———. "Jim Jeffries . . . Warhorse of Yesteryear," *Wail! . . . The CBZ Journal,* April 2001.

———. "Joe Choynski . . . 'Clever, Shifty, and Explosive." *Wail! . . . The CBZ Journal,* May 2002.

———. "Tommy Burns: He of the Terrible Right Hand," *Wail! . . . The CBZ Journal,* February 2004.

Callis, Tracy, Chuck Hasson, and Mike DeLisa. *Philadelphia's Boxing Heritage, 1876–1976.* Charleston, S.C., 2002.

Capeci, Dominic J., Jr., and Martha Wilkerson. "Multifarious Hero: Joe Louis, American Society and Race Relations During World Crisis, 1935–1945." *Journal of Sport History* 10, no. 3 (Winter 1983).

Captain, Gwendolyn. "Enter Ladies and Gentlemen of Color: Gender, Sport, and the Ideal of African American Manhood and Womanhood During the Late Nineteenth and Early Twentieth Centuries." *Journal of Sport History* 18, no. 1 (Spring 1991).

Chaplin, Ralph. *Wobbly: The Rough-and-Tumble Story of an American Radical.* Chicago, 1948.

Chicago Vice Commission. *The Social Evil in Chicago.* Chicago, 1911.

Choynski, Joe. "I Fought 'Em All." *Fight Stories,* 1930.

Coady, Robert. "Arthur Cravan vs. Jack Johnson." *The Soil* 1, no. 4 (April 1917).

Cochran, Charles. *Showman Looks On.* London, 1945.

Cooper, Henry. *The Great Heavyweights.* Secaucus, N.J., 1978.

Corbett, Jim. *The Roar of the Crowd: The True Tale of the Rise and Fall of a Champion.* New York, 1976.

Corn, Elliott J. *The Manly Art: Bare-Knuckle Prize Fighting in America.* Ithaca, N.Y., 1986.

Corri, Eugene. *Gloves and the Man.* London, 1928.

———. *Thirty Years a Referee.* London, 1915.

Curley, Jack (with Frank Graham). *Memoirs of a Promoter* (in 24 installments). *The Ring,* May 1930–April 1932.

Dartnell, Fred. *"Seconds Out!" Chats About Boxers, Their Trainers and Patrons.* New York, 1924.

Decoy, Robert H. *The Big Black Fire.* Los Angeles, 1969.

Deghy, Guy. *Noble and Manly: The History of the National Sporting Club.* London, 1956.

Dempsey, Jack (with Barbara Piatelli Dempsey). *Dempsey.* New York, 1977.

Diamond, Wilfrid. *Kings of the Ring.* London, 1954.

Donovan, Mike. *The Roosevelt That I Know and Recollections of the Most Famous American Fighting Men.* New York, 1909.

Duberman, Martin. *Paul Robeson: A Biography.* New York, 1989.

Erbstein, Charles E. *The Show-Up: Stories Before the Bar.* Chicago, 1926.

Ehrman, Pete. "The White Hope Who Outsped Jack Johnson." *Wail! . . . The CBZ Journal,* October 2002.

Etter, Roberta, and Stuart Schneider. *Halley's Comet: Memories of 1910.* New York, 1985.

Farr, Finis. *Black Champion: The Life and Times of Jack Johnson.* New York, 1964.

———. "Black Hamlet of the Heavyweights." *Sports Illustrated,* June 15, 1959.

Fields, Armond. *James J. Corbett: A Biography of the Heavyweight Boxing Champion and Popular Theater Headliner.* Jefferson, N.C., 2001.

Fleischer, Nat. *50 Years at Ringside.* New York, 1958.

———. *Fighting Furies: Story of the Golden Era of Jack Johnson, Sam Langford and Their Negro Contemporaries.* New York, 1939.

———. "Fleischer Bought Confession but Didn't Believe It." *The Ring,* January 1969.

———. "Johnson, Craftiest Boxer." *The Ring,* August 1946.

———. *The Michigan Assassin: The Saga of Stanley Ketchel.* New York, 1946.

Fleischer, Nat, and Sam Andre. *A Pictorial History of Boxing.* Secaucus, N.J., 1975.

Forte, Gilbert. "The One Who Was Best of All." *Boxing & Wrestling,* March 1955.

Fox, Richard F. *Life and Battles of Jack Johnson.* New York, 1910.

Fullerton, Hugh. *Two Fisted Jeff.* New York, 1929.

Gaddis, Thomas E. *Birdman of Alcatraz: The Story of Robert Stroud.* New York, 1955.

Gains, Larry. *The Impossible Dream.* Toronto, 1976.

Gilmore, Al-Tony. *Bad Nigger! The National Impact of Jack Johnson.* Port Washington, N.Y., 1975.

Gilmore, Robert K. "An Ozarks Melodrama: The Killing of Stanley Ketchel." *Ozarkswatch,* Winter 1993.

Goodwin, Nat C. *Nat Goodwin's Book.* Boston, 1914.

Goodwin, Ruby Berkley. *It's Good to Be Black.* Garden City, N.Y., 1953.

Gorn, Elliott J. *The Manly Art: Bare-Knuckle Prize Fighting in America.* Ithaca, N.Y., 1986.

Gottschild, Brenda Dixon. *Waltzing in the Dark: African American Vaudeville and Race Politics in the Swing Era.* New York, 2001.

Gravely, Vernon. "Willus Britt: More Than Just a Manager." *The Ring,* June 1954.

Greene, Casey Edward, and Shelly Henley Kelly, eds. *Through a Night of Horrors: Voices from the 1900 Galveston Storm.* College Station, Tex., 2000.

Hales, Douglas. *A Southern Family in White and Black: The Cuneys of Texas.* College Station, Tex., 2003.

Haley, Melissa. "Storm of Blows." *Common-place* 3, no. 2 (January 2003).

Harlan, Louis R. *Booker T. Washington: The Making of a Black Leader, 1856–1901.* New York, 1972.

———. *Booker T. Washington: The Wizard of Tuskegee, 1901–1915.* New York, 1983.

Harrison, Carter H. *Stormy Years: The Autobiography of Carter H. Harrison, Five Times Mayor of Chicago.* New York, 1935.

Hayes, Frank. *Champions of the Ring.* London, 1910.

Heinz, W. C. *What a Time It Was.* New York, 2001.

Heinz, W. C., and Nathan Ward, eds. *The Book of Boxing.* New York, 1999.

Heller, Peter. *"In This Corner . . . !" 42 World Champions Tell Their Stories.* New York, 1994.

Hetherington, John. *Australians: Nine Profiles.* Melbourne, 1960.

Hietala, Thomas R. *The Fight of the Century: Jack Johnson, Joe Louis and the Struggle for Racial Equality.* London, 2002.

Holtzman, Jerome. *No Cheering in the Press Box.* New York, 1954.

Horn, Robert. "Two Champions and Enemies." *Sports Illustrated,* May 14, 1990.

Igoe, Hype. "Li'l Arthur's Lean Days." *The Ring,* undated clipping.

Inglis, William. *Champions Off Guard.* New York, 1932.

Isenberg, Michael T. *John L. Sullivan and His America.* Urbana, Ill., 1988.

Jacobs, Jim. "Don't Tell Me Jack Johnson Took a Dive." *Boxing Illustrated and Wrestling News,* November 1961.

Jay, Ricky. *Jay's Journal of Anomalies.* New York, 2003.

Jeffries, James J. *My Life and Battles.* New York, 1910.

Jervis, James, and Leo R. Flack. *A Jubilee History of the Municipality of Botany, 1888–1938.* Sydney, 1938.

Johnson, Jack. "A Champion Remembers." *Fight Stories.* December 1930.

———. "A Champ Recalls." *The Ring,* July 1946.

———. "Getting Mine." Leavenworth *New Era,* October 29, 1920.

———. "How I Whipped Mr. Jeffries." Los Angeles *Times,* July 5, 1931.

———. "How Ketchel Tried to Double Cross Me." *Boxing & Wrestling,* July 1957.

———. "Jack Johnson Discourses on Timing and Feinting—and Gives Some Hints." *Souvenir of the Tommy Burns–Jack Johnson Boxing Contest.* Sydney, 1910.

———. *Jack Johnson—In the Ring and Out.* New York, 1927.

———. *Jack Johnson—In the Ring and Out.* Gilbert Odd Edition, London, 1977. (Reprint with appendixes.)

———. "Johnson's Story of His Victory." *Boxing,* July 16, 1910.

———. "Mason-Dixon Line Retards Heavy." Syndicated newspaper article, 1929.

———. *Ma Vie et Mes Combats* (in 14 installments). *La Vie au grand air,* 1910.

———. *Mes Combats.* Paris, 1914.

———. "Mes Débuts dans le noble art." *La Boxe et Les Boxeurs,* April 5, 1923.

———. "Mes Premiers Combats." *La Vie au grand air,* 1910 (precise date not given).

Johnson, Jack, and Bill Sims. *Jack Johnson, The Man with Boxing Instructions and Health Hints.* Chicago, 1932.

Johnson, Mrs. Irene. "Jack Johnson Was a Fine Gentleman." *Boxing & Wrestling,* February 1957.

Johnson, James Weldon. *Along This Way.* New York, 2000.

Kahn, Roger. *A Flame of Pure Fire: Jack Dempsey and the Roaring 20's.* New York, 1999.

Kammer, David J. "TKO in Las Vegas: Boosterism and the Johnson-Flynn Fight." *New Mexico Historical Review* 61 (October 1986).

Kaye, Andrew M. " 'Battle Blind': Atlanta's Taste for Black Boxing in the Early Twentieth Century." *Journal of Sport History* 28, no. 2 (Summer 2001).

Kenney, William Howland. *Chicago Jazz: A Cultural History.* New York, 1993.

Kramer, William M., and Norton B. Stern. "San Francisco's Fighting Jew." *California Historical Quarterly,* Winter 1974.

Land, Barbara, and Myrick Land. *A Short History of Reno.* Reno, Nev., 1995.

Langley, Tom. *The Life of Peter Jackson: Champion of Australia.* London, 1974.

Langum, David J. *Crossing over the Line: Legislating Morality and the Mann Act.* Chicago, 1994.

Lardner, John. *White Hopes and Other Tigers.* New York, 1947.

———. "Yesterday's Graziano." *Sport*, April 1948.

Lardner, Rex. *The Legendary Champions*. New York, 1972.

Larson, Erik. *Isaac's Storm: A Man, a Time, and the Deadliest Hurricane in History*. New York, 2000.

Leddig, Arthur. "Myth and Fact: The Reception of the Birth of a Nation." *Film History* 16, 2004.

"Leonce." "Jack Johnson: Colored Champion of the World." *Lone Hand*, December 1, 1908.

Levy, Eugene. *James Weldon Johnson: Black Leader, Black Voice*. Chicago, 1973.

Lewis, David Levering. *W. E. B. Du Bois: Biography of a Race, 1868–1919*. New York, 1993.

Liebling, A. J. (ed. by Fred Warner and James Barbour). *A Neutral Corner: Boxing Essays*. New York, 1990.

Lindberg, Richard. *Chicago by Gaslight: A History of Chicago's Netherworld, 1880–1920*. Chicago, 1996.

———. *Chicago Ragtime: Another Look at Chicago, 1880–1920*. South Bend, Ind., 1985.

Lindsay, Lionel. *Comedy of Life: An Autobiography by Sir Lionel Lindsay, 1874–1961*. Sydney, 1967.

Lomax, Alan. *Mister Jelly Roll*. New York, 1950.

London, Jack (ed. by James Banke). *Stories of Boxing*. Dubuque, Iowa, 1992.

Louis, Joe (with Edna Rust and Art Rust, Jr.). *Joe Louis: My Life*. New York, 1978.

Lucas, Bob. *Black Gladiator: A Biography of Jack Johnson*. New York, 1970.

Lynch, Bohun. *Knuckles and Gloves*. London, 1922.

Lyon, Harris Merton. "In Reno Riotous." *Hampton's Magazine*, September 1910.

Mason, Herbert Molloy, Jr. *Death from the Sea: Our Greatest Natural Disaster, The Galveston Hurricane of 1900*. New York, 1972.

Mayer, Al. "When Jack Johnson Clobbered Luis Firpo." *Boxing & Wrestling*, July 1957.

McCaffery, Dan. *Tommy Burns: Canada's Unknown World Heavyweight Champion*. Toronto, 2000.

McCallum, John Dennis. *The Encyclopedia of World Boxing Champions Since 1882*. Radnor, Pa., 1975.

———. *The World Heavyweight Boxing Championship: A History*. Radnor, Pa., 1974.

McComb, David G. *Galveston: A History*. Austin, Tex., 1986.

McGehee, Richard V. "The Dandy and the Mauler in Mexico: Johnson, Dempsey, et al., and the Mexico City Press, 1919–1927." *Journal of Sport History* 23, no. 1 (Spring 1996).

McIntosh, Hugh D. "The Pride of the Blacks, Effect of Johnson's Victory on the Coloured Race." *Boxing*, August 20, 1910.

McLaglen, Victor. *Express to Hollywood*. New York, 1934.

McLean, Alec. "Who Will Be the Next Heavyweight Champion of the World? The Remarkable Story of Jack Johnson, His Early Struggles, His Winning of the World's Championship and a Glimpse of His Probable Successor." *Baseball Magazine*, January–March 1912.

Mead, Chris. *Champion: Joe Louis, Black Hero in White America*. New York, 1985.

Mee, Bob. *Bare Fists: The History of Bare-Knuckle Prize-Fighting*. Woodstock, N.Y., 2002.

Meunier, Claude. *Ring noir: Quand Apollinaire, Cendrars et Picabia Découvraient les Boxeurs Nègres*. Paris, 1992.

Mews, Stuart. "Puritanicalism, Sport and Race: A Symbolic Crusade of 1911." In G. J. Cuming and Derek Baker, eds., *Popular Belief and Practice*, Cambridge, England, 1972.

Miller, Max. *Reno*. New York, 1941.

Miller, Patrick B. "The Anatomy of Scientific Racism: Racial Responses to Black Athletic Achievement." *Journal of Sport History* 25, no. 1 (Spring 1998).

Morgan, Dan. "Strange but True!" *The Ring*, February 1982.

Morgan, Dan (as told to John McCallum). *Dumb Dan*. New York, 1953.

Morgan, Denise C. "Jack Johnson: Reluctant Hero of the Black Community." *Akron Law Review* 32, no. 3 (Winter 1999).

Mumford, Kevin J. *Interzones: Black/White Sex Districts in Chicago and New York in the Early Twentieth Century*. New York, 1977.

Myler, Patrick. *Gentleman Jim Corbett: The Truth Behind a Boxing Legend*. London, 1998.

Nagler, Barney. *Brown Bomber*. New York, 1972.

Nathan, Daniel A. "Sugar Ray Robinson, the Sweet Science, and the Politics of Meaning." *Journal of Sport History* 26, no. 1 (Spring 1999).

Neal, Larry. "Uncle Rufus Raps on the Squared Circle." *Partisan Review*, Spring 1972.

Nicholson, Kelly Richard. *A Man Among Men: The Life and Ring Battles of Jim Jeffries, Heavyweight Champion of the World*. Salt Lake City, 2002.

Nolan, William F. *Barney Oldfield: The Life and Times of America's Legendary Speed King*. Carpinteria, Calif., 2002.

Nott, Rick. "Barney Oldfield, Jack Johnson and the AAA." Forthcoming in *Afro-American Life in New York History*.

O'Dare, Kain. *Philosophy of the Dusk*. New York, 1929.

Odem, Mary E. *Delinquent Daughters: Protecting and Policing Adolescent Female Sexuality in the United States, 1885–1920*. Chapel Hill, N.C., 1995.

Oldfield, Barney. "Wide Open All the Way." *Saturday Evening Post*, September 19, 1925.

"Old Time." "Famous Fights I Have Seen. *Fight Stories*, 1930.

Osofsky, Gilbert. *Harlem: The Making of a Ghetto*. New York, 1963.

Ottley, Roi. *The Lonely Warrior: The Life and Times of Robert S. Abbott*. Chicago, 1955.

Palmer, Joe. *Recollections of a Boxing Referee*. London, 1927.

Pegler, Westbrook. "Are Wrestlers People?" In *The Bedside Esquire*, New York, 1940.

Peiss, Kathy. *Cheap Amusements: Working Women and Leisure in Turn-of-the-Century New York*. Philadelphia, 1986.

Phelon, William A. "Fitzsimmons and the White Hopes." *Baseball Magazine* 4 (February 1914).

———. "The Kings of the Roped Arena." *Baseball Magazine* 6 (February 1913).

———. "Where Boxing Stands Today." *Baseball Magazine* 3 (January 1914).

Preston, Sir Harry. *Leaves from My Unwritten Diary*. London, n.d.

Quarles, Benjamin. "Peter Jackson Speaks of Boxers." *Negro History Bulletin*, November 1954.

Queensberry, the Tenth Marquess of. *The Sporting Queensberrys*. London, 1945.

Rice, Grantland. *Sport Lights of 1923*. New York, 1924.

Rickard, Mrs. Tex. *Everything Happened to Him: The Story of Tex Rickard*. New York, 1936.

Roberts, James B., and Alexander G. Skutt. *The Boxing Register: International Boxing Hall of Fame Official Record Book*. Ithaca, N.Y., 2002.

Roberts, Randy. "Heavyweight Champion Jack Johnson: His Omaha Image, a Public Reaction Study." *Nebraska History* 57, no. 2 (Summer 1970).

———. *Jack Dempsey: The Manassa Mauler*. New York, 1979.

———. *Papa Jack: Jack Johnson and the Era of White Hopes*. New York, 1983.

Rosen, Ruth. *The Lost Sisterhood: Prostitution in America, 1900–1918*. Baltimore, Md., 1992.

Rudensky, (Morris) Red. *The Gonif . . . Red Rudensky*. Blue Earth, Minn., 1970.

Ruhl, Arthur. "The Fight in the Desert." *Collier's*, July 23, 1910.

Runyon, Damon. "The Havana Affair." *Boxing Illustrated*, 1992.

Rutter, Jon David. *White Hopes: Heavyweight Boxing and the Repercussions of Race*. Ph.D. Diss., University of Texas at Austin, 2001.

Sackler, Howard. *The Great White Hope*. New York, 1968.

Sammons, Jeffrey T. *Beyond the Ring: The Role of Boxing in American Society*. Urbana, Ill., 1998.

———. " 'Race' and Sport: A Critical Historical Examination." *Journal of Sport History* 21, no. 3 (Fall 1994).

Samuels, Charles. *The Magnificent Rube: The Life and Gaudy Times of Tex Rickard*. New York, 1957.

Shaler, N. S. "Science and the African Problem." *Atlantic Monthly*, July 1890.

Siler, George. *Inside Facts on Pugilism*.

Sklaroff, Lauren Rebecca. "Constructing G.I. Joe Louis: Cultural Solutions to the 'Negro Problem' During World War II." *Journal of American History*, December 2002.

Smith, Kevin R. *Black Genesis: The History of the Black Prizefighter, 1760–1870*. New York, 2003.

———. *Boston's Boxing Heritage: Prizefighting from 1882 to 1955*. Charleston, S.C., 2002.

Soutar, Andrew. *My Sporting Memories*. London, 1934.

Spielman, Ed. *The Mighty Atom: The Life & Times of Joseph Greenstein*. London, 1980.

Streible, Dan. *Fight Pictures*. Forthcoming from Smithsonian Institution Press.

———. "Race and the Reception of Jack Johnson Fight Films." In Daniel Bernardi, ed., *The Birth of Whiteness: Race and the Emergence of U.S. Cinema*. New Brunswick, N.J., 1996.

Strong, L. A. G. *Shake Hands and Come Out Fighting*. London, 1938.

Stump, Al. "The Rowdy Reign of the Black Avenger." *True: The Man's Magazine*, January 1963.

Thurber, James. "Big Boy." *New Yorker*, May 4, 1929.

Tully, Jim. *A Dozen and One*. New York, 1943.

———. "Famous Negroes of the Ring." *Vanity Fair*, April 1927.

Van Court, DeWitt. *The Making of Champions in California*. San Francisco, 1926.

Van Every, Edward. *Muldoon: The Solid Man of Sport*. New York, 1929.

Van Orden, Kate. *Music and the Cultures of Print*. New York, 2002.

Wamsley, Kevin B. "Celebrating Violent Masculinities: The Boxing Death of Luther McCarty." *Journal of Sport History* 25, no. 3 (Fall 1998).

Ward, Geoffrey C. *American Originals: The Private Worlds of Some Singular Men and Women*. New York, 1991.

———. *Baseball: An Illustrated History*. New York, 1994.

Washburn, Charles. *Come into My Parlor: A Biography of the Aristocratic Everleigh Sisters of Chicago*. New York, 1934.

Waters, Ethel, with Charles Samuels. *His Eye Is on the Sparrow*. New York, 1951.

Wells, Jeff. *Boxing Day: The Fight That Changed the World.* New York, 1998.

White, Shane, and Graham White. *Stylin': African American Expressive Culture.* Ithaca, N.Y., 1998.

Wiggins, David K. " 'Great Speed but Little Stamina': The Historical Debate over Black Athletic Superiority." *Journal of Sport History* 16, no. 2 (Summer 1989).

———. "Peter Jackson and the Elusive Heavyweight Championship." *Journal of Sport History* 12, no. 2 (Summer 1985).

Wiggins, William H. Jr. "Boxing's Sambo Twins: Racial Stereotypes in Jack Johnson and Joe Louis Newspaper Cartoons, 1908 to 1938." *Journal of Sports History* 15, no. 3 (Winter 1988).

———. "Jack Johnson as Bad Nigger: The Folklore of His Life." *The Black Scholar,* January 1971.

Wignall, Trevor. *The Story of Boxing.* London, 1923.

Wilson, Raymond. "Another White Hope Bites the Dust: The Jack Johnson–Jim Flynn Heavyweight Fight in 1912." *Montana: The Magazine of History* 29, no. 1 (January 1979).

SOUVENIR PROGRAMS

Souvenir of the Tommy Burns–Jack Johnson Boxing Contest. Sydney, 1908.

The Referee Jeffries–Johnson Official Souvenir Edition. San Francisco, July 4, 1910.

Café de Champion Souvenir Program. Chicago, 1912.

Jess Willard–Jack Johnson Souvenir Program. Havana, 1915.

INDEX

Abbott, Robert S., 201, 236
aboriginal people, 130
Abrams, Zeke, 53, 64–5, 70, 71
Adams, Alice, 62*n*
Addams, Jane, 303
Afro-American Ledger (newspaper), 200
Ahrens, Abe, 148, 177
Aitken, Abe, 82*n*
Aldrich, Alice Phillips, 303
Aldrich, G. B., 308*n*
Alexander, Jane, 429*n*
Ali, Muhammad, 87*n*, 427, 429*n*
Allen, Fred, 416
Allen, Henry J., 413*n*
Allen, Julia, 177, 237, 238, 239, 338
American Automobile Association Contest
    Board, 239, 241–2, 243
American Burlesque Association, 424
Amsterdam News, 439, 441, 445
Anderson, A. V., 406, 411, 414, 415–16
Anderson, Louis B., 417
Anderson, W. G., 317, 323, 324, 325
Andlauer, W. A., 415–16, 417, 418
Anthony, Daniel Read, Jr., 416
Armand, Frank S., 391
Armstrong, Bob, 38, 43, 183, 199, 200, 207, 211,
    211*n*, 374
Armstrong, Henry, 24*n*
Armstrong, Louis, 217, 419
Arrudi, Fermin, 274–5
Aschuler, Samuel L., 404
Ashburn, Maj. P. M., 225
Ashworth, Mr. and Mrs., 88, 89
As the World Rolls On (film), 418*n*
Astor, Vincent, 416
Atkinson, Brooks, 428–9, 443
Attell, Abe, 38, 41, 42, 207, 211
Austin, Junius Caesar, 448
Austin, Mary, 22, 38–9, 48, 99
Australian Star (newspaper), 117–18
Automobile magazine, 240
automobile racing, 239–44

Bachrach, Benjamin, 315, 316–17, 327–8, 333,
    334, 336–8, 340, 342, 344, 347, 347*n*, 356
Baden-Powell, Sir Robert, 269
Baer, Max, 439, 441
Baker, Josephine, 436
Bakersfield *Daily Californian*, 41, 53
Baldwin, Linton, 443
Baldwin, Matthew S., 317, 347
Baltimore *Afro-American*, 157

Baltimore *American*, 183, 187–8, 197, 204–5*n*,
    382–3
Baltimore *Sun*, 76*n*
Banks, Ada, 287, 294, 296, 303
Barron, Jim, 87–8*n*
Barry, Dave, 436
Barrymore, Ethel, 173
Barton, George A., 154
battles royal, 24–5, 35
Beach, Rex, 193, 194, 195–6, 198, 199, 203, 205,
    207
Beardsley, David, 427–8
Beauscholte, Jack, 35
Bedford, Randolph, 129
Beerly, Gustav, 250
Belmont, August, 175
Bendy, Ernest, 435
Bennett, William S., 191
Berger, Sam, 134, 134*n*, 154, 156–7, 170, 185, 211
Bernau, Herman, 13, 36
Bertelli, C. F., 354
Bettinson, Arthur Frederick "Peggy," 107, 115,
    124, 143
Between Rounds (Eakins), 27*n*
Biddle, Anthony Joseph Drexel, 150–1*n*
Biddle, W. I., 418
Bielaski, A. Bruce, 311, 313, 347, 371
Binga, Jesse, 417
Birth of a Nation, The (film), 371–2
Black, Julian, 437, 440
Black Boy (Dazey and Tully), 428–9
Blackburn, Jack, 79, 437–8
Blake, Eubie, 170
Blanchard, Josephine B., 403*n*
Blease, Cole, 321
Bloom, Ike, 299
Blumenberg, Milton W., 232
Boddington, Clem, 446
Bolden, Mabel, 289, 291
Bond, Virginia, 153
Bonfils, Frederick G., 171–2
Boston *Post*, 82
Bottoms, William, 415, 417, 419, 420, 424
Botwen, Morris, 442
boxing
    beginning of modern boxing era, 19
    "fakery" charge against black boxers, 67*n*
    interstate shipment of prizefight films, ban
        on, 283*n*
    violence resulting from racially mixed fights,
        60–1, 216–18
    "white hope" search, 234, 258–9, 274–5

PHOTOGRAPHIC CREDITS

p. 1: Gary Phillips Collection; pp. 2–3: Gary Phillips Collection; p. 3 inset: Gary Phillips Collection pp. 4–5: Pugilistica.com Boxing Memorabilia, Dave Bergin; p. 5: Gary Phillips Collection; p. 6 inset top: Collection of Ben Hawes; inset bottom: Gary Phillips Collection; pp. 6–7: Gary Phillips Collection; p. 8 top: Antiquities of the Prize Ring; bottom: Library of Congress; p. 9: Pugilistica.com Boxing Memorabilia, Dave Bergin; pp. 10–11: Corbis; p. 11: National Archives at College Park; p. 12: Corbis; p. 13: Brown Brothers; pp. 14–15: Brown Brothers; p. 15: Boston Public Library, Print Department; p. 16: Gary Phillips Collection; p. 17 top: Culver Pictures; bottom: Nevada Historical Society; p. 18 top and bottom: Nevada Historical Society; p. 19: Nevada Historical Society; p. 20 inset: David Schaye; pp. 20–21: Chicago Historical Society; p. 21 inset: Culver Pictures; p. 22: Craig Hamilton, JO Sports, Inc; p. 23: John Liffmann Collection; p. 24: National Archives at College Park; p. 25 top: Bill Loughman Collection; bottom: Collection of Ben Hawes; p. 26 top: Antiquities of the Prize Ring; bottom: Getty Images; pp. 26–27: Library of Congress; p. 28: Kevin Smith; pp. 28–29 top: Corbis; bottom: John Liffmann Collection; pp. 30–31: Brown Brothers; p. 31 inset: Gary Phillips Collection; p. 32: Brown Brothers